**W9-BZK-739**

# southeastern europe

# southeastern europe

## A GUIDE TO BASIC PUBLICATIONS

### paul l. horecky

**EDITOR**

**THE UNIVERSITY OF CHICAGO PRESS**
**CHICAGO & LONDON**

The research reported herein was performed pursuant to a
contract between the American Council of Learned Societies and
the United States Department of Health, Education,
and Welfare, Office of Education (under provisions
of Section 602, Title VI, P.L. 85-864.) Copyright is claimed
until 31 December 1976. Thereafter all portions of this work
will be in the public domain.


*Standard Book Number 226-35190-4*
*Library of Congress Catalog Card Number 73–110336*
THE UNIVERSITY OF CHICAGO PRESS, CHICAGO 60637
THE UNIVERSITY OF CHICAGO PRESS, LTD., LONDON
© *1969 by the American Council of Learned Societies. All rights reserved*
*Published 1969. Printed in the United States of America*

# contents

# Contents

# preface

## CONCEPT AND PURPOSE

In the summer of 1966 the Subcommittee on East Central and Southeast European Studies (American Council of Learned Societies and the Social Science Research Council) initiated a two-pronged survey of language and area studies and of the corresponding bibliographic resources in the field. The first stage of this investigation has already come to a conclusion earlier this year with the publication of *Language and Area Studies: East Central and Southeastern Europe*, under the editorship of Charles Jelavich. The second stage was assigned to me, with a mandate for the compilation of two separate books containing a highly selective and judiciously evaluated inventory of the most important publications relating to these two areas. The present guide on Southeastern Europe and its companion volume on East Central Europe bring the entire survey to fruition.

This book deals with the peoples and countries of Southeastern Europe — Albania, Bulgaria, Greece, Romania, and Yugoslavia. Turkey, which since the end of World War I has had but a residual foothold on European soil, is rarely considered in the context of current Southeast European area studies and academic curricula and, consequently, remains outside the purview of our bibliographic survey. Of course, works dealing with the Ottoman period are included where relevant.

The bulk of the territory of Southeastern Europe is taken up by the Balkan Peninsula. Although Romania is situated to the north of the geographic borderline of this peninsula, the country is generally regarded as a component of Europe's Southeast. The whole region is inhabited by close to sixty million people of varied ethnic backgrounds, tongues, and creeds, who, in the course of their tangled and turbulent historical experience, have built up a record of noteworthy cultural and intellectual contributions. The factors of strategic location, absence of protective barriers of nature, and ethnic complexity have often turned this area into a battleground for the ambitions and rivalries of great powers and a target of recurrent foreign interference and even extended occupation. Periods of peace and tranquillity have constituted only sporadic interludes in its history. Most of the nations in this part of the world spent a good deal of their historical past in the Roman, Byzantine, and Ottoman empires, and, while there exist vast differences in their discrete historical destinies, they share the marked impress on their national existence and society of centuries-long Turkish overlordship.

With the decline of Ottoman rule in the nineteenth and twentieth centuries, various movements for cultural renaissance and political emancipation emerged and ultimately led the way to the establishment of national states. Yet the neighboring Austrian and Russian Empires found themselves only too ready to move into the vacuum created by Turkey's disintegration, and their power policies, spurred by divisiveness and the territorial aspirations of the Balkan nations themselves, brought new tensions and conflicts to the area and were instrumental in precipitating the outbreak of the First World War.

In the more recent past, the largely agricultural societies of this region have undergone profound institutional, economic, and social transformations in their quest for modernization and industrialization. World War II and its aftermath witnessed the extension of communist rule to four countries of Southeastern Europe, with concomitant revolutionary changes in the fabric of Balkan society. It was in Yugoslavia that the great schism in the communist world originated, and the manifestation of Titoism, postulating an independent and separate path toward socialism, ushered in the era of polycentrism within the communist camp. A wide spectrum of disparate and autochthonous forms of political and socioeconomic organizations are discernible on the contemporary scene of Southeastern Europe, ranging from Albania, Eastern Europe's outpost of Chinese communism, to reform-minded and neutralist Yugoslavia and to Western-oriented Greece groping for political and social stability. Obviously, then, this part of the world deserves close study and intimate understanding, and it is our hope that this present guide may contribute to such a goal.

The complexities and obvious limitations of an undertaking such as ours — which requires sifting the most essential writings on the present and past of a multinational and multilingual conglomerate — can be graphically illustrated by a few rough statistics. The aggregate book output for the past fifty years in and about the area under scrutiny may well be in excess of 600,000 titles. Suppose that a mere 20 percent of this total is of continuing research value, the agonizing problem still persists of selecting for this current guide some 5,000 out of a potential reservoir of at least 120,000 publications. The plethora of printed information available on the area can be illustrated by a few random figures just on certain types of publications which are limited to specific periods, events, or languages. Thus, Léon Savadjian's *Bibliographie balkanique* fills eight volumes, recording writings that were published in English, French, German, and Italian between 1920 and 1938. Similarly, *Bibliographie d'études balkaniques*, an annual recently inaugurated by the Bulgarian Academy of Sciences, contains 1,951 listings of materials published on the area in 1966 alone and covering the period of up to 1939 only. The literature on the assassination in 1913 of the Austrian archduke in Sarajevo has reportedly grown to well over four thousand titles.

Inexorable limitations of time, manpower, and funds dictated that the essential record of knowledge of such enormous proportions be telescoped into one single volume. High selectivity was the obvious modus operandi toward that end. In facing the prospect, I found solace in an idea of the Spanish philosopher Ortega y Gasset, who some thirty years ago envisioned the role of the future librarian as that of a sensitive filter standing between man and the unending flood of print. When espousing such an assignment, the bibliographer must assume cheerfully — so to say as an occupational hazard — the task of navigating the perilous channel between the Scylla of too much and the Charybdis of too little — especially since such a voyage makes no provision for travel insurance against the slings and barbs of the critic who may doubt the wisdom of the course charted.

We profess candidly that we have not been able to conjure up either a magic formula for miniaturizing knowledge or a technique for a foolproof selection process. But, despite these reservations, we venture to hope that we did manage to come up with a relatively concentrated distillate of information which can be reconstituted into a panoramic and synoptic view of the area. This guide traces general contours, as would a large-scale map, the further exploitation of which is best served by reference to more detailed small-scale maps. To translate this thought into the present context, it would be very desirable if in the future the data of this bibliography could be expanded through a series of specialized subject bibliographies.

Keeping in mind the need of maximizing the informational potentiality of our guide, we have given generous coverage to bibliographic material, both in separate chapters and in the context of specific subjects. Such bibliographic sources should be regarded as a sort of master key to a wealth of other literature which could not be explicitly included here. Thus, with proper exploration, only very few targets of bibliographic search should, in the final analysis, remain terra incognita.

In a situation marked by an unprecedented proliferation of printed information and by the evolvement of the study of the area from a single discipline to a constantly widening complex of subspecialties, a far-reaching degree of multidisciplinary teamwork was the obvious answer to the problem posed by a selective approach. Thus, this work embodies the collective subject and area expertise of many specialists from this country and abroad. It was our common aim to base the selection of publications on scholarly and informational merits only and to reflect the character of the individual entries in thoughtful and restrained comment. The design and structure of the guide, including allocation of space by language and subject, as well as the overall direction of the project, were my responsibilities. Our editorial policy endeavored to preserve as much as possible the authentic style and format of the contributors' presentation, subject to the needs of bibliographic consistency. When major alterations, expansions, or contractions appeared indicated for reasons of balanced coverage or topical coherence, I strove, circumstances permitting, to resolve such questions with the advice and consent of the contributor concerned.

This guide addresses itself to a multiple audience — the general reader, the researcher, the student, the teacher, and the librarian. It is our hope that it may serve several useful functions: as a study aid to those who wish to work on one or more aspects of the area; as a classroom tool for the more advanced investigation of the area; as a medium for the development of concentrated library collections at the growing number of educational institutions which are extending their programs in the field; and, finally, as a basis for determining important out-of-print material and identifying hitherto neglected domains of published research.

## SCOPE AND ORGANIZATION

*Scope.* This volume records basic books, periodicals, and, occasionally articles of special pertinence, on the lands and peoples of Albania, Bulgaria, Greece, Romania, and Yugoslavia. The subject coverage focuses on the political, socioeconomic, and intellectual life in the respective areas of Europe. The bibliography lists writings in languages indigenous to the countries concerned, as well as in other languages in which significant contributions to the knowledge of the area have been made. Among the latter, the emphasis is on English-language publications. In determining the relative language representation we were guided both by the relevance of the material and by the presumed linguistic capabilities of the book's potential reading public. In keeping with the intended function of this bibliography as an area research aid, its temporal reach spans primarily the more recent period of statehood of the various countries, but the background and general historical development leading up to the present are given consideration. Although we have aimed at maximum currency of coverage up to the production stage, we are reconciled to the idea that onrushing events and never-resting printing presses set distinct limitations to such a goal. As a rule, the latest imprints included are those which were available for physical inspection in 1968.

*Methodological Approach.* For each country the material is structured under eight or nine major sectors of knowledge, which are subdivided into more specialized categories as suggested by the particularities of the respective country. The availability of a substantial body of information offering a total view of the area or segments thereof counseled the inclusion of an introductory overview.

The intertwined and stratified character of knowledge, particularly in its application to the study of an area, renders the strict delineation of a discipline an arduous task. The Great Divide between political thought and history, philosophy, economics, jurisprudence, psychology, sociology, and international affairs is all too fluid and changeable. How can a precise boundary be drawn between the societal and political systems of a country? Is there a readily identifiable demarcation line between the national characteristics of a people and the makeup of its society? In the face of such uncertainties the reader will be well advised not to limit his bibliographic investigation to the seemingly indicated chapter or section heading but to refer in case of need to kindred and contiguous topical sections.

To improve subject control we have followed the practice — notwithstanding a very acute shortage of space in this volume — of including in two or more subject contexts such identical titles as deal significantly with several subjects. Such multiple listings sometimes bear divergent assessments by different contributors — a fact which underscores the inherently subjective and personal nature of book evaluation, as well as the versatility of coverage by some publications. The prefatory table of contents, detailed statements of content at the beginning of major chapters, and an extensive author-title-subject index should guide the reader and enhance reference use.

*Entries.* We have endeavored to keep the form of entry as succinct and nontechnical as is consistent with the need for clear bibliographic identification of a title. Basically, the Library of Congress bibliographic style was followed because it permits ready referrals to, and collation with, the widely used Library of Congress printed cards and catalogs. Occasional departures from this procedure were thought advisable in the interests of economy of space and simplified presentation. English translations are given for titles cited in the Slavic languages and in Albanian, Hungarian, and Romanian. Alternate versions of authors' names are indicated parenthetically. The consecutively numbered lead entries are followed by annotative comments, often accompanied by additional citations of collateral writings. Within subject groups, entries usually are in alphabetical order. Divergent methods, such as arrangement by chronology or topical affinity, are explained in footnotes wherever they are employed.

The Cyrillic alphabet is transliterated according to Library of Congress practices and so is the Greek alphabet except for minor modifications noted in the transliteration table at the beginning of this volume.

## ACKNOWLEDGMENTS

My foremost thanks go to the team of distinguished contributors and consultants on foreign-language publications who, notwithstanding many pressing professional commitments, spiritedly responded to my call and joined forces in our venture. Their names are mentioned individually in the roster of participants which appears elsewhere in this book. I was very fortunate to benefit in this enterprise from the invaluable help of Frederick B. Mohr and Peter J. Watters, who served as Assistant Editors. Their editorial experience and devotion to our undertaking were material assets in melding a mass of raw material into a homogeneous entity. Robert G. Carlton reviewed the manuscript and made helpful suggestions for improvement. In addition, he undertook the task of preparing the detailed index. The chapter on General Reference Aids and Bibliographies for Yugoslavia owes many a contribution to Eric A. Kovacic. Barbara A. Burkey, Constance Carter, and Ruth M. Miller helped with the preparation of prefatory matter. The aforementioned assistants are on the staff of the Library of Congress.

In various phases of our undertaking the need arose to seek ad hoc advice on specific questions from specialists here and abroad. Among those who gave generously of their thought and time were Dušan Biber (Institute of Social Sciences, Belgrade); Slobodan Jovanović (until recently with the National Library in Belgrade); John Nicolopoulos (State University of New York in Albany); Vladimir Pregelj (Library of Congress); Marin V. Pundeff (San Fernando Valley State College); and Matko Rojnić (National and University Library in Zagreb). I am much indebted to Mathias W. Bernath (Südost-Institut, Munich) for making possible the participation of his staff in recommending pertinent German-language materials for final selection by the subject compilers.

A veritable key aide on the team, to whom I am greatly obliged, is Martha L. Rose, who, undaunted by a spate of drafts in a Babel of languages and a profusion of diacritical marks, exhibited both initiative and dispatch in preparing the final manuscript for the printers. Basil Nadraga and Gerald F. Stowell checked many an item in this volume against the pertinent catalogs and bibliographic sources. And finally, my wife, Emily I. Horecky, has once again — as perennially — borne with my involvement in such an undertaking. Beyond this, she was of truly indispensable assistance in taking a most active hand in a vast variety of editorial and administrative endeavors.

The present volume was sponsored by the Subcommittee on East Central and Southeast European Studies under the dynamic chairmanship of Charles Jelavich (Indiana University), who was the moving spirit in activating the overall project. Gordon B. Turner, Vice President of the American Council of Learned Societies, guided the operational aspects of this project, and I am profoundly grateful to him for his unflagging support and generous understanding of our needs and problems. Finally, I should like to add my own very great appreciation to the sponsoring bodies for according me complete freedom of action in planning and executing this undertaking.

PAUL L. HORECKY

Alexandria, Virginia
January 1969

# participants

## CONTRIBUTORS

ALEXANDER ADAMOVITCH (Yugoslavia: Law) is a staff member of the Library of Congress. He was formerly a member of the Yugoslav bar and an associate of the Mid-European Studies Center of the Committee for a Free Europe, New York. He has also served as a Legal Analyst, Mid-European Law Project, Library of Congress; a Legal Assistant in the Civil Division of the United States Department of Justice; and a foreign law consultant.

JELISAVETA STANOJEVICH ALLEN (Yugoslavia: Fine Arts) was born in Belgrade, Yugoslavia, and studied art history at the University of Belgrade. She was on the staff of the National Museum, Belgrade, and the Institute for Protection of Monuments in Serbia. She is presently a cataloger and classifier at Dumbarton Oaks Center for Byzantine Art in Washington, D.C., and recently received a M.S.L.S. from the Catholic University of America.

GEORGE G. ARNAKIS (Greece: History) is Professor of History at the University of Texas and Director of the Center for Neo-Hellenic Studies. He has taught history at Pierce College (Athens, Greece), the University of Missouri in Kansas City, the University of Kansas, the University of Chicago, and Texas Christian University. The recipient of ACLS, Guggenheim, and Fulbright Fellowships at various times between 1952 and 1963, Dr. Arnakis has contributed many articles to journals and authored or edited more than a dozen books in Greek and in English.

ROBERT AUTY (Yugoslavia: Languages) is a Fellow of Brasenose College and Professor of Comparative Slavonic Philology, Oxford University. He was previously Fellow of Selwyn College and Lecturer in Slavonic Studies, Cambridge University; and Professor of Comparative Philology of the Slavonic Languages, London University. His writings include *Old Church Slavonic Texts and Glossary* (Athlone Press, 1959-60); and journal articles, principally on Czech, Serbo-Croatian, Slovak, Slovenian, and Old Church Slavonic.

ELIZABETH BEYERLY (Overview: General Reference Aids and Bibliographies) is completing her doctorate in international relations at the Institut universitaire de hautes études internationales, Geneva. With Master's degrees from

Columbia University in Russian language and literature and in library science, she has served, mainly as a Slavic specialist, in government and university libraries and at the World Health Organization. She has contributed articles to professional journals concerned with Russian and East European librarianship and documentation.

JOSEF BROŽEK (all sections on Psychology) is Research Professor at Lehigh University, Department of Psychology, of which he was Chairman from 1959 to 1963. His current interest, on which he has written copiously, is the history of psychology, with special reference to the Slavic countries and the USSR. He has served in editorial capacities for professional journals.

DAVID E. BYNUM (Yugoslavia: Literatures, with Albert B. Lord; Folklore; Theater) teaches South Slavic languages and literatures and Slavic folklore at Harvard University, where he is Assistant Professor of Slavic Languages and Literatures. He is also Assistant Curator of the Milman Parry Collection in the Harvard College Library.

JOHN C. CAMPBELL (Overview: Politics and Government. Yugoslavia: Diplomacy and Foreign Relations) is Senior Research Fellow of the Council on Foreign Relations and serves also as a consultant to the Department of State. His governmental service included the positions of Deputy Director of the Office of East European Affairs in the State Department and member of the Policy Planning Staff. He is a frequent contributor to professional journals and the author of several books including *Tito's Separate Road; America and Yugoslavia in World Politics* (Harper and Row, 1967).

ROBERT G. CARLTON, Assistant Editor and contributor (Romania: General Reference Aids and Bibliographies) is an Area Specialist with the Slavic and Central European Division of the Library of Congress. Co-compiler of *The USSR and Eastern Europe: Periodicals in Western Languages* (Library of Congress, 1967), he has also edited *Newspapers of East Central and Southeastern Europe in the Library of Congress* (Washington, 1965) and *Latin America in Soviet Writings: a Bibliography* (Baltimore, Johns Hopkins Press, 1966).

MANOLIS CHATZIDAKIS (Greece: Fine Arts) served as Director of the Byzantine Museum in Athens and was formerly the Director of the Benaki Museum. He has participated in excavations of Christian antiquities in Delphi, Ilissos, and Kaisariani. He is the author of several books including *Byzantine Monuments in Attica and Boeotia* (Athens' Editions, 1956), *Les icônes de Saint-Georges des Grecs* (Venice, N. Pozza, 1962), and of numerous articles in scholarly journals.

JAMES F. CLARKE (Overview: The Intellectual and Cultural Life — Bulgaria: The Intellectual and Cultural Life) has contributed on Balkan subjects to various books and journals, including the *Foreign Affairs Bibliographies* and the American Historical Association's *Guide to Historical Literature* (Macmillan, 1961). He has taught history at several universities and was formerly employed in the Library of Congress, Department of State, and other government agencies.

The REV. DEMETRIOS J. CONSTANTELOS (Greece: Religion; Education) was born in Greece but received his advanced education in the United States, including a doctorate from Rutgers University. He is currently Associate Professor of History at the Holy Cross Theological School, Brookline, Massachusetts, and Visiting Associate Professor of History at Boston College. His writings include *The Greek Orthodox Church* (Seabury Press, 1967) and *Byzantine Philanthropy and Social Welfare* (Rutgers University Press, 1967).

ADONIS G. M. DECAVALLES (Greece: Modern Greek Theater and Cinema) has taught at Fairleigh Dickinson University since 1961, where he is presently Associate Professor of Comparative Literature and Modern Poetry. His publications include *Nimoule-Gondokoro* (1949), *Akis* (1950), which are two books of original Greek verse, *A Short History of Modern Greek Literature* (Athens, 1953), and numerous contributions to Greek and American literary journals. Dr. Decavalles is also executive editor of *The Charioteer, a Review of Modern Greek Culture*.

L. A. D. DELLIN (Bulgaria: Economy) is currently Professor of Economics and Political Science and Director of the Graduate Institute of Russian and East European Studies at the University of Vermont. He studied at the Universities of Sofia and Vienna, obtained his doctorate from Genoa University, and in 1967/68 was a Fulbright research scholar at the University of Munich. He is the editor of *Bulgaria* (Praeger, 1957) and author of articles on Eastern Europe and communism.

ANDREW ELIAS (Yugoslavia: Demography) is a Senior Statistician with the Foreign Demographic Analysis Division, U.S. Bureau of the Census. His writings include the following publications of the U.S. Bureau of the Census: *The Labor Force of Yugoslavia* (1965), *The Labor Force of Czechoslovakia: Scope and Concepts* (1963), and *The Magnitude and Distribution of Civilian Employment in the U.S.S.R., 1928-1959* (1961), which he coauthored with M. S. Weitzman.

STEPHEN FISCHER-GALATI (Romania: The People; History) was born in Bucharest, Romania, and educated at Harvard University, where he received A.B., M.A., and Ph.D. degrees. Currently Professor of East-Central European History at the University of Colorado and managing editor of the *East European Quarterly*, he is the author and editor of several books and articles on East European history.

RADU R. FLORESCU (Romania: The Intellectual and Cultural Life [Excluding Language, Literature, Music]) is Associate Professor of East European History at Boston College and was a Fulbright Exchange Professor in Bucharest, Romania, 1967/68. The author of *The Struggle Against Russia in the Romanian Principalities, 1821-54* (Munich, 1963), Dr. Florescu has contributed articles to such journals as the *Slavonic and East European Review*, *History Today*, the *Journal of Central European Affairs*, and the *Journal of Modern History*.

HOURMOUZIS G. GEORGIADIS (Greece: Economy) has served as an economic consultant to the United Nations, a senior economic specialist to the Chase Manhattan Bank, and is presently Associate Professor in the Graduate School of Economics of New York University. He is also a staff member of the National Bureau of Economic Research, where he is conducting a study evaluating the competitive position of the United States in the world economy. Dr. Georgiadis is the author of *Balance of Payments Equilibrium* (University of Pittsburgh Press, 1964) and several articles in professional journals.

JOEL M. HALPERN (Yugoslavia: The People; The Society) is an Associate Professor of Anthropology at the University of Massachusetts in Amhurst. Specializing in the study of peasant society and related problems of migration and urbanization, he is the author of *A Serbian Village* (2d rev. ed., Harper and Row, 1967), *The Changing Village Community* (Prentice-Hall, 1967), and numerous articles in scholarly journals. A second book on Yugoslav peasant society is scheduled to be published in 1969 by Holt, Rinehart, and Winston.

ERIC P. HAMP (Albania: The Intellectual and Cultural Life, sections A-D) is Professor and Chairman of Linguistics as well as Director of the Center for Balkan and Slavic Studies at the University of Chicago. He was a visiting professor at the Universities of Beogard and Copenhagen, a U.S. cultural exchange lecturer in Romania, and a visiting research scholar at the University of Athens. He has served on various committees concerned with Southeast European affairs, including the American Committee, Association internationale d'études du sud-est européen (AIESEE).

KEITH HITCHINS (Romania: Legal History, Government and Politics) is Associate Professor of History at the University of Illinois. His specialty is Romanian history and civilization, and he has spent three years in Romania pursuing his research. He is the author of several articles on the nationality question in Transylvania and of the forthcoming book, *The Rumanian National Movement in Transylvania, 1780-1849*.

GEORGE W. HOFFMAN (Overview: Geographic Aspects; The People. Bulgaria: The Land; The People. Greece: The Land; The People. Romania: The Land. Yugoslavia: The Land) is Professor of Geography at the University of Texas. Author of *The Balkans in Transition* (Van Nostrand, 1963), coauthor of *Yugoslavia and the New Communism* (Twentieth Century Fund, 1962), and editor of *A Geography of Europe* (2d ed., Ronald Press, 1961), Dr. Hoffman has contributed numerous articles to professional journals both in the United States and abroad. He has been a recipient of several academic awards.

PAUL L. HORECKY, Chief Editor of this book and contributor of chapters on Yugoslavia, is Assistant Chief, Slavic and Central European Division, Library of Congress. His publications include *East Central Europe* (University of Chicago Press, 1969); *Russia and the Soviet Union* (University of Chicago Press, 1965); *Basic Russian Publications* (University of Chicago Press, 1962); *Libraries and Bibliographic Centers in the Soviet Union* (Indiana University Publications, 1959); and other monographs and articles on cultural affairs of the USSR and Eastern Europe.

GHITĂ IONESCU (Romania: Diplomacy and Foreign Relations; Military Affairs; Mass Media; Society) received his doctorate in law and political science from Bucharest University. In 1944 he served as General Secretary of the Romanian Armistice Commission and is presently a Fellow of the London School of Economics and editor of *Government and Opposition; a Quarterly of Comparative Politics*. His books include *Communism in Rumania* (Oxford University Press, 1964), *The Break-up of the Soviet Empire in Eastern Europe* (Penguin Books, 1965), and *The Politics of the European Communist States* (Praeger, 1967).

BARBARA JELAVICH (Yugoslavia: Co-compiler, History) is Professor of History at Indiana University. Her writings include *A Century of Russian Foreign Policy 1814-1914* (Lippincott, 1964); *Russia and the Rumanian National Cause, 1858-1859* (Bloomington, 1959); *Russia and Greece during the Regency of King Othon 1832-1835* (Argonaut, 1962); *Russia and the Greek Revolution of 1843* (Munich, 1966); and articles on Russian and Balkan foreign policy. With Charles Jelavich she coedited *Russia in the East 1876-1880* (E. J. Brill, 1959).

CHARLES JELAVICH (Yugoslavia: Co-compiler, History is Professor of History at Indiana University. His writings include *Tsarist Russia and Balkan Nationalism* (University of California Press, 1958), (with Barbara Jelavich) *The Balkans in Transition* (University of California Press, 1963), (with Barbara Jelavich) *The Balkans* (Prentice-Hall, 1965), and articles on Balkan history.

CHARILAOS G. LAGOUDAKIS (Greece: Diplomacy and Foreign Relations; Military Affairs; Nationalities; Mass Media and Public Opinion) is a foreign affairs specialist in the Department of State. Formerly, he served as Professor and Head of the Department of History at Athens College. In 1967 the Center for Research in Social Systems of the American University published his *Anatomy of the Communist Insurgency in Greece (1946-49) and of the Greek Uprising in Cyprus* (1955-58). In recent years he has been lecturing at the Foreign Service Institute and the National War College.

IVO J. LEDERER (Overview: Diplomacy and Foreign Relations) has taught at Princeton and Yale Universities and is presently Professor of History at Stanford University. His writings include *Yugoslavia at the Paris Peace Conference: A Study in Frontiermaking* (Yale University Press, 1963), *The Versailles Settlement. Was It Foredoomed to Failure?* (Heath, 1960), and the forthcoming *Nationalism in Eastern Europe*, of which he is coeditor with Peter F. Sugar. He is a member of the Conference on Slavic and East European Studies and other professional organizations.

KAETHE LEWY (Overview: Co-compiler, the Jews in Southeastern Europe) is Head of Bibliographic Services and Serials Catalogue, Jewish National and University Library, Jerusalem, and is a Lecturer in General Bibliography, Graduate Library School, Hebrew University, Jerusalem. She is editor of *Union List of Serials in Israel Libraries* (Jerusalem, 1964-67) and author of *Guide to General Bibliographies and Reference Books* (Hebrew University, Graduate Library School, 1967). She is a contributor to the professional library journal of Israel.

ANTON LOGORECI (Albania: History; Intellectual and Cultural Life, sections G, H) is a political commentator on communist affairs with a West European broadcasting organization in London. He has written articles on Eastern Europe published in a number of British and American journals and encyclopedias.

ALBERT B. LORD (Yugoslavia: Literatures, with David E. Bynum) is Professor of Slavic and of Comparative Literature at Harvard University. He teaches courses in South Slavic languages and literatures, oral epic poetry, and folklore. Dr. Lord is an Honorary Curator of the Milman Parry Collection of Oral Literature in the Harvard College Library and is the author of scholarly publications in his specialties.

JOHN M. MONTIAS (Overview: The Economy. Romania: The Economy) is Professor of Economics at Yale University. His academic honors include both Ford and Guggenheim Fellowships. Dr. Montias has written *Central Planning in Poland* (Yale University Press, 1962) and *Economic Development in Communist Rumania* (M.I.T. Press, 1967). His articles have appeared in

*Foreign Affairs, Journal of Political Economy, American Economic Review,* and numerous other scholarly journals.

ELEZ NDREU (Albania: General Reference Aids, Bibliographies and Survey Works) has published several articles on Albanian literature and Balkan linguistics. He teaches Albanian at the Defense Language Institute in Monterey, California.

GEORGE E. PERRY (Greece: General Reference Aids and Bibliographies) is Head, Slavic Room, Slavic and Central European Division, Library of Congress. He has served since June 1966 as Secretary of the Slavic and East European Subsection, Association of College and Research Libraries, American Library Association.

MICHAEL B. PETROVICH (Overview: History. Bulgaria: History. Yugoslavia: History of Thought, Culture and Scholarship; Religion; Education) is Professor of History at the University of Wisconsin and one of the University's specialists in Russian and Balkan history. His writings include *The Emergence of Russian Panslavism, 1856-79* (Columbia University Press, 1956) and articles in such journals as the *Political Science Quarterly, American Slavic and East European Review,* and the *Journal of Central European Affairs.* Dr. Petrovich is also the translator of three books by Milovan Djilas.

VLADIMIR N. PREGELJ (Yugoslavia: General and Descriptive Works) is Analyst in International Trade and Finance in the Legislative Reference Service, Library of Congress, specializing in the field of East European economic conditions and relations. He has lived, traveled, and received part of his education in Yugoslavia. Mr. Pregelj was a lecturer at Fordham University and has written several studies on East-West trade for the use of the United States Congress.

MARIN V. PUNDEFF (Bulgaria: General Reference Aids and Bibliographies; The State) is Professor of History at San Fernando Valley State College. His works include *Bulgaria: A Bibliographic Guide* (Library of Congress, 1965) and *History in the USSR* (Hoover Institution Publications, 1967). He has contributed numerous chapters to books as well as articles to leading professional journals in the United States and abroad. A former staff member of the Library of Congress, he served in 1963 as Consultant in Bulgarian Affairs to the Library.

IRWIN T. SANDERS (Overview: Society) is Vice-President of Education and World Affairs in New York City. Dr. Sanders' specialization in sociology and Balkan affairs encompasses an extensive academic career (including the American College in Sofia, Bulgaria, in the 1930s, and, more recently, Harvard and Columbia), governmental assignments (e.g., as Agricultural Attaché to the U.S. Embassy, Belgrade, Yugoslavia), and service on scholarly committees concerned with Eastern Europe. His books include *Rainbow in the Rock: The People of Rural Greece* (Harvard University Press, 1962) and *Balkan Village* (University of Kentucky Press, 1948).

ROBERT SCHWANKE (Albania: The Land; The People; The State; The Economy) is a graduate of the Institute for Balkan Studies, Vienna, and of the Austrian Historical Institute. Since 1962 he has been Chief of the Division for Balkan Archives in ths Austrian State Archives. Dr. Schwanke is also a member of the Austrian Institute on Eastern and Southeastern Europe, specializing in regional studies, law, and economic and cultural life.

THEOFANIS G. STAVROU (Greece: General and Descriptive Works) is Associate Professor of Russian and Near Eastern History at the University of Minnesota. He is the author of *Russian Interests in Palestine 1882-1914, a Study of Religious and Educational Enterprise* (Thessalonike, Institute for Balkan Studies, 1963) and of several articles on religious and intellectual history for professional journals and for *Threskeutike kai ethike egkyklopaideia* [Religious and Ethical Encyclopedia], a twelve-volume work published in Greece.

TRAIAN STOIANOVICH (Yugoslavia: The National Question; The Agrarian Question) is a Professor in the Department of History, Rutgers University. His writings include *A Study in Balkan Civilization* (Knopf, 1967) and articles in the *Journal of Economic History, Comparative Studies in Society and History, Slavic Review,* and *Annales (E.S.C.).* Dr. Stoianovich was also a contributor to Charles and Barbara Jelavich's *The Balkans in Transition* (University of California Press, 1963).

VIRGILIU STOICOIU (Romania: The Legal System) is a Legal Specialist in the European Law Division of the Library of Congress. A former lawyer in Bucharest, his writings include the *Legal Sources and Bibliography of Romania* (Praeger, 1964) and articles on various legal subjects published in journals in the United States and abroad.

RUTH TRONIK (Overview: Co-compiler, The Jews in Southeastern Europe) is Assistant Head of the Bibliographic Services and Serials Catalogue, Jewish National and University Library, Jerusalem. She is editor of *Bibliographie d'ouvrages hébraiques traduits en Français* (Jerusalem, Ministère des affaires étrangères, 1966) and other bibliographies published in the professional library journal of Israel.

CONSTANTINE A. TRYPANIS (Greece: Language, Literature, Folklore, History of Thought and Culture) is University Professor of Classics at the University of Chicago. From 1947 to 1968 he was Professor of Medieval and Modern Greek Literature and Language at Oxford University. His numerous books include *Pompeian Dog* (London, 1964; New York, Chilmark Press, 1965); *Medieval and Modern Greek Poetry* (Oxford University Press, 1951), *The Stones of Troy* (Faber and Faber, 1957), and the forthcoming *Sancti Romani Melodi Carmina,* vol. 2. Active in many professional organizations, Dr. Trypanis is also a Nominator for the Nobel Prize for Literature of the Swedish Academy.

EMANUEL TURCZYNSKI (Romania: Language; Literature; Folklore) was born in Romania, and has taught Romanian language, literature, and history at the University of Munich since 1949. He is the author of *Die deutsch-griechischen Kulturbeziehungen* (R. Oldenbourg, 1959) and has contributed many articles on Southeast European history and literature to periodicals in Germany, Austria, Greece, and the United States. He is a member of the Präsidium of the Südosteuropa-Gesellschaft, Munich.

MILOŠ VELIMIROVIĆ (all sections on music in this volume) is Professor of History of Music, University of Wisconsin. Specializing in the history of Byzantine music and its relationship to the music of the Slavic countries, his publications include *Byzantine Elements in Early Slavic Chant* (Munksgaard, 1960) and "Liturgical Drama in Byzantium and Russia," in volume 16 of *Dumbarton Oaks Papers.* He is Chairman of the International Committee for an Inventory of Old Slavic Musical Manuscripts, and joint editor with Egon Wellesz of the biannual *Studies in Eastern Chant* (Oxford University Press).

WAYNE S. VUCINICH (Yugoslavia: Politics and Government; Military Affairs; Public Opinion) is Professor of History, Stanford University. During the Second World War he served with the Office of Strategic Services and Department of State. He is the author of *Serbia Between East and West* (Stanford University Press, 1954) and *The Ottoman Empire: In Record and Legacy* (Van Nostrand, 1965), and editor of the *Russian Peasant in Nineteenth Century Russia* (Stanford University Press, 1968). Dr. Vucinich has also written many shorter studies in the field of East European history.

BENJAMIN N. WARD (Yugoslavia: The Economy) is on the faculty of the University of California at Berkeley.

STEPHEN G. XYDIS (Greece: Law; Politics and Government) is an Associate Professor at Hunter College. He has formerly served as a senior information officer, United Nations Secretariat, and done free lance work for the United States Information Agency and the Voice of America. His publications include *Cyprus: Conflict and Conciliation 1954-58* (Ohio State University Press, 1967), *Greece and the Great Powers 1944-1947* (Thessalonike, Institute for Balkan Studies, 1963), and articles in scholarly journals.

CONSTANTINE A. YERACARIS (Greece: Society) is Professor of Sociology and Director of the Training Program in the Social Sciences (NIMH) at the State University of New York at Buffalo. He holds a law degree from the University of Athens and a Ph.D. in sociology from the University of Chicago. The author of articles on demography and social change, Dr. Yeracaris is currently completing an empirical study on political factors and acceptance of innovations in a Greek community.

## CONSULTANT

GERTRUD KRALLERT-SATTLER (Consultant on German-language publications) is a historian who received her doctor's degree from the University of Vienna. She is a research librarian at the Südost-Institut München. Dr. Krallert-Sattler is the editor of *Südosteuropa-Bibliographie* (München, Oldenbourg, 1956–).

## ASSISTANT EDITORS

ROBERT G. CARLTON (see above)

FREDERICK B. MOHR is Publications Coordinator for the Aerospace Technology Division of the Library of Congress and editor of that Division's monthly *Foreign Science Bulletin*. He has edited a variety of scientific and technical reports and monographs, the most recent being *Air Transportation 1975 and Beyond: A Systems Approach* (The M.I.T. Press, 1968).

PETER J. WATTERS is a management analyst on the staff of the Office of the Director, Reference Department, Library of Congress. He formerly served on the editorial staff of the Aerospace Technology Division, Library of Congress, and was chief editor of the *ATD Press*, a daily abstract bulletin reporting developments in Soviet science and engineering.

# slavic transliteration

| Russian | | | Ukrainian | | | White Russian | | | Bulgarian | | | Serbian* | | |
|---|---|---|---|---|---|---|---|---|---|---|---|---|---|---|
| А | а | a | А | а | a | А | а | a | А | а | a | А | а | a |
| Б | б | b | Б | б | b | Б | б | b | Б | б | b | Б | б | b |
| В | в | v | В | в | v | В | в | v | В | в | v | В | в | v |
| Г | г | g | Г | г | h | Г | г | h | Г | г | g | Г | г | g |
| — | | | Ґ | ґ | g | Ґ | ґ | g | — | | | — | | |
| Д | д | d | Д | д | d | Д | д | d | Д | д | d | Д | д | d |
| — | | | — | | | — | | | — | | | Ђ | ђ | đ |
| Е | е | e | Е | е | e | Е | е | e | Е | е | e | Е | е | e |
| — | | | Є | є | ie | — | | | — | | | — | | |
| Ё | ё | ë | — | | | Ё | ё | io | — | | | — | | |
| Ж | ж | zh | Ж | ж | zh | Ж | ж | zh | Ж | ж | zh | Ж | ж | ž |
| З | з | z | З | з | z | З | з | z | З | з | z | З | з | z |
| И | и | i | И | и | y | — | | | И | и | i | И | и | i |
| I | i | ī | І | і | i | I | i | i | — | | | — | | |
| — | | | Ї | ї | ï | — | | | — | | | — | | |
| Й | й | ĭ | Й | й | ĭ | Й | й | ĭ | Й | й | ĭ | — | | |
| — | | | — | | | — | | | — | | | Ј | ј | j |
| К | к | k | К | к | k | К | к | k | К | к | k | К | к | k |
| Л | л | l | Л | л | l | Л | л | l | Л | л | l | Л | л | l |
| — | | | — | | | — | | | — | | | Љ | љ | lj |
| М | м | m | М | м | m | М | м | m | М | м | m | М | м | m |
| Н | н | n | Н | н | n | Н | н | n | Н | н | n | Н | н | n |
| — | | | — | | | — | | | — | | | Њ | њ | nj |
| О | о | o | О | о | o | О | о | o | О | о | o | О | о | o |
| П | п | p | П | п | p | П | п | p | П | п | p | П | п | p |
| Р | р | r | Р | р | r | Р | р | r | Р | р | r | Р | р | r |
| С | с | s | С | с | s | С | с | s | С | с | s | С | с | s |
| Т | т | t | Т | т | t | Т | т | t | Т | т | t | Т | т | t |
| — | | | — | | | — | | | — | | | Ћ | ћ | ć |
| У | у | u | У | у | u | У | у | u | У | у | u | У | у | u |
| — | | | — | | | Ў | ў | ŭ | — | | | — | | |
| Ф | ф | f | Ф | ф | f | Ф | ф | f | Ф | ф | f | Ф | ф | f |
| Х | х | kh | Х | х | kh | Х | х | kh | Х | х | kh | Х | х | h |
| Ц | ц | ts | Ц | ц | ts | Ц | ц | ts | Ц | ц | ts | Ц | ц | c |
| Ч | ч | ch | Ч | ч | ch | Ч | ч | ch | Ч | ч | ch | Ч | ч | č |
| — | | | — | | | — | | | — | | | Џ | џ | dž |
| Ш | ш | sh | Ш | ш | sh | Ш | ш | sh | Ш | ш | sh | Ш | ш | š |
| Щ | щ | shch | Щ | щ | shch | — | | | Щ | щ | sht | — | | |
| Ъ | ъ | '' | — | | | — | | | Ъ | ъ | ŭ or '' | — | | |
| Ы | ы | y | — | | | Ы | ы | y | — | | | — | | |
| Ь | ь | ' | Ь | ь | ' | Ь | ь | ' | Ь | ь | ' | — | | |
| Ѣ | ѣ | ie | — | | | — | | | Ѣ | ѣ | ie | — | | |
| Э | э | ė | — | | | Э | э | ė | — | | | — | | |
| Ю | ю | iu | Ю | ю | iu | Ю | ю | iu | Ю | ю | iu | — | | |
| Я | я | ia | Я | я | ' ia | Я | я | ia | Я | я | ia | — | | |
| Ѳ | ѳ | f | — | | | — | | | — | | | — | | |
| Ѵ | ѵ | ẏ | — | | | — | | | — | | | — | | |
| — | | | — | | | — | | | ѫ | ǔ | | — | | |

\* Transliteration of Macedonian is the same as that for Serbian, except that the following additional letters are present in Macedonian and are transliterated as shown:

$$\text{Ѓ ѓ} = \acute{g}; \quad \text{Ќ ќ} = k'; \quad \text{Ѕ ѕ} = dz.$$

# GReek alphabet and transliteration

| Name of Letter | Greek Alphabet | | Transliteration |
|---|---|---|---|
| Alpha | A | α | a |
| Beta | B | β | v(b) |
| Gamma | Γ | γ | g |
| Delta | Δ | δ | d |
| Epsilon | E | ε | e |
| Zeta | Z | ζ | z |
| Eta | H | η | ē |
| Theta | Θ | θ | th |
| Iota | I | ι | i |
| Kappa | K | κ | k |
| Lambda | Λ | λ | l |
| Mu | M | μ | m |
| Nu | N | ν | n |
| Xi | Ξ | ξ | x |
| Omicron | O | o | o |
| Pi | Π | π | p |
| Rho | P | ρ | r |
| Sigma | Σ | σ | s |
| Tau | T | τ | t |
| Upsilon | Υ | υ | y |
| Phi | Φ | φ | ph |
| Chi | X | χ | ch |
| Psi | Ψ | ψ | ps |
| Omega | Ω | ω | ō |

Note: The letter group τκ (at the beginning of the word) is transliterated here as G; Mπ as B; and the diphthongs au, ευ, ηυ are rendered as au, eu, ēu. The Greek spiritus asper ʻ is expressed by the letter H. Occasional exceptions were thought indicated, particularly in the interest of expressing proper names more customarily.

# PART ONE

# OVERVIEW of the southeast european area

# 1

# GENERAL REFERENCE AIDS AND BIBLIOGRAPHIES*

*by Elizabeth Beyerly*

## A. BIBLIOGRAPHIC AIDS

### 1. Bibliography of Bibliographies

1. Borov, Todor, *and others.* Die Bibliographie in den europäischen Ländern der Volksdemokratie; Entwicklung und gegenwärtiger Stand. Leipzig, Verlag für Buch- und Bibliothekswesen, 1960. 165 p. (Bibliothekswissenschaftliche Arbeiten aus der Sowjetunion und den Ländern der Volksdemokratie in deutscher Übersetzung, Reihe B, 3)

An East German translation of a Bulgarian original. Analysis by country (except for Greece and Yugoslavia) of bibliographical work from 1918 to the late 1950s. Contains a list of useful current reference works, including selected subject bibliographies and indexing journals. An appendix lists bibliographies published in East Germany since 1945.

For a detailed discussion of the historical evolution of national bibliographies in Eastern Europe, *see*:

Natsional'naia bibliografiia v stranakh iugovostochnoi Evropy (The national bibliography in the countries of Southeastern Europe). *In* Simon, Konstantin R. Istoriia inostranoi bibliografii (History of foreign

---

* The arrangement in this chapter is by language and by chronological and topical affinity of the publications listed.

3

bibliography). Moskva, Izdatel'stvo Vsesoiuznoi knizhnoi palaty, 1963. p. 473-482.

2. In 1962-1963 the Library of the Academy of Sciences of the USSR and the Fundamental Library of Social Sciences cooperated in issuing bibliographies of bibliographies relating to Bulgaria, Czechoslovakia, Hungary, Poland, Romania, and Yugoslavia. The individual volumes are of 15 to 50 pages in length and list from 100 to 400 references to bibliographies published in these countries during 1945-1960. For the separate volumes relevant here, *see*:

Akademiia nauk SSSR. *Biblioteka.* Bibliografiia bolgarskikh bibliografii o Bolgarii; literatura, opublikovannaia v 1945-1960 gg. (Bibliography of Bulgarian bibliographies about Bulgaria; literature published in 1945-1960). Moskva, 1962. 23 p.

————. . . . iugoslavskikh bibliografii o Iugoslavii; . . . (. . . of Yugoslav bibliographies about Yugoslavia; . . .). Moskva, 1962. 19 p.

————. . . . rumynskikh bibliografii o Rumynii; . . . (of Romanian bibliographies about Romania; . . . ). Moskva, 1963. 15 p.

3. New York. Public Library. *Slavonic Division.* A Bibliography of Slavonic Bibliography in English. New York, New York Public Library, 1947. 11 p.
   Contains 14 general Slavic, 15 Czech, 16 Polish (as well as Russian) bibliographies of English-language references.

4. Teich, Gerhard. Bibliographie der Bibliographien Südosteuropas. Ein Beitrag zur Bibliographie über den Gesamtraum Südosteuropa sowie über Albanien, Griechenland und die Türkei. *In* Zotschev, Theodor, *ed.* Wirtschaftswissenschaftliche Südosteuropa-Forschung; Grundlagen und Erkenntnisse. München, Südosteuropa-Verlagsgesellschaft, 1963. p. 177-213.

## 2. Area Bibliographies

5. Novaia literatura po evropeiskim stranam narodnoi demokratii (New literature concerning the European countries of peoples' democracies). 1-12; 1948-1959. Moskva, Akademiia nauk SSSR. Monthly.
   International coverage, emphasizing works published in Eastern Europe, of monographs and journal articles concerning socio-economic, political, and cultural problems. Since 1960 this has been superseded by separate series for each of the East European countries, e.g.:
   Novaia literatura po Bolgarii (New literature on Bulgaria). 1960– Moskva. Monthly.
   Novaia literatura po Iugoslovii (. . . Yugoslavia). 1960– Moskva. Monthly.

Novaia literatura po Rumynii (. . . Romania). 1960– Moskva. Monthly.

*See also*, for publications of more general content:

Novaia literatura po obshchim voprosam evropeiskikh sotsialisticheskikh stran (New literature on the common problems of the European socialist countries). 1964– Moskva. Monthly.

Novaia literatura po obshchim problemam slavianovedeniia (New literature on general problems of Slavic studies). 1966– Moskva. 6 times yearly.

6. American Bibliography of Russian and East European Studies. 1956– Bloomington, Indiana University Press. Annual.

Title varies: 1956-1959, *American Bibliography of Slavic and East European Studies*. Lists titles of monographs and journal articles concerning the humanities and, since 1957, the social sciences, in the USSR and Eastern Europe in English (1956-1960 in the United States and Canada only, 1961– in English and published outside Eastern Europe) or written by persons living in the United States. Each volume appears approximately two years after the date to which it refers. Entries are grouped by broad subject arrangement. Author index.

Continues on a current basis the work by Robert F. Byrnes (*see* entry no. 15). A more restricted, specialized bibliography is:

U.S. *Department of State. Office of Intelligence Research and Analysis.* External Research: Eastern Europe. 1952-1968. Washington, D.C. Semiannual. The April issue lists research in progress and the October one, completed research. Publications principally in the field of international affairs, reporting results of research undertaken by private American scholars.

7. L'URSS et les pays de l'Est; revue des revues. 1– 1960– Paris, Centre Nationale de la Recherche Scientifique. Quarterly.

Appears in two parts. The first (Bulletin analytique) contains summaries of major articles published in Soviet and East European journals on legal, economic, and social problems. The second (Repertoire systematique) is an index to the contents of about 20 Soviet and 20 East European periodicals. Sponsored by the Centre de Recherche sur l'URSS et les pays de l'Est of the Université de Strasbourg. May be compared with *Notes et études documentaires*, issued since 1945 by the Direction de Documentation in Paris, certain numbers of which are devoted to Eastern Europe.

8. Turczynski, Emanuel. Deutsche Beiträge zur Geschichte und Landeskunde Südosteuropas. East European Quarterly, January, 1968: 297-340.

A knowledgeable and informative bibliographic essay surveying the more relevant German literature on a variety of aspects, past and present, of Southeastern Europe. *See also*:

Teich, Gerhard. Bibliographie der Bibliographien Südosteuropas. *See* entry no. 4.

9. Wissenschaftlicher Dienst Südosteuropa. 1– 1952– München, Südost-Institut. Monthly.

> German summaries and partial translations, mainly of articles published in Southeastern Europe, concerning current economic and political developments.

10. To supplement information in current bibliographies consult the extensive bibliographic sections and book reviews in the following journals: Canadian Slavic Studies. Revue canadienne d'études slaves. 1– 1967– Montreal, Loyola College. Quarterly.

> Revue des études slaves. 1921– Paris. Annual. This contains a "Chronique bibliographique" which lists monographs and journal articles in Eastern Europe and elsewhere, emphasizing language, literature, and historical topics.

> Slavic Review. 1940– Seattle, Washington. Quarterly. A subject, author, and book review index for the period 1941-1964 has been compiled by L. Charbonneau.

> Slavonic and East European Review. 1922– London. Semiannual. Contains many biographical references and extensive book reviews, largely of publications issued outside East Europe.

> Berlin. Freie Universität. *Osteuropa-Institut.* Bibliographische Mitteilungen, 1952– Irregular. Bibliographies on special subjects, including sciences and the humanities.

> Zeitschrift für Ostforschung. 1952– Marburg/Lahn, Johann Gottfried Herder-Institut. Quarterly.

> Osteuropa. 1951– Stuttgart, Deutsche Gesellschaft für Osteuropakunde. Monthly. This and the preceding publication contain numerous bibliographical references, chiefly to works in the German language.

11. Hillgruber, Andreas.   Südosteuropa im zweiten Weltkrieg; Literaturbericht und Bibliographie. Frankfurt am Main, Bernard und Graefe, 1962. 150 p. (Schriften der Bibliothek für Zeitgeschichte, 1)

> The bibliographic section lists about 2,000 titles of monographs and journal articles published both in Eastern Europe and elsewhere in the period 1945-1961. Emphasis is on the military and political aspects of Eastern Europe during the Second World War, especially on Germany's role in the area.

12. Moscow. Publichnaia biblioteka.   Strany Evropy. Chast' 1: Sotsialisticheskie strany; rekomendatel'nyi ukazatel' literatury (The countries of Europe. Part 1: The socialist countries; suggested reading list). Moskva, Kniga, 1965. 92 p.

> Contains 324 annotated references to monographs and journal articles published in the USSR and also in Eastern Europe in the period 1956 to 1964. Two-thirds of the references concern the humanities, and materials on social sciences are included only for the years 1962-

1964. An earlier edition, covering material published during 1945-1955, appeared as *Evropeiskie strany narodnoi demokratii na puti k sotsializmu; rekomendatel'nyi ukazatel' literatury* (The European peoples' democracies on the road to socialism; suggested reading list) (Moskva, 1956, 112 p.).

13. Südosteuropa-Bibliographie. Bd. 1– 1945/50– München, R. Oldenbourg, 1956–

*See also* entries no. 482 *and* 1540.

Each volume provides a five-year bibliographic survey of monographs and journals published in or relating to Eastern Europe. Volume 1 covered the period from 1945 to 1950, volume 2, 1951-1955, and volume 3, 1956-1960. Each volume consists of two parts, one listing materials on Slovakia, Romania, and Bulgaria, and the other on Yugoslavia, Hungary, Albania, and Southeast Europe as a whole. From 3,000 to 4,500 entries are contained in each volume, principally in the social sciences. Author indexes. *See also*:

Munich. Osteuropa-Institut. Ost- und Südosteuropa im westlichen Schrifttum der Nachkriegszeit; ein bibliographischer Leitfaden für Dozenten und Hörer an Volkshochschulen. München, Im Auftrage des Deutschen Volkshochschulverbandes und der Deutschen Gesellschaft für Osteuropakunde, 1956. 113 p. Annotated bibliography of materials on Eastern Europe published outside that area and intended for students and teachers of adult education. References are principally to German and English language materials.

14. East European Accessions Index. v. 1-11, 1951-1961. Washington, D.C., Library of Congress, 1951-1961. Monthly.

*See also* entries 36 *and* 1566.

While primarily an accessions index of monographs( 1944–) and journals (1950–) published in Eastern Europe and received by the Library of Congress and some 100 major American libraries, the index listed an annual average of 100,000 titles (in English translation) of monographs and of articles in journals published in the Baltic and East European countries. Arranged by country of publication, with subdivision by broad subject categories. Author indexes.

For general sources on serials, with abundant coverage of the area, see:

Union List of Serials in Libraries of the United States and Canada. 3d ed. Edited by Edna Brown Titus. New York, H. W. Wilson, 1965. 5 v.

List of the Serial Publications of Foreign Governments, 1815-1931. Edited by Winifred Gregory. New York, H. W. Wilson, 1932. 720 p.

15. Byrnes, Robert F. Bibliography of American Publications on East Central Europe, 1945-1957. Bloomington, Indiana, 1958. 213 p. (Indiana University Publications, Slavic and East European Series, 12)

*See also entry* no. 489.

Contains titles of about 2,800 monographs and journal articles published mainly in the United States, but with a few Canadian imprints, concerning East European humanities and to a lesser extent the social sciences. Arranged by country, with broad subject subdivisions. Author index. Continued by *American Bibliography of Russian and East European Studies* (see entry 6). Byrnes has also contributed to a selective listing of about 350 English language monographs on Eastern Europe considered important for American colleges and universities in:

American Universities Field Staff. A Select Bibliography: Asia, Africa, Eastern Europe, Latin America. New York, 1960. p. 325-353. Additional entries on Eastern Europe are included in supplements which appeared in 1961, 1963, 1965, and 1967.

Other English language materials from the late 1950s to mid-1960s may be found in the bibliographic section of *Focus on Eastern Europe* (see entry 45).

16. Spector, Sherman D. *and* Lyman Legters. Checklist of Paperbound Books on Russia and East Europe. Albany, University of the State of New York, 1966. 79 p.

Pages 53-72 list publications relating to Eastern Europe.

17. Halpern, Joel M., John A. McKinstry, *and* Dalip Saund. Bibliography of Anthropological and Sociological Publications on Eastern Europe and the USSR (English Language Sources). Los Angeles, Russian and East European Studies Center, University of California, 1961. 142 p. (Russian and East European Studies Center Series, v. 1, no. 2)

About one-third of the monographs and journal articles listed refer to the ecology, archaeology, linguistics, and social change of the Slavs and the peoples of the Balkans. Materials are mostly from the late 1940s through the 1950s. For a bibliography on Slavic civilization containing references in German, Russian, and other Slavic languages, *see*:

Adamczyk, A. Literaturübersicht. *In*: Diels, Paul. Die slavischen Völker. Wiesbaden, O. Harrassowitz, 1963. p. 311-357.

A similar bibliographic survey is:

Lencek, Rado L. A Bibliographical Guide to the Literature on Slavic Civilization. New York, Columbia University, Department of Slavic Languages, 1966. 52 p.

18. Sztachova, Jirina. Mid-Europe; a Selective Bibliography. New York, Mid-European Studies Center, 1953. 197 p.

Contains mainly titles of monographs published in West European languages in the period from 1930 to the 1950s concerning the political, historical, and, to a lesser degree, economic development of Eastern Europe. Arranged by broad subjects, with subdivision by countries. Author index. For a bibliography of unpublished works sponsored by the Mid-European Studies Center, *see*:

Free Europe Committee. Index to Unpublished Studies Prepared for Free Europe Committee, Inc.; Studies 1-378. New York, 1958.

21 p. The index is also included as part of the February 1953 issue of the *East European Accessions Index (see* entry 14). Arranged numerically by author and subject of reports. May also be compared with the *External Research: Eastern Europe* (entry 6), issued by the State Department.

19. U.S. *Library of Congress. Division of Bibliography.* The Balkans; a Selected List of References. Compiled by Helen Conover. Washington, D.C., 1943. 5 v.

About 2,400 references, mostly to monographs published in Western European languages during the years 1918-1940 and available in American libraries. One volume lists material on the Balkans as a whole and the others treat separately of Albania, Bulgaria, Romania, and Yugoslavia. Author and subject index.

20. Savadjian, Léon, *ed.* Bibliographic balkanique. Paris, Revue des Balkans, 1931-1939. 8 v.

Contains entries, a few of which are annotated, for French, English, Italian, and German monographs and journal articles published in the Balkan countries as well as elsewhere in the period 1920-1938, chiefly on historical and political subjects. Includes some information on socioeconomic, statistical, and biographical problems and on general reference works. May be used in conjunction with the German *Bibliographische Vierteljahrshefte der Weltkriegsbücherei* for the years 1934-1944. Also to be noted is:

Howard, H. Essai d'une bibliographie américaine sur les Balkans. Les Balkans (Athens), no. 1, 1930: 462-471.

For a bibliography of contemporary writings on the Balkans up to the Second World War *see*:

Bibliographie d'études balkaniques. 1966– Sofia, Académie des sciences, Institut d'études balkaniques, 1968–. Inaugurating a planned annual bibliography this 347-page volume was prepared under the chief editorship of Professor Nikolai Todorov by his associates at the Institute of Balkan Studies in Sofia. The focus is on books and articles published in 1966 in numerous countries and languages, primarily on the history, humanities, and legal developments in the Balkan countries from the fifteenth century up to the beginning of the Second World War. The 1,951 entries are organized according to the International Decimal Classification System. Indexes of persons and of subjects and geographic names are appended. This publication provides a very useful documentation aid for the study of Balkan affairs.

21. Breslau. Osteuropa-Institut. Osteuropäische Bibliographie. Breslau, Pribatsch's Buchhandlung, 1921-1928. Annual.

*See also* entry no. 1528.

Lists titles of monographs and journal articles in Russian and the languages of Western and Eastern Europe published in 1920-1923. Author indexes.

22. Kerner, Robert J. Slavic Europe; a Selected Bibliography in the West-

ern European Languages, Comprising History, Languages and Literatures. Cambridge, Harvard University Press, 1918. 402 p.

Of the 4,500 entries, mostly for monographs published before 1914, approximately 2,800 refer to Slavic languages (other than Russian), literature, and history. Titles are those of monographs published prior to 1914. Arranged by ethnic group, with subject subdivisions. Author index.

## 3. Dictionaries

23. Bibliographie der Wörterbücher erschienen in der Deutschen Demokratischen Republik, Rumänischen Volksrepublik, Tschechoslowakischen Sozialistischen Republik, Ungarischen Volksrepublik, Union der Sozialistischen Sowjetrepubliken, Volksrepublik Bulgarien, Volksrepublik China, Volksrepublik Polen, 1945-1961. Edited by D. Rymsza-Zalewska and I. Siedlecka. Warszawa, Wydawnictwa Naukowo-Techniczne, 1965. 248 p.

In two sections, the first of which lists monolingual, and the second, bilingual dictionaries. Entries are arranged by Universal Decimal Classification. Language, author, subject, and title indexes. Editorial material in Russian and German. Supplement: *Bibliographie der Wörterbücher . . . , 1962-1964* (Warszawa, Wydawnictwa Naukowo-Techniczne, 1968, 166 p.)

24. Lewanski, Richard C.   A Bibliography of Slavic Dictionaries. New York, New York Public Library, 1959-1963. 3 v. (Contents: v. 1: Polish; v. 2: Belorussian, Bulgarian, Czech, Kashubian, Lusatian, Old Church Slavic, Macedonian, Polabian, Serbocroatian, Slovak, Slovenian, Ukrainian; v. 3: Russian)

Each volume lists monolingual and multilingual dictionaries, as well as dictionaries of abbreviations, pseudonyms, slang, and dialects. Author and subject indexes. *See also*:

Kiss, L.   Die erklärenden Wörterbücher der slawischen Sprachen. Studia Slavica (Budapest), v. 9, 1963: 74-122. Analysis of outstanding monolingual dictionaries published by national academies in the Slavic countries.

## 4. Bibliographies of Serials

25. For lists of periodicals published in the countries and languages of Eastern Europe, *see*:

U.S. *Bureau of the Census.*   Bibliography of Social Science Periodicals and Monograph Series: Albania, 1944-1961. Washington, D.C., 1962. 12 p. (Foreign Social Science Bibliographies. Series P-92, no. 6)
*See also* entry no. 272.

————. Bibliography of Social Science Periodicals and Monograph Series: Bulgaria, 1944-1960. Washington, D.C., 1961. 36 p. (Foreign Social Science Bibliographies. Series P-92, no. 2)
*See also* entry no. 488.

————.   Bibliography of Social Science Periodicals and Monograph

Series: Rumania, 1947-1960. Washington, D.C., 1961. 27 p. (Foreign Social Science Bibliographies. Series P-92, no. 1)
*See also* entry no. 1546.

————. Bibliography of Social Science Periodicals and Monograph Series: Yugoslavia, 1945-1963. Washington, D.C., 1965. 152 p. (Foreign Social Science Bibliographies. Series P-92, no. 18)

For each volume, titles of periodicals published after the Second World War are arranged under broad subject headings in the social sciences. Each volume contains subject, title, author, and issuing agency indexes.

26. U.S. *Library of Congress. Slavic and Central European Division.* The USSR and Eastern Europe: Periodicals in Western Languages. Compiled by Paul L. Horecky and Robert G. Carlton. 3d ed. Washington, D.C., 1967. 89 p.

Entries are grouped by country and include English and other West European language periodicals issued in the East European countries as well as those appearing elsewhere which refer to these countries. All subjects, with the exclusion of those in the natural or technical sciences, are included. Library of Congress call numbers are given, as are addresses of publishers.

27. For a short-title list of periodicals published in Eastern Europe and of Western periodicals concerning Eastern Europe which are available in British libraries, *see*:

Fyfe, J., *comp.* List of Current Acquisitions of Periodicals and Newspapers Dealing With the Soviet Union and the East European Countries. Economics of Planning (Oslo), v. 4, 1964: 185-199. *See also*:

Eckhardt, T. Balkanzeitschriften. *In*: Österreichische Osthefte, v. 9, 1967: 230-233. Analysis of French and English language publications in Greece, Bulgaria, and Romania dealing with Balkan topics. Similar information for the period prior to the Second World War may be found in the *Bibliographie balkanique* (v. 1, p. 10, 218; v. 2, p. 93) (*see* entry 20).

28. U.S. *Library of Congress. Slavic and Central European Division.* Newspapers of East Central and Southeastern Europe in the Library of Congress. Edited by Robert G. Carlton. Washington, D.C., 1965. 204 p.

*See also* entry no. 1547.

Entries are arranged by country and include about 800 newspaper titles published in Eastern Europe and available in the Library of Congress. Place, language, and title indexes.

A shorter list of holdings is:

Periodicals and Newspapers Concerning East-Central and East Europe in the Library of the Hoover Institution on War, Revolution, and Peace, 1958; a Checklist. Stanford University, 1958. 22 p. This mimeographed list includes brief titles of 314 journals and newspapers, many published outside East Europe, largely by émigré groups.

29. Paris. Bibliothèque nationale. *Département des périodiques.* Périodiques slaves en caractères cyrilliques; état des collections en 1950. Edited and compiled by E. Belin de Ballu. Paris, 1956. 2 v. Supplément, 1951-1960. Paris, 1963. 497 p. Addendum et errata: Paris, 1965. 223 p.

> The list, predominantly of Russian language periodicals, also includes titles of Bulgarian and Serbian periodicals available in Paris libraries. A partial continuation of:
> Unbegaun, Boris O. Catalogue des périodiques slaves et relatifs aux études slaves des bibliothèques de Paris. Paris, Champion, 1929. 221 p.

30. Current periodicals concerning the whole of Eastern Europe or the Balkans include:

> Balkan Studies. 1960– Thessaloniké. Semiannual.
> *See also* entries no. 1004 *and* 1204.
>
> East European Quarterly. 1967– Boulder, Colorado, University of Colorado. Quarterly.
>
> Études balkaniques. 1965– Sofiia. Irregular.
>
> Les études balkaniques tchécoslovaques. 1966– Prague, Universita Karlova. Irregular.
>
> Revue des études sud-est européennes. 1963– Bucureşti. Quarterly (irregular).
>
> Zeitschrift für Balkanologie. 1962– Wiesbaden, Harrassowitz. Semiannual.
>
> Südost-Forschungen. 1936– München. Annual.
>
> Südosteuropa-Jahrbuch. 1957– München. Annual.
>
> Österreichische Ost-Hefte. Mitteilungsorgan der Arbeitsgemeinschaft Ost. 1959– Wien. Bimonthly.
>
> Ost-Probleme. 1949– Bonn. Biweekly (weekly until 1956).

## 5. Dissertations

31. Dossick, Jesse J. Doctoral Dissertations on Russia, the Soviet Union, and Eastern Europe Accepted by American, Canadian, and British Universities. Slavic Review, v. 24, 1965: 752-761; v. 25, 1966: 710-717; v. 26, 1967: 705-712.

> Lists about 50 theses concerning the humanities and social sciences in Eastern Europe. No such coverage available before 1965, but compare with:
> Aronson, H. I. American Doctoral Dissertations in the Fields of Slavic and East European Languages. Slavic Review, v. 22, 1963: 1-8, 449-450. Lists 139 theses presented in the United States from 1921 to 1961.

In general, dissertations in the field of Slavic languages and literatures and in the fields of East European history should be approached through the relevant subject bibliographies.

32. Hanusch, G.   Osteuropa-Dissertationen. Jahrbücher für Geschichte Osteuropas, Neue Folge. v. 1, 1953, no. 4, supplement: 1-44; v. 2, 1954, no. 2, supplement: 45-72; v. 3, 1955, no. 1, supplement: 74-114; v. 4, 1956, no. 3, supplement: 115-152; v. 6, 1958, no. 4, supplement: 153-194; v. 8, 1960, no. 2, supplement: 195-239.

Theses in all fields of the humanities and social sciences submitted to German-speaking universities in Western Europe and to universities in Northern Europe and the United States during 1945-1960.

## 6. Library Catalogs, Services, and Accession Records

33. Cyrillic Union Catalog in Microprint. New York, Readex Microprint Corp., 1962.

A microprint reproduction of the Cyrillic Union Catalog of the Library of Congress, listing monographs in Russian, Ukrainian, Belorussian, Bulgarian, and Serbian, reported as of 1956 by 186 cooperating libraries in the United States and Canada. Entries arranged separately by author, subject, and title.

34. New York. Public Library. *Slavonic Division.*   Dictionary Catalog of the Slavonic Collection of the New York Public Library. Boston, G. K. Hall, 1959. 26 v.

A photographic reproduction of the original catalog entries, 60 percent of which are in the Cyrillic alphabet, mainly in the fields of Slavic languages and literature. Included are many translations from Slavic languages and original works in Western languages, as well as references to journal articles not indexed elsewhere. Alphabetical arrangement by authors, titles, and subjects. *See also*:

Rosenthal, H.   A List of Russian, Other Slavonic, and Baltic Periodicals in the New York Public Library. *In*: New York. Public Library. Bulletin, v. 20, 1916: 339-372.

35. Jena. Universität. Bibliothek.   Slavica-Auswahl-Katalog der Universitätsbibliothek Jena; ein Hilfsbuch für Slawisten und Germanoslavica-Forscher. Edited by O. Feyl. Weimar, H. Böhlaus Nachfolger, 1956-1959. 2 v. in 3. (Claves Jenenses, 4-6)

A similar East German catalog of Slavic holdings is:

Gotha (City). *Landesbibliothek.*   Slavica Katalog der Landesbibliothek Gotha. Edited by Helmut Claus. Berlin, Akademie Verlag, 1961. 531 p. (Quellen und Studien zur Geschichte Osteuropas, Bd. 10)

In West Germany there is:

Johann Gottfried Herder-Institut, *Marburg. Bibliothek.*   Bibliothek des Johann Gottfried Herder-Instituts; alphabetischer Katalog. Boston, G. K. Hall, 1964. 5 v. A photographic reproduction of a catalog which includes numerous East European, particularly Slavic, monographs and journals, reflecting in part the holdings of the former Preussische Staatsbibliothek in Berlin.

36. Accession Records: Supplementing the regular Slavica catalogs of the various libraries are the accession lists reporting new additions both of monographs and journals published in the countries of Eastern Europe. Such lists include:

> East European Accessions Index. Washington, D.C., Library of Congress. Monthly. v. 1-11, 1951-1961. *See also* entries no. 14 *and* 1566.

> British Museum. *Department of Printed Books.*   Catalogue of Printed Books. Accessions: Slavonic, Hungarian, etc. London, 1931-1947.

> Munich. Bayerische Staatsbibliothek.   Slavica Neuerwerbungen. 1– 1950– Annual.

> Berliner Titeldrucke. Neue Folge. Zugänge aus der Sowjetunion und den europäischen Ländern der Volksdemokratie. Berlin, Deutsche Staatsbibliothek, 1954-1959. 6 v. in 5.

37. Library Service: Moscow. Publichnaia biblioteka. Biblioteko-vedenie i bibliografiia za rubezhom (Library service and bibliography outside of the USSR). 1958– Irregular.

> Numbers 1-2, 5-6, 8, 10, and 20 deal with library service in various countries of Eastern Europe and describe cooperation of these countries with the USSR in library matters. *See also*:
> Moscow. Vsesoiuznaia gosudarstvennaia biblioteka inostrannoi literatury.   Inostrannye periodicheskie izdaniia po bibliografii i bibliotekovedeniiu, imeiushchiesia v bibliotekakh Moskvy i Leningrada (Foreign bibliography and library service journals available in the libraries of Moscow and Leningrad). Moscow, Vsesoiuznaia knizhnaia palata, 1959. 169 p. Includes most East European publications in the field. Arranged alphabetically. Country and subject indexes.

38. Buist, Eleanor, *and* Robert F. Byrnes.   Area Programs for the Soviet Union and East Europe; Some Current Concern of the Libraries. *In*: Chien, Ts'un-hsün, *and* H. W. Winger, *eds.* Area Studies and the Library. Proceedings of the 30th Annual Conference of the University of Chicago Graduate Library School, May 20-22, 1965. Chicago, University of Chicago Press, 1966. p. 108-127.

> Cooperation among the libraries of the countries of Eastern Europe is discussed in:
> Lavrova, M. A.   Mezhdunarodnaia bibliograficheskaia konferentsiia v Varshave (The international bibliographic conference in Warsaw). Sovetskaia bibliografiia, vyp. 49, 1958: 84-89.

39. Kjellberg, Lennert.   Slavistik för bibliotekarier. Lund, Distribution Bibliotekstjänst, 1963. 76 p. (Svenska bibliotekariesamfundet. Skriftserie, 5)

> Useful information for librarians on Cyrillic script and on title description of Slavic imprints and series. Includes a brief comparative

morphology of Slavic languages. G. G. Firsov's article "Tsentralizo-vannaia katalogizatsiia v sotsialisticheskikh stranakh" (Centralized cataloging in the socialist countries), *Sovetskaia bibliografiia*, vyp. 45, 1957, p. 91-101, discusses cataloging rules and printed catalogs in Eastern Europe.

## B. THE STATE OF AREA RESEARCH

### 1. Bibliographies

40. Hillgruber, Andreas.    Literaturbericht. *In his*: Südosteuropa im zwei-ten Weltkrieg; Literaturbericht und Bibliographie. Frankfurt am Main, Bernard und Graefe, 1962. p. 11-35.

Contains information on research concerning the area of Southeast Europe conducted in both Western and Eastern Europe and in the United States. The emphasis is on research from a military and politi-cal viewpoint operative through the Second World War. For addi-tional information concerning Slavic research *see*:

Kaloeva, I. A., *comp.*    Sovetskoe slavianovedenie; literatura o zarubezhnykh slavianskikh stranakh na russkom iazyke, 1918-1960 (Soviet Slavic research; literature about other Slavic countries in Rus-sian). Moskva, Izd-vo Akademii nauk SSSR, 1963. 401 p. Covers the literature published during 1918-1960, with a supplement for the years 1961-1962. More than 10,000 entries referring to scholarly works on area study, including the Soviet approach to theoretical problems of world socialism and international scholarly cooperation as well as many references to political, economic, and cultural affairs in the in-dividual Slavic countries. Includes a section on reference works and bibliographies. Author index.

For a bibliography of Balkan studies in Czechoslovakia *see*:

Bibliographie des études balkaniques en Tchécoslovaquie 1945-1965. Bibliografie československé balkanistiky 1945-1965. Prague, Akadémie tchécoslovaque des sciences, Institut d'histoire des pays socialistes européens, 1966. 117 p.

Cronia, Arturo.    La conoscenza del mondo Slavo in Italia; bilancia storico-bibliografico di un millennio. Padova, Officine grafiche Stediv, 1958. 792 p. Bibliography of Italian works on Slavic research and area study.

## 2. Analyses, Guides, and Surveys of Library Collections

41. Ornstein, Jacob.    Slavic and East European Studies; Their Develop-ment and Status in the Western Hemisphere. Washington, D.C., De-partment of State, External Research Staff, Office of Intelligence Research, 1957. 65 p. Bibliography: p. 61-65. (External Research Paper, no. 129)

Contains analysis mainly of the state of Slavic language study, largely in the United States. Additional relevant information is contained in:

Manning, Clarence A.    A History of Slavic Studies in the United States. Milwaukee, Marquette University Press, 1957. 117 p. Bibliography: p. 109-113. (Marquette Slavic Studies, 3) Deals with the evolution of area study in the United States, primarily in the period before the Second World War.

Horna, Dagmar, ed. Current Research on Central and Eastern Europe. New York, Mid-European Studies Center, Free Europe Committee, 1956. 251 p. (Mid-European Studies Center Publication no. 28) Survey of the nature and extent of area study between the end of the Second World War and 1955, emphasizing work conducted by the Mid-European Studies Center. Lists 1,400 topics, mostly in history and politics.

A major survey, prepared by leading American scholars and edited by Charles Jelavich, is scheduled for publication in 1969 by the University of Chicago Press under the title: *Area and Language Studies: East Central and Southeastern Europe.*

42. U.S. *Department of State. External Research Staff.* Language and Area Study Programs in American Universities. Washington, D.C., 1964. p. 99-124.

A summary of the area study programs at the graduate level which are offered by American universities.

Analyses of area study programs in the United States are also contained in reports issued by separate institutions. *See*, among others:

Smal-Stocki, Roman. The Slavic Institute of Marquette University, 1949-1961. Milwaukee, Wisconsin, Slavic Institute, Marquette University, 1963. 37 p. (Marquette University, Milwaukee. Slavic Institute. Papers, no. 11)

Thomson, J. M., ed. Report on Research and Publications, 1947-1962. Bloomington, Indiana, Russian and East European Institute, 1963. 39 p.

43. For guides to and surveys of area studies in a number of the countries of Europe, *see*:

Bulgaria:

Savova, Elena, ed. Les études balkaniques et sud-est européennes en Bulgarie; guide de documentation. Sofia, Académie bulgare des sciences, Bibliothèque centrale, 1966. 184 p. *See also* entries no. 510 *and* 894. Basically a guide to the structure and administration of the general research activities of the Bulgarian Academy of Sciences and of institutions of higher learning, to archives, museums, libraries, and documentation centers, and to Bulgarian reference works. The guide is the result of a series of suggestions by the International Committee of the International Association for the Study of South-East Europe. A similar guide for Romania is understood to be planned for 1968.

Great Britain:

Jopson, N. B., *and others.* The School of Slavonic and East European Studies; the First Forty Years, 1922-1962. Slavonic and East European Review, 1966, no. 102: 1-30.

Germany (West):

Berlin, Freie Universität. *Osteuropa-Institut.* Tätigkeitsbericht, 1951-1966. Berlin, 1967. 59 p. A description of the work of this institute, together with lists of its publications and of the activities of its staff members. The institute's publications are also described in its *Veröffentlichungen, 1952-1967* (Berlin, 1967, 26 p.).

Deutsche Gesellschaft für Osteuropakunde. Fünfzig Jahre Osteuropa-Studien; zur Geschichte der Deutschen Gesellschaft zum Studium Osteuropas und der Deutschen Gesellschaft für Osteuropakunde. Stuttgart, 1963. 48 p. The evolution of the society's research from 1913 to 1945 and from its reconstitution under a somewhat different name in 1949 to 1963. Contains a list of the society's publications and of its annual conferences. *See also*:

Hacker, Jens. Osteuropa-Forschung in der Bundesrepublik. Das Parlament. Beilage "Aus Politik und Zeitgeschichte," September 14, 1960: 591-622.

Munich. Osteuropa-Institut. Studienführer durch die Münchener Institutionen der Ost- und Südosteuropaforschung. München, Sagner, 1967. 104 p.

Romania:

Cândea, V. Les études sud-est européennes en Roumanie. Bucarest, Comité national roumain d'études du Sud-Est européen, 1966. 266 p.

Switzerland:

La Suisse, l'URSS et l'Europe Orientale. Revue économique et sociale (Lausanne). Numéro spécial, avril 1963. 164 p.

44. For descriptions of collections and facilities in various libraries with Slavic and East European collections *see* especially:

Horecky, Paul L. The Slavic and East European Resources and Facilities in the Library of Congress. Slavic Review, v. 23, 1964: 309-327.

Pulaska, Jadwiga. The Slavonic Division of the New York Public Library. New York, 1953. 52 p.

Mach, Otto. Osteuropa-Dokumentation; ein Ausschnitt aus der Sondersammlungsarbeit. Dokumentation, Fachbibliothek, Werksbücherei, v. 7, 1958, no. 2: 60-63. Describes the East European resources of the Bayerische Staatsbibliothek.

Lewanski, Richard C. European Library Directory. Florence, Leo S. Olschki, 1967. 774 p. The arrangement is geographical, by country, and then by city. Contains detailed coverage of East Central European (Southeast European) countries.

45. Focus on Eastern Europe. Intercom, v. 7, no. 4, 1965. 64 p.

Concise guide to recent U.S. ideas, programs, public opinion, teaching aids, and services in the field of Eastern Europe. Includes bibliography.

46. Ruggles, Melville, *and* Vaclav Mostecky. Russian and East European Publications in the Libraries of the United States. New York, Columbia University Press, 1960. 396 p. (Columbia University Studies in Library Service, 11)

Quantitative analysis of American library resources, including suggestions for possible improvement of existing service. *See also*:
Ash, Lee.   Subject Collections. New York, Bowker, 1961. p. 203.
A survey of East European materials in American libraries.

## C. REFERENCE AIDS FOR AREA STUDIES

### 1. General Surveys, Handbooks, and Encyclopedias

47. Savadjian, Léon, *ed*.   Encyclopédie balkanique permanente. Paris, Société génerale d'imprimerie et d'édition, 1936. 1 v.

Contains historical, political, and socioeconomic information for Albania, Bulgaria, Greece, Romania, Turkey, and Yugoslavia. Arranged by countries. Based on Eastern and Western European sources, including many not available in the United States. Subject index.

48. Byrnes, Robert F., *ed*.   The United States and Eastern Europe. Englewood Cliffs, N.J., Prentice-Hall, 1967. 176 p. Maps.

A panoramic view of the major aspects of domestic and foreign affairs, present and past, of the eight European countries with communist-type governments. This collection of eight essays, authored by distinguished experts in the respective fields, was prepared as a background for American Assembly meetings on this subject throughout the United States.

49. Fischer-Galati, Stephen, *ed*.   Eastern Europe in the Sixties. New York, Praeger, 1963. 239 p. (Praeger Publications in Russian History and World Communism, no. 137)

*See also* entries no. 144 and 221.

Essays by 10 specialists on social, economic, domestic, and international political problems. For similar information published in Great Britain and France, *see*:

Singleton, Frederick B.   Background to Eastern Europe. Oxford, New York, Pergamon Press, 1965. 226 p.

Paraf, P.   Les démocraties populaires: Albanie, Bulgarie, Hongrie, Pologne, Roumanie, Tchechoslovaquie, Yougoslavie, République Démocratique Allemande. Paris, Payot, 1962. 229 p.

50. Liess, Otto R.   Südosteuropa. Befund und Deutung. Wien, Wollzeilen Verlag, 1968. 399 p. Maps, bibliography.

A rather elementary and chatty though informative survey.

51. Markert, Werner, *ed*.   Jugoslawien. Köln, Böhlau, 1954. 400 p. (Osteuropa-Handbuch, 1) Bibliography: p. 353-372.

*See also* entry no. 2176.

This handbook provides an extensive geographical, economic, historical, and social survey of Yugoslavia, principally in the period after the Second World War, based on literature from Eastern and Western Europe and the United States. *See also*:

Südosteuropa-Jahrbuch. 1957– München, R. Oldenbourg. Annual

contributions by experts, primarily relating to cultural, historical, and socioeconomic problems. Reflect reports presented to the Internationale Hochschulwoche sponsored by the Südosteuropa-Gesellschaft.

Matl, Josef. Südslawische Studien. München, R. Oldenbourg, 1965. 598 p. (Südosteuropäische Arbeiten, 63)

Britz, N., ed. Wiener Südostbuch. 1959– Wien, Wiener Forschungsstelle der Österreicher aus dem Donau-, Sudeten- und Karpatenraum. Annual. Relates principally to cultural and historical ties between Austria-Hungary and the Slavs of Eastern Europe.

52. Strakhovsky, Leonid, ed.   A Handbook of Slavic Studies. Cambridge, Mass., Harvard University Press, 1949. 753 p.

Chapters written by specialists, chiefly on the history and literature of the Slavs. Intended for the reader not familiar with the Slavic languages. Includes bibliographies of materials in Western European languages and a comparative historical chronology. See also:

Rouček, Joseph S.   Slavonic Encyclopedia. New York, Philosophical Library, 1949. 1445 p. Alphabetically arranged, unsigned articles, mainly of historical and biographical value. No bibliographies. Based, as is Strakhovsky, on data through the mid-1940s.

For English-language data of the mid- and late 1930s, see:

Handbook of Central and East Europe. Zürich, Central European Times Publishing Co., 1932-1937. 6 v.

Royal Institute of International Affairs. Information Department. South-Eastern Europe; a Political and Economic Survey. London, 1939. 203 p. Illus., maps, diagrs.

For data of the 1920s, see:

Great Britain. Foreign Office. Historical Section.   Handbooks. Prepared under the Direction of the Historical Section of the Foreign Office . . . London, His Majesty's Stationery Office. 1920. Numbers 2, 3, 5-8, 11-14, 17-23, 43-46, and 51 of this series, which are often known as the "Peace Handbooks," are devoted to the countries and areas of Eastern Europe.

53. Petrov, Fedor N., ed.   Balkanskie strany (The Balkan countries). Moskva, Sovetskaia entsiklopediia, 1946. 548 p.

Information on economics, history, population, nationalities, and languages, based mostly on Russian data of the years between the First and Second World Wars. For a Yugoslav view, mainly historical and cultural, see:

Balkanski institut, Beograd.   Knjiga o Balkanu (A book about the Balkans). Beograd, Izdanje Balkanskog instituta, 1936-1937. 2 v. Illus., maps, ports.

## 2. Guidebooks and Gazetteers

54. The geographical names of places in Eastern Europe employed by agencies of the United States government may be found in:

U.S. Office of Geography.   Albania; Official Standard Names Approved by the United States Board on Geographic Names. 2d ed.

Washington, D.C., U.S. Government Printing Office, 1961. 207 p. (U.S. Board on Geographic Names. Gazetteer no. 8)

————. Bulgaria; Official Standard Names Approved by the United States Board on Geographic Names. Washington, D.C., U.S. Government Printing Office, 1959. 293 p. (U.S. Board on Geographic Names. Gazetteer no. 44)

————. Greece; Official Standard Names Approved by the United States Board on Geographic Names. Washington, D.C., U.S. Government Printing Office, 1955. 404 p. (U.S. Board on Geographic Names. Gazetteer no. 11)
See also entry no. 971.

————. Rumania; Official Standard Names Approved by the United States Board on Geographic Names. Washington, D.C., U.S. Government Printing Office, 1960. 450 p. (U.S. Board on Geographic Names. Gazetteer no. 48)
See also entry no. 1582.

————. Yugoslavia; Official Standard Names Approved by the United States Board on Geographic Names. Washington, D.C., U.S. Government Printing Office, 1961. 495 p. (U.S. Board on Geographic Names. Gazetteer no. 55)

55. Kane, Robert S.   Eastern Europe, A to Z; Bulgaria, Czechoslovakia, East Germany, Hungary, Poland, Romania, Yugoslavia, and the Soviet Union. Garden City, N.Y., Doubleday, 1968. 348 p. Maps.
An up-to-date travel guide written in somewhat breezy style and intended primarily for the American tourist with little or no knowledge of the area.
Other tourist and background information is contained in the richly illustrated *Yugoslavia, Rumania, Bulgaria, Albania* volume of the "Illustrated Library of the World and Its Peoples" series (New York, Greystone Press, 1965, 216 p.).
For the period prior to the Second World War, *see* the following volume of the French "Guide bleu" series:
Monmarché, Marcel.   Roumanie, Bulgarie, Turquie. Paris, Hachette, 1933. 702 p. Illus., maps.

## 3. Congresses and Meetings

There is no bibliography of congresses exclusively devoted to the area of Eastern Europe and the Balkans. A selected list of published proceedings of such meetings is offered here, including both national and international gatherings.

56. Balkanologen-Tagung, *Munich, 1962*.   Die Kultur Südosteuropas: ihre Geschichte und ihre Ausdrucksformen. Wiesbaden, O. Harrassowitz; München, Südosteuropa-Verlagsgesellschaft, 1964. 337 p. Illus., maps. (Südosteuropa-Schriften, Bd. 6)

*See also* entry no. 245.

Reports in German, English, French, or Italian. Includes bibliographical references. The cultural, mainly linguistic, problems of the Balkans are stressed in:

Colloque internationale de civilisations balkaniques, *Sinaia, Rumania, 1962.*    Actes. Organisé par la Commission nationale roumaine pour l'UNESCO . . . n.p., UNESCO, 1962. 210 p.

57. In 1966, the first Congrès international des études balkaniques et sud-est européennes met in Sofia under the sponsorship of the Association internationale d'études du sud-est européen. The proceedings of this congress have been published as *Resumés des communications* . . . (Sofia, 1966–). The parent organization also publishes a quarterly *Bulletin.*

The International Congress of Slavists meets every five years. The fifth congress was held in Sofia in 1963 and the sixth in Prague in 1968. Its work is chiefly devoted to the problems of individual and comparative linguistics and to literature.

Conferences are also held by national organizations concerned with East European or Slavic studies. In the United States, the American Association for the Advancement of Slavic Studies holds a conference every three years, and a number of its regional bodies meet in the intervals. In West Germany the Südosteuropa-Gesellschaft meets in its annual conference (Tagung), the papers of which are published as the *Südosteuropa-Jahrbuch* (*see* entry 65).

## 4. Reproductions and Translations

58. Ouvrages cyrilliques concernant les sciences sociales et humaines; liste des reproductions disponibles. Paris, Mouton, 1964-1965. 2 v. (Cahiers du monde russe et soviétique. Supplément, 1-2)

Although predominantly devoted to material in the Russian language, Supplement 2 also lists publications in Bulgarian and Serbian, copies of which are available in photographic reproduction or in microforms.

59. Materials published in Eastern Europe are made available in other languages through a number of translation services. No such service in the United States deals exclusively with East European sources. However, extensive translations may be found in:

U.S. *Joint Publications Research Service.*    Selected Translations from East European Political Journals and Newspapers. 1958– Irregular. (*Its* JPRS/DC)

———.    Political Translations on Eastern Europe. 1962– Irregular. Emphasis on political and military problems, industrial development, and economics. Distribution of these reports in the United States is the subject of:

Lucas, R., *and* G. Caldwell. JPRS Translations. College and Research Libraries, v. 25, 1964: 103-110. For guides to the contents of JPRS publications, *see*:

East Europe; a Bibliography-Index. 1962– New York, Research and Microfilm Publications. Monthly. Formerly issued in Annapolis, Md., by T. E. Kyriak, this is "a complete bibliographic listing of the most recent JPRS translations relevant to . . . Albania, Bulgaria, Czechoslovakia, East Germany, Hungary, Poland, Romania and Yugoslavia."

A numerical index to the microprinted JPRS reports is provided by M. E. Poole's *Index to Readex Microprint Edition of JPRS Reports* (New York, Readex Microprint Corporation, 1964, 137 p.).

60. Material from Eastern Europe relating to the social sciences is also made available by the International Arts and Sciences Press of White Plains, New York. Journals and monographs published by this firm are listed in its catalog, *Translations in the Social Sciences* (White Plains, New York, 1967, 24 p.).

For English-language summaries from the press of Southeastern Europe, *see*:

U.S. *Joint Publications Research Service.* Press Information Report on Albania. 1960– Washington, D.C., Irregular.

————. Summary of the Bulgarian Provincial Press. 1958– Washington, D.C. Biweekly.

Rumanian Press Review. 1946– Bucharest. Irregular. Published by the U.S. and British Embassies.
*See also* entry no. 1569.

U.S. *Joint Publications Research Service.* Summary of the Rumanian Provincial Press. 1958– Washington, D.C., Weekly.

Joint Translation Service. Summary of the Yugoslav Press. 1949– Belgrade. Daily.

61. Wiener Quellenhefte zur Ostkunde. Reihe: 1. Kultur; 2. Landeskunde; 3. Recht; 4. Technik; 5. Wirtschaft. 1958-1968. Wien, Arbeitsgemeinschaft Ost. Quarterly.

German translations, chiefly from journal articles published in the USSR and Eastern Europe. Extensive bibliographical citations from the original sources.

For journals devoted primarily to abstracts and summaries of Eastern European publications, *see* entries 7 and 9.

## 5. Publishing and Copyright

62. Böhmer, Alois. Copyright in the USSR and Other European Countries under Communist Governments; Selective Bibliography with Digest and Preface. South Hackensack, New Jersey, Published for the Copyright Society of the USA by F. B. Rothman, 1960. 62 p.

Contains 91 brief annotations on copyright in East European countries other than the Soviet Union together with a selected bibliography of literature on the subject published outside Eastern Europe.

63. For publishing activity in Eastern Europe, reference may be made to the following:

Bulgaria:
Sofiia. Bulgarski bibliografski institut.   Knigi i periodichni izdaniia v. N. R. Bulgariia; statisticheski materiali (Books and periodical publications in the Bulgarian Peoples Republic; statistical materials). 1956– Sofiia.

Bulgaria. *Tsentralno statistichesko upravlenie.*   Knigoizdavane i pechat v Narodna Republika Bulgariia; statisticheski sbornik (Book publishing and the press in the Bulgarian Peoples Republic). 1962/63– Sofiia.

Rumania:
Delegation of U.S. Book Publishers Visiting Rumania.   Book Publishing and Distribution in Rumania. Report of the Delegation of U.S. Book Publishers Visiting Rumania, October 1-10, 1965 . . . New York, American Book Publishers Council, American Textbook Publishers Institute, 1966. 60 p.
*See also* entry no. 1580.

Yugoslavia:
Delegation of U.S. Book Publishers Visiting Yugoslavia.   The Book Industry of Yugoslavia. New York, American Book Publishers Council and American Textbook Publishers Institute, 1964. 41 p. *See also* entry no. 2156.

Uzelac, Iliija.   L'édition, la presse, la radio et le film dans la République fédérative populaire de Yougoslavie. Beograd, Édition "Jugoslavija," 1955. 58 p.

Deset godina izdavačke djelatnosti štampe, bibliotekarstva i radia N. R. Bosne i Hercegovina, 1945-1955 (Ten years of publishing activity, librarianship, and radio in Bosnia and Hercegovina). Sarajevo, 1955. 58 p. Illus., ports.

## 6. Monographic Series

64. The following series issued in the United States should be noted as periodically contributing handbooks or survey studies of Eastern Europe:

Praeger Series on East Central Europe under the Communists.

Begun in New York in the mid-1950s under the general guidance of Robert F. Byrnes and later of Stephen Fischer-Galati and in cooperation with Radio Free Europe. The series contains handbooks mainly on geographical, demographic, economic, and political problems of the individual countries of Eastern Europe in the period after the Second World War. Each volume includes bibliographies. *See also* the Southeast Europe series of the American Universities Field Staff (New York, 1952–), the individual volumes of which contain reports written by experts on current socioeconomic and political topics.

Other series published in the United States are chiefly devoted to linguistic and historical research on Slavic Eastern Europe. Note especially the following:

Russian and East European Studies. 1– 1960– Los Angeles, University of California.

California Slavic Studies. 1– 1960– Berkeley, University of California Press.

Harvard Slavic Studies. 1– 1953– Cambridge, Mass., Harvard University Press.

Indiana Slavic Studies. 1– 1956– Bloomington, Indiana University Press.

Florida State University Slavic Papers. 1– 1966– Tallahassee, Florida State University, Center for Slavic and East European Studies.

65. Among the many series issued in Germany may be noted the *Südosteuropa-Jahrbuch*, *Südosteuropa-Schriften*, and *Südosteuropa-Studien*, all issued by the Südosteuropa Gesellschaft in Munich. The Südost-Institut, also in Munich, issues *Südosteuropäische Arbeiten*, which emphasize historical studies.

In Switzerland the Schweizerisches Ost-Institut since 1958 has issued its *Schriftenreihe* (now *Materialien*), which comprise mainly bibliographic surveys, with much attention to Hungary in the period after the Second World War.

## 7. Directories and Biographic Information

66. Little (Arthur D.) Inc.   Directory of Selected Research Institutes in Eastern Europe. Prepared by Arthur D. Little, Inc. for the National Science Foundation. New York, Columbia University Press, 1967. 445 p.

A descriptive guide to the location and type of research institutes, academies and universities in Bulgaria, Czechoslovakia, Hungary, Poland, Romania, and Yugoslavia. The emphasis is on biological and physical science institutes. The address, name of director, and titles of selected institute publications are given. Name and subject index. *See also*:

Leska, M.   Instytucje Naukowo badawcze w państwach demokracji ludowych (Scientific research institutes in the peoples' democracies). Warszawa, Centralny Instytut Informacji Naukowo-Technicznej i Ekonomicznej, 1961. 106 p.

67. National Science Foundation.   The Eastern European Academies of Sciences; a Directory. Washington, National Academy of Sciences–National Research Council, 1963. 148 p.

Names of social scientists and academicians are included. Brief biographical information provided. Supplementary information on university studies in general and Eastern Europe in particular can be located in:

Moscow. Universitet. *Biblioteka*.   Universitetskoe obrazovanie v SSSR i za rubezhom; bibliograficheskii ukazatel' russkoi i inostrannoi literatury za 1950-1960 gg. (University education in the USSR and abroad. Bibliography of Russian and foreign literature for 1950-1960). Edited by G. G. Krichevskii and E. A. Nersesova. Moskva, Izdatel'stvo Moskovskogo universiteta, 1966. 645 p. Author and subject indexes.

68. Who's Who in Eastern Europe. n.p., 1962. 2 v. (looseleaf). Ports.
> May be supplemented by:
> International Who's Who. London, International Who's Who Publishing Company, 1910– For the period prior to the Second World War, *see*:
> Who's Who in Central and East Europe. Edited by Stephen Taylor. Zurich, Central European Times Publishing Co., 1933-34, 1935-36. 2 v.
> The Near East Yearbook and Who's Who; a Survey of the Affairs . . . of Yugoslavia, Roumania, Bulgaria, Greece and Turkey, 1931/32. Edited by H. T. M. Bell. London, The Near East, Ltd., 1931. 1 v.

69. Wurzbach, Constantin.    Biographisches Lexikon des Kaiserthums Österreichs, enthaltend die Lebensskizzen der denkwürdigen Personen, welche seit 1750 in den Österreichischen Kron-Ländern geboren wurden oder darin gelebt und gewirkt haben. Wien, Kaiserlich-Königliche Hof- und Staatsdruckerei ,1856-1891. 60 v. Fold. geneal. tables.
> A classic containing over 24,000 biographies for the period from 1750 to the 1850s, including Austria's East European crown lands.

70. Kleine slavische Biographie. Edited by A. Schmaus. Wiesbaden, O. Harrassowitz, 1958. 832 p.
> Contains 3,500 short biographies of outstanding personalities and titles of their principal works. Emphasis is on representatives of the cultural life. For mainly political biographical data, *see*:
> Brown, James F.    The New Eastern Europe; the Khrushchev Era and After. New York, Praeger, 1966. Appendix 1, p. 239-256; Appendix 2, p. 257-289. Appendix 1 provides data on state and party officials, and appendix 2, on other East European personalities.

71. Thierfelder, F.    Männer am Balkan, von Alexander dem Grossen bis Josip Tito. Graz, Verlag Styria, 1961. 355 p. Illus.
> Contains 23 long biographies, mostly of past historical personalities. Even more historical is the approach in:
> Gabriel, A. L.    Pannonian Portraits: Biographies of Great Danubian Figures. New York, Sheed and Ward, 1957.

# 2

# GEOGRAPHIC ASPECTS
# OF THE AREA

*by George W. Hoffman*

72. American Geographical Society of New York. Research Catalogue. Boston, G. K. Hall, 1962. 15 v.

> A major research bibliography including books, periodicals, monographs, and documents in all languages, mainly since 1923. Albania, Greece, Romania, and Yugoslavia are covered in v. 10. For other basic reference works in the field *see:*
>
> > Bibliographie géographique internationale. Paris, Association de géographes français. v. 1– 1891– Each annual volume of this bibliography includes coverage of Southeastern Europe.
> >
> > Harris, Chauncy D., *and* Jerome D. Fellmann. International List of Geographical Serials. Chicago, 1960. 189 p. (University of Chicago, Department of Geography. Research Paper no. 63) Includes lists of all known geographic periodicals and nonperiodical serials: Bulgaria: p. 16-17; Greece: p. 68; Romania: p. 96-98; Yugoslavia: p. 151-152.

73. Birot, Pierre. Les Balkans. *In* Birot, Pierre, and Jean Dresch. La Méditerranée et le Moyen-Orient. v. 2. La Méditerranée orientale et le Moyen-Orient. Paris, Presses universitaires de France, 1956. 123 p. Illus., plates, maps.

> Topical discussion of the geography of the Balkans.

74. Blanc, André. Géographie des Balkans. Paris, Presses universitaires de France, 1965. 124 p. Maps.

> Survey of the cultural geography of Bulgaria, Albania, Greece, European Turkey, and Yugoslavia.

75. Bowman, Isaiah. The New World; Problems in Political Geography. 4th ed. Yonkers-on-Hudson, N.Y. and Chicago, Ill., World Book Company, 1928. 803 p. Maps, diagrs.

> The political geographical impact of the First World War is surveyed in chapters 12 and 14-18.

76. Chataigneau, Y., *and* Jules Sion.   Les pays Balkaniques. *In* Vidal de la Blache, Paul M. J., *and* L. Gallois, *eds*. Géographie universelle. v. 7, part 2. Paris, A. Colin, 1934. p. 395-595.
Regional geographic study of Yugoslavia, Albania, Bulgaria, and Greece.

77. Cvijić, Jovan.   La péninsule balkanique, géographie humaine. Paris, A. Colin, 1918. 528 p. Illus., maps.
*See also* entries no. 219 *and* 2266.
Detailed discussion of the geography of the Balkans. A classic study by the renowned Serbian geographer.

78. East, William G.   The Danube Routeway. *In his* An Historical Geography of Europe. 4th ed. London, Methuen; New York, Dutton, 1950. p. 368-391.
An historical geography with strong political emphasis, surveying the Danube at various periods in history. Fifth edition published in 1966.

79. Hoffman, George W.   The Balkans in Transition. Princeton, N.J., Van Nostrand, 1963. 124 p. Maps, tables. Bibliography: p. 109-111.
*See also* entry no. 119.
Political geographic survey of Bulgaria, Albania, Yugoslavia, and Northern Greece.

80. Hoffman, George W.   The Problem of the Underdeveloped Regions in Southeast Europe: a Comparative Analysis of Romania, Yugoslavia, and Greece. *In*: Association of American Geographers. Annals, v. 57, Dec. 1967: 637-666.
Discussion of the great regional disproportion among the countries. Compares the problems and evaluates steps taken toward their solution.

81. Kostanick, Huey L.   The Geopolitics of the Balkans. *In* Jelavich, Charles, and Barbara Jelavich, *eds*. The Balkans in Transition; Essays on the Development of Balkan Life and Politics Since the Eighteenth Century. Berkeley, University of California Press, 1963. p. 1-55.
Political geographic discussion of the Balkan countries.

82. Krebs, Norbert.   Die geographische Struktur der südslawischen Länder. Geographische Zeitschrift, v. 47, no. 6, 1941: 241-256.
A scholarly article, oriented toward political geography.

83. Maull, Otto.   Länderkunde von Südeuropa: die südosteuropäische Halbinsel. *In* Enzyklopaedie der Erdkunde. Edited by Oskar Kende. Leipzig, F. Deuticke, 1929. p. 299-532.
Survey of general geography of the region, with strong anthropogeographic emphasis. Coverage includes Greece, Bulgaria, Albania, European Turkey, and Yugoslavia.

84. May, Jacques M.   The Ecology of Malnutrition in Central and South-

eastern Europe: Austria, Hungary, Rumania, Bulgaria, Czechoslovakia. New York, Hafner Pub. Co., 1966. 290 p. Maps. (*His* Studies in Medical Geography, v. 6; Food Geography Series, 4)

Survey of food resources, diet types, nutritional disease patterns, and agricultural policies.

85. Newbigin, Marion I.   Geographical Aspects of the Balkan Problem, in Their Relation to the Great European War. New York, G. P. Putnam's Sons, 1915. 243 p. Maps, diagrs.

Political geography of the Balkans, with emphasis on the changes brought about by the First World War.

86. Pounds, Norman J. G.   Eastern Europe. Chicago, Aldine Pub. Co., 1969. 912 p. Plates, illus., maps, bibliographies.

An up-to-date reference work on the geography of Eastern Europe (exclusive of Greece). See also:

Osborne, Richard H.   East-Central Europe; an Introductory Geography. New York, Praeger, 1967. 384 p. Maps. Covers seven countries of Central and Southeast Europe (except East Germany and Greece). British edition: *East-Central Europe: a Geographical Introduction to Seven Socialist States* (London, Chatto and Windus, 1967, 384 p.).

*See also*:

Hall, Elvajean, *and* Calvin L. Criner.   Picture Map Geography of Eastern Europe. Illustrated by Thomas R. Funderburk. Philadelphia, Lippincott, 1968. 155 p. Illus.

87. Pounds, Norman J. G., *and* Robert C. Kingsbury.   An Atlas of European Affairs. New York, London, Frederick A. Praeger, 1964. 135 p.

Twelve political maps (with text) refer specifically to Southeast Europe. For a useful small black-and-white atlas, with text, *see*:

Adams, Arthur E.   An Atlas of Russian and East European History. New York, Praeger, 1967. 204 p. Maps. Serviceable general reference tools on cartographic materials are:

American Geographic Society of New York. Map Department. Index to Maps in Books and Periodicals. Boston, G. K. Hall, 1968. 10 v.

Bibliographie cartographique internationale. 1937– Paris, Comité national français de géographie. Annual.

88. Shackleton, Margaret R.   South Central Europe. *In her* Europe, a Regional Geography. 7th ed., rev. under the direction of W. Gordon East. New York, F. A. Praeger, 1964. p. 378-447. Illus., charts, maps.

Standard survey of the regional geography of South Central Europe.

89. Wanklyn, H. G.   The Eastern Marchlands of Europe. London, G. Philip & Son, 1941. 356 p. Illus. (maps), diagr.

Regional geography with emphasis on historical and political developments. Yugoslavia is discussed in part 3.

# 3

# the people

General 90-98

The Jews in Southeastern Europe 99-116

## A. GENERAL

*by George W. Hoffman*

90. Cvijić, Jovan.   Die ethnographische Abgrenzung der Völker auf der Balkanhalbinsel. Petermanns geographische Mitteilungen (Gotha), v. 59, 1913: 113-118, 185-189, 244-246.
    Ethnographic divisions on the Balkan Peninsula are described.

91. Cvijić, Jovan.   The Zones of Civilization of the Balkan Peninsula. The Geographical Review (New York) v. 5, June 1918: 470-482.
    Analysis of the impact of Old Balkan or Modified Byzantine civilization, Turco-Oriental influences, Western influences, and the patriarchal regime.

92. Fisher, Jack C.   Planning the City of Socialist Man. Journal of the American Institute of Planners (Cambridge, Mass.), v. 28, Nov. 1962: 251-265.
    Examines socialist planning objectives in the light of existing urban reality. Postulates three categories of contemporary East European urban areas.

93. Földes, László, *ed.*   Viehzucht und Hirtenleben in Ostmitteleuropa; ethnographische Studien. Budapest, Verlag der Ungarischen Akademie der Wissenschaften, 1961. 699 p. Illus., maps, diagrs., plans, profiles, tables.
    Animal husbandry and peasant life in Hungary and Southeast Europe are discussed.

94. Gavazzi, Milovan.   Die kulturgeographische Gliederung Südost-europas. Südost-Forschungen (München), v. 15, 1956: 5-21.
    Plea for order in the cultural geographic divisions of southeast Europe.

29

95. Hartl, Hans, *ed.*   Bevölkerungsentwicklungen in Südosteuropa; Jugoslawien, Ungarn, Rumänien. München, R. Oldenbourg, 1964. 77 p.
Untersuchungen zur Gegenwartskunde Südosteuropas, 5)

> Analysis of population changes in Yugoslavia, Hungary, and Ro-
> mania. For an American study on the subject, *see* entry 96.

96. Scott, James L.   Projections of the Population of the Communist
Countries of Eastern Europe, by Age and Sex, 1965-1985. Washing-
ton, D.C., Bureau of the Census, 1965. 59 p. (International Population
Reports, Series P-91, no. 14)

> Contains, among others, population estimates and projections for
> Albania, Bulgaria, Romania, and Yugoslavia, and examines the main
> implications of the projections.

97. Soulis, George C.   The Gypsies in the Byzantine Empire and the
Balkans in the Later Middle Ages. Dumbarton Oaks Papers (Washington, D.C.), v. 15, 1961: 141-165.

> A critical examination of the historical evidence of the presence of
> Gypsies in Byzantine territory before their migration to Central and
> Eastern Europe.

98. Wilhelmy, Herbert. Völkische und koloniale Siedlungsformen der
Slawen. Geographische Zeitschrift (Leipzig), v. 42, 1936: 81-97.

> Valuable contribution to the geography of settlement types.

## B. THE JEWS IN SOUTHEASTERN EUROPE

### by Kaethe Lewy and Ruth Tronik

### 1. General Publications

99. The American Jewish Yearbook. 1899– Philadelphia, New York.
American Jewish Committee and Jewish Publication Society of
America.

> An authoritative compendium of demographic, civic, political,
> religious, and cultural data concerning Jews in the United States and
> around the world. Each yearbook presents surveys of Jewish com-
> munities in various countries. They begin with a review of the general
> situation in a particular country followed by details on the Jewish
> community. Most issues also include special articles of an historic
> nature, such as two articles by Elias Schwarzfeld in volume 3, 1901/02,
> on the Jews of Romania: "The Jews of Roumania from the Earliest
> Times to the Present Day" (p. 24-62) and "Roumania Since the Berlin
> Treaty" (p. 63-87). These two articles form the only general outline
> of the history of Romanian Jewry in English.

100. Franco, Moïse.   Essai sur l'histoire des Israélites de l'Empire Ottoman depuis les origines jusqu'à nos jours. Paris, A. Durlacher, 1897.
296 p.

> A general history of the Jews of the Turkish Empire of which

Balkan Jewry formed a part. Special attention is paid to their literature. The standard work until now for the history of the Jews in the
Ottoman Empire is the Hebrew work by Salomon A. Rosanes, *Divre
yeme Yisrael be-Togarma* (Histoire des Israélites de Turquie [Turquie,
Hongrie, Serbie, Bulgarie, Bosnie, Albanie et Grèce] et de l'Orient
[Syrie, Palestine, Egypte, etc.] Sophia, Tel Aviv, Jerusalem, 1930-
1945, 6 v.). It covers the period from the 14th to the 20th century
and includes documentary chapters on specific places or events and
special chapters on Hebrew typography. Although a very comprehensive work, it is not always reliable.

101. Loeb, Isidore.  La situation des Israélites en Turquie, en Serbie et
en Roumanie. Paris, J. Baer, 1877. 471 p.

A good study by a competent historian on the status of the Jews
in the Balkans during the second half of the 19th century. Many
documents.

102. Meyer, Peter, *and others.*  The Jews in the Soviet Satellites. Syracuse,
N.Y., Syracuse University Press, 1953. 637 p.

A collection of surveys on the situation of the Jews in five Soviet-
Bloc countries up to the spring of 1953. Each survey begins with a
review of the situation of the Jews before the Second World War
and during the Nazi occupation, but mainly deals with the communist
attitude toward Jewish problems and the effect of the Soviet system
on Jewish life. Based on communist sponsored Jewish publications,
official documents, and Jewish press from the West. Excellent extensive bibliographical notes. "Rumania" by Nicolas Sylvain, p. 493-556;
"Bulgaria" by Peter Meyer, p. 559-629.

Another publication based on similar sources is *Rumanian Jewry
in the Postwar Period* (New York, Institute of Jewish Affairs, World
Jewish Congress, 1952, 16, 14 p.), a brief, factual account on Romanian Jews in the period 1945 to 1951. Valuable for information
on changes within the political parties of Romanian Jews under
communist pressure.

103. Schmelz, Uziel O., *comp.*  Jewish Demography and Statistics; Bibliography for 1920-1960. Jerusalem, Hebrew University, Institute of
Contemporary Jewry, 1961. 2 v. Addenda.

A very useful extensive bibliography listing approximately 5,000
items relating to Jewish communities throughout the world. Includes
books and articles in many languages, adding English translations of
titles in lesser-known languages. Demography is used here in a wide
sense to include health, economy, education, social matters, and community organization. Author index in Addenda. The editor calls this
publication a "first draft; not for publication or circulation," and a
definitive edition is planned. A third volume with new material up
to 1966 and an addendum for 1920-1960 is to be published in 1968.
For material on the Balkan countries in general *see* under Europe;
other pertinent listings are Albania, Bulgaria, Greece, Romania and
Yugoslavia.

Another bibliography, narrower in scope, is *Jews in the Communist World; a Bibliography, 1945-1962* (New York, Pro Arte, 1963, 125 p.) by Randolph L. Braham and Mordecai M. Hauer. This selected bibliography of books and articles lists 845 entries. Part A lists references to non-English literature, with titles in lesser-known languages translated into English. Part B supplements an earlier compilation by Braham entitled *Jews in the Communist World; a Bibliography 1945-1960* (New York, Twayne Publishers, 1961, 64 p.), which listed materials in English only.

## 2. Bulgaria

104. Evreĭski vesti (Jewish news). 1944– Sofiia. Irregular.

Organ of the Central Board of the Social, Cultural, and Educational Association of Jews in the People's Republic of Bulgaria. Consists of current news on political, cultural, and economic problems of Bulgarian Jewry and contains some articles by the well-known historian of Bulgarian Jewry, Eli Eškenazí. Also has selections of literary works of Jews from Bulgaria and other countries. Anti-Zionist orientation.

105. Grinberg, Natan, *ed.* Dokumenti (Documents). Sofiia, Tsentralnata Konsistoriia na Evreitie v Bulgariia, 1945. 200 p. Illus.

A collection of documents (in Bulgarian) from the Archives of the Commissariat for Jewish Affairs published by the Jewish Consistory of Sofia. The documents deal with deportations of Bulgarian Jews during the Second World War and are accompanied by brief explanations. A detailed study of the holocaust in Bulgaria is the Hebrew work of Benjamin Arditti, *Yehude Bulgaria bishnot ha-mishtar ha-Nazi, 1940-1944* (Les Juifs de Bulgarie sous le régime Nazi, 1940-1944) (Holon, Israel, 1962, 436 p.). This book includes an introductory chapter on the history of the Jews in Bulgaria, facsimiles of documents, personal narratives, and an extensive bibliography in several languages.

106. Mézan, Saül. Les Juifs espagnols en Bulgarie. v. 1: Histoire, statistique, ethnographie. Édition d'essai. Sofia, Ivria, 1925. 150 p.

This somewhat elementary work remains the only history of the Sephardic Jews of Bulgaria in a Western language. Not completed.

Authoritative articles on the history of Bulgarian Jewry (particularly by S. A. Rosanes, the well-known historian of Balkan Jewry) may be found in *Evreiska tribuna; dvumesechno spisanie za obshtestven zhivot i kulturu* (Jewish tribune; bimonthly revue of social life and culture) (Ruse, 1926-1929?).

See also *Godishnik* of the Obshtestvena Kulturno-Prosvetna Organizatsiia na Evreite v Narodna Republika Bulgariia, Tsentralno Rukovodstvo (Annual of the Central Board of the Social, Cultural, and Educational Association of Jews in the People's Republic of Bulgaria) (Sofiia, 1966–). This heavily politicized publication concentrates on recent history. Contents and summaries in English, French, German, Russian, and Spanish.

### 3. Greece

107. Emmanuel, Isaac S.   Histoire des Israélites de Salonique. v. 1: (140 av. J.-C. à 1640); histoire sociale, économique et littéraire de la Ville Mère en Israël, contenant un supplément: L'histoire de l'industrie des tissus des Israélites de Salonique. Thonon, Paris, Lipschutz, 1935-1936. 304, 64 p. Plates.

A comprehensive history of the Jewish community of Saloniki. Emphasis on the role of the Jews in the economic activities of the city. Not completed. Another work on the same subject, larger but less reliable, covering the period from ancient times to 1669, is Joseph Nehama's *Histoire des Israélites de Salonique* (Paris, Durlacher, 1935-1959, 5 v.).

108. Galanté, Abraham.   Histoire des Juifs de Rhodes, Chio, Cos, etc. Istanbul, Société anonyme de papeterie et d'imprimerie (Fratelli Haim), 1935. 177 p. Illus.

————.   Appendice à l'Histoire des Juifs de Rhodes, Chio, Cos., etc. et fin tragique des communautés juives de Rhodes et de Cos, œuvre du brigandage hitlérien. Istanbul, Kâğit ve basim işleri, 1948. 76 p. Facsims.

A history of the Jews of Rhodes from ancient times through the 20th century, covering all aspects of their social, cultural, religious, and economic life. A special chapter gives information on Lemnos, Metelin, Cassos, Castellorizo, Halki, Patmos, Calymnos, Symi, Carpathos, Leros, and Nyssiros. The appendix contains details on the Italian and Nazi occupation and on the deportation of the Jews of Rhodes and Cos during the Second World War.

109. Molho, Michael, *ed.*   In memoriam; hommage aux victimes juives des Nazis en Grèce. Salonique, Buenos Aires, 1948-1953. 3 v. Illus.

Volumes 1 and 2 deal with the holocaust of Greek Jewry, including details on deportations and life in concentration camps. Facsimiles of German anti-Jewish orders are appended. Volume 3 is a pictorial history of the Jewish cemetery of Saloniki, preceded by an introduction. Another publication by the same author is "Le judaïsme grec en général et la communauté juive de Salonique en particulier entre les deux guerres mondiales," *Homenaje a Millás-Vallicrosa*, v. 2 (Barcelona, Consejo Superior de Investigaciones Científicas, 1956, p. 73-107), a succinct history of the Jews of Greece from ancient times until their extermination by the Nazis, with special emphasis on Saloniki during the period 1914 to 1940.

### 4. Romania

110. Berkowitz, Joseph.   La question des Israélites en Roumanie; étude de son histoire et des divers problèmes de droit qu'elle soulève. Paris, Jouve, 1923. 795 p. Bibliography: p. 9-18.

*See also* entry no. 1626.

Well documented account of the Jewish problem in Romania from its rise in the 19th century until just after the First World War. There is introductory material on the history of Romanian Jewry before the 19th century, but the focus is on the impact of the Convention of Paris and the Congress of Berlin on the status of Jews in Romania. Written from a legal point of view. Doctoral dissertation, University of Paris.

An excellent source book on the political aspects of the position of Romanian Jews in the 19th century is *Jewish Disabilities in the Balkan States; American Contributions Toward Their Removal, With Particular Reference to the Congress of Berlin* (New York, American Jewish Committee, 1916, 169 p.) by Max J. Kohler and Simon Wolf. The book is divided between commentary and source material.

111. Carp, Matatias. Cartea neagrǎ; suferinţele evreilor din România, 1940-1944 (Black book; the suffering of the Jews in Romania. 1940-1944). Bucureşti, Socec, 1946-1948. 3 v. Illus., facsims.
*See also* entry no. 1734.

An important collection of official reports, letters, and other documents on the persecution of Rumanian Jewry in 1940-1944. Volume 1: The Iron Guard Legion and Its Rebellion; volume 2: The Pogrom of Jassy; volume 3: Transnistria.

For a history of Jewish communities in Bukovina since the 14th century, particularly detailed and documented for the period between the World Wars and during the holocaust, see *Geschichte der Juden in der Bukowina,* edited by Hugo Gold (Tel-Aviv, "Olamenu," 1958-62, 2 v., illus., ports.), which also devotes much space to Zionist movements.

112. Societatea istoricǎ Iuliu Barasch. Analele (Annals). Bucureşti, 1887-1889. 3 v.

The society was founded in order to collect documents concerning Romanian Jewish history and folklore. Articles in the *Analele* deal with the history of Romanian Jewry from its beginnings through the 19th century.

## 5. Yugoslavia

113. The Crimes of the Fascist Occupants and Their Collaborators against the Jews in Yugoslavia. Belgrade, Federation of Jewish Communities of the Federative People's Republic of Yugoslavia, 1957. 42, 245 p. Illus., facsims., ports.

Findings of the Yugoslav State Commission for Investigation of Crimes of the Occupants and Their Collaborators. Details on concentration camps, forced labor camps, and anti-Jewish laws. In Serbo-Croatian, with an introduction and detailed summary in English. Originally published without English summary as *Zločini fašističkih okupatora i njihovih pomagača protiv Jevreja u Jugoslaviji* (Beograd, Izdanje Saveza Jevrejskih Opština Jugoslavije, 1952, 245 p.).

114. Jevrejski pregled (The Jewish review). 1950– Beograd, Savez Jevrejskih Opština Jugoslavije.

Organ of the Federation of Jewish Communities of Yugoslavia.
Volumes 1-9 have title *Bilten* (Bulletin). Current political and cultural
events in the Jewish communities of Yugoslavia and their relations
with Jewish communities in other countries, particularly Israel. List
of contents and summaries of the more important articles in English
with title *The Jewish Review.*

For material on current and past history of Yugoslavian Jewry
written by noted scholars and publicists, and short literary works on
Jewish subjects, mainly by Yugoslavian writers, see *Jevrejski almanah*
(Jewish almanac) (1954–, Beograd, Savez Jevrejskih Opština Jugoslavije).

115. Levy, Moritz.    Die Sephardim in Bosnien; ein Beitrag zur Geschichte
der Juden auf der Balkan-Halbinsel. Sarajevo, D. A. Kajon, 1911.
127 p. Illus., ports.

An account of Jewish life in Bosnia mainly during the 18th and
19th centuries, describing education, taxation, disabilities, political
status, and economic and religious life. Based on Jewish community
records (some of which are quoted) and official documents of the
Turkish administration.

116. Spomenica 400 godina od dolaska Jevreja u Bosnu i Hercegovinu,
1566-1966 (Memorial book celebrating the 400th anniversary of the
arrival of Jews in Bosnia and Hercegovina, 1566-1966). Sarajevo,
1966. 364 p. Illus., facsims., ports.

A comprehensive collection of essays by noted historians, men of
letters, and scientists in Serbo-Croatian with a short summary in
English and French. Divided into three parts: historical — a survey
of the life and activities of the Jewish community during its 400
years; biographical — sketches on outstanding personalities; and literary — samples of folklore and literary and scientific works of Jewish
writers from Bosnia and Hercegovina.

# 4

# history*

## by Michael B. Petrovich

117. Đorđevic (Djordjevic), Dimitrije. Révolutions nationales des peuples balkaniques, 1804-1914. Edited by Jorjo Tadić. Translated by Margita Ristić. Beograd, Institut d'histoire, 1965. 250 p.
   *See also* entry no. 169.
   > A survey of Balkan national revolutions, by a Yugoslav historian.
   > *See also*:
   > Les peuples de l'Europe du Sud-Est et leur rôle dans l'histoire (XVᵉ-XXᵉ ss.). Sofia, Edition de l'Académie bulgare des sciences, 1966. 154 p.

118. Forbes, Nevill, *and others.* The Balkans; a History of Bulgaria, Serbia, Greece, Rumania, Turkey. Oxford, The Clarendon Press, 1915. 407 p. 3 fold. maps.
   > A somewhat disjointed and outdated survey, but still useful to the general reader. The authors include Nevill Forbes (Bulgaria and Serbia), Arnold J. Toynbee (Greece), D. Mitrany (Romania), and D. G. Hogarth (Turkey). Coverage extends from earliest times to the First World War.

119. Hoffman, George W. The Balkans in Transition. Princeton, N.J., Van Nostrand, 1963. 124 p. Maps, tables. Bibliography: p. 109-111.
   *See also* entry no. 79.
   > A small but very informative volume by a geographer from the University of Texas who has a broad interest in and personal acquaintance with the area. Coverage is limited to Albania, Bulgaria, and Yugoslavia. The first two chapters deal with the land and peoples, chapter 3 discusses the political territorial framework, chapter 4 is devoted to the social and economic transformation, and the last chapter "focuses on the political-geographical role of the major factors that contributed to the transition in the Balkans."

120. Iorga (Jorga), Nicolae. Histoire des états balkaniques jusqu'à 1924. Paris, J. Gamber, 1925. 575 p.

36

A useful survey of Balkan history since the Ottoman conquest, by a distinguished Romanian historian.

121. Jelavich, Charles, *and* Barbara Jelavich, *eds.*   The Balkans in Transition; Essays on the Development of Balkan Life and Politics since the Eighteenth Century. Berkeley and Los Angeles, University of California Press, 1963. 451 p. Maps., diagrs., tables, bibliography.
*See also* entries no. 150, 161, *and* 222.
Papers presented by 13 scholars from the United States and Great Britain at a conference on "The Transformation of the Balkans Since the Ottoman Era," held in 1960 at the University of California, Berkeley. Almost all these essays cut across national lines to treat the Balkans as a whole. Subjects covered include geography, foreign and domestic policy, economics, culture, literature, and historiography.

122. Jelavich, Charles, *and* Barbara Jelavich.   The Balkans. Englewood Cliffs, N.J., Prentice-Hall, 1965. 148 p.
A brief but useful survey of Albania, Bulgaria, Greece, Romania, and Yugoslavia. Presents basic facts about the geography, peoples, and history of the area through the period of Ottoman rule, and then stresses internal developments in the 19th and 20th centuries, especially nationalism, economic problems, communism, and interference by the Great Powers. The list of suggested readings in the back enhances the book's usefulness, especially for students and general readers. For similar brief surveys which are especially adapted to college survey courses in world history, *see also* Wesley M. Gewehr's *The Rise of Nationalism in the Balkans, 1800-1930* (Hamden, Conn., Archon Books, 1967, 137 p.), a reprint of a 1931 volume in the Holt Bershire Studies in European History; and Leften S. Stavrianos' *The Balkans, 1815-1914* (New York, Holt, Rinehart and Winston, 1963, 135 p.), a handy survey of Balkan history in the 19th and early 20th centuries.

123. Kostich, Dragoš D.   The Land and People of the Balkans; Albania, Bulgaria, Rumania, and Yugoslavia. Philadelphia, Lippincott, 1962. 160 p. Illus. (Portrait of the Nations Series)
An elementary, well-illustrated survey. See also *The World and Its Peoples; Yugoslavia, Rumania, Bulgaria, Albania* (New York, Greystone Press, 1965, 216 p.), a lavishly illustrated elementary guide to these four Balkan countries covering the land, people, history, fine arts, literature, theater, music, and film. *See also* Edmund O. Stillman's *The Balkans* (New York, Time Inc., 1964, 160 p.), a profusely illustrated introduction to Yugoslavia, Albania, Romania, and Bulgaria. These volumes are suitable for secondary school libraries as well as for the general reader.

124. Miller, William.   The Balkans: Roumania, Bulgaria, Servia, and Montenegro, with New Chapters Containing Their History from 1896 to 1922. 3d ed. London, T. F. Unwin, 1923. 538 p. Front. (port.), illus., 2 fold. maps.

Separate histories of the four nations, with a final section on Albania. Though dated, the volume is still of use to the general reader.

125. Miller, William.   The Ottoman Empire and Its Successors, 1801-1927; with an Appendix, 1927-1936. Cambridge (Eng.), The University Press, 1936. 644 p. Maps.

This work by a distinguished British scholar is still one of the more useful books in the field. Beginning with the Ottoman Empire in the Napoleonic period, it weaves together international and domestic politics in 22 informative chapters, all of which deal with the Balkan peoples. The author, a specialist on Greece, has given due attention to the other Balkan peoples. With the exception of the sections on Greek history, the work is based largely on secondary sources in Western languages.

126. Newman, Bernard.   Balkan Background. London, Robert Hale, Limited, 1944. 288 p. Front., illus. (maps), plates, ports., facsims. New York, Macmillan, 1945. 354 p. Illus. (maps).

An introduction to the Balkans, written for the general public by a knowledgeable journalist. Separate chapters on the six Balkan countries, including Turkey.

127. Nikitin, Sergei A., ed.   Istoriia iuzhnykh i zapadnykh slavian. Moskva, Izd-vo Moskovskogo universiteta, 1957. 573 p. Fold. map (in pocket).

This symposium of leading Soviet scholars in the field of Slavic history contains many chapters that deal with the Balkan Slavs from earliest times to the end of the Second World War. The book was intended as a text for a university course.

128. Ristelhueber, René.   Histoire des peuples balkaniques. Paris, A. Fayard, 1950. 503 p.

A popular survey. After a brief, broad description of the Balkan peoples and their historical background, concentrates on the 19th and 20th centuries, through the Soviet-Yugoslav schism in 1948.

129. Schevill, Ferdinand.   The History of the Balkan Peninsula and the Near East; a History from the Earliest Times to the Present Day. New York, Harcourt, Brace, 1922. 558 p. Maps (2 double; incl. front.).

Long the standard work in English on Balkan history. Though superseded by Stavrianos's work (see entry no. 135), it still deserves to be read, especially in view of the fact that half of this large volume deals with medieval and early modern history, while the second half deals entirely with the 19th and early 20th centuries. A revised edition of this work, prepared with the collaboration of Wesley M. Gewehr, was published under the title *The History of the Balkan Peninsula, From the Earliest Times to the Present Day* (New York, Harcourt, Brace, 1933, 614 p., maps).

130. Seton-Watson, Hugh.   The East European Revolution. London, Methuen; New York, Praeger, 1956. 435 p. Bibliography, illus.

*See also* entries no. 179 *and* 331.

A sequel to the author's earlier work (see entry no. 131), this book takes up the history of Eastern Europe through five years of the Second World War and five years of what the author calls "Sovietisation." It deals in large patterns such as the resistance movements, the communist seizure of power, economic problems, social and religious policy, the state and the Communist Party machine, and international problems. Includes a special chapter on "The Greek Exception."

131. Seton-Watson, Hugh.    Eastern Europe between the Wars, 1918-1941. Hamden, Conn., Archon Books, 1962. 422 p. Illus., maps, tables. 1965. 250 p.

*See also* entries no. 156 *and* 178.

A remarkable survey by a leading British scholar with a personal and varied acquaintance with Eastern Europe that is scarcely matched in the West. Written under trying conditions during the Second World War, this is not a scholarly book from the standpoint of detailed coverage or apparatus. Its greatest merit lies precisely in its being an informative synthesis of the important strands and forces in East European history. It is useful to have the Balkan countries treated within the general framework of the East European "*Zwischenland.*" First published in 1945.

132. Seton-Watson, Robert W.    The Rise of Nationality in the Balkans. London, Constable, 1917. 308 p. 4 fold. maps. Bibliography: p. 285-295.

A standard work by Britain's leading observer of East European affairs in his generation. Written during the First World War, the book was designed to give English readers an informative historical survey of the region in which the war began. It has withstood the test of time remarkably well.

133. Sloane, William M.    The Balkans; a Laboratory of History. New York, Eaton & Mains, 1914. 322 p. Maps.

Published in the first year of the First World War and just after the Balkan Wars, this survey by an American scholar stresses the rise of Balkan nationalisms in an international Great-Power setting. Except for its emphasis on the Turks, it has been largely superseded.

134. Stadtmüller, Georg.    Geschichte Südosteuropas. München, R. Oldenbourg, 1950. 527 p. Maps. Bibliography: p. 423-468.

*See also* entry no. 163.

Emphasizes the ancient, medieval, and early modern history of Southeast Europe, including the Czechs and the entire Danube Valley. Of its 24 chapters, only the last four deal with the 19th century, and almost nothing is said about the 20th century. The book stresses the German role in the history of the area. There is an interesting appendix on the development of scholarship concerning Southeast European history and an extensive bibliography which is especially useful for its references to German works.

The Südosteuropa-Gesellschaft and its role in planning and executing the Third Reich's blueprint for the New Order in Southeastern Europe is the subject of Dietrich Orlow's *The Nazis in the Balkans* (University of Pittsburgh Press, 1968, 235 p., bibliography).

135. Stavrianos, Leften S.   The Balkans Since 1453. New York, Rinehart, 1958. 970 p. Illus., ports., maps, facsims. Bibliography: p. 873-946.
    *See also* entry no. 165.
    Written by an American scholar with a feel for his subject, this vast synthesis is undoubtedly the standard work in English on modern Balkan history, and supersedes all previous general accounts. The approach is both topical and chronological. Its treatment of the Ottoman period is more from the standpoint of Ottoman institutions and affairs than of the domestic history of the Balkan peoples, a gap which reflects a fault of traditional Balkan native historiography. The chapters dealing with the last two centuries are especially useful. An excellent bibliography is included.

136. Wolff, Robert L.   The Balkans in Our Time. Cambridge, Mass., Harvard University Press, 1956. 618 p. Maps, tables. (Russian Research Center Studies, 23)
    *See also* entries no. 159 *and* 181.
    A *tour de force* by an author who combines a scholarly background with personal acquaintance gained in the O.S.S. during the Second World War. While the first third presents a very useful summary of the leading events of Balkan history up to 1939, the chief usefulness of the book lies in its full and critical treatment of the Balkan communist countries between 1939 and 1955. Reprint edition: 1967 (New York, W. W. Norton).

# 5

# politics and government

*by John C. Campbell*

137. Armstrong, Hamilton Fish.  Where the East Begins. New York,
Harper, 1929. 139 p. Illus.
> Together with the same author's *The New Balkans* (New York,
> Harper, 1926, 179 p.), presents the essentials of Balkan politics and
> international problems of the 1920s.

138. Beitzke, Günther.  Das Staatsangehörigkeitsrecht von Albanien, Bulgarien und Rumänien. Frankfurt, Metzler, 1951. 111 p. Nachtrag;
1956. 31 p. (Sammlung geltender Staatsangehörigkeitsgesetze. Band 5,
5a)
> History and interpretation of the law of citizenship from 1832 to
> 1956. Includes pertinent provisions of the laws and regulations in
> German translation. Bibliography.

139. Brown, James F.  The New Eastern Europe: The Khrushchev Era
and After. New York, Praeger, 1966. 306 p.
> Basically a political analysis, with some attention to economic
> development and international relations. Nationalism is a main theme.

140. Brzezinski, Zbigniew K.  The Soviet Bloc, Unity and Conflict. Rev.
and enl. ed. Cambridge, Mass., Harvard University Press, 1967.
599 p. Bibliography: p. 559-576. (Russian Research Center Studies,
37)
> *See also* entry no. 172.
> Indispensable study of the politics of communism in Eastern Eu-
> rope, with due attention to the Balkans. Previous editions appeared
> in 1960 and 1961.

141. Burks, R. V.  The Dynamics of Communism in Eastern Europe.
Princeton, Princeton University Press, 1961. 244 p. Maps, tables.
> *See also* entry no. 1135.

A stimulating and in many ways original work throwing light on the nature of Balkan communist parties and the character of their public support. Especially good on Greece.

142. East Central Europe Under the Communists. Edited by Robert F. Byrnes. New York, Praeger, 1956-1957. 7 v.

Comprehensive survey, country by country, covering political as well as many other aspects. The Balkan volumes are on Romania, Bulgaria, Yugoslavia, and Albania. The quality of individual contributions varies considerably.

143. Fejtö, François.   Histoire des démocraties populaires. Paris, Editions du Seuil, 1952. 446 p. Illus.

One of the best studies of the Soviet takeover and the Stalinist period in Central Europe and the Balkans.

144. Fischer-Galati, Stephen, ed.   Eastern Europe in the Sixties. New York, Praeger, 1963. 239 p. (Praeger Publications in Russian History and World Communism, no. 137)

See also entries no. 49 and 221.

A collaborative work, topically organized, with a substantial section on politics and government by Andrew Gyorgy. An earlier symposium is The Satellites in Eastern Europe, edited by Henry L. Roberts (Philadelphia, American Academy of Political and Social Sciences, 1958, 230 p., Its Annals, v. 317).

145. Gluckstein, Ygael.   Stalin's Satellites in Europe. Boston, Beacon Press, 1952. 333 p.

A solid study by an Israeli political scientist.

146. Gsovski, Vladimir, and Kazimierz, Grzybowski, eds.   Government, Law, and Courts in the Soviet Union and Eastern Europe. London, Stevens; New York, Praeger, 1959. 2 v. Bibliography: p. 1945-2009.

See also entries no. 629 and 2395.

A massive study prepared by émigré scholars covering many aspects of law in the context of the existing political systems. All communist countries in the Balkan area are included.

147. Gyorgy, Andrew.   Governments of Danubian Europe. New York, Rinehart, 1949. 376 p. Bibliography: p. 352-365.

A systematic exposition of the political situation of the early postwar period. Four Balkan countries are included.

148. The Hoover Institution at Stanford University has initiated, under the editorship of Jan F. Triska, a monographic series, Integration and Community Building in Eastern Europe, focusing on the relations of communist-governed countries of East and Southeast Europe with each other and with the other communist-type states. Two monographs, on The Development of Socialist Yugoslavia, by M. George Zaninovich and The People's Republic of Albania, by Nicholas C.

Pano, appeared in 1968 (Baltimore, Johns Hopkins Press), and two additional volumes on Bulgaria and Romania are scheduled for 1969. The constitutions of Albania, Bulgaria, Romania, and Yugoslavia are contained in Jan F. Triska's *Constitutions of the Communist-Party States* (Stanford, Hoover Institution, 1968, 541 p.).

149. Ionescu, Ghita.   The Politics of the European Communist States. New York, Praeger, 1967. 303 p. Bibliography: p. 291-296.
   *See also* entry no. 1868.
      Analysis of the structure of political power in the Balkan and other Eastern European states, breaking new ground in its appreciation of realities ignored both by Marxist theorists and by most Western students of communist politics.
      For the organization, tactics, and equipment of the armies of the Warsaw Pact member states *see*:
      Wiener, Friedrich.   Die Armeen der Ostblockstaaten. 2d ed. München, J. F. Lehmanns Verlag, 1967. 224 p. Illus., maps. Bibliography: p. 198-200.

150. Jelavich, Charles, *and* Barbara Jelavich, *eds.*   The Balkans in Transition: Essays on the Development of Balkan Life and Politics Since the Eighteenth Century. Berkeley and Los Angeles, University of California Press, 1963. 451 p. Maps, diagrs., tables, bibliography.
   *See also* entries no. 121, 161, *and* 222.
      Although a collection of essays by different authors, the book has a unity often lacking in similar works, makes good use of a topical rather than country-by-country approach, and relates politics to factors of history, culture, and social phenomena.

151. Kertesz, Stephen D., *ed.*   The Fate of East Central Europe: Hopes and Failures of American Foreign Policy. Notre Dame, University of Notre Dame Press, 1956. 463 p.
      The most substantial part of the book is devoted to political developments in individual countries, including four Balkan states. The story is carried further in a sequel edited by Professor Kertesz entitled *East Central Europe and the World* (Notre Dame, University of Notre Dame Press, 1962, 386 p.). Robert Lee Wolff, Stavro Skendi, and Stephen Fischer-Galati are among the contributors.

152. Macartney, C. A., *and* Alan W. Palmer.   Independent Eastern Europe: a History. New York, St. Martin's Press, 1962. 499 p. Illus.
      A substantial work on the politics of the interwar period, especially good on Hungary and the Balkans, areas on which the authors are recognized authorities.

153. Mitrany, David.   Marx Against the Peasant: A Study in Social Dogmatism. Chapel Hill, University of North Carolina Press, 1951. 301 p. Bibliography: p. 270-286.
   *See also* entry no. 224.

The communist-agrarian issue discussed as an integral part of the politics of Eastern Europe, especially the Balkans. A pioneering book.

154. Pribichevich, Stoyan.   World without End: the Saga of Southeastern Europe. New York, Reynal and Hitchcock, 1939. 408 p. Map. Bibliography: p. 393-402.

   A general book written with a journalist's flair and at the same time useful to the scholar.

155. Rouček, Joseph S.   Balkan Politics: International Relations in No Man's Land. Stanford, Stanford University Press, 1948. 298 p. Maps, bibliography.

   Although uneven in quality, this is one of the few books devoted specifically to Balkan politics in the interwar period and covering all countries.

156. Seton-Watson, Hugh. Eastern Europe between the Wars, 1918-1941. 3d ed. Hamden, Conn., Archon Books, 1962. 425 p. Illus.

   Probably the best balanced book on the interwar period. A companion volume, *The East European Revolution* (3d rev. ed., New York, Praeger, 1956, 435 p.), is also soundly conceived and informative. The interpretations are personal, but also realistic, reflecting the author's long acquaintance with the Balkan area. First published in 1945.

157. South-Eastern Europe; a Political and Economic Survey. London, Royal Institute of International Affairs, Oxford University Press, 1939. 203 p. Illus., maps.

   *See also* entries no. 131 *and* 178.

   Essentially a handbook, but gives a good picture of the politics of the individual Balkan states. Later information, including the early postwar period, is contained in the subsequent but less satisfactory volume edited by Reginald R. Betts entitled *Central and South-East Europe, 1945-1948* (London, New York, Royal Institute of International Affairs, 1950, 227 p.). A Soviet survey, useful for comparison, is *Balkanskie strany* (The Balkan countries), edited by F. N. Petrov (Moscow, Ogiz, 1946, 548 p.).

158. Stavrianos, Leften S.   Balkan Federation: A History of the Movement toward Balkan Unity in Modern Times. Hamden, Conn., Archon Books, 1964. 338 p. Bibliography: p. 314-332.

   *See also* entry no. 164.

   A thorough, scholarly work notable for its treatment of the theme of union or federation in nationalist and socialist movements as well as on the governmental level. The general subject is also dealt with by Theodore I. Geshkoff in *Balkan Union: A Road to Peace in Southeastern Europe* (New York, Columbia University Press, 1940, 345 p.); A. Papanastasiou in *Vers l'Union Balkanique* (Paris, Centre européen de la dotation Carnegie, 1934, 284 p.); and Robert Joseph Kerner and Harry Nicholas Howard in *The Balkan Conferences and the Balkan Entente, 1930-1935* (Berkeley, University of California Press, 1936, 271 p.).

159. Wolff, Robert L.   The Balkans in Our Time. Cambridge, Mass., Harvard University Press, 1956. 618 p. Maps, tables. (Russian Research Center Studies, No. 23)

*See also* entries no. 136 *and* 181.

The most informative and judicious account in English of Balkan history and politics from the First World War to the early '50s. Reprint edition: 1967 (New York, W. W. Norton).

# 6

# διplomacy anδ
# foreign relations

*by Ivo J. Lederer*

General 160-165
To 1918 166-171
Since 1918 172-182

## A. GENERAL

160. Barker, Elisabeth.   Macedonia, Its Place in Balkan Power Politics.
London, New York, Royal Institute of International Affairs, 1950.
129 p. Maps.
*See also* entry no. 2571.
> A succinct, and by far the best, synthesis of the neuralgic issue of
> modern Balkan politics.

161. Jelavich, Charles, *and* Barbara Jelavich, *eds.*   The Balkans in Transition: Essays on the Development of Balkan Life and Politics since
the Eighteenth Century. Berkeley and Los Angeles, University of California Press, 1963. 451 p. Maps, diagrs., tables, bibliography.
*See also* entries no. 121, 150, *and* 222.
> A series of essays on Balkan life and politics since the 18th century,
> originally presented as papers at a conference held at the University
> of California (Berkeley) in 1960. While not primarily concerned
> with diplomatic developments, these essays represent a landmark in
> the historical treatment of the region by focusing on the Balkans as
> a whole rather than on individual states or societies. The collection
> provides essential historical background. Particularly relevant are
> the chapters on the geopolitics of the area by Huey L. Kostanick, the
> Ottoman view of the Balkans by Stanford J. Shaw, the role of Russia
> in Balkan modernization by Cyril E. Black, the influence of the West
> by L. S. Stavrianos, and heritage and continuity by John C. Campbell.

162. Novak, Grga.   Jadransko more u sukobima i borbama kroz stoljeća
(The Adriatic in conflicts and struggles through the centuries). Beograd, 1962. 586 p.

An important general history of the "Adriatic world" from antiquity through 1941, covering the classic struggles between Venetian, Ottoman, Austrian, and South Slav interests. The geopolitical interests of Italy between the two world wars are treated in the last sections of the book. The author is a distinguished scholar and president of the Yugoslav Academy of Arts and Sciences.

163. Stadtmüller, Georg.   Geschichte Südosteuropas. München, R. Oldenbourg, 1950. 527 p. 23 maps. Bibliography: p. 423-468.
*See also* entry no. 134.
   A general history of the region, by a distinguished German historian. Coverage extends from antiquity through the 19th century, with some emphasis on the period from the late Middle Ages through the Counterreformation. On the whole a reliable work, although tending to view developments from a German and Central European standpoint.

164. Stavrianos, Leften S.   Balkan Federation: A History of the Movement toward Balkan Unity in Modern Times. Hamden, Conn., Archon Books, 1964. 338 p. Bibliography: p. 314-332.
*See also* entry no. 158.
   A basic study of intra-Balkan diplomacy and relationships from the beginning of the 19th century to the Second World War. Richly documented, this monograph argues that great-power diplomacy has for over a century tended to keep the Balkan states apart rather than to harmonize their differences.

165. Stavrianos, Leften S.   The Balkans since 1453. New York, Rinehart, 1958. 970 p. Illus., ports., maps, facsims. Bibliography: p. 873-946.
*See also* entry no. 135.
   Indubitably the best general history of the area. Written as a textbook, this massive work is nonetheless rich in documentation (much of it first made available through the author's researches) and original interpretations. Stavrianos challenges the traditional Balkan view that Turkish oppression was the root of the region's problems. The book is most readable and contains a valuable bibliography.

## B. TO 1918

166. Albertini, Luigi.   The Origins of the War of 1914. Translated and edited by Isabella M. Massey. London, New York, Oxford University Press, 1952-57. 3 v. Fold. maps. Includes bibliographies.
   The most detailed study of the subject, the result of 20 years of painstaking labor by a distinguished liberal member of the Italian Senate. In volume 1 the author surveys the European political trends from 1878 to 1914. Volume 2 sifts the facts pertinent to the Sarajevo assassination and the Austrian mobilization. Volume 3 is devoted entirely to the final two weeks of the July crisis of 1914. This massive study offers more reliable data on the diplomacy of the Balkan states from 1878 to 1914 than any other work.

167. Cataluccio, Francesco.   Balcani e Stretti Nella Politica Russa (1700-1909). Firenze, Soc. Editrice Universitaria, 1950. 107 p. Bibliographical footnotes.

A useful synthesis by an Italian scholar and specialist in modern history and international relations. Essentially a carefully researched essay, this study presents a judicious interpretation of the role of the Balkans and the Straits in Russia's search for access to the Mediterranean (1699-1815), the struggle against the Ottoman Empire (1815-1878), and the Russian-Austro-Hungarian rivalry (1878-1909). *See also* the more extensive works of J. A. R. Marriott, M. S. Anderson, and S. M. Goriainov.

168. Danev, S.   Ocherk na diplomaticheskata istoriia na Balkanskitie derzhavi (Outline of the diplomatic history of the Balkan Peninsula). Sofiia, 1931. 133 p.

A series of lectures by a former president of the Sobranie, Bulgarian prime minister, and well-known student of Balkan diplomatic history. One of the few general treatises on the diplomacy of the entire region by a Balkan author. *See also*:

Stojanović, Mihailo D.   The Great Powers and the Balkans, 1875-1878. Cambridge (Eng.), University Press, 1939 (reprinted 1968). 296 p.

169. Đorđević, Dimitrije.   Revolutions nationales de peuples balkaniques, 1804-1914. Translated by Margita Ristić. Beograd, Institut d'histoire, 1965. 250 p.

*See also* entry no. 117.

A concise history, by a prominent Yugoslav scholar, of the Balkan national liberation movements in the 19th century. Though somewhat weak on the Romanian side, this work is carefully researched and well documented and contains a useful discussion of the social economic, and political bases of the liberation movements.

170. Helmreich, Ernst C.   The Diplomacy of the Balkan Wars, 1912-1913. Cambridge, Mass., Harvard University Press, 1938. 523 p. Maps. Bibliography: p. 469-495.

The classic account of the diplomatic side of the Balkan conflicts, fully documented, objective, and readable, with a useful bibliography. The documentation published since 1938 has not rendered this work obsolete. Students of the subject should also consult Edward C. Thaden's *Russia and the Balkan Alliance of 1912* (University Park, Pennsylvania State University Press, 1965, 192 p., map), Viktor A. Zhebokritskii's *Bolgariia vo vremia balkanskikh voin* (Bulgaria in the time of the Balkan wars) (Kiev, Gos. universitet, 1961, 300 p.), and *Bolgariia nakanune balkanskikh voin* (Bulgaria on the eve of the Balkan wars) (Kiev, Gos. universitet, 1960, 248 p.).

171. Sumner, Benedict H.   Russia and the Balkans, 1870-1880. Hamden, Conn., Archon Books, 1962. 724 p. Illus. Includes bibliography.

First published in 1937 by the Oxford University Press. A seminal study of Russian-Balkan relations, focusing on the critical decade of the 1870s. This work remains a classic despite the publication of additional documentation over the past three decades. It is essential for an understanding of Balkan geopolitics, the Treaty of San Stefano, the Congress of Berlin, and Russian-Austro-Hungarian-Serbian, and Bulgarian diplomatic interests. Contains a valuable annotated bibliography.

## C. SINCE 1918

172. Brzezinski, Zbigniew K.   The Soviet Bloc, Unity and Conflict. Rev. and enl. ed. Cambridge, Mass., Harvard University Press, 1967. 599 p. Bibliography: p. 559-576. (Russian Research Center Studies, 37)

*See also* entry no. 140.

The standard work on the subject, by a leading specialist on Soviet foreign policy and East European affairs. The Balkan states and the problem of Titoism are placed in the larger context of East-West tensions.

173. International Conference on World Politics. *5th, Noordwijk, Netherlands, 1965.*   Eastern Europe in Transition. Edited by Kurt London. Baltimore, Johns Hopkins Press, 1966. 364 p.

Includes valuable critical essays on nationalism, communism, polycentrism, the role of national minorities, the Romanian "national deviation," and Western influences in Eastern Europe.

174. Kerner, Robert J., *and* Harry N. Howard.   The Balkan Conferences and the Balkan Entente, 1930-1935; a Study in the Recent History of the Balkan and Near Eastern Peoples. Berkeley, University of California Press, 1936. 271 p. Front., ports., maps.

The basic monograph on the subject, by two distinguished American specialists on East European and Near Eastern affairs. Richly documented.

175. Kertesz, Stephen D., *ed.*   East Central Europe and the World: Developments in the Post-Stalin Era. Notre Dame, Ind., University of Notre Dame Press, 1962. 386 p. Map (on lining papers), tables.

The editor of this volume, a former Hungarian diplomat, is a well-known specialist on contemporary diplomacy and head of International Studies at the University of Notre Dame. The papers of this symposium include a useful survey of recent developments in Romania, Bulgaria, Albania, and Yugoslavia, as well as balanced assessments of American, West European, Chinese, and Soviet policies.

176. Laqueur, Walter, *and* Leopold Labedz, *eds.*   Polycentrism, the New Factor in International Communism. New York, Praeger, 1962. 259 p. (Praeger Publications in Russian History and World Communism, No. 116)

This excellent collection was originally published in a special issue of *Survey* (1962), a journal of Soviet and East European studies. It includes judicious interpretive discussions of the origins of polycentrism, intercommunist diplomacy, the nature of coexistence within the bloc, revisionism and Yugoslavia, a chapter on the Balkans as a unit, and a separate paper on Albania.

177. Lukacs, John A. The Great Powers and Eastern Europe. New York, American Book Company, 1953. 878 p. Maps.

A detailed account of the role of Eastern Europe in European diplomacy between 1917 and 1945. An epilogue covers the period up to 1952. The diplomacy of the Balkan states receives a good deal of attention and is placed in the larger East European and continental contexts. Includes a useful bibliographic note.

178. Seton-Watson, Hugh.   Eastern Europe Between the Wars, 1918-1941. 3d ed. Hamden, Conn., Archon Books, 1962. 425 p. Illus.
*See also* entries no. 131 *and* 156.

Written toward the close of the Second World War and originally published in 1945, this is a valuable study of interwar developments in Eastern Europe by a distinguished British historian. Balkan developments appear within the larger East European picture. The author is somewhat overcritical of the internal policies of the interwar governments of the region. The concluding two chapters on "Small Power Imperialism" and "International Experience, 1918-1941" are particularly valuable.

179. Seton-Watson, Hugh.   The East European Revolution. 3d ed. London, Methuen; New York, Praeger, 1956. 435 p. Bibliography, illus.
*See also* entries no. 130 *and* 331.

A continuation of the author's previous study on the interwar period, this work deals with the German conquest and occupation of Eastern Europe during the Second World War, the entry of Soviet power into the region, and the communization of the area. As with the earlier work, the Balkans are placed in the larger East European setting. Contains a very good separate chapter on the Greek civil war.

180. Skilling, H. Gordon.   Communism, National and International; Eastern Europe after Stalin. Toronto, University of Toronto Press, 1964. 168 p.

The author is a well-known analyst of contemporary communism, educated at Toronto, Oxford, and London, and now Director of Russian and East European Studies at Toronto. In this carefully researched essay, he devotes considerable attention to the Balkan scene and ends with a discussion of the special situation of Romania.

181. Wolff, Robert L.   The Balkans in Our Time. Cambridge, Mass., Harvard University Press, 1956. 618 p. Maps, tables. (Russian Research Center Studies, 23)
*See also* entries no. 136 *and* 159.

A thorough treatment of Balkan problems during the Second World

War and the period of Sovietization. The author, a distinguished historian and specialist on Byzantine and medieval history, headed the Balkan Section, Research and Analysis Branch, O.S.S., during the war and was eyewitness to many of the wartime events dealt with in this work. The book contains a brief but serviceable bibliographical essay.

182. Xydis, Stephen G.   Greece and the Great Powers, 1944-1947; Prelude to the Truman Doctrine. Thessalonike, Institute for Balkan Studies, 1963. 758 p. Illus., maps. Bibliography: p. 721-738.

*See also* entries no. 1117 *and* 1241.

The best scholarly work on the subject, by the leading Western specialist on modern Greece. This massive work is richly documented and objective in its interpretations and it includes a useful documentary appendix and good working bibliography. The interested reader may supplement this work by reference to Edgar O'Ballance's *The Greek Civil War, 1944-1949* (New York, Praeger, 1966, 237 p., maps).

# 7

# the economy

*by John M. Montias*

Books and Articles 183-213
Serials 214-217

## A. BOOKS AND ARTICLES

183. The Balkan States; I. Economic; a Review of the Economic and Financial Development of Albania, Bulgaria, Greece, Roumania, and Yugoslavia since 1919. Specially prepared for, and with the assistance of, the Information Department of the Royal Institute of International Affairs. London, Oxford University Press, 1936. 155 p. Map, tables.

A carefully compiled summary of economic developments in the Balkans in the interwar period, especially useful for its domestic and international financial data.

184. Basch, Antonín. The Danube Basin and the German Economic Sphere. New York, Columbia University Press, 1943. 275 p. Tables. Bibliography: p. 261-265.

An informative and competent account of the breakdown of East European trade relations during the early 1930s and the subsequent economic penetration of Hungary and the Balkans by Nazi Germany. More detailed information on Germany's trade with Hungary and the Balkans may be found in N. Montchiloff's *Ten Years of Controlled Trade in South-Eastern Europe* (Cambridge, The University Press, 1944, 89 p.).

185. Bodnar, Artur. Gospodarka europejskich krajów socjalistycznych; zarys rozwoju w latach 1950-1975 (The economy of the European socialist states; an outline of development in the years 1950-1975). Warszawa, Książka i wiedza, 1962. 390 p. Illus., bibliography.

The most informative survey of the Eastern European economies to have come out of the region itself. The abundant data are collated from a wide variety of published sources, not all easily accessible in the West. The analysis is fairly superficial but, within limits, objective.

186. Economic Development in S.E. Europe, including Poland, Czecho-

slovakia, Austria, Hungary, Roumania, Yugoslavia, Bulgaria, and Greece. With an introduction by Professor David Mitrany. London, PEP, distributed by Oxford University Press, 1945. 165 p.

A highly condensed, well-documented survey of economic conditions in Eastern Europe in the 1930s. Also contains sketches of possible future plans for the postwar period.

187. Feiwel, George R., *ed.*    New Currents in Soviet-type Economies: A Reader. Scranton, International Textbook Company, 1968. 629 p.

Contains, in addition to material on the Soviet Union, 20 essays on economic organization and development in Eastern Europe, most of which originally appeared in journal articles. Every East European economy, except Yugoslavia and Albania, receives detailed treatment in at least one article. Most of the essays on individual countries deal with current economic reforms. Of exceptional importance is the reprint in the above volume of:

Ernst, Maurice. Postwar Economic Growth in Eastern Europe (A Comparison with Western Europe). Washington, D.C., U.S. Government Printing Office, 1966. 220 p. Illus., maps. (New Directions in the Soviet Economy; Studies Prepared for the Subcommittee on Foreign Economic Policy of the Joint Economic Committee, Congress of the United States, Part 4)

188. Grossman, Gregory, *ed.*    Money and Plan: Financial Aspects of East European Economic Reforms. Berkeley, University of California Press, 1968. 188 p.

Instructive essays by qualified specialists on money and credit and on the financial aspects of economic reforms in Soviet-type economies. Also includes an article on the operation of the International Bank for Economic Cooperation of CEMA. For recent surveys of the East European financial systems, *see also*:

Fox, Ursula. Das Bankwesen der europäischen Volksdemokratien. Wiesbaden, Betriebswirtschaftlicher Verlag Gabler, 1967. 209 p.

Beiträge zum Bank- und Devisenrecht in Südosteuropa, München, Südosteuropa-Verlagsgesellschaft, 1965. 135 p.

189. Grossman, Gregory, *ed.*    Value and Plan; Economic Calculation and Organization in Eastern Europe. Berkeley, University of California Press, 1960. 370 p. Tables. Includes bibliographical references.

A collection of essays, including, in addition to the papers on the Soviet economy that represent the bulk of the book, contributions on Poland's price-setting problems and Yugoslavia's institutional reforms. The papers by L. Hurwicz and B. Ward explore theoretical problems common to all Soviet-type economies. For recent surveys *see*:

Economic Development for Eastern Europe. Edited by M. C. Kaser. London, Macmillan; New York, St. Martin's Press, 1968. 329 p.

Thalheim, Karl C., *ed.*    Wirtschaftsreformen in Osteuropa. Köln, Verlag Wissenschaft und Politik, 1968. 309 p.

Grossman, Gregory. Economic Reform: The Interplay of Economics and Politics. *In* Burks, R. V., *ed.* The Future of Communism in Europe. Detroit, Wayne State University Press, 1968. p. 103-140.

190. Hertz, Friedrich Otto.   The Economic Problem of the Danubian
States. London, V. Gollancz, 1947. 223 p.
    Devoted mainly to the problems of Austria and Hungary after the
    breakdown of the Dual Monarchy. The Balkan economies receive
    only superficial treatment.
    On trade restrictions in the 1920s, see the classic study Economic
    Nationalism of the Danubian States by L. Pasvolsky (New York, Mac-
    millan, 1928, 609 p., maps).

191. Jahn, Georg M., and W. M. v. Bissing, eds.   Die Wirtschaftssysteme
der Staaten Osteuropas und der Volksrepublik China; Untersuchungen
der Entstehung, Entfaltung und Wandlung sozialistischer Wirtschaftssysteme. Berlin, Duncker und Humblot, 1961-62. 2 v. Illus. Includes
bibliographies. (Schriften des Vereins für Socialpolitik, n. F., Bd. 23)
    Contains lengthy and detailed essays on the economies of Czecho-
    slovakia, East Germany ("Mitteldeutschland"), Hungary, Romania,
    Bulgaria, Albania, and Yugoslavia (as well as China and the USSR).
    The essays, on the whole, are more descriptive than analytical, but
    the material is well presented and carefully compiled.

192. Karcz, Jerzy F., ed.   Soviet and East European Agriculture. Berkeley,
University of California Press, 1967. 445 p.
    Only the last three papers in this conference volume deal with
    Eastern Europe: Joel M. Halpern's demographic and sociological study
    of the Yugoslav peasantry, George Lazarcik's statistical analysis of
    Czechoslovak agriculture, and Andrzej Korbonski's essay on socialized
    and private agriculture in Poland. Together with the shorter com-
    ments of their discussants, these papers represent one of the more
    significant contributions to the scant literature on the postwar agri-
    cultural problems of Eastern Europe.
    For recent statistical data see the following publications of the
    U.S. Dept. of Agriculture, Economic Research Service: Indices of
    Agricultural Production in Eastern Europe and the Soviet Union,
    1950-68 (Washington, D.C., 1969, 22 p. ERS-Foreign 273); and
    Agricultural Statistics of Eastern Europe and the Soviet Union, 1950-
    66 (Washington, D.C., 1969, 110 p. ERS-Foreign 252).

193. Lipták, Julius.   Pol'nohospodárstvo v socialistických krajinach (Agriculture in the socialist countries). Bratislava, Vydavatel'stvo politickej
literatury, 1963. 405 p.
    This survey of agricultural trends in Eastern Europe by an econo-
    mist of the region delves into some of the technical problems of
    agriculture but is short on economic analysis. See also the same au-
    thor's Mezinárodní dělba práce v zemědělství zemí RVHP (The
    international division of labor in agriculture in the countries of
    CEMA) (Praha, Nakladatelství politické literatury, 1965, 319 p.; bib-
    liography: p. 316-320). This more recent book, while it is nominally
    devoted to intra-CEMA specialization in farm products, also contains
    a good deal of information on the output and consumption of food-
    stuffs and agricultural products in individual East European countries.

194. Mandelbaum, Karl.   The Industrialization of Backward Areas. Oxford, B. Blackwell, 1945. 111 p. Tables, diagrs. (Oxford University Institute of Statistics, Monograph No. 2)

Prepared with the assistance of J. R. L. Schneider. Following a short description of the development problems of Eastern Europe, focused on the surplus-labor hypothesis, the author formulates an aggregative plan for the industrialization of the region, relying on projections and on sectoral allocations of investment resources in line with derived demand. Mandelbaum's methodology thus diverges essentially from the teleological principles underlying Soviet-style long-term planning in the early 1950s. Second edition published in 1955.

195. Marczewski, Jan.   Planification et croissance économique des démocraties populaires. Paris, Presses universitaires de France, 1956. 2 v. Bibliography: v. 2, p. 551-560.

Broad panorama of the East European economic scene. The volume on growth is limited essentially to the targets and achievements under the first long-term plans (four to six years) in the People's Democracies. The volume on planning draws mainly from pre-1956 accounts of the Polish experience. For a recent French survey, *see*:

George, Pierre.  L'économie de l'Europe centrale slave et danubienne. 3d ed. Paris, Presses universitaires de France, 1968. 128 p. Ill., maps.

196. Miller, Margaret S., *ed.*   Communist Economy under Change; Studies in the Theory and Practice of Markets in Competition in Russia, Poland, and Yugoslavia. London, Published for the Institute of Economic Affairs by A. Deutsch, 1963. 272 p. Bibliographies: p. 254-266.

A study of economic reforms in the USSR, Poland, and Yugoslavia. The authors concentrate on the malfunctions of centralized schemes and on the potential benefits of market-type decentralization.

197. Montias, John M.   Economic Nationalism in Eastern Europe: Forty Years of Continuity and Change. Journal of International Affairs, v. 20, Jan. 1966: 45-71.

An attempt to link East European trade trends before and after the Second World War, with special emphasis on exchanges by broad commodity groups. Compares the character of economic nationalism under prewar capitalism and under communist conditions.

198. Montias, John M.   Inflation and Growth: The Experience of Eastern Europe. *In* Baer, W., *and* I. Kerstenetsky, *eds.* Inflation and Growth in Latin America. Chicago, Irwin, 1964. p. 216-249.

Describes monetary planning via the synthetic balances and surveys the monetary experiences of the East European countries. Special emphasis is placed on the inflationary pressures released by the political and economic disturbances of 1956 in Poland and Hungary. For further information on monetary reforms after the Second World War, *see* Henri Wronski's *Le rôle économique et social de la monnaie dans les Démocraties Populaires: La réforme monétaire polonaise*

*1950-1953* (Paris, M. Rivière et Cie, 1954, 181 p.). For a Soviet survey of monetary institutions in various Eastern European countries, throughout which financial statistics are thinly scattered, see also *Banki i kredit v stranakh narodnoi demokratsii* (Banks and credits in the people's democratic countries) by V. Bochkova and others (Moskva, Gosfinizdat, 1961, 323 p., illus., bibliography).

199. Novozámsky, Jiří.   Vyrovnávání ekonomické úrovně zemí RVHP (The leveling of economic levels among the countries of CEMA). Praha, Nakladatelství politické literatury, 1964. 172 p. Bibliographical footnotes.

A short but important book dealing with the levels of development, rates of growth, and foreign-trade policies of CEMA members. The author argues that disparities in development will be gradually reduced as the less developed countries surpass the more developed in their rates of growth of national income per capita, but warns against the sanguine view that all members will attain communism at exactly the same time.

Pryor, Frederic L., *and* George J. Staller.   The Dollar Values of the Gross National Product in Eastern Europe. Economics of Planning, v. 6, no. 1, 1966: 1-26. Independent calculations, based upon sectoral estimates, of the national incomes of East European countries in 1955.

200. Pryor, Frederic L.   The Communist Foreign Trade System. Cambridge, M.I.T. Press, 1963. 296 p. Bibliography: p. 289-293.

The only available treatment *in extenso* of the relation between central planning and foreign-trade decisions in Soviet-type economies. The author's evidence for the description of foreign-trade planning methods is drawn mainly from East Germany. Contains very useful statistical information on East European trade. For institutional details on the organization of foreign trade in Eastern Europe, *see also*:

Hermes, Theodor.   Der Aussenhandel der Ostblockstaaten. Hamburg, Cram, de Gruyter, 1958. 177 p.

201. Pryor, Frederic L.   Public Expenditures in Communist and Capitalist Nations. Homewood, Ill., Richard D. Irwin, 1968. 543 p.

A sophisticated analysis and comparison of government expenditures on defense, education, and welfare in the Soviet Union and Eastern Europe and in capitalist countries.

202. Rosenstein-Rodan, P. N.   Problems of Industrialization of Eastern and South-Eastern Europe. The Economic Journal, v. 53, June 1943: 202-211.

This influential article by a well-known specialist on economic development contains a plea for the rapid industrialization of Eastern Europe, which the author considers to be the best, if not the only, means for absorbing the surplus labor of the region.

203. Sanders, Irwin T., *ed.*   Collectivization of Agriculture in Eastern

Europe. Lexington, University of Kentucky Press, 1958. 214 p. Maps, tables. Includes bibliographical references.

*See also* entry no. 227.

Completed before the onset of full-scale collectivization in Eastern Europe. Generally obsolete, but still the only multicountry survey in English of the first stages of collectivization in the region.

204. Spulber, Nicolas.    The Economics of Communist Eastern Europe. Cambridge, Technology Press of M.I.T., 1957. 525 p. Illus.

Ten years after its publication, this was still the only comprehensive English-language survey of the economies of Eastern Europe, even though it appeared before most of the official statistical yearbooks of the East European countries were issued on a regular basis (after an interruption of nearly a decade). Still authoritative on the nationalization of industry and trade, on reparation payments, and on other early postwar events.

205. Spulber, Nicolas.    The State and Economic Development in Eastern Europe. New York, Random House, 1966. 179 p. "Bibliographical essay": p. 153-173.

Three essays on the economic history of Eastern Europe, chiefly devoted to the development of the region prior to the onset of communist rule. Basic themes treated in the essays include the role of the state in industrial progress, the expanding web of credit relations, and the generation of an entrepreneurial class in Eastern Europe. A good selection of growth statistics and an annotated bibliography add to the value of the book.

206. Suranyi-Unger, Theo.    Studien zum Wirschaftswachstum Südosteuropas. Stuttgart, Gustav Fischer Verlag, 1964. 216 p. Bibliographical footnotes.

A valuable analysis of economic growth in Hungary, Romania, Bulgaria, and Albania, stressing the synthetic, and especially the financial, aspects of development (budget policy, sectoral allocation of investments, distribution of national income, etc.).

207. Svennilson, Ingvar.    Growth and Stagnation in the European Economy. Geneva, United Nations Economic Commission for Europe, 1954. 342 p. Diagrs., tables.

A synthesis of the quantitative aspects of European economic development in the interwar period, corroborating the pessimistic appraisal of P. N. Rosenstein-Rodan, K. Mandelbaum, and others on the performance of the East European economies during this period.

208. *United Nations. Economic Commission for Europe.*    Economic Survey of Europe in 1961. Part 2. Some Factors in Economic Growth in Europe during the 1950s. Geneva, 1964. 283 p.

A simple econometric analysis of the contribution of labor, capital, and technical progress to growth in Eastern and Western Europe during the 1950s. The study is marred, in the case of Eastern Europe, by the undiscriminating use of official statistics of national income and industry. The same criticism applies to the otherwise highly informative and useful annual surveys of economic development in the Eastern European countries prepared by the Secretariat of the Economic Commission for Europe.

209. Warriner, Doreen.  Economics of Peasant Farming. 2d ed. New York, Barnes and Noble, 1965. 208 p. Illus., maps.
    *See also* entry no. 230.
        First published in 1939. Essays by a well-known specialist on peasant problems, overpopulation, rural standards of living, efficiency of farming operations, and labor conditions in Eastern Europe.

210. Warriner, Doreen, *ed.*  Contrasts in Emerging Societies; Readings in the Social and Economic History of South-Eastern Europe in the Nineteenth Century. Bloomington, Indiana University Press, 1965. 402 p. Maps, bibliographical footnotes.
    *See also* entry no. 229.
        A judicious selection of annotated readings on Hungary, Romania, Bulgaria, and the regions now making up Yugoslavia, chiefly based upon 19th century writings but also containing a few extracts from documents of the 18th century.

211. Wellisz, Stanislaw.  The Economies of the Soviet Bloc; a Study of Decision Making and Resource Allocation. New York, McGraw-Hill, 1964. 245 p. Bibliographical footnotes.
        A systematic analysis of the sources of static inefficiency in central planning. The author particularly deplores the absence of rational prices. Based almost entirely on Polish sources.

212. Zagoroff, S. D., Jenö Végh, *and* Alexander D. Bilimovich.  The Agricultural Economy of the Danubian Countries, 1935-1945. Stanford, Calif., Stanford University Press, 1955. 478 p. Illus., maps.
        Technical and competent essays on agricultural conditions in Bulgaria, Hungary, Romania, and Yugoslavia before and during the Second World War. Also contains a general survey of agriculture in the Balkans, together with an economic and statistical analysis of land reforms after the First World War.

213. Zaleski, Eugène.  Les courants commerciaux de l'Europe Danubienne au cours de la première moitié du vingtième siècle. Paris, Librairie générale de droit et de jurisprudence, 1952. 564 p. Diagrs. Bibliography: p. 553-561.
        A sound analysis of trade trends among the Danubian states in the first half of the 20th century. The discussion of multilateral European exchanges is particularly enlightening.
        Brown, Alan A., and Egon Neuberger, *eds.*  International Trade and Central Planning: Analysis of Economic Interactions. Berkeley, University of California Press, 1968, 455 p. Contains five eassys on the

foreign trade of Eastern Europe (by A. A. Brown, N. Spulber, J. M. Montias, and Peter Wiles) together with short discussions by specialists on the subject. Other articles by E. Neuberger, A. Bergson, and H. G. Johnson analyze the nature of foreign trade relations in Soviet-type economies. By far the best source of analytical material on the subject.

## B. SERIALS

214. The American Review of Soviet and Eastern European Foreign Trade. 1965– White Plains, N.Y. Bimonthly.

This journal, published by the International Arts and Sciences Press, contains translations of articles from Soviet and East European journals on specialization in CEMA, the effects of economic reforms on the conduct and practice of foreign trade, and numerous other economic problems arising from the external economic relations of the communist countries.

215. Eastern European Economics. 1962– White Plains, N.Y. Quarterly.

This periodical, published by the International Arts and Sciences Press, contains translated articles from East European economic journals, selected by American scholars. From time to time an entire issue is taken up with a single source, such as J. Timár's "Planning the Labor Force in Hungary" v. 4. no. 3, 1966, 145 p.), prepared and translated by the National Planning Office in Budapest with an introduction by Lynn Turgeon. Articles on economic growth and on institutional reforms are featured.

216. Osteuropa-Wirtschaft. 1956– Stuttgart. Quarterly.

Economic developments in the USSR and East Central Europe.

217. Quarterly Economic Review. Eastern Europe, South. 1956– London, Economist Intelligence Unit. Quarterly.

Surveys economic developments in Albania, Bulgaria, Hungary, and Romania.

# 8

# the society

*by Irwin T. Sanders*

218. Brailsford, Henry N.   Macedonia: Its Races and Their Future. London, Methuen, 1906. 336 p. Illus., maps.

A very informative description of Macedonia under Ottoman rule at the turn of the century.

219. Cvijić, Jovan.   La péninsule balkanique. Paris, A. Colin, 1918. 528 p. Illus., maps.

*See also* entries no. 77 *and* 2266.

An excellent baseline study, somewhat pro-Serbian, of ethnic types, migrations, material culture, and habitat.

220. Ehrenburg, Il'ia G.   European Crossroad: A Soviet Journalist in the Balkans. New York, Knopf, 1947. 177 p.

The Balkans in Soviet perspective by a perceptive writer. Translated from the Russian by Anya Markov.

221. Fischer-Galati, Stephen, *ed.*   Eastern Europe in the Sixties. New York, Praeger, 1963. 239 p. (Praeger Publications in Russian History and World Communism, no. 137)

*See also* entries no. 49 *and* 144.

The Balkan countries, exclusive of Greece, are included in sections on the new social order, the planned economy, and the politics of coexistence.

222. Jelavich, Charles, *and* Barbara Jelavich, *eds.*   The Balkans in Transition: Essays on the Development of Balkan Life and Politics since the Eighteenth Century. Berkeley and Los Angeles, University of California Press, 1963. 451 p. Maps, diagrs., tables, bibliography.

*See also* entries no. 121, 150, *and* 161.

Authoritative essays on modernization and social change.

223. Ladas, Stephen P.   The Exchange of Minorities: Bulgaria, Greece, and Turkey. New York, Macmillan, 1932. 849 p. Illus., maps. Bibliography: p. 831-832.

*See also* entries no. 708, 1202, *and* 1341.
Shows the close connection between nationality problems and political events in the Balkans.

224. Mitrany, David.    Marx against the Peasant: A Study in Social Dogmatism. Chapel Hill, University of North Carolina Press, 1951. 301 p. Bibliography: p. 270-286.
*See also* entry no. 153.
Excellent background for understanding peasant reactions to collectivization in the Balkans and elsewhere in Eastern Europe.

225. Mosely, Philip E.    The Peasant Family: The Zadruga or Communal Joint-Family in the Balkans and Its Recent Evolution. *In* Ware, C. F., *ed*. The Cultural Approach to History. New York, Columbia University Press, 1940. p. 95-108.
*See also* entry no. 2694.
Based on actual field research in the 1930s.

226. Rouček, J. S., *ed*.    Moscow's European Satellites. *In* American Academy of Political and Social Science. Annals, v. 271, September, 1950: 1-253.
Discussion of various social trends by U.S. specialists on Eastern Europe, not including Greece.

227. Sanders, Irwin T., *ed*.    Collectivization of Agriculture in Eastern Europe. Lexington, University of Kentucky Press, 1958. 214 p. Maps, tables. Includes bibliographical references.
*See also* entry no. 203.
Treats East European peasantries, Soviet strategy in collectivization, and agricultural collectivization in Bulgaria, Czechoslovakia, Hungary, Romania, and Yugoslavia.

228. Shotwell, James T.    A Balkan Mission. New York, Columbia University Press, 1949. 180 p. Illus.
A prominent historian's personal impressions of the Balkan countries except Albania.

229. Warriner, Doreen, *ed*.    Contrasts in Emerging Societies; Readings in the Social and Economic History of South-Eastern Europe in the Nineteenth Century. Bloomington, Indiana University Press, 1965. 402 p. Maps, bibliographic footnotes.
*See also* entry no. 210.
Basic background for understanding social changes in the twentieth century. Selected and translated by G. F. Cushing and others.

230. Warriner, Doreen.    Economics of Peasant Farming. 2d ed. New York, Barnes and Noble, 1965. 208 p. Illus., maps.
*See also* entry no. 209.
A classic study of rural conditions in the 1930s.

# 9

# intellectual and cultural life

*by James F. Clarke*

## A. GENERAL

231. Diels, Paul. Die slavischen Völker. Mit einer Literaturübersicht von Alexander Adamczyk. Wiesbaden, Harrassowitz, 1963. 381 p. Fold. maps. Bibliography: p. 311-358. (Veröffentlichungen des Osteuropa-Institutes München, Bd. 11)

Includes the best and most complete concise survey of all aspects of the intellectual and cultural life of the Balkan Slavs. It is the last, posthumously published, work of the author of the important *Altkirchenslavische Grammatik* (2d ed., Heidelberg, Carl Winter, 1963, 2 pts. in 1), first edition, 1932-1934. Of related interest is:

Koschmieder, E. *and* Alois Schmaus, *eds.* Münchner Beiträge zur Slavenkunde. Festgabe für Paul Diels. München, Isar Verlag, 1953. 329 p. Illus., ports. (Veröffentlichungen des Osteuropa-Institutes München, Bd. 4)

232. Geyer, Dietrich. Wissenschaft in kommunistischen Ländern. Tübingen, Rainer Wunderlich Verlag Hermann Leins, 1967. 309 p.

A collection of papers, originally read at the University of Tübingen, on numerous aspects of study and research in the humanities and social sciences.

233. Il'inskii, Grigorii A.   Opyt sistematicheskoi Kirillo-Mefod'evskoi bibliografii (Attempt at a systematic Cyrillo-Methodian bibliography). Edited and supplemented by Mikhail G. Popruzhenko and Stoian Romanski. Sofiia, P. Glushkov, 1934. 302 p.

Published under the auspices of the Bulgarian Academy of Sciences. The 3,385 items listed here are augmented by some 900 more in *Kirilometodievska bibliografiia za 1934-1940* (Cyrillo-Methodian bibliography for 1934-1940) by Mikhail Popruzhenko and Stoian Romanski (Sofiia, Durzh. pechatnitsa, 1942, 169 p.), and in "Bulgarska kirilometodievska bibliografiia za perioda 1944-1962" (Bulgarian Cyrillo-Methodian bibliography for the period 1944-1962) by Ivan Duĭchev and others in *Khiliada i sto godini slavianska pismenost, 863-1963* (1100 years of Slavic writing) (Sofiia, 1963, p. 515-541). Also *Bibliografski pregled na slavianskitie kirilski iztochnitsi za zhivota i deinost'ta na Kirila i Methodiia* (Bibliographical survey of Slavic Cyrillic sources for the life and activity of Cyril and Methodius) by Mikhail Popruzhenko and Stoian Romanski (Sofiia, Pridvorna pechatnitsa, 1935).

234. Stoianovich, Traian.   A Study in Balkan Civilization. New York, Knopf, 1967. 215 p. Bibliography: p. 199-215. (Borzoi Studies in History)

Although this study fits none of the categories of Balkan intellectual and cultural life, it touches on all. The author tries to find common denominators to define "Balkan" and in so doing ranges over the whole of time and history. The highly selective bibliography is noteworthy.

235. Zimmermann, Werner G.   Valtazar Bogišić, 1834-1908. Ein Beitrag zur südslawischen Geistes- und Rechtsgeschichte im 19. Jahrhundert. Wiesbaden, Steiner, 1962. 530 p. (Veröffentlichungen des Instituts für europäische Geschichte, Mainz, 22)

*See also* entry no. 2402.

An excellent study of the life and work of the lawyer, codifier, social thinker, and leader of the Slavophile movement.

## B. LANGUAGES

236. Jagić, Vatroslav.   Entstehungsgeschichte der kirchenslavischen Sprache. Berlin, Weidmann, 1913. 540 p.

A much revised and enlarged edition, first published in 1900 in the *Denkschriften* of the Vienna Academy, by the foremost authority at that time. His *Istoriia slavianskoi filologii* (History of Slavic philology) (Sanktpeterburg, 1910, 961 p., Entsiklopediia slavianskoi filologii, vyp. 1) also still has much value as does his contribution in the *Cambridge Medieval History*, v. 4 (1923), ch. 7B, "The Conversion of the Slavs." The same subject is covered in brief in the second edition, v. 4, ch. 2 (1967) by Dimitri Obolensky.

237. Lunt, Horace G.  Old Church Slavonic Grammar. 2d rev. ed. 'S-Gravenhage, Mouton, 1959. 143 p. (Slavistic Printings and Reprintings, 3)

> A structural linguistic textbook description, the Introduction (p. 1-14) gives a concise summary of the history and bibliography of the subject. More historical is *Geschichte der altkirchenslavische Sprache* by Nikolaas van Wijk (Berlin, W. de Gruyter, 1931 [only v. 1 was published], Grundriss der slavischen Philologie und Kulturgeschichte, Bd. 8).

238. Miklosich, Franz, *Ritter von*.  Die türkischen Elemente in den südost- und osteuropäischen Sprachen. Rev. ed. Wien, In Commission bei F. Temsky, 1889-1890. 2 v. Bibliography: v. 2, 191-194. (*In* K. Akademie der Wissenschaften, Wien, Philosophisch-historische Classe. Denkschriften, Bd. 37, 38)

> First published in 1884, this is the most extensive treatment of the subject by a leading South Slav (Slovene) Slavic scholar of the 19th century.

239. Sandfeld, Kristian.  Linguistique balkanique. Problèmes et résultats. Paris, E. Champion, 1930. 242 p. (Collection linguistique, publiée par la Société de linguistique de Paris, 31)

> A Danish philologist who took a doctorate in Balkan linguistics in 1900, Sandfeld is also author of *Der Schwund des Infinitivs im Rumänischen und den Balkansprachen* (Leipzig, Johann Ambrosius Barth, 1902; Institut für rumänische Sprache, Jahresbericht, 9, p. 75-131). See also *Des traits linguistiques communs aux langues balkaniques* (*Revue des études slaves* [Paris], v. 5, 1925: 38-57) by A. M. Selishchev, who is a noted Russian authority.

## C. LITERATURES

240. Léger, Louis.  Serbes, Croates, et Bulgares. Études historiques, politiques et littéraires. Paris, J. Maisonneuve, 1913. 222 p.

> Essays mostly literary and cultural on the 18th and 19th centuries. Léger was a pioneer French Slavist and literary historian. For a recent Bulgarian study *see*:
> Le développement des littératures du sud-Est européen en relation avec les autres littératures de la fin du XVIII° siècle à nos jours. Edited by A. Mirambel and E. Georgiev. Sofia, Edition de l'Académie bulgare des sciences, 1966. 74 p.

241. Lord, Albert B.  Nationalism and the Muses in Balkan Slavic Literature. *In* Jelavich, Charles, *and* Barbara Jelavich, *eds*. The Balkans in Transition. Berkeley and Los Angeles, The University of California Press, 1963. p. 258-296.

This informative essay, largely on the 19th century, may be supplemented by the too brief survey by Clarence A. Manning, "The Literature of the Balkan Slavs," in *A Handbook of Slavic Studies*, edited by Leonid Strakhovsky (Cambridge, Mass., Harvard University Press, 1949), p. 512-531, including a selected bibliography, p. 526-531.

242. Murko, Matthias.   Geschichte der älteren süd-slavischen Literaturen, Leipzig, C. F. Amelang, 1908. 248 p. Bibliography: p. 220-225. (Die Literaturen des Ostens, Bd. 5, Abt. 2)

See also entry no. 2786.

A penetrating student of West and South Slav culture and literature, Murko also wrote "Die südslavischen Literaturen," in *Die osteuropäischen Literaturen und die slawischen Sprachen*, v. 1, pt. 9 (Berlin-Leipzig, 1908), p. 194-244. On Murko's work there is "Zum 100. Geburtstag Matthias Murkos: Matthias Murkos Leistung und Bedeutung für die Südostforschung" by Josef Matl and "Matthias Murko und die Prager Südosteuropa-Forschung," by Walther Wünsch, in *Südost-Forschungen* (Munich), v. 20 (1961).

## D. FOLKLORE

243. Leskien, August, *ed. and tr.*   Balkanmärchen aus Albanien, Bulgarien, Serbien und Kroatien. Jena, E. Diederichs, 1919. 332 p. (Die Märchen der Weltliteratur, Bd. 11)

Leskien was the author of one of the first and most widely used and imitated Church Slavic grammars, *Handbuch der altbulgarischen (altkirchenslavischen) Sprache* (7th rev. ed., Heidelberg, C. Winter, 1955, 351 p.), first published in 1871; and the more elaborate *Grammatik der altbulgarischen (altkirchenslavischen) Sprache* (2d and 3d eds., Heidelberg, C. Winter, 1919, 260 p., Sammlung slavischer Lehr- und Handbücher, 1. Reihe, Grammatiken, 1)

244. Skendi, Stavro.   Albanian and South Slavic Oral and Epic Poetry. Philadelphia, American Folklore Society, 1954. 221 p. Bibliography: p. 215-221. (Memoirs of the American Folklore Society, v. 44)

A Columbia dissertation, this is a thorough description and analysis of comparative elements.

## E. HISTORY OF THOUGHT AND CULTURE

245. Balkanologen-Tagung, *München, 1962.*   Die Kultur Südosteuropas: ihre Geschichte und ihre Ausdrucksformen. Wiesbaden, Harrassowitz; München, Südosteuropa-Verlagsgesellschaft, 1965. 337 p. Illus., maps. (Südosteuropa-Schriften, Bd. 6)

See also entry no. 56.

Twenty-three papers given at an international conference held by the Südosteuropa-Gesellschaft, Munich, in 1962 and edited by Günther Reihenkron and Alois Schmaus. A similar volume is *Völker und*

*Kulturen Südosteuropas; kulturhistorische Beiträge*, edited by Balduin Saria (München, Südosteuropa-Verlagsgesellschaft, 1959, 284 p., illus., maps; Südosteuropa-Schriften, 1). Both reflect the German tendency to view Southeastern Europe as an extension of Central Europe.

246. Dvornik, Francis.   The Slavs; Their Early History and Civilization. Boston, American Academy of Arts and Sciences, 1956. 394 p. Bibliography: p. 341-371. (Survey of Slavic Civilization, v. 2)

This and much of Dvornik's work relates to Cyril and Methodius and the medieval culture of the Balkans. His extensive bibliographies are especially noteworthy. Bio-bibliographical information on Dvornik is in *Harvard Slavic Studies*, v. 2 (Cambridge, Mass., Harvard University Press, 1954), edited by Horace G. Lunt.

247. Gesemann, Gerhard.   Kultur der Südslaven (Bulgaren, Serben, Kroaten, Slowenen). *In* Handbuch der Kulturgeschichte, no. 37. Wildpark-Potsdam, Athenaion, 1937.

Among Gesemann's other monographs on South Slav culture is *Heroische Lebensform. Zur Literatur- und Wesenskunde der balkanischen Patriarchalität* (Berlin, Wiking-Verlag, 1943, 371 p.).

248. Iorga, Nicolae (Nicholas).   Le caractère commun des institutions du Sud-Est de l'Europe. Paris, J. Gamber, 1929. 138 p.

Widely ranging essays on the continuity of Balkan institutions and customs. Among his many similar lectures at the Sorbonne, is *Byzance après Byzance: continuation de "l'Histoire de la vie byzantine"* (Bucharest, 1935, 272 p.), which reflects a Romanian and Greek point of view.

249. Thierfelder, Franz.   Ursprung und Wirkung der französischen Kultureinflüsse in Südosteuropa. Berlin, Duncker und Humblot, 1943. 226 p. (Frankreich in deutscher Sicht, Heft 1)

Descriptive work, including a short bibliography.

250. Valjavec, Fritz.   Geschichte der deutschen Kulturbeziehungen zu Südosteuropa. München, R. Oldenbourg, 1953-1968? 5 v. (Südosteuropäische Arbeiten, 41-45)

The first four volumes cover the medieval, Reformation and Counterreformation, Enlightenment and 19th century periods. The fifth volume is bibliography and index. Valjavec was the longtime director of the important Südost-Institut in Munich. A more restricted but excellent work is *Die Bedeutung der Reformation und Gegenreformation für das geistige Leben der Südslaven* by Matthias Murko (Prag und Heidelberg, Druck der Česká grafická unie a. s. v Praze; C. Winter in Heidelberg, 1927, 184 p.), reprint from *Slavia*, v. 4-5.

# F. RELIGION

251. Amand de Mendietta, Emmanuel.   La presqu'île des caloyers: Le

Mont-Athos. Paris, Desclée, de Brouwer, 1955. 388 p. Fold. map. Bibliography: p. 360-385.

Of special significance is the bibliography. Many aspects of Mt. Athos are included in *Le Millénaire de Mont Athos, 963-1963 Études et mélanges* (Chevetogne, Editions de Chevetogne, 1963-64, 2 v., illus., ports., maps; bibliography: v. 2, p. 337-483).

252. Attwater, Donald. The Christian Churches of the East. v. 2: Churches not in Communion with Rome. Milwaukee, Bruce Pub. Co., 1948. 290 p. Illus.

This factual description, first published separately in 1937, may be compared with a Protestant view, *The Churches of Eastern Christendom* by J. B. Kidd (London, The Faith Press, 1927, 541 p., front., plates, ports., bibliography), and a Greek Orthodox, *Geschichte der orientalischen Kirchen von 1453-1898* by A. D. Kyriakos (Leipzig, A. Deichert [G. Böhne], 1902, 280 p.), translated from the third volume of the second edition (Athens, 1898), first published in 1872.

253. Golubinskii, Evgenii E. Kratkii ocherk istorii pravoslavnykh tserkvei bolgarskoi, serbskoi i rumynskoi ili moldovskoi (Short sketch of the history of the Orthodox churches of Bulgaria, Serbia and Romania or Moldavia). Moskva, 1871. 732 p.

Long the standard Russian history, it may be supplemented with *Kratka istoriia na suvremennitie pravoslavni tsurkvi*, v. 2 *Bulgarska, Ruska i Surbska* (Short history of the contemporary Orthodox churches. v. 2. Bulgarian, Russian and Serbian) by Ivan Snegarov (Sofiia, Universitetska pechatnitsa, 1946, 472 p.; Universitetska biblioteka, no. 299). Snegarov is the foremost Bulgarian church historian.

254. Obolensky, Dimitri. The Bogomils, a Study in Balkan Neo-Manichaeism. Cambridge, University Press, 1948. 317 p. Fold. map. Bibliography: p. 290-304.

A thorough well-documented study with a full bibliography, principally focused on Bulgaria. An exhaustive analysis and translation of one of the chief sources for Bogomilism is *Le traité contre les Bogomiles de Cosmas le Prêtre* by Henri Charles Puech and André Vaillant (Paris, 1945, 348 p.; Travaux publiés par l'Institut d'études slaves, 21)

255. Sas-Zaloziecky, Wladimir. Die byzantinische Baukunst in den Balkanländern und ihre Differenzierung unter abendländischen und islamischen Einwirkungen; Studien zur Kunstgeschichte der Balkanländer. München, R. Oldenbourg, 1955. 147 p. Illus., plates. Bibliography: p. 111-134. (Südosteuropäische Arbeiten, 46)

A study of styles and their interchange and continuity. Although more restricted, an excellent work is *Early Byzantine Churches in Macedonia and Southern Serbia. A Study of the Origins and Initial Development of Early Christian Art*, by Ralph F. Hoddinott (London and New York, St. Martin's Press, 1963, 262 p., illus., 72 plates [part col.], fold. maps, plans).

256. Spinka, Matthew.   A History of Christianity in the Balkans; a Study in the Spread of Byzantine Culture among the Slavs. Chicago, The American Society of Church History, 1933. 202 p. Bibliography: p. 189-191. (Studies in Church History, v. 1)
    *See also* entry no. 2940.

    Post-medieval material from a Greek point of view is contained in *Studies and Documents Relating to the History of the Greek Church and People under Turkish Domination* by Theodore H. Papadopoullos (Brussels, Wetteren, 1952, 507 p.; Bibliotheca Graeca aevi posterioris, 1). Informative is the documented study by George G. Arnakis, "The Role of Religion in the Development of Balkan Nationalism," in *The Balkans in Transition*, edited by Charles and Barbara Jelavich (Berkeley and Los Angeles, University of California Press, 1963, p. 115-144.

## G. EDUCATION AND RESEARCH

257. Kerner, Robert J.   Social Sciences in the Balkans and in Turkey; a Survey of Resources for Study and Research in These Fields of Knowledge. Berkeley, University of California Press, 1930. 137 p.
    *See also* entry no. 1288.

    Of value for its description of activity generated after the First World War. An excellent though brief survey is "Historical Studies in the Balkans" by George C. Soulis in *The Balkans in Transition*, edited by Charles and Barbara Jelavich (Berkeley and Los Angeles, University of California Press, 1963, p. 421-438).

258. Spuler, Berthold.   Die Minderheitenschulen der europäischen Türkei von der Reformzeit bis zum Weltkrieg. Breslau, Priebatsch's Buchhandlung, 1934. 100 p. (Schriften des Osteuropa-Institutes in Breslau, neue Reihe, Heft 8)

259. Tsourkas, Cleobule.   Les débuts de l'enseignement philosophique et de la libre pensée dans les Balkans. La vie et l'oeuvre de Théophile Corydalée (1570-1646). 2d rev. ed. Thessalonika, Institute for Balkan Studies, 1967. 441 p. 24 plates.

    Of interest for Greek schools with special reference to Romania and to philosophy. Of great related interest with respect to Greek and other schools at the end of the 18th century is *The Life and Adventures of Dimitrije Obradović, Who as a Monk Was Given the Name of Dositej, Written and Published by Himself*, edited and translated by George R. Noyes (Berkeley, University of California Press, 1953, 340 p., illus., map; University of California Publications in Modern Philology, v. 39). It includes an exhaustive introduction by the editor and a full bibliography (p. 317-320).

## G. THE FINE ARTS AND MUSIC

260. L'Art byzantin chez les Slaves. Les Balkans. Premier recueil dédié à

la mémoire de Théodore Uspenskij. Paris, Paul Geuthner, 1930. 2 v. Illus., plates, plan, facsims., diagrs. (Orient et Byzance. Études d'art mediéval, 4)

> Planned as a Festschrift, it includes contributions by many of the foremost authorities. In addition to general and special contributions it has chapters on Bulgaria, Serbia, and Romania. An appendix comprises a complete catalog of the art work and bibliography of these three areas, p. 417-454.

261. Grabar, André.   Recherches sur les influences orientales dans l'art balkanique. Paris, Société d'édition Les Belles Lettres; London, New York, H. Milford, Oxford University Press, 1928. 150 p. Illus., plan, plates, facsims. (Publications de la Faculté des lettres de l'Université de Strasbourg, fasc. 43)

> Grabar is one of the foremost authorities on medieval (Byzantine) Balkan art. A group of distinguished specialists (Kurt Weitzmann, Manolis Chatzidakis, Kruste Miatev, and Svetozar Radojčić) have combined to produce *Frühe Ikonen. Sinai, Griechenland, Bulgarien, Jugoslawien* (Wien u. München, Schroll, 1965, 220 p. of illus., 174 plates [part col.], bibliographies).

262. Palikarova Verdeil, R.   La musique byzantine chez les Bulgares et les Russes (du IXᵉ au XIVᵉ siècle). Copenhague, E. Munksgaard; Boston, Byzantine Institute, 1953. 249 p. Illus., facsims. (Monumenta musicae byzantinae. Subsidia, v. 3)

> The scope of this work is somewhat broader than the title. It includes musical notations and an extensive bibliography. For a recent symposium *see*:
>
> Volksmusik Südosteuropas. Edited by W. Wünsch. München, R. Trofenik, 1966. 167 p. Illus., music. (1. Balkanologentagung, Graz, 1964)

# PART TWO

# ALBANIA

# 10

# GENERAL
# REFERENCE AIDS,
# BIBLIOGRAPHIES,
# AND SURVEY WORKS

*by Elez Ndreu*

## A. BIBLIOGRAPHIES

263. Albanesische Bibliographie. Compiled by Franz Manek, G. Pekmezi, and A. Stolz. Wien, Selbstverlag des Vereins "Dija," 1909. 147 p.
   Approximately 1,700 entries, arranged by date of publication except for 113 which are not dated, cover the period from 900 B.C. to 1909. Although it is incomplete, this bibliography provides many useful references in the humanities and the social sciences. Entries are in Albanian, English, French, German, Greek, Italian, and Latin, with annotations in German. Author and subject indexes, as well as separate lists of Albanian newspapers and journals and of various bibliographies on Albania.

264. Bartl, Peter. Albanica Monacensia. Verzeichnis der in München selbständigen Veröffentlichungen über Albanien. München, Albanien-Institut d. Univ. München, 1963. 83 p.
   553 entries in alphabetical order.

265. Biblioteka Kombëtare. Bibliografia e Republikës Popullore të

73

Shqipërisë; Vepra origjinale dhe përkthime (Bibliography of the People's Republic of Albania; original works and translations). 1958–Tiranë. Quarterly.

Includes original Albanian works, translations, and foreign language publications. According to the Biblioteka Kombëtare (National Library), a bibliography of all Albanian publications from 1945 to 1957, now in mimeographed form, will be published in 1968. For a supplemental bibliography listing articles from Albanian periodicals, *see* the following:

Biblioteka Kombëtare. Bibliografia e Republikës Popullore të Shqipërisë; artikuj të revistave shqipe (Bibliography of the People's Republic of Albania; articles from Albanian periodicals). 1961–Tiranë. Monthly.

266. Çoba, A., *and* Z. Prela. Albanica; Vepra të botuara në shek. XVI-XVIII. (Albanica; works published from the 16th to the 18th centuries). Tiranë, Biblioteka Kombëtare, 1965. 108 p.

This highly selective bibliography lists 294 entries covering the period 1473 to 1799. Arranged chronologically according to publication date, it lists only books in the collection of the National Library in Tirana. Most of the entries are in Italian, with others in English, French, German, Greek, and Latin. Annotations are in Albanian. Contains many important references on Albanian linguistics, ethnography, history and geography, and travelogues. An index of authors and titles is included.

267. Indogermanisches Jahrbuch. 1913-1955. Berlin. Annual.

The volumes for 1917, 1918, 1920, 1922, 1924, 1926-1942, 1948, 1951, 1955 contain bibliographies, compiled successively by Norbert Jokl, Carlo Tagliavini, and Karl Gurakuqi, listing approximately 3,700 titles relating to Albanian subjects which appeared between 1916 and 1948. Entries in the last three volumes are limited to Albanian and Balkan linguistics. Annotations are in German or Italian.

268. Kastrati, Jup. Bibliografi Shqipe (29. XI. 1944 - 31. XII. 1958). (Albanian bibliography, 29 Nov. 1944 - 31 Dec. 1958). Tiranë, N. Sh. B. "Naim Frashëri," 1959. 498 p.

This bibliography lists all Albanian books published in Albania from November 1944 to November 1958. Included are some 2,400 entries which are arranged according to subject or discipline, with entries under each discipline listed for the most part alphabetically by author. Although this bibliography is by its nature nonselective, it is a valuable reference tool for research into contemporary Albanian subjects. Contains an index of authors and names of persons and a very useful history of bibliographies on Albania, with listings of both foreign and Albanian works.

269. Kersoupolos, Jean G. Bibliographie, No. 1. Albanie. Ouvrages et articles des revues parus de 1555 à 1934. *In* Les Balkans, Supplément V, 1934: 377-424; 651-712.

1,000 entries arranged alphabetically by author, some of which are annotated in French. Although extremely weak in the areas of belles-lettres, the arts, and cultural affairs, this bibliography lists very useful references in the social sciences. On pages 379-382 is a convenient list of periodicals which are cited.

270. Lambertz, Maximilian, *and others, comps.* Albanische Bibliographie. *In* Südosteuropa-Bibliographie. München, R. Oldenbourg, 1956– Band I, Teil 2, 1945-1950: 183-195; Band II, Teil 2, 1951-1955: 363-382.

The first section includes 215, and the second, 292 entries for publications in the fields of history, the social sciences, and the arts. A continuation covering the years 1956-1960 was issued in 1967.

271. Legrand, Émile Louis Jean. Bibliographie albanaise; description raisonnée des ouvrages publiés en albanais ou relatifs à l'Albanie, du quinzième siècle a l'année 1900. Completed and published by Henri Guys. Paris, H. Welter, 1912. 228 p.

A very good selective list of publications on Albania from 1474 to 1900. Some 724 entries, including works in Albanian, Greek, and Western European languages, are arranged chronologically. Under each year, entries are listed alphabetically by author. Annotations are in French. Emphasis is given to bibliographies, language, linguistics and philology, literature, folklore, geography, ethnography, history, politics, theology, and religion. Author, publisher, subject, and name indexes are included. For a supplement to this bibliography, covering the period from 1900 to 1910, *see*:

Guys, Henri. Bibliographie albanaise. Description raisonée des ouvrages publiés en albanais ou relatifs à l'Albanie de 1900 à 1910. Tirana, K. Luarasi, 1938. 56 p.

272. U.S. *Bureau of the Census.* Bibliography of Social Science Periodicals and Monograph Series: Albania, 1944-1961. Washington, D.C., 1962. 12 p. (Foreign Social Science Bibliographies. Series P-92, no. 6)
*See also* entry no. 25.

This bibliography includes 40 periodicals and monograph series in the general area of the social sciences which were published in Albania from 1944 to 1961, covering a variety of subjects. Entries are arranged first by discipline and then alphabetically by issuing agency or by title. Descriptive annotations in English are provided, but no attempt has been made to evaluate the contents. Indexes for subjects, authors, titles, and issuing agencies are also included.

273. U.S. *Library of Congress. Division of Bibliography.* The Balkans. v. 2. Albania; a Selected List of References. Compiled by Helen F. Conover under the direction of Florence S. Hellman. Washington, D.C., 1943. 24 p.

A highly selective list of primarily Western language publications. Some 239 entries are divided into the following categories: bibliographies, official publications, general (surveys, description, travel), the land (geography, geology, etc.), history and politics, economics, people (ethnology, religion, culture, etc.), and language. The first volume of this series, *The Balkans. v. 1. General*, which treats Albania as one of the component parts of the larger Balkan picture, is a useful supplement to this specialized volume.

## B. GENERAL PERIODICALS*

274. Albania. E përkohëshme shqip. Revue albanaise. v. 1-11, v. 12, no. 1: mars 1897-1909. Bruxells, 1897-1902; London, 1902-1909. Monthly.

Founded by the well-known Albanian writer and literary critic Faik Konica, this periodical was the most important Albanian publication of the time and remains a very significant collection of studies on Albanian literature and language, history, folklore, and sociology. It established essay writing as an important genre in Albanian literature for the first time. Among the contributors, which included some foreign as well as many Albanian writers and scholars, are N. Frashëri, G. Fishta, A. Çajupi, H. Pedersen, and Asdreni. Articles are in Albanian and French. Issues frequently contain bibliographical surveys.

The following periodicals, all of which are general in nature, also contain extremely valuable contributions to Albanological studies:

Belgrade. Univerzitet. *Seminar za arbanasku filologiju.* Arhiv za arbanasku starinu, jezik i etnologiju (Archive for Albanian antiquity, language and ethnology). 1-3, 1923-1926. Beograd. Annual. Edited by Henrik Barić, this periodical contains studies in Serbo-Croatian, Slovenian, French, and German. Some issues contain first-rate critical bibliographies.

Gjurmime Albanologjike (Albanological Research). 1962– Priština. Irregular. First three volumes (1962, 1965, 1966) published by the Department of Albanology of the University of Belgrade at Priština. Now published by the Institute of Albanology in Priština, this periodical covers a variety of aspects of Albanian cultural affairs.

Hylli i Dritës (The star of light). 1913-1914; 1921-1924; 1930-1944. Shkodër. Monthly. Founded by the great Albanian poet and writer, Father Gjergj Fishta, and published by the Franciscans, this periodical played an outstanding role in the development of Albanological studies of all kinds — language, literature, history, folklore, politics, religion, sociology, etc. Bibliographies are included.

Leka. 1929-1944. Shkodër. Monthly. Published by the Society of Jesus in Shkodër (Scutari), this periodical offers illuminating articles in Albanian and Italian on Albanian documents, history, language, literature, folklore, etc.

Përparimi (Progress). 1955– Priština. Monthly. Published by the Autonomous Region of Kossovo-Metohija, Yugoslavia, this periodical

* For periodicals on Albania in Western European languages refer to *The USSR and Eastern Europe; Periodicals in Western Languages* (*see* entry no. 26).

is devoted to cultural and political topics as they relate to the Albanian people of Kossovo-Metohija and of Albania.

Shêjzat. Le Pleiadi. 1957– Roma. Bimonthly. Articles in Albanian, Italian, French, and German are included in this excellent periodical devoted to Albanian belles-lettres and Albanological studies. Ernest Koliqi and Martin Camaj founded and continue to edit Shêjzat.

Studi albanesi. 1931-1936. Roma, Istituto per l'Europa orientale. Annual. This serial offers studies in Italian on Albanian archaeology, history, geography, culture, etc.

275. Revista d'Albania. 1940-1943. Milano, R. Accademia d'Italia, Istituto per gli studi di politica internazionale. Quarterly.

This review contains important articles and studies by well-known Italian and Albanian scholars and writers. Nearly all issues contain bibliographical surveys for the quarterly period of publication, among which the most significant are the thoroughly annotated lists compiled by Carlo Tagliavini on linguistics: I (1940): fascicolo 2, p. 198-228; fascicolo 4, 416-424; II (1941): fascicolo 2, p. 181-190; fascicolo 3, p. 277-285; fascicolo 4, p. 397-413; III (1942): fascicolo 4, p. 252-262; IV (1943): fascicolo 2, p. 115-122.

276. Studia Albanica. 1964– Tiranë. Semiannual.

A publication of the Institute of History and Language of the University of Tirana, with articles in French, English, Russian, German, and Italian. The majority of the contributors are Albanian. Despite the fact that the articles occasionally contain biased political allusions, this is a valuable review for those without knowledge of Albanian who wish to do research in Albanology.

277. Tirana. Universiteti Shtetëror. Buletin. Seria shkencat shoqërore (Bulletin. Social sciences series). 1957-1963. Tiranë. Quarterly.

A scholarly journal containing articles and critical reviews of books. Résumés in French. Previously appeared as:

Buletin i Institutit të Studimeve (Bulletin of the Institute of Research). 1947. Tiranë.

Buletin i Institutit të Shkencave (Bulletin of the Institute of Sciences). 1948-1952. Tiranë.

Buletini për shkencat shoqërore (Bulletin of social sciences). 1952-1957. Tiranë. Quarterly.

Superseded by two quarterlies in Albanian, Studime historike (Studies on history) and Studime filologjike (Studies on philology) and, in other languages, by the semiannual Studia Albanica (see entry no. 276).

A bibliography of the contents for the years 1947-1963 is contained in no. 4 of 1963.

## C. OTHER REFERENCE TOOLS

278. Albania. Drejtoria e Statistikës. Anuari Statistikor i R. P. Sh. (Statistical yearbook of the People's Republic of Albania). 1958– Tiranë.

Statistical compilation containing information on many aspects of the society and economy, including territorial divisions, population, industry, agriculture, transport and communications, commerce, foreign trade, education and culture, and public health.

279. Frashëri, Kristo, *ed.* Rilindja Kombëtare Shqiptare; me rastin e 50 vjetorit të shpalljes së Pavarësisë Kombëtare, 1912 — 28 Nëndor — 1962 (Albanian national renaissance: on the occasion of the 50th anniversary of national independence, November 28, 1912-1962). Tiranë, N. Sh. B. "Naim Frashëri," 1962. 120 p. Illus., ports., facsims.

An album illustrating, by photographic and documentary materials, Albanian history from 1840 to 1912, which has been termed the "Albanian national renaissance." It is divided into topical chapters, with each recounting specific events and highlighting leading historical personages chronologically. Fairly detailed running captions are given in Albanian, English, French, and Russian. The materials have been culled primarily from the Central Archives of History and from the National Library in Tirana, which are rarely visited by foreign scholars. An interesting and informative volume which has no counterpart among Western publications.

280. Kunze, Horst. Das Bibliothekswesen in Albanien seit 1945. München, Südosteuropa-Verlagsgesellschaft, 1960. 18 p. (Hausdrucke der Südosteuropa-Gesellschaft, Heft 1)

281. Permanent Committee on Geographical Names for British Official Use. A Gazetteer of Albania. London, 1946. 210 p. "Sources of information": p. xiv-xix.

A gazetteer listing place names and geographic coordinates for regions, populated places and topographic features within Albania. Maps are included. Although it is somewhat out of date, this gazetteer is still a most useful and accurate source of information.

Another gazetteer is the U.S. Office of Geography's *Albania: Official Standard Names Approved by the U. S. Board on Geographic Names*, 2d ed. (Washington, D.C., U.S. Government Printing Office, 1961, 207 p.).

## D. SURVEYS AND DESCRIPTIVE WORKS

282. Albania. *Ministrija e punve të mbrendshme.* Shqipënija më 1937 (Albania in 1937). Tiranë, Shtypshkronja "Kristo Luarasi," 1937. 272 p.

Issued in connection with the celebration of 25 years of independence.

283. Albania. Shqipria më 1927. L'Albanie en 1927. By Teki Selenica. Tiranë, Shtypshkronja "Tirana," 1928. 573 p.

A government-sponsored general survey written by a high official in the Ministry of Interior in Albania in 1927 with detailed information on Albanian politics, society, history, and economy as well as copious statistical data on the various administrative subdivisions of Albania. The statistical information is important, particularly since no other source offers such a complete survey for the period. However, some sections of the author's commentary, especially that treating of the history of Albania, are subjective and unreliable.

284. Durham, Mary Edith.    High Albania. London, Edward Arnold, 1909. 352 p. Illus., fold. map.

An important book, based on an eight-month tour in 1907 and previous visits in Northern Albania, striving "to give the national points of views, the aims and aspirations, the manner and customs of High Albania." It offers a perceptive view of the social customs, living habits, folklore, and traditions of Northern Albanian tribes, including lively descriptions of the cities and countryside of Northern Albania, and a good deal of historical information and intelligent speculation on the political future of Albania. A most worthwhile general introduction to Albanian life in the early 20th century. For additional information on specific aspects of Albanian life in the period, *see* the author's other books: *The Burden of the Balkans* (London, Edward Arnold, 1905); *The Struggle for Scutari* (London, Edward Arnold, 1914); *Some Tribal Origins, Laws and Customs of the Balkans* (London, George Allen & Unwin, 1928); and *Twenty Years of Balkan Tangle* (New York, Putnam, 1929).

285. Hahn, Johann Georg von.    Albanesische Studien. Wien, Aus der kaiserlich-königlichen Hof- und Staatsdruckerei, 1853. 3 v.

An important collection of studies by the founder of modern German research on the geography, history, folklore, and language of Albania. Volume 1 is a book of travels with data on the folklore, genesis, and history of the Albanian people; volume 2 contains a grammar of the Tosk dialect; and volume 3 is an Albanian-German dictionary.

*See also* the following work by the same author: *Reise durch die Gebiete des Drin und Wardar. Denkschriften.* Vienna, Kaiserliche Akademie der Wissenschaften, 1867-1869. 2 v. (Denkschriften, Bd. 15, 16, 2. Abth.)

286. Kostallari, Androkli, *ed.*    Konferenca e Parë e Studimeve Albanologjike (15-21 Nëndor 1962) (The first conference of Albanological studies, November 15-21, 1962). Published by the Instituti i Historisë dhe i gjuhësisë, Universiteti Shtetëror i Tiranës. Tiranë, 1965. 740 p.

Addresses, reports, papers, and discussions held during the First Conference of Albanologists in Tirana in 1962. The bulk of the book consists of scholarly papers emphasizing Albanian language and history. Among the contributors are Franz Babinger, Eqrem Çabej, Selman Riza, Vittore Pisani, Stuart E. Mann, Justin Rrotta, and Karl Treimer. A valuable book despite the absence of some Albanologists resident outside Albania. Illustrations and errata pages are included.

287. Skendi, Stavro, *ed.*    Albania. New York, Published for the Mid-European Studies Center of the Free Europe Committee by Frederick A. Praeger, 1956. 389 p. Bibliography: p. 355-370.
*See also* entries no. 332 *and* 450.

The most useful general survey in English of contemporary Albania (up to the year 1955). Includes a brief résumé of Albania's history and detailed information on the politics, economics, society, and culture of Albania, with short biographical sketches of leading figures of the communist regime, a chronology of important events from 1944 to 1955, and a list of treaties and agreements undertaken by the Albanian government from 1947 to 1955.

288. Swire, Joseph.    King Zog's Albania. London, Robert Hale, 1937. 302 p. Map. Bibliographical note: p. 285-286.
*See also* entry no. 339.

The author, a competent and knowledgeable journalist who was a Fellow of the Royal Geographical Society and a member of the Royal Institute of International Affairs, offers an interesting and well-informed personal view of Albania. The bibliographical note supplements the fairly extensive, annotated bibliography appended to Swire's historical work, *Albania: The Rise of a Kingdom* (New York, Richard R. Smith, 1930).

# 11

# the land

*by Robert Schwanke*

Journals and Reference Works 289-290
Monographs and Special Aspects 291-303

## A. JOURNALS AND REFERENCE WORKS

289. Italy. *R. Ufficio geologico.* Bibliografia geologica e geografico-fisica della regione albanese. Suppl. ad vol. LXIV (1939) del Bolletino (del R. Ufficio geologico d'Italia). 2d ed. Roma, Istituto poligrafico dello Stato, 1941. 106 p. Maps.

> This bibliography, edited by M. Magnani, contains about 1,354 titles of books and articles on Albania and the bordering areas in line with the then prevailing political situation.

290. Tirana. Universiteti Shtetëror. Buletin. Seria Shkencat natyrore (Bulletin of the State University of Tirana, Natural Science Series). 1957– Tiranë. Quarterly.

> Supersedes Tirana University's *Buletin Institutit i Shkencavet* (Bulletin of the Institute of Sciences), 1947-1951, and *Buletin për shkencat natyrore* (Bulletin of the natural sciences), 1952-1956. It contains papers on geography and biology. Summaries in French are provided.

## B. MONOGRAPHS AND SPECIAL ASPECTS

291. Bourcart, Jacques. Les confins albanais administrés par la France 1916-1920: contribution à la géographie et la géologie de l'Albanie moyenne. Revue de géographie, v. 10, 1922: 1-307.

> Contains not only geological, geographic, geobotanical, and anthropogeographic information, but also statistical data on population, housing, and the like. Also included is a map (1:200,000) for the area of Albania occupied by French forces during the First World War.

292. Demiri, Mustafa, *and* Ilja Mitrushi. Die Flora und Fauna Albaniens. Die Presse der Sowjetunion (Presseamt beim Ministerpräsidenten der Regierung der DDR), 1957, no. 9: 199-203.

> A rather brief survey, but sufficient for an overall orientation on the flora and fauna. Translated from *Priroda* (v. 9, no. 8, 1957: 71-80).

*See also* Mitrushi's *Drurët e shkurret e Shqipërisë; përhapja, kultivimi, dobia dhe përdorimi i tyre* (Trees and shrubs of Albania; their distribution, cultivation, usefulness, and utilization) (Tiranë, Instituti i shkencave, 1955, 604 p.). One of the features of this work is the provision of Latin, Russian, German, French, and English equivalents for botanical names.

293. Isidorov, Cvetko G.   Klima e Shqipërisë (The climate of Albania). Tiranë, Instituti i shkencave, 1955. 159 p. Illus.
> This monograph contains extensive tabular material.

294. Louis, Herbert.   Albanien; eine Landeskunde, vornehmlich auf Grund eigener Reisen. Stuttgart, Engelhorn, 1927. 164 p. Map. Bibliography: p. 154-158. (Geographische Abhandlungen, 2d ser., no. 3).
> The author participated in the 1923-1924 topographic survey of the country and provides within the framework of an essentially topographical study numerous other geographical observations.

295. Louis, Herbert.   Karte von Albanien, 1:200,000 auf Grund der österreichischen Kriegsaufnahmen. Wien, Hauptvermessungsabteilung, 1939. 2 sheets.
> The Italian Institute of Military Geography issued a map with a scale of 1:50,000 in 94 sheets between 1929 and 1939; it also exists in the form of a German reprint at the original scale (Berlin, Generalstab des Heeres, Abteilung für Kriegskarten- und Vermessungswesen). Maps with a scale of 1:200,000 were distributed in Albania in 1965 to schools and government offices. Outside Albania, only a school wall-map is commercially available. It has a scale of 1:250,000 and is entitled *Shqipëria* (Albania) (Tiranë, NISH Mjete mesimore e sportive).

296. Markgraf, Friedrich.   Pflanzengeographie von Albanien, ihre Bedeutung für Vegetation und Flora der Mittelmeerländer. Stuttgart, Schweizerbart, 1932. 132 p. Illus., map. Bibliography: p. 125-130. (Bibliotheca botanica, no. 105)
> This work, containing numerous tables and a map (1:400,000), combines a summary of earlier publications with the results of the author's 1924 and 1928 field trips. It emphasizes the significance of autochthonous Albanian flora for clarifying problems in the field of Balkan and Mediterranean geobotany.

297. Mukeli, Raqi.   Elemente të hidrologjise së Shqipërisë (Elements of the hydrology of Albania). v. 1. Tiranë, UShT. 1960. 260 p.
> This study relies on the research so far published on Albanian hydrology. It attempts to develop basic information for the efficient utilization of the water resources, for the construction of power plants, for irrigation, and for the water supply for the population. Because of its statistical data it should find wide use. Summaries in French are provided.

298. Mźik, Hans.   Beiträge zur Kartographie Albaniens nach orientalischen

Quellen. *In* Nopcsa, Ferencz. Geographie und Geologie Nordalbaniens. Budapest, Edidit Institutum Regni Hungariae Geologicum, 1929. p. 625-629.

In addition to this historical contribution on the cartography of Albania, *see also* Nopcsa's "Zur Geschichte der okzidentalen Kartographie Nordalbaniens," published in the same work (p. 651-703), which carries an account of the publication of Herbert Louis' map in 1928.

299. Nopcsa, Ferencz.   Geographie und Geologie Nordalbaniens. Budapest, Edidit Institutum Regni Hungariae Geologicum, 1929. 703 p. Illus., tables, diagrs., maps. Bibliography: p. 518-525.

This work combines material on the geography of northern Albania that was collected between 1903 and 1916. With regard to Nopcsa's activities, *see also* Gert Robel's *Franz Baron Nopcsa und Albanien. Ein Beitrag zu Nopcsas Biographie* (Wiesbaden, Harrassowitz, 1966, 191 p. [Albanische Forschungen, 5]).

300. Nowack, Ernst.   Geologische Übersicht von Albanien. Erläuterungen zur geologischen Karte 1:200,000. Innsbruck, 1929. 229 p.

Of Nowack's numerous works, this is the clearest presentation with regard to the map it describes.

301. Penningsfeld, Franz.   Zur Kenntnis der Böden Albaniens. Berlin, Reichsamt für Bodenforschung, 1942. 135 p. Illus., maps, tables. Bibliography: p. 129-135.

Soil maps with scales of 1:1,000, 1:2,500, 1:5000, and 1:10,000 are presented. A brief history of Albanian soil research can be found in the first two chapters of Faik Bajraktari's *Tokat e Shqipërisë dhe rruget për ngritjen e pjellorisë së tyre* (Soils of Albania and ways to improve their yield) (Tiranë, Min. Bujq., 1960, 251 p.).

302. Pumo, E., *and* A. Papa.   Harta e re gjeologjike e Shqipërisë dhe vlera e saj për studimin, kerkimin dhe shfrytëzemin e pasurive nëntokësore të vendit (The new geological map of Albania and its value for the study and utilization of the mineral resources of that country). Ekonomia Popullore, v. 12, 1965, no. 2: 36-47.

A good survey of the present status of the geological cartography. In addition to Nopcsa, Bourcard, Nowack, and Zuber (*Carta tettonica dell'Albania*, Roma, 1940), the data in Z. A. Mishunin's *Geotektonicheskaia karta raionov Albanii* (1953) were relied on in the preparation of the new Albanian geological map (1:200,000). *See* annotation to entry no. 295.

303. Società geografica italiana, *Rome*.   L'Albania. Bologna, Zanichelli, 1943. 445 p. Illus., maps., diagrs. Bibliography: p. 413-426.

A contemporary area study of Albania, prepared between 1939 and 1941 by Professors Bruno Castiglioni (geography), Ferdinando Milone (economy and population), and Aldo Sestini (individual districts) under the auspices of the Italian Geographic Society. It also includes Greek and Yugoslav territories incorporated into Albania at that time.

# 12

# the people

*by Robert Schwanke*

Journals and Reference Works 304-305

Monographs and Special Aspects 306-315

## A. JOURNALS AND REFERENCE WORKS

304. Etnografia Shqiptare (Albanian ethnography). 1962– Tiranë. Irregular.
A scientific section for ethnography has been in existence at Tirana University since 1947, and it has collected significant ethnological materials. Prior to 1962, ethnological studies appeared in the *Social Sciences Series Bulletin* of the University (entry no. 305). This new serial, of which three issues have already been published, looks toward the publication of an ethnographic atlas and records pertinent materials for this purpose. Summaries of various articles are provided in French and Russian. For a good survey of Albanian culture (with a bibliography through 1943) *see* Eqrem Çabej's "Albanische Volkskunde" in *Südost-Forschungen*, 25 (1966), p. 333-387.

305. Tirana. Universiteti Shtetëror. Buletin. Seria shkencat shoqërore (Bulletin of the State University of Tirana, Social Science Series). 1957– Tiranë. Quarterly.
This journal for social sciences was combined until 1952 with the one for the natural sciences. It covers primarily the fields of archaeology, ethnography, history of art, economics, and statistics. In 1962, a new publication on ethnography was begun (entry no. 304). In 1964, the *Studime historike* (Historical studies) and the *Studime filologjike* (Philological studies) split off. A complete index for the years 1947 to 1963 can be found in number 4 of the 1963 volume. Summaries in French are provided for most articles. Important articles from these two journals have appeared since 1964 in English, French or German translation in *Studia Albanica*, published semiannually by the University of Tirana.

## B. MONOGRAPHS AND SPECIAL ASPECTS

306. Adhami, S. Monumente të kultures në Shqiperi (Cultural monuments of Albania). Tiranë, Ministria e Arësimit, 1958. 176 p.

Describes mostly classical, but also medieval and early modern, cultural monuments relating to the history of Albanian culture.

307. Fallmerayer, Jacob Philipp.   Das albanesische Element in Griechenland. *In* Bayerische Akademie der Wissenschaften. *Historische Klasse. Abhandlungen*, v. 8, 1860: 417-489, 657-736; v. 9, 1866: 1-110.

    The ethnic origin of the Albanian people early became a subject of much controversy. Fallmerayer opposes the nationalistic views set forth by the Greek Nikokles in 1855 as not being scientifically founded. Demetrios S. Constantopoulos tried to justify Greek claims for Albanian territory in his study *Zur Nationalitätenfrage Südosteuropas; eine rechtssoziologische Untersuchung der griechischen Minderheit in Albanien als Voraussetzung ihrer völkerrechtlichen Stellung* (Würzburg, Triltsch, 1940, 227 p.). On the fate of Albanian culture in Greece, *see* Johannes Irmscher's "Die Albaner bei der Gründung des griechischen Staates," *Studia Albanica*, v. 1, 1964: 223-243.

308. Haberlandt, Arthur.   Kulturwissenschaftliche Beiträge zur Volkskunde von Montenegro, Albanien und Serbien. Ergebnisse einer Forschungsreise in den von den k. u. k. Truppen besetzten Gebieten. Sommer 1916. Wien, Gerold, 1917. 187 p. Illus., tables. Bibliography: p. 171-183. (Zeitschrift der österreichischen Volkskunde, Ergänzungsband 12)

    Although only pages 41 to 138 deal directly with Albania, adjacent areas, which are largely inhabited by Albanians, are also described. An account of the Arumani should also be noted.

309. Kostallari, Androkli.   Le développement des études albanologiques en Albanie. Problèmes nouveaux et tâches nouvelles. Studia Albanica, v. 1, 1964, no. 1: 5-46.

    Provides a survey of studies undertaken in Albania in the fields of history, archaeology, ethnography, folklore research, and linguistics.

310. Nopcsa, Ferencz.   Albanien; Bauten, Trachten und Geräte Nordalbaniens. Berlin, de Gruyter, 1925. 257 p. Illus. Bibliography: p. 240-246.

    Since Hahn's *Albanesische Studien* (Wien, 241 p.) appeared in 1853, scholarship has paid special attention to Albanian housing. Nopcsa, however, was the first to produce a systematic work on this subject. On Hahn, *see* Gerhard Grimm's *Johann Georg von Hahn, (1811-1869); Leben und Werk* (Wiesbaden, Harrassowitz, 1964, 385 p. [Albanische Forschungen, Bd. 1]).

311. Praschniker, Camillo, *and* Arnold Schober.   Archäologische Forschungen in Albanien und Montenegro. Wien, Hölder, 1919. 104 p. Illus., maps. (Schriften der Balkankommission der Akademie der Wissenschaften. Antiquarische Abteilung, 8)

    *See also* entry no. 455.

    Publishes the findings of the archaeological members of a scholarly expedition sent to Albania during the First World War. With regard to Italian archaeological excavations, *see* Luigi M. Ugolini's *L'antica Albania, nelle ricerche archeologiche italiane* (Roma, Ente nazionale Industrie turistiche, 1927, 96 p.). For an account of French excavations, *see* Léon Rey's *Albania* (Paris, 1925-39, 6 v.). Current archaeological findings have been reported since 1945 in the Bulletin (Social Science Series) of the University of Tirana (*see* entry no. 305).

312. Seiner, Franz.   Ergebnisse der Volkszählung in Albanien in dem von den österreichisch-ungarischen Truppen 1916-1918 besetzten Gebiete. Wien, Hölder, 1922. 116 p. Maps (Akademie der Wissenschaften in Wien. Schriften der Balkankommission. Linguistische Abteilung, 13)

> Contains the results of the first official census. Later results may be found in *Shqipria më 1927* (Albania in 1927) (Tiranë, Shtypshkronja "Tirana," 1928, 573 p.), edited by Teki Selenica, and in *Shqipria më 1937* (Albania in 1937). From 1945, a census has been taken every five years. Censuses for the 1945-1960 period are reported in *Annuari Statistikor i R.P.Sh.* (Statistical annual of the People's Republic of Albania), published by the Drejtoria e Statistikës in Tirana.

313. Selishchev, Afanasiĭ Matveevich.   Slavianskoe naselenie v Albanii (Slavic population in Albania). Sofiia, Izd. Makedonskogo nauchnogo instituta, 1931. 352 p. Map.

> An account of the Slavic, specifically of the Bulgarian, minority in Albania on the basis of an analysis of its cultural history and linguistic heritage.

314. Urban, Martin.   Die Siedlungen Südalbaniens. Öhringen, Rau, 1938. 198 p. (Tübinger geographische und geologische Abhandlungen, 2d ser., no. 4)

> This profusely illustrated linguistic doctoral dissertation supplements the work by Nopcsa on the north. Both together provide a well-rounded account of the research on Albanian settlement. Urban has included some of his arduous preliminary investigations on the indigenous character of Albanian settlements, on the distribution of minorities, and on population density — subjects on which, at the time the book appeared, there was a dearth of material.

315. Weninger, Josef.   Rassenkundliche Untersuchungen an Albanern. Ein Beitrag zum Problem der dinarischen Rasse. Wien, Anthropologische Gesellschaft, 1934. 67 p. (Rudolf Pöchs Nachlass, Ser. A, no. 4)

> While Weninger based his study on data gathered in an internment camp in 1918, another anthropologist, Carleton S. Coon, undertook field studies in Albania itself in 1929-1930. His study appeared under the title "The Mountains of Giants; a Racial and Cultural Study of the North Albanian Mountain Ghegs" (*Papers of the Peabody Museum of Archaeology and Ethnology*, Harvard University, v. 23, no. 3, 1950).

# 13

# hISTORy

*by Anton Logoreci*

316. Amery, Julian. Sons of the Eagle; a Study in Guerilla War. London, Macmillan, 1948. 354 p. Plates, ports., maps.
    *See also* entry no. 363.
    A vivid account of the experiences of a British officer attached to the monarchist resistance movement in Albania during the Second World War.

317. Babinger, Franz. Das Ende der Arianiten. München, Beck, 1960. 94 p. (Sitzungsberichte der Bayerischen Akademie der Wissenschaften. Phil.-hist. Kl. 1960, H. 4)
    A study of Skanderbeg's brother-in-law, Konstantin Arianiti, papal protégé and diplomat of Emperor Maximilian I.

318. Babinger, Franz. Rumelische Streifzüge. Berlin, Reichsdruckerei, 1938. 62 p.
    Revised and enlarged edition of two studies published in 1930 and 1931: Ewlija Tschelebi's "Reisewege in Albanien" and "Die Gründung von Elbasan."

319. Bourcart, Jacques. L'Albanie et les Albanais. Paris, Bossard, 1921. 264 p. Illus.
    Work of a French scholar who lived in Albania during the First World War.

320. Davies, Edmund F. Illyrian Venture; the Story of the British Military Mission to Enemy-Occupied Albania, 1943-44. London, Bodley Head, 1952. 246 p. Illus.
    Written by the officer who led the mission.

321. Dedi, V., *and others.* Dokumenta e materiale historike nga lufta e popullit Shqiptar për liri e demokraci, 1917-41 (Historical documents and materials on the struggle of the Albanian people for freedom and democracy, 1917-41). Tiranë, 1959. 555 p.

*See also* entry no. 346.

A highly selective collection of documents and papers accompanied by an account of the period written from the communist point of view.

322. Durham, Mary E.    The Burden of the Balkans. London, Edward Arnold, 1905. 331 p. Illus., map.

An account of travels in Albania during 1903-1904 by a well-informed British observer of Balkan affairs. The work, written in a popular form, contains a good deal of reporting on contemporary events.

323. Durham, Mary E.    The Struggle for Scutari. London, Edward Arnold, 1914. 320 p. Illus.

A personal account of the movement to dislodge the Serbian and Montenegrin troops from the town of Scutari, which had been assigned to Albania after the Balkan wars.

324. Frasheri, Kristo.    The History of Albania. Tirana, 1964. 343 p. Illus., ports.

A survey of Albanian history in communist interpretation.

325. Gegaj, Athanase.    L'Albanie et l'invasion Turque au XV$^e$ siècle. Louvain, Bibliothèque de l'Université, 1937. 169 p. Illus., bibliography.

A good historical essay on the invasions of Albania by the Turks during the fifteenth century.

326. Godart, Justin.    L'Albanie en 1922; l'enquête de la Société des nations. Paris, La Flèche, Dépôt des publications de la conciliation internationale, 1922. 374 p.

A French diplomat's sympathetic account of the political and diplomatic developments after the First World War leading to Albania's admission to the League of Nations.

327. Griffith, William E.    Albania and the Sino-Soviet Rift. Cambridge, Mass., M.I.T. Press, 1963. 423 p. Bibliographical footnotes.

*See also* entry no. 349.

A fully documented analytical work on Albania's role in the quarrel between Russia and China with useful historical background.

328. Historia e Shqipërisë (History of Albania). Tiranë, Universiteti Shtetëror i Tiranës, 1959-1965. 2 v. Bibliography: v. 1, p. 495-508.

Volume 1, edited by Selim Islami and Kristo Frashëri, provides a general survey from the earliest times to 1839 with both Marxist and Albanian nationalist coloring. Volume 2, edited by Aleks Buda and others, covers the 1839-1944 period.

329. Noli, Fan S.    George Castrioti Scanderbeg, 1405-1468. New York, International Universities Press, 1947. 250 p. Bibliography: p. 165-180.

A biography of the leader of Albanian resistance against the Turks, it is a scholarly work written from an Albanian nationalist point of view. Includes a valuable critical bibliography.

330. Robinson, Vandeleur.    Albania's Road to Freedom. London, Allen & Unwin, 1941. 135 p. Illus.
    A British journalist's account of the country's development and problems under the rule of King Zog.

331. Seton-Watson, Hugh.    The East European Revolution. 3d ed. London, Methuen; New York, Praeger, 1956. 435 p. Bibliography, illus.
    *See also* entries no. 130 *and* 179.
    A good history of the region from 1941 to 1955, with sections on Albania. The second edition was published in 1952; the first, in 1950.

332. Skendi, Stavro, *ed.*    Albania. New York, Praeger, 1956. 389 p. Maps. Bibliography: p. 355-370. (Praeger Publications in Russian History and World Communism, no. 46)
    *See also* entries no. 287 *and* 450.
    A good comprehensive work which contains a general survey of Albanian history from the earliest times up to 1955.

333. Skendi, Stavro.    The Albanian National Awakening, 1878-1912. Princeton, Princeton University Press, 1967. 498 p. Bibliography: p. 475-488.
    The most thorough and scholarly work on this vital period.

334. Skendi, Stavro.    Beginnings of Albanian Nationalist and Autonomous Trends: The Albanian League, 1878-1881. American Slavic and East European Review, April 1953: 219-232.
    Important essay by a distinguished scholar. A sequel to it is Skendi's "Albanian Political Thought and Revolutionary Activity, 1881-1912," *Südostforschungen*, v. 13, 1954: 159-199.

335. Skendi, Stavro.    The Political Evolution of Albania, 1912-1944. New York, Mid-European Studies Center of the National Committee for a Free Europe, 1954. 20 p.
    Useful brief survey of the country's political development between independence and the advent of the communist regime. Mimeographed.

336. Stadtmüller, Georg.    Forschungen zur albanischen Frühgeschichte. Pest, Királyji Magyar Tudomány-Egyetem, 1941. 196 p. (*Archivum Europae Centro-Orientalis*, 7)
    *See also* entry no. 393.
    A valuable study on the history of Albania and the genesis of the Albanian people from pre-Roman times to the 13th century, by a distinguished German scholar. A reprint of this edition, with an introduction on the results of research during the last 30 years and an updated bibliography, was published in 1966 (Wiesbaden, Harrassowitz, 221 p., maps, Albanische Forschungen, 2).

337. Šufflay, Milan von.   Städte und Burgen Albaniens hauptsächlich
während des Mittelalters. Wien, Hölder-Pichler-Tempsky, 1924. 82 p.
(Denkschriften der Akademie der Wissenschaften in Wien. Phil.-hist.
Kl. 63, Abh. 1)
> The first social history of the Albanian people in the later middle
> ages, giving a lively description of Italian-Albanian-Slavic-Byzantine
> syncretism of the social and economic life in the cities and of the
> social conditions of the mountain tribes.

338. Swire, Joseph.   Albania, the Rise of a Kingdom. London, Williams
and Norgate, 1929. 560 p. Illus., maps, diagrs. Bibliography: p. 525-
535.
> A political history of Albania from 1878 to 1928; useful, if some-
> what pedestrian.

339. Swire, Joseph.   King Zog's Albania. London, Robert Hale, 1937.
302 p. Map. Bibliography: p. 285-286.
> See also entry no. 288.
> Written by a British journalist who visited the country in the 1920s
> and 1930s, the work contains a good deal of simple historical infor-
> mation.

340. Thallóczy, Ludwig von, ed.   Illyrisch-albanische Forschungen. München, Leipzig, Duncker und Humblot, 1916. 2 v. Maps.
> See also entry no. 356.
> A basic work covering in volume 1 the history of Albania up to
> the end of the 19th century.

341. Thallóczy, Ludwig von, Josef K. Jireček, and Milan von Šufflay,
eds.   Acta et diplomata res Albaniae mediae aetatis illustrantia.
Vindobonae, 1913. 2 v. Map.
> A collection of medieval documents in Latin dealing with the period
> between 344 to 1406.

# 14

# the state

*by Robert Schwanke*

Law 342-345
Politics and Government 346-356
Diplomacy and Foreign Relations 357-362
Military Affairs 363-366
Mass Media 367-370

## A. LAW

342. Constitution of the People's Republic of Albania. Tirana. 1964. 39 p.

The more important Albanian codes are available in a separate 687-page volume of *Kodifikimi* (Collections), entitled *Kodet I* (Codes I) and published in Tirana in 1961. It covers the constitution, civil law, civil procedure, criminal law, criminal procedure, family law, and tariff law. A translation of the family code into German appeared in *WGO; Die wichtigsten Gesetzgebungsakte in den Ländern Ost-Südosteuropas* . . . , v. 7, 1965, no. 6: 337-359.

343. Drejtësia popullore (People's justice). Tiranë. 1947– Bimonthly.

This organ of the Supreme Court and the Procurator usually includes a chapter on Albanian court decisions. Provides running commentaries and treatises on Albanian legislation and court decisions. The most important articles have been noted since 1957 in *Wiener Quellenhefte zur Ostkunde, Reihe Recht*.

344. Gazeta zyrtare e Republikës Popullore të Shqipërisë (Official gazette of the People's Republic of Albania). Tiranë. Irregular.

Its interwar precursor was entitled *Fletorja zyrtare* (Official gazette). A convenient reference work is the official *Kodifikimi i përgjithëshëm i legjislacionit në fuqi të RPSh* (General collection of the legislation in force for the People's Republic of Albania) (Tiranë, 1958, 3 v.), with supplements for the years 1958-1962. For information in German on current Albanian legislation see *Wiener Quellenhefte zur Ostkunde, Reihe Recht* (Wien, 1957-1967), *Jahrbuch für Ostrecht* (München, 1960), *WGO; Die wichtigsten Gesetzgebungskate in den Ländern Ost-*

91

*Südosteuropas* . . . (Hamburg, 1959–), and *Dokumentation, Gesetze und Verordnungen Osteuropas* (Wien, Österreichisches Ost- und Südosteuropa-Institut, 1957–).

345. Gjeçov, Stefano C.   Codice di Lek Dukagjini ossia Diretto consue-tudinario delle Montagne d'Albania. Translated by Paolo Dodaj. Roma, 1941. 327 p. (Reale Accademia d'Italia. Centro studi per l'Albania, 2)

A translation of the complete collection of Albanian customary law, which was compiled before 1914 and published in Shkodra in 1933 after the compiler's death. Surveys of customary law are also presented in *Illyrisch-albanische Forschungen* (Wien, 1916) and in *Studi Albanesi, Studi e Testi*, volumes 1 and 3 of which were published in Rome in 1941 and 1969, respectively. The latter volume contains an important study by G. Valentini, entitled "La legge delle montagne albanesi nelle relazioni della missione volante 1880-1932. *See also* G. Valentini's important post-1945 contributions in the Albanian literary journal *Shêjzat* (Pleiades) and Margaret Hasluck's *The Unwritten Law of Albania* (Cambridge, Engl., 1954, 285 p.), which combines meaningfully her own observations with an account of the provisions of the customary law. More attention has been paid in Albania to this subject recently, as evidenced by many articles in *Buletin i Universitetit* (University bulletin) and in *Drejtësia popullore* (People's justice).

## B. POLITICS AND GOVERNMENT

346. Dedi, V., *and others.*   Dokumenta e materiale historike nga lufta e popullit Shqiptar për liri a demokraci, 1917-1941 (Documents and historical materials on the fight of the Albanian people for freedom and democracy, 1917-1941). Tiranë, Botim i Drejtorisë së Arkivave Shtetërore të R.P. Sh., 1959. 555 p.

*See also* entry no. 321.

This collection, published under the auspices of the Albanian State Archives, contains 574 documents, most of which are Albanian. Bibliographical references are appended.

347. Frashëri, Sami B.   Was war Albanien, was ist es, was wird es werden. Gedanken und Betrachtungen über die unser geheiligtes Vaterland bedrohenden Gefahren und deren Abwendung. Translated from the Turkish by A. Traxler. Vienna, Hölder, 1913. 69 p.

Presents the basic ideas of a cultural leader of the Albanian revival of 1899. Of interest as an example of Albanian self-evaluation, and for the author's ideas on a modern government.

348. Giannini, Amadeo.   L'Albania dall'independenza all'unione con l'Italia (1913-1939). 4th ed. Milano, Istituto per gli Studi di Politica Internazionale, 1940. 379 p. Bibliography: p. 367-377.

A well-documented account, from the Italian viewpoint, of the in-

creasingly closer relations between Albania and Italy prior to the
Second World War. *See also* the memoirs of Francesco Jacomoni di
San Savino, *La politica dell'Italia in Albania* (Bologna, Capelli, 1965,
380 p. [Testimoni per la storia del nostro tempo, 39]).

349. Griffith, William E.    Albania and the Sino-Soviet Rift. Cambridge,
Mass., M.I.T. Press, 1963. 423 p. Bibliographical footnotes.
*See also* entry no. 327.

Analysis of Albanian-Soviet relations prior to November 1962.
Of particular significance for an understanding of domestic developments such as Hoxha's decisive 1961 speech. Includes the texts of
34 important documents. For the subsequent relations of Albania
with world communism, see *The Sino-Soviet Rift* (London, Allen &
Unwin, 1964, 508 p. [Library of International Studies, 4], by the
same author.

350. Hoxha, Enver.    Rapport sur l'activité du comité central du Parti du
travail presenté au V^e congrès du PTA 1^er novembre 1966. Tirana,
Frashëri, 1966. 254 p.

The reports of the First Party Secretary at party congresses reflect
the decisive changes in Albanian policies. English, French, and Ger-
man translations are included in some cases. For selected earlier
reports by Hoxha *see* William J. Griffith's work listed in entry no. 349.
So far 2 volumes of Hoxha's collected works have been published
(Tiranë, Naim Frashëri, 1968). For compilations by subject, see *Die
Wahrheit über die sowjetisch-albanischen Beziehungen* (Tirana, Naim
Frashëri, 1964, 172 p.), *Die marxistisch-leninistische Ideologie wird
über den Revisionismus siegen* (Tirana, Frashëri, 2 v.), and *Die
Belgrader Revisionistenclique* (Tirana, Frashëri, 1964, 355 p.).

351. Kotini, Dhimitër, *and others, eds.*    Qeveria e përkohëshme e Vlorës
dhe veprimtaria e saj (28.11.1912-22.1.1914) (Vlora's provisional
government and its activities, November 28, 1912 to January 22,
1914). Tiranë, Botim i Drejtorisë së Arkivave shtetërore të R.P. Sh.,
1963. 383 p.

This collection, issued under the auspices of the Albanian State
Archives, contains translations of 399 Turkish, French, German, and
Italian documents. Bibliographical references are appended.

352. Partia e Punës së Shqipërisë. *Komitet Qëndror.*    Information Bulletin. v. 1– 1949– Tirana.

Reprints important party statements on domestic and foreign policy.
Also available in French as *Bulletin d'information.*

353. Partia e Punës së Shqipërisë. *Instituti i Historisë.*    Dokumenta
kryesore të Partisë së Punës së Shqipërisë (Basic documents of the
Party of Labor of Albania). Tiranë, 1960-1961. 2 v.

Volume 1 covers the period 1941-1948, and volume 2, 1949-1956.
A history of the Party of Labor of Albania has recently appeared
under the title *Historia e Partisë së Punës të Shqipërisë* (Tiranë, Naim
Frashëri, 1968, 453 p.).

354. Le procès contre le complot organisé pour liquider la Republique
Populaire d'Albanie. Tirana, 1961. 447 p.
   Preceded by similar publications on the trials of agents in 1950-52.
   *See also* Th. Bare's comprehensive survey, *Provokacionet dhe kom-
   plotet kundra R.P.Sh. në vitet 1945-56* (Provocations and plots
   against the People's Republic of Albania in the years 1945-56) (Tiranë,
   1966, 199 p.).

355. Rruga e partisë. Organ teorik dhe politik i Komitetit Qendror të PPSh
(The Party's road. Theoretical and political organ of the Central Committee of the Party of Labor of Albania). v. 1– 1953– Tiranë. Monthly.
   Provides complete texts of speeches on domestic policies, as well
   as articles on current ideological and practical problems.

356. Thallóczy, Ludwig von, *comp.* Illyrisch-albanische Forschungen.
München, Leipzig, Duncker und Humblot, 1916. 2 v. 5 maps (1 fold.).
   *See also* entry no. 340.
   The articles by Thallóczy himself ("Probleme der Einrichtung Al-
   baniens") and by Topia ("Das Fürstentum Albanien") represent sig-
   nificant contributions on the domestic history of Albania.

## C. DIPLOMACY AND FOREIGN RELATIONS

357. Dedijer, Vladimir. Jugoslovensko-albanski odnosi, 1939-1948
(Yugoslav-Albanian relations, 1939-1948). Beograd, Borba, 1949.
225 p. Illus.
   *See also* entry no. 2574.
   Outlines the domestic and foreign policies of the Albanian parti-
   sans and of postwar Albania. *See also* M. Đilas' *Conversations with
   Stalin* (New York, Harcourt, Brace and World, 1962, 211 p.), which
   gives more consideration to the Albanian position. Italian translation:
   *Il sangue tradito, relazioni jugoslavo-albanesi, 1938-1949* (Varese [?],
   Editoriale periodici italiani, 1949, 221 p., illus.).

358. Dokumenta mbi miqësine shqiptaro-sovjetike (Documents on Albanian-Soviet friendship). Tiranë, Universiteti Shtetëror i Tiranës,
1957. 551 p.
   This important publication, prepared for the 40th anniversary of
   the October Revolution by the University of Tirana, the Institute for
   Party History, and the Society for Soviet-Albanian Friendship, contains 251 documents, speeches, and newspaper articles pertaining to
   the period 1905-1957.

359. Gardiner, Leslie. The Eagle Spreads His Claws: a History of the
Corfu Channel Dispute and of Albania's Relations with the West,
1945-1965. Edinburgh, London, Blackwood, 1966. 286 p. Map on
endpapers.
   An account of the international naval incident involving Albania
   and Great Britain, with a detailed presentation of the debate in the

U.N. General Assembly and before the International Court of Justice at The Hague, over the issue of free passage through the Corfu Channel. *See also*:

The Hague. International Court of Justice.    Affaire du Détroit de Corfu. Alexandrie, 1949. 42 p.

360. Livre blanc sur la politique hostile du gouvernement de la Republique Populaire d'Albanie envers la R.P.F.J. Belgrade, 1961. 166 p.

A publication of the State Secretariat for Foreign Affairs, presenting the Yugoslav point of view on political relations between 1948 and 1961 (Documents 1-82), and discusses Yugoslav economic policies directed against Albania (Documents 83-111).

361. Self, George M.    Foreign Relations of Albania. Chicago, The University of Chicago Library, Dept. of Photographic Reproduction, 1946.

Film copy of typewritten manuscript of an unpublished dissertation. *See also* a dissertation by Sander Bushati entitled *Die Entstehung des Fürstentums Albanien* (Universität Wien, 1940, 166 p.).

362. Umiltà, Carlo.    Jugoslavia e Albania; memorie di un diplomatico. Milano, Garzanti, 1947. 201 p.

Provides insight into the Italian administration of Yugoslav-Albanian territories during the Second World War.

## D. MILITARY AFFAIRS

363. Amery, Julian.    Sons of the Eagle; a Study in Guerilla War. London, Macmillan, 1948. 354 p. Plates, ports., maps.

*See also* entry no. 316.

A lively study by a member of the British Military Mission to Albania. Based in part on the English journalist J. Swire's account of the Zog regime entitled *Albania, the Rise of a Kingdom* (London, Williams and Nogate, 1929, 560 p.). Includes a discussion of Amery's own experiences during a seven-month stay.

Brigadier Edmund F. "Trotsky" Davies' *Illyrian Venture, The Story of the British Military Mission to Enemy-Occupied Albania, 1943-44* (London, Bodley Head, 1952, 246 p., illus.) is more concerned with the author's fate than with the Albanians', since he was captured within one year of his arrival in Albania.

364. Kasneci, L.    Steeled in the Heat of Battle; a Brief Survey of the History of the National Liberation War of the Albanian People, 1941-44. Tiranë, Frashëri, 1966. 127 p.

*See also* a volume issued by the Institute for Party History entitled *Storm Brigade of the National Liberation War* (Tiranë, 1963, 455 p.).

365. Kronikë ë ditëve të stuhishme (Chronicle of stormy days). Edited by L. Kasneci and others. Tiranë, M.M.P., Section for Military History, 1962. 479 p.

A record of events and participants in the Partisan war (1942-44). Includes Party and General Staff documents, plans of operations, and biographies. See also *La bataille pour la libération de Tirana* (Tiranë, Naim Frashëri, 1966, 126 p.) by Mehmet Shehu, on the final phase of the war.

366. Shehu, Mehmet.   On the Experience of the National Liberation War and on the Development of the National Army. Tiranë, Naim Frashëri, 1963. 109 p.

This report stresses the advantages of guerrilla warfare in a mountainous country like Albania, points out the differences between Albanian and Yugoslav military doctrine, and emphasizes the basic disagreements with the Soviet Union.

## E. MASS MEDIA

367. Alia, Ramiz.   De l'elévation du rôle de la littérature et des arts pour l'éducation communiste des masses. *In* Partia e Punës së Shqipërisë. Bulletin d'information, v. 17, no. 4, 1965: 4-45.

Alia makes the interesting point that a country that has complete control of its public media must still rely on ideologically unacceptable foreign films and books in order to supplement its own inadequate Production. See also *Education for Communism: School and State in the People's Republic of Albania*, by John I. Thomas (Stanford, Calif., Hoover Institution Press, 1969, 131 p.)

368. Biblioteka Kombëtare.   Bibliografia kombëtare e Republikës Popullore të Shqipërisë. Artikujt e periodikut shqip (Articles published in Albanian periodicals). 1961– Tiranë.

*See also* Kenneth E. Olson's survey "The Press of Albania" in his *The History Makers* (Baton Rouge, Louisiana State University Press, 1966, p. 333-340).

369. Biblioteka Kombëtare. Bibliografia kombëtare e Republikës Popullore të Shqipërisë.   Libri Shqip (Albanian books). 1959– Tiranë.

370. Kastrati, Jup.   Bibliografië shqipe e shtypit, 1848-1946 (Albanian press bibliography, 1848-1946). Tiranë, Biblioteka Kombëtare, 1946.

A work in manuscript form.

Since 1945 a daily bulletin, *Nouvelles d'Albanie*, has been issued by the Albanian Press Agency. In addition, broadcasts from Radio Tirana are published in *Radio Free Europe, Albania Monitoring*. The only adequate treatise on the Albanian press is in Skendi's *Albania* (p. 125-137). Albanian propaganda publications for domestic and foreign consumption are listed in the national bibliography (*see* entries 265 and 268). The illustrated propaganda semimonthly *New Albania* is also published in Albanian, Chinese, French, Russian, and Arabic.

# 15

# the economy

*by Robert Schwanke*

Journals and Reference Works 371-374

Special Subjects 375-385

## A. JOURNALS AND REFERENCE WORKS

371. Albania. *Drejtoria e Statistikës.* Vjetari statistikor i R.P.Sh. (Statistical yearbook of the People's Republic of Albania). 1963– Tiranë.

Has sections on general data, climate, elections, population, manpower, industry, agriculture, construction, transportation, domestic trade, foreign trade, national income and finance, education and culture, public health, and international data. Supersedes *Anuari statistikor i R.P.Sh.* (Statistical annual of the People's Republic of Albania), 1958-1961. For pre-1945 statistics, *see Annuario del Regno di Albania* (Milano, 1940), *Shqipria më 1927* (Albania in 1927) (Tiranë, 1928, 573 p.), and *Shqipenia më 1937* (Albania in 1937) (Tiranë, 1937).

372. Buletin i punimeve shkencore të ekonomisë së peshkimit (Bulletin of scientific works on the fishing economy). 1959– Tiranë.

Has summaries in French. Serves as a sound basis for the study of the Albanian fishing economy, about which little was known during the interwar period. Pre-1959 articles on this subject can be found in Tirana State University's Natural Sciences Series Bulletin (entry no. 290).

373. Ekonomia Popullore (National economy). 1954– Tiranë. Bimonthly.

Journal of the principal Albanian economic organizations. Unfortunately, it lacks summaries in other languages. Indispensable for following the economic trends of this country. In recent issues, theoretical subjects predominate.

374. Tirana. *Instituti i larte shtetëror i bujqësisë.* Buletin i shkencave bujqësore (Bulletin of agricultural sciences). 1961– Tiranë. Quarterly.

Has Russian, English, and French summaries. Only French résumés are given in *Anuar i studimeve shkencore bujqësore* (Yearbook of agricultural scientific studies) (1961–, Tiranë).

## B. SPECIAL SUBJECTS

375. Albanien; Referat über die Bodenkultur. Wien, Staatsdruckerei, 1914. 83 p.

> Contains the results of a study commission on soil conservation sent to Albania in 1913.

376. Calmès, Albert.   La situation économique et financière de l'Albanie Annex du rapport présenté au Conseil par le Comité financier de la Commission économique et financière provisoire sur sa huitième session). Genève, 1922. 31 p. Map. (Société des Nations. Commission économique et financière, Comité financier, C 706 M 417. 1922 II Annex I C-652, 1922 II, EFS 343 A 195)

> An impressive account of the poor conditions existing in the agricultural sector of the Albanian economy.

377. The Development of Agriculture in the People's Republic of Albania. Tirana, Naim Frashëri, 1962. 53 p.

> Includes data to 1960 and planned goals to 1965. Only useful as a starting point for further investigation.

378. Geço, Pandi. Gjeografia ekonomike e Shqipërisë (Economic geography of Albania). Tiranë, Drejt. e Bot. Shkollore, 1965. 220 p. Illus., maps.

> This textbook for schools of higher education is also available in a shorter edition in English. The English translation by Harilla Papajorgji is *The Development of Socialist Industry and Its Prospects in the People's Republic of Albania* (Tirana, 1964, 146 p.). The English edition contains statistical information to 1963 and planning goals to 1965. This is one of the most informative and useful of Albanian propaganda publications.

379. Hamiti, Zenel. Historiku i vajgurorit në Shqiperi (History of petroleum in Albania). Tiranë, Naim Frashëri, 1966. 164 p.

> This pamphlet, although reflecting a somewhat one-sided point of view, provides a good survey of the development of the petroleum industry and suffices as a source of basic information on this important branch of the economy. Contains statistical data to 1964.

380. Italie et Albanie. n.p., 1946. 209 p. Illus.

> An Italian white paper on Italian aid to Albania, Albanian reparations claims, and Italian reconstruction in 1944-1946. Contains parts of the Calmès report (entry no. 376).

381. Lorenzoni, Giovanni.   La questione agraria albanese; studi, inchiesti e proposte per una reforma agraria in Albania. 2d ed. Bari, 1930. 200 p.

An interesting juxtaposition of the proposals of an Italian expert with enacted regulations. For an analysis of land reform after 1945 and the rise of the collectives through 1956, see the study by Vasil Xhai and Kristo Cevi entitled *Regjimi juridik i tokës në Shqipëri* (Legal basis of landholding in Albania) (Tiranë, Botim. i. Min. së bujq., 1956, 148 p.). A popular and progagandistic treatment of the subject can be found in *Land Reform in the People's Republic of Albania* (Tirana, Committee for Cultural Relations with the Outside World, 1961, 48 p.).

382. Schwanke, Robert. Die Verwirklichung der Sowjetwirtschaft in Albanien. *In* Jahn, Georg, *and* W. M. Frhr. von Bissing, *eds*. Die Wirtschaftssysteme der Staaten Osteuropas und der Volksrepublik China. v. 2. Berlin, Duncker und Humblot, 1962. p. 243-326.

Attempts to provide a survey of economic development and a forecast to 1965. In the same vein are pages 198-254 of *Albania*, edited by Stavro Skendi (New York, Praeger, 1956; London, Atlantic Press, 1957). For the period of the 1966-1970 plan, compare Mehmet Shehu's *Bericht über die Direktive des 5. Parteitages der Partei der Arbeit Albaniens für den 4. Fünfjahrplan der wirtschaftlichen und kulturellen Entwicklung der VR Albanien in den Jahren 1966-1970. Erstattet auf dem 5. Parteitag der PAA. 5. November 1966* (Tirana, Naim Frashëri, 1966, 147 p.).

383. Sheri, Fiqri, *and* Shero Mami. Nje përshkrim i shkurtër i historikut të statistikës në vendin tonë (A brief account of the history of statistics in our country). Ekonomia Popullore, v. 9, no. 4, 1962: 54-68.

Contains a good survey of statistical publications on Albania, beginning with the Venetian land records of the 15th century and including Austrian, French, and Italian statistics of the period of the First World War. Censuses after 1918 stress demography and public health, but also include not very reliable economic data on agriculture and foreign trade.

384. Silaev, E. D. Albaniia; ekonomiko-geograficheskaia kharakteristika (Albania; economic-geographic characteristics). Moskva, Geografizdat, 1953. 174 p. Illus., maps.

Covers the period to 1950 and has plan data to 1955. In addition, Silaev in *Ekonomia popullore* (1960, no. 4: 61-78) has dealt with the problems inherent in regional economic-development in Albania, particularly with respect to intensification of agriculture.

385. Zavalani, Dalib. Die landwirtschaftlichen Verhältnisse Albaniens. Berlin, P. Parey, 1938. 151 p. Maps, diagrs. Bibliography: p. 149-151.

The best study of agricultural conditions in Albania before the Second World War. It is still cited frequently in Albanian publications. Summaries in German, English, French, and Spanish are provided.

# 16

# the society

*by Robert Schwanke*

Journals and Reference Works 386-387
Monographs and Other Works 388-392

## A. JOURNALS AND REFERENCE WORKS

386. Shëndetësia popullore (National health). 1953–(?) Tiranë. Ministria e shëndetësisë. Bimonthly.

387. Veliu, Shevqet, *and others.*   Fjaluer terminologjik serbokroatisht-shqip (Terminological dictionary; Serbo-Croatian-Albanian). Prishtinë, Rilindja, 1961. 404 p. Bibliography: p. 5-7.

    Also contains terms in the fields of social sciences, geography, biology, and medicine.

## B. MONOGRAPHS AND OTHER WORKS

388. Hoxha, Enver.   Sur la situation économique et culturelle de la campagne et les mesures pour son essor ultérieur (Rapport présenté a la réunion du plenum du CC du PTA le 6 juin 1963). *In* Partia e Punës së Shqipërisë. Bulletin d'information, v. 15, no. 2, 1963: 5-91.

    An analysis of rural social conditions and Party instructions for their quick improvement.

389. Hoxha, Fejzi.   Njoftime historike mbi zhvillimin e mjekësisë në Shqiperi (Historical documentation on the development of medicine in Albania). Tiranë, Kateder të Terapisë, 1962. 215 p.

    The treatment includes the development of the medical service through 1959, living and housing conditions, contagious diseases, and the establishment of health agencies before 1945 and their development after that date. The appendix contains short biographies of Albanian physicians.

390. The Labor Code of the People's Republic of Albania. *In* Partia e

Punës së Shqipërisë. Bulletin d'information, v. 17, 1966: 29-45. (Special issue)

This Albanian labor code is a typical example of the type of comprehensive legislation now passed in Albania. Also published in a French-language version.

391. State Social Insurance in the People's Republic of Albania. Tirana, Naim Frashëri, 1963. 55 p.

A propaganda pamphlet providing basic information, using pre-1962 statistics. For the new social security act, *see* "The State Social Insurance Law of the People's Republic of Albania" in the special issue cited in entry no. 390.

392. Tirana. Universiteti Shtëteror. Fjalë të urta të Popullit tonë (Proverbs of our people). Tiranë, Naim Frashëri, 1958. 212 p.

Contains about 3,200 proverbs arranged under subject headings, such as love, labor, life, society. A shorter collection in German, compiled and translated by Nikolaus Rotta, is entitled *Albanische Sprichwörter und Redensarten* (Wien, Roller, 1914, 56 p.).

# 17

# ıntellectual anð
# cultuʀal lıfe

## A. SCHOLARSHIP AND ALBANOLOGY

### by Eric P. Hamp

393. Stadtmüller, Georg. Forschungen zur albanischen Frühgeschichte.
2d enl. ed. Wiesbaden, Harrassowitz, 1966. 221 p. Maps (Albanische
Forschungen, Bd. 2)
   *See also* entry no. 336.
   Philologically based discussion of the "Albanian question" of
   antiquity. Based on a rich bibliography. First published in 1941.

394. Jokl, Norbert. Albanisch. *In*: Streitberg, W., *ed.* Die Erforschung
der indogermanischen Sprachen (Geschichte der indogermanischen
Sprachwissenschaft seit ihrer Begründung durch Franz Bopp). Strassburg, Karl J. Trübner, 1917. v. 3. p. 109-154.
   Brief chronicle of philological scholarship, including monuments
   of the language, provenience of the Albanians, Balkan relations,
   dialects, etymology, historical phonology, morphology, and syntax.
   *See also* Jokl's article, "Albaner" (Sprache), on pages 84-94 of
   *Reallexikon der Vorgeschichte*, v. 1 (Berlin, W. de Gruyter, 1924),

* The arrangement in sections A-E is by topical coherence and affinity.

edited by Max Ebert, which emphasizes prehistory. For a detailed listing of Jokl's writings *see* the obituary published by C. Tagliavini in *Indogermanisches Jahrbuch*, v. 28, 1949, p. 296–301.

395. Grimm, Gerhard.   Johann Georg von Hahn (1811-1869): Leben und Werk. Wiesbaden, O. Harrassowitz, 1964. 385 p. Fold. col. maps, port. (Albanische Forschungen, Bd. 1)

Hahn was the founder of systematic Albanian philology and folklore. The classic early study of Albanian philology and ethnology was his *Albanesische Studien* (Wien, Aus der kaiserlich-königlichen Hof- und Staatsdruckerei, 1853, 347, 169, 241 p., illus., fold. col. map). Volume 1: Ethnography; volume 2: Grammar, texts and translation; volume 3: Glossary, Albanian-German, German-Albanian.

396. Roques, Mario. Recherches sur les anciens textes albanais avec huit fac-similés. Paris, P. Geuthner, 1932. 45 p. Plates (facsims.).

A careful, well-annotated catalog of the early documents. For the earliest lexical material, *see* Franciscus Blanchus' *Le dictionnaire albanais de 1635* (Paris, P. Geuthner, 1932–).

## B. LANGUAGE

### by *Eric P. Hamp*

### 1. Grammar

397. Pekmezi, Georg.   Grammatik der albanesischen Sprache (Laut- und Formenlehre). Wien, Gerold, 1908. 294 p.

Though superficial, still one of the best Albanian grammars from the standpoint of coverage, accessibility, sophistication. Considerable synchronic detail and some dialect coverage, but rather outdated comparative treatment. A minor classic of this era (with interesting specimen texts), now of limited use, is Gustav Meyer's *Kurzgefasste albanesische Grammatik* (Leipzig, Breitkopf und Härtel, 1888, 105 p.).

398. Lambertz, Maximilian.   Lehrgang des Albanischen. Berlin, Deutscher Verlag der Wissenschaften, 1954-1959. 3 v.

Volume 1, Albanisch-deutsches Wörterbuch (228 p.) is useful because it presents the contemporary standard language as well as the official orthographic regulations; volume 2 (to be used with great care) is a 251-page Albanian chrestomathy; and volume 3 (267 p.), rather poorly arranged, is a grammar. Not among this scholar's best work, but nothing better is readily accessible. His *Albanisches Lesebuch* (Leipzig, O. Harrassowitz, 1948, 2 v.) contains an unevaluated bibliography, a sketchy grammatical outline, and useful texts with translation. His article on conditional constructions (*Indogermanische Forschungen*, v. 34, 1914: 44-208) is a major contribution to the study of Albanian syntax.

399. Dodbiba, L., *and* S. Spasse.   Gramatika e gjuhës shqipe. I. Fillimet e sintaksës, fonetika, morfologjia (Grammar of the Albanian language.

I. Elements of syntax, phonetics, morphology). 3d ed. Tiranë, Ministria e Arësimit dhe e Kulturës, 1955. 286 p.

Didactic question and explanation method. Standard language textbook for fifth and sixth grades. *See also* volume 2 of this series, *Sintaksa* (Syntax), by M. Domi, 3d ed. (Tiranë, Ministria e Arësimit dhe e Kulturës, 1957, 235 p.), which employs discursive commentary for natives on selected passages. Leonard D. Newmark's *Structural Grammar of Albanian* (Bloomington, Indiana University Press, 1957, 130 p.), a sketch with methodological interest, contains an annotated bibliography.

400. Domi, M.    Gramatika e gjuhës shqipe. II. Sintaksa për shkollat pedagogjike (Grammar of the Albanian language. II. Syntax for normal schools). Tiranë, Drejtoria e botimeve shkollore, 1964. 203 p.

401. Cipo, K.    Gramatika shqipe (Albanian grammar). Tiranë, Instituti i Shkencavet, Ndërmarrja shtetërore e botimeve dhe shpërndarjes, 1949. 192 p.

A traditional treatment of phonology and morphology. *See also* his *Sintaksa* (Syntax) (Tiranë, Instituti i Shkencavet, 1952, 125 p.). Discursive treatment under traditional rubrics.

These two books are better suited in arrangement for scholars and non-natives than the ones by Dodbiba-Spasse and Domi listed in the preceding two entries.

## 2. Dictionaries

402. Tirana. Instituti i shkencavet.    Fjalor i gjuhës shqipe (Dictionary of the Albanian language). Tiranë, Instituti i shkencavet, sekcioni i gjuhës e i letërsisë, 1954. 648 p.

The official current standard language. Useful even for those who do not read Albanian. Photo-reprint (1965) available from Rilindja Prishtinë. For a good bibliography of earlier dictionaries, *see* Henrik Barić's *Rečnik srpskoga ili hrvatskoga i arbanaskoga jezika* (Dictionary of the Serbo-Croatian and Albanian language) (Zagreb, Izdavački zavod Jugoslavenske Akademije, 1950, A-O, all published).

403. Leotti, Angelo.    Dizionario albanese-italiano. Roma, Istituto per l'Europa orientale, 1937. 1710 p. (Publicazioni dell' "Istituto per l'Europa orientale," Roma. Ser. 5. Grammatiche e dizionari, 3)

The fullest Tosk Albanian (the basis of the current standard of Albania) bilingual dictionary in a Western language.

404. Mann, Stuart E.    An Historical Albanian-English Dictionary. 2d ed. London, Longman's, Green, 1948. 601 p.

Not really historical; no citations are included. Reviewed by N. Jokl in *Indogermanisches Jahrbuch*, 24, 1940, 243-245. *See also* the same author's *An English-Albanian Dictionary* (Cambridge, The University Press, 1957, 434 p.), which is primarily concerned with the Geg dialect, the prewar standard, and is hence now of most use for the Kosovë (Yugoslavia) standard. Photo-reprint, Rilindja Prishtinë, 1966. In this connection, *see* Sokol Dobroshi's *Fjaluer serbokroatisht-shqip* (Serbo-Croatian-Albanian dictionary) (Prishtinë, Mustafa Bakija, 1953, 757 p.).

405. Tirana. Instituti i Shkencavet. Russko-albanskii slovar' (Russian-Albanian dictionary). Moskva, Gosudarstvennoe izdatel'stvo inostran-nykh i natsional'nykh slovarei, 1954. 636 p.

A useful bilingual dictionary of the contemporary language. *See also* Vedat Kokona's *Fjalor frengjisht-shqip* (French-Albanian dictionary) (Tiranë, 1966, 372 p.) and *Bŭlgarsko-albanski rečnik* (Bulgarian-Albanian dictionary), prepared by the Bŭlgarska akademiia na naukite, Sofiia, Institut za bŭlgarski ezik (Sofiia, 1959, 871 p.).

406. Kristoforidhi, Konstandin. Lexikon tēs albanikēs glōssēs (Dictionary of the Albanian language). Athēnai, Sakellaríou, 1904. 502 p.

Old and incomplete, but valuable as the sole compilation of Geg and Tosk dialect forms with precise provenience. Transcribed into modern orthography by A. Xhuvani, with some revisions, as *Fjalor shqip-greqisht* (Albanian-Greek dictionary) (Tiranë, Univ. shtetëror i Tiranës, Instituti i historisë e i filologjisë, 1961, 397 p.).

### 3. Dialects

407. Lambertz, Maximilian. Die Mundarten der albanischen Sprache und ihre Erforschung. Leipziger Vierteljahrsschrift für Südosteuropa, v. 7, 1943: 123-160.

General and informative, but rather out of date. For a more recent report on certain particular studies by the same author, *see* "Die Mundarten der albanischen Sprache (Heutiger Stand der Forschung)," in *Südost-Forschungen*, v. 16, 1957: 430-435. The work within Albania of the 1950s and '60s is covered in various articles in the Tirana *Buletin* and successor journals, and especially Jorgji Gjinari's "Essai d'une démarcation dialectale de la langue albanaise," in *Studia Albanica* (Tiranë), v. 3, 1966, no. 2: 31-50.

408. Cimochowski, Wacław. Le dialecte de Dushmani: description de l'un des parlers de l'Albanie du Nord. Poznań, Nakładem Poznańskiego Towarzystwa Przyjaciół Nauk z zasiłkiem Ministerstwa Szkół Wyższych i Nauki, 1951. 233 p.

A north Geg dialect. The fullest dialect description available. A detailed review and restatement by Eric P. Hamp appeared in *Language*, v. 29, 1953: 500-512.

409. Elezović, Gl. Glasovne osobine arbanaškog dijalekta Debra i njegove okoline (The phonetic characteristics of the Albanian dialect of Debar [Dibrë] and its environs). Srpski dijalektološki zbornik (Beograd), v. 11, 1950: 227-300.

Based on 94 song texts collected and published by Haki Stërmilli in *Visaret e kombit* (Treasures of the nation), XIV, 1944. The only substantial treatment of a dialect verging on the Macedonian area.

410. Pedersen, Holger.    Albanesische Texte mit Glossar. Leipzig, S. Hirzel, 1895. 207 p. and corrigenda.

Analysis of the southernmost Tosk dialect, on the Greek-Albanian border. Source for much of the early factual knowledge of spoken Albanian among Western scholars. Translations of the texts are found in the same author's *Zur albanesischen Volkskunde* (Kopenhagen, S. Michaelsens Nachf. [E. Møller], 1898, 125 p.).

411. Haebler, Claus.    Grammatik der albanischen Mundart von Salamis. Wiesbaden, O. Harrassowitz, 1965. 178 p. (Albanische Forschungen, Bd. 3)

Taxonomic phonological and morphological description of the contemporary Greek-Albanian (Arvanítika) dialect of Salamis, Attica. Reviewed in *Südost-Forschungen* (München, v. 25, 1966: 525-526.

412. Giordano, Sac. Emanuele.    Fjalor i Arbëreshvet t'Italisë (Dictionary of the Albanian [Arbresh] dialects of Italy). Bari, Edizioni Paoline, 1963. 592 p. Tables.

Includes a good list of writers and of Italo-Albanian literature, and the most accurate available table of Arbresh villages. Strong on the dialect of Frascineto. Employs a standardized orthography, which obscures many interesting phonetic points.

## 4. Historical-Comparative Studies

413. Meyer, Gustav.    Albanesische Studien. Wien, C. Gerold's Sohn, 1883-1897. 6 v.

Volume 1 (1883), on noun plural formations, is now superseded by Fiedler's unpublished dissertation (Humboldt-Universität). Volume 2 (1884), on the numerals, is quite out of date. Volume 3 (1892) is still important as the basic treatment of Albanian comparative phonology. Volumes 5 and 6 (1896-1897) comprise useful dialect texts.

414. Jokl, Norbert.    Linguistisch-kulturhistorische Untersuchungen aus dem Bereiche des Albanischen. Berlin und Leipzig, W. de Gruyter, 1923. 366 p. (Untersuchungen zur indogermanischen Sprach- und Kulturwissenschaft, 8)

Important for etymology and aspects of Albanian cultural history as reflected in the language. Extensive but dispersed discussion of historical phonology and morphology.

415. Camaj, Martin.    Albanische Wortbildung. Die Bildungsweise der älteren Nomina. Wiesbaden, O. Harrassowitz, 1966. 175 p. (Albanische Forschungen, Bd. 6)

Includes extensive references to earlier work. One half of the monograph is devoted to the fate of Indo-European Ablaut and vowel alternation, and the remainder deals primarily with affixal etymology.

416. Meyer, Gustav. Etymologisches Wörterbuch der albanesischen Sprache. Strassburg, K. J. Trübner, 1891. 526 p. (Sammlung indogermanischer Wörterbücher, 3)

> Though out of date, still the only basic etymological work; where pertinent, Tagliavini's *Lessico etimologico* and other more recent literature should also be consulted.

417. Tagliavini, Carlo. L'albanese di Dalmazia; contributi alla conoscenza del dialetto ghego di Borgo Erizzo presso Zara. Firenze, L. S. Olschki, 1937. 317 p. Illus. (inc. map). (Biblioteca dell' "Archivum romanicum," diretta da Giulio Bertoni, Ser. II: Linguistica, v. 22)

> Introduction, texts with translation, lessico etimologico, and appendix on verbs. Also on the dialect of this village (now Arbanasi) is Idriz Ajeti's *Istorijski razvitak gegijskog govora Arbanasa kod Zadra* (Sarajevo, 1961, 164 p.). For lexical etymology, *see also* N. Jokl's "Zur Erforschung der albanischen Mundart von Borgo Erizzo in Dalmazien," in *Archivum romanicum*, v. 24, 1940: 101-137, and E. P. Hamp's "Albanian Corrigenda to Pokorny's IEW," *Indogermanische Forschungen*, v. 67, 1962: 142-150.

418. Çabej, Eqrem. Studime rreth etimologjisë së gjuhës shqipe (Studies on the etymology of the Albanian language). *In*: Tirana. Universiteti Shtetëror. Buletin. Seria shkencat shoqërore. Studime filologjike, 1960–

> A partial etymological dictionary in installments. Includes abundant references to earlier literature and fresh philological forms.

419. Hamp, Eric P. The Position of Albanian. *In* Conference on Indo-European Linguistics, University of California, Los Angeles, 1963. Ancient Indo-European Dialects; Proceedings. Edited by Henrik Birnbaum and Jaan Puhvel. Berkeley, University of California Press, 1966. p. 97-121.

> Review of scholarship on the relation of Albanian to its neighbors and to its sister Indo-European languages; includes a selective bibliography on these topics.

## C. LITERATURE

### by Eric P. Hamp

420. Shuteriqi, Dhimitër S., K. Bihiku, *and* M. Domi, *eds.* Historia e letërsisë shqipe (History of Albanian literature). Tiranë, Universiteti Shtetëror i Tiranës, Instituti i historisë dhe i gjuhësisë, 1959– Illus., ports., facsims.

> Two volumes published to date, with coverage up to the interwar period. The most complete work of its kind.

421. Mann, Stuart E. Albanian Literature; an Outline of Prose, Poetry, and Drama. London, Bernard Quaritch, 1955. 121 p.

> Extremely brief; only two pages are devoted to the postwar period.

422. Bihiku, Koço.   An Outline of Albanian Literature.   Translated by
Ali Cungu. Tirana, Naim Frashëri State Pub. House, 1964. 146 p.
> Informative treatment of the postwar period, with coverage of
> current views and trends.

423. Schirò, Giuseppe.  Storia della letteratura albanese.  Milano, Nuova
Accademia, 1959. 267 p. Col. plate, fold. col. map. (Thesaurus Lit-
terarum, Sezione 1)
> Strong on the Albanian of Italy, an important phase of this litera-
> ture. Covers primarily the earlier periods. The author is the younger
> Giuseppe Schirò.

424. Lambertz, Maximilian.   Die Volksepik der Albaner. Halle (Saale),
M. Niemeyer, 1958. 184 p.
> Twenty translations of selected short epic poems of Mujo and
> Halil, with the most complete discussion to date of the content, struc-
> ture, style, and metrics of the north Geg folk epic. Reviewed by
> E. Çabej in Lingua Posnaniensis, v. 8: 288-292.

425. Fishta, Gjergj.   Die Laute des Hochlandes (Lahuta e Malcis). Translated by Max Lambertz. München, R. Oldenbourg, 1958. 312 p.
(Südosteuropäische Arbeiten, 51)
> The most admired work (North Geg dialect) of all Albanian litera-
> ture. A recent edition of the original is Lahuta e Malcís (Romë,
> Komiteti "Shqipëria e Lirë," 1958, 702 p.). Both works include brief
> notes.

426. Catholic Church. Liturgy and Ritual. Missal. Albanian.   Il "messale"
di Giovanni Buzuku: riproduzione e trascrizione. Edited by Namik
Ressuli. Città del Vaticano, Biblioteca Apostolica Vaticana, 1958.
406 p. (Vatican. Biblioteca Vaticana. Studi e testi, 199)
> A unique printed copy comprising the oldest substantial document
> of the language. Includes an index of the Latin passages which the
> missal translates. For a critical commentary on this edition, see
> G. Markelaj's article in Quaderni dell'Istituto di Glottologia di Bo-
> logna, v. 3, 1958: 35-52. Studies on Buzuku's work and times by
> Çabej and Rrota have appeared in the Buletin (Tirana), 1955-1956.

427. De Rada, Girolamo.  I canti di Milosao: traslitterazione, varianti
delle edizioni a stampa e traduzione. Edited by Giuseppe Gradilone.
Firenze, Leo S. Olschki, 1965. 134 p. (Studi albanesi, studi e testi, v. 1)
> A recent edition of one of the works of this important 19th cen-
> tury poet.

428. Librandi, Vincenzo.  Grammatica albanese con le poesie rare di
Variboba. 2d ed. Milano, U. Hoepli, 1928. 381 p.
> The initial grammatical portion is worthless, but the poetic texts
> with Italian translations are serviceable, despite inaccuracies and
> misreadings. The earliest independent original body of literature in
> the language, by a native of S. Giorgio Albanese, in Calabria. See

M. Lambertz (*Zeitschrift für vergleichende Sprachforschung aus dem Gebiete der Indogermanischen Sprachen*, v. 74, 1956: 47-122, 185-224) for a valuable glossary based on reinspection of a photocopy of original printing, introducing, however, its own errors.

429. Kodra, Ziaudin, *ed.* Gavril Darë i Riu, Kënka e sprasme e Balës (Gavril Dara the Younger, the last song of Bala). Tiranë, Ndërmarrja shtetërore e botimeve, 1955. 136 p.

Nineteenth century romantic epic, from Palazzo Adriano in Sicily. Not an ideal edition. Reviewed by E. P. Hamp in *Kratylos*, 5, 1960: 104-105.

## D. FOLKLORE

### by Eric P. Hamp

430. Lambertz, Maximilian. Die Volkspoesie der Albaner. Eine einführende Studie. Sarajevo, Studnička, 1917. 80 p. (Zur Kunde der Balkanhalbinsel. II. Quellen und Forschungen, Hft. 6)

Introduction to the content and form of heroic poems, love poems, marriage poems, and funeral lamentations, with an appendix on nursery rhymes.

431. Lambertz, Maximilian. Albanische Volksmärchen (und andere Texte zur albanischen Volkskunde). Wien, Hölder-Pichler,Tempsky, 1922. 255 p. (Schriften der Balkankommission der Akademie der Wissenschaften in Wien. Linguist. Abt., 12)

Sixty-one folk tales, with translations. Includes an introduction on the forms of Albanian folk tales and a review of previous literature.

432. Instituti i Folklorit. Mbledhës të hershëm të folklorit shqiptar, 1635-1912 (Collection of Albanian folklore in the past, 1635-1912). Edited by Z. Sako and others. Tiranë, Instituti i Folklorit, 1961-1962. 3 v. Ports., facsims.

A rich republication in modern orthography, based on most of the earlier sources of folk literature. Includes short glossaries and indexes of names.

433. Instituti i Folklorit. Folklor shqiptar (Albanian folklore). Edited by Z. Sako and others. Tiranë, 1963– Illus.

Part I, *Proza popullore* (Prose folk literature), v. 1-4 (1963-1966), 488 texts, includes much new material, as well as 19th and 20th century sources. Brief glossaries in each volume.

434. Çetta, Anton. Tregime popullore (Folk tales). v. 1. Prishtinë, Rilindja, 1963. 331 p.

Prose texts in a northern Kosovë dialect (Drenicë).

435. Fouríkēs, P. A. ῾E ᾽en ᾽Attikḗ ῾ellēnalbanikḗ diálektos (The Greek-

Albanian [Avanítika] dialect of Attica). 'Athēna, v. 44, 1932: 28-76; v. 45, 1933: 49-181.

The basic source-work on the Attica dialects. For a brief linguistic commentary, see E. P. Hamp's "On the Arvanítika Dialects of Attica and Megarid," in *Balkansko ezikoznanie*, v. 3, 1961, no. 2: 101-107.

436. Haxhihasani, Qemal, *ed.* Këngë popullore legjendare (Legendary folk poetry). Tiranë, Institut i Shkencavet. 1955. 332 p.

———. Këngë popullore historike (Historical folk poetry). Tiranë, Instituti i Shkencavet, Instituti i historisë dhe i gjuhësisë, 1956. 408 p.

Collected from various published and unpublished sources. Includes brief notes and a glossary. *See also* his *Këngë Popullore historike, 1878-1912* (Tiranë, 1962).

437. Ruches, Pyrrhus J. Albanian Historical Folksongs, 1716-1943. Chicago, Argonaut, 1967. 123 p. Bibliography: p. 119-123.

A survey of oral epic poetry from southern Albania, with original texts.

438. Instituti i Shkencavet. Këngë popullore lirike (Lyrical folk poetry). Tiranë, 1955. 348 p.

Folk songs on a wide range of topics.

439. Dheri, Eftim, *and others, eds.* Këngë popullore (Folk songs). Tiranë, Instituti i Folklorit, 1964. 134 p.

———. 250 këngë popullore dasme (250 wedding songs). Tiranë, Instituti i Folklorit, 1966. 168 p.

The first is a selection of 104 songs, with music, from many genres. The second includes songs homophonic and polyphonic, from various regions of the country.

## E. ETHNOGRAPHY AND FOLK MUSIC

### by Eric P. Hamp

440. Zojzi, Rrok, *and others, eds.* Etnografia shqiptare I (Albanian ethnography I). Tiranë, Universiteti Shtetëror i Tiranës, Instituti i historisë dhe i gjuhësisë, Sektori i etnografisë, 1962. 308 p.

Essays on regionalism, material culture, marriage, etc.

441. Sokoli, Ramadan. Folklori muzikor shqiptar; morfologjia (Albanian musical folklore; morphology). Tiranë, Instituti i Folklorit, 1965. 283 p. Music.

General exposition of rhythm, melody, verse metrics, polyphony. Includes an ethnomusicological glossary and 347 transcribed melodies, with lyrics.

442. Antoni, Lorenc. Folklori muzikuer shqiptar (Albanian musical folklore). Prishtinë, Shtëpija botuese Milladin Popoviq, 1956–

Volume 1 includes metrical analysis, musical transcription, and texts of 105 songs from Prizren, Gjakovë, and Skopje. Volume 2 covers 106 songs from various parts of Kosovë, and volume 3, 37 from Metohja, 8 from Crna Gora, 2 from Srbija, and 63 from Makedonija.

443. Stockmann, Doris, Wilfried Fiedler, *and* Erich Stockmann. Albanische Volksmusik. Muzika popullore shqiptare. v. 1. Berlin, Akademie-Verlag, 1965. 302 p. Map, music. (Deutsche Akademie der Wissenschaften zu Berlin. Veröffentlichungen des Instituts für deutsche Volkskunde, Bd. 36)

Detailed musicological, musico-ethnological, and textual analysis of 30 (primarily narrative and lyric) songs of the Çams who settled near Vlorë from the region of Greek Epirus south of Igoumenitsa. Includes a good review of scholarship on Albanian folk music through 1957 by E. Stockmann, musicological analysis and transcriptions by D. Stockmann, and texts and translation, with analysis of content, style, metrics, and comparative notes on diction, motifs, etc. by W. Fiedler.

444. Agolli, Nexhat. Valle popullore (Folk dances). Tiranë, Instituti i Folklorit, 1965. 114 p.

Based on freshly collected materials from west-central Albania, between the Shkumbi and Seman rivers. Formal analysis, verbal description with sketches, music, lyrics where appropriate, and typology of 14 dances. Includes an introduction on performance, style, structure, movements, accompaniment, dress, and notation.

## F. MUSIC

### *by Miloš Velimirović*

445. Di Salvo, Bartolomeo. Albania. *In* Enciclopedia della musica, v. 1. Milano, Ricordi, 1963. p. 33-34.

The only article on Albanian music in which an attempt at surveying the role of Albanians is made. Special stress is laid on Albanian church music and Albanian settlements in Italy. Bibliography, such as it is, covers primarily studies on folk music. In another distinguished musicological encyclopedia, *Die Musik in Geschichte und Gegenwart; allgemeine Enzyklopädie der Musik*, edited by F. Blume (v. 1, Kassel, Bärenreiter-Verlag, 1949, cols. 282-285), there is an article on Albanian music by Yuri Arbatsky which is worthless. The best survey of studies in folk music is that by Erich Stockmann, "Zur Sammlung und Untersuchung albanischer Volksmusik," *Acta Musicologica*, XXXII, 1960, p. 102-109.

446. Music. *In* Skendi, Stavro, *ed.* Albania. New York, Frederick A. Praeger for the Mid-European Studies Center of the Free Europe Committee, 1956. p. 320-322.

This brief essay is, as far as is known, the only source of information about the beginnings of artistic music in Albania. A brief list of composers and their works is included which indicates that artistic music only began to develop after 1944. Reports about events in Albania periodically published in *Osteuropa; Zeitschrift für Gegenwartsfragen des Ostens* (Stuttgart, Deutsche Verlags-Anstalt, 1951–, monthly) contain occasionally references to music; e.g., the October 1955 issue includes data on the number of theaters, operatic performances, etc. (p. 722). For a treatment on Albanian folk music *see*: Stockmann, Doris, *and others.* Albanische Volksmusik. Berlin, Akademie-Verlag, 1965– The first volume is titled *Gesänge der Çamen.*

## G. THE FINE ARTS

### by Anton Logoreci

### 1. Art History, Surveys, and Guides

447. Arti në Republikën Popullore të Shqipërisë (Art in the Albanian People's Republic). Berlin, Deutscher Zentralverlag, 1953. 63 p. Illus.

   A survey (in Albanian, Russian, and French) of painting, sculpture, archaeology, folk art, music, and drama. Propagandistic in tone. Sponsored by the Albanian Committee for Foreign Cultural Relations.

448. Rey, Léon.   Guide de l'Albanie. Paris, Office du Tourisme en Albanie, 1930. 158 p.

   Despite its date of publication, this work, by an eminent French archaeologist who worked in Albania between the two world wars, contains excellent notes on the history of towns, churches, buildings, works of art, and archaeological sites.

449. Sestieri, Pellegrino, *and* Margherita Abbruzzese.   Albania. *In* Encyclopedia of World Art. v. 1. New York, Toronto, London, McGraw-Hill, 1959. p. 182–187.

   Brief scholarly notes on centers of artistic, archaeological, and architectural interest.

450. Skendi, Stavro, *ed.*   Albania. New York, Praeger, 1956. 389 p. Maps. (Praeger Publications in Russian History and World Communism, no. 46)

   *See also* entries no. 287 *and* 332.

   This work provides the only readily available information in English on the development of the fine arts, drama, and music (p. 317–322).

451. Ugolini, Luigi.   Albania: Arte. *In* Enciclopedia Italiana di Scienze, Lettere ed Arti. v. 2. Roma, Istituto Giovanni Treccani, 1929. p. 127–128.

   Brief survey of archaeological sites, buildings, and crafts by an eminent Italian archaeologist who directed important excavations in Albania between the two world wars.

## 2. Folk and Decorative Art

452. Nopcsa, Ferencz.   Haus und Hausrat im katholischen Nordalbanien. Sarajevo, 1912. 90 p. Illus.

A study of domestic architecture, furniture, crafts, costumes, and agricultural implements of northern Albania by a well-known Hungarian scholar. A later and more detailed study by Nopcsa is his *Albanien, Bauten, Trachten und Geräte Nordalbaniens* (Berlin, Leipzig, W. de Gruyter, 1925, 257 p.).

## 3. Archaeology

453. Patsch, Carl.   Das Sandschak Berat in Albanien. Wien, Hölder, 1904. 200 columns. Illus., map. (Schriften der Balkankommission der Akademie der Wissenschaften in Wien. Antiquar. Abt. 3)

One of the standard works about archaeology and historical geography of central Albania.

454. Praschniker, Camillo.   Muzakhia und Malakastra. Archáologische Untersuchungen in Mittelalbanien. Wien, Hőlder, 1920. 234 p. Illus.

Reprint of the "Jahreshefte des Österreichischen Archäologischen Instituts," v. 21-22, offering the results of investigations of Apollonia and Byllis in 1917-1918. The studies mark an important advance in the knowledge of the history of Albania during the pre-Roman and Roman periods.

455. Praschniker, Camillo, *and* Arnold Schober.   Archäologische Forschungen in Albanien und Montenegro. Wien, Hölder, 1919. 104 p. Illus., map (Schriften der Balkankommission der Akademie der Wissenschaften. Antiquar, Abteilung, 8)

*See also* entry no. 311.

Focuses on the archaeological investigation of Doclea, Scutari, Lissus, Elbasan, and Berat.

456. Rey, Léon.   Seize années de fouilles en Albanie. Revue de Paris, v. 66, August, 1939: 685-696.

Review of the excavations of a group of French archaeologists in Pojan, ancient Apollonia, a Greek colony founded in 588 B.C., written by the director of the group.

457. Ugolini, Luigi M.   Albania antica. V. 1. Ricerche Archeologiche. Roma, Società Editrice d'Arte Illustrata, 1927. 204 p. Illus.

A leading Italian archaeologist's account of his first visit to Albania in 1924, in which he describes the country's most important archaeological centers. This preliminary survey led to the very successful excavations that Ugolini himself was to direct in subsequent years.

458. Ugolini, Luigi M.   Albania antica. V. 2. L'Acropoli di Fenice. Milano, Roma, Treves-Treccani-Tumminelli, 1932. 245 p. Illus.

During 1926-1937, Ugolini carried out a series of excavations at Fenice (Feniki) in southern Albania, where he discovered Illyrian, Greek, Roman, and Byzantine remains. In this work, the Italian archaeologist gives a full report of his findings.

459. Ugolini, Luigi M.    Butrinto. Il Mito d'Enea, Gli Scavi. Roma, Istituto Grafico Tiberino, 1937. 203 p. Illus.

This work tells the story of Ugolini's crowning achievement in Albania — the excavations carried out at Butrinto, the old Greek settlement of Buthrotum opposite the island of Corfu. The digging revealed a number of well-preserved relics of Greek, Roman, Byzantine, and Venetian civilizations. The most widely known single discovery made there is a Hellenic sculptured head, the so-called "Goddess of Butrinto," which is now in Rome.

# H. RELIGION

## by Anton Logoreci

460. Benna, A. N.    Studien zum Kultusprotektorat Österreich-Ungarns in Albanien im Zeitalter des Imperialismus 1888-1918. *In* Austria. *Staatsarchiv*. Mitteilungen, v. 7, 1954: 13-46.

Essay on the protection of Albanian Catholics by the Habsburg Empire.

461. Borgia, Nilo.    I monaci basiliani d'Italia in Albania, appunti di storia missionaria, secoli XVI-XVIII, periodo secondo (1692-1769). Roma, Reale Accademia d'Italia, Centro di studi per l'Albania, 1942. 201 p.

A survey of the work of Italian Catholic missionaries in Albania during the 17th and 18th centuries.

462. Hasluck, Frederick W.    Christianity and Islam Under the Sultans. Oxford, Clarendon Press, 1929. 2 v. Illus., map.

Parts of this extensive survey deal with the Bektashi and Sunni sects in Albania.

463. Hasluck, Margaret.    The Nonconformist Moslems of Albania. Contemporary Review, v. 127, May 1925: 599-606.

A short essay on the Bektashi sect by a well-informed writer on Albania.

464. Ippen, Theodor.    Das religiöse Protektorat Österreich-Ungarns in der Türkei. Die Kultur, v. 111, 1902: 298-310.

An Austrian scholar's and diplomat's essay on the protection of Albanian Catholics under Turkish rule exercised by the Habsburg Empire from the end of the 17th century to the early part of the 19th century. For a biography of Ippen, who served as Austrian Consul General in Scutari from 1897 to 1904, *see*:

Wernicke, Anneliese.    Theodor Anton Ippen. Ein österreichischer

Diplomat und Albanienforscher. Wiesbaden, Harrassowitz, 1967. 147 p. Maps. (Albanische Forschungen, 7)

465. Rossi, E.    Saggio sul dominio turco e l'introduzione dell'Islam in Albania. Rivista d'Albania, v. 111, 1942: 200-213.

An essay on the introduction of Mohammedanism in Albania by a specialist on Turkish history.

466. Skendi, Stavro.    Crypto-Christianity in the Balkan Area under the Ottomans. Slavic Review, v. 26, no. 2, June 1967: 227-246.

An essay which includes a survey of Albanian crypto-Christians under Turkish rule.

467. Skendi, Stavro.    Religion in Albania During the Ottoman Rule. Südost Forschungen, v. 15, 1956: 311-327.

The best short introduction in English to a complex subject by a distinguished scholar. Chapter 18 of Skendi's *Albania* (entry no. 287) includes a short survey of religious trends from the beginning of the Christian era to 1953. It is the only information available in book form on the changes undergone by religious bodies during the first nine years of the Albanian communist regime.

468. Stadtmüller, Georg.    Die Islamisierung bei den Albanern. Jahrbücher für Geschichte Osteuropas, v. 3 (Neue Folge), 1955: 404-429.

Essay by a well-known German scholar on the conversion of parts of Albania to Islam under Ottoman rule.

469. Sufflay, Milan von.    Die Kirchenzustände im vortürkischen Albanien. Die Orthodoxe Durchbruchszone im katholischen Damme. *In* Thallóczy, Ludwig von, *ed.* Illyrisch-Albanische Forschungen. v. 1. München, Leipzig, Duncker und Humblot, 1916. p. 188-282.

An important contribution to the history of the Christian churches in pre-Ottoman Albania.

# PART THREE

# BULGARIA

# 18

# GENERAL
# REFERENCE AIDS
# and
# BIBLOGRAPHIES

by *Marin V. Pundeff*

## A. BIBLIOGRAPHIES

### 1. Bibliographies of Bibliographies; History of Bibliography

470. Bibliografiia na bŭlgarskata bibliografiia, knigoznanie i bibliotechno delo (Bibliography of Bulgarian bibliographies, the book trade, and librarianship). 1965– Sofiia.

> The Cyril and Methodius National Library in Sofia in 1965 initiated this annual series listing all Bulgarian bibliographies published individually or in books and articles. Coverage began with 1963. Bibliographies published from 1945 to 1962 were listed in the *Godishnik na Bulgarskiia bibliografski institut* (Yearbook of the Bulgarian Bibliographic Institute), Sofiia, of which nine volumes (1948-1963) appeared.

471. Trenkov, Khristo. Spetsialna bibliografiia; teoriia, organizatsiia, metodika (Subject bibliography; theory, organization, methodology). Sofiia, Nauka i izkustvo, 1958. 235 p.

119

The last part of this volume (p. 145-200) is a thorough survey of the development and present state of Bulgarian subject bibliography. Existing bibliographies in all fields are cited and discussed.

472. Tsvetanov, Tsenko. Bŭlgarska bibliografiia; istoricheski pregled i dneshno sŭstoianie (Bulgarian bibliography; survey of its history and present state). Sofiia, Nauka i izkustvo, 1957. 180 p.

Surveys the development of general and subject bibliography in Bulgaria during the century since the compilation of the first bibliography by Ivan Shopov in 1852.

## 2. Current and Continuing General Bibliographies

473. Bŭlgarski knigopis (Bulgarian bibliography). 1897– Sofiia. Biweekly.

This is the national bibliography of Bulgaria, legislated into existence 21 years ago to reflect the books and periodicals published in the country and deposited in the National Library in Sofia. Through the years, its title, coverage, and frequency have varied; for the most recent discussion of these changes see *Sovetskaia bibliografiia* (Soviet bibliography), no. 4, 1966: 91-98. It covers books intended for wide distribution. Publications for limited distribution (official publications, dissertations, books for the blind, etc.) have been listed since 1962 in quarterly supplements.

## 3. Bibliographic Guides; Special and Institutional Bibliographies

474. Almanakh na Sofiiskiia universitet Sv. Kliment Okhridski; zhivotopisni i knigopisni svedendiia za prepodavatelite (Almanac of the St. Kliment of Okhrida University in Sofia; biographic and bibliographic data on the teaching staff). 2d ed. Sofiia, 1940. 726 p.

An indispensable guide to the bibliographies of the teaching staff of the University of Sofia from its founding in 1888 to 1939. The first edition (1929) should also be consulted.

475. Borov, Todor, *ed.* Tipov katalog za masovi biblioteki (Standard catalog for public libraries). Sofiia, Nauka i izkustvo, 1957. 241 p.

A bibliography of basic books recommended for public libraries in Bulgaria. Later additions will be found in *Anotiran tipov katalog za masovite biblioteki* (Annotated standard catalog for public libraries) (Sofiia, Nauka i izkustvo, 1961, 423 p.).

476. Kovachev, Asen S. Bibliografiia na Sofiiskiia universitet "Sv. Kliment Okhridski, 1904-1942 (Bibliography of the St. Kliment of Okhrida University in Sofia, 1904-1942). Sofiia, 1943. 366 p.

A full bibliography of the numerous publications of Bulgaria's leading institution of higher education from the time it attained university status to 1942. It is supplemented by *Katalog na universitetskite izdaniia, 1943-1946* (Catalog of university publications, 1943-1946) (Sofiia, 1947, 31 p.) and *Bibliografiia na izdaniiata na Sofiiskiia uni-*

*versitet, 1947-1955* (Bibliography of the publications of the University of Sofia, 1947-1955) (Sofiia, 1956, 108 p.).

477. Pogorelov, Valerii A.   Opis na starite pechatani bŭlgarski knigi, 1802-1877 g. (Bibliography of old Bulgarian printed books, 1802-1877). Sofiia, 1923. 795 p.

> A list of Bulgarian incunabula. Library of Congress holdings of such books, some not listed in Pogorelov, are discussed by Charles Jelavich in the Library's *Quarterly Journal of Current Acquisitions*, v. 14, May 1957: 77-94.

478. Pundeff, Marin V.   Bulgaria; a Bibliographic Guide. Washington, D.C., Library of Congress, 1965. 98 p.

> *See also* entry no. 724.

> The only comprehensive guide to the sources of knowledge about Bulgaria in existence. The 1,243 titles discussed represent general and subject bibliographies, reference aids, and major works in various fields and languages. Reprinted in 1968 by Arno Press, New York.

479. Sofia. Narodna biblioteka "Kiril i Metodii."   Opis na rukopisite i staropechatnite knigi na Narodnata biblioteka v Sofiia (Bibliography of manuscripts and old imprints in the National Library in Sofia). Sofiia, 1910-1964. 3 v. (555, 553, 499 p.)

> This is in effect a printed catalog of the Slavic manuscripts at the National Library in Sofia. Holdings of other libraries in the country are surveyed in *Izvestiia* (News) of the National Library and the Library of the University of Sofia, v. 3, 1963.

480. Stoianov, Man'o.   Bŭlgarska vŭzrozhdenska knizhnina; analitichen repertoar na bŭlgarskite knigi i periodichni izdaniia, 1806-1878 (Publications of the Bulgarian revival; an analytical list of Bulgarian books and periodicals, 1806-1878). Sofiia, Nauka i izkustvo, 1957-1959. 2 v. (664, 958 p.)

> An exhaustive bibliography of publications from the period of the national revival, providing full information on the books and contents of periodicals published from the appearance of the first printed book in modern Bulgarian to the liberation of the country in 1878.

481. Subeva, E., *and* M. Stancheva.   Opis na izdaniiata na Bŭlgarskata akademiia na naukite, 1869-1953 (Bibliography of the publications of the Bulgarian Academy of Sciences, 1869-1953). Sofiia, Bŭlgarska akademiia na naukite, 1956. 535 p.

> A full bibliography of the publications of the leading scholarly institution in the country from its founding in 1869 to 1953. It may be supplemented by *Katalog na izdaniiata na BAN* (Catalog of publications of the Bulgarian Academy of Sciences) issued by the Academy for 1870-1944, 1945-1955, 1956-1957, and 1958, and by the bibliographic information provided in the Academy's *Spisanie na Bulgarskata akademiia na naukite.*

482. Südosteuropa-Bibliographie. Bd. 1– 1945/50– München, R. Oldenbourg, 1956–
    *See also* entries no. 13 *and* 1540.
    A continuing comprehensive bibliography of publications in various
languages on Southeastern Europe. Bulgaria is treated in volume 1,
pages 57-91, covering 1945-1950, volume 2, pages 383-493, covering 1951-1955, and volume 3, pages 39-199, covering 1956-1960.
Earlier Western publications can be found in the following: U.S. Library of Congress, *Division of Bibliography, The Balkans; a Selected
List of References* (Washington, D.C., 1943); Léon Savadjian, ed.,
*Bibliographie balkanique* (Paris, 1931-1939); Robert J. Kerner, *Slavic
Europe; a Selected Bibliography in the Western European Languages*
(Cambridge, Mass., 1918).

483. Teodorov-Balan, Aleksandŭr. Bŭlgarski knigopis za sto godini,
1806-1905 (Bulgarian bibliography for one hundred years, 1806-
1905). Sofiia, 1909. 1667 p.
    This is the largest single bibliography of Bulgarian books, listing
15,258 titles. Numerous additions and corrections were made by
Nikola Nachov in *Sbornik za narodni umotvoreniia i narodopis* (Collection for folklore and ethnography), v. 26, and in *Sbornik na Bulgarskata akademiia na naukite* (Collection of the Bulgarian Academy
of Sciences), v. 3 (1914) and v. 17 (1925).

## 4. Bibliographies and Indexes of Periodical Literature

484. Bŭlgarski periodichen pechat; bibliografski biuletin . . . (The Bulgarian periodical press; a bibliographic bulletin for . . . ). Sofiia,
Narodna Biblioteka "Kiril i Metodii," 1967–.
    The first issue of a projected annual list of all newspapers, journals,
and serial publications in Bulgaria covering 1965. Similar earlier bibliographies for 1947, 1950, 1945-1950, 1951, 1953, 1954, and 1955
are listed on page six of that issue. A general bibliography of serial
publications for 1944-1964 is being prepared by the National Library
to extend for the postwar period D. Ivanchev's *Bŭlgarski periodichen
pechat, 1844-1944* (entry no. 485).

485. Ivanchev, Dimitŭr P. Bŭlgarski periodichen pechat, 1844-1944;
anotiran bibliografski ukazatel (Bulgarian periodicals, 1844-1944; an
annotated bibliographic index). Sofiia, Nauka i izkustvo, 1962-1966.
2 v.
    An exhaustive alphabetical list of 8,120 Bulgarian journals and
newspapers published from 1844 to 1944. It provides information on
the history, editors, contributors, and political orientation of each
periodical.

486. Letopis na periodichniia pechat (Bibliography of the periodical press).
1952– Sofiia. Biweekly.
    A selective monthly list of articles and books reviews in Bulgarian
journals and newspapers, issued by the National Library in Sofia. Also

useful is *Osvedomitelen biuletin za po-vazhni statii po teoretichni, politicheski, vŭtreshnopartiini, stopanski i kulturni vŭprosi* (Information bulletin on the more important articles on theoretical, political, intra party, economic, and cultural questions), issued monthly by the research unit of the Sofia Party Committee of the Bulgarian Communist Party.

487. Mikhov, Nikola V.   Bibliographie des articles de périodiques allemands, anglais, français et italiens sur la Turquie et la Bulgarie. Sofia, 1938. 686 p.

A basic bibliography of 10,044 works on Turkey and Bulgaria published in Western periodicals from 1715 to 1891.

488. U.S. *Bureau of the Census.*   Bibliography of Social Science Periodicals and Monograph Series: Bulgaria, 1944-1960. Washington, 1961. 36 p. (Foreign Social Science bibliographies, Series P-92, no. 2)
*See also* entry no. 25.

A bibliography of postwar serials received by the Library of Congress.

### 5. Bibliographies of Materials Published outside Bulgaria

489. Byrnes, Robert F.   Bibliography of American Publications on East Central Europe, 1945-1957. Bloomington, Ind., 1958. 213 p. (Indiana University Publications, Slavic and East European Series, 12)
*See also* entry no. 15.

The basic bibliography for works on Bulgaria published in the United States after the war. Publications in the succeeding years are listed in the annual *American Bibliography of Russian and East European Studies* (Bloomington, Ind., 1958–).

490. Iordanov, Petŭr.   La Bulgaria in Italia; bibliografia delle pubblicazioni italiane sulla Bulgaria, 1870-1942. Roma, 1943. 86 p.

The basic Italian bibliography on Bulgaria.

491. Kersopoulos, Jean G.   Bulgarie: ouvrages et articles de revues parus de 1613 à 1937. Athènes, 1937. 180 p.

The most comprehensive bibliography of Bulgaria in French. It is supplemented by the bibliographic sections in the annual *Revue des études slaves* (Paris, 1921–).

492. Novaia literatura po Bolgarii (New literature on Bulgaria). 1960–
Moskva. Monthly.

A monthly bibliography of books and articles on Bulgaria issued by the Fundamental Library of the Social Sciences of the Soviet Academy of Sciences. It lists annually about 3,000 titles in Russian, Bulgarian, and other languages. Soviet publications on Bulgarian subjects are listed in I. A. Kaloeva's *Sovetskoe slavianovedenie; literatura o zarubezhnykh slavianskikh stranakh na russkom iazyke, 1918-1960* (Soviet Slavic studies; literature on non-Soviet Slavic countries in the

Russian language, 1918-1960) (Moskva, Izd-vo Akademii nauk SSSR, 1963, 402 p.), and its supplement for 1961-1962 (Moskva, 1963, 261 p.). A current bibliography of Soviet writings on Bulgaria is maintained in the bimonthly *Sovetskoe slavianovedenie* (Soviet Slavic studies) (1965–, Moskva).

493. Saenger, Mathilde.   Verzeichnis deutsch-sprachiger Bücher über Bulgarien. *In* Bulgaria-Jahrbuch 1942 der Deutsch-Bulgarischen Gesellschaft Berlin. Leipzig, 1942. p. 335-382.

> This basic list of books in German on Bulgarian subjects is supplemented by Part 5, "Bulgarien," of *Europa-Bibliographie* (Leipzig, 1942, 113 p.) and by a list published in *Bulgaria-Jahrbuch* (Frankfurt, v. 6, 1962: 157-170). German-language dissertations are listed in A. Scherer's *Südosteuropa-Dissertationen 1918-1960* (Wien, Böhlau, 1968, 221 p.).

494. Szolginiowa, Wanda.   Bulgaria w pismiennictwie polskim (1944-1963) (Bulgaria in Polish publications, 1944-1963). Warszawa, Biblioteka Narodowa, 1965. 216 p.

> A bibliography of postwar works on Bulgaria in Polish.

495. Traikov, Veselin.   Bŭlgariia v chuzhdata literatura, 1954-1963. Bibliografski ukazatel (Bulgaria in foreign publications, 1954-1963; a bibliographic index). Sofiia, Narodna biblioteka "Kiril i Metodii," 1965. 219 p.

> A bibliography of 3,022 titles published by non-Bulgarians and Bulgarians outside Bulgaria on all aspects of the country's life. Another volume, for the 1944-1953 decade was published in 1968. The years after 1963 are being covered by the library's annual series *Bŭlgariia v chuzhdata literatura; bibliografski ukazatel.*

## B. ENCYCLOPEDIAS AND HANDBOOKS

496. Danchov, Nikola G., *and* I. G. Danchov.   Bŭlgarska entsiklopediia (Bulgarian encyclopedia). Sofiia, 1936. 1720 p.

> The only Bulgarian encyclopedia of the interwar period. It has continuing value as a source of information on personalities and developments of that period.

497. Dellin, L. A. D., *ed.*   Bulgaria. New York, Praeger, 1957. 457 p. Bibliography.

> A handbook of information on various aspects of Bulgarian life as of 1956. A handbook with more recent data is *Bulgarien* by Christo Ognjanoff (Nürnberg, Glock und Lutz Verlag, 1967, 496 p.).

498. Desev, Boris.   Spravochno-bibliografski izdaniia (Reference and bibliographic publications). Sofiia, Nauka i izkustvo, 1960. 182 p.

> Bulgarian and non-Bulgarian reference works used in Bulgaria are cited and discussed. Similar information through 1966 is provided in

Khristo Trenkov's *Spravochno-bibliografska rabota i metodika na preporuchitelnata bibliografiia v masovite i uchilishtnite biblioteki* (Reference and bibliographic work and methodology of recommended bibliography in the public and school libraries) (Sofiia, Nauka i izkustvo, 1967, 156 p.).

499. Kazasov, Dimo. Bŭlgariia; pŭtevoditel (Bulgaria; a guide). Sofiia, Nauka i izkustvo, 1963. 377 p.

A handbook of useful information on all aspects of life in Bulgaria and all areas of the country. For a recent guide to Sofia *see* Stoiko Kozhukharov's *Sofia* (Sofia, Foreign Languages Press, 1967, 140 p.).

500. Kratka bŭlgarska entsiklopediia (Concise Bulgarian encyclopedia). Sofiia, Bŭlgarska akademiia na naukite, 1963–

This is the only major up-to-date Bulgarian encyclopedia, in five volumes.

501. Marinov, Aleksi. Bŭlgariia; povŭrkhnina, narod i kultura (Bulgaria; land, people, and culture). Sofiia, "Khudozhnik," 1931. 378 p. Illus., maps. Bibliography: p. 378.

A handbook useful for its data on the interwar period.

502. Rusinov, Spas. Bulgaria: Land, Economy, Culture. Sofia, Foreign Languages Press, 1965. 245 p.

A handbook of basic data published for foreigners in Bulgaria. Also available in French and German. Recent travel guides include *Bulgarie* in the series "Les guides Nagel" Geneva, Nagel, 2d rev. ed., 1968, 496 p.) and *Bulgarien* (München, Grieben Verlag, 1967, 210 p., "Grieben-Reiseführer," Bd. 290).

## C. STATISTICAL PUBLICATIONS

503. Dzherova L., *and* N. Toteva. Bibliografiia na bŭlgarskata statisticheska literatura, 1878-1960 (Bibliography of Bulgarian statistical literature, 1878-1960). Sofiia, 1961. 105 p.

*See also* entry no. 723.

An exhaustive bibliography of official statistical publications (general census statistics, annual abstracts, etc.) as well as writings on statistics in Bulgaria.

504. Statisticheski godishnik na Narodna Republika Bŭlgariia (Statistical yearbook of the People's Republic of Bulgaria). Sofiia, 1947/48– Tsentralno statistichesko upravlenie.

*See also* entry no. 727.

The basic statistical publication of Bulgaria, issued from 1909 to 1942 under the title *Statisticheski godishnik na Tsarstvo Bŭlgariia* (Statistical yearbook of the Kingdom of Bulgaria). The text is provided with French and, in recent years, English translations. The 1956 and

1961 editions have been translated by the U.S. Joint Publications Reserch Service as *Statistical Yearbook of the People's Republic of Bulgaria, 1956* (New York, 1958, 153 p.) and *Statistical Yearbook of the Bulgarian People's Republic, 1961* (Washington, D.C., 1962, 925 p.).

505. Statisticheski izvestiia (Statistical news). 1957– Sofiia. Quarterly.

506. Statisticheski spravochnik na NR Bŭlgariia (Statistical manual of the People's Republic of Bulgaria). Sofiia, 1958– Annual.

A pocket-size manual of general statistical data issued by the Central Statistical Office in Sofia.

## D. DICTIONARIES (BILINGUAL)

507. The following dictionaries are listed in alphabetical order of the second language.

English: Atanasova, T., *and others.* Angliisko-bŭlgarski rechnik (English-Bulgarian dictionary). Sofiia, Bŭlgarska akademiia naukite, 1966-1967. 2 v. (828, 800 p.).

Chakalov, Gocho G., *and others.* Bŭlgarsko-angliiski rechnik (Bulgarian-English dictionary). Sofiia, Nauka i izkustvo, 1961. 982 p.

French: Tomov, T. S., *and others.* Frensko-bŭlgarski rechnik (French-Bulgarian dictionary). Sofiia, Bŭlgarska akademiia na naukite, 1964. 1247 p.

Stefanova, L., *and others.* Bŭlgarsko-frenski rechnik (Bulgarian-French dictionary). Sofiia, Nauka i izkustvo, 1964. 976 p.

German: Arnaudov, Ia., *and others.* Nemsko-bŭlgarski rechnik (German-Bulgarian dictionary). Sofiia, Bŭlgarska akademiia na naukite, 1965. 2 v.

Dorich, A., *and others.* Bŭlgarsko-nemski rechnik (Bulgarian-German dictionary). 2d ed. Sofiia, Narodna prosveta, 1962. 562 p.

Italian: Nurigiani, Giorgio. Italiano-bŭlgarski rechnik (Italian-Bulgarian dictionary). Plovdiv, 1942. 506 p.

Russian: Chukalov, Sava K. Pulen rusko-bŭlgarski rechnik (Complete Russian-Bulgarian dictionary). Sofiia, 1951. 1234 p.

Bernshtein, S. B. Bolgarsko-russkii slovar' (Bulgarian-Russian dictionary). Moskva, Sovetskaia entsiklopediia, 1966. 768 p.

Spanish: Neikov, T., *and others.* Ispansko-bŭlgarski rechnik (Spanish-Bulgarian dictionary). Sofiia, Nauka i izkustvo, 1964. 948 p.

## E. OTHER REFERENCE AIDS

508. Atanasov, Petŭr. Nachalo na bŭlgarskoto knigopechatane (The beginning of Bulgarian printing). Sofiia, Nauka i izkustvo, 1959. 240 p.

A history of Bulgarian printing. It is supplemented by S. Kutinchev's *Pechatarstvoto v Bŭlgariia do osvobozhdenieto* (Printing in Bulgaria to the Liberation) (Sofiia, 1920, 287 p.).

A survey of the Bulgarian press from the first Bulgarian journal "Luboslovie" (1844) up to the present is offered in the following study: Borchoukov, G., *and* Vl. Topentcharov. Histoire de la presse bulgare. Journalisme (Strasbourg), no. 26, 1966: 99-120.

509. Pundeff, Marin V.    Sources for Bulgarian Biography. *In* U.S. Library of Congress. Quarterly Journal, v. 24, no. 2, April 1967: 97-102.

The article provides information on the existing sources for biographical research on prominent Bulgarians in various fields of endeavor.

510. Savova, Elena, *ed.*    Les études balkaniques et sud-est européenes en Bulgarie; guide de documentation. Sofia, Académie bulgare des sciences, Bibliothèque centrale, 1966. 184 p.

*See also* entries no. 43 *and* 894.

A useful guide to institutions, research facilities, and major tools of Balkan studies in Bulgaria. Published by the Bulgarian National Committee for Balkan Studies and the Central Library of the Bulgarian Academy of Sciences for the First International Congress of Balkan Studies in 1966. The guide lists scholarly organizations, institutes, institutions of higher learning, archives, libraries, and publishing houses (with addresses, names of directors, and much other information) as well as reference works and relevant periodicals.

511. Subeva, Emiliia, *ed.*    Nauchni uchrezhdeniia v Bŭlgariia, 1966; spravochnik (Scientific institutions in Bulgaria, 1966; a guide). Sofiia, 1967. 188 p.

A guide to academies, institutions of higher education, research institutes, principal archival repositories, libraries, and learned societies in Bulgaria, issued by the Center for Scientific Information and Documentation of the Central Library of the Bulgarian Academy of Sciences. Includes data, as of December 31, 1966 (in some cases as of the end of March, 1967), on key personnel, address, organization, and publications of each institution.

For a useful source of information on the organization, collections, and facilities of all types of libraries, *see*:

Sofia. Narodna biblioteka. Nauchno-metodichen otdel po bibliotekoznanie i preporuchitelna bibliografiia. *Spravochnik na bibliotekete v Bŭlgariia* (A guide to libraries in Bulgaria). Sofiia, 1963. 389 p.

The best guide to archival holdings in Bulgaria is Mariia Kuzmanova's *Istoriia na arkhivite i organizatsiia na arkhivnoto delo v Bŭlgariia* (History of archives and organization of archive-keeping in Bulgaria) (Sofia, Nauka i izkustvo, 1966, 259 p.). For current information, see *Isvestiia na dŭrzhavnite arkhivi* (Bulletin of the state archives). Sofia, 1957–

512. U.S. *Library of Congress. Slavic and Central European Division.* Bulgarian Abbreviations; a Selective List. Washington, D.C., 1961. 326 p.

A useful list of abbreviations commonly used in Bulgarian publications. English translations are provided. The list should be used together with Boris Damianov's *Kratŭk rechnik na nai-upotrebiavanite sŭkrashteniia v bŭlgarskiia ezik* (A concise dictionary of abbreviations most frequently used in Bulgarian) (Sofiia, Bŭlgarska akademiia na naukite, Tsentŭr za nauchna informatsiia i dokumentatsiia, 1965, 71 p.).

# 19

# the land

*by George W. Hoffman*

Survey Studies and Atlases 513-524

Serials 525-527

Regional Studies and Special Aspects 528-536

## A. SURVEY STUDIES AND ATLASES

513. Beshkov, Anastas S.   Volksrepublic Bulgarien; Natur und Wirtschaft. Berlin, Verlag Wirtschaft, 1960. 191 p. Illus., maps. Bibliography: p. 190-191.

See also entry no. 745.

A brief economic geography. *See also*:

Gŭlŭbov, Zh. S., *and others*.   Fizicheskaia geografiia Bolgarii (Bulgaria's physical geography). Translated by A. I. Dvoriadkina. Moska, Izd-vo inostrannoi literatury, 1960. 361 p. Illus.

514. Bulgaria. *Upravlenie geodeziia i kartografiia.*   Ucheben geografski atlas (Geographic study atlas). Chief editor, Zh. Baikov. Sofiia, 1959. 114 p. Maps, tables.

An excellent atlas, covering physical, social, and economic aspects of Bulgaria. Index of place names.

515. Bŭlgariia; khristomatiia po ikonomicheska geografiia (Bulgaria; a reader in economic geography). v. 2. Compiled by Veliu Velev and others. Sofiia, Narodna prosveta, 1961. 472 p. Illus.

Topical and regional description emphasizing economic geography.

516. Chankov, Zhecho.   Geografski rechnik na Bŭlgariia (Geographical dictionary of Bulgaria). Sofiia, Nauka i izkustvo, 1958. 537 p. Bibliography: p. 526-537.

A convenient source of reference.

129

517. Chataigneau, Y., *and* Jules Sion.   La Bulgarie. *In* Chataigneau, Y., and Jules Sion, *eds.* Geographic universelle, v. 7, part 2. Paris, Armand Colin, 1934. p. 486-508.
    Survey of regional geography of Bulgaria.

518. Fichelle, Alfred.   Bulgaria. *In* Larousse Encyclopedia of Geography. v. 1. General editor, Pierre Deffontaines, assisted by Mariel Jean-Brunhes Delamarre. New York, Prometheus Press, 1961. p. 295-300.
    Survey of regional geography of Bulgaria.

519. Geografiia na Bŭlgariia, t. 1: Fizicheska geografia (Geography of Bulgaria, v. 1: physical geography). Prepared by I. P. Gerasimov and others. Sofiia, Bŭlgarska akademiia na naukite, 1966. 548 p. Illus., maps.
    The standard and most detailed survey. Includes a brief regional analysis.

520. Geografiia na Bŭlgariia; t. 2: Ikonomicheska geografiia (Geography of Bulgaria; v. 2: economic geography). Prepared by A. Beshkov and others. Sofiia, Bŭlgarska akademiia na naukite, 1961. 570 p. Illus., maps.
    The standard and most detailed survey of the subject.

521. Ishirkov, Anastas T.   Bulgarien, Land und Leute. Leipzig, Parlapanoff, 1916-1917. 2 v. Illus., maps. (Bulgarische Bibliothek, 1-2)
    Excellent descriptive geography of Bulgaria. The first volume is devoted to physical geography, and the second, to anthropogeography.

522. Jireček, Josef K.   Das Fürstenthum Bulgarien. Wien, Tempsky, 1891. 573 p. Illus.
    *See also* entry no. 775.
    Detailed description of all important regions of Bulgaria.

523. Kanitz, Felix P.   Donau-Bulgarien und der Balkan: Historisch-geographisch-ethnographische Reisestudien aus den Jahren 1860-1879. 2d ed. Leipzig, Rengersche Buchhandlung, 1882. 3 v. Illus., maps.
    Detailed description of land and people in the 19th century.

524. Penkov, Ignat, *and* Todor D. Khristov.   Ikonomicheska geografiia na Bŭlgariia (Economic geography of Bulgaria). 2d ed. Sofiia, Nauka i izkustvo, 1964. 518 p. Illus., maps, plans, bibliographies.
    A detailed study of economic geography. For an English translation of an earlier work by the same author *see:*
    Penkov, Ignat, *and* Milka Penkova.   Economic Geography of the People's Republic of Bulgaria. 2nd rev. ed. New York, U.S. Joint Publications Research Service, 1958. 497 p. Illus., maps, diagrs., tables. (JPRS/NY-547) Bibliography: p. 452-455. Translation of a basic economic geography.

## B. SERIALS

525. Bŭlgarska akademiia na naukite, Sofiia. *Geografski institut.* Izvestiia (Proceedings of the Geographical Institute, Bulgarian Academy of Sciences). 1951– Sofiia. Irregular.
Summaries in Russian and French.

526. Bŭlgarsko geografsko druzhestvo, *Sofia.* Izvestiia (Transactions of the Bulgarian Geographical Society). 1933– Sofiia. Annual.
Includes summaries in French, German, or Russian.

527. Geografiia; nauchno-populiarno spisanie (Geography; a popular scientific journal). 1950– Sofiia. 10 issues a year.
Popular publication of the Bulgarian Geographical Society.

## C. REGIONAL STUDIES AND SPECIAL ASPECTS

528. Barten, H.   Die Landschaften Bulgariens. Zeitschrift für Erdkunde, v. 9, March 1941: 143-170.
Regional geographic description of Bulgaria.

529. Gellert, Johannes F.   Mittelbulgarien; das kulturgeographische Bild der Gegenwart. Berlin, Junker u. Dünnhaupt, 1937. 294 p. Tables, maps, plans.
Description of the lowlands of southern Bulgaria, the basins of the Sub-Balkans, and Sredna Gora. The author has also written a physicogeographical study of the same region: *Oberflächengestaltung und Morphotektonik Mittelbulgariens und ihre Beziehung zur Morphotektonik der Balkanhalbinsel* (Leipzig, Hirzel, 1936, 66 p.).

530. Iordanov, Tianko.   Ikonomgeografski problemi na selkskoto stopanstvo v Pazardzhishko-Plovdivskoto pole i ogradnite mu zemi (Economic-geographic problems of agriculture in the Pazardzhik-Plovdiv plain and surrounding areas). *In* Bŭlgarska akademiia na naukite, Sofiia. Geografski institut. Izvestiia, v. 7, 1963: 91-181.
Contribution to an understanding of Bulgarian agriculture, based on field investigations in the fertile Maritsa Lowlands.

531. Khristov, Todor D.   Geografiia na promishlenostta v Bŭlgariia (Geography of industrial production in Bulgaria). Sofiia, Nauka i izkustvo, 1962. 288 p. Illus., bibliography.
General survey of the geographical character of Bulgarian industry.

532. Louis, Herbert.   Morphologische Studien in Südwest-Bulgarien. Stuttgart, Verlag von J. Engelhorns Nachf., 1930. 119 p. Tables, plates, maps.
An essential contribution to the knowledge of the Struma and Mesta valleys, the mountain regions of Pirin and Rila, and the adjacent regions of the Rhodopes.

533. Marinov, Khristo T.   Geografsko razpredelenie na promishlenostta v Bŭlgariia i neratsionalnite prevozi (Geographic distribution of industry in Bulgaria and unrationalized transportation). Sofiia, Nauka i izkustvo, 1959. 189 p. Illus., bibliography.

534. Marinov, Khristo T.   Osnovni vŭprosi na geografskoto razpredelenie na proizvodstvoto i ikonomicheskoto raĭonirane (Basic problems of geographic distribution and economic regionalization). Varna, Dŭrzhavno izdatelstvo, 1963. 313 p. Maps, diagrs.
    Sophisticated treatment of general location theory, based on economic geography.

535. Natsionalen komitet po geografiia. Problemi na geografiiata v NR Bŭlgariia; sbornik ot statii po sluchai XX mezhdunaroden geografski kongres, London, 1964 (Problems of geography in the People's Republic of Bulgaria; collection of articles on the occasion of the XX International Geographic Congress, London, 1964). Sofiia, Nauka i izkustvo, 1964. 246 p.
    Articles on various aspects of Bulgarian geography.

536. Stoianov, Nikolai, and B. Stefanov.   Flora na Bŭlgariia (Flora in Bulgaria). 3d rev. ed. Sofiia, Univ. pechatnitsa, 1948. 1361 p. (Universitetska biblioteka, No. 360)
    Basic reference book on the flora of Bulgaria.

# 20

# the people

*by George W. Hoffman*

537. Bulgaria. *Ministerstvo na vŭnshnite raboti.* The Bulgarian Question and the Balkan States. Sofia, State Printing Press, 1919. 304 p. Maps, facsims, tables.
*See also* entry no. 701.
Material prepared for the Paris Peace Conference in 1919.

538. Bulgaria. *Tsentralno statistichesko upravlenie.* Preboiavane na naselenieto na 1. dekemvri 1956 god.; obshti rezultati (Population census as of Dec., 1956; general results). Sofiia, Nauka i izkustvo, 1959-1961. 4 v.

————. Statistika za dvizhenieto na naselenieto v NR Bŭlgariia za perioda 1947-1959 g. (Statistics concerning the population movement for the period 1947-1959). Sofiia, Nauka i izkustvo, 1961. 577 p.

————. Returns of the 1 December 1965 Population Census in the People's Republic of Bulgaria. Sofiia, Central Statistical Office, 1966. 111 p.
Three important sources of recent demographic information. For other basic demographic materials *see:*
Chankov, Zhecho. Naselenieto na Bŭlgariia (Bulgaria's population). Sofiia, 1935. 278 p.
Mikhov, Nikola V. Naselenieto na Turtsiia i Bŭlgariia prez XVIII i XIX v.; bibliografsko-statistichni izsledvaniia (The population of Turkey and Bulgaria in the 18th and 19th centuries; bibliographic-statistical studies). Sofiia, 1915-1966. 5 v.

539. Hoffman, George W. Transformation of Rural Settlement in Bulgaria. Geographical Review, v. 54, January 1964: 45-64.
Historical-geographical discussion of the transformation of rural settlements in Bulgaria, up-dating earlier settlement theories.

540. Kostanick, Huey L. The Turkish Resettlement of Bulgarian Turks, 1950-53. Berkeley, University of California Press, 1957. 65-163 p.

Illus., maps, diagr., tables. Bibliography: p. 145-146. (University of California Publications in Geography, v. 8, no. 2)
*See also* entry no. 806.

541. Ishirkov (Ischirkoff), Anastas I.   Die Bevölkerung in Bulgarien und ihre Siedlungsverhältnisse. Translated by A. Kassner. Petermanns Geographische Mitteilungen (Gotha), 57, 1911: 117-122, 179-185.

    A survey of the historical-geographical development of Bulgarian settlements and the structure of such settlements. Includes a discussion of the position of minorities in Bulgaria.

542. Penkov (Penkoff), Ignat.   Die Siedlungen Bulgariens, ihre Entwicklung, Veränderungen und Klassifizierung. Geographische Berichte, Heft 17, December 1960: 211-227.

    Detailed survey by a well-known Bulgarian geographer.

543. Prochazka, Zora.   The Labor Force of Bulgaria. Washington, D.C., Bureau of the Census, 1962. 38 p. (International Population Statistics Reports. Series P-90, no. 16)

    Presents data on the size, composition, and growth of the Bulgarian labor force from 1934 to 1959. Demographic factors which influence changes in the working population are discussed.

    *See also* entry no. 769.

544. Waltscheff (Vŭlchev), Todor.   Bevölkerungsbewegung Bulgariens nach dem Weltkrieg. Leipzig, Fock, 1932. 102 p. Tables.

    Survey of the refugee movement after the First World War. Includes a discussion of the rehabilitation of refugees and the demographic and social changes caused by them.

545. Wilhelmy, Herbert.   Hochbulgarien. Kiel, Schmidt und Klaunig, 1935-1936. 2 v. Illus., maps, plans. Bibliography: v. 1, p. 291-308; v. 2, p. 203-220. (Schriften des Geographischen Instituts der Universität Kiel, Bd. IV, Bd. V, Heft 3)

    *See also* entry no. 780.

    Volume 1, *Die ländlichen Siedlungen und die bäuerliche Wirtschaft,* is a detailed survey of rural settlements and the agricultural economy. Volume 2, *Sofia, Wandlungen einer Grosstadt zw. Orient und Okzident,* is a historical-geographical analysis of Sofia.

# 21

# history

*by Michael B. Petrovich*

## A. GENERAL HISTORY

546. Akademiia nauk SSSR. *Institut slavianovedeniia.* Istoriia Bolgarii (History of Bulgaria). Moskva, Izd-vo Akademii nauk SSSR, 1954-55. 2 v.

> This survey, in Russian, of Bulgarian history from earliest times to 1955 is the work of the Institute of Slavic Studies of the Soviet Academy of Sciences and was intended to supply a "Marxist-Leninist" interpretation. The first volume ends with the Great October Revolution in Russia in 1917, and the second volume is divided roughly evenly between the period 1917-1941 and the period following the Second World War, with the emphasis on the latter. It may be taken to represent the official Soviet view at the time.

547. Buchan, John, *ed.* Bulgaria and Rumania. Boston, New York, Houghton Mifflin, 1924. 321 p.

> More than half of this volume is devoted to a popular survey of Bulgarian history from earliest times to the first years after the First World War. Lady Grogan wrote the historical part, G. C. Logio described Bulgaria during the war, and H. J. Fisher supplied the section on the Bulgarian economy. Though it has no scholarly pretensions, this work may still be read with profit by readers who are restricted to English accounts.

548. Bŭlgariia; khiliada godini, 927-1927 (One thousand years of Bul-

135

garia, 927-1927). v. 1. Sofiia, Izd-vo na Ministerstvoto na naradnoto prosveshtenie, 1930. 1023 p. Illus.

See also entry no. 813.

This massive anniversary volume commemorating the millenium of Tsar Simeon's state contains chapters topically and chronologically arranged from A.D. 927 to San Stefano Bulgaria in 1878. Though written in a nationalist spirit, this symposium brings together the writings of some of Bulgaria's outstanding scholars, and despite the ceremonial circumstances surrounding this volume, the contributions are generally serious scholarly works.

549. Bŭlgarska akademiia na naukite. *Institut za bŭlgarska istoriia.* Istoriia na Bŭlgariia (History of Bulgaria). 2d rev. ed. Sofiia, Nauka i izkustvo, 1961-1964. 3 v.

This edition replaces the hastily written two-volume edition of 1954-1955 and is intended to be the latest official survey history of Bulgaria from earliest times to 1963 as interpreted by the Marxist historians of the Historical Institute of the Bulgarian Academy of Sciences. This edition differs markedly from the first, in large part as the result of criticism by "specialists and readers," to bring it in line with "the latest achievements of Bulgarian and Soviet historical science."

550. Derzhavin, Nikolai S.    Istoriia Bolgarii (History of Bulgaria). Moskva, Izd-vo Akademii nauk SSSR, 1945-1948. 4 v.

Until the appearance of the two-volume work published by the Soviet Academy of Sciences in 1954-1955, this was the only general survey of Bulgarian history by a Soviet scholar. Volume 1 is devoted to early medieval Bulgarian history and bears the imprint of Marr's linguistic theories, since repudiated in the Soviet Union. Volume 2 deals with the First and Second Bulgarian Empires, 679-1393. Volume 3 takes up the period of Ottoman rule to the middle of the 19th century. The last volume treats the liberation from the Turks in 1878. Though superseded, this work still contains much that is useful.

551. Evans, Stanley G.    A Short History of Bulgaria. London, Lawrence and Wishart, 1960. 254 p. Bibliography.

The author, an English clergyman who visited Bulgaria in 1950 as a journalist, here gives a sketchy account of Bulgarian history in six chapters, extending to the mid-1950s. This book was meant to fill the gap in English since the 1924 volume edited by Buchan. It is based largely on sources in Western languages. The tone is very friendly to the communist regime. The most useful part of the book may well be its bibliography.

552. Hýbl, František.    Dějiny národa bulharského (History of the Bulgarian People). Praha, Nakl. Historického klubu, 1930. 2 v.

This very good Czech synthesis has the additional advantage of going beyond Jireček's work (*see* entry 553).

553. Jireček, Josef K.   Geschichte der Bulgaren. Prag, Tempsky, 1876. 584 p.

Written by the great Czech pioneer of Balkan studies and minister of education in Bulgaria, this is the first complete scholarly survey of Bulgarian history. It surveys Bulgarian history up to 1872. It has withstood the test of time and has become a standard work in several languages. It first appeared in Czech, in sections, then in the present German edition, than in a Russian edition (Odessa, 1878) — thoroughly revised by the author — and in several Bulgarian translations and emendations. (Tŭrnovo, 1886; Sofiia, 1929; Sofiia, 1939).

554. Kosev, Dimitŭr, H. Hristov, and D. Angelov.   A Short History of Bulgaria. Sofia, Foreign Languages Press, 1963. 461 p.

This survey from earliest times to the early 1960s may be taken to represent the prevailing Bulgarian Marxist interpretation of Bulgarian history. It is the only Bulgarian history in English to appear after the Second World War that was written by Bulgarians. Full of information, it is increasingly colored by ideological and political considerations as it progresses into recent history. Also available in other Western languages.

555. MacDermott, Mercia.   A History of Bulgaria, 1393-1885. London, Allen and Unwin, 1962. 354 p.

Based largely on Bulgarian sources, this volume is rather more substantial in depth of coverage than any exisiting history of Bulgaria in English. It is centered around the theme of Ottoman subjugation and the national liberation movement. The author sees the present Bulgaria as the fulfillment of that liberation.

556. Mishev, Dimitŭr.   The Bulgarians in the Past, Pages from the Bulgarian Cultural History. Lausanne, Librairie Centrale des Nationalités, 1919. 478 p.

See also entry no. 891.

This survey from earliest times to the liberation from the Turks is a Bulgarian nationalist's view of the highlights of the general cultural and social development of his people. It is still useful to the general English reader, especially for the period of the national rebirth in the late 18th and 19th century, though rather one-sided.

557. Mitev, Iono.   Kratka istoriia na bŭlgarskiia narod (Short history of the Bulgarian People). Sofiia, Nauka i izkustvo, 1951. 626 p.

A popular account from earliest times to the anti-Fascist uprising of September 9, 1944, which emphasizes the more recent "period of capitalism" after 1878. The author has tried to give a Marxist interpretation. Frequent footnote references to Stalin's works, in addition to the works of other communist leaders, identify the book as a product of the Stalin era.

558. Monroe, Will S.   Bulgaria and Her People, with an Account of the

Balkan Wars, Macedonia, and the Macedonia Bulgars. Boston, 1914.
410 p.
> This is the first American survey of Bulgaria. About a third is de-
> voted to history. It is especially interesting with respect to the author's
> treatment of two subjects of which he had personal knowledge — the
> Balkan Wars and American activities in Bulgaria. The writer is very
> pro-Bulgarian.

559. Mutafchiev, Petŭr.   Istoriia na bŭlgarskiia narod (History of the Bulgarian People). 2d ed. Sofiia, Khemus, 1943-1944. 2 v.
> Written by a distinguished Bulgarian historian of the pre–World
> War II generation, this survey of Bulgarian medieval history represents
> one of the most solid synthetic efforts of pre-communist Bulgarian
> historiography. The author's right-wing nationalism has made this
> book unacceptable in Bulgaria today, but its scholarly worth is un-
> deniable. He added nothing to Zlatarskii's political account, but in-
> cluded more cultural and social history, as well as his own interpreta-
> tions. When the author's death cut short this work (he reached the
> year 1323 in his writings), Ivan Duĭchev completed the last section
> to include the last Bulgarian rulers before the Ottoman conquest.
> Duĭchev also prepared this posthumous edition.

560. Pastukhov, Ivan.   Bŭlgarska istoriia (Bulgarian history). Sofiia, Izd-vo
Khemus, 1942-1943. 2 v.
> This is a popular history and quite useful, especially for its empha-
> sis on social history. It also has an extensive bibliography.

561. Scipkovensky, Minco.   La Bulgaria, XVI secoli di storia, a Boris III,
zar dei Bulgari. Milano, 1931. 382 p.
> A Bulgarian history for Italians, written in an era of Italian-
> Bulgarian political amity. For another later work in Italian *see* Carlo
> A. Ferrario's *Storia dei Bulgari* (Milano, 1940, 279 p.).

562. Songeon, Guérin.   Histoire de la Bulgarie depuis les origines jusqu'à
nos jours, 485-1913. Paris, Nouvelle librairie nationale, 1913. 480 p.
> A useful textbook account which stresses the pre-Ottoman period.

563. Zlatarski, Vasil N., *and* N. Stanev.   Geschichte der Bulgaren. Leipzig, 1918. 2 v.
> This joint effort by two outstanding Bulgarian historians long
> served as the most competent account of Bulgarian history in any
> Western language since Jireček's work. The first volume covers the
> period 679-1396, and the second volume deals with the Ottoman
> period and the new Bulgarian state until 1917.

## B. MEDIEVAL HISTORY

564. Beševliev (Beshevliev), Veselin, *and* Johannes Irmscher, *eds.*   Antike
und Mittelalter in Bulgarien. Berlin, Akademie-Verlag, 1960. 363 p.
Plates, map. (Berliner byzantinische Arbeiten, 21)

*See also* entry no. 886.

The value of the first part lies in six bibliographical surveys of Bulgarian historiography, byzantinology, epigraphy, numismatics, and classic philology. The second and third parts deal with the ancient and medieval history of Sofia and the old towns situated at the Danube.

565. Litavrin, G. G.  Bolgariia i Vizantiia v XI-XII vv. (Bulgaria and Byzantium in the XI-XII centuries). Moskva, Akademiia nauk SSSR, 1960. 470 p.

This book by a Soviet scholar deals with a little known period, the Byzantine conquest of Bulgaria from 1018 to 1185.

566. Nicolaus I, *the Great, Saint, Pope.*  Responsa Nicolai I. Papae ad consulta Bulgarorum (anno 866). Sofia, 1939. 152 p.

This is the Latin original and Bulgarian translation of one of the earliest and most important sources of early Bulgarian history, the replies of Pope Nicholas I to the Bulgarian Prince Boris in 866, at the time of Bulgaria's official conversion to Christianity, when Boris was negotiating with both Rome and Constantinople.

567. Runciman, *Sir* Steven.  A History of the First Bulgarian Empire. London, Bell, 1930. 337 p.

This is an admirable piece of scholarship by a distinguished English scholar who has made thorough use of Byzantine and Western sources as well as the Bulgarian literature on the subject. This book takes up Bulgarian history from the coming of the Bulgars to the Balkans in the seventh century to 1018, when the Bulgarian lands were annexed by the Byzantine Empire.

568. Sergheraert, G.  Les Bulgares de la Volga et les Slaves du Danube; le problème des races et les barbares. Paris, G. P. Maisonneuve, 1939. 294 p.

Writing under the pseudonym Christian Gerard, the author deals with the Volga Bulgars to 1552 and with the Danubian Bulgarians to 893. He takes up the later period in his book *Symeon le Grand 893-927* (Paris, Maisonneuve, 1960, 197 p.), published under his own name. The author was a professor in a French school in Bulgaria.

569. Snegarov, Ivan.  Dukhovno-kulturni vrŭzki mezhdu Bŭlgariia i Rusiia prez srednite vekove, X-XV v. (Spiritual and cultural ties between Bulgaria and Russia during the Middle Ages, 10th-15th centuries). Sofiia, Sinodalno kn-vo, 1950. 96 p.

A disappointingly brief treatment of an important subject, which is of as much interest to the Russian as to the Balkan scholar. It is another reminder of how much early Russian culture owed to the Balkan Slavs.

570. Tsenov, Gancho.  Die Abstammung der Bulgaren und die Urheimat der Slaven. Berlin, 1930. 358 p.

A work by a Bulgarian scholar on the origin and earliest history of the Bulgars and Balkan Slavs. *See also* his *Geschichte der Bulgaren*

*und der anderen Südslaven . . . bis zum Ende des neunten Jahr-*
*hunderts* (Berlin, 1935, 272 p.).

571. Wolff, Robert Lee.   The Second Bulgarian Empire; Its Origin and
History to 1204. Speculum, v. 24, April 1949: 167-206.

> Despite its brevity, this is the best account in English of the origins
> and early history of the Second Bulgarian Empire (1186-1393). The
> author, a professor at Harvard University, deals with this controversial
> question up to 1204.

572. Zlatarski, Vasil N.   Istoriia na bŭlgarskata dŭrzhava priez sriednitie
viekove (History of the Bulgarian state during the Middle Ages). Sofiia,
1918-1940. 3 v. in 4.
*See also* entry no. 2318.

> Undoubtedly the most massive and authoritative work on Bulgarian
> medieval history by Bulgaria's foremost academic historian. This
> work extends to the year 1280 and was interrupted by the author's
> death. It emphasizes political history.

## C. THE OTTOMAN PERIOD

573. Angelov, Dimitŭr S.   Agrarnite otnosheniia v severna i sredna Makedoniia prez XIV vek (Agrarian relations in northern and central
Macedonia in the 14th century). Sofiia, Bŭlgarskata akademiia na
naukite, 1958. 256 p.

> An important work on the economic history of northern and central
> Macedonia in the century of the Ottoman conquest.

574. Hajek, Alois.   Bulgarien unter der Türkenherrschaft. Stuttgart-Berlin-
Leipzig, Deutsche Verlags-Anstalt, 1925. 330 p.

> The best monograph on the period of Turkish domination, with
> emphasis on the political and military events of the 19th century, by
> a scholar of the "Forschungsinstitut für Osten und Orient" (today
> Institut für Ost- und Südosteuropäische Geschichte) in Vienna. For
> the internal conditions and circumstances of life *see also* the author's
> review of the travel literature: "Die Bulgaren im Spiegel der Reiselitera-
> tur des 16. bis 19. Jahrhunderts" in *Bulgaria-Jahrbuch 1942* (Leipzig):
> 47-99.

575. Leo, Michel.   La Bulgarie et son peuple sous la domination otto-
mane, tels que les ont vus les voyageurs anglo-saxons (1586-1878);
découverte d'une nationalité. Sofia, Nauka i izkustvo, 1949. 335 p.

> A very useful contribution consisting of a collection of impressions
> of Bulgaria by English travelers between 1586 and 1878.

576. Milev, Nikola.   Katolishkata propaganda v Bŭlgariia priez XVII
viek (Catholic propaganda in Bulgaria during the 17th century). Sofiia,
1914. 194 p.

> This is an important work by a Bulgarian scholar whose assassina-

tion in 1925 cut short a promising career. Based on some 190 letters and reports which he found in Vienna in 1911-1912, this work centers around the activity of the first Roman Catholic bishop in Bulgaria, Peter Solinat of Bosnia, and his successor. For a later work on this subject by an even more distinguished Bulgarian scholar, *see* Ivan Duĭchev's *Il cattolicesimo in Bulgaria nel sec. XVII secondo i processi informativi sulla nomina dei vescovi cattolici* (Roma, 1937, 202 p.).

577. Snegarov, Ivan.   Kulturni i politicheski vrŭzki mezhdu Bŭlgariia i Rusiia prez XVI-XVIII v. (Cultural and political ties between Bulgaria and Russia during the 16th-18th centuries). Sofiia, Sinodalno kn-vo, 1953. 129 p.

> This is a sequel to the author's earlier work (*see* entry 569) in which he dealt with the Middle Ages. This work emphasizes Russia's interest in Bulgaria and its help to Bulgarian Christians under Ottoman rule. The author is obviously a Russophile.

578. Snegarov, Ivan.   Turskoto vladichestvo prechka za kulturnoto razvitie na Bŭlgarskiia narod i drugite balkanski narodi (Turkish rule, an impediment to the cultural development of the Bulgarian people and the other Balkan peoples). Sofiia, Bŭlgarska akademiia na naukite, 1958. 241 p.

> This was a reply to those Turkish scholars who, on the 500th anniversary of the Ottoman conquest of Constantinople, stressed the positive aspects of Ottoman rule in the Balkans. The author vigorously contests this theory and stresses the regressive influence of Turkish rule on the Bulgarian economy and cultural life.

## D. RENAISSANCE AND LIBERATION, 1762-1878

579. Akademiia nauk SSSR.   Osvobozhdenie Bolgarii ot turetskogo iga; sbornik statei (The liberation of Bulgaria from the Turkish yoke; collection of articles). Moskva, Akademiia nauk SSSR, 1953. 321 p.

> This is one of several Soviet and Bulgarian publications dealing with Bulgaria's liberation from the Turks as a result of the Russo-Turkish War of 1877-1878. All of these stress the theme of Russian-Bulgarian ties. There is much good material in these studies. *See also* the work by the Akademiia nauk SSSR, *Osvobozhdenie Bolgarii ot turetskogo iga; dokumenty* (Liberation of Bulgaria from the Turkish yoke; documents) (Moskva, 1961-1967, 3 v.); *Osvobozhdenieto na Bŭlgariia ot Tursko igo 1878-1958; sbornik statii* (Liberation of Bulgaria from the Turkish yoke, 1878-1958; collection of articles) (Sofiia, Bŭlgarska Komunisticheska partiia, (1958, 679 p.); P. K. Fortunatov, *Voina 1877-1878 gg. i osvobozhdenie Bolgarii* (The war of 1877-1878 and the liberation of Bulgaria) (Moskva, Gos. uchebno-pedagog. izd-vo, 1950, 179 p.; the latter is also available in German under the title *Der Krieg 1877-1878 und die Befreiung Bulgariens* [Berlin, 1953]); N. I. Beliaev, *Russko-turetskaia voina 1877-1878 gg.* (The Russo-Turkish war of 1877-1878) (Moskva, Voenn, izd-vo, 1956, 463 p.);

and Georgi Georgiev and V. Topalov, *Kratka istoriia na osvoboditelnata voina, 1877-1878; pregled na voennite deistviia* (A short history of the War of Liberation, 1877-1878; survey of military operations) (Sofiia, BKP, 1958, 516 p.).

580. Arnaudov, Mikhail P.   Tvortsi na bŭlgarskoto vŭzrazhdane (Protagonists of the Bulgarian revival). 2d enl. ed. Sofiia, Bŭlgarska misŭl, 1942. 159 p.

A standard work on the Bulgarian cultural rebirth of the late 18th and early 19th centuries, by a nationalist scholar of the old school. Arnaudov has written many separate monographs, mostly biographical, dealing with this subject. For another general account, see his *Bŭlgarskoto vŭzrazhdane* (The Bulgarian revival) (Sofiia, Ministerstvo na narodnoto prosveshtenie, 1944, 206 p.). Arnaudov gives 10 biographical sketches, from Paisii to Ivan Bogorov, in his *Bŭlgarski obrazi* (Bulgarian profiles) (Sofiia, Khemus, 1944, 422 p.).

For a biographic study of Vasil Levsky presented against the background of Bulgaria's struggle for independence from the Ottoman Empire, *see*:

MacDermott, Mercia.   The Apostle of Freedom. London, Allen and Unwin, 1968. 407 p.

581. Bŭlgarska akademiia na naukite. *Institut za istoriia.*   Paisii Khilendarski i negovata epokha. Sbornik ot izsledvaniia po sluchai 200-godishninata ot istoriia slavianobŭlgarska 1762-1962 (Paisii of Hilendar and his age; a collection of studies on the occasion of the 200th anniversary of the Slaveno-Bulgarian history 1762-1962). Sofiia, 1962. 647 p.

*See also* entry no. 863.

This is an impressive collection of 17 scholarly articles on various aspects of the life of Father Paisii and his pioneer history of the Bulgarian people. This volume corrects and brings up to date the literature on this popular subject and adds a Marxist interpretation. The contributors are associates of the Institute of History of the Bulgarian Academy of Sciences and range from Marxists such as Kosev and Khristov to the eminent non-Marxist historian Ivan Duĭchev, who, with Veselin Traikov, contributes an excellent bibliographical article.

The best scholarly edition — issued by the Bulgarian Academy of Sciences — of Father Paisii's patriotic version of Bulgarian history, written in 1762 is *Istoriia slavenobolgarskaia* (Slaveno-Bulgarian history) (Sofiia, Dŭrzh. pechatnitsa, 1914, 91 p.). A recent popular edition was prepared by Petŭr Dinekov and published as *Slavianobŭlgarska istoriia* (Sofiia, Bulgarski pisatel, 8th ed., 1963, 120 p.)

582. Gandev, Khristo.   Faktori na bŭlgarskoto vŭzrazhdane, 1600-1830 (Factors in the Bulgarian renaissance, 1600-1830). Sofiia, 1943. 303 p.

A major work by a specialist in the period of the Bulgarian Renaissance. The author begins his analysis over a century earlier than is traditional and traces the various factors that produced the modern national awakening in Bulgaria.

583. Harris, David.    Britain and the Bulgarian Horrors of 1876. Chicago, University of Chicago Press, 1939. 437 p.

This thorough study by an American scholar is mainly interested in the British responses to the massacres of Bulgarians which followed the uprisings of 1875-1876, but the book is also useful for the student of Bulgarian history. For another book on the same subject, *see* Walter G. Wirthwein's *Britain and the Balkan Crisis, 1875-1878* (New York, Columbia University Press, 1935, 433 p.). A primary source in this area is the famous tract by William E. Gladstone, *Bulgarian Horrors and the Question of the East* (London, J. Murray, 1876, 64 p.).

584. Kinov, Ivan.    Vŭoruzhenata borba na bŭlgarskiia narod sreshtu osmanskoto gospodstvo (The armed struggle of the Bulgarian people against Ottoman rule). Sofiia, Dŭrzhavno voenno izd-vo, 1961. 403 p.

This work, by a specialist in military history, details the various uprisings of the Bulgarian people against Ottoman rule.

585. Kosev, Dimitŭr.    Novaia istoriia Bolgarii; kurs lektsii (Modern history of Bulgaria; lectures). Moskva, Izd-vo inostrannoi literatury, 1952. 522 p. Bibliography: p. 472-521.

A convenient account, in Russian, by a distinguished Bulgarian Marxist historian, based on his lecture course, first published in Bulgarian. This survey extends from the latter half of the 18th century to the establishment of the Bulgarian state after the liberation from the Turks.

586. Natan, Zhak.    Bŭlgarskoto vŭzrazhdane (The Bulgarian renaissance). 4th ed. Sofiia, Bŭlgarski pisatel, 1949. 543 p.

A provocative and scholarly analysis of the modern Bulgarian rebirth by an eminent Marxist scholar. This authoritative work is also available in Russian under the title *Bolgarskoe vozrozhdenie* (Moskva, 1949). Fifth edition: 1950.

587. Nikov, Petŭr.    Vŭzrazhdane na bŭlgarskiia narod; tsŭrkovno-natsionalni borbi i postizheniia (Renaissance of the Bulgarian people; church-national struggles and achievements). Sofiia, S. Slavchev, 1929. 351 p.

Written by the succesor to Zlatarski's chair, this major work is based on a rich variety of primary sources, both Bulgarian and Western, among the latter especially the Vienna archives. Here for the first time is described the influence of the British and Austrian envoys at the Porte, and of the Hellenic Kingdom and the Patriarch of Constantinople. Especially valuable is Nikov's description of Bulgarian social and ecclesiastical life, 1860 to 1872.

588. Penev, Boian.    Nachalo na bŭlgarskoto vŭzrazhdane (The beginnings of the Bulgarian renaissance). Sofiia, Khemus, 1946. 95 p.

Written by a leading historian of Bulgarian literature, this brief but important work attempts to describe the historical and intellectual environment which gave rise to modern Bulgaria's cultural rebirth in the 18th century and later. While Penev gives much attention to political, economic, and social factors, he also stresses the role of individual personalities.

589. Shishmanov, Ivan D.   Ot Paisiia do Rakovski; statii po bŭlgarskoto vŭzrazhdane (From Paisiĭ to Rakovski; articles on the Bulgarian renaissance). Sofiia, Ministerstvo na narodnoto prosveshtenie, 1943. 401 p.

Written by the founder of Bulgarian literary history, and by a man who was himself, until his death in 1928, an important figure in Bulgarian cultural development, this collection of articles gives the highlights of the Bulgarian rebirth as seen by one of its greatest interpreters.

590. Stanev, Nikola.   Bŭlgariia pod igo; vŭzrazhdane i osvobozhdenie, 1393-1878 (Bulgaria under the yoke; renaissance and liberation, 1393-1878). 3d ed. Sofiia, S. Atanasov, 1947. 495 p.

This is a popular yet authoritative account of Bulgarian history under the double yoke of Turkish political rule and Phanariot Greek ecclesiastical control, written from a nationalist point of view. Most of the book is devoted to the period from the 18th century rebirth to the Treaty of San Stefano and the Congress of Berlin in 1878. It unfortunately lacks both footnotes and bibliography.

591. Stoianov, I.   Vŭzrazhdane na bŭlgarskiia narod (The renaissance of the Bulgarian nation). Sofiia, 1931. 190 p.

A survey of the preliberation period which is useful because of its treatment of economic development.

592. Stoyanoff, Zachary (Zakhari Stoianov).   Pages from the Autobiography of a Bulgarian Insurgent. London, Edward Arnold, 1913. 316 p. *See also* entry no. 861.

The English translation of the first portion of a classic in Bulgarian literature and historiography by a participant in the 1876 uprising. For the Bulgarian original, *see* his *Zapiski po bŭlgarskite vŭztaniia* (Plovdiv, Sofiia, 1884-1892, 3 v.). For a more recent edition see the three-volume collection of Stoianov's *Sŭchineniia* (works), published in Sofiia (Bulgarski pisatel, 1965-1966).

593. Todorov, Goran D.   Vremennoto rusko upravlenie v Bŭlgariia prez 1877-1879 (The Russian provisional administration in Bulgaria during 1877-1879). Sofiia, Bŭlgarska komunisticheska partiia, 1958. 459 p.

A very competent monograph concerning the important but little-studied period of Russian administration in Bulgaria during and just after the Russo-Turkish War of 1877-1878, by a Bulgarian communist scholar who bases his work largely on Bulgarian and Russian archival materials, though he includes an impressive bibliography of secondary works as well. However, the author unduly ignores Western sources and is generally too eager to show Russian actions in the best light.

594. Zarev, Pantelei. Bŭlgarskoto vŭzrazhdane (The Bulgarian renaissance). Sofiia, Nauka i izkustvo, 1950. 200 p.

This Marxist interpretation stresses changes in the economic and social structure as the mainsprings of the Bulgarian national awakening in the 18th and 19th centuries.

## E. FROM 1878 TO 1918

595. Ancel, Jacques. L'unité de la politique bulgare, 1870-1919. Paris, Éditions Bossard, 1919. 75 p.

A French scholar's indictment of modern Bulgarian imperialism, written under the impress of the Balkan Wars and the First World War.

596. Beaman, A. Hulme. H. M. Stambuloff. London, Bliss, Sands, and Foster, 1895. 240 p.

Though old, this work has not been superseded in any Western language and is still useful, even if the author was an admirer of his subject. For a Bulgarian study, *see* Dimitŭr I. Marinov's *Stefan Stambolov i noveishata ni istoriia* (Stefan Stambolov and our recent history) (Sofiia, 1909, 722 p.).

597. Black, Cyril E. The Establishment of Constitutional Government in Bulgaria. Princeton, Princeton University Press, 1943. 344 p.

An indispensable American study of Bulgarian internal developments from 1878 to 1885, based on British and Austrian archives as well as other sources, including Bulgarian materials. The book includes a very helpful background chapter, a bibliographical essay, and English translations of the Bulgarian Constitution of 1879, the Statute of the Council of State, and the Amendments to the Constitution proposed in 1883.

598. Corti, Egon C. Alexander von Battenberg. London, Cassell, 1954. 319 p.

A translation of the German original, *Alexander von Battenberg: Sein Kampf mit den Zaren und Bismarck* (Wien, R. W. Seidel und Sohn, 1920, 351 p.), this is an informative biography of modern Bulgaria's first ruler.

599. Girginov, Aleksandŭr A. Bŭlgariia pred Velikata voina (Bulgaria before the Great War). Plovdiv, Kh. G. Danov, 1932. 315 p.

A Bulgarian study of Bulgaria on the eve of 1914 and its involvement in the First World War. The author was a general and chairman of the commission on military history attached to the War Ministry. For some other works in this area *see* Georgi I. Kapchev's *La débâcle nationale bulgare devant la Haute-cour* (Paris, 1925, 278 p.), Tushe Vlakhov's *Otnosheniiata mezhdu Bŭlgariia i Tsentralnite sili po vreme na voinite 1912-1918 g.* (Relations between Bulgaria and the Central Powers during the wars of 1912-1918) (Sofiia, Bŭlgarska Komunisticheska partiia, 1957, 289 p.), and entries no. 604 and 608 below.

600. Girginov, T.   Istoricheski razvoi na sǔvremenna Bǔlgariia (Historical development of contemporary Bulgaria). Sofiia, 1934-35. 2 v.

One of the best surveys of modern Bulgarian history to appear between the two world wars. The second volume is particularly useful because of its treatment of economic development, education, justice, the press, and political parties to 1912.

601. Hajek, Alois.   Bulgariens Befreiung und staatliche Entwicklung unter seinem ersten Fürsten. München, R. Oldenbourg, 1939. 411 p.

A sequel to Hajek's work on the Turkish rule in Bulgaria, this less valuable but useful work is a natural companion to Cyril Black's book (*see* entry no. 597), especially since Hajek stresses the role of the Great Powers.

602. Knodt, Josef.   Ferdinand der Bulgare. Die Balkanmission eines Prinzen aus dem Hause Sachsen-Koburg und Gotha-Kohary, 1878-1918. Bielefeld, Bechauf, 1947. 237 p.

A German biography of modern Bulgaria's second ruler. For a work in English *see* Hans Roger Madol's *Ferdinand of Bulgaria: the Dream of Byzantium* (London, Hurst & Blackett, 1933, 296 p.), which is a "court" biography, but based on German Foreign Ministry archives. The original, in German, is entitled *Ferdinand von Bulgarien. Der Traum von Byzanz* (Berlin, Universitas-Verlag, 1931, 309 p.), and there is a French translation entitled *Ferdinand de Bulgarie: la rêve de Byzance* (Paris, 1937). *See also* John Macdonald's *Czar Ferdinand and His People* (New York, Frederick A. Stokes, 1913, 344 p.), which is well-informed but partial to Ferdinand.

603. Krachunov, Krǔstiu.   Velikite dǔrzhavi i Bǔlgariia, 1886-1887 (The Great Powers and Bulgaria, 1886-1887). Sofiia, 1928. 232 p.

A standard Bulgarian diplomatic history of an important time, just after the unification of Bulgaria. For a more general account, in French, *see* his *La politique extérieure de la Bulgarie, 1880-1920* (Sofia, 1932).

604. Kuhne, Victor.   Bulgaria Self-Revealed. London, 1919. 292 p.

"Thanks to M. Victor Kuhne," the preface states with misplaced confidence, "there are no longer any grounds for anyone taking up the cudgels on behalf of Bulgaria." This book is a denunciation of Bulgaria's aspirations and policies which led it to become an ally of the Central Powers in the First World War. The author's method is to assemble his ammunition from Bulgarian newspapers and statements.

605. Ormandzhiev, Ivan.   Nova i nai-nova istoriia na bǔlgarskiia narod (Modern and contemporary history of the Bulgarian people). Sofiia, 1945. 664 p.

A very useful account by a nationalist historian.

606. Radev, Simeon.   Stroitelite na sǔvremenna Bǔlgariia (The builders of contemporary Bulgaria). Sofiia, Pechatnitsa P. Glushkov, 1911. 2 v.

A massive work and a very rich, though not always reliable, history of Bulgaria from 1879 to 1886, during the reign of Prince Alexander, based on a variety of primary sources as well as secondary accounts, by a Bulgarian diplomat.

607. Stanev, Nikola.    Nai-nova istoriia na Bŭlgaria, 1878-1920 (Contemporary history of Bulgaria, 1878-1920). Sofiia, 1925. 2 v. in 1.

This is an outstanding history of Bulgaria since the liberation from the Turks. For a later edition, *see* his *Istoriia na nova Bŭlgariia, 1878-1928* (History of New Bulgaria, 1878-1928) (Sofiia, Izd-vo Chipev, 1929, 520 p.). It is largely concerned with political history and lacks any scholarly apparatus.

608. Todorov, Petŭr.    Pogromite na Bŭlgariia (Bulgaria's disasters). Sofiia, Pech. Knipegraf, 1930. 2 v. in 1.

This is a broad treatment of Bulgaria's unsuccessful wars between 1912 and 1918, which includes some previously unpublished documents. It is especially useful in its description of the dispute leading to the renewal of hostilities in 1913, the role of the Macedonian organizations, and the struggle over the separate peace in 1918.

## F. FROM 1918 TO 1944

609. Busch-Zantner, Richard.    Bulgarien. 2d ed. Leipzig, Goldman, 1943. 238 p.

See also entry no. 641.

A German view of Bulgarian politics, surprisingly well balanced for a wartime book.

610. Desbons, Georges.    La Bulgarie après le Traité de Neuilly. Paris, Librairie des sciences politiques et sociales, Marcel Rivière, 1930. 462 p.

A fervent defense of Bulgaria's case for revision of the Treaty of Neuilly, by a Frenchman with personal experience in Bulgaria. The book is full of good information, despite its pleading.

611. Dimitrov, Mikhail.    Poiava, razvitie i ideologiia na fashizma v Bŭlgariia (Appearance, development, and ideology of fascism in Bulgaria). Sofiia, 1947. 110 p.

See also entry no. 644.

A study of fascism in Bulgaria by an old left-wing intellectual.

612. Gentizon, Paul.    Le Drame bulgare. Paris, Payot, 1924. 238 p.

A French journalist's account of Bulgarian events from the reign of Tsar Ferdinand to Stamboliiski in the years just after the First World War.

613. Kazasov, Dimo.    Burni godini, 1918-1944 (Stormy years, 1918-1944). Sofiia, Naroden pechat, 1949. 783 p.

See also entry no. 646.
The memoirs of a Bulgarian politician of changing affiliations.

614. Kosev, Dimitŭr.   Septemvriĭskoto vŭstanie v 1923 godina (The September uprising in 1923). Sofiia, Bŭlgarska akademiia na naukite, 1954. 353 p.
The most scholarly of many communist accounts of the communist revolt of September 1923.

615. Nikolaev, N. P.   Le Règne et la mort de Boris III, roi des Bulgares, 1894-1918-1943; quatre esquisses. Uppsala, 1952. 118 p.
An adulatory biography of the monarch who ruled Bulgaria from 1918 to 1943. For similar works see also Nicolai P. Kamtchiyski's Boris III, roi de Bulgarie, et son pays (Sofia, I. Davidov, 1936, 199 p.); Nencho Iliev's Boris III, König der Bulgaren (Sofia, 1943, 252 p.); and the collection of several essays by admirers which was edited by N. P. Nikolaev, La destinée tragique d'un roi (Uppsala, Almquist and Wiksells, 1952, 232 p.).

616. Nurigiani, Giorgio.   Dieci anni di vita blugara (1920-1930). Sofia, 1931. 224 p.
An account of the first decade of Bulgaria's history after the Treaty of Neuilly, by an Italian who lived in Bulgaria.

617. Petkov, Nikola D.   Aleksandŭr Stamboliĭski; lichnost i idei (Alexander Stamboliĭski; personality and ideas). 2d ed. Sofiia, S. T. Charŭkchiev, 1946. 380 p.
See also entry no. 647.
A biography of the ill-fated leader of Bulgaria's Agrarian Union by an admiring follower and himself a party leader till his execution by the communists. This work is also available in Serbian (Beograd, 1933, 287 p.). For another biography, also in Serbian, see Kosta Todorov's Stamboliski (Beograd, Jugo-istok, 1937, 170 p.). An important source for the Agrarian Union itself is the work by one of its moderate leaders, Marko Turlakov, Istoriia, printsipi i taktika na Bŭlgarskiia Zemedelski Naroden Sŭiuz (History, principles, and tactics of the Bulgarian Agrarian Union) (Stara Zagora, 1929, 418 p.). See also Prokopi Kiranov's Bŭlgarskoto zemedelsko dvizhenie (Bulgarian agrarian movement) (Sofiia, 1927).

618. Swire, Joseph.   Bulgarian Conspiracy. London, Hale, 1939. 356 p.
See also entry no. 648.
This is the most complete Western study on IMRO — the Internal Macedonian Revolutionary Organization — and the role of Macedonian revolutionaries and refugees in Bulgarian politics between the two world wars. The author was a British correspondent residing in Bulgaria.

619. Tadzher, Zh.   Nova Bŭlgariia (New Bulgaria). Sofiia, 1922. 688 p.

Especially useful for the period after the First World War, when Bulgaria was governed by the Agrarian Union.

620. Todorov, Kosta.    Balkan Firebrand; the Autobiography of a Rebel, Soldier, and Statesman. Chicago, New York, Ziff-Davis, 1943. 340 p.
*See also* entry no. 649.

Absorbing memoirs by a leftist leader of the Agrarian Union, who describes events in Bulgaria between the two world wars, and particularly his relations with the communists.

621. Todorov, Kosta.    Politička istorija savremene Bugarske. Beograd, Sloga, 1938. 363 p.

Written by the exiled leftist Agrarian leader, this is a popular survey of Bulgarian history from 1878 to 1938, in Serbian, and intended for the Yugoslav reading public. It is especially interesting in the more recent period, of which the author has personal knowledge.

# 22

# the state

*by Marin V. Pundeff*

## A. LAW

### 1. Official Publications, Bibliographies, and Indexes

622. Bulgaria. Vŭrkhoven Sŭd. Sbornik postanovleniia i tŭlkuvatelni resheniia na Vŭrkhovniia Sud na NR Bŭlgariia, 1953-1963 (Collection of decrees and interpretive decisions of the Supreme Court of the People's Republic of Bulgaria, 1953-1963). Sofiia, Nauka i izkustvo, 1965. 528 p.

   This basic collection of the decisions of the Bulgarian Supreme Court is continued by annual supplements of the decisions of the Court's criminal and civil law divisions.

623. Bŭlgarska akademiia na naukite, *Sofiia. Institut za pravni nauki.*

Bibliografiia na bŭlgarskata pravna literatura (1944-1963) (Bibliography of Bulgarian legal literature [1944-1963]). Sofiia, 1965. 128 p.
    A bibliography of 3,440 Bulgarian legal writings published since the introduction of the new legal system in 1944.

624. Dŭrzhaven vestnik (State gazette). 1879– Sofiia.
    The official gazette of Bulgaria, in which laws, treaties, administrative regulations, and other official materials are promulgated. From 1950 to 1962 its function was fulfilled by *Izvestiia na Prezidiuma na Narodnoto Sŭbranie* (News of the Presidium of the National Assembly). The legislative background of the laws enacted is found in the stenographic record of the National Assembly, *Stenografski dnevnitsi*, issued since 1879. The decisions and directives of the Council of Ministers are also published in *Sbornik postanovleniia i razporezhdeniia na Ministerskiia suvet* (Collection of decisions and directives of the Council of Ministers) (1950–, Sofiia, monthly).

625. Maksimov, Khr.    Spravochnik po zakonodatelstvoto na Narodna Republika Bŭlgariia (Index of the laws of the People's Republic of Bulgaria). Sofiia, Nauka i izkustvo, 1957. 606 p.
    A detailed index, arranged by subject of the laws of Bulgaria issued from September 9, 1944, when the new legal system was introduced, to June 30, 1957, and published in *Dŭrzhaven vestnik* and *Izvestiia na Prezidiuma na Narodnoto Subranie*. The indexing has been continued for the period from July 1, 1957, to December 31, 1963, under the same title, by Liuben Dimitrov and Zdravko Chalukov (Sofiia, Nauka i izkustvo, 1965, 210 p.). Laws issued since January 1, 1964, can be located through the table of contents and the subject index of each annual volume of *Dŭrzhaven vestnik*.

626. Sipkov, Ivan.    Legal Sources and Bibliography of Bulgaria. New York, Praeger, 1956. 199 p.
    A bibliography of publications in which Bulgarian laws were promulgated or collected from 1879 to 1955; indexes; and writings on all fields of Bulgarian law in Bulgarian, Russian, and Western languages. Additional information on the bibliography of Bulgarian legal literature is contained in Khr. Trenkov's *Spetsialna bibliografiia* (see entry no. 471).

## 2. The Legal System

627. Aleksiev, Serafim.    Valutni prestŭpleniia (Foreign exchange violations). Sofiia, Nauka i izkustvo, 1965. 162 p. Bibliography: p. 156-157.

628. Avramov, Liusien, *and* Vitali Tadzher.    Avtorsko pravo na Narodna Republika Bŭlgariia (Copyright law of the People's Republic of Bulgaria). Sofiia, Nauka i izkustvo, 1965. 320 p. Bibliography: p. 312-314.

629. Gsovski, Vladimir, *and* Kazimierz Grzybowski, *eds.*    Government, Law, and Courts in the Soviet Union and Eastern Europe. London,

Stevens; New York, Praeger, 1959. 2 v. Bibliography: p. 1945-2009. *See also* entries no. 146 *and* 2395.

Contains chapters on Bulgaria by a number of authors under the general topics "The Regime and the Origin," "Administration of Justice," "New Substantive Criminal Law," "Sovietization of Civil Law," "Worker and Factory," and "Land and Peasant."

630. Konstantinov, Dimitŭr I.   Persönliches Eigentum und Erbrecht in der Volksrepublik Bulgarien. Sofia, Fremdsprachenverlag, 1962. 45 p.

This publication on personal ownership and inheritance law in Bulgaria is supplemented by Ivan Sipkov's article "Postwar Nationalizations and Alien Property in Bulgaria" in the *American Journal of International Law*, v. 52, no. 3, July, 1958: 469-494.

631. Kozhukharov, A.   Sbornik grazhdanski zakoni (Collection of civil laws). Sofiia, Nauka i izkustvo, 1956. 800 p.

A major collection of civil law enactments currently in effect.

632. Kutikov, Vladimir.   Mezhdunarodno chastno pravo na Narodna Republika Bŭlgariia (Private international law of the People's Republic of Bulgaria). Sofiia, Nauka i izkustvo, 1958. 439 p.

This is a treatise on conflicts of laws as approached from the provisions of Bulgarian law, by a professor at the University of Sofia. Its extensive bibliography lists both Bulgarian and non-Bulgarian sources on the subject. A more recent treatise on one aspect of the subject is *Priznavane i dopuskane izpŭlnenie na chuzhdestranni sŭdebni resheniia v NRB* (Recognition and admission to execution of foreign court decisions in the People's Republic of Bulgaria), by Tsoniu Damianov (Sofiia, Nauka i izkustvo, 1963, 202 p.).

633. Pravna misŭl (Juridical thought). 1957– Sofiia. Bimonthly.

Organ of the Institute of Law of the Bulgarian Academy of Sciences. The institute also publishes the irregular *Izvestiia* (Communications) (1954–, Sofiia).

634. Sotsialistichesko pravo (Socialist law). 1952– Sofiia. 10 no. per year.

Official organ of the Bulgarian Ministry of Justice. Provides a running bibliography of Bulgarian legal literature in addition to authoritative interpretive articles.

635. Spasov, Boris, *and* Angel Angelov. Dŭrzhavno pravo na Narodna Republika Bŭlgariia (Constitutional law of the People's Republic of Bulgaria). 2d rev. ed. Sofiia, Nauka i izkustvo, 1968. 515 p.

This textbook for university students reflects the status of constitutional law as of June 1, 1967. Another useful work, also intended as a textbook, is *Osnovi na dŭrzhavata i pravoto na NR Bŭlgariia* (Foundations of state and law of the People's Republic of Bulgaria) by Mikhail Genovski and Dimitŭr Dimitrov (4th ed., Sofiia, Nauka i izkustvo, 1964-1965, 2 v.).

## B. POLITICS AND GOVERNMENT

### 1. Bibliographies

636. Narodnaia Respublika Bolgariia; istoricheskaia bibliografiia (People's Republic of Bulgaria; a historical bibliography). Moskva, Izd-vo Akademii nauk SSSR, 1954-1958. 2 v. (675, 856 p.)

   A joint Soviet-Bulgarian product, this comprehensive bibliography contains the titles of all Bulgarian and Soviet publications on political developments in Bulgaria from 1944 to 1952.

637. Pundeff, Marin, ed.   Bulgaria. In Hammond, Thomas T., ed. Soviet Foreign Relations and World Communism; a Selected, Annotated Bibliography of 7,000 Books in 30 Languages. Princeton, Princeton University Press, 1965. p. 298-311.

   A selected bibliography of 117 works dealing primarily with the Bulgarian Communist Party and postwar politics.

638. Tsolov, I., V. Kovachev, and I. Dancheva.   Istoriia na BKP, 1885-1944; bibliografiia. Materiali, publikuvani sled 9 septemvri 1944 g. (History of the Bulgarian Communist Party, 1885-1944; bibliography of materials published after September 9, 1944). Sofiia, Bŭlgarska komunisticheska partiia, 1965. 566 p.

   Current bibliographic information is supplied by Izvestiia of the Institute of History of the Bulgarian Communist Party (1957-).

### 2. History of the Bulgarian Communist Party

639. Materiali po istoriia na Bŭlgarskata komunisticheska partiia, 1925-1962 g. (Materials on the history of the Bulgarian Communist Party, 1925-1962). Sofiia, Bŭlgarska komunisticheska partiia, 1966. 520 p.

   This publication, complemented by another volume under the same title for the period 1885-1925 (Sofiia, BKP, 1966, 264 p.) is issued as an instructional aid and serves as the official history of the party in Bulgarian. It has appeared in ten substantially differing versions since 1952. Its 1959 edition is available in Russian translation as Istoriia Bolgarskoi kommunisticheskoi partii (History of the Bulgarian Communist Party) (Moskva, Gospolitizdat, 1960, 391 p.). Current research on the subject in Bulgaria appears in Izvestiia (Communications) of the Institute of History of the Bulgarian Communist Party (1957-) and Izvestiia of the Higher Party School of the Central Committee (1957-). See also The Fight for Socialism in Bulgaria, prepared by the Institut po istoriia na Bulgarskata Komunisticheska partiia under the chief editorship of I. Vŭlov (Sofia, Bulgarian Communist Party Pub. House, 1965, 301 p., illus.).

640. Rothschild, Joseph.   The Communist Party of Bulgaria; Origins and Development, 1883-1936. New York, Columbia University Press, 1959. 354 p.

A first-rate study of the earlier history of the Bulgarian Communist Party in the general context of Bulgarian politics.

## 3. POLITICS, 1918-1941

641. Busch-Zantner, Richard.    Bulgarien. 2d ed. Leipzig, Goldmann, 1943. 238 p.
    *See also* entry no. 609.
    A view of Bulgarian politics on the eve of the Second World War. The first edition was published in 1941.

642. Danubian Group of Economic Experts.    Danubian Studies. I. Chronology of Political and Economic Events in the Danube Basin, 1918-1936. Bulgaria. Paris, International Institute of Intellectual Cooperation, League of Nations, 1938. 120 p.
    *See also* entry no. 740.

643. Dimitrov, Georgi M.    Agrarianism. *In* Gross, Feliks, *ed.* European Ideologies; a Survey of 20th Century Political Ideas. New York, Philosophical Library, 1948. 1075 p.
    A statement of the ideology of the Bulgarian Agrarian movement by one of the successors of Stamboliĭski, at present in exile in the United States.

644. Dimitrov, Mikhail.    Poiava, razvitie i ideologiia na fashizma v Bŭlgariia (Appearance, development, and ideology of fascism in Bulgaria). Sofiia, 1947. 110 p.
    *See also* entry no. 611.
    A brief discussion of fascism in Bulgaria by a left-wing intellectual.

645. Jackson, George D., Jr.    Comintern and Peasant in East Europe, 1919-1930. New York, Columbia University Press, 1966. 339 p. Bibliography: p. 321-328.
    *See also* entry no. 2539.
    Contains a chapter on communism and the Agrarian movement in Bulgaria in 1919-1923, when the peasant leader, Alexander Stamboliiski, was in power.

646. Kazasov, Dimo.    Burni godini, 1918-1944 (Stormy years, 1918-1944). Sofiia, Naroden pechat, 1949. 783 p.
    *See also* entry no. 613.
    The memoirs of a politician of changing affiliations, active during this period and beyond.

647. Petkov, Nikola D.    Aleksandŭr Stamboliĭski; lichnost i idei (Alexander Stamboliĭski; personality and ideas). 2d ed. Sofiia, S.T. Charŭkchiev, 1946. 380 p.
    *See also* entry no. 617.
    A political portrait of the peasant leader by one who himself be-

came a leader of the peasant movement and was executed by the communist regime in 1947. The first edition of this work was published in 1930 (Sofiia, 342 p.), and was followed by a Serbian edition in 1933 (Beograd, 287 p.).

648. Swire, Joseph. Bulgarian Conspiracy. London, Hale, 1939. 356 p. *See also* entry no. 618.

A detailed account of the role of the Internal Macedonian Revolutionary Organization (IMRO) in Bulgarian politics in the interwar period.

649. Todorov, Kosta. Balkan Firebrand; the Autobiography of a Rebel, Soldier, and Statesman. Chicago, New York, Ziff-Davis, 1943. 340 p. *See also* entry no. 620.

The memoirs of a close associate of Stamboliiski.

650. Turlakov, Marko. Istoriia, printsipi i taktika na Bŭlgarskiia Zemedelski Naroden Sŭiuz (History, principles, and tactics of the Bulgarian Agrarian People's Union). Stara Zagora, 1929. 418 p.

A history of the Agrarian Union from its founding in 1899 to 1923 by one of its moderate leaders. Contains the Union's statutes and program.

## 4. The Second World War

651. Bozhinov, Voin. Politicheskata kriza v Bŭlgariia prez 1943-1944 (The political crisis in Bulgaria during 1943-1944). Sofiia, Bŭlgarska akademiia na naukite, 1957. 170 p.

A study of the efforts of the last noncommunist governments of Bulgaria to extricate the country from the war. The author had access to the files of the Bulgarian foreign ministry and was able to develop important details of the armistice negotiations between Bulgaria and the Western Powers in Istanbul, Ankara, and Cairo in 1944.

652. Gorenenski, Nikifor. Vŭorŭzhenata borba na bŭlgarskiia narod za osvobozhdenie ot khitleristkata okupatsiia i monarkho-fashistkata diktatura, 1941-1944 g. (The armed struggle of the Bulgarian people for liberation from the Hitlerite occupation and the monarcho-fascist dictatorship, 1941-1944). Sofiia, BKP, 1958. 336 p.

A substantial study of the communist efforts to mount and maintain a resistance movement during the Second World War. It may be supplemented by *Bolgarskii narod v bor'be protiv fashizma (nakanune i v nachal'nyi period vtoroi mirovoi voiny)* (The Bulgarian people in the struggle against fascism [on the eve and during the initial period of the Second World War]) by L. B. Valev (Moskva, Nauka, 1964, 372 p.).

653. Govori radiostantsiiata "Khristo Botev," 23 iuli 1941-22 septemvri 1944 (This is radio station "Khristo Botev," July 23, 1941, to September 22, 1944). Sofiia, BKP, 1950-1952. 7 v.

The record of broadcasts by Georgi Dimitrov, Vasil Kolarov, and other Bulgarian communists over the wartime radio station operated from Soviet territory and directed by Vulko Chervenkov.

## 5. Politics, 1944 to the Present

654. Bŭlgarska komunisticheska partiia. *Kongres.* Stenografski protokol (Stenographic minutes of the Congresses of the Bulgarian Communist Party). Sofiia, 1948-1967. 5 v.

The record of the proceedings of the Fifth (first postwar) Congress of the Bulgarian Communist Party in 1948, the Sixth in 1954, the Seventh in 1958, the Eighth in 1962, and the Ninth in 1966. Each volume contains the party statutes as amended at the time. The reports to the congresses of the party secretaries (Dimitrov, 1948; Chervenkov, 1954; Zhivkov, 1958, 1962, and 1966) are available separately in translations in Western languages.

655. Bŭlgarskata rabotnicheska partiia (komunisti) v rezoliutsii i resheniia na kongresite, konferentsiite i plenumite na TsK (The Bulgarian Workers' Party [Communists] in the resolutions and decisions of its congresses, conferences, and the plenums of the Central Committee). Sofiia, 1947-1965. 5 v.

The official collection of the decisions and policy statements of the Bulgarian Communist Party adopted from its founding in 1891 to 1962.

656. Dimitrov, Georgi.    Sŭchineniia (Works). Sofiia, Bŭlgarska komunisticheska partiia, 1951-1955. 14 v.

This complete edition of Dimitrov's writings is indexed by Elena Savova in *Spravochnik kŭm sŭchineniiata na Georgi Dimitrov* (Index to the works of Georgi Dimitrov) (Sofiia, BKP, 1957, 366 p.). There are several collections of selected writings in Western languages: *Selected Speeches and Articles* (London, Wishart, 1951, 275 p.); *Selected Works, 1910-1949* (Sofia, Foreign Languages Press, 1960, 427 p.); and *Ausgewählte Schriften* (Berlin, Dietz, 1956).

657. Kostov, Traicho.    Izbrani statii, dokladi, rechi (Selected articles, reports, speeches). Sofiia, Bŭlgarskata komunisticheska partiia, 1965. 962 p.

The posthumous edition of the writings of a former secretary of the party, executed for Titoism in 1949. The record of his trial is in *The Trial of Traicho Kostov and His Group* (Sofia, 1949, 644 p.).

658. Kŭncheva, Pavlina.    Vŭlko Chervenkov; bio-bibliografiia, 1900-1950 (Vulko Chervenkov; bibliography, 1900-1950). Sofia, 1950. 71 p.

The biobibliography of Chervenkov, who succeeded Dimitrov as secretary-general of the Bulgarian Communist Party (1949-1954) and Kolarov as prime minister (1950-1956).

659. Kurella, Alfred.    Dimitroff contra Göring. Nach Berichten Georgi

Dimitroffs über den Reichstagsbrandprozess 1933. Berlin, Dietz, 1964. 347 p.

A communist account of the Leipzig trial of 1933 at which Dimitrov was charged, along with others, with setting the Reichstag on fire. (He was acquitted.)

660. Novo vreme (New times). 1897– Sofiia. Monthly.

The principal organ of the Bulgarian Communist Party, devoted mainly to theoretical questions.

661. Savova, Elena.   Georgi Dimitrov; letopis na zhivota i revoliutsionnata mu deĭnost (Georgi Dimitrov; chronicle of his life and revolutionary activity). Sofiia, Bŭlgarska akademiia na naukite, 1952. 803 p.

This is the basic source on the life and activity of Georgi Dimitrov, the leader of the Bulgarian Communist Party, secretary-general of the Comintern from 1935 to 1943, and Bulgarian prime minister from 1946 to 1949. A brief biography in English is *Georgi Dimitrov, a Biographical Sketch*, by Stella Blagoeva, daughter of the founder of Bulgarian orthodox Marxism, Dimitŭr Blagoev (Sofia, Foreign Languages Press, 1965, 217 p.).

662. Savova, Elena.   Vasil Kolarov; bio-bibliografiia po sluchaĭ 70-godishninata mu 16 iuli 1947 (Vasil Kolarov; a biobibliography on the occasion of his 70th birthday, July 16, 1947). Sofiia, 1947. 180 p.

The biobibliography of the Bulgarian communist leader, secretary-general of the Comintern from 1922 to 1924, and Dimitrov's successor as prime minister in 1949-1950. His principal writings are available in *Izbrani proizvedeniia* (Selected works) (Sofiia, Bŭlgarska komunisticheska partiia, 1954-1955, 3 v.).

663. The Trial of Nikola D. Petkov Before the Sofia Regional Court; Record of the Judicial Proceedings, August 5-15, 1947. Sofia, 1947. 631 p.

The official record of the trial of the agrarian leader which led to his execution in 1947. For an analysis of the trial and its background, *see* M. Padev's *Dimitrov Wastes No Bullets; Nikola Petkov, the Test Case* (London, Eyre and Spottiswoode, 1948, 160 p.).

664. Zhivkov, Todor.   Speeches, Reports, Articles. Sofia, Foreign Languages Press, 1964. 3 v.

A collection of the writings of Todor Zhivkov, who succeeded Chervenkov as party secretary in 1954 and became prime minister in 1962.

### 6. The Military

665. Armeĭski pregled (Armed forces review). Sofiia. Monthly.

666. Atanasov, Shteriu.   Bŭlgarskoto voenno izkustvo prez kapitalizma (Bulgarian military art in the age of capitalism). Sofiia, Dŭrzhavno voenno izdatelstvo, 1959. 387 p.

A discussion by a communist general of the wars of 1877-1878, 1885, 1912-1913, and 1915-1918. An earlier volume by Atanasov, *Bŭlgarskoto voenno izkustvo prez feodalizma* (Bulgarian military art in the age of feudalism) (Sofiia, Dŭrzhavno voenno izdatelstvo, 1958, 646 p.), discusses the wars of medieval Bulgaria to the Turkish conquest in 1393.

667. Bŭlgarska komunisticheska partiia.   Rabotata na BKP v armiiata, 1941-1944 g.; dokumenti i materiali (The work of the Bulgarian Communist Party in the army, 1941-1944; documents and materials). Sofiia, 1959. 614 p.

668. Bŭlgarski voenen knigopis (Bulgarian military bibliography). 1955– Sofiia. Bimonthly.

669. Iz opita na politiko-vŭzpitatelnata rabota v Bŭlgarskata narodna armiia; sbornik statii (From the experience in the work of political indoctrination in the Bulgarian people's army; a collection of articles). Sofiia, Dŭrzhavno voenno izdatelstvo, 1960. 272 p.
   An analysis of the work of indoctrination since 1944.

670. Khristov, F.   Voenno-revoliutsionnata deĭnost na Bŭlgarskata komunisticheska partiia, 1912-1944 (The military revolutionary activity of the Bulgarian Communist Party, 1912-1944). Sofiia, Dŭrzhavno voenno izdatelstvo, 1959. 237 p.
   A history of the activity of the Bulgarian Communist Party in the armed forces before the assumption of control in 1944.

671. Kinov, Ivan.   Kratka istoriia na voennoto izkustvo (Concise history of the art of war). Sofiia, Dŭrzhavno voenno izdatelstvo, 1960, 2 v.
   Includes a discussion of Bulgarian military history to 1945. The author was Bulgarian chief of staff to 1949 and subsequently was superintendent of the Bulgarian Military Academy.

672. Kinov, Ivan.   Marksistko-leninskoto uchenie za voinata i armiiata (The Marxist-Leninist doctrine on war and the army). Sofiia, Dŭrzhavno voenno izdatelstvo, 1958. 322 p.
   An authoritative Bulgarian statement of the communist doctrine on war and the armed forces. Also of interest is *Partizanskata voina* (Partisan warfare) by S. Mitev and Kh. Kovachev (Sofiia, Dŭrzhavno voenno izdatelstvo, 1966, 184 p.).

673. Narŭchnik na voenniia agitator (Handbook of the armed forces agitator). Sofiia. Biweekly. Continued since 1966 as *Voenen agitator*.

674. Otechestvenata voina na Bŭlgariia, 1944-1945 (The patriotic war of Bulgaria, 1944-1945). Sofiia, Dŭrzhavno voenno izdatelstvo, 1961-1966. 3 v.
   The official history of Bulgaria's operations against Germany in

1944-1945. A brief treatment by Colonel Ivan Kirchev entitled *Otechestvenata voina, 1944-1945* (Sofiia, 1946, 111 p.) is available in French translation as *La guerre patriotique, 1944-45* (Sofia, 1946, 95 p.).

675. 15 godini Bŭlgarska narodna armiia, 1944-1959 (15 years of the Bulgarian people's army, 1944-1959). Sofiia, 1959. 207 p.

A commemorative volume marking the 15th anniversary of the assumption of control by the Communist Party over the Bulgarian armed forces.

676. Popov, Ivan T.   Krila na Rodinata; stranitsi iz istoriiata na bŭlgarskata aviatsiia (Wings of the fatherland; pages from the history of the Bulgarian air force). Sofiia, Dŭrzhavno voenno izdatelstvo, 1958. 200 p.

677. Popov, Vasil, *and* Stoian Stoianov. Stranitsi iz istoriiata na Bŭlgarskiia voenno-morski flot (Pages from the history of the Bulgarian naval forces). Sofiia, Dŭrzhavno voenno izdatelstvo, 1958. 184 p.

678. 75 godini Morsko uchilishte; iubileen sbornik (75 years of the Naval Academy; anniversary collection). Sofiia, Dŭrzhavno voenno izdatelstvo, 1956. 167 p.

679. Stoichev, Ivan K.   Stroiteli i boini vozhdove na bŭlgarskata voiska, 1878-1941 (Builders and battle leaders of the Bulgarian army, 1878-1941). Sofiia, 1941.

Contains brief biographical sketches of prominent military leaders.

680. Tashev, Tasho V.   Otechestvenata voina na Bŭlgariia, 1944-1945; bibliografiia (The patriotic war of Bulgaria, 1944-1945; a bibliography). Sofiia, Dŭrzhavno voenno izdatelstvo, 1966. 338 p.

A bibliography of over 2,000 Bulgarian publications on Bulgaria's participation in operations against Germany in the last stages of the Second World War.

681. U.S. *War Dept.*   Order of Battle and Handbook of the Bulgarian Armed Forces. Washington, D.C., 1943. 131 p.

A translation of Bulgarian prewar military regulations.

682. Voenno-istoricheski sbornik (Review of military history). 1927– Sofiia. Bimonthly.

Contains bibliographic information.

683. Zhekov, N. T.   Bŭlgarskoto voinstvo, 1878-1928 g. (The Bulgarian military, 1878-1928). Sofiia, 1928. 557 p.

A detailed history of the Bulgarian military establishment and the wars of 1885, 1912-1913, and 1915-1918, by the Bulgarian commander-in-chief in the First World War. Contains statistics, texts of laws and orders, and other data.

## C. DIPLOMACY AND FOREIGN RELATIONS

### 1. Collections of Treaties

684. Genov, Georgi P.    Actes et traités internationaux concernant la Bulgarie. Sofia, 1940. 464 p.

A collection of 32 principal treaties involving Bulgaria, from the treaty of Kuchuk-Kainardzhi in 1774 to the Salonika Accord in 1938. Parallel texts in French and Bulgarian are provided. Treaties signed by Bulgaria are normally published in *Dŭrzhaven vestnik*.

685. Kesiakov, B. D., *ed.*    Prinos kŭm diplomaticheskata istoriia na Bŭlgariia (A contribution to the diplomatic history of Bulgaria). Sofiia, 1925-1926. 3 v.

A collection of treaties involving Bulgaria, from the Treaty of Berlin in 1878 to 1925. A supplementary index (Sofiia, 1936, 158 p.) lists treaties signed from 1926 to 1935.

686. Kutikov, Vladimir, *ed.*    Sbornik na mezhdunarodni aktove i dogovori (Collection of international acts and treaties). Sofiia, 1948. 648 p.

Intended as a general aid for students of international law, the collection contains a number of treaties signed by Bulgaria between 1918 and 1948, including the peace treaty of 1947. The authentic English text of the peace treaty is in *Treaty of Peace With Bulgaria* (U.S. Department of State, Treaties and Other International Acts Series, 1650).

687. Stefanova, Slava.    Mezhdunarodni aktove i dogovori, 1648-1918 (International acts and treaties, 1648-1918). Sofiia, Nauka i izkustvo, 1958. 484 p.

A general collection for teaching purposes. Includes treaties affecting Bulgaria.

### 2. Diplomatic History

688. Altŭnov, Ivan.    Iztochniiat vŭpros i Nova Turtsiia s osoben ogled kŭm interesite na Bŭlgariia (The Eastern Question and New Turkey, with special reference to the interests of Bulgaria). Sofiia, 1926. 519 p.

A history of what remained of the Eastern Question after the First World War. The author taught international law for many years at the University of Sofia and served in the Bulgarian Foreign Ministry.

689. Bulgaria. *Ministerstvo na vŭnshnite raboti.*    Diplomaticheski dokumenti po namesata na Bŭlgariia v evropeĭskata voĭna (Diplomatic documents on Bulgaria's intervention in the European war). Sofiia, 1920-1921, 2 v.

A collection of documents from Bulgarian archives concerning the policy of King Ferdinand's government in the First World War, published by the government of Alexander Stamboliiski, who had opposed the intervention on Germany's side.

690. Genov, Georgi P.   Bulgaria and the Treaty of Neuilly. Sofia, 1935. 186 p.

A statement of the Bulgarian case against the peace treaty that Bulgaria signed at Neuilly in 1919.

691. Genov, Georgi P.   Bŭlgariia i Obshtestvoto na narodite (Bulgaria and the League of Nations). Sofiia, 1938. 174 p.

692. Genov, Georgi P.   Iztochniiat vŭpros; politicheska i diplomaticheska istoriia (The Eastern Question; a political and diplomatic history). Sofiia, 1925-1926. 2 v.

A comprehensive history of the Eastern Question and Bulgaria's place in it by a professor of international law at the University of Sofia during the interwar period. Genov was a leading exponent of the nationalist viewpoint.

693. Geshov, Ivan E.   The Balkan League. London, 1915, 141 p.

The memoirs of the Bulgarian prime minister under whom the war against Turkey in 1912 was arranged and fought.

694. Hyde, Arthur M.   Diplomatic History of Bulgaria, 1870-1886. Urbana, University of Illinois, 1931. 172 p.

A diplomatic history of Bulgaria from the establishment of the Bulgarian Exarchate to the crisis of the unification of the two Bulgarias.

695. Krachunov, Krŭstiu.   Sanstefanskiiat mir (izgrazhdane i razrushavane na velika Bŭlgariia) (The San Stefano Peace [erection and demolition of Greater Bulgaria]). Sofiia, 1932. 136 p.

A study of the diplomacy of the San Stefano Treaty, which created Greater Bulgaria before it was torn down by the Congress of Berlin. Krachunov is also the author of numerous other studies of Bulgaria's foreign relations from 1878 to 1941. See also entry no. 603.

696. Madzharov, Mikhail I.   Diplomaticheskata podgotovka na nashite voĭni (The diplomatic preparation for our wars). Sofiia, 1932. 371 p.

A study of the diplomacy of the wars of 1912-1913 and 1915-1918, based in large measure on the author's personal recollections and materials. Madzharov was Bulgaria's elder statesman until his death in 1944 and Bulgarian minister to London during the Balkan Wars.

697. Radoslavov, Vasil.   Bulgarien und die Weltkrise. Berlin, 1923. 312 p.

A personal account by the Bulgarian prime minister during the First World War.

698. Sarailiev, Georgi V.   Le Conflit gréco-bulgare d'octobre 1925 et son règlement par la Société des nations. Amsterdam, 1927. 165 p.

A study of the frontier incident and ensuing Greek invasion of Bulgarian areas in 1925.

699. Vasev, Slavcho, *and* Krum Khristov.   Bŭlgariia na mirnata konfer-

entsiia, Parizh — 1946 (Bulgaria at the peace conference, Paris — 1946). Sofiia, 1947. 368 p.

A journalistic report of the discussion of the terms for Bulgaria at the peace conference after the Second World War. More scholarly is the study of Voin Bozhinov. *Zashtitata na natsionalnata nezavisimost na Bŭlgariia, 1944-1947* (The defense of the national independence of Bulgaria, 1944-1947) (Sofiia, Bŭlgarska akademiia na naukite, 1962, 295 p.). Bozhinov's study, however, clearly reflects the fact that in the postwar period Bulgarian foreign relations were essentially a matter of Soviet foreign policy.

## 3. Irredentist Issues and Population Exchanges

700. Altŭnov, Ivan.   La Thrace interalliée. Sofia, 1921. 188 p.

A monograph on the Allied regime in Western Thrace after the First World War before it was permanently assigned to Greece in 1923.

701. Bulgaria. *Ministerstvo na vŭnshnite raboti.*   The Bulgarian Question and the Balkan States. Sofia, State Printing Press, 1919. 304 p. Maps, facsims., tables.

*See also* entry no. 537.

The official statement of Bulgarian claims after the First World War.

702. Die Bulgaren in ihren historischen, ethnographischen und politischen Grenzen. Berlin, 1917. 74 p. Maps.

An official presentation of the background, mainly geographic, of Bulgaria's claims in the First World War.

703. Derzhavin, N. S.   Les rapports bulgaro-serbes et la question macédonienne. Lausanne, 1918. 163 p.

A view of the Bulgarian-Serbian dispute over Macedonia, by a noted Russian Balkanist and Bulgarianist.

704. Ishirkov, Anastas.   Les Bulgares en Dobroudja; aperçu historique et ethnographique. Berne, 1919. 189 p.

A statement of the Bulgarian claims to Dobruja, by a noted professor of geography and ethnography at the University of Sofia.

705. Ivanov, Ĭordan.   Les Bulgares devant le Congrès de la Paix; documents historiques, ethnographiques et diplomatiques. Berne, 1919. 304 p.

An able presentation of the Bulgarian claims after the First World War by a professor at the University of Sofia.

706. K'osev, Dino G.   Istoriia na makedonskoto natsionalno revoliutsionno dvizhenie (History of the Macedonian national revolutionary movement). Sofiia, NS OF, 1954. 552 p.

A history of the Macedonian question by a Macedonian communist working in Bulgaria.

707. Krainikovski, Asen I.    La Question de Macédoine et la diplomatie européenne. Paris, Rivière, 1938. 339 p.

708. Ladas, Stephen P.    The Exchange of Minorities: Bulgaria, Greece, and Turkey. New York, Macmillan, 1932. 849 p. Illus., maps. Bibliography: p. 831-832.
   *See also* entries no. 223, 1202, *and* 1341.
   A detailed study of the population exchanges arranged and carried out after the First World War. The study by Andre Wurfbain, *L'échange gréco-bulgare des minorités ethniques* (Lausanne, 1930, 217 p.), should also be consulted.

709. Mazedonisches wissenschaftliches Institut.    Die Wahrheit über Mazedonien. Sofia, 1941. 93 p. Map.
   A review of the evidence supporting the Bulgarian claims in the Second World War.

710. Mojsov, Lazo.    Bŭlgarskata rabotnicheska partiia (komunisti) i makedonskoto natsionalno prashanie (The Bulgarian Workers' Party [Communist] and the Macedonian national question). Skopje, 1948. 275 p.
   A view of the changing policies of the Bulgarian Communist Party toward the Macedonian problem, by a Macedonian communist working in Yugoslavia. Serbo-Croatian edition: Beograd, Borba, 1948, 320 p.
   A more recent examination is provided by Dimitar Mitrev in *BKP i Pirinska Makedoniia* (The Bulgarian Communist Party and Pirin Macedonia) (Skopje, Kultura, 1960, 152 p.).

711. Nédeltchev, Christo.    Le problème de la Thrace occidentale. Paris, Jouve, 1943. 150 p.
   A review of the question of Western Thrace, created by the assignment of the area to Greece after the First World War. The study by Stantcho Djoumalieff, *L'accès de la Bulgarie à la mer Égée; étude historique et juridique* (Paris, 1936, 204 p.), should also be consulted.

712. Tchilinghiroff, St.    Le pays de la Morava suivant des témoignages serbes; études d'histoire et d'ethnographie avec une carte hors texte. Berne, 1917. 243 p. Map.
   A Bulgarian statement of the basis of the Bulgarian claims to the Morava region. A second, enlarged edition appeared in Bulgarian in 1942, *Pomoraviia po srŭbski svidetelstva* (Pomoravia according to Serbian sources) (Skopie, 1942, 287 p.).

713. Wilkinson, Henry R.    Maps and Politics; a Review of the Ethnographic Cartography of Macedonia. Liverpool, University Press, 1951. 366 p. Illus., maps, diagrs. Bibliography: p. 333-349.
   *See also* entries no. 2229 *and* 2522.
   Reviews the ethnographic maps produced by various specialists and interested parties in the Macedonian question in the 19th and 20th centuries. Other British publications on the Macedonian question

are listed in Hristo Andonov-Poljanski's *Britanska bibliografiia za Makedoniia* (British bibliography on Macedonia) Skopje, 1966, 512 p.).

## D. MASS MEDIA AND PUBLIC OPINION

714. Bulgaria. *Upravlenie za kinematografiia. Dŭrzhaven kino-arkhiv.* Kinoizkustvoto v Bŭlgariia; filmografii i drugi spravochni materiali The film art in Bulgaria; filmography and other reference materials). Sofiia, Nauka i izkustvo, 1960. 128 p.

A weak art in Bulgaria, film-making has nevertheless been employed for internal propaganda in the country's 2,400 motion picture theaters and on television. For an up-to-date English-language presentation *see Presentday Bulgarian Cinema* (Sofia, Sofia Press, 1969, 153 p.) by M. Racheva.

715. Narŭchnik na agitatora (The agitator's manual). 1945– Sofiia. Weekly.

Issued by the Department of Propaganda and Agitation of the Central Committee of the Bulgarian Communist Party to guide the work of the party propagandists.

716. Podgotovkata na propagandistite (The training of propagandists). Sofiia, Bŭlgarska komunisticheska partiia, 1966. 86 p. (Biblioteka na propagandista, no. 6)

717. Popoff, Haralan.    I was a Communist Prisoner. Grand Rapids, Mich., Zondervan, 1966. 287 p. Illus., maps.

An account of personal experiences under communism by one of the 15 Bulgarian Protestant pastors tried in 1949 on charges of spying for the U.S. and released in 1961.

718. Nikolov, Tsanko.    Rabotata na BKP sled Aprilskiia plenum za vŭzpitanieto na komunistite, 1956-1962 (The work of the BCP after the April plenum concerning the education of the communists, 1956-1962). Sofiia, Bŭlgarska komunisticheska partiia, 1964. 341 p.

Reflects the work of ideological reorientation within the party undertaken after the ouster of Vulko Chervenkov as prime minister and party leader in April, 1956.

719. Politicheska prosveta (Political education). 1966– Sofiia. Monthly.

Issued by the Central Committee of the Bulgarian Communist Party "for the thousands of propagandists" of the party.

720. Radio Free Europe. *Audience Research Section.*    The Psycho-political Climate in Bulgaria; a Survey Based on a Sample of Bulgarian Refugees and Visitors. Munich, 1960. 92 p.

*See also* Kenneth E. Olson's survey "The Newspapers of Bulgaria" in his *The History Makers* (Baton Rouge, Louisiana State University Press, 1966, p. 341-351).

721. Shamliev, Barukh, *and others.*    Spravochnik na agitatora; tsifri i fakti

(Handbook of the agitator; figures and facts). Sofiia, Bŭlgarska komunisticheska partiia, 1963, 362 p.

Materials for internal propaganda. See also *Spravochnik na propagandista i agitatora, 1967* (Handbook for agitators and propagandists) by Todor Ganchev and others (Sofiia, BKP, 1967, 334 p.).

722. Vodenicharov, Tinko, *and* A. Petkov.    Spravochnik na aktivista (1961-1965 g.) (Handbook of the activist [1961-1965]). Sofiia, Bŭlgarska komunisticheska partiia, 1966. 570 p.

A collection of party and government materials to guide the work of internal propaganda and public opinion molding. Earlier materials are collected in *Spravochnik na aktivista* (Sofiia, BKP, 1961, 1051 p.).

# 23

# the economy

by L. A. D. Dellin

## A. BIBLIOGRAPHIES

723. Dzherova, L., *and* N. Toteva. Bibliografiia na bŭlgarskata statisticheska literatura, 1878-1960 (Bibliography of Bulgarian statistical literature, 1878-1960). Sofiia, 1961. 105 p.
    *See also* entry no. 503.
    A compilation of statistical sources.

724. Pundeff, Marin V. Bulgaria; a Bibliographic Guide. Washington, D.C., Library of Congress, 1965. 98 p.
    *See also* entry no. 478.
    A general bibliographic guide based primarily on the holdings of the Library of Congress, containing a section on the Bulgarian economy (p. 43-49).
    Several entries relating to economics may also be found in Ivan Sipkov's *Legal Sources and Bibliography of Bulgaria* (New York, Praeger, 1956, 199 p.), no. 18 in the series Praeger Publications in Russian History and World Communism.

725. Trenkov, Khristo. Bibliografski izvori po stopanski nauki (Biblio-

166

graphic sources in economics). *In* Varna, Bulgaria. Visshe institut za narodno stopanstvo. Izvestiia, no. 2, 1961: 82-106.

Bibliography of economic sources published before 1960. A more extensive, but also more specialized, bibliography by the same author containing economic sources published between 1945 and 1948 is *Spetsialna bibliografiia; teoriia, organizatsiia metodika* (Special bibliography, theory, organization, methodology) Sofiia, Nauka i izkustvo, 1958, 235 p.).

726. Svishtov, Bulgaria. Visshe uchilishte za stopanski i sotsialni nauki. *Institut za stopanski izsledvaniia.* Stopanska i sotsialna knizhnina v Bŭlgariia; bibliografiia na bulgarskite knigi i statii ot nachaloto do dnes, 1850-1945 (Economic and social literature in Bulgaria; a bibliography of Bulgarian books and articles from the beginning to the present, 1850-1945). Svishtov, 1948. 951 p.

*See also* entry no. 779.

This bibliography was compiled by the Svishtov Institute for Economic Research and contains the major Bulgarian-language sources on the country's economy — from economic history to social policies. It is a valuable reference guide to publications up to 1945.

## B. STATISTICS

727. Statisticheski godishnik na Narodna Republika Bŭlgariia (Statistical yearbook of the People's Republic of Bulgaria). 1947/48– Sofiia, Tsentralno statistichesko upravlenie.

*See also* entry no. 504.

The official statistical yearbook. Translations in English are available for the 1956, 1960, and 1961 editions through the U.S. Joint Publications Research Service. Since 1958, a pocket edition has been published as *Statisticheski spravochnik na NR Bŭlgariia* (Statistical handbook of the People's Republic of Bulgaria).

728. Statisticheski godishnik na Tsarstvo Bŭlgariia (Statistical yearbook of the Bulgarian Kingdom). 1909-1942. Sofiia, Glavna direktsiia na statistikata. Annual.

The official statistical yearbook of Bulgaria up to 1942. Entries are in both Bulgarian and French.

## C. PERIODICALS

729. Bŭlgarska akademiia na naukite, *Sofia. Ikonomicheski institut.* Izvestiia (News). 1954– Sofiia. Quarterly.

An official publication of the Economics Institute, Bulgarian Academy of Sciences.

730. Bŭlgarsko ikonomichesko druzhestvo, *Sofia.* Spisanie. Pokazalets. (Bulletin. Index). Pt. 1, 1896-1927; pt. 2, 1927-1946. Sofiia. Monthly.

The most distinguished Bulgarian economic journal of the pre-1946 period.

731. Ikonomicheska misŭl (Economic thought). 1956– Sofiia. Quarterly 1956; bimonthly 1957; 10 no. a year 1958–

The official theoretical economics journal of the Economics Institute, Bulgarian Academy of Sciences.

The Bulgarian Chamber of Commerce has issued *Economic News of Bulgaria* monthly since 1960.

732. Planovo stopanstvo i statistika (Planned economy and statistics). 1946– Sofiia. Monthly.

The major economic journal of the State Planning Commission and the Central Statistical Administration, containing articles primarily on applied economics and statistics.

## D. NATIONAL INCOME

733. Chakalov, Asen.    Natsionalniiat dokhod i razkhod na Bŭlgariia, 1924-1945 (The national income and expenditures of Bulgaria, 1924-1945). Sofiia, 1946. 158 p. Summary and list of statistical tables in English. Bibliography: p. 14-16.

A noted Bulgarian statistician analyzes national income data for the 20-year period. An English translation of a previous study by the same author is *National Income of Bulgaria* (Sofia, Sofia University, 1937, 128 p.). May be supplemented by Prokopi Kiranov's *Natsionalniiat dokhod na Bŭlgariia, 1939, 1944, 1945* (The national income of Bulgaria for 1939, 1944, and 1945 (Sofiia, Dŭrzh. pechatnitsa, 1946, 100 p.).

734. Kovachev, Zdravko.    Sŭzdavane, razpredelenie i izpolzvane na natsionalniia dokhod u nas (Creation, distribution, and use of our national income). Varna, Dŭrzhavno izdatelstvo, 1962. 115 p. Illus. Bibliography: p. 112-113.

A theoretical-statistical study of aggregate economics.

## E. ECONOMIC HISTORY

735. Natan, Zhak.    Stopanska istoriia na Bŭlgariia (Economic History of Bulgaria). Sofiia, Nauka i izkustvo, 1957. 570 p. Bibliography: p. 561-562.

A massive work by an academician and noted economic historian interpreting Bulgaria's economic history from the Marxist viewpoint. The Russian-language edition is *Istoriia ekonomicheskogo razvitiia Bolgarii* (History of the economic development of Bulgaria) (Moskva, Inoizdat, 1961, 498 p.). A more balanced, but older, treatment is Natan's *Ikonomicheska istoriia na Bŭlgariia sled Osvobozhdenieto* (Economic history of Bulgaria since the liberation) (Sofiia, Bratstvo, 1938, 185 p.).

736. Sakazov, Ivan.   Bulgarische Wirtschaftsgeschichte. Translated from the Bulgarian by Otto Müller-Neudoff. Berlin, W. de Gruyter, 1929. 294 p. Bibliography at end of each chapter.

> A competent treatment of Bulgaria's economic development through the late '20s. Other works covering various periods of prewar Bulgarian economic history are Max Brabec's *Bulgarien und seine Volkswirtschaft* (Wien, Harbauer, 1924, 48 p.) and Franz Joseph von Battenberg's *Die volkswirtschaftliche Entwicklung Bulgariens von 1879 bis zur Gegenwart* (Leipzig, Veit, 1891, 202 p.).

## F. GENERAL ECONOMIC STUDIES AND ECONOMIC GEOGRAPHIES

### 1. Prior to the Second World War

737. Blagoev, Dimitŭr.   Ikonomicheskoto razvitie na Bŭlgariia, industriia ili zemedelie (The economic development of Bulgaria, industry or agriculture). Sofiia, 1950. *His* izbrani proizvedeniia, v. 1.

> An early Bulgarian Marxist expounds his views on the economic development of Bulgaria, opting for industry. The original essay was published in 1903. Blagoev's major work of a general character is *Prinos kum istoriiata na sotsializma v Bŭlgariia* (Contribution to the history of socialism in Bulgaria) (Sofiia, 1906), also reprinted in his selected works.

738. Chakalov, Asen.   Formi, razmer i deĭnost na chuzhdiia kapital v Bŭlgariia (Forms, volume, and activity of foreign capital in Bulgaria). Sofiia, Bŭlgarska akademiia na naukite, 1962. 139 p.

> A discussion of the role of foreign capital in Bulgaria from 1878 to 1945. Based on substantial selected data but interpreted one-sidedly.

739. Danailov, Georgi T.   Les effets de la guerre en Bulgarie. Paris, Les presses universitaires de France, 1932. 752 p. Map.

> A massive study on the difficult post-World War I problems of the Bulgarian economy by a noted Bulgarian academician and statesman. For supplementary information on the same period, *see* Kosta D. Spisarevski's *La Bulgarie au travail, cinquante ans après* (Marseille, Societé anonyme du sémaphore de Marseille, 1929, 276 p.).

740. Danubian Group of Economic Experts.   Danubian Studies. I. Chronology of Political and Economic Events in the Danubian Basin, 1918-1936. Bulgaria. Paris, International Institute of Intellectual Cooperation, League of Nations, 1938. 120 p.
*See also* entry no. 642.

> A useful reference work including tables of major events and legislation of the interwar period.

741. Kosaroff, Theodore S.   La dette publique extérieure de la Bulgarie: 1879-1932. Paris, Sirey, 1933. 338 p.

The impact of foreign loans on Bulgaria's economic development is competently documented by a Bulgarian author. Another source treating the same general topic is J. P. Koszul's *Les efforts de réstauration financière de la Bulgarie: 1922-1931* (Paris, Alcan, 1932, 468 p.).

742. Iaranov, Atanas.    La Bulgarie économique. Lausanne, Petter, Giesser et Held, 1919. 108 p. Map, diagrs., bibliography.

A Bulgarian economist reviews the country's development prior to the First World War. His major work is *Stopanskata politika na Bŭlgariia ot 1878 do 1928 godina* (The economic policy of Bulgaria from 1878 to 1928) (Sofiia, Khudozhnik, 1934, 392 p.). A complementary source is Kiril G. Popov's *La Bulgarie économique, 1879-1911* (Sofia, 1920, 520 p.).

743. Pasvolsky, Leo.    Bulgaria's Economic Position, with Special Reference to the Reparation Problem and the Work of the League of Nations. Washington, D.C., The Brookings Institution, 1930. 409 p. Maps, diagrs. (The Institute of Economics of the Brookings Institution. Publication no. 39)

An authoritative study of the post–World War I period of the Bulgarian economy, with useful statistics and evaluations by a former director of the Brookings Institution. An enlarged Bulgarian edition is *Stopanska Bŭlgariia* (Economic Bulgaria) (Sofiia, 1932).

## 2. After the Second World War

744. Stanev, Liuben.    Dŭrzhaven i finansov kontrol v NR Bŭlgariia (State and financial control in the People's Republic of Bulgaria). Sofiia, Nauka i izkustvo, 1962. 389 p. Bibliography: p. 387-389.

The role of the government in the economy of present-day Bulgaria is discussed in technical detail.

745. Beshkov, Anastas S.    Volksrepublik Bulgarien; Natur und Wirtschaft. Berlin, Verlag Die Wirtschaft, 1960. 191 p. Illus., maps. Bibliography: p. 190-191.

*See also* entry no. 513.

A well-known Bulgarian economic geographer provides a description of the geography and economy of the country. Among his older works is *Stopansko-geografsko podelenie na Bŭlgariia* (Economic-geographic division of Bulgaria) (Sofiia, 1934).

746. Konstantinov, Fedor T.    Bolgariia na puti k sotsializmu (Bulgaria on the road to socialism). 2d rev. and enl. ed. Moskva, Gospolitizdat, 1953. 382 p.

Bulgarian development under the communist regime presented and interpreted by a Soviet specialist.

747. Lazarov, Kiril.    Ikonomicheskoto razvitie na Narodna Republika Bŭlgariia (The economic development of the People's Republic of Bulgaria). Sofiia, Nauka i izkustvo, 1961. 441 p. Illus., bibliography.

A presentation by a Marxist economist and postwar Minister of Finance interpreting Bulgaria's economic development under communism. A Russian translation is available as *Ekonomicheskoe razvitie Narodnoi Respubliki Bolgarii* (Moskva, 1963, 277 p.).

748. Rochlin, R. P.   Die Wirtschaft Bulgariens seit 1945. Berlin, Duncker & Humblot, 1957. 144 p. Maps, tables. Bibliography: p. 129-130.
A critical treatment of the contemporary Bulgarian economy, with comparative statistical data. The same author analyzes the economic system of Bulgaria in an article "Das bulgarische Wirtschaftssystem" in *Die Wirtschaftssysteme der Staaten Osteuropas und der Volksrepublik China*, volume 2, edited by Georg Jahn (Berlin, Duncker & Humblot, 1962), p. 189-242.

749. Sergeev, Sergei D., *and* A. F. Dobrokhotov.   Narodnaia Respublika Bolgariia; ekonomika i vneshniaia torgovlia (The People's Republic of Bulgaria; economy and foreign trade). Moskva, Vneshtorgizdat, 1962. 271 p. Illus.
The Bulgarian economy, with particular emphasis on foreign trade, is discussed by two Soviet authors.

750. Spulber, Nicolas.   Planned Economy: 1947-1957. *In* Dellin, L. A. D., *ed.* Bulgaria. New York, Praeger, 1957. p. 268-275. (Praeger Publications in Russian History and World Communism, no. 47)
A noted American specialist on Soviet-type economics analyzes the structure and performance of the Bulgarian postwar economy. The same author treats that country's national income and gross national product in the same source (p. 276-286).

751. Bulgaria: *In:* United Nations. *Economic Commission for Europe*. Economic Survey of Europe in 1960. Geneva, 1961. Chapter 6, B, p. 16-40.
Includes an analytical discussion of Bulgaria's postwar economic development — its industry, agriculture, and foreign trade — along with statistical data.

752. Valev, E. B.   Bolgariia: ekonomiko-geograficheskaia kharakteristika (Bulgaria: economic-geographic characteristics). 2d rev. and enl. ed. Moskva, Geografizdat, 1957. 472 p. Illus., maps. Bibliography: p. 459-470.
Economic-geographic data and evaluations by a Soviet specialist. The first edition appeared in 1949.

## G. AGRICULTURE

753. Jankoff, Dimiter A.   Labor Cooperative Farms in Bulgaria. New York, Mid-European Studies Center of the National Committee for a Free Europe, 1953. 17 p. (*Its* Mimeographed Series, No. 1)
A short monograph on the establishment and performance of col-

lective farms in communist Bulgaria. A more specialized treatment by the same author is *Bulgarian Agricultural Producers' Cooperatives* (New York, Mid-European Studies Center, 1954, 21 p.).

754. Jones, B. D., *and* Dimiter A. Jankoff.    Agriculture. *In* Dellin, L. A. D., *ed*. Bulgaria. New York, Praeger, 1957. p. 287-312. (Praeger Publications in Russian History and World Communism, no. 47)

A discussion of Bulgarian agricultural development under communism.

755. Kazandzhiev, Minko.    Osnovi na ikonomikata na sotsialisticheskoto selsko stopanstvo (Foundations of the economics of socialist agriculture). Sofiia, Nauka i izkustvo, 1958. 404 p. Bibliography: p. 397-400.

A discussion from an official point of view of the main characteristics and development of socialist agriculture during the communist period. A supplementary source is Stancho Cholakov's *Ikonomika na sotsialisticheskoto selsko stopanstvo* (The economics of socialist agriculture) (Sofiia, Tekhnika, 1961, 203 p.).

756. Mollov, Ianaki S., *ed*.    Pogled vurkhu sotsialno-ikonomicheskata struktura na bŭlgarskoto zemedelsko stopanstvo (A look at the socioeconomic structure of Bulgarian agriculture). Sofiia, 1936. 158 p.

This most valuable symposium, edited by a Bulgarian professor, examines the pre–World War II structure of Bulgarian agriculture. The German translation is *Die sozialökonomische Struktur der bulgarischen Landwirtschaft* (Berlin, Internazionale Konferenz der Landwirtschaft, 1936, 196 p.).

757. Vladov, Dimo, *ed*.    Ikonomika i organizatsiia na TKZS i DZS (Economics and organization of cooperative labor farms and state farms). Sofiia, Bŭlgarska komunisticheska partiia, 1962. 559 p.

The structure and performance of the two farm types in communist Bulgaria are analyzed and interpreted from an official point of view. A previous edition was published in 1959. To be supplemented by a more recent English-language presentation of Bulgarian provenance: Organization and Management of Co-operative Farms in Bulgaria. Edited by Alexander Rizov and Marguerite Alexieva. Sofia, Sofia Press, 1968. 380 p.

## H. INDUSTRY AND TRANSPORTATION

758. Gerschenkron, Alexander.    Some Aspects of Industrialization in Bulgaria. *In his* Economic Backwardness in Historical Perspective, a Book of Essays. Cambridge, Mass., Belknap Press of Harvard University Press, 1962. p. 198-234.

An essay by a well-known economic historian presenting the dilemma of Bulgaria's prewar governments and critical of what he considers their inability to meet the challenge of industrialization.

759. Iubileen sbornik: 50 godini b. d. zheleznitsi (Jubilee collection: 50 years of Bulgarian state railways). Sofiia, 1938. 469 p. Illus., map.
    A collection of articles on the 50th anniversary of the first Bulgarian railroad. It is useful for its discussion of the important role of railways in the country's economic development.

760. Kaltscheff, Anton.    Die Industrialisierung Bulgariens. Leipzig, 1939. 80 p.
    A brief survey of the industrialization of Bulgaria. More specific aspects of prewar Bulgarian industrial development are treated by W. W. Rondeff in *Die Entwicklung der bulgarischen Industrie unter besonderer Würdigung der fördernden Gesetzgebung* (Hildburghausen, 1938, 102 p.) and R. G. Rustcheff in *Die fabrikmässige Textilindustie Bulgariens: Entwicklung und wirtschaftliche Bedeutung* (Leipzig, 1938, 161 p.).

761. Nikolchov, V., *ed.*    100 godini bŭlgarska industriia, 1834-1937: nachalo, razvitie i znachenie (One hundred years of Bulgarian industry, 1834-1937: origin, development, and significance). Sofiia, 1937. 103 p.
    A collection of articles on Bulgaria's industrialization from the period of Turkish domination to the late '30s. The same subject is treated in English by Dimiter Popov in *One Hundred Years of Bulgarian Industry* (Sofia, Union of Bulgarian Industrialists, 1937).

762. Rangeloff, Grigor.    Transportation and Communications, *In* Dellin, L. A. D., *ed.* Bulgaria. New York, Praeger, 1957. p. 365-384. (Praeger Publications in Russian History and World Communism, no. 47)
    Discusses developments in the contemporary transportation and communications systems.

763. Toshev, Dinko.    Industrialnata politika na Bŭlgariia sled pŭrvata svetovna voĭna (The industrial policy of Bulgaria after the First World War). Varna, 1943. 224 p. Bibliography: p. 215-222.
    A general treatment of Bulgaria's industrialization in the period following the First World War. The same author discusses related subjects in his *Prinos za izuchavane industrialnata politika na Bŭlgariia ot osvobozhdenieto do Balkanskata voina* (Contribution to the study of the industrial policy of Bulgaria from the liberation to the Balkan War) (Varna, 1941, 180 p.) and *Razvitie na edrata industriia v Bŭlgariia pri sistemata na protektsionizma* (Development of heavy industry in Bulgaria under the system of protectionism) (Varna, 1946, 212 p.).

764. Wszelaki, Jan.    Industry. *In* Dellin, L. A. D., *ed.* Bulgaria. New York, Praeger, 1957. p. 313-332. (Praeger Publications in Russian History and World Communism, no. 47)
    A discussion of communist industrial policy and performance by the various branches of industry by a noted specialist on East Central European economics.

## I. LABOR

765. Dellin, L. A. D.    Labor. *In his* Bulgaria. New York, Praeger, 1957. p. 228-250. (Praeger Publications in Russian History and World Communism, no. 47)

A treatment of contemporary Bulgarian labor policies, trade unions, and the status of labor. The author discusses the social security system for the corresponding period in the same source (p. 258-266). See also *Trade Unions and Labor Legislation in Bulgaria* (New York, Mid-European Studies Center, 1953, 30 p.), in which the same author discusses the development of Bulgaria's labor movement and labor legislation from the establishment of the Bulgarian state to the death of Stalin.

766. Dimitrov, Georgi.    Sindikalnoto dvizhenie v Bŭlgariia (The Syndicalist movement in Bulgaria). *In his* Sŭchineniia (Works), v. 1. Sofiia, Bŭlgarska komunisticheska partiia, 1951. p. 283-357.

The noted Bulgarian communist leader discusses the Bulgarian labor movement in revolutionary terms. The same topic is also treated by Dragoi Kodzheikov and others in *Revoliutsionnoto profsŭiuzno dvizhenie v Bŭlgariia; kratŭk istoricheski ocherk* (The revolutionary trade union movement in Bulgaria: a short historical sketch) (Sofiia, Profizdat, 1957, 291 p.).

767. Ianulov, Iliia.    Sotsialnoto zakonodatelstvo v Bŭlgariia (Social legislation in Bulgaria). Sofiia, 1938. 370 p.

A Bulgarian professor discusses the main features of the rather advanced social security system of interwar Bulgaria. The same author treats labor legislation under communism in *Ikonomicheskite osnovi na kodeksa na truda i negovoto vŭzdeistvie vŭrkhu sotsialisticheskoto izgrazhdane u nas* (The economic foundations of the Labor Code and its impact on socialist construction in Bulgaria) (Sofiia, Bŭlgarska akademiia na nakite, 1956, 190 p.).

768. Lazard, Max.    Compulsory Labor Service in Bulgaria. Geneva, International Labor Office, 1922. 158 p. (International Labor Office. Studies and Reports, Series B: Economic Conditions, no. 12)

A study on behalf of the International Labor Office devoted to a characteristic institution which was introduced in lieu of military service, restricted by the 1919 Peace Treaty, in order to train Bulgarian youth.

769. Prochazka, Zora.    The Labor Force of Bulgaria. Washington, D.C., Bureau of the Census, 1962. 38 p. (International Population Statistics Reports, Series P-90, no. 16)

*See also* entry no. 543.

An analysis, with statistical data, of the manpower resources and occupational strata of Bulgaria. More recent data will be found in *Naselenieto i rabotnata sila v Bŭlgariia* (Population and labor force in Bulgaria) by Minko Minkov (Sofiia, Bŭlgarska akademiia na naukite, 1966, 257 p.).

## J. TRADE

770. Gabensky, Ivanko.    Trade. *In* Dellin, L. A. D., *ed*. Bulgaria. New York, Praeger, 1957. p. 333-364. (Praeger Publications in Russian History and World Communism, no. 47)

Bulgarian domestic and foreign trade under communism is analyzed by a former Bulgarian official. For a recent presentation of Bulgarian provenance *see Bulgaria's Foreign Trade* by Lŭchezar Avramov (Sofia, Foreign Languages Press, 1963, 177 p.).

771. Stefanoff, Ivan.    The Foreign Trade of Bulgaria after the World War. Sofia, State University, 1938. 117 p. (Sofia. Universitet. Statisticheski institut za stopanski prouchivaniia. Trudove)

The interwar foreign trade pattern is analyzed by an economic expert.

772. Steptschitsch, Georg P.    Strukturwandlungen im Aussenhandel Bulgariens. Leipzig, 1939. 110 p.

A discussion of the interwar orientation of Bulgaria's foreign trade toward Germany and of its causes and effects.

For recent statistical data on foreign trade *see*: Bulgaria. '*Tsentralno statistichesko upravlenie*. Vŭnshna tŭrgoviia na Narodna Republika Bŭlgariia; statisticheski daniia 1950-1967 (The foreign trade of the People's Republic of Bulgaria; statistical data, 1950-1967). Sofiia, 1968. 253 p. Illus.

# 24

# the society

*by Marin V. Pundeff*

*(With the exception of Section G)*

## A. BIBLIOGRAPHIES AND GENERAL DESCRIPTIONS

773. Bolgariia. *In* Iovchuk, M. T., *ed.* Marksistsko-leninskaia filosofiia i sotsiologiia v SSSR i evropeiskikh sotsialisticheskikh stranakh (Marxist-Leninist philosophy and sociology in the USSR and the European socialist countries). Moskva, Nauka, 1965. p. 409-427.

 A review of Bulgarian communist writings on sociological theory and problems after 1944.

774. Haucke, Kurt. Bulgarien. Land, Volk, Geschichte, Kultur, Wirtschaft, Bayreuth, Gauverlag, 1942. 180 p. Maps, illus.

 An introduction to Bulgaria before the Second World War.

775. Jireček, Josef K. Das Fürstenthum Bulgarien. Wien, Tempsky, 1891. 573 p. Illus.

 *See also* entry no. 522.

 A handbook by the great historian of Bulgaria, now only of historical value.

776. Markham, Reuben H. Meet Bulgaria. Sofia, 1931. 309 p. Illus.

 *See also* entry no. 814.

An effective depiction of the Bulgaria of the interwar years, by an American missionary and longtime resident of the country.

777. Sanders, Irwin T.    Balkan Village. Lexington, University of Kentucky Press, 1949. 291 p.
A sociological study of Bulgarian rural life based on observations in the village of Dragalevtsi, near Sofia.

778. Schütze, Gladys H.    Where East is West; Life in Bulgaria. Boston, Houghton-Mifflin, 1933. 320 p.
The flavor of Bulgarian society before the Second World War is conveyed by a visitor.

779. Svishtov, Bulgaria. Visshe uchilishte za stopanski i sotsialni nauki. *Institut za stopanski izsledvaniia.*    Stopanska i sotsialna knizhnina v Bŭlgariia; bibliografiia na bŭlgarskite knigi i statii ot nachaloto do dnes, 1850-1945 (Economic and social literature in Bulgaria; a bibliography of Bulgarian books and articles from the beginning to the present, 1850-1945). Svishtov, 1948. 951 p.
*See also* entry no. 726.
An exhaustive bibliography of the Bulgarian literature on all aspects of society and social problems published before 1945.

780. Wilhelmy, Herbert.    Hochbulgarien. Kiel, Schmidt und Klaunig, 1935-1936. 2 v. Illus., maps, plans. Bibliography: v. 1, p. 291-308; v. 2, p. 203-220. (Schriften des Geographischen Instituts der Universität Kiel, Bd. IV, Bd. V, Heft 3)
*See also* entry no. 545.
A treatise in cultural geography offering much sociological information on rural life in northern Bulgaria and urban life in Sofia.

## B. THE NATIONAL CHARACTER

781. Avramov, Petŭr.    Bŭlgarskata komunisticheska partiia i formirane na sotsialisticheskata inteligentsiia (The Bulgarian Communist Party and the formation of the socialist intelligentsia). Sofiia, BKP, 1966. 276 p.
An analysis of the process of the creation of a new intellectual stratum in Bulgaria since 1944. The booklet by N. Filchev, *The Intelligentsia in Bulgaria* (Sofia, Foreign Languages Press, 1964, 114 p.), also contains useful information.

782. Khadzhiĭski, Ivan.    Bit i dushevnost na nashiia narod (Way of life and psychology of our people). 2d ed. Sofiia, 1966. 460 p.
A penetrating inquiry into Bulgarian national and class psychology. A two-volume first edition was published in 1945.

783. Khadzhiĭski, Ivan.    Optimistichna teoriia za nashiia narod; studiĭ i statiĭ (An optimistic theory about our people; studies and articles). Sofiia, Bŭlgarski pisatel, 1966. 431 p.

A collection of the writings of Ivan Khadzhiiski (1907-1944), an incisive sociologist and analyst of the Bulgarian social scene and national character.

784. Kosturkov, S.   Vŭrkhu psikhologiiata na bŭlgarina (On the psychology of the Bulgarian). Sofiia, 1949. 233 p.
    Insights from the author's experience as a prominent Bulgarian politician.

785. Panov, T.   Psikhologiia na bŭlgarskiia narod (Psychology of the Bulgarian people). Sofiia, 1914. 306 p.
    An attempt to deal with the subject of national psychology and character.

786. Pundeff, Marin V.   Bulgaria. In Sugar, Peter F., and Ivo Lederer, eds. Nationalism in Eastern Europe. Seattle, University of Washington Press. In press.
    An examination of the sources, manifestations, and evolution of Bulgarian nationalism.

## C. WOMEN AND YOUTH

787. Bŭlgarska komunisticheska partiia. BKP za mladezhta (The Bulgarian Communist Party on youth). Sofiia, Narodna mladezh, 1955. 263 p.
    A collection of party documents on the youth movement, issued from 1893 to 1955.

788. Bŭlgarski naroden zhenski suiuz.   Bŭlgarski zhenski sŭiuz (Po sluchaĭ 30-godishninata mu), 1901-1931 (The Bulgarian Women's Union [on the occasion of its 30th anniversary], 1901-1931). Sofiia, 1931. 140 p.
    Useful for the history of the feminist movement in Bulgaria.

789. Dimitrov, Stoian, and Kostadin Popov.   Drugar na komsomolskiia aktivist (Vademecum of the Komsomol activist). Sofiia Narodna mladezh, 1962. 284 p.
    A handbook for Communist Youth Union activists.

790. Paskaleva, Virzhiniia.   Bŭlgarkata prez Vŭzrazhdaneto; istoricheski ocherk (The Bulgarian woman during the national revival; a historical outline). Sofiia, Bŭlgarska komunisticheska partiia, 1964. 315 p. Bibliography: p. 286-292.
    See also entry no. 913.
    Presents the historical background (to 1878) of the strong feminist movement in Bulgaria.

791. Vodenicharova, Zdravka, and Neviana Popova.   100 godini ot osnovavaneto na pŭrvite druzhestva na zhenite v Bŭlgariia (100 years since the founding of the first women's associations in Bulgaria). Sofiia, 1957. 139 p.

## D. HEALTH AND SOCIAL INSURANCE

792. Bulgaria. *Ministerstvo na narodnoto zdrave i sotsialnite grizhi.* Spravochnik po organizatsiia na zdraveopazvaneto (A reference book on the organization of health services). Sofiia, Nauka i izkustvo, 1952. 714 p.

    A comprehensive collection of official materials.

793. Kolarov, Petŭr V., *ed.* Petnadeset godini narodno zdraveopazvane (Fifteen years of public health service). Sofiia, Meditsina i fizkultura, 1959. 393 p.

    A review of public health measures taken from 1944 to 1959, by the then minister of public health. Of historical interest is *The Public Health Services in Bulgaria* by Ivan Golosmanoff (Lyon, 1926, 74 p.).

794. Red Cross. *Bulgaria.* Iubileĭna kniga; kratŭk pogled vŭrkhu istoriiata, zadachite i deĭnostta na Bŭlgarskoto d-vo Cherven krŭst, 1885-1935 (Anniversary volume; a concise review of the history, goals, and activity of the Bulgarian Red Cross, 1885-1935). Sofiia, 1936. 318 p.

    A detailed history. More recent information is provided in *Bŭlgarskiiat Cherven Krŭst; tseli, razvitie i deĭnost* (The Bulgarian Red Cross; purposes, development, and activity) by G. Gospodinov and G. Angelov (Sofiia, Meditsina i fizkultura, 1964, 164 p.).

795. Spasov, Khristo, *and* Georgi Lisev. Rŭkovodstvo po obshtestveno osiguriavane v NRB (A guide to social insurance in the People's Republic of Bulgaria). Sofiia, Profizdat, 1962. 288 p.

    A handbook on social security. The system is outlined for the foreign reader in *Les pensions en République Populaire de Bulgarie* (Sofia, Editions en langues étrangères, 1962, 71 p.).

## E. SOCIAL PROBLEMS

796. Boichev, Iordan. Preodoliavane na razlichiiata mezhdu grada i seloto v NRB (Overcoming the differences between city and countryside in the People's Republic of Bulgaria). Sofiia, Bŭlgarska komunisticheska partiia, 1964. 136 p.

    A discussion of one of the few areas of social tension that the communists admit to exist.

797. Bŭlgarska akademiia na naukite, *Sofia. Institute po filosofiia.* Izgrazhdane i razvitie na sotsialisticheskoto obshtestvo v Bŭlgariia (Construction and evolution of the socialist society in Bulgaria). Sofiia, Bŭlgarska akademiia na naukite, 1962. 488 p.

    A collection of studies on contradictions between mental and physical labor, city and countryside, social problems, role of the Communist Party, etc.

798. Iakhiel, Niko. Gradŭt i seloto; sotsiologicheski aspekti (City and countryside; sociological aspects). Sofiia, BKP, 1965. 275 p.

An effort to map out problems for sociological research. Russian translation: *Gorod i derevnia* (Moskva, "Progress," 1968, 269 p.).

799. Karadzhov, Kiril S. Za protivorechiiata v sotsialisticheskoto obshtestvo (On the contradictions in socialist society). Sofiia, Nauka i izkustvo, 1965. 243 p.

800. Karanfilov, Efrem. Senki ot minaloto; ochertsi i eseta za niakoi ostatutsi ot burzhoazniia moral v sotsialisticheskoto obshtestvo (Shadows from the past; sketches and essays on remnants of the bourgeois morality in socialist society). 2d rev. and enl. ed. Sofiia, Narodna mladezh, 1963. 271 p.

801. Markov, Marko V. Sotsialno-klasovite izmeneniia v perioda na izgrazhdane na razvito sotsialistichesko obshtestvo (Social and class changes during the period of the building of an advanced socialist society). Sofiia, BKP, 1965. 191 p.

A discussion of changes in the social classes under communism. Markov's earlier work, *Kŭm vŭprosa za klasovite izmeniia v NRB* (On the question of class changes in the People's Republic of Bulgaria) Sofiia, BKP, 1960, 174 p.), should also be consulted.

802. Mikhailov, Stoian. Likvidiraneto na protivopolozhnostta mezhdu umstveniia i fizicheskiia trud (Liquidation of the contradiction between mental and physical labor). Sofiia, Bŭlgarska akademiia na naukite, 1959. 219 p.

A penetrating, detailed examination of the problem in Bulgaria.

803. Semov, Mois I. Prichini za ostatŭtsite ot burzhoazniia moral v nasheto obshtestvo (Causes for the remnants of bourgeois morality in our society). Sofiia, Nauka i izkustvo, 1965. 234 p.

804. Smatrakalev, Mikhail I. Khuliganstvoto kato obshtestveno opasno deianie (Hooliganism as a socially dangerous act). Sofiia, Nauka i izkustvo, 1967. 176 p.

An examination of the Bulgarian manifestations of a worldwide problem.

805. Toshev, Dinko, *and others*. Vŭprosi na zhilishtnoto stroitelstvo v NR Bŭlgariia (Problems of housing construction in the People's Republic of Bulgaria). Sofiia, Bŭlgarska akademiia na naukite, 1959. 198 p.

A discussion of the housing problem in Bulgaria since 1944. Also of interest is *Planirane na bŭlgarskoto selo* (Planning the Bulgarian village) by Liuben Tonev and others (Sofiia, Bŭlgarska akademiia na naukite, 1956, 288 p.).

## F. MINORITIES

806. Kostanick, Huey L.   The Turkish Resettlement of Bulgarian Turks, 1950-53. Berkeley, University of California Press, 1957. 65-163 p. Illus., maps, diagr., tables. Bibliography: p. 145-146. (University of California Publications in Geography, v. 8, no. 2)

    *See also* entry no. 540.

    A monograph on the resettlement of over 150,000 Turks expelled from Bulgaria in 1950-1951.

807. Mizov, Nikolai.   Isliamut v Bŭlgariia (Islam in Bulgaria). Sofiia, BKP, 1965. 232 p. Bibliography.

    Written from the standpoint of combating Islam as a religion, this study contains some data on the Moslem groups in Bulgaria (Turks, Gypsies, converted Bulgarians, and Tatars).

808. Pandurski, V., *and others*.   NR Bŭlgariia i religioznite izpovedaniia v neia (The People's Republic of Bulgaria and the religious denominations in it). Sofiia, Sinodalno izdatelstvo, 1966. 123 p.

    Provides up-to-date data on principal minorities in Bulgaria, traditionally defined on the basis of religion (Turks, Jews, and others). The text is also in English, French, German, and Russian. For prewar data, *see* A. Girard's *Les minorités nationales, ethniques et religieuses en Bulgarie* (Paris, 1932, 206 p.).

## G. PSYCHOLOGY

*by Josef Brozek*

809. Geron, Ema.   Psikhologiia (Psychology). Rev. and enl. ed. Sofiia, Meditsina i fizkultura, 1965. 434 p. Illus., bibliography.

    A textbook for the students of the "G. Dimitrov" Higher Institute of Physical Culture. Psychological aspects of athletics are emphasized.

810. Geron, Ema, *and* Nikola Popov.   Razvitie na visshata nervna deĭnost v preduchilishtna vŭzrast (Development of higher nervous activity during the preschool period). Sofiia, Narodna prosveta, 1966. 136 p. Illus. Bibliography: p. 124-129.

    A research monograph on the development of motor and verbal responses. Extensive summaries in Russian and German.

811. Zhekova, Stoianka, Dimka Stoitseva, *and* Stefan Chonov.   Detska psikhologiia (Child psychology). Sofiia, Narodna prosveta, 1963. 196 p. Illus. Bibliography: p. 195-196.

    A textbook for teachers' colleges. Refers to the publications of Bulgarian authors such as V. Ivanov, K. Kondov, V. Tomova-Manova, G. T. Nastev, M. N. Shardakov, and, in particular, Gencho D. Pir'ov, author of *Detska psikhologiia* (Child psychology) (Sofiia, Nauka i izkustvo, 1950, 452 p.), and *Detska psikologiia s defektologiia* (Child psychology, normal and abnormal) (2d rev. ed., Sofiia, Nauka i izkustvo, 1959, 556 p., bibliography).

# 25

# intellectual and cultural life

*by James F. Clarke*
*(Except for Section J)*

## A. GENERAL WORKS ON CULTURE

812. Bŭlgariia. *In* Kratka bŭlgarska entsiklopediia (Concise Bulgarian encyclopedia). v. 1. Sofiia, Bŭlgarska akademiia na naukite, 1963. p. 321-405. Bibliography.

Planned for five volumes, this encyclopedia supersedes earlier works. The selections and coverage reflect current ideological tastes. Under "Bulgaria" are included education, learning, cultural institutions, folk arts, literature, architecture, fine arts, music, theater, and cinema.

813. Bŭlgariia; Khiliada godini 927-1927 (One thousand years of Bulgaria, 927-1927). v. 1. Sofia, Ministerstvoto na narodnoto prosveshtenie, 1930. 1023 p. Illus.

*See also* entry no. 548.

Consisting of syntheses by the foremost authorities, about half the volume deals with the intellectual and cultural past of Bulgaria. Only one volume was published.

814. Markham, Reuben H.    Meet Bulgaria. Sofia, 1931. 390 p. Illus.

*See also* entry no. 776.

Best popular introductions to all aspects of Bulgarian life before the Second World War. Chapters on religion, art, literature, education, and theater. For the postwar period, there are brief sections on religion, education, literature and the arts in *Bulgaria*, edited by L. A. D. Dellin (New York, Praeger, 1957, p. 182-227) and related bibliography (p. 427-430). *See also* the series of articles in *Survey* (no. 39, Dec. 1961: 80-151).

## B. LANGUAGE

### 1. History

815. Damerau, Norbert.    Die russische Lehnwörter in der neu-bulgarischen Literatursprache. Wiesbaden, Harrassowitz, 1960. 148 p. (Osteuropa-Institut an der Freien Universität Berlin, Veröffentlichungen. Bd. 24)

Only direct borrowings from Russian are included and listed, p. 61-148.

816. Georgiev, Vladimir.    Bŭlgarska etimologiia i onomastika (Bulgarian etymology and onomastics). Sofiia, Bŭlgarska akademiia na naukite, 1960. 179 p. Map.

Georgiev, one of Bulgaria's most prominent scholars and a comparative linguist who specializes in classical and pre-classical languages, here gives special place to names of rivers. A more general work is his *Vuprosi na bŭlgarskata etimologiia* (Problems in Bulgarian etymology) (Sofiia, 1958, 158 p.).

817. Mirchev, Kiril.    Istoricheska gramatika na bŭlgarskiia ezik (Histori-

cal grammar of the Bulgarian language). 2d ed. Sofiia, Nauka i izkustvo, 1963. 275 p. Bibliography: p. 266-271.

Mirchev, who holds the chair of Bulgarian language at Sofia University, is also author of *Istoriia na bŭlgarskiia ezik* (History of the
Bulgarian language) (Sofia, Nauka i izkustvo, 1950, 162 p.).

818. Mladenov, Stefan.   Geschichte der bulgarischen Sprache. Berlin, de
Gruyter, 1929. 354 p. Map, bibliography. (Grundriss der slavischen
Philologie und Kulturgeschichte, 6)

The best history of the Bulgarian language, it has full bibliographies
at the ends of sections. For Mladenov, who began writing in 1901,
there is *Ezikovedski izsledovaniia v chest na akademik Stefan Mladenov*
(Linguistic researches in honor of Academician Stefan Mladenov),
edited by Vladimir Georgiev (Sofiia, Bŭlgarska akademiia na naukite,
1957, 653 p.). This is an enormous work with contributions on Bulgarian, Slavic, and general linguistics. *See also* Ekaterina Mikhailova's
*Stefan Mladenov. Biobibliografski prinos* (Stefan Mladenov. Biobibliographical contribution) (Sofiia, Bŭlgarska akademiia na naukite, 1955,
308 p.).

819. Tsonev, Ben'o.   Istoriia na bŭlgarskii ezik (History of the Bulgarian
language). Sofiia, Sofiĭski universitet, 1919-1937. 3 v.

A basic work comprising Tsonev's university lectures. Volumes 2
and 3 were published posthumously and edited by Stefan Mladenov.
Volume 1-A (529 p.) was republished in 1940; it is edited by Mladenov
and Kiril Mirchev (Universitetska biblioteka, 203) and includes an
extensive review of sources.

## 2. Grammars

820. Andreichin, Liubomir D.   Osnovna bŭlgarska gramatika (Basic
Bulgarian grammar). Sofiia, Hemus, 1944. 559 p.

A standard grammar, with newer editions. Andreichin, Director of
the Bulgarian Language Institute, Bulgarian Academy of Sciences,
has also published, with K. Popov and M. Ivanov, *Sŭvremenen bŭlgarski ezik* (The contemporary Bulgarian language) (Sofiia, 1955-
1957, 2 v.). Important older grammars are *Gramatika na bŭlgarskiia
ezik* by S. Mladenov (with Stefan Pop Vasilev) (Sofiia, Kazanlŭshka
Dolina, 1939, 440 p.) and *Nova bŭlgarska gramatika* (New Bulgarian grammar) by Aleksandŭr Teodorov-Balan (Sofiia, 1940).

821. Beaulieux, Léon.   Grammaire de la langue bulgare. 2d rev. ed. Paris,
Institut d'études slaves, 1950. 415 p. (Collection de grammaires de
l'Institut d'études slaves, IV)

One of the best foreign-language grammars, it was done with the
collaboration of Stefan Mladenov, It retains the 1923 orthography
used in the first edition of 1933. A less advanced grammar, with vocabulary, is Enrico Damiani's *Corso di lingua bulgara, teoretico-
pratico* (Roma, Edizioni Universitarie, 1942, 419 p.).

822. Ginina, Stefana Ts., Tsvetana N. Nikolova, *and* Liuba A. Sakazova. A Bulgarian Textbook for Foreigners. Sofia, Nauka i Izkustvo, 1965. 409 p. Illus., map.

> Progressively scaled, practical, elementary grammar translated from a Bulgarian text (Sofiia, 1963) designed for foreign students at Sofia University.

823. Lord, Albert B.    Beginning Bulgarian. The Hague, Mouton, 1962. 165 p.

> The author is an authority on South Slav languages and literatures. For American students there is also *Bulgarian Basic Course* (Washington, D.C., Department of State, Foreign Service Institute, 1961, 2 v., offset) and *Reader* (1962), keyed to tapes and informant, both by Carlton T. Hodge and associates. The Army Language School, Monterey, California, has also produced a *Bulgarian Basic Course*, mimeographed in 7 volumes (1959-1960).

### 3. Onomastics

824. Mikov, Vasil.    Proizkhod i znachenie na imenata na nashite gradove i sela, reki, planini i mesta (Origin and meaning of the names of our towns and villages, rivers, mountains, and localities). Sofiia, 1943. 316 p. Bibliography: p. 270-271. (Nauka i znanie, 1)

> Informative though lacking in scholarly apparatus. Mikov also authored *Izvori za istoriiata i geografiiata na nashite gradove i sela* (Sources for the history and geography of our towns and villages) (Sofiia, Pechatnitsa "Kultura," 1935, 107 p.).

825. Werner, Waltraud.    Die männlichen Personennamen in den bulgarischen Volksliedern; ein Beitrag zur bulgarischen Anthroponymie. Wiesbaden, Harrassowitz, 1965. 171 p. Map, bibliography. (Osteuropa-Institut an der Freien Universität Berlin. Slavische Veröffentlichungen, 33)

> Bulgarian onomastics has been concerned largely with place names. This is a pioneer study of 1,341 male names in folksongs. A study of female names is promised.

### 4. Dictionaries (Monolingual)

826. Andreichin, Liubomir D., *and others*.    Bŭlgarski tŭlkoven rechnik (Bulgarian explanatory dictionary). 2d ed. Sofiia, Nauka i izkustvo, 1963. 1022 p.

> The first such dictionary to be completed (1st edition, 1955). A more ambitious work by Stefan Mladenov (with A. Teodorov-Balan) is *Bŭlgarski tŭlkoven rechnik s ogled kŭm narodnite govori* (Bulgarian explanatory dictionary with reference to vernacular dialects), v. 1 (Sofiia, D. Stefanov, 1951, 1126 p.). Volume 2 is in press.
>
> A widely used thesaurus is *Bŭlgarski sinonimen rechnik* (Bulgarian dictionary of synonyms), compiled by Liuben N. Nanov (Sofiia, Nauka i izkustvo, 5th ed., 1968, 628 p.).

827. Andreichin, Liubomir, *and others.*  Pravopisen rechnik na bŭlgar-skiia ezik (Orthographic dictionary of the Bulgarian language). 6th ed. Sofiia, Nauka i izkustvo, 1965. 424 p.

Another standard dictionary of this type is Stoian Romanski's *Pravopisen rechnik na bŭlgarskiia knizhoven ezik, s posochvane izgo-vora i udarenieto na dumite i poiasnenie na chuzhdite dumi* (Ortho-graphic dictionary of the Bulgarian literary language, with a guide to the pronunciation and accentuation of words and explanation of for-eign words), 2d ed. (Sofiia, Nauka i izkustvo, 1954, 677 p.). Both dic-tionaries follow the orthographic reform of February 17, 1945.

For a textbook of orthography see *Bŭlgarski pravopis* (Bulgarian orthography) by Mosko D. Moskov (Sofiia, Nauka i izkustvo, 2d rev. and enl. edition, 1969, 364 p.).

828. Bŭlgarska akademiia na naukite, *Sofia. Institut za bŭlgarski ezik.* Bulgarski etimologichen rechnik (Bulgarian etymological dictionary). Compiled by Vladimir Georgiev and others. Sofiia, 1962–

In 1941, Stefan Mladenov published *Etimologicheski i pravopisen rechnik na bŭlgarskiia knizhoven ezik* (Etymological and orthographic dictionary of the Bulgarian literary language) (Sofiia, Danov, 704 p.), based on the 1923 orthography.

829. Gerov, Naĭden.   Rechnik na bŭlgarskiia ezik, s tŭlkuvanie rechite na bŭlgarski i na ruski (Dictionary of the Bulgarian language, with defi-nitions in Bulgarian and Russian). Plovdiv, 1895-1904. 5 v. Supple-ment by Teodor Panchev: Plovdiv, 1908.

Gerov (1823-1900), one of the most important personalities of the Bulgarian national revival, who also collected folk songs, devoted 50 years to collecting terms for his dictionary of the spoken language, which comprises 78,620 main entries. Definitions include excerpts from folk songs and other folklore material.

830. Milev, Aleksandŭr, *and others.*   Rechnik na chuzhdite dumi v bŭl-garskiia ezik (Dictionary of foreign words in the Bulgarian language). 2d ed. Sofiia, Nauka i izkustvo, 1964. 755 p.

Also of value is Stefan Mladenov's *Rechnik na chuzhdite dumi v bŭlgarskiiat ezik, s obiasneniia za poteklo i sŭstav* (Dictionary of foreign words in the Bulgarian language with explanations of origin and composition), 3d enl ed. (Sofiia, 1947, 491 p.). On the perennial issue of language purity, there is Mosko Moskov's *Borbata protiv chuzhdite dumi v bŭlgarskiia knizhoven ezik* (The battle against foreign words in the Bulgarian literary language) (Sofiia, Bŭlgarska akademiia na naukite, 1958, 147 p.), covering the subject from Peter Beron to Teodorov-Balan.

831. Romanski, Stoian, *ed.*   Rechnik na sŭvremenniia bŭlgarski knizhoven ezik (Dictionary of the contemporary Bulgarian literary language). Sofiia, Bŭlgarska akademiia na naukite, 1954-59. 3 v.

See also *Ezikovedsko-etnograski izsledvaniia v pamet na akademik Stoian Romanski* (Linguistic-ethnographic researches in memory of

Academician Stoian Romanski), edited by Vladimir Georgiev (Sofiia, Bŭlgarska akademiia na naukite, 1960, 981 p.).

## 5. Dialectology

832. Mazon, André.   Contes slaves de la Macédoine sud-occidentale; étude linguistique; textes et traductions; notes de folklore. Paris, Champion, 1923. 236 p. (Travaux publiés par l'Institut d'études slaves, 1)

————.   Documents, contes et chansons slaves de l'Albanie du Sud. Paris, Droz, 1936. 462 p. Illus. (Bibliothèque d'études Balkaniques, 5). Part 2, with Maria Filipova-Bajrova. Pièces complémentaires. Paris, Institut d'études slaves, 1965. 181 p. (Bibliothèque d'études slaves, 8)

————, and André Vaillant.   L'Evangéliaire de Kulakia; un parler slave du Bas-Vardar. Paris, Librairie Droz, 1938. 358 p. (Bibliothèque d'études balkaniques, 6)

Spendid studies of Western Bulgarian (Macedonian) dialects. Mazon was one of France's finest Slavists.

833. Miletich, Liubomir.   Das Ostbulgarische. Wien, Holder, 1903. 302 cols. Map. (Kaiserliche Akademie der Wissenschaften. Schriften der Balkankommission. Linguistische Abteilung I. Südslavische Dialektstudien, 2)

————.   Die Rhodopenmundarten der bulgarischen Sprache. Wien, 1912. (Südslavische Dialekstudien, 6)

Miletich (1863-1937) was Bulgaria's first outstanding philologist. He was the recipient of two Festschriften, the first after 25 years of literary activity (Sofiia, 1912, 414 p.), listing 177 publications. The second was *Sbornik v chest na Prof. L. Miletich* (Collection in honor of Prof. L. Miletich) (Sofiia, Makedonski nauchen institut, 1933, 687 p.), with a bibliographical review by Stoian Romanski.

834. Selishchev, Afanasiĭ M.   Polog i ego bolgarskoe naselenie; istoricheskie, etnograficheskie i dialektologicheskie ocherki severozapadnoi Makedonii (Polog and its Bulgarian inhabitants; historical, ethnographic, and dialectological sketches of northwestern Macedonia). Sofiia, Makedonski nauchen institut, 1929. 439 p. Illus., maps.

————.   Makedonskie kodiki XVI-XVIII vekov. Ocherki po istoricheskoi etnografii i dialektologii Makedonii (Macedonian codices of the 16th-19th centuries; sketches on the historical ethnography and dialectology of Macedonia). Sofiia, Makedonski nauchen institut, 1933. 262 p.

One of the best Soviet Slavists, Selishchev's first work on Macedonian dialectology was published in Kazan in 1918.

835. Stoĭkov, Stoĭko.  Bŭlgarska dialektologiia (Bulgarian dialectology). Sofiia, Nauka i izkustvo, 1956. 220 p.

Stoikov is the ranking speech and dialect specialist at the University and Academy. Among his other works is *Uvod v bŭlgarskata fonetika* (Introduction to Bulgarian phonetics) (Sofiia, Bŭlgarska akademiia na naukite, 1955, 174 p.). He is also coauthor of a four-volume Bulgarian dialect atlas being compiled in cooperation with the Soviet Academy's Slavistics Institute (1964–).

## C. LITERATURE
### 1. Reference and Survey Works

836. Borriero-Picchio, Lavinia.  Storia della letteratura bulgara con un profilo della letteratura paleoslava. Milano, Nuova Academia editrice, 1957. 279 p. Bibliography: p. 265-270. (Storia delli letteratura di tutto il mondo)

A competent survey which barely gets as far as the 19th century. Another Bulgarian specialist, Enrico Damiani, wrote a short *Sommario di storia della letteratura bulgara della origini ad oggi* (Roma, 1942, 111 p.).

837. Bozhkov, Stoĭko, *and others, eds.*  Istoriia na bŭlgarskata literatura (History of Bulgarian literature). Sofiia, Bŭlgarska akademiia na naukite, 1962– Illus.

A major collective undertaking by the Academy, involving leading specialists and using a biographical approach. Projected for four volumes; v. 1-2 published so far. Volume 1 on old Bulgarian literature (453 p.) includes essays on 16 writers from Cyril and Methodius to Iosif Bradati, along with general introductions to periods and corresponding bibliography, mostly Bulgarian and Russian (p. 425-438). Volume 2 on the literature of the rebirth (658 p.) covers 16 authors from Paisii to Nesho Bonchev, with some general chapters and bibliography, mostly Bulgarian (p. 624-638).

838. Konstantinov, Georgi, Tsvetan Minkov, *and* Stefan Velikov.  Bŭlgarski pisateli: biografii, bibliografiia (Bulgarian writers: biographies, bibliography). Sofiia, Bŭlgarski pisatel, 1961. 788 p.

Supersedes earlier, similar works by Konstantinov, an industrious compiler, literary historian, and popularizer. Among his works is a good survey, *Stara bŭlgarska literatura ot sv. Kiril i Metodi do Paisii Khilendarski* (Old Bulgarian literature from Sts. Cyril and Methodius to Paisii Khilendarski) (Sofiia, Hemus, 1946, 255 p.), and *Nova bŭlgarska literatura ot Paisii Khilendarski do Ivan Vazov* (Modern Bulgarian literature from Paisii Khilendarski to Ivan Vazov) (Sofiia, Hemus, 1947, 486 p.), with several variations of title and date.

839. Manning, Clarence A., *and* Roman Smal-Stocki.  The History of Modern Bulgarian Literature. New York, Bookman Associates, 1960. 198 p.

The only survey in English, it actually sketches all of Bulgarian literature and includes a selection of Bulgarian poetry (p. 167-186). The last part, since the Second World War, is understandably thin, and there is an odd Ukrainian flavor. *See also* Dimitri Shishmanov's *A Survey of Bulgarian Literature*, translated by Clarence A. Manning (Williamsport, Pa., Bayard Press, 1932, 40 p.).

840. Minkov, Tsvetan, Boniu Angelov, *and* Stoĭko Bozhkov. Bŭlgarska literatura (Bulgarian literature). 3d ed. Sofiia, Narodna prosveta, 1958. 531 p.

A popular survey by three prominent authorities.

841. Tsanev, Georgi. Rechnik na bŭlgarskata literatura (Dictionary of Bulgarian literature). Sofiia, Bŭlgarska akademiia na naukite, 1966–

Tsanev in charge of the section on Bulgarian literature of the Academy's Institute of Literature, is the author of several works of literary criticism. Volume 1: A-K.

## 2. The Old Bulgarian Literature

842. Angelov, Bozhan, *and* Mikhail Genov. Stara bŭlgarska literatura v primeri, prevodi i bibliografiia (Old Bulgarian literature in examples, translations, and bibliography). Sofiia, Paskalev, 1922. 608 p.

A rich collection on the ninth-eighteenth centuries by two well-known literature historians. Another useful anthology, in Bulgarian translation, is Ivan Duĭchev's *Iz starata bŭlgarska knizhnina* (From Old Bulgarian literature) (2d ed., Sofiia, Hemus, 1943, 1944, 2 v.). The translations are from original sources, comprising literary and historical monuments from the first and second Bulgarian empires. Exhaustive bibliographical notes are included.

843. Angelov, Dimitŭr, *and others, eds.* Khiliada i sto godini slavianska pismenost, 863-1963; sbornik v chest na Kiril i Metodiĭ (One thousand, one hundred years of Slavic writing; collection in honor of Cyril and Methodius). Sofiia, Bŭlgarska akademiia na naukite, 1963. 543 p. Illus.

In one of the most important of such anniversary volumes, 25 Bulgarian and one Russian scholar deal with important aspects and consequences of the work of Cyril and Methodius. Of particular interest are Asen Vasiliev's "Obrazi na Kiril i Metodii v chuzhdoto i nasheto izobrazitelno izkustvo" (Portraits of Cyril and Methodius in foreign and domestic fine arts) (p. 393-488); and "Bŭlgarska kirilometodievska bibliografiia za perioda 1944-1962." (Bulgarian Cyrillo-Methodian bibliography for the period 1944-1962) by Ivan Duichev and others.

844. Cronia, Arturo. Saggi di letteratura bulgara antica; inquadramento storico e versioni. Roma, Istituto per l'Europa orientale, 1936. 130 p.

Anthology by an Italian Slavic specialist.

845. Dinekov, Petŭr. Stara bŭlgarska literatura (Old Bulgarian literature). Sofiia, 1951-1953. 2 v.

Dinekov, titular head of pre-Liberation literature at the Academy and the University, has authored many studies of literary history and criticism and of folklore. A collection of 20 critical essays ranging over all of Bulgarian literature is *Literaturni vŭprosi* (Literary questions) (Sofiia, Narodna kultura, 1963, 377 p.).

846. Duĭchev, Ivan, *ed.* Letopisŭt na Konstantin Manasi (Chronicle of Konstantin Manasses). Sofiia, Bŭlgarska akademiia na naukite, 1963. 415 p. (Pametnitsi na starata bŭlgarska pismenost, 1)

An excellent facsimile of the Vatican copy of the Middle Bulgarian translation, edited by the foremost Bulgarian medievalist-historian, with learned introduction. A splendid companion volume is Duichev's *The Miniatures of the Chronicle of Manasse* (Sofiia, Bŭlgarski Houdozhnik, 1963, 137 p.), in which all 69 of the miniatures are reproduced in color. Includes critical introductions and notes. Duichev is currently working on a definitive critical edition of the chronicle.

See also Henri Boissin's *Le Manassès moyen-bulgare, étude linguistique* (Paris, Droz, 1946, 119 p.).

847. Georgiev, Emil. Kiril i Metodi, osnovopolozhnitsi na slavianskite literaturi (Cyril and Methodius, founders of the Slavic literatures). Sofiia, Bŭlgarska akademiia na naukite, 1956. 293 p.

————. Raztsvetŭt na bŭlgarskata literatura v IX-X v. (The flowering of Bulgarian literature in the 9th and 10th centuries). Sofiia, Bŭlgarska akademiia na naukite, 1962. 345 p.

————. Literatura na izostreni borbi v srednovekovna Bŭlgariia (The literature of sharpened struggle in medieval Bulgaria). Sofiia, Bŭlgarska akademiia na naukite, 1966. 320 p.

These fully documented monographs form a trilogy by a specialist in early Slavic and Bulgarian literature. For Georgiev's latest findings see *Kiril i Metodii. Istinata za suzdatelite na bŭlgarskata i slavianska pismenost* (Cyril and Methodius. The Truth about the Founders of Bulgarian and Slavic Letters). Sofiia, Nauka i izkustvo, 1969, 366 p.).

848. Ivanov, Ĭordan. Bogomilski knigi i legendi (Bogomil books and legends). Sofiia, Bŭlgarska akademiia na naukite, 1925. 387 p.

————. Starobŭlgarski razkazi; tekstove, novobŭlgarski prevodi i belezhki (Old Bulgarian tales; texts, modern Bulgarian translations, and notes). Sofiia, 1935. 322 p.

————. Bŭlgarski starini iz Makedoniia (Bulgarian antiquities throughout Macedonia). 2d ed. Sofiia, Bŭlgarska akademiia na naukite, 1931. 671 p. Illus.

The first of these books is a survey with texts and analyses of Bulgarian (Slavic) dualistic writings. The latter part covers dualism in Bulgarian folklore. One of the best works of Ivanov (1872-1947), the greatest authority on Bulgarian language, literature, and folklore.

The third (Bulgarian antiquities), twice as large as the first edition (1908), contains shorter literary and historical texts and inscriptions from the 9th to the 19th centuries.

849. Turdeanu, Émile.  La littérature bulgare du XIVe siècle et sa diffusion dans les pays roumains. Paris, Droz, 1947. 188 p. Bibliography: p. 166-178. (Travaux publiés par l'Institut d'études slaves, 22)

An important monograph. Turdeanu specializes in Slavic literature and culture in the Romanian principalities.

### 3. More Recent Bulgarian Literature

#### a. Surveys, Studies, Anthologies

850. Andreichin, Liubomir, *and* Petŭr Dinekov, *eds.*  Ezik i stil na bŭlgarskite pisateli; izsledvaniia i ocherki (Language and style of Bulgarian writers; studies and sketches). Sofiia, Bŭlgarska akademiia na naukite, 1962. 648 p.

Some distinguished contributions dealing with writers from P. R. Slaveikov to Vasil Kolarov.

851. Arnaudov, Mikhail, *ed.*  Bŭlgarski pisateli: zhivot, tvorchestvo, idei; iliustrovana literaturno-istoricheska biblioteka (Bulgarian writers: life, works, ideas; illustrated literary-historical library). Sofiia, Fakel, 1929-1930. 6 v.

Sketches of 40 modern writers from Paisii to Elin Pelin by various authors.

852. Dimov, Georgi.  Bŭlgarskata literaturna kritika prez vŭzrazhdaneto (Bulgarian literary criticism during the revival). Sofiia, Bŭlgarska akademiia na naukite, 1965. 405 p.

A substantial work on the origins of literary criticism, including essays on seven leading exponents.

853. Dinekov, Petŭr.  Vŭzrozhdenski pisateli (Revival writers). Sofiia, Nauka i izkustvo, 1962. 363 p.

Critical essays on 15 literary figures of the national revival, a sequel to his earlier (1942) *Pŭrvi vŭzrozhdentsi* (The first revivers) (Sofiia, 1944, 178 p.), dealing with the "Damascene" writers. Similar ground is covered on a broader scale by Khristo Gandev, head of the Ethnographic Institute and Museum in his *Faktori na bŭlgarskoto vŭzrazhdane, 1600-1830* (Factors in the Bulgarian renaissance, 1600-1830) (Sofiia, Bŭlgarska kniga, 1943, 303 p.).

854. Dontchev, Nikolai.  Études bulgares. Première Série. Sofia, Chipev, 1938. 231 p.

Most of Dontchev's work first appeared as articles in *La Bulgarie* and other Sofia journals. This includes "Influences étrangères dans la littérature bulgare" (*La Bulgarie*, 1934, 141 p.), a documented study, and *Esquisse d'un tableau de la nouvelle littérature bulgare* (Sofia, 1935, 74 p.).

855. Dragnewa, Ziwka, *ed.* and *tr.*   Neue bulgarische Erzähler. München, Langen-Müller, 1936. 172 p.

Contains a postscript by the noted South Slavist Gerhard Gesemann. *See also* a similar anthology by Valerie Dashkova-Dumas entitled *Conteurs bulgares d'aujourd'hui; recits, contes, nouvelles, choisis et adaptés* (Sofia, 1937), with a preface by Nikolai Dontchev.

856. Koneski, Blaže.   Towards the Macedonian Renaissance. Skopje, Nova Makedonija, 1962. 94 p.

A polemical argument for considering writers from Macedonia in the context of the post-1944 Macedonian literary language and literature and not part of Bulgarian literature. A similar line is taken by Horace Lunt in "A Survey of Macedonian Literature," *Harvard Slavic Studies*, v. 1 (Cambridge, Harvard University Press, 1953), p. 363-396. For the traditional view *see* Siméon Radev's *La Macédoine et la renaissance bulgare au XIXe siècle* (Sofia, 1918, 315 p.).

857. Penev, Boian.   Istoriia na novata bŭlgarska literatura (History of modern Bulgarian literature). Sofiia, Ministerstvo na narodnoto prosveshtenie, 1930-1936. 4 v.

A second-generation Bulgarian scholar, Penev's university lectures were edited after his early death (1927) by Boris Iotsov, with Penev's very full bibliographical notes. Dealing with the national revival on a broad scale, volume 1 is devoted to underlying origins. The last volume scarcely reaches the Liberation. Also posthumously published was Penev's *Bŭlgarska literatura; kratŭk istoricheski pregled* (Bulgarian literature; short historical survey) (Plovdiv, Danov, 1930, 206 p.; 3d ed., Sofiia, 1946, 254 p.), consisting of lectures given in Poland. *See also* Penev's *La renaissance bulgare,* translated by S. Petrova (Sofia, La Bulgarie, 1933, 64 p.).

858. Petkanova-Toteva, Donka.   Damaskinite v bŭlgarskata literatura (The Damascenes in Bulgarian literature). Sofiia, Bŭlgarska akademiia na naukite, 1965. 259 p. Illus. Bibliography: p. 237-259.

A significant body of writings overlapping the beginning of modern Bulgarian literature. The author lists all texts and editions from the 17th to the 19th centuries, both in Bulgaria and abroad.

859. Pinto, Vivian.   Bulgarian Prose and Verse; a Selection with an Introductory Essay. London, University of London, Athlone Press, 1957. 211 p.

The bulk of this volume consists of an anthology of 25 modern writers in the original Bulgarian. The author, who took a doctorate in Bulgarian literature at the University of London in 1952, is the foremost English authority on modern Bulgarian literature.

860. Salvini, Luigi.   La letteratura bulgara dalla liberazione alla prima guerra balcanica (1878-1912). Roma, Istituto per l'Europa orientale, 1936. 213 p. (Pubblicazioni, 30)

A documented survey by the author of several works on Bulgaria, including *Canti popolari bulgari* (Roma, 1931, 70 p.).

861. Stoyanoff, Zachary (Zakhari Stoianov). Pages from the Autobiography of a Bulgarian Insurgent. London, Edward Arnold, 1913. 316 p.
*See also* entry no. 592.
Portion of a classic of Bulgarian prose, cherished as much for literature as for history. First published in three volumes (1884-1892). It covers the author's exploits during 1875-1876.

862. Yovkov, Yordan (Iordan Iovkov). Short Stories. Translated by Marco Mincoff and Marguerite Alexieva. Sofia, Foreign Languages Press, 1965. 239 p.
One of the best short story tellers in modern Bulgarian literature.

### b. Individual Authors

863. Paisiĭ Khilendarski.
Angelov, Boniu S., *ed.* Istoriia slavenobŭlgarskaia; Nikiforov prepis ot 1772 (The Slaveno-Bulgarian history; the Nikifor copy of 1772). Sofiia, Bŭlgarska akademiia na naukite, 1961. 208 p.
Most complete edition, comprising the texts of Paisii's manuscript (1762), the first known copy by Sofronii (1765), and the Nikifor copy (1772). Angelov is also the author of *Sŭvremennitsi na Paisii* (Paisii's contemporaries) (Sofiia, Bŭlgarska akademiia na naukite, 1963-1964, 2 v.), comprising 15 writers and texts.

Clarke, James F. Father Paisii and Bulgarian History. *In* S. H. Hughes, *ed.*, Teachers of History. Ithaca, Cornell University Press, 1954. p. 258-283.
The only study in English, touching on bibliographical aspects to 1870. Bibliographical problems relating to the first decades of printed Bulgarian literature are reviewed by the same author in "The Russian Bible Society and the Bulgarians," *Harvard Slavic Studies*, v. 3, 1955: 67-103.

Dinekov, Petŭr. Paisiĭ Khilendarski; Slaviĭanobŭlgarska istoriia (Paisii Khilendarski; Slavo-Bulgarian history). Sofiia, Bŭlgarski pisatel, 1963. 144 p. Illus. Bibliography: p. 133-144.
Anniversary edition in modern Bulgarian translation with excerpts from two similar contemporary histories. Dinekov has been editing Paisii since 1938.

Ivanov, Iordan, *ed.* Istoriia slavenobolgarskaia sobrana i narezhdena Paisiem ieromonakhom v leto 1762 (The Slaveno-Bulgarian history gathered and arranged by the priest-monk Paisii in the year 1762). Sofiia, Bŭlgarska akademiia na naukite, 1914. 91 p. Illus.
*The editio princeps* of Paisii's final draft, identified by Ivanov, comprising 82 pages in this edition.

Bŭlgarska akademiia na naukite. *Institut za istoriia.* Paisiĭ Khilendarski i negovata epokha. Sbornik ot izsledvaniia po sluchai 200- godishninata ot istoriia slavianobŭlgarska 1762-1962. (Paisiĭ Khilendarski and his age; a collection of studies on the occasion of the 200th anniversary of the Slaveno-Bulgarian history 1762-1962). Sofiia, 1962. 647 p. *See also* entry no. 581.

Among the 17 widely ranging studies in this collection, edited by Dmitŭr Kosev and others, half concern Paisii's written work. Among these are Man'o Stoianov's first complete description of all known Paisii manuscripts (p. 577-598) and a review by V. Traikov and I. Duichev of all printed references to Paisii (p. 605-644). Of special interest is Asen Vasiliev's monograph on 18th century Bulgarian painting (p. 465-556, with 65 plates). Summaries in German or French are provided.

Here also may be noted *200 Jahre Paisij, 1762-1962* (Frankfurt, Deutsche-Bulgarische Gesellschaft, 1962, 172 p.).

864. Vazov, Ivan M.   Pŭlno sŭbranie sŭchineniiata na Ivan Vazov (Complete collection of Ivan Vazov's works). Sofiia, Paskalev, 1921-1922. 28 v.

The collected works of Bulgaria's most prolific and popular author. The first English translation of Vazov's *Pod Igoto* (Under the yoke) was published in London in 1894. Several editions of a new translation by M. Aleksieva and T. Atanasova were published in Sofia in 1955, 1960, and 1964. *See* also his *Selected Stories* (Sofia, Foreign Languages Press, 1967, 181 p.). An analysis of three of Vazov's novels is offered in Wolfgang Gesemann's *Die Romankunst Ivan Vazovs; Epische Studien* (München, Sagner, 1966, 131 p., Slavistiche Beiträge, 16).

Biographic and bibliographic works:

Christophorov, Petr.   Ivan Vazov; la formation d'un écrivain bulgare (1850-1921). Paris, Droz, 1938. 245 p. Bibliography: p. 212-238. (Travaux publiés par l'Institut d'études slaves, 17) Complete biography including a chronological list of Vazov's works, 1870-1921 (p. 212-235) and bibliography (p. 236-238).

Moscow.   Vsesoiuznaia gosudarstvennaia biblioteka inostrannoi literatury.   Ivan Vazov; bibliograficheskii ukazatel' (Ivan Vazov; a bibliographic list). Prepared by L. P. Likhachev. Moskva, Izd-vo knizhnoi palaty, 1962. 174 p.

865. Sofronii Vrachanski.

Kiselkov, V. S.   Sofronii Vrachanski; zhivot i tvorchestvo (Sofronii Vrachanski; life and work). Sofiia, Bŭlgarska akademiia na naukite, 1963. 229 p. Illus.

A thoroughly critical study by the author of many works of literary history.

Léger, Louis, *translator*.   La Bulgarie à la fin du XVIIIe siècle; mémoires de Sofrony. *In* École des langues orientales vivantes; IIe serie. 9. Mélanges orientaux. Paris, 1883. p. 389-429.

Apparently still the only translation in a Western language. Léger was the first French Slavist to deal extensively with Bulgarian literature. See also *Sbornik v chest i v pamet na Lui Lezhe, 1843-1923* (Collection in honor of and in memory of Louis Léger, 1843-1923), edited by Ben'o Tsonev and others (Sofiia, Dŭrzhavna pechatnitsa, 1925, 325 p.).

Nicheva, Keti.  Ezikŭt na Sofronieviia "Nedelnik" v istoriiata na bŭlgarskiia knizhoven ezik (The language of Sofronii's "Nedelnik" in the history of the Bulgarian literary language). Sofiia, Bŭlgarska akademiia na naukite, 1965. 247 p.
A thorough study of the first printed book (1806).

Oreshkov, Pavel N.  Avtobiografiia na Sofronii Vrachanski (Autobiography of Sofronii Vrachanski). Sofiia, Bŭlgarska akademiia na naukite, 1914. 119 p. (Bŭlgarska biblioteka, 9)
The original text with modern Bulgarian translation. A handsomely illustrated modern Bulgarian edition is *Zhitie i stradanie* (Life and sufferings) (Sofiia, Bŭlgarski pisatel, 1966, 53 p.).

# D. FOLKLORE

## 1. Survey Studies and Anthologies

866. Angelov, Bozhan, and Khristo Vakarelski.   Senki iz nevidelitsa; kniga na bŭlgarskata narodna balada (Shades from nowhere; a book of the Bulgarian popular ballad). Sofiia, Dŭrzhavna pechatnitsa, 1936. 496 p.

————.   Trem na bŭlgarskata narodna istoricheska epika ot Momchila i Krali Marko do Karadzhata i Khadzhi Dimitra (Course of Bulgarian folk historical epic from Momchil and Krali Marko to Karadzhata and Khadzhi Dimitŭr). Sofiia, Chipev, 1939. 552 p.

————.   Kniga na narodnata lirika ot sedenkite i khorata do semeinite radosti i nevoli (Book of folk lyricism from evening gatherings and dances to family joys and adversities). Sofiia, 1946. 462 p.
An important trilogy with full notes and references by an expert folklorist and a leading ethnographer. For a bio-bibliography of Angelov *see* "Bozhan Angelov" in *Literaturni statii* (Literary articles), edited by Ivan Bogdanov (Sofiia, Bŭlgarski pisatel, 1960), p. 5-20.
Vakarelski's notable Bulgarian ethnography has recently become available in a German translation, *Deutsche Volkskunde* (Berlin, De Gruyter, 1969, 451 p., maps, music, plates).

867. Arnaudov, Mikhail, *and others, eds.*   Bŭlgarsko narodno tvorchestvo (Bulgarian folk creation). Sofiia, Bŭlgarski pisatel, 1961-1965. 13 v.
A definitive collection. Each large volume (averaging around 700 pages) comprises a separate category of folklore poetry and prose, with a separate title page and a specialist editor, and with extensive introduction and notes.

868. Arnaudov, Mikhail.   Ocherki po bŭlgarskiia folklor (Outlines of Bulgarian folklore). Sofiia, Ministerstvo na narodnoto prosveshtenie, 1934. 695 p.

Basic history and analysis of the various categories of folklore and folk customs. Arnaudov, Bulgaria's most prolific scholar and editor, since before the First World War has been producing massive biographies of leading writers and churchmen of the revival period, voluminous anthologies of folklore material, and monographs on literature and folklore. Among his most recent works is *Baladni motivi v narodnata poezia: I. Pesenta za delba na dvama bratia* (Ballad motifs in folk poetry: I. The song about partition between two brothers) (Sofiia, Bŭlgarska akademiia na naukite, 1964, 399 p.).

869. Bernard, Henry, E. J. Dillon, *and* Pencho Slaveikov.   The Shade of the Balkans; Being a Collection of the Bulgarian Folksongs and Proverbs. London, David Nutt, 1904. 327 p.

In this collaboration, Dillon did the history and language, and the noted poet Slaveikov, a sketch of Bulgarian folksongs (p. 25-87). A small English anthology, compiled and translated by Elizabeth Mincoff-Marriage, is *Bulgarian Folksongs* (Sofia, 1945, 88 p.).

870. Dinekov, Petŭr.   Bŭlgarski folklor (Bulgarian folklore). Sofiia, Bŭlgarski pisatel, 1959–

An important work, planned for two volumes, by the folklore authority second only to Arnaudov.

871. Dinekov, Petŭr, *ed.*   Deloto na bratiia Miladinovi; bŭlgarski narodni pesni subrani ot bratiia Miladinovtsi Dimitriia i Konstantina i izdadeni ot Konstantina (The work of the Miladinov brothers; Bulgarian folksongs collected by the Miladinov brothers Dimitŭr and Konstantin and published by Konstantin). Sofiia, Bŭlgarski pisatel, 1961. 692 p.

Fourth anniversary edition of the most important 19th century collection, containing 674 songs gathered in Macedonia and originally published in Zagreb in 1861. An earlier edition was edited by Arnaudov (Sofiia, 1942, 571 p.), who also wrote their biography, *Bratiia Miladinovi* (The brothers Miladinov) (Sofiia, Bŭlgarska akademiia na naukite, 1943, 319 p.).

872. Dozon, August, *ed. and tr.*   Bŭlgarski narodni pesni (Bulgarian folksongs). Paris, Maisonneuve, 1875. 423 p. French translation, p. 147-332.

French consul in the Balkans, Dozon was ordered to investigate the controversy over the authenticity of Verkovich's *Veda Slavian* (Belgrad, 1874). He concluded in favor of Verkovich and against Louis Léger, who was eventually vindicated. Dozon also published translations of Serbian folk songs. On the Verkovich hoax, *see* I. D. Shishmanov's "Glück und Ende einer berühmten literarischen Mistification: Veda Slovena," in *Archiv für slavische Philologie*, v. 25, 1903.

873. Gesemann, Gerhard, *tr.*   Zweiundsiebzig Lieder des bulgarischen Volkes. Berlin, Wiking-Verlag, 1944. 146 p.

Put into German verse by a distinguished folklorist. An earlier German anthology is that of Pentscho Slawejkoff (Pencho Slaveikov),

*Bulgarische Volkslieder*, translated by Georg Adam (Leipzig, Parlapa-noff, 1919, 123 p.).

874. Ivanov, Iordan.   Bŭlgarski narodni pesni (Bulgarian folksongs). So-fiia, Bŭlgarska akademiia na naukite, 1959. 308 p.

> The noted scholar Ivanov, who lectured on folklore at the University, was working on this study when he died in 1947. Résumé in French.

875. Obreschkoff, Christo (Khristo Obreshkov).   Das bulgarsche Volkslied. Bern, Haupt, 1937. 106 p.

> Study based on about 5,500 folksongs.

876. Slaveĭkov, Pencho P., *comp.*   Kniga na pesnite; bŭlgarski narodni pesni (Book of songs; Bulgarian folk songs). Sofiia, Paskalev, 1922. 444 p.

> Anthology by Bulgaria's greatest poet, son of P. R. Slaveikov.

877. Strausz, Adolph, *ed. and tr.*   Bulgarische Volksdichtungen. Wien, Leipzig, Graeser, 1895. 518 p.

> Included are 169 songs, preceded by an extensive critical introduction reviewing all earlier Bulgarian folksong collections and the several categories of songs. Strausz also published *Die Bulgaren; ethnographische Studien* (Leipzig, 1898, 477 p.).

## 2. Proverbs and Tales

878. Craver, Elena Borikova.   Bulgarian Folk Tales. New York, Washington, Hollywood, 1964. 184 p.

> Collected from childhood memory and by correspondence. Well written.

879. Slaveĭkov, Petko R., *comp.*   Bŭlgarski pritchi ili poslovitsi (Bulgarian parables or proverbs). New edition by Mikhail Arnaudov. Sofiia, 1954. 643 p.

> Slaveikov, one of the earliest folklorists, published his collection in 1890. He had begun work on it in 1844. It is of lasting value.

## 3. Folk Music

880. Djoudjeff, Stoyan (Stoian Dzhudzev).   Rythme et mesure dans la musique populaire bulgare. Paris, Champion, 1931. 364 p. Bibliography: p. 360-364.

> A leading folk musicologist, Professor Dzhudzhev is author of a four-volume work on the theory of folk music (Sofiia, 1954-1961).

881. Katsarova, Raina D.   Bulgarian Folk Dances. Sofia, Science and Art, 1958. 167 p.

> Katsarova, one of the younger authorities on folk dance, is also author of *Dances of Bulgaria* (New York, Crown, 1951, 40 p.) and has published also in French and German.

882. Kremenliev, Boris A.   Bulgarian-Macedonian Folk Music. Berkeley, Los Angeles, University of California Press, 1952. 165 p. Bibliography: p. 144-155.

Comprehensive musicological analysis with over 200 musical examples. Full, unselective bibliography.

883. Stoin, Vasil, *comp.*   Narodni pesni ot Timok do Vita (Folk songs from the Timok to the Vit). Sofiia, Ministerstvo na narodno prosveshtenie, 1929. 1134 p.

An enormous work with scores of 4,076 folk songs and dances and a variety of indexes. Stoin was chief of the music division of the Ethnographic Museum. His other collections cover the rest of the country.

## E. THOUGHT, PHILOSOPHY, LEARNING

884. Arnaudov, Mikhail.   Istoriia na Sofiĭskiia universitet sv. Kliment Okhridski prez pŭrvoto mu polustoletie, 1888-1938 (History of St. Clement of Okhrid Sofia University during its first half century, 1888-1938). Sofiia, Pridvorna pechatnitsa, 1939. 647 p.

A companion to this is *Almanakh na Sofiiskiia universitet sv. Kliment Okhridski; zhivotopisni i knigopisni svedeniia za prepodavatelite* (Almanac of Sofia University; biographical and bibliographical information on the faculty) (Sofiia, 1940, 726 p.). About 700 faculty members, 1888-1939, are included. For a review of the University's history *see* Marin Pundeff's "The University of Sofia at Eighty," *Slavic Review*, September, 1968, p. 438-446.

885. Arnaudov, Mikhail.   Liuben Karavelov; zhivot, delo, epokha, 1834-1879 (Liuben Karavelov; life, work, epoch, 1834-1879). Sofiia, Bŭlgarska akademiia na naukite, 1964. 864 p.

The many-faceted life of Karavelov is minutely described by Bulgaria's most distinguished biographer. Includes his ideology and literary accomplishments. The preface is dated 1952; the manuscript was revised in 1959. The editor, Pantelei Zarev, asks the reader to overlook the author's ideological lapses.

886. Beševliev, Veselin, *and* Johannes Irmscher, *eds.*   Antike und Mittelalter in Bulgarien. Berlin, Akademie Verlag, 1960. 363 p. Plates, map. (Berliner byzantinische Arbeiten, 21)

*See also* entry no. 564.

Includes progress reports on Bulgarian research in various related fields, such as Ivan Duichev on medieval studies. The editors are leading classical specialists in Sofia and East Berlin, respectively. For status reports by qualified Bulgarian specialists on the prewar situation in a score of fields, see *Bulgaria; Jahrbuch 1940/41 der Deutsch-Bulgarischen Gesellschaft*, edited by Kurt Haucke (Berlin, Leipzig, 1941, 331 p.).

887. Dimitrov, Mikhail, *and others, eds.*   Georgi Stoĭkov Rakovski;

vŭzgledi, deinost i zhivot (Georgi Stoĭkov Rakovski; his ideas, work, and life). v. 1. Sofiia, Bŭlgarska akademiia na naukite, 1964. 439 p.

Seventeen contributors make the most of one of the chief architects of the Bulgarian national revival in fully documented studies. Table of contents also in English, French, and German.

888. Dimov, Georgi, *ed.* Ivan D. Shishmanov; izbrani sŭchineniia. I. Bŭlgarsko vŭzrazhdane. II. Folklor i etnografiia, literaturna teoriia, istoriia i kritika, statii po obshestveni i kulturni vŭprosi (Ivan D. Shishmanov; selected works. I. Bulgarian revival. II. Folklore and ethnography, literary theory, history and criticism, articles on public and cultural questions). Sofiia, Bŭlgarska akademiia na naukite, 1965-1966. 2 v. Bibliography: p. 505-515.

Shishmanov is Bulgaria's foremost scholar. No one did more than he to set the high level of new Bulgaria's intellectual and cultural life, as minister of education and especially as founder of the *Sbornik za narodni umotvoreniia, nauka i knizhnina* (Collection for folklore, learning, and literature (1889–). The collection contains many of his own many-sided contributions to scholarship. *See also* Georgi Dimov's *Ivan Shishmanov; literaturno-kriticheski ocherk* (Ivan Shishmanov, literary-critical survey) (Sofiia, 1964, 240 p.).

889. Grozev, Groziu. Istoriia na bŭlgarskata filosofiia (History of Bulgarian philosophy). Sofiia, Nauka i izkustvo, 1957-1959. 2 v.

More properly a textbook history of thought, the author, who teaches history of philosophy at the University of Sofia, begins with the ninth century. Volume 2 covers the Liberation to September 9, 1944. Although admitting a preference for Marxism, Grozev includes representatives of opposing points of view.

890. Khristov, Khristo, *and* Kiril Vasilev. Dimiter Blagoev; Lebensabriss. Sofia, Fremdsprachen Verlag, 1960. 113 p.

The collected works of the founder of the Bulgarian Communist Party are available in 20 volumes (Sofiia, 1957-1964). His bibliography was edited by Todor Borov and Khristo Khristov, and published as *Dimitŭr Blagoev; bibliografiia* (Sofiia, Nauka i izkustvo, 1954, 305 p.).

891. Mishev, Dimitŭr. The Bulgarians in the Past; Pages from the Bulgarian Cultural History. Lausanne, Librairie centrale des Nationalités, 1919. 478 p.

*See also* entry no. 556.

A poor translation of the Bulgarian original (Sofiia, Iskra, 1916, 492 p.), which, however, comes closest to a cultural history of Bulgaria. The author, long associated with the Bulgarian Exarchate, also used the name Draganof.

For a survey of Bulgarian contributions to European culture *see* Emil Georggiev's *Bulgarische Beiträge zur europäischen Kultur* (Sofia, Sofia-Press, 1968, 126 p., illus.).

892. Pavlov, Todor.   Izbrani proizvedeniia (Selected works). Sofiia, Bŭlgarska akademiia na naukite, 1957–
    Pavlov, first postwar Academy president, high Party member, and
    ranking Marxist philosopher, has expressed himself on a wide range
    of historical, literary, and other Bulgarian topics. See his "Some
    Topical Problems of Philosophy in Bulgaria," in *Political Transla-
    tions on Eastern Europe* (JPRS), no. 149, December 18, 1964.

893. Raleva, O., *comp.*   Bŭlgarskata akademiia na naukite sled 9 septemvri 1944; spravochna kniga (The Bulgarian Academy of Sciences
after September 9, 1944; reference book). Sofiia, Bŭlgarska akademiia
na naukite, 1958. 325 p. Bibliography: p. 307-311.
    A variety of useful information including a biobibliography of mem-
    bers and historical notes on the Academy (completely reorganized after
    1947) and its components.
    A wealth of statistical data for the period 1961-1964 is presented in:
    Bulgaria. *Tsentalno statistichesko upravlenie pri Ministerski suvet.*
    Obrazovanieto i naukata v Narodna republika Bulgariia (Education
    and learning in the People's Republic of Bulgaria). Sofiia, 1965. 621 p.

894. Savova, Elena, *ed.*   Les études balkaniques et sud-est européennes en
Bulgarie; guide de documentation. Sofia, Académie Bulgare des Sciences. Bibliotèque centrale, 1966. 184 p.
    *See also* entries no. 43 *and* 510.
    Invaluable descriptive directory of Bulgarian institutes, schools of
    higher learning, libraries, museums, archives, presses, etc., and their
    key personnel, together with a selected basic Bulgarian bibliography
    for the principal social sciences and humanities. The editor, a dis-
    tinguished bibliographer, is Director of the Academy Library. There
    is almost nothing "Balkan," in spite of the title.

895. Sbornik v chest na Akademik Aleksandŭr Teodorov-Balan po sluchai
devetdeset i petata mu godishnina (Volume in honor of Academician
Alexander Teodorov-Balan on the occasion of his 95th birthday).
Sofiia, Bŭlgarska akademiia na naukite, 1955. 435 p.
    Forty-seven mainly linguistic contributions for a scholar whose
    active career spanned almost the whole of modern Bulgaria. He was
    famous for his campaign for language purity, and for *Bŭlgarski
    knigopis za sto godini* (Bulgarian bibliography for 100 years) (Sofiia,
    1909, 1667 p.).

## F. RELIGION (OTHER THAN JUDAISM)

896. Antonoff, Nicolas, *and* Marin V. Pundeff.   Bulgaria; Churches and
Religion. Washington, D.C., Library of Congress, 1951. 53 p. (Mid-
European Law Project)

897. Duĭchev, Ivan.   Il cattolicesimo in Bulgaria nel secolo XVII secondo

i processi informativi sulla nomina del vescovi cattolici. Roma, 1937. 202 p. (Orientalia Christiana Analecta, 111)

Duichev is the chief authority on Roman Catholic-Bulgarian history. Another important work is his *Sofiiskata katolishka arkhiepiskopiia prez XVII vek; izuchavane i dokumenti* (The Sofiia Catholic Archdiocese in the 17th century; studies and documents) (Sofiia, 1939, 203 p.), which includes 47 documents in Italian, an Italian summary, and references and bibliography (p. 158-184). Another excellent archival study is by the late historian Nikola Milev, *Katolishkata propaganda v Bulgariia priez XVII viek* (Catholic propaganda in Bulgaria during the 17th century) (Sofiia, 1914, 193 p.), which includes the Bulgarian Paulicians. These were also the object of special attention by the philologist Liubomir Miletich in a number of studies.

898. Fermendžin, Eusebius, *ed.* Acta Bulgariae ecclesiastica ab a. 1565 usque ad a. 1799. Zagreb, 1887. (Monumenta spectantia historiam Slavorum meridionalium, 18)

Important collection of sources for the history of Roman Catholicism in Bulgaria.

899. Girard, André. Les minorités nationales, ethniques et réligieuses en Bulgarie. Paris, 1932. 203 p.

A dissertation.

900. Hall, William W. Puritans in the Balkans; the American Board Mission in Bulgaria, 1878-1918. Sofia, 1938. 280 p. Bibliography: p. 273-280. (Studia historico-philologica serdicensia. Supplementi, 1)

A Yale dissertation, this is a factual narrative with introductory chapters describing the period before 1878. *See also* James F. Clarke's "Protestantism and the Bulgarian Church Question in 1861" in *Essays in the History of Modern Europe*, edited by D. C. McKay (New York, Harper, 1936), p. 79-97.

901. Kiril, *Patriarkh.* Katolicheskata propaganda sred Bŭlgarite prez vtorata polovina na XIX vek. 1859-1865 (Catholic propaganda among the Bulgarians during the second half of the 19th century, 1859-1865). Sofiia, Sinodalno izdatelstvo, 1962. 472 p.

On the author as historian, *see* Irenaeus Doens, "Patriarch Kiril, Kirchenhistoriker Bulgariens," in *Österreichische Osthefte*, v. 7, no. 4, 1965: 322-331. For a Catholic view, *see* Ivan Sofranov's *Histoire du mouvement bulgare vers l'Église catholique au XIX siècle. I. 1855-65* (Rome, Bibliothèque catholique bulgare, 1960, 400 p.).

902. Mach, Richard von. The Bulgarian Exarchate, Its History and the Extent of Its Authority in Turkey. London, 1907. 105 p.

Translation of *Der Machtbereich des bulgarischen Exarchats in der Türkei* (Leipzig, 1906) by a longtime Balkan scholar.

The establishment of the Exarchate is described in enormous biographies of the first two exarchs: Patriarch Kiril's *Eksarkh Antim*

(1816-1888) (Sofiia, Sinodalno knigoizdatelstvo, 1956, 953 p.), and M. Arnaudov's *Eksarkh Iosif* (1870-1915) (Sofiia, Sv. Sinod na bŭlgarskata tsŭrkva, 1940, 666 p.). These are two of several biographies of churchmen authored by Patriarch Kiril and Arnaudov.

903. Nemeth, Julius. Die Türken von Vidin; Sprache, Folklore, Religion. Budapest, Akadémiai Kiadó, 1965. 419 p. (Bibliotheca Orientalis Hungarica, 10)

> In the first part the author describes the Turkish dialect; in the second part, the folk literature, customs, and popular religion of this minority.

904. Sharenkoff, Victor N. A Study of Manichaeism in Bulgaria, with Special Reference to the Bogomils. New York, Columbia University Press, 1927. 83 p.

> Includes translated selections from the principal Bogomil writings. In Bulgaria, among others, Dimitŭr Angelov, the Byzantine historian, has written *Bogomilstvoto v Bŭlgariia. Proizkhod sŭshtnost i razprostranenie* (Bogomilism in Bulgaria; origin, nature, and spread) (2d ed.: Sofiia, 1961, 196 p.).

905. Slijepčević, Đoko M. Die bulgarische orthodoxe Kirche 1944-1956. München, Oldenbourg, 1957. 67 p. (Untersuchungen zur Gegenwartskunde Südosteuropas, 1)

> Review of developments since the communist takeover, with special reference to the new church constitution of December 31, 1950.

906. Vŭrgov, Khristo V. Konstitutsiia na bŭlgarskata pravoslavna tsŭrkva; istoriia i razvoi na ekzarkhiĭskiia ustav, 1871-1921 (Constitution of the Bulgarian Orthodox Church; history and development of the exarchate statute). Sofiia, Dŭrzhavna pechatnitsa, 1920. 630 p.

907. Zankow (Tsankov), Stefan. Die Grundlagen der Verfassung der bulgarischen orthodoxen Kirche. Zürich, Leemann, 1918. 156 p.

————. Die Verwaltung der bulgarischen orthodoxen Kirche. Halle, 1920.

> In the first of these two books, history, constitution, and church-state relations are considered. Tsankov, a prominent Bulgarian theologian and ecumenical thinker, also wrote *The Eastern Orthodox Church* (2d ed.: Paris, Student Christian Movement Press, 1930).

## G. EDUCATION

908. Apanasewicz, Nellie M., *and* Seymour M. Rosen. Education in Bulgaria. Washington, D.C., U.S. Government Printing Office, 1965. 27 p. (U.S. Office of Education, Studies in Comparative Education)

> See also Irwin T. Sanders' "Communist-Dominated Education in Bulgaria: a Study in Social Relationships" in *American Slavic and East European Review*, v. 15, 1956: 364-381. For a critical examina-

tion of the postwar system of general education to the eighth grade, including the 1959 reforms, *see* Peter John Georgeoff, *The Social Education of Bulgarian Youth.* Minneapolis, Minn., University of Minnesota Press, 1968. 329 p.

909. Atanasov, Zhecho, *and* Petŭr Dinekov, *eds.* Petŭr Beron; izsledvaniia i materiali (Peter Beron; studies and materials). Sofiia, Bŭlgarska akademiia na naukite, 1962. 241 p. Illus. Bibliography: p. 189-236.

> Beron, author of the first school book, was also the foremost pre-liberation scientist. An older work, edited by Khristo Negentsov and N. T. Balabanov is *Sbornik Dr. Petŭr Beron; po sluchai stogodishninata na Ribniia Bukvar, 1824-1924* (Collection on Dr. Peter Beron; on the occasion of the centennial of the first primer, 1824-1924) (Sofiia, Dŭrzhavna pechatnitsa, 1925, 148 p.). The work contains a bibliographical description of his scientific works in French (p. 141-148).

910. Black, Floyd H. The American College of Sofia. Boston, Trustees of the Sofia American Schools, 1958. 95 p.

> The last president of the school gives its history from 1860 to 1942.

911. Chakŭrov, Naĭden, *and* Zhecko Atanasov. Istoriia na obrazovanieto i pedagogicheskata misŭl v Bŭlgariia (History of education and pedagogical thought in Bulgaria). 2d ed. Sofiia, Nauka i izkustvo, 1962. 432 p.

> One of several such books by two prominent professors of education. A standard work. *See also* Marin Pundeff's article "80 Jahre Universität Sofia (Österreichische Osthefte, v. 10, no. 6, 1968, p. 329-339).

912. Chilingirov, Stiliian. Bŭlgarski chitalishta predi osvobozhdenieto; prinos kŭm istoriiata na bŭlgarskoto vŭzrazhdane (Bulgarian reading rooms before the liberation; contribution to the history of the Bulgarian rebirth). Sofiia, Ministerstvo na narodnoto prosveshtenie, 1930. 683 p.

> The multifaceted activity of the adult education clubs with descriptions of 131 of them. The standard work.

913. Paskaleva, Virzhiniia. Bŭlgarkata prez vŭzrazhdaneto; istoricheski ocherk (The Bulgarian woman during the revival; historical sketch). Sofiia, Bŭlgarska komunisticheska partiia, 1964. 314 p. Bibliography: p. 286-292.

> *See also* entry no. 790.

> A straightforward account largely of female education and teachers by one of the most promising younger historians. A German summary is provided.

914. Russell, William F. Schools in Bulgaria, with Special Reference to the Influence of the Agrarian Party on Elementary and Secondary

Education. New York, Teachers College, Columbia University, 1924. 101 p. (Studies of the International Institute, 1)

> Largely the views and policies of Stoian Omarchevski, Minister of Education in Aleksandŭr Stamboliiski's government. Omarchevski himself contributed on "Bulgaria" to the *Educational Yearbook*, edited by I. L. Kandel (Teachers College, Columbia University, 1931, p. 97-124; 1937, p. 59-84).

915. Tschauschov, Slave P.    Die Entwicklung des bulgarischen Bildgungswesens. Halle, 1944. 120 p.

> One of many similar works in German or French, mostly dissertations.

## H. THE FINE ARTS

### 1. General Works

916. Draganov, Kŭncho I., Mikhail G. Raĭchev, *and* Stancho R. Stanchev. Muzei i pametnitsi v Narodna Republika Bŭlgariia; vodach (Museums and monuments in the People's Republic of Bulgaria; a guide). Sofiia, Nauka i izkustvo, 1959. 655 p. Illus.

> Organized regionally.

917. Filov, Bogdan.    Geschichte der altbulgarischen Kunst bis zur Eroberung des bulgarischen Reiches durch die Türken. Berlin, de Gruyter, 1932. 100 p. Illus. (Grundriss der slavischen Philologie und Kulturgeschichte, 10)

————.    Geschichte der bulgarischen Kunst unter der Türkenherrschaft und in der neueren Zeit. Berlin, de Gruyter, 1933. 94 p. Illus.

> Originally published in English, French, and German in 1919 (*Early Bulgarian Art*, Bern, Haupt, 86 p., illus.) and reprinted in a French edition *L'ancien art bulgare* (Paris, Alcan, 1922). An enlarged second edition was published in Bulgarian (Sofiia, 1924, 128 p.). Filov pioneered the history of Bulgarian art. One of Bulgaria's most distinguished scholars, he was executed in 1944.

918. Krŭstev, Kiril, *and* Vassil Zakhariev.    Old Bulgarian Painting. Translated by Alexander Rizov. Sofia, Bŭlgarski hudozhnik, 1961. 47 p. Illus.

> Excellent album. Bulgarian editions were published in 1959 and 1961. A German edition was published in 1960. Krŭstev was responsible for the medieval portion and Zakhariev, himself a distinguished artist, for the Ottoman and national revival periods. On Zakhariev, author of other works on art history, *see* P. Datscheff's *Vasil Zakhariev* (Dresden, Verlag der Kunst, 1961).

### 2. Painting

#### a. Medieval

919. Grabar', Andrei (André Grabar).    La peinture religieuse en Bul-

garie. Paris, Geuthner, 1928. 396 p. Illus. (Orient et Byzance, 1)
> Grabar is the foremost authority on medieval Bulgarian and Balkan painting.

920. Medieval Bulgarian Culture; the Art of the Medieval Bulgarian Capitals Pliska, Preslav, and Turnovo. Sofia, Bŭlgarski hudozhnik, 1963. 280 p. Illus.
> To commemorate the eleven-hundredth anniversary of the Bulgarian (Slavic) script. Not to be confused with *Medieval Bulgarian Culture* (Sofia, Foreign Language Press, 1964, 139 p.), an odd collection of monographic articles by leading art historians.

921. Miiatev, Krŭstiu.   Boianskite stenopisi; monografiia (The Boiana frescoes; monograph). Sofiia, Bŭlgarski khudozhnik, 1961. 91 p. Illus.
> A fine album by a distinguished author deceased in 1966. German translation by Michail Matliev as *Die Wandmalereien in Bojana* (Dresden, Verlag der Kunst, 1961, 95 p.).

922. Monumenta artis Bulgariae.
> This important illustrated series by the Bulgarian Academy of Sciences includes the following volumes:

> 1. Grabar', Andrei (André Grabar).   L'église de Boiana. Sofia, 1924.

> 2. Rachenov, A.   Églises de Mesembria. Sofia, 1932.

> 3. Filov, Bogdan.   Les miniatures de l'évangile du roi Jean Alexandre à Londres. Sofia, 1934.

> 4. Miatev, Kiril.   Die Keramik von Preslav. Sofia, 1936.

923. Panaĭotova, Dora.   Peintures murales bulgares du XIVe siècle. Translated by Stoian Tzonev and Nicolas Pouliev. Sofia, Langues étrangères, 1966. 217 p. Illus.
> The author is a qualified architect and art historian.

924. United Nations Education, Scientific, and Cultural Organization. Bulgaria: Medieval Wall Paintings. Greenwich, Conn., 1962. 26 p. Illus. (UNESCO World Art Series, 17)
> Splendid reproductions of 12th to 15th century frescoes from Bachkovo, Boiana, Zemen, Ivanovo, Tŭrnovo, and Kremikovtsi. Text by André Grabar and Krŭstiu Miiatev.

### b. Modern

925. Mavrodinoff, Nikola.   Modern Bulgarian Art. Sofia, Ministry of Information and Arts, 1946. 49 p. Illus.
> Confined to pictorial art since the 18th century. Mavrodinov was director of the National Museum and author of numerous works on art history, among them *Izkustvoto na bŭlgarskoto vŭzrazhdane* (Art of the Bulgarian revival) (Sofiia, Nauka i izkustvo, 1957, 458 p.).

926. Toncheva, Mara.   Bŭlgarsko vŭzrazhdane. Zhivopis i grafika (The

Bulgarian revival; painting and graphics). Sofiia, Bŭlgarski khudozhnik, 1962. 113 p. Illus.

> A splendid work by an artist, professor, and productive art historian.
> The revival period greatly attracts historians of art as it does those of
> literature.

927. Vasiliev, Asen.  Bŭlgarski vŭzrozhdenski maistori; zhivopistsi, rez-
bari, stroiteli (Bulgarian revival masters; painters, wood carvers,
builders). Sofiia, Nauka i izkustvo, 1965. 748 p. Illus. Bibliography:
p. 693-697.

> Vasiliev himself is the master of premodern art history, especially
> ecclesiatical and monastic.

## 3. Architecture

928. Bichev, Milko.  Architecture in Bulgaria from Ancient Times to
the Late Nineteenth Century. Translated by Alexander Rizov. Sofia,
Foreign Language Press, 1961. 80 p. Illus.

> Extends to the liberation (1878).

929. Studies in Bulgaria's Architectural Heritage.   Sofia, Bulgarian
Academy of Sciences, Institute of Urbanism and Architecture, 1952–

> Monographic series published in Bulgarian, German, and English.
> Volume 4, by Georgi Stoĭkov, deals with the Church of Boiana (1954,
> 87 p.). Volume 6, by Khristo Khristov and others, deals with the his-
> tory, architecture, frescoes, and wood carvings of the Rila Monastery
> (1959, 318 p.).

## 4. Folk Art

930. Veleva, Maria G., *and* E. I. Lepavtsova.   Bulgarian Folk Costumes.
v. 1. Bulgarian Folk Costumes of North Bulgaria in the Nineteenth
and Early Twenties Centuries. Sofia, Bulgarian Academy of Sciences,
1961. Illus., map.

> The Bulgarian original was published in 1960; there is also a French
> edition. The bulk of this volume consists of color plates of sketches
> of male and female costume, followed by extensive notes on dress
> and hair styles. On the art of embroidery *see* Rositsa Chukanova's
> *Bulgarische Volkstickerei: West Bulgarien* (Sofia, Bŭlgarski khudozh-
> nik, 1957, 135 col. plates). The compiler was herself an accomplished
> master of the art.

## I. THEATER AND CINEMA

931. Derzhavin, Konstantin N.   Bolgarskii teatr; ocherk istorii (Bulgarian
theater; outline of history). Moscow, Leningrad, Izkustvo, 1950. 458
p. Illus.

> A useful survey by the son of N. S. Derzhavin, long a Soviet au-
> thority on Bulgaria.

932. Ionova, Violette, *tr.* Le centième anniversaire du théâtre bulgare, 1856-1956. Sofia, Nauka i izkustvo, 1956. 160 p.

A more elaborate anniversary volume is *Sto godini bŭlgarski teatur, 1856-1956* (100 years of Bulgarian theater, 1856-1956), edited by D. P. Mitov, Pencho Penev, and Liubomir Tenev (Sofiia, Nauka i izkustvo, 1956, 354 p.). It includes historical and critical essays and reminiscences of prominent artists. Professor Penev has written extensively on theatrical history; the other editors, on criticism.

933. Kino-izkustvoto v Bŭlgariia; filmografiia i drugi spravochni materiali (The cinema art in Bulgaria; filmography and other reference materials). Sofiia, Nauka i izkustvo, 1960. 128 p.

934. Popov, Ivan P. Minaloto na bŭlgarskiia teatŭr (The past of the Bulgarian theater). Sofiia, 1939-1960. 5 v.

Most extensive body of materials on the modern theater by a former actor.

## J. MUSIC

### by Miloš Velimirović

### 1. Reference Aids

935. Braschowanow, Stojan. Bulgarische Musik. *In* Musik in Geschichte und Gegenwart; allgemeine Enzyklopädie der Musik. Friedrich Blume, *ed.* v. 2. Kassel, Bärenreiter-Verlag, 1950. cols. 453-461.

The first section of this article deals with folk music. Sections 2 ("Kunstmusik") and 3 ("Die mehrstimmige Tonkunst") are of primary importance for musicologists. This is the most extensive presentation of Bulgarian music in any of the Western languages in any of the available encyclopedias. The coverage ends, however, with the year 1950, at a time when a new outburst of publications was about to begin.

Similar in scope is the article "Bulgaria" by Dieter Lehmann in *Enciclopedia della musica*, v. 1 (Milano, Ricordi, 1963), p. 338-339.

936. Bŭlgariia. XX-Muzika (Bulgaria [pt.] 20-Music). *In* Kratka bŭlgarska entsiklopediia, v. 1. Sofiia, Bŭlgarska akademiia na naukite, 1963. p. 398-400.

A survey of the history of Bulgarian music as well as of contemporary activities.

937. Entsiklopediia na bŭlgarskata muzikalna kultura (Encyclopedia of Bulgarian musical culture). Chief editor, Venelin Krŭstev. Sofiia, Bŭlgarska akademiia na naukite, 1967. 465 p. Illus., notes.

The most comprehensive one-volume collection of materials on music in Bulgaria. This work, first-rate in execution, consists of two parts: The first (p. 9-160) contains essays on a multitude of aspects of Bulgarian music; the second (p. 163-459) is an alphabetical dictionary, many entries of which are followed by extensive bibliographies.

938. Kamburov, Ivan D. Iliustrovan muzikalen rechnik (An illustrated musical dictionary). Sofiia, 1933.

## 2. Serials

939. Bŭlgarska akademiia na naukite, *Sofia. Institut za muzika.* Izvestiia (News). 1952– Sofiia. Irregular.

Originally intended as an annual publication, the volumes published so far are as follows: v. 1, 1952, 218 p.; v. 2/3, 1956 (covering 1955), 543 p.; v. 4, 1957, 271 p.; v. 5, 1959, 307 p.; v. 6, 1959, 251 p.; v. 7, 1961 (covering 1960), 260 p.; v. 8, 1962, 257 p.; v. 9, 1963, 227 p.; v. 10, 1964, 276 p., and v. 11, 1965, 235 p. The studies deal more or less equally with folk music and artistic music; some are truly outstanding. Among the most interesting studies are those by L. Brashovanova on Kukuzeles (v. 6) and by S. Lazarov on a medieval musical manuscript (v. 7).

940. Bŭlgarska muzika (Bulgarian music). 1948– Sofiia. 10 issues a year. Title varies: 1948-1953, *Muzika.*

941. Coover, James B. A Bibliography of East European Music Periodicals; I. Bulgaria. *In* Fontes Artis Musicae. v. 3. Kassel, Bärenreiter-Verlag, 1956. p. 223-226.

A listing of 57 periodicals dealing with music.

## 3. History of Music

942. Ivanov, A. T. Chitalishteto — sredishte na muzikalna deĭnost (Reading rooms — centers for musical activity). *In* Sto godini Narodno chitalishte-Svishtov (One hundred years of the Svishtov People's Reading Room). Svishtov, 1958. p. 367-426.

An analysis of the role of public libraries as gathering places in which vocal and instrumental talent was developed.

943. Krŭstev, Venelin. Ocherki vŭrkhu razvitieto na bŭlgarskata muzika (Outline of the development of Bulgarian music). v. 1. Sofiia, Nauka i izkustvo, 1954. 376 p. Illus., ports., music.

Covers the period from the Middle Ages to the 20th century. The second volume, so far as is known, has not yet appeared. The same author recently edited a volume entitled *Izbrani stranitsi iz bŭlgarskoto muzikalno nasledstvo* (Selected pages from the Bulgarian musical heritage) (Sofiia, 1963).

944. Krŭstev, Venelin. Puti razvitiia bolgarskoĭ muzykal'noĭ kul'tury v period XII-XVIII stoletiĭ (The path of development of Bulgarian musical culture in the period from the 12th to the 18th century). *In* Lissa, Zofia, *ed.* Musica Antiqua Europae Orientalis. Warszawa, Państwowe Wydawnictwo Naukowe, 1966. p. 45-65.

945. Petrov, Stoian V. Ochertsi po istoriia na bŭlgarskata muzikalna kul-

tura (Essays on the history of musical culture in Bulgaria). v. 1. Sofiia, Nauka i izkustvo, 1959. Illus., ports., music.

## 4. Special Aspects, Personalia

946. Krŭstev, Venelin.   Dobri Khristov; populiaren ocherk (Dobri Khristov; popular sketch). Sofiia, Nauka i izkustvo, 1961. 65 p. Port. (Biblioteka "Bŭlgarski kompozitori," 3)

> One of a series of monographs about individual composers. In the same series is Andrei Andreiev's book on Panaiot Pipkov (1952, 52 p.).

947. Sagaev, Liubomir.   Bŭlgarskoto operno tvorchestvo (Bulgarian operas). Sofiia, Nauka i izkustvo, 1958. 160 p. Illus., ports.

> Bulgarian operatic productions usually receive thorough coverage in any surveys of the history of music in Bulgaria. This monograph, however, is the only survey of opera through recent times. The beginnings of operatic life in Bulgaria are discussed in a dissertation (Vienna Univesity, 1950) by Evgeniia Pancheva: *Die Entwicklung der Oper in Bulgarien von ihren Anfängen bis 1915, unter Berücksichtigung der ersten Nationalopern* published in German in Vienna (1962). Another dissertation (Köln, 1944) by Krŭstju Mirsky, *Die Anfänge des bulgarischen Theaters bis zur Bildung der ersten Berufstruppe (1841-1883)*, appears to have remained unpublished. Sagaev's book concentrates on the work of G. Atanasov (p. 67-104); the period after Atanasov is covered in one chapter (p. 105-143).

948. Stŭrshenov, Bogomil. Bŭlgarskoto simfonichno izkustvo (Bulgarian symphonic art). Sofiia, Suiuz na bŭlgarskite kompozitori, 1964. 63 p.

> The first monograph dealing exclusively with a description of symphonies by Bulgarian composers.

# part four

# GREECE

The transliteration of the Greek alphabet presents a thorny problem. Of the several transliteration systems in use, each has its shortcomings, and none has found general acceptance. As a pragmatic expedient, we have followed here the system of the Library of Congress, with certain departures suggested by our consultants. The transliteration table at the beginning of this book should orient the reader and enable him to reconstruct the original Greek version of listings.

# 26

## GENERAL
## REFERENCE AIDS
## AND
## BIBLIOGRAPHIES

*by George E. Perry*

### A. BIBLIOGRAPHIES

#### 1. Bibliographies of Bibliographies

949. Phousaras, G. I.   Vivliographia tōn Hellēnikōn vivliographiōn, 1791-1947 (Bibliography of Greek bibliographies, 1791-1947). Athēnai, Vivliopōleion tēs "Hestias," 1961. 284 p.

Includes bibliographies on Greek subjects or composed by Greeks. Contains 1,616 entries arranged in eight subject categories. Indexes of authors, subjects, date of publication, and place of publication are provided.

#### 2. Bibliographies of Monographs, Periodicals, and Newspapers

950. Bulletin analytique de bibliographie hellénique. v. 6– 1945– Athènes, 1947–

Frequency varies. Issued by the Institut français d'Athènes. Published with delay, the volume covering 1962 having been published in 1966.

213

Each volume consists of two parts, the first listing monographic literature with the title in the original language preceded by its French
translation, with most entries annotated. Periodicals are listed in the
second part, with the contents of most issues described in detail. Arrangement is by subject. Index of names in each volume. Volumes 1-5
(covering 1940-1944) and volume 6, fascicle 2-3 (dealing with periodicals issued in 1945) not yet published.

951. Deltion Hellēnikēs vivliographias (Bulletin of Greek bibliography).
1960– Athēnai, Ek tou Ethnikou Typographeiou. Quarterly.

Published also in English under the title *Greek Bibliography*, and
in French as *Bulletin de bibliographie hellénique*. Although the three
editions have the same numbering, they are not published simul-
taneously, and there is some variation in content among them. Eighteen
numbers of the Greek language edition have appeared to date, covering the period from 1959 to 1964. Lists books published in Greece
and books about Greece published abroad. Some periodical and annual publications are also listed. Coverage is selective, the emphasis
being on materials reflecting Greek achievements in the arts and
sciences. The material is arranged by the Dewey decimal classification.
Author and other indexes with each volume.

952. Dēmaras, Kōnstantinos Th. (C. Th. Dimaras), Aikaterinē Koumarianou
(C. Coumariano), *and* Loukia Droulia. La Grèce moderne et sa littérature; orientation bibliographique en allemand, anglais, français,
italien. Athènes, 1966. 81 p.

Lists Western-language works on Modern Greece and its cultural
life as well as translations of Greek works. Includes a listing of periodicals in English, French, and German devoted entirely or in part to
Greek studies. Author index. Sponsored by Comité national hellénique
de l'Association internationale d'études du sud-est européen. New
enlarged edition: *Modern Greek Culture; a Selected Bibliography, in
English, French, German, Italian*. Thessaloniki, Institute for Balkan
Studies, 1968. 137 p.

See also *Quinze ans de bibliographie historique en Grèce (1950-
1964), avec une annexe pour 1965* (Athènes, 1966, 266 p.), which lists
chronologically 5,500 selected monographs and reprints of periodical
articles in Greek and in Western languages. Greek titles are translated
into French. Author and subject indexes.

953. Ghinēs (Nkinēs), Dēmētrios S., *and* Valerios G. Mexas. Hellēnikē
vivliographia, 1800-1863. Anagraphē tōn kata tēn chronikēn tau-
tēn periodon hopou dēpote Hellēnisti ekdothentōn vivliōn kai entypōn
en genei (Greek bibliography, 1800-1863. Record of books and printed
matter in general published in Greek anywhere during this period).
Athēnai, Grapheion Dēmosieumatōn tēs Akadēmias Athēnōn, 1939-
1957. 3 v. (Pragmateiai tēs Akadēmias Athēnōn, tomos 11)

A continuation of Legrand (entry no. 956). Contains about 10,939
titles arranged chronologically, and within each year alphabetically
by title. Name index for the entire work in volume 3.

For additions to the Greek bibliography for 1800-1863, *see* articles in the periodical *Ho Eranistēs*, v. 1, 1963, p. 51-55, 243-265; v. 2, 1964, p. 127-134, 249-252; and v. 3, 1965, p. 119-124, 199-214, 249-270. Newspapers and periodicals for 1811-1863 are listed in:

Ghinēs (Nkinēs), D. S. Katalogos Hellēnikōn ephēmeridōn kai periodikōn 1811-1863 (Catalog of Greek newspapers and periodicals, 1811-1863). 2d ed. Athēnai, Kentron Neoellēnikōn Hereunōn V.I.E., 1967. 33 p.

954. Greece. *Genikon symvoulion vivliothēkōn.* Hellēnikē vivliographia; katalogos tōn en tēi Ethnikēi vivliothēkēi kata nomon katatetheimenōn antitypōn. Etos 1930; teuchos 1-9, 1931-39 (Greek bibliography; catalog of materials deposited according to law in the National Library. Year 1930; no. 1-9, 1931-39). Athēnai, Typographeion S. K. Vlastou, 1934-1940. 10 v. (Genikon symvoulion vivliothēkōn tēs Hellados. [Dēmosieumata] 5-6, 8-9, 11, 14-15, 17-18)

————. Katalogos tōn en tēi Ethnikēi vivliothēkēi kai tēs Voulēs kata nomon katatetheimenōn antitypōn. Symplērōmatikon teuchos tōn etōn 1930-1934 (Catalog of materials deposited according to law in the National Library and the Library of the Chamber of Deputies. Supplementary number for the years 1930-1934). Athēnai, Ek tou Ethnikou Typographeiou, 1937. 107 p. (Genikon symvoulion vivliothēkōn tēs Hellados. [Dēmosieumata] 13)

Issued by the General Council of Libraries of Greece, listing books and periodicals published from 1930 through 1939. Entries grouped under 13 subject headings. Author and subject indexes for each volume.

955. Koromēlas, Dēmētrios A. Catalogue des livres publiés en Grèce depuis 1868 jusqu'en 1872. Athènes, Impr. A. Coromilas, 1878. 172 p.

————. Catalogue des livres publiés en Grèce depuis 1873 jusqu'à 1877. Athènes, Impr. A. Coromilas, 1878. 232 p.

The volume for 1868-1872 contains about 650 entries, that for 1873-1878 approximately 1,250 entries. Arrangement in both is chronological, and within each year entries are arranged by classes. Both volumes list monographs and periodicals; a 10-page newspaper section is included in the volume for 1873-1877. Author and title index in each volume. Titles in French translation only. Coverage has gaps.

956. Legrand, Émile L. J. Bibliographie hellénique, ou Description raisonnée des ouvrages publiés en grec par des Grecs aux xve et xvie siècles. Paris, E. Leroux, 1885-1906. 4 v.

————. Bibliographie hellénique, ou Description raisonnée des ouvrages publiés par des Grecs au dix-septième siècle. Paris, A. Picard et fils, 1894-1896; J. Maisonneuve, 1903. 5 v.

————. Bibliographie hellénique, ou Description raisonnée des ouvrages publiés par des Grecs au dix-huitième siècle, œuvre posthume complétée et publiée par mgr. Louis Petit et Hubert Pernot. Paris, Garnier frères, 1918-1928. 2 v.

Lists works published from 1476 to 1790. Detailed annotations and extensive biographical data are included.

For a recent supplement, *see* Manousakas, M. I., Prosthēkai kai symplērōseis eis tēn Hellēnikēn Vivliographian tou E. Legrand (Symvolē prōtē) (Additions and supplements to the Greek Bibliography of E. Legrand [First contribution]). *In*: Akadēmia Athēnōn. Mesaiōnikon Archeion. Epetēris. v. 7, 1957: 34-83. Supplements to Legrand by other investigators are also cited therein.

An important supplement to Legrand's bibliography for the 18th Century appeared in 1964: Ladas, Geōrgios G., *and* Athanasios D. Chatzēdēmos. *Hellēnikē vivliographia. Symvolē sto dekato ogdoo aiōna* (Greek bibliography. A contribution to the 18th century). Athēnai, 1964. 31, 282 p.

957. Legrand, Émile L. J.    Bibliographie ionienne; description raisonnée des ouvrages pub. par les Grecs des Sept-Îles ou concernant ces îles du quinzième siècle à l'année 1900. Oeuvre posthume complétée et pub. par Hubert Pernot. Paris, E. Leroux, 1910. 2 v.

————. Bibliographie ionienne. Suppléments [par] Nakis Pierris, à la description raisonnée des ouvrages publiés par les Grecs des Sept-Îles ou concernant ces îles du quinzième siècle a l'année 1900. Athènes, 1966. 293 p.

Outstanding examples of regional bibliographies, dealing with the Ionian Islands. For bibliographies of other Greek regions, published prior to 1947 and too numerous to be cited here, *see* chapter 5, pages 124-130 of Phousaras, entry no. 949.

958. Mager (Mayer), Kōstas.    Historia tou Hellēnikou typou (History of the Greek press). Athēnai, A. Dēmopoulos, 1957-1960. 3 v.

*See also* entry no. 1248.

Contains a wealth of bibliographical data on Greek newspapers published from 1790 to 1959. Important newspapers are described in detail, while others are listed according to place and date of publication. Brief biographies of noted Greek journalists are given. Greek periodicals are also listed. For additional reference works on the Greek press, *see*:

Thōmopoulos, Sōz. Hē peri typou kai dēmosiographias Hellēnikē vivliographia. Autoteleis ekdoseis, 1831-1967 (Greek bibliography on the press and journalism. Self-contained publications, 1831-1967). Athēnai. 1967. 31 p.

959. Politēs, Nikolaos G.    Hellēnikē vivliographia. Katalogos tōn en Helladi, ē hypo Hellēnōn allachou ekdothentōn vivliōn apo tou etous 1907 (Greek bibliography. Catalog of books published since 1907 in Greece or by Greeks elsewhere). Athēnai, Thessalonikē, 1909-1932. 3 v.

Lists books and periodicals for the period 1907 through 1920. Entries are arranged by subject, and alphabetically within each subject. Author index in each volume.

960. U.S. *Library of Congress. Division of bibliography.* Greece: A Selected List of References. Compiled by Ann Duncan Brown and Helen Dudenbostel Jones. Washington, D.C., 1943. 101 p.
*See also* entry no. 1289.

A catalog of English, French, German, and Italian publications on Modern Greece presented in broad subject groups. Author and subject indexes.

See also *War and Postwar Greece; an Analysis Based on Greek Writings,* prepared by Floyd A. Spencer (Washington, D.C., European Affairs Division, Library of Congress, 1952, 175 p.), basically a bibliographical survey of political, economic, and social writings, mainly in Greek, on war and postwar Greece.

### 3. Bibliographies of Foreign Hellenica

961. Horváth, Endre. Magyar-Görög bibliografia. Houngroellēnikē vivliographia (Hungarian-Greek bibliography). Budapest, Kir. M. Pázmány Péter Tudományegyetemi Görög Filológiai Intézet, 1940. 95 p. Magyar-Görög Tanulmányok, 12)

A bibliographical record of Hungarian-Greek intellectual and cultural relations in modern times. Includes 497 works of Greeks living in Hungary and by Hungarian neo-Hellenists. Text in Hungarian and in Modern Greek.

A similar publication is James K. Demetrius' *Greek Scholarship in Spain and Latin America* (Chicago, Argonaut, 1965, 144 p.), which is primarily a bibliography on classical Greek scholarship, but also deals with Byzantine and Modern Greek studies.

## B. CATALOGS AND COLLECTION SURVEYS

962. American School of Classical Studies at Athens. *Gennadius Library.* Catalogue. Boston, G. K. Hall, 1968. 7 v.

The Gennadius Library contains 50,000 volumes on Greece, from antiquity to the present, with special emphasis on the medieval and modern periods (to 1900). Its catalog consists of approximately 106,000 cards arranged by author, added entries, and selected subject entries.

963. Cincinnati. University. *Library.* The Modern Greek Collection in the Library of the University of Cincinnati: A Catalogue. Edited by Niove Kyparissiotis. With a foreword by Carl W. Blegen. Athens, Hestia Press for the University of Cincinnati, 1960. 387 p.

A catalog of an important Modern Greek collection; 4,447 entries arranged by the Greek alphabet. *See also* Peter William Topping's "Modern Greek Studies and Materials in the United States," *Byzantion,* v. 15, 1940/41, p. 414-442.

## C. ENCYCLOPEDIAS

964. Eleutheroudakē synchronos enkyklopaideia, meta plērous lexikou tēs Hellēnikēs glōssēs. Ekdosis tritē, eksynchronismenē dia symplērōmatos kata tomon (Modern encyclopedia of Eleutheroudakes, with a complete dictionary of the Greek language. 3d ed., updated by a supplement in each volume). Athēnai, Enkyklopaidikai ekdoseis N. Nikas kai Sia E.E. [1965-1967] 12 v.

First and second editions (Athēnai, Ekdotikos oikos Eleutheroudakē, 1927-1931 and 1962-1965, respectively, both 12 v.) have title *Eleutheroudakē enkyklopaidikon lexikon.* Contents of second and third editions are identical.

An important Greek encyclopedia; about 400,000 entries provide concise information. Each volume consists of two parts: the first part is a reprint of the corresponding volume of the first edition; the second part is a supplement containing new entries as well as corrections and additions to existing entries. The supplementary material is also available separately in three volumes.

The following abridged version was published recently: *Eleutheroudakē neon epitomon enkyklopaidikon lexikon. Mikrē enkyklopaideia eikonographēmenē* (New abridged encyclopedic dictionary of Eleutheroudakes. A concise illustrated encyclopedia) (Athēnai, Enkyklopaidikai ekdoseis N. Nikas kai Sia E.E., 1967-1968, 2 v.).

See also *Neōteron enkyklopaidikon lexikon* (Modern encyclopedic dictionary), 2d ed. (Athēnai, Ekdosis tēs enkyklopaidikēs epitheōrēseōs "Hēlios," 1957-1962, 18 v.), a popularized encyclopedia. Volume 7 deals with Greece. A supplement to the entire work is included in v. 18, p. 913-1044. First edition: 1948-1955, 18 v.

965. Megalē Hellēnikē enkyklopaideia. Ekdosis deutera, enēmerōmenē dia symplērōmatōn (The great Greek encyclopedia. 2d ed., updated by supplements). Athēnai, Ekdotikos organismos "Ho Phoinix," 1956–1965. 24 v.

————. Symplērōma (Supplement). Athēnai, Ekdotikos organismos "Ho Phoinix," 1957-1963. 4 v.

*See also* entry no. 1506.

The basic encyclopedia of Modern Greece. The second edition is essentially identical with the first edition, 1926-1934, except that volume 10, devoted to Greece, has been considerably revised; it examines the Greek world from prehistoric times to the present and is a self-contained reference work with a detailed index. Contains lengthy articles, bibliographies, and numerous biographies.

## D. BIOGRAPHIC MATERIALS

For additional biographic data consult the encyclopedias listed in the preceding section.

966. Hellēnikon Who's Who, 1965 (Greek Who's Who, 1965). 2d ed.

Athēnai, Ekdotikos Organismos Hellēnikon Who's Who, 1965. 709, 48 p.

Biographical data on approximately 2,700 Greek personalities in various fields of endeavor. A supplement includes biographical sketches of about 200 prominent living Cypriots. Indexes group personalities according to professional activity. The second edition, in which 600 biographies are published for the first time, expands, but does not completely supersede, the first edition of this work published in 1962; it contained approximately 2,500 entries.

967. Mega Hellēnikon viographikon lexikon (The great Greek biographical dictionary). Athēnai, Ekdosis "Viomēchanikēs Epitheōrēseōs," 1958–

Contains lengthy biographies of persons, living and dead, prominent in the cultural, political, social and, particularly, economic life of Modern Greece. Each volume contains an index of biographies, a name index and indexes of terms arranged by subject. The first series, consisting of five volumes, includes 400 biographies; in addition, 15,000 names are cited therein. Publication of the second series, also in five volumes, has commenced.

968. Sathas, Kōnstantinos N.   Neoellēnikē philologia. Viographiai tōn en tois grammasi dialampsantōn Hellēnōn, apo tēs katalyseōs tēs Vyzantinēs Autokratorias mechri tēs Hellēnikēs ethnegersias (1453-1821). (Modern Greek literature. Biographies of Greeks who distinguished themselves in the letters, from the dissolution of the Byzantine Empire to the Greek national uprising [1453-1821].) Athēnai, Ek tēs typographias tōn teknōn Andreou Koromēla, 1868. 761 p.

This biobibliographical catalog should be used in conjunction with two supplements to it by Andronikos K. Dēmētrakopoulos: *Prosthēkai kai diorthōseis eis tēn Neoellēnikēn philologian Kōnstantinou Satha* (Additions and corrections to the Modern Greek Literature of Konstantinos Sathas) (Leipzig, 1871, 119 p.), and *Epanorthōseis sphalmatōn paratērēthentōn en tēi Neoellēnikēi philologiai tou K. Satha meta kai tinōn prosthēkōn* (Corrections of errors observed in the Modern Greek Literature of K. Sathas with some additions also) (Trieste, 1872, 53 p.).

969. Vretos, Andreas Papadopoulos.   Neoellēnikē philologia, ētoi Katalogos tōn apo ptōseōs tēs Vyzantinēs Autokratorias mechri enkathidryseōs tēs en Helladi vasileias typothentōn vivliōn par' Hellēnōn eis tēn homiloumenēn, ē eis tēn archaian hellēnikēn glōssan (Modern Greek literature, or a catalog of books published by Greeks in the vernacular or in ancient Greek from the fall of the Byzantine Empire to the establishment of a kingdom in Greece). Athēnai, typois kai analōmasi L. D. Vilara kai V. P. Lioumē, 1854-1857. 2 v.

1,272 entries. The first volume lists ecclesiastical works published between 1476 and 1832 while the second includes literary and scientific works for the same period. The arrangement is chronological. Each volume has a biographical section. First edition: 1845. An unpublished third edition, listing 1,599 entries is kept in the Greek national archives (Genika Archeia tou Kratous).

*See also* Iōsēph De Kigallas' *Schediasma katoptrou tēs neoellēnik. philologias* (Outline of a mirror of Modern Greek literature) (Hermoupolis, Ek tēs typographias Georgiou Polymerē, 1846, 110 p.), which lists alphabetically 632 men of letters and their works from 1550 to 1838; however, the biographical data are meager and the descriptions of titles are incomplete.

970. Zaviras (Zabiras), Geōrgios I.   Nea Hellas ē Hellēnikon theatron ekdothen hypo Georgiou P. Kremou (Modern Greece or Greek theater edited by Georgios P. Kremos). Athēnai, Typois Ephēmeridos tōn Syzētēseōn, 1872. 561 p.

A pioneer work containing biobibliographies of approximately 500 Greek writers from the fall of Constantinople to 1804. Biographical data on each author are followed by bibliographical data on his published and unpublished works. Author index prepared by the editor (p. 555-561).

## E. OTHER REFERENCE WORKS

### 1. Gazetteers

971. U.S. *Office of Geography*.   Greece; Official Standard Names Approved by the United States Board on Geographic Names. Washington, D.C., U.S. Government Printing Office, 1955. 404 p. (U.S. Board on Geographic Names. Gazetteer no. 11)

*See also* entry no. 54.

A gazetteer containing about 15,600 entries for places and features in Greece, including Crete, the Dodecanese, and other Greek islands.

The British equivalent is *A Gazetteer of Greece* (London, Royal Geographical Society, 1942, 161 p.), containing approximately 20,000 entries.

### 2. General Statistical Publications

972. Statistikē epetēris tēs Hellados. Statistical Yearbook of Greece. 1930– Athēnai, Ethnikon Typographeion.

Title varies. Volumes for 1930-1939 have title and text in Greek and French. Publication suspended 1940-1953. Volumes for 1954 to date have title and text in Greek and English.

# 27

# General and
# Descriptive Works

*by Theofanis G. Stavrou*

Picture Books 973-978
Guide Books 979-983
General Works 984-986
Characteristics of the People 987-993
Travel Accounts and Descriptions 994-1003
Periodicals 1004-1008

## A. PICTURE BOOKS

973. Bon, Antoine.   En Grèce. Paris, Paul Hartman, 1937. 130 p. Illus.
     A collection of 122 photographs in black and white, all of them of
     historic monuments and scenes of towns and villages on the mainland
     and on the islands. It contains an informative introduction by Fernand
     Chapouthier of the French School in Athens. With some variations,
     reduction in size, and some new photographs, the same team published
     *Retour en Grèce* (Paris, Paul Hartman, 1938, 136 photographs).

974. Kinross, John Patrick Douglas Balfour, *Baron*.   Portrait of Greece.
     With photographs in colour by Dimitri. London, Max Parrish, 1956.
     127 p.
     Eight delightful essays, illustrated with 37 colored photographs,
     touching on the important chapters of Greek history and visiting the
     most representative parts of Greece. The chapter "Shrines of Byzan-
     tium" includes a section with good photographs of Mount Athos. For
     a greater number of pictures, some excellent, of the Holy Mountain
     *see* John Julius Cooper's (Viscount Norwich) and Reresby Sitwell's
     *Mount Athos* (New York, Harper and Row, 1966, 191 p.).

975. Lacretelle, Jacques de, *and others*.    The Greece I Love. London, George Proffer, 1961. 130 p. Illus.

   A marvelous combination of photography and text by four distinguished Frenchmen. It contains 100 gravure pictures, 12 in color, of historic monuments, occupations, and customs, accompanied by commentary.

   Similar, but with a greater variety of pictures depicting cultural monuments and the modern scene, is *This Is Greece*, a book of photographs by Otto Siegner with a preface by Hans Obergethmann (Munich-Pullach, Ludwig Simon, no date, 239 p.).

   Numerous other picture books on Greece have appeared in the last decade. Some good examples are as follows: *Eternal Greece*, with text by Rex Warner and 93 pictures in photogravure and 6 color plates by Martin Hürlimann, revised edition (New York, Viking Press, 1961, 176 p.); C. Kerenyi's *Greece in Color*, with introduction by Lord Kinross and photographs by R. G. Hoegler (London, Thames and Hudson, 1957; New York, Viking Press, 1967, 99 p.), translated from the German by Daphne Woodward. This latter volume includes an article by Kerenyi explaining the peculiar character of Greek light and the effect it had on some of the great literary figures of the past.

976. Roux, Jeanne, *and* Georges Roux.    Greece. Translated from the French by Lionel and Miriam Kochan. With 264 heliogravure illustrations by Bernard Aury and others. New York, Oxford University Press, 1965. 302 p.

   An absorbing and up-to-date album compiled by two longtime residents of Greece. The illustrations include significant sites and monuments as well as sculpture and pottery exhibited in the various museums throughout Greece. There are also photographs depicting the rapid evolution which the country has experienced in recent years. The text reveals erudition and a keen understanding of the Greek people.

977. Spelios, Thomas.    Pictorial History of Greece. New York, Crown, 1967. 328 p. Illus. Bibliography: p. 320-323.

   This is a balanced panoramic pictorial view of Greek history and culture from ancient times to the present. Profusely and successfully illustrated (1,000 illustrations), the contents range from politics to poetry and from the mainland and its islands to the Greeks in the Diaspora. Especially valuable and well done are the sections on the Byzantine, the Ottoman, and the modern periods. Together they constitute a chronicle of the political, social, cultural, and economic evolution of modern Greece. Consultant for the Byzantine period was John Rexine; text for the Ottoman and modern periods was by Harry J. Psomiades. The collection is also rich in portraits of national figures.

978. This is Greece, as Photographed by Members of the American School of Classical Studies at Athens and Their Friends. New York, Hastings House, 1941. 128 p. Illus.

   The photographs in this volume, some of them rare, were provided by 75 members and friends of the American School of Classical Studies at Athens as part of their contribution toward aid to Greece during the Second World War. These photographs represent the Greece of the interwar years, which was partly destroyed by the war and partly changed by the advancing modernization of the country since the war.

## B. GUIDE BOOKS

979. Baedeker, Karl, *Firm.*    Griechenland: Handbuch für Reisende. Leipzig, Karl Baedeker, 1904. 438 p. Illus., maps.

> Though dated, this typical Baedeker volume is detailed and informative for Greece at the turn of the century. It contains a panoramic view of Athens, 11 maps, and 19 plans. An English translation, entitled *Greece; Handbook for Travellers*, was published in 1905 (New York, Scribner's).

980. Boulanger, Robert.    Greece. Translated from the French by M. N. Clark and J. S. Hardman. Paris, Hachette, 1964. 921 p. Illus., maps. (Hachette World Guides)

> This is a completely revised edition of the *Hachette World Guide to Greece*. It is by far the most comprehensive one-volume guide available and is geared to serve the needs of all tourists, lay and scholarly. General information is printed in bold type, and specialized information, usually of a more scholarly nature, in smaller type.
>
> Of almost equal value and scope is *Greece* by O. Merlier and others, with a preface by Jacques de Lacretelle of the French Academy (New York, Nagel Publishers, 1962, 958 p.). In addition to basic information, both volumes include large color folding maps and plans of chief cities and sites.

981. Greek Tourism. Athens, Hellenews Almanacs, 1965. 210 p. Illus.

> This has been an annual publication since 1961. The 1965 edition is an excellent example of how the heavy traffic of tourism has forced the Greeks to approach their number one industry with some relaxation, sophistication, and business-like calculation. Topically arranged, the almanac provides a wealth of information about the country and the services available. It also includes authoritative chapters on the economy, literature, theater, folk dance, handicraft, etc. Richly and representatively illustrated.

982. Bradford, Ernle.    The Greek Islands; a Travel Guide. New York, Harper and Row, Colophon Edition, 1966. 269 p.

> Originally appearing under the slightly different title, *The Companion Guide to the Greek Islands* (1963), this book is an intimate account and guide to 46 Greek islands to which the author sailed in his boat.

983. Pentreath, Guy.    Hellenic Traveller; a Guide to the Ancient Sites of Greece. New York, Crowell, 1964. 338 p. Illus., map.

> This engaging guidebook to all the major and many of the lesser known sites has special chapters on such topics as Byzantine Greece,

the Orthodox Church, the outlines of Greek architecture, sculpture, and vases. A glossary of technical terms is included.

## C. GENERAL WORKS

984. Dēmaras, Kōnstantinos Th. (C. Th. Dimaras). Historia tēs neoellēnikēs logotechnias (History of modern Greek literature). 2d ed. Athēnai, Ikaros, 1955. 478 p. Accompanied by a supplement in a separate volume, contains notes and tables. 140 p.

    *See also* entry no. 1373.

    The best work on the intellectual and literary history of modern Greece. In addition to discussing the evolution of modern Greek literature, it is a guide to Greek life and ideology as revealed in the works of the leading Greek writers. The work has recently been translated into French.

985. Miller, William. Greece. London, Ernest Benn, 1928. 351 p. Bibliography: p. 340-341.

    *See also* entry no. 1061.

    Miller's scholarly contributions on medieval and modern Greek history and culture are a landmark in modern Greek studies. This particular work is a masterly summary of the ideas and themes discussed in his more detailed studies. It touches upon practically all the significant issues of modern Greece. Miller's best-known work on modern Greece is *A History of the Greek People (1821-1921)*, with an introduction by G. P. Gooch (London, Methuen, 1922, 184 p.). *See also* Edward S. Forster's *A Short History of Modern Greece (1821-1956)*, revised and enlarged by Douglas Dakin (London, Methuen, 1958, 268 p.). For a very recent work see *Modern Greece* (New York, Praeger, 1968, 426 p., illus., map, bibliography) by John K. Campbell and Philip Sherrard.

986. Paparrēgopoulos, Kōnstantinos. Historia tou hellēnikou ethnous (History of the Greek people). 6th ed. rev. by Paulos Karolides. Athēnai, Eleutheroudakēs, 1932. 8 v. Illus., maps, tables, bibliography.

    *See also* entries no. 1062 *and* 1410.

    The historical unity of the Greek people from antiquity to 1827 is the theme of this ambitious study by the father of modern Greek historiography. Dated in some details, it is still remarkable both for its analysis and synthesis. Professor Karolides' edition brought the story to 1930. There is also a one-volume abridged edition of this work prepared under the general supervision of Ap. B. Daskalakēs, bringing the story up to date: *Epitomos historia tou hellēnikou ethnous* (Abridged history of the Greek people) (Athēnai, 1955, 1048 p.).

## D. CHARACTERISTICS OF THE PEOPLE

987. Bent, James T. The Aegean Islands: The Cyclades, or Life among

the Insular Greeks. New and enl. ed. Edited by A. N. Oikonomides. Chicago, Argonaut, 1966. 592 p. Illus., maps, bibliography.

The first edition of this classic appeared in 1885 under the title *The Cyclades, or Life among the Insular Greeks*. The author, a notable 19th century traveler, treats in great detail and in their historical and geographic perspective, modern folklore, religious traditions, and everyday customs and occupations in 19 Aegean islands. The new edition contains an introduction to Cycladic archeology and folklore, along with appendixes and an index.

988. Burn, Andrew R.   The Modern Greeks. London, New York, Nelson, 1944. 55 p.

The author, a classical scholar and representative of the British Council in Greece in 1940-1941, introduces the modern Greeks as the worthy descendants of their illustrious ancestors. Written partly to counter German propaganda about the Greeks during the Second World War, it elaborates on the essence of modern Greek civilization and modern Greek character, emphasizing the virtues which assert themselves in time of national crisis.

989. Hammond, Peter.   The Waters of Marah; the Present State of the Greek Church. London, Rockliff, 1956. 186 p. Illus.

*See also* entry no. 1430.

A lucid and authoritative description of the state, role and relevance of the Greek Church in contemporary Greek society.

990. Kazantzakēs, Nikos.   Report to Greco. Translated from the Greek by P. A. Bien. New York, Simon and Schuster, 1965. 512 p.

In this intellectual and spiritual autobiography of the best known of Modern Greek writers, Kazantzakis recaptures the synthesis of modern Greek life and attitudes based on the clashes and interaction of Greek and West European ideas and values. Some of the author's other works which mirror modern Greek life are *Freedom or Death* (New York, Simon and Schuster, 1955, 433 p.) and *The Greek Passion* (New York, Simon and Schuster, 1959, 432 p.), both translated by Jonathan Griffin, and *The Fratricides*, translated by Athena Gianakas Dallas (New York, Simon and Schuster, 1964, 254 p.).

991. Lancaster, Osbert.   Classical Landscape with Figures. Boston, Houghton Mifflin Co., 1949. 224 p. Illus., map.

A remarkable achievement, capturing in text, pen drawings, and water colors, the flavor of Greek life in town and country in the immediate postwar period.

992. Sanders, Irwin T.   Rainbow in the Rock; the People of Rural Greece. Cambridge, Harvard University Press, 1962. 363 p. Illus.

*See also* entries no. 1046, 1295, *and* 1460.

Probably the most significant study on postwar rural Greece, it covers every phase of Greek village life, particularly the cultural and socioeconomic changes which rural Greece has experienced since the war. This study is a model for others who wish to study other phases of Greek life in transition.

Equally successful and exemplary in scholarship, but dealing with a narrower topic, is J. K. Campbell's *Honour, Family, and Patronage; a Study of Institutions and Moral Values in a Greek Mountain Community* (Oxford, Clarendon, 1964, 393 p.). This is a socioanthropologic study of the Sarakatsani, a group living in the Zagori villages in Epirus, among whom the author lived for two years (1954 and 1955).

993. Theotokas, Giōrgos.   Argō. Translated from the Greek by E. Margaret Brooke and Ares Tsatsopoulos. London, Methuen, 1951. 357 p.

This celebrated novel presents the most comprehensive picture of Greek life during the interwar years. Political, ideological, psychological, and social problems and attitudes of the modern Greeks are skillfully and purposefully portrayed in the novel's main characters.

## E. TRAVEL ACCOUNTS AND DESCRIPTIONS

### 1. General

994. Weber, Shirley Howard.   Voyages and Travels in Greece, the Near East, and Adjacent Regions Made Previous to the Year 1801. Princeton, The American School of Classical Studies at Athens, 1953. 208 p. (Catalogs of the Gennadius Library, II)

This catalog includes a bibliography of treatises on Greek travels. The travels are arranged chronologically but two good indexes make every reference readily traceable. There are separate classifications for topographical and descriptive accounts, books largely or entirely pictorial, and a rather unique and interesting group of descriptive books, the *Proskynētaria*, pilgrim descriptions of holy places and shrines. *See also* the same author's *Voyages and Travels in the Near East Made During the XIX Century* (Princeton, American School of Classical Studies at Athens, 1952, 252 p., Catalogs of the Gennadius Library, I). Both volumes are invaluable guides to the rich travel literature on Greece.

995. Wegner, Max, *comp.*   Land der Griechen: Reiseschilderungen aus sieben Jahrhunderten. Berlin, de Gruyter, 1955. 336 p. Illus., map.

This convenient handbook provides excerpts of descriptions and impressions of Greece by numerous European travelers, especially German, to Greece and the Levant from the 14th century to the 20th. The usefulness of the volume is enhanced by a detailed chronological listing of travelers and their accounts in the major European languages during the last seven centuries. Understandably, the greatest number of this vast travel literature on Greece appeared in the 19th century, when the Greek War of Independence and Philhellenism brought Greece increasingly to the attention of Europeans.

Terence Spencer's standard work *Fair Greece! Sad Relic; Literary Phihellenism from Shakespeare to Byron* (London, Weidenfeld and Nicolson, 1954, 312 p., illus.) surveys the contributions by pre-19th century European travelers to the rise of Philhellenism in Europe, especially in Great Britain. Different in scope and purpose but still useful because it draws attention to significant European travel accounts is the essay by James M. Osborn, "Travel Literature and the Rise of Neo-Hellenism in England," published in the *Bulletin of the New York Public Library*, v. 57, 1963, p. 229-300.

*See also* Philip Sherrard's *The Pursuit of Greece* (London, John Murray, 1964, 291 p.), which is a skillful arrangement of quotations from travelers to Greece reflecting the attraction and the puzzle that Greek studies and the Greeks have been to the Western world from earliest times to the present. It also includes a list of distinguished travel accounts.

More specific in nature is James Morton Paton's *Chapters on Medieval and Renaissance Visitors to Greek Lands* (Princeton, The American School of Classical Studies at Athens, 1951, 212 p.), which is a collection of sources and descriptions of Greece and the islands by the best-known medieval and Renaissance travelers. The accounts appear in the original language with copious notes by the editor. An excellent historical source, the collection was published posthumously, and it is preceded by a rather elementary but still useful lecture on Turkish Athens which the author delivered before his death.

## 2. Before Independence (to 1830)

996. Chandler, Richard.   Travels in Greece: or an Account of a Tour Made at the Expense of the Society of Dilettanti. Oxford, Clarendon Press, 1776. 304 p. Maps.

This account appears again as volume 2 of the author's *Travels in Asia Minor and Greece* (London, 1825, 370 p.). The latter edition includes an introductory account of the author, an English scholar of the classics. He spent a year in Greece (1765-1766) visiting and describing places of ancient renown in Attica and Peloponnesus.

997. Leake, William M.   Travels in the Morea. London, John Murray, 1830. 3 v. Illus.

————.   Peloponnesiaca: a Supplement to the Travels in the Morea. London, J. Rodwell, 1846. 432 p. Illus., maps.

————.   Travels in Northern Greece. London, J. Rodwell, 1835. 4 v. Illus., maps.

Of all the 19th century travelers to Greece, Leake is indisputably the most venerated. Finlay referred to him as the man "whose long and laborious exertions" helped clear "the ancient history of Greece from obscurity and the modern from misrepresentation." He covered Northern and Southern Greece (in 1804, 1805, and 1806) thoroughly and, though a classical scholar, his interest ranged widely from descriptions of geography and topography to descriptions of customs and the language of the people to detailed commentaries on colorful individuals such as Ali Pasha of Jannina.

998. Pouqueville, François C. H. L. de.   Voyage en Morée, à Constantinople, en Albanie, et dans plusieurs autres parties de l'Empire Ottoman, pendant les années 1798, 1799, 1800 et 1801. Paris, Gabon, 1805. 3 v.

————.   Voyage dans la Grèce comprenant la description ancienne et moderne de l'Épire, de l'Illyrie grecque, de la Macedoine cisaxienne, d'une partie de la Triballie, de la Thessalie, de l'Acarnanie, de l'Étolie ancienne et Épictète, de la Locride Hesperienne, de la Doride, et du Péloponèse; avec des considérations sur l'archéologie. Paris, Didot, 1820. 5 v. Reprinted in 1826-1827.

   Pouqueville's detailed accounts are most valuable for the historian of 18th and early 19th century Greece. The author served as Consul General of France at the court of Ali Pasha at Jannina from 1805 to 1815, and after that at Patras.

   Pouqueville's works enjoyed wide popularity and were translated into German and Italian. In English there are abbreviated editions, *Travels in Epirus, Albania, Macedonia and Thessaly* (London, Phillips, 1820, 122 p.), and *Travels in Greece and Turkey, Comprehending a Particular Account of the Morea, Albania etc., a Comparison Between the Ancient and Present State of Greece, and an Historical and Geographical Description of the Ancient Epirus* (London, Colburn, 1820, 482 p.).

### 3. After Independence (1830–)

999. Bremer, Fredrika.   Greece and the Greeks: The Narrative of a Winter Residence and Summer Travel in Greece and its Islands. Translated by Mary Howitt. London, Hurst and Blackett, 1863. 2 v.

   Packed with firsthand information about the life of the Greeks at home, in the city, and in the country. The author, Swedish by nationality, was both persistent and observant, and Greek politics, education, the position of women, etc., attracted her attention.

   Similar in nature is the account by the American Samuel J. Barrows: *The Isles and Shrines of Greece* (Boston, Roberts, 1898, 389 p.).

1000. Porfirii, *Bishop of Chigirin.*   Puteshestvie v Meteorskie i Osoolimpiiskie monastyri v Fessalii v 1859 godu (Travels to the monasteries of the Meteora and of Ossa and Olympus in the year 1859). Edited by P. A. Syrku. Sanktpeterburg, Izd. Imp. akademii nauk, 1896. 614 p.

   Of the 19th century Russian travelers, Porfirii was the most indefatigable and passionate. His description of the Meteora monasteries is a classic, and its value to historians is still great. Under special missions, Porfirii travelled extensively in the Orthodox East and especially to Mount Athos, leaving rich accounts of the monasteries and his experiences there. *See also* his *Pervoe puteshestvie v Afonskie monastyri i skity . . . v 1845-46 godu* (First journey to the monasteries and sketes of Mount Athos in the year 1845-46) (Kiev, 1877-

1880, 2 v.); and *Vtoroe puteshestvie po sviatoi gore Afonskoi v gody 1858, 1859 i 1861* (Second journey to the holy Mount Athos in the years 1858, 1859, and 1861) (Moskva, 1880).

For a colorful and informative description of the Meteora and Athos monasteries, *see also* the English account by Robert Curzon (Lord Zouche), *Visits to Monasteries in the Levant* (Ithaca, Cornell University Press, 1955, 349 p., illus., facsim.). This latest edition is a reissue of a classic work which first appeared in 1849 and which went through several editions in the 19th century, in time acquiring the sobriquet "a gentleman's book."

## 4. Contemporary

1001. Fermor, Patrick Leigh.    Mani: Travels in the Southern Peloponnese. London, John Murray, 1958. 320 p. Illus.

Fermor's *Mani* and its companion *Roumeli: Travels in Northern Greece* (London, John Murray, 1966, 248 p.), are exciting descriptions of mainland Greece. The author concentrated on the most inaccessible or least visited places and communities of Northern and Southern Greece. The value of this work is likely to increase with the passing of time.

The Greek islands have evoked a large amount of contemporary travel literature. A. t'Serstevens' *Le périple des archipels grecs* (Paris, Arthaud, 1963, 353 p.) is an informative general account with 28 original drawings by Amandine Doré and 76 photographs. Less ambitious, but expertly told is the story of a voyage through the Aegean by Göran Schildt, *In the Wake of Ulysses,* translated from the Swedish by Alan Blair (New York, Dodd Mead, 1953, 229 p.). A classic description by Lawrence Durrell is *Prospero's Cell; a Guide to the Landscape and Manners of the Island of Corcyra* (London, Faber and Faber, 1945, 142 p.). The last is also published together in one volume with Durrell's *Reflections on a Marine Venus; a Companion to the Landscape of Rhodes* (New York, Dutton, 1960).

1002. Kazantzakēs, Nikos.    Journey to the Morea. Translated from the Greek by F. A. Reed. New York, Simon and Schuster, 1965. 190 p. Illus.

Kazantzakēs' extensive travels and descriptions of Greece form a peculiar journey in time and space, searching to understand his homeland and his roots. *Journey to the Morea* is one of his most successful ones. *See also* his *Report to Greco* (entry no. 990), from which the *Journey to the Morea* is really extracted. *See also* Greek-American Elias Kulukundis' *The Feast of Memory: A Journey to the Greek Islands* (New York, Holt, Rinehart, and Winston, 1967, 241 p.), which blends the history and flavor of the Dodecanese Islands with the author's own life experiences in the new world.

Finally, Henry Miller's *The Colossus of Maroussi* (San Francisco, Colt, 1941, 244 p.) is an unconventional narrative by the American writer describing Greek character and attitudes.

1003. Spunda, Franz.   Griechenland, Fahrten zu den alten Göttern. Leipzig, Insel-Verlag, 1938. 415 p. Illus.

A sympathetic and comprehensive account of modern Greece, including the Islands. Reprinted in 1943 by the same publisher.

## F.  PERIODICALS

1004. Balkan Studies. 1960– Thessalonikē. Semiannual.
See also entries no. 30 and 1204.

A semiannual publication of the Institute for Balkan Studies in Thessalonica. International in scope, it publishes articles on Greece and the Balkans in Greek and Western European languages.

1005. Byzantinisch-neugriechische Jahrbücher; internationales wissenschaftliches Organ. 1920-1925, Berlin; 1926–, Athens. Irregular.

This serious journal was under the editorship of the noted Byzantinist and Modern Greek scholar Nikos Beēs. Operating on an international level, the journal has made significant contributions to Byzantine and Modern Greek studies, despite interruptions during and after the Second Word War.

Less international in scope is Epetēris Hetaireias Vyzantinōn Spoudōn (Yearbook of the Society for Byzantine Studies) (1924–, Athēnai), which also deals with post-Byzantine themes. It is a good reference source for works on medieval and modern Greece. For the modern period, see also L'Hellénisme contemporain (1935–, Athènes).

1006. Nea Hestia (New hearth). 1927– Athēnai. Monthly.

The best-known Greek literary journal. Historical and especially literary subjects predominate. It carries a regular bibliography of new Greek publications on a variety of subjects. Leading literary figures of modern Greece served as its editors, and many contemporary young authors had their works first appear in Nea Hestia. Especially useful are the commemorative volumes which deal either with eminent individuals or significant events in Greek history.

1007. Neos Hellēnomnēmōn (Modern Greek Recorder). 1904-1927. Athēnai. Quarterly.

This was basically the personal journal of the eminent modern Greek historian Spyridōn Lambros, which some consider as his crowning achievement. Lambros edited the first 14 volumes (1904-1917). After his death, the journal continued under the supervision of K. Dyobouniotou, utilizing material left by Lambros. There is an index to the whole set published by Charitake (Athēnai, 1930, 604 p.).

This journal appeared as continuation of an older journal Hellēnomnēmōn (Recorder) (1843-1853, Athēnai, 12 v.).

1008. Parnassos (Parnassus). 1877-1894. Athēnai. 17 v.

Sponsored by the famous Philological Society, Parnassos, this is a rich journal for modern Greek studies. The Society continued its publication efforts after termination of Parnassos in 1894, with its *Epetēris* (Yearbook) (1896-1917, Athēnai, 13 v.) and after some interruption from 1937. See also *Ho en kōnstantinoupolei hellēnikos philologikos syllogos, syngramma periodikon* (Journal of the Philological Society of Constantinople) (1863-1921, Konstantinoupolis, 33 v.).

# 28

# the land

*by George W. Hoffman*

1009. Baxevanis, John.   The Port of Thessaloniki. Thessalonikē, Institute for Balkan Studies, 1963. 99 p.
    Descriptive study of the port of Thessalonike, its facilities and administration, geographic orientation, and traffic flow. Concluding discussions of the port's prospects.

1010. Bon, Antoine.   Greece. *In* Larousse Encyclopedia of Geography — Europe. New York, Prometheus Press, 1961. p. 323-334.
    Survey of the regional geography of Greece.

1011. Chataigneau, Y., *and* Jules Sion.   La Grèce. *In* Chataigneau, Y., *and* Jules Sion, *eds.* Géographie universelle. v. 7, part 2. Paris, Armand Colin, 1934. p. 512-575.
    Survey of the regional geography of Greece.

1012. Chombart de Lauwe, Jean.   Problems of Agricultural Co-operation; Case Study in Greece. Paris, Organization for Economic Co-operation and Development, 1964. 136 p.
    Report of a team of experts who studied the agricultural cooperative movement. Lists the strong and weak points of the movement and suggests certain changes.

1013. Fischer, Eric.   Greece. *In* Hoffman, George W., *ed.* A Geography of Europe, Including Asiatic U.S.S.R. 2d ed. New York, Ronald Press Co., 1961. p. 469-507.
    Detailed regional survey of Greece within the general setting of Southern Europe.

1014. Füldner, Eckhart.   Agrargeographische Untersuchungen in der Ebene von Thessaloniki. Frankfurt am Main, Verlag Waldemar Kramer, 1967. 146 p. Maps, plates. (Frankfurter Geographische Hefte, 44)
    Changes of the physical and human geography in the plain of

Thessalonike, especially since the liberation from the Turks. Special emphasis is on agricultural changes.

1015. Hellēnikē geōgraphikē hetaireia, *Athens*. Deltion (Bulletin). 1924– Irregular.
Official publication of the Greek Geographical Society.

1016. Hoffman, George W.   Thessaloniki: The Impact of a Changing Hinterland. East European Quarterly, Mar. 1968: 1-27.
Study in historical geography, investigating the changing relationship between the port and the city of Thessalonike and its hinterland.

1017. International Bank for Reconstruction and Development. The Development of Agriculture in Greece. Report of a Mission Organized by the International Bank for Reconstruction and Development With the Cooperation of the Food and Agriculture Organization of the United Nations. Washington, D.C., 1966. 123 p.
A detailed discussion of the importance of agriculture to the economy, prepared to assist the Greek Government in formulating and implementing agricultural policies.

1018. Kasperson, Roger E.   The Dodecanese: Diversity and Unity in Island Politics. Chicago, University of Chicago, 1966. 184 p. Maps, photos, statistical tables. (University of Chicago. Department of Geography. Research Paper No. 108)
A detailed study of the effects of selected economic, social, and political experiences upon political diversity and unity in the Dodecanese Islands.

1019. Kayser, Bernard, *and others*.   Développement régional et régionalisation de l'espace en Grèce. Tiers monde (Paris), v. 6, Oct.-Dec. 1965: 1003-1004.
Brief analysis of development plans and political influences on regional development.

1020. Kayser, M. B.   Les transformation de la Grèce du Nord. Bulletin de l'Association de géographes français, no. 324-325, May-June 1964: 59-70.
Discussion of social and economic changes in northern Greece.

1021. Kirsten, Ernst, *and* Wilhelm Kraiker.   Griechenlandkunde; ein Führer zu klassischen Stätten. Heidelberg, Carl Winter Universitätsverlag, 1956. 2d ed. 519 p. Illus., maps (one fold.).
Up-to-date coverage of archeological research, with general and background information included in the first and last chapters.

1022. Kolias, Geōrgios T.   Historikē geōgraphia tou Hellēnikou chōrou (Historical geography of the Greek area). Athēnai, 1948. 340 p. Maps.

A publication of the Ministry of Reconstruction in three parts: the spread of the Greeks in the Mediterranean and in Europe throughout history; the political geography; and the economic geography.

1023. Megas, Geōrgios A.   Geōgraphia tēs Hellados (Geography of Greece). Athēnai, 1939. 228 p. Illus., maps.
A textbook.

1024. Myres, John L.   Geographical History in Greek Lands. Oxford, Clarendon Press, 1953. 381 p. Illus., maps. "A select list of the works of John Linton Myres": p. 351-381.
In addition to geographical history per se, covers such general topics as "Ancient Geography in Modern Education" and "The Value of Ancient History."

1025. Newbigin, Marion I.   Greece and Albania. In Church, R. J. Harrison, ed. Southern Europe, a Regional and Economic Geography of the Mediterranean Lands. 3d rev. ed. London, Methuen; New York, E. P. Dutton, 1949. p. 311-388.
Brief regional study, with emphasis on economic geography.

1026. Philippson, Alfred.   Die griechischen Landschaften; eine Landeskunde. Frankfurt am Main, Vittorio Klostermann, 1950-1959. 4 v. Maps.
Historical geography, considered a classic.

1027. Philippson, Alfred.   Das Klima Griechenlands. Bonn, Ferd. Dummlers Verlag, 1948. 238 p. Map.
A detailed discussion of the climate of Greece, by a world-renowned geographer.

1028. Schultze, Joachim H.   Neugriechenland. Eine Landeskunde Ostmakedoniens und Westthrakiens mit besonderer Berücksichtigung der Geomorphologie, Kolonistensiedlung und Wirtschaftsgeographie. Gotha, Justus Perthes, 1937. 447 p. Plates, maps (part fold.), plans, diagrs. (Petermanns geographische Mitteilungen, Ergänzungsheft Nd. 233)
Detailed regional geography, with special attention given to the new settlements.

1029. Vooys, A. C. de.   Western Thessaly in Transition. Tijdschrift van het Koninklijk Nederlandsch Aardrijkskundig Genootschap, v. 76, Jan. 1959: 31-54.
Discussion of the trend during the last few years toward greater differentiation in agricultural production.

# 29

# the people

*by George W. Hoffman*

1030. Baxevanis, John. Population, Internal Migration and Urbanization in Greece. Balkan Studies (Thessalonikē), v. 6, 1965, no. 1: 83-98.

Population data, rural-to-urban migration in Greece, hierarchy of urban settlements.

1031. Greece. *Ethnikē Statistikē Hypēresia.* Apotelesmata tēs apographēs plēthysmou-katoikiōn tēs 19 Martiou 1961 (Results of the population and housing census of 19 March 1961). Sample Elaboration; v. 5, Internal Migration. A: 9 Population. Athēnai, 1963. 54 p.

Data on internal migration, employment status, age, sex, region, etc. are presented and analyzed.

1032. Greece. *Ethnikē Statistikē Hypēresia.* Dēmographikai ropai kai mellontikai proektaseis tou plēthysmou tēs Hellados (Demographic trends and population projections of Greece). Athēnai, 1966. 78 p. Illus., map.

Emigration trends since the Second World War, analysis of emigration and of its impact on the Greek economy. The study concludes that Greece can expect population stagnation or decline because of high emigration and low birth rate.

1033. Greece. *Ethnikē Statistikē Hypēresia.* Statistikē epetēris tēs Hellados (Statistical yearbook of Greece). Athēnai, 1964.

Compilation, in Greek and English, of useful demographic and economic data from the 1961 census, with comparative statistics for other European countries.

1034. Greece. *Ethnikē Statistikē Hypēresia.* Statistical Summary of Greece. Athens, 1955.

Compilation of demographic and economic data from the 1951 census, in Greek and English.

1035. Kayser, Bernard. Géographie humaine de la Grèce; éléments pour

l'étude de l'urbanisation. Paris, Presses Universitaires de France, 1964. 147 p. Tables, maps, bibliography.
*See also* entry no. 1319.
Detailed study of the distribution of Greece's population, the impact of emigration, and changes brought about by internal migration.

1036. Kayser, Bernard, *and* Kenneth Thompson.    Economic and Social Atlas of Greece. Athens, National Statistical Service of Greece, 1964. 350 p. 1 v. (unpaged). Illus., maps, diagrs.
*See also* entry no. 1317.
Very valuable reference atlas, based on the 1960 census data.

1037. Lambiri, Jane (Ioanna).    Social Change in a Greek Country Town; the Impact of Factory Work on the Position of Women. Athens, Center of Planning and Economic Research, 1965. 163 p. (Research Monograph Series, 13)
*See also* entry no. 1306.
The town of Megara, with its new textile factory, is analyzed to demonstrate the impact of new occupation roles in a traditional society.

1038. Mears, Eliot G.    Greece Today; the Aftermath of the Refugee Impact. Stanford University, Calif., Stanford University Press, 1929. 336 p. Front. (double map), illus. (maps), plates, diagrs. "Chronology": p. xv-xxii. Bibliography: p. 303-315.

1039. Miller, William.    Greek Life in Town and Country. London, G. Newnes, Ltd., 1905. 310 p. Illus., 28 pl. (incl. front.).
Penetrating description of Greek urban life 60 years ago.

1040. Moore, Wilbert E.    Economic Demography of Eastern and Southern Europe. Geneva, League of Nations, 1945. 299 p. Illus. (maps), diagrs.
Useful analysis for Greece, presented in a general European context.

1041. Organization for Economic Cooperation and Development.    Manpower Policy and Problems in Greece, Paris, 1965. 51 p. (OECD Reviews of Manpower and Social Policies, 3)
Basic study of future manpower needs and related social policies.

1042. Organization for Economic Cooperation and Development. *Mediterranean Regional Project.*    Country Reports: Greece. Paris, 1965. 195 p. Illus.
*See also* entry no. 1310.
Study of requirements for the expansion and improvement of education in Greece.

1043. Pentzopoulos, Dēmētres.    The Balkan Exchange of Minorities and

Its Impact upon Greece. Paris, Mouton, 1962. 293 p. Illus. (Publications of the Social Sciences Center, Athens, 1)

>A detailed discussion of the international conventions relating to the refugee problem and the impact of the refugees on Greek social and economic life.

1044. Pepelasis, Adamantios A., *and* Kenneth Thompson.    Agriculture in a Restrictive Environment: The Case of Greece. Economic Geography, v. 36, Apr. 1960: 145-157.

>Brief analysis of the problems faced in modernizing Greek agriculture. Emphasis on environmental problems, reclamation, and institutional changes.

1045. Pepelasis, Adamantios A., *and* Pan A. Yotopoulos.    Surplus Labor in Greek Agriculture, 1953-1960. Athens, Center of Economic Research, 1962. 187 p. (Research Monograph Series, no. 2)

>Analysis of the relationship between the size of the agricultural population and employment opportunities in general.

1046. Sanders, Irwin T.    Rainbow in the Rock; the People of Rural Greece. Cambridge, Mass., Harvard University Press, 1962. 363 p. Illus.

>*See also* entries no. 992, 1295, *and* 1460.

>The first study on Greek village life to cover social changes over a period of more than 50 years.

1047. Thompson, Kenneth.    Farm Fragmentation in Greece. Athens, Center of Economic Research, 1963. 263 p. Illus. Bibliography: p. 261-263 (Research Monograph Series, 5)

>*See also* entry no. 1274.

>The author takes the position that farm fragmentation represents a liability to the Greek economy and that more effective land consolidation measures are called for.

1048. Valaoras, Vassilios G.    A Reconstruction of the Demographic History of Modern Greece. Milbank Memorial Fund Quarterly (New York), v. 38, 1960: 115-139.

>Useful demographic profiles for Greece up to the 1950 census, with natality statistics through 1960.

# 30

# history

*by George G. Arnakis*

General Histories 1049-1063

The Ottoman Period, 1453-1821 1064-1073

The Greek Revolution and Independence, 1821-1833 1074-1096

Political and Diplomatic History, 1833-1914 1097-1107

Greece Since 1914 1108-1117

## A. GENERAL HISTORIES

1049. Driault, Édouard, *and* Michel Lhéritier.   Histoire diplomatique de la Grèce de 1821 à nos jours. Paris, Les Presses Universitaires de France, 1925-26. 5 v. Maps, bibliographies.
> *See also* entry no. 1213.
> Brilliant and vivid literary style in the French tradition of popular history, but poorly proofread and lacking depth. Moreover, it contains avoidable errors. It should be used with caution. It should be supplemented by the brief and balanced account of S. Th. Laskaris entitled *Diplōmatikē historia tēs Hellados, 1821-1914* (Diplomatic history of Greece, 1821-1914) (Athēnai, 1947, 267 p.).

1050. Finlay, George.   A History of Greece from Its Conquest by the Romans to the Present Time, B.C. 146 to A.D. 1864. Rev. and enl. ed. Oxford, Clarendon Press, 1877. 7 v.
> *See also* entry no. 1408.
> Beginning with a study of the Greek Revolution published in 1861, Finlay expanded the scope of his work till it covered the Roman, Byzantine, Ottoman, and national Greek periods, up to the establishments of the Glücksburg dynasty. The author, who lived most of his life in Greece, had an anti-Greek bias, which is evident not only in the narrative of events of his own time, but also in his Byzantine historiography.

1051. Forster, Edward S.   A Short History of Modern Greece, 1821-1956.

Revised and enlarged by Douglas Dakin. New York, Praeger, 1957. 268 p. Illus.

See also entry no. 1164.

Intended for the general reader, this book is a brief and methodical account, but it rarely comes to grips with the problems of Greek history. Dakin added material dealing with the recent period.

Also of interest to the general reader are the following: *Modern Greece: a Chronicle and Survey, 1800-1931,* by John Mavrogordato (New York, 1931); *Greece,* by Harold W. Gomme (London, 1945); and *Histoire de la Grèce Moderne,* by N. G. Svoronos (Paris, 1953).

1052. Gaitanides, Johannes.   Griechenland ohne Säulen. München, List, 1955. 374 p. Illus., maps. Bibliography: p. 359-365.

A well-informed and balanced account of Greek history and culture 10 years after the war, with chapters describing earlier periods. For an equally good treatment 20 years after the war, see *Griechenland,* by Isidora Rosenthal-Kamarinea with the collaboration of Panajotis Kamarineas (Nürnberg, Glock und Lutz, 1965, 328 p.).

1053. Greece. *In* Encyclopedia Americana. v. 13. New York, Americana, 1958. p. 389-418.

Important résumé and background information on modern Greek history are presented in three articles: 1. "Greece: History of the Byzantine Period, 330-1453" by G. G. Arnakis (p. 389-399). 2. "Greece: History of the Turkish Period, 1453-1821" by M. B. Sakellariou and N. Svoronos (p. 404-413). 3. "Greece: Modern History" by L. S. Stavrianos (p. 415-418).

For a detailed historical account of the rise and fall of the Ottoman Empire and of the emergence of the Balkan States see *The Ottoman Empire and the Balkan States* by George G. Arnakis (Austin, Texas, The Pemberton Press, 1969, 452 p., maps, bibliography). Two continuation volumes which are to cover the periods 1900-1940 and 1940-1960, respectively, are scheduled to appear in 1970.

1054. Hertzberg, Gustav F.   Geschichte Griechenlands seit dem Absterben des antiken Lebens bis zur Gegenwart. Gotha, Perthes, 1876-1879. 4 v.

Covers the period from 395 to 1878. From the point of view of scholarship, it ranks as high as Hopf and higher than either Mendelssohn-Bartholdy or George Finlay.

1055. Heurtley, W. A., *and others.*   A Short History of Greece from Early Times to 1964. New York, Cambridge University Press, 1965. 202 p. Maps. Bibliography: p. 184-187.

Concise and well written, this volume not only gives a clear chronological survey of Greek history, but, more important, suggests the great need for specialized studies in medieval and modern Greek history.

1056. Historikē kai ethnologikē hetaireia tēs Hellados. Deltion (Bulletin

of the Historical and Ethnological Society of Greece). 1883– Athēnai. Annual.
One of the basic historical journals.

1057. Hopf, Carl H. F. J.   Geschichte Griechenlands vom Beginn des Mittelalters bis auf unsere Zeit. New York, Burt Franklin, 1960. 2 v. (Burt Franklin Research and Source Works, Series no. 17)
History of the Greek area from 395 to 1821. Important for establishing the continuity of the Greek historical and cultural tradition as opposed to Fallmerayer's theory of Slavic predominance in the Middle Ages in Southern Greece. The post-Byzantine period is too condensed and sketchy to satisfy the 20th century reader. First published in Leipzig in 1867-1868.

1058. Kordatos, Giannēs K.   Historia tēs neōterēs Helladas (History of modern Greece). Athēnai, 20ᵒˢ Aiōnas, 1957-1958. 5 v. Bibliography.
The first important attempt to interpret modern Greek history in terms of Marxism, this work deviates from the standard presentation of such pivotal matters as the Greek Revolution, the First World War, and the Greek campaign in Asia Minor. The author, secretary of the Communist Party of Greece in the early 1920s, was a prolific writer on all periods of Greek history, but all his works bear the imprint of his political views and are written in a polemic tone. The fifth volume of the work takes the reader to the establishment of the Hellenic Republic in 1924.

1059. Lambros (Lampros), Spyridon P.   Historia tēs Hellados (History of Greece). Athēnai, Eleftheroudakis, 1886-1902. 6 v. Illus., maps.
More comprehensive than Paparrēgopoulos with regard to the late Byzantine and Ottoman periods, it lacks the critical judgment and the depth of the former scholar. The narrative takes us to the reign of King Othon.

1060. Mendelssohn-Bartholdy, Karl.   Geschichte Griechenlands von der Eroberung Konstantinopels durch die Türken im Jahre 1453 bis auf unsere Tage. Leipzig, Hirzel, 1870-1874. 2 v. (Staatengeschichte der neuesten Zeit, 15 Bd.)
A narrative of historical events from 1453 to 1835. Outdated in part, and not entirely free of errors, it is still useful but should be followed with caution.

1061. Miller, William.   Greece. London, Ernest Benn, 1928. 351 p. Bibliography: p. 340-341.
See also entry no. 985.
Contains a balanced résumé of modern Greek history from 1821 to 1920, followed by "The Constantinist Restoration and the Asia Minor Catastrophe, 1920-24" and "The Greek Republic, 1924-28." There are also chapters on Greek politics, the church, press, education, commerce, and the armed forces. Essentially a revised version of the author's *A History of the Greek People* (1821-1921) (London,

Methuen, 1922). The older volume includes a discussion of the Cretan and Macedonian questions. Miller, an English correspondent in Athens, was regarded as the successor to the work of Finlay but he lacked the latter's anti-Greek bias. Miller was a sincere philhellene and he viewed the Greek Republic (1924-35) favorably.

1062. Paparrēgopoulos, Kōnstantinos. Historia tou hellēnikou ethnous (History of the Greek nation). 6th ed. rev. by Paulos Karolides. Athēnai, Eleutheroudakēs, 1932. 8 v. Illus., maps, tables, bibliography.

    *See also* entries no. 986 *and* 1410.

    The author, who is regarded as the greatest historian of modern Greece, sets out to prove the historical continuity of the Greek people and culture from antiquity to modern times. His monumental work closes with the year 1827. The editor, Karolides, continues the narrative to 1930, inserting long excerpts from his own works, especially from his *Historia tōn Hellēnōn kai tōn loipōn laōn tēs Anatolēs* (History of the Greeks and of the other peoples of the [Near] East) (Athēnai, 1922-1929, 7 v.). Important supplementary readings to fill the gaps in Karolides' account include George Aspreas' *Politikē historia tēs neōteras Hellados* (Political history of modern Greece) (Athēnai, 1922-1930, 3 v.), and Dionysios A. Zakythēnos' *Politikē historia tēs neōteras Hellados* (Political history of modern Greece), 2d ed. (Athēnai, 1965, 118 p.).

1063. Vakalopoulos (Bakalopoulos), Apostolos E. Historia tou Neou Hellēnismou (History of modern Greece). v. 1– Thessalonikē, 1961–
    *See also* entry no. 1411.

    The three volumes published thus far in this projected five-volume work are up-to-date and authoritative contributions to the history of Greece of the Late Byzantine and Early Ottoman periods. The entire series, when completed, will constitute as definitive a history of modern Greece as one could expect in our time. Volume 1 will appear in English translation in the *Byzantine Series* of Rutgers University Press.

## B. THE OTTOMAN PERIOD, 1453-1821

1064. Arsh, Grigorii L. Albaniia i Epir v kontse XVIII–nachale XIX v. (Albania and Epirus at the end of the 18th and the beginning of the 19th century). Moskva, Izd-vo Akademii nauk, 1963. 366 p. Fold. map. Bibliography: p. 344-352.

    Deals with the Napoleonic period in northwestern Greece, Ali Pasha, etc. Presents a wealth of heretofore untapped Russian archival source material. By the same author, a leading specialist in 18th and 19th century Balkan history, *see:*

    Tainoe obshchestvo "Filiki Eteriia"; iz istorii bor'by Gretsii za sverzhenie osmanskogo iga (The secret society Philike Hetairia; from the history of the struggle of Greece for the overthrow of the Osman

yoke). Moskva, Nauka, 1965. 126 p. Illus., ports. Bibliography:
p. 126-127.

1065. Alexandrēs, Kōnstantinos.   Hē anabiōsis tēs thalassias mas dyna-
meōs kata tēn Tourkokratian (The revival of our naval power during the Turkish domination). Athēnai, Historical Service of the Royal
Navy, 1960. 416 p.

Based upon archival material, especially the records of the Island
of Hydra (most prominent in the pre-1821 period among the Aegean
Islands), this is the most authentic work on the subject of the growth
of the Greek navy in modern times. The author is a naval expert who
has written much on historical subjects.

1066. Botzaris, Notis.   Visions Balkaniques dans la préparation de la
Revolution Grecque (1789-1821). Genève, Librairie E. Droz, 1962.
280 p. Map. Bibliography: p. 271-278. (Études d'histoire économique, politique et sociale, 38)

A study of the influences of the French Revolution and the European Enlightenment as seen in the activities of Rhigas, Korais, and
other leaders of the Greek struggle for independence.

1067. Chaconas, Stephen G.   Adamantios Korais: a Study in Greek Nationalism. New York, Columbia University Press, 1942. 151 p. Bibliography: p. 167-178.

Emphasizes the cultural importance of Korais' literary work, but
includes information on the political situation in his time. Supplementary reading should include the detailed work of A. B. Daskalakēs
entitled *Ho Adamantios Koraēs kai hē eleutheria tōn Hellēnōn*
(Adamantios Korais and the freedom of the Greeks) (Athēnai, 1965,
656 p.).

Korais' works are now available in new editions: *Adamantios
Koraēs, Hapanta ta prōtotypa erga* (Adamantios Korais; collected
original works), edited by G. Valetas (Athēnai, 1964-1965, 2 v.),
and *Adamantios Koraēs, Allēlographia* (Adamantios Korais, correspondence), edited by K. Th. Dēmaras and others (v. 1–, Athēnai,
Hestia, 1964–), two volumes of which have appeared to date.

1068. Daskalakēs, Apostolos B.   Rhigas Velestinlis; la Revolution française et les préludes de l'indépendance hellénique. Paris, 1937. 230
p. Maps, illus. Bibliography: p. 199-226.

————.   Meletai peri Rhēga Velestinlē (Studies of Rhigas of Vele-
stino). Athēnai, 1964. 513 p.

Two very important works, the second including the material of
the first, concerning the first national leader of Greece and his attempts to prepare the ground for Greek independence.

Of equal importance is L. I. Vranousēs' *Rhēgas* (Athēnai, 1953,
406 p. Vasikē Vivliothēkē 10). It contains Rhigas' works, with an
excellent introduction.

1069. Kandēlōros, Takēs Ch.   Ho armatolismos tēs Peloponnēsou, 1500-

1821 (The Institution of Armatoli in the Peloponnesus, 1500-1821). Athēnai, 1924. 444 p.

Though in some respects controversial, this is still the main work on the subject of the militia which was recruited from the Greeks by the Ottoman administrators.

1070. Papadopoullos, Theodore H.   Studies and Documents Relating to the History of the Greek Church and People under Turkish Domination. Brussels, 1952. 507 p. Facsims. (Bibliotheca Graeca aevi posterioris, 1) Bibliography: p. xi-xxiv.
*See also* entry no. 1437.

Important material on the status and internal organization of the Greek Orthodox Church (Patriarchate of Constantinople) and its relations with the Ottoman Empire. An 18th century narrative poem, entitled "Planosparaktēs" (Destroyer of fallacies), published herein for the first time, typifies the mentality of the Greek Church at the crossroads between the post-Byzantine era and the era of Enlightenment. The poem deals with particular aspects of ecclesiastical relations and certain dogmatic controversies of lesser importance.

1071. Prōtopsaltēs, Emmanouēl G.   Hē Philikē Hetairia (The Society of Friends). Athēnai, Akadēmia Athēnōn, 1964. 295 p. Illus.

Commemorating the 150th anniversary of the founding of the secret society that prepared the Greek Revolution, this impressive volume contains information published for the first time and includes important documents in facsimiles and in transcripts. Other works on the subject that are still in print are as follows:

Kandēlōros, Takēs Ch.   Hē Philikē Hetairia, 1814-1821 (The Society of Friends, 1814-1821). Athēnai, 1926.

Mexas, Valerios G.   Hoi Philikoi (The members of the Society of Friends). Athēnai, 1937. A list of the known members, with essential informatioin on each.

Melas, Spyros.   Hoi Philikoi (The members of the Society of Friends). Athēnai, Bires, n.d. Biographical sketches.

Enepekidēs, Polychronēs K.   Rhēgas, Hypsilantēs, Kapodistrias. Athēnai, Hestia, 1965. Important biographical information on the leader of the Society, Alexander Ypsilantis, with new material from Viennese and other archives.

1072. Sphyroeras, Vasilios.   Hoi Dragomanoi tou Stolou (The Dragomans of the fleet). Athēnai, 1965. 190 p. Bibliography: p. 175-180.

The only study of the office of the chief assistants to the Kapudan Pasha (high admiral of the Ottoman Empire, who was also governor of the Aegean Islands). The history of the office is traced and the Dragomans are presented in chronological order, with the significance indicated of each one in the affairs of the Ottoman Empire and of the Greek nation.

1073. Zakythēnos, Dionysios A.   Hē Tourkokratia: Eisagōgē eis tēn neōteran historian tou Hellēnismou (The Turkish domination: introduction to the modern history of Hellenism). Athēnai, 1957. 104 p.

Brief but incisive work on the significance of the fall of the Byzantine Empire in relation to the formation of the Greek people and institutions.

## C. THE GREEK REVOLUTION AND INDEPENDENCE, 1821-1833

1074. Arnakis, George G., *ed.*    Americans in the Greek Revolution. Austin, Texas, Center for Neo-Hellenic Studies, 1966– Illus., maps.

The corpus of the writings of the American philhellenes who took part in the Greek Independence War or actively helped the cause of Greek freedom in the 1820s. Volume 1, comprising the journals and related documents of George Jarvis, and volume 2, containing the writings of Samuel G. Howe, have been published to date. Altogether seven volumes are to be published.

1075. Barth, Wilhelm, *and* Max Kehrig-Korn.    Die Philhellenenzeit: Von der Mitte des 18. Jahrhunderts bis zur Ermordung Kapodistrias am 9. Okt. 1831. München, Hüber, 1960. 286 p. Bibliography: p. 267-277.

Biographical information on the philhellenes, with an introduction on German philhellenism. Part of a larger work prepared by Barth, but not finished and no longer extant.

*See also* Bernard Vonderlage's *Die Hamburger Philhellenen* (Göttingen, Gerstung und Lehman, 1940, 116 p.), and Johannes Irmscher's *Der Philhellenismus in Preussen als Forschungsanliegen* (Berlin, Akademie Verlag, 1966, 73 p.).

1076. Dakin, Douglas.    British and American Philhellenes during the War of Greek Independence, 1821-1833. Thessaloniki, Institute for Balkan Studies, 1955. 247 p. Illus., map, bibliography.

Draws attention to some of the less well-known volunteers in the Greek Revolution and utilizes archival material.

1077. Daskalakēs, Apostolos B.    Hē prōtē ethnosyneleusis kai to politeuma tēs Epidaurou (The first National Assembly and the Constitution of Epidaurus). *In* Epistēmonikē Epetēris tēs Philosophikēs Scholēs tou Panepistēmiou Athēnōn (Scholarly yearbook of the School of Philosophy of the University of Athens). 2d series, v. 16, 1966: 43-140.

Detailed study of the establishment of the first central government and an analysis of the constitution of 1822.

1078. Dēmakopoulos, Geōrgios D.    Hē dioikētikē organōsis kata tēn Hellēnikēn Epanastasin, 1821-1827 (Administrative organization during the Greek Revolution). Athēnai, 1966. 285 p. Maps. Bibliography: p. 17-29; p. 276-277.

The best work so far dealing with the subject of administration prior to the arrival of Kapodistrias.

1079. Hofmann, Georg.   Das Papsttum und der griechische Freiheitskampf (1821-1829): Quellenausgabe mit Einführung. Roma, Pontificium Institutum Orientalium Studiorum, 1952. 209 p. (Orientalia Christiana Analecta, 136)

Important for the study of the attempted rapprochement of the Greek government and the Holy See and the role of the Knights of Malta during the Greek Revolution. *See also* the introduction of Eugène Dalleggio in *Les philhellènes et la Guerre de l'Indépendance: 138 lettres inédites de J. Orlando et A. Louriotis* (Athènes, Collection de l'institut français d'Athènes, 1949).

1080. Kaldis, William P.   John Capodistrias and the Modern Greek State. Madison, State Historical Society of Wisconsin, 1963. 126 p.

Background of the Greek Question and the problems of administration of Greece from 1827 to 1831, with an analysis of the personality of President Capodistrias.

*See also* the following two books: Alexandros J. Despotopoulos' *Ho Kybernētēs Kapodistrias kai hē apeleutherōsis tēs Hellados* (President Capodistrias and the liberation of Greece) (Athēnai, 1954, 222 p.), and Helenē Koukou's *Iōannēs Kapodistrias: Ho anthrōpos, ho agōnistēs* (John Capodistrias: the man, the fighter) (Athēnai, 1965, 77 p.).

1081. Kokkinos, Dionysios, A.   Hē Hellēnikē Epanastasis (The Greek Revolution). 3d ed. Athēnai, Melissa, 1956-1960. 12 v. Illus., maps.

A monumental work, the most complete of its kind, in which the presentation of historical facts is combined with the techniques of creative writing — such as descriptions of landscapes, stories of human interest and anecdotes, and excerpts of reported or imagined dialogues. The index (v. 12, p. 601-735) is hard to use because it is arranged volume by volume, each volume with its own list of names. The narrative ends with the liberation of the Acropolis of Athens in January 1833.

1082. Larrabee, Stephen A.   Hellas Observed: the American Experience of Greece, 1775-1865. New York, New York University Press, 1957. 357 p. Illus., map. Bibliography: p. 335-343.

Well-written and scholarly presentation of American philhellenism before, during, and after the War of Independence.

*See also* E. M. Earl's "American Interest in the Greek Cause, 1821-1827," *American Historical Review*, v. 33, no. 1, Oct. 1927: 44-57; and Myrtle A. Cline's *American Attitude toward the Greek War of Independence, 1821-1828* (Atlanta, 1930, 231 p.).

1083. Makriyannis (Makrygiannēs), Iōannēs.   The Memoirs of General Makriyannis. Edited and translated by H. A. Lidderdale. London, Oxford University Press, 1966. 234 p. Illus., maps.

Makriyannis was one of the most liberal leaders of the period of revolution and independence and also one of the staunch opponents of Othon's absolutist tendencies. The account is fascinating in its directness and simplicity and in its expressions of the people's sense of justice and freedom.

Other memoirs of heroes of the Greek Revolution have not been translated. A 20 volume set of Greek original narratives (memoirs, biographies, and autobiographies) was edited by Emmanouël G. Prōtopsaltēs and published in Athens, under the title *Apomnēmoneumata Agōnistōn tou 21* (Memoirs of the fighters of 1821) (Athēnai, Athēnaikē Vivliothēke, 1955-1957). Prōtopsaltēs also edited the papers of Alexander Mavrokordatos and other leaders, under the auspices of the Academy of Athens.

1084. Nonnenberg-Chun, Marie.   Der französische Philhellenismus in den zwanziger Jahren des vorigen Jahrhunderts. Berlin, Ebering, 1909. 234 p. (Romanische Studien, 10)

A basic study of the French philhellenic movement in literature and political life.

1085. Papadopoulos, Stephanos I.   Hē Epanastasē stē Dytikē Sterea Hellada (The Revolution in Western Sterea Hellas). Thessalonikē, 1962. 232 p. Map (Epistēmonikē Epetēris Philosophikēs Scholēs, 8)

Covers the period from April 1826 to December 1832. In addition to military events, the book deals with the political situation in Greece and the diplomacy of the Greek Question. Summary in French.

Equally important is a work by Domna N. Dontas, *The Last Phase of the War of Independence in Western Greece (December 1827 to May 1829)* (Thessaloniki, Institute for Balkan Studies, 1966, 187 p.).

1086. Phillips, W. Alison.   The War of Greek Independence, 1821 to 1833. London, Smith and Elder, 1897. 424 p. Map.

Intended for the general reader, this volume is largely based upon the work of George Finlay, without his prejudices.

Of a similar nature, though much shorter, is Christopher M. Woodhouse's *The Greek War of Independence: Its Historical Setting* (London, New York, Hutchinson University Library, 1952). For the diplomatic history of the struggle, the English-speaking reader will have to rely upon Charles W. Crawley's *The Question of Greek Independence: A Study of British Policy in the Near East, 1821-1833* (Cambridge, Cambridge University Press, 1930).

1087. Prevelakēs, Eleutherios.   Hē ekstrateia tou Ivraēm Pasa stēn Argolida (The campaign of Ibrahim Pasha in Argolis). Athēnai, Aetos, 1950. 129 p.

Brief but scholarly description of operations in the area around Nauplia in 1825.

1088. Prokesch von Osten, Anton.   Geschichte des Abfalls der Griechen vom türkischen Reiche im Jahre 1821 und der Gründung des hellenischen Königreiches. Wien, Gerold, 1867. 6 v.

Important for the role of the Great Powers in Greece's struggle for independence. The author has a pro-Austrian bias.

1089. Rothpletz, Emil. Zur Geschichte des Philhellenismus im 19. Jahrhundert: Die Griechenbewegung in der Schweiz während des hel-
lenistischen Freiheitskampfes, 1821-1830. Affoltern, Aehren Verlag, 1948. 110 p.
    Important for the study of Swiss philhellenic activities during the
Greek Revolution. *See also* Emil Rothpletz's *Der schöfflisdörfer
Philhellene Johann Jakob Meyer (1798-1826): Ein Beitrag zur Geschichte der Griechenbewegung in Europa während des griechischen
Freiheitskrieges (1821-1829)* (Basel, E. Birkhäuser, 1931).

1090. Stamatopoulos, Takēs. Ho esōterikos agōnas prin kai kata tēn
Epanastasin tou 1821 (The internal struggle before and during the
Revolution of 1821). Athēnai, 1957-64. 2 v.
    A detailed account of the civil strife of the Greeks, with descrip-
tions of the personalities involved, and adequate analysis of issues.
The author rejects the theories of class struggle as presented by
Kordatos (entry no. 1058).

1091. Todorov, Nikolai. Filiki Eteriia i bŭlgarite (Philikē Hetairia and
the Bulgarians). Sofiia, Bŭlgarska akademiia na naukite, 1965. 169 p.
Facsims., map. Bibliography: p. 142-146.
    Contribution of the study of the Greek national awakening in the
first quarter of the 19th century in the Danubian area, and its repercussions on other Balkan peoples. Excellent use of new sources.

1092. Trikoupēs, Spyridōn. Historia tēs Hellenikēs Epanastaseōs (History of the Greek Revolution). 3d ed. Athēnai, Aslanēs, 1888. 4 v.
    The first important history of Greece's War of Independence writ-
ten by a Greek. The account is rich in detail at times, but somewhat
uncritical. The author tries, usually with success, to maintain a
neutral position in the presence of the rivalries of Greece's political
factions. Today the importance of Trikoupēs' work is mainly literary,
representing a vital stage in the development of Greek historiography.

1093. Turczynski, Emanuel. Die deutsch-griechischen Kulturbeziehungen
bis zur Berufung König Ottos. München, Oldenbourg, 1959. 284 p.
Map. (Südosteuropäische Arbeiten, 48)
    Based on materials in Central European archives and libraries, this
is essentially a study of the influence of the Greek communities in
Germany, Austria, Hungary, and the Danubian Principalities through
trade relations and the educational development of the Greeks
through the ideas of German Enlightenment.

1094. Vasdravellēs, Iōannēs K. Hoi Makedones eis tēn Epanastasin tou
1821 (Macedonians in the Revolution of 1821). 3d ed. Thessalonikē,
Hetaireia Makedonikōn Spoudōn, 1967. 323 p. Illus.
    The only book on the subject and also a product of excellent
scholarship. In the first chapter, the author sketches the career of
prerevolutionary warriors; in the second, he introduces the associates of Rhigas; and in the next four chapters he deals with the

participation of Macedonians in the first stage of the Greek Revolution (in the Danubian Principalities), the uprisings in the Chalkidic Peninsula, the Revolution in the Olympus area, and the descent of the Macedonian warriors into Southern Greece during the last stage of the Revolution. The term "Macedonian" is used as a regional term, and the people thus identified were Greeks, ethnically and culturally.

1095. Woodhouse, Christopher M.    The Battle of Navarino. London, Hodder and Stoughton, 1965. 191 p. Illus., maps. Bibliography: p. 183-185.

Scholarly treatment of the diplomatic background of the battle of Navarino, which marked the beginning of the active intervention of Great Britain, France, and Russia and opened the way for Greek independence.

1096. Zamanos, E.    Hē ekstrateia tou Dramali hypo to phōs historiko-stratiōtikēs ereunēs (The expedition of Dramali in the light of historical and military research). Athēnai, 1964. 255 p.

Analysis of the military facts connected with the first large-scale attempt of the Ottoman Empire to crush the revolution in the Peloponnesus (1822).

## D. POLITICAL AND DIPLOMATIC HISTORY, 1833-1914

1097. Arnakis, George G., ed.    American Consul in a Cretan War — William J. Stillman. Austin, Texas, Center for Neo-Hellenic Studies, 1966. 146 p. (American Interest in the Cretan Struggle, 1866-1869, v. 1)

Important eyewitness account of the first two years of the Cretan struggle, with firsthand reports from the diplomatic side scenes.

Supplementary reading should include the following: Nikolaos Tsirintanēs' *Hē politikē kai diplōmatikē historia tēs en Krētēi ethnikēs epanastaseōs, 1866-1868* (Political and diplomatic history of the national revolution in Crete, 1866-1868) (Athēnai, 1951, 3 v.); J. D. Mourellos' *Historia tēs Krētēs* (History of Crete), v. 1 (Herakleion, 1950); J. P. Mamalakis' *Ho agōnas tou 1866-1869 gia tēn Henōsē tēs Krētēs* (The struggle of 1866-1869 for the union of Crete) (Thessalonikē, 1942, 3 v.); Nicholas B. Tomadakis' *The Cretan Revolt, 1866-1869* (Canea, Literary Society Chrysostomos, 1966, 21 p.).

1098. Bower, Leonard, *and* Gordon Bolitho.    Otho I, King of Greece: A Biography. London, Selwyn and Blount, 1939. 263 p. Illus. Bibliography: p. 245-246.

A good survey of the area of King Othon. A critical view of Othon's reign is given by Dēmētrēs Phōtiadēs in *Ho Othōnas — Hē Monarchia* (Othon — the monarchy) (Athēnai, Vivlioekdotikē, 1963, 384 p.). For a more objective, if sympathetic view, *see* A. Skandamēs' *Hē Triakontaetia tēs Vasileias tou Othōnos I* (The 30 years of the reign of Othon I) (Athēnai, 1961, 1046 p.).

1099. Cassavetti, Demetrius J.    Hellas and the Balkan Wars. London, Unwin, 1914. 368 p. Illus., maps.

Best account of the role of Greece in solving the Macedonian Question. A slight pro-Greek bias is discernible. Supplementary reading should include Ernst C. Helmreich's *The Diplomacy of the Balkan Wars, 1912-1913* (Cambridge, Mass., Harvard University Press, 1938, 523 p). Based upon archival material, this book concentrates on the role of the other Balkan allies and seeks to minimize Bulgaria's responsibility in the outbreak of the Second Balkan War.

1100. Dakin, Douglas.    The Greek Struggle in Macedonia, 1897-1913. Thessalonikē, Institute for Balkan Studies, 1966. 538 p. Illus.

Richly documented, detailed account of the Macedonian Question and Greece's involvement, from the aftermath of Greek defeat by Turkey to the victorious conclusion of the Balkan Wars. Describes individual leaders.

Also important from the point of view of Greek national aspirations is George B. Zotiades' *The Macedonian Controversy* (Thessalonikē, Institute for Balkan Studies, 1954, 92 p.).

1101. Dontas, Domna N.    Greece and the Great Powers, 1863-1875. Thessalonikē, Institute for Balkan Studies, 1966. 223 p. Bibliography. *See also* entry no. 1211.

Essentially a study of the Cretan Question during the years 1866-1869, this book provides adequate information for an understanding of what preceded and what followed that great upheaval in the Near East. Well documented from the Archives of the Greek Ministry of Foreign Affairs and from other depositories.

Also important with special reference to the Cretan Question is Geōrgios Papantōnakēs' *Hē diplōmatikē historia tēs Krētikēs Epanastaseōs tou 1866* (Diplomatic history of the Cretan Revolution of 1866) (Athēnai, 1926).

1102. Jelavich, Barbara, *ed.*    Russia and Greece during the Regency of King Othon, 1832-1835. Thessalonikē, Institute for Balkan Studies, 1962. 155 p. Illus., bibliography.

Concise introduction to the Greek Question in the early 1830s, followed by documentary material — mainly instructions to the Russian minister at the court of Munich, revealing Russia's efforts to maintain a predominant influence over Greece.

1103. Jelavich, Barbara.    Russia and the Greek Revolution of 1843. Munich, Oldenbourg, 1966. 124 p. (Südosteuropäische Arbeiten, 65)

Survey of Greece's domestic politics in relation to the diplomacy of the Great Powers, followed by diplomatic dispatches of the Bavarian minister at St. Petersburg and the Austrian minister at Athens (Prokesch-Osten).

1104. Korisis, Hariton.    Die politischen Parteien Griechenlands. Ein neuer

Staat auf dem Weg zur Demokratie, 1821-1910. Hersbruck, Nürnberg, Pfeiffer, 1966. 230 p. Bibliography: p. 213-225.
*See also* entry no. 1140.

Critical analysis of economic and social factors in the development of modern Greece and the historical evolution of her political parties from her independence to the rise of Venizelos.

1105. Pournaras, Dēmētrios.    Charilaos Trikoupēs — Hē zoē kai to ergon tou (Charilaos Trikoupis — his life and work). Athēnai, 1950. 2 v. (Historikē Vivliothēkē, 3-4)

The only biography of Greece's great statesman of the 19th century, written after the Second World War, in popular style, but rich in detail and accurate. The author's attitude is one of admiration and his purpose is educative.

1106. Prevelakēs (Prevelakis), Eleutherios.    British Policy towards the Change of Dynasty in Greece, 1862-1863. Athens, 1953. 194 p. Bibliography: p. 172-185.
*See also* entry no. 1228.

Based upon Foreign Office and other archival material, this penetrating study sheds light on the side scenes of the dethronement of King Othon.

1107. Sergeant, Lewis.    New Greece. London, Paris, New York, Cassell, Petter, Galpin, 1878. 423 p. Maps. Bibliography: p. 417-418.

Important for its detailed descriptions of 19th century Greece. The author has firsthand knowledge, but his material is not well organized. More systematic, though less detailed, is his *Greece in the Nineteenth Century: a Record of Hellenic Emancipation and Progress, 1821-1897* (London, Fisher Unwin, 1897, 400 p.).

Equally important is the recent work by Anthony Petropulos, *Politics and Statecraft in the Kingdom of Greece* (Princeton, N.J., Princeton University Press, 1968, 646 p.).

## E. GREECE SINCE 1914

1108. Abbott, George F.    Greece and the Allies, 1914-1922. London, Methuen, 1922. 242 p.
*See also* entry no. 1208.

Lucid and well written account, with a Constantinist bias. Also sympathetic to King Constantine's position are the following: Paxton Hibben's *Constantine I and the Greek People* (New York, Century, 1920, 592 p); S. Phocas-Cosmetatos' *L'Entente et la Grèce pendant la Grande Guerre* (Paris, Societé mutuelle d'édition, 1926, 2 v.); A. F. Frangoulis' *La Grèce et la crise mondiale* (Paris, 1926-1927, 2 v.).

For the Venizelist point of view, the best book in English is still Herbert A. Gibbons' *Venizelos* (Boston, New York, Houghton Mifflin, 1920, 384 p.).

Archival material in support of the Venizelist version of the crisis is included in Polychronēs Enepekidēs' *Hē doxa kai ho dichasmos — Apo ta mystika archeia tēs Viennēs, 1908-1916* (Glory and dissension — from the secret archives of Vienna, 1908-1916) (Athēnai, Birēs, 1962, 404 p.).

1109. Daphnēs, Grēgorios.   Hē Hellas metaxy dyo polemōn, 1923-1940 (Greece between the two wars, 1923-1940). Athēnai, Ikaros, 1955. 2 v. Bibliography: v. 2, p. 477-479.
*See also* entries no. 1169 *and* 1210.
The most complete and reliable account of the interwar period in Greece, with special attention to domestic affairs.

1110. O'Ballance, Edgar.   The Greek Civil War, 1944-1949. New York, Praeger, 1966. 237 p. Maps. Bibliography: p. 225-227.
*See also* entry no. 1189.
Fair-minded account by a military man who is also a military historian. While the military operations are described clearly and critically, there is little more than a superficial examination of the political forces behind the conflict.
Equally important and more penetrating is D. George Kousoulas' *Revolution and Defeat: the Story of the Greek Communist Party* (London, New York, Oxford University Press, 1965, 306 p.).

1111. Pallis, Alexander A.   Greece's Anatolian Venture — and After: a Survey of the Diplomatic and Political Aspects of the Greek Expedition to Asia Minor (1915-1922). London, Methuen, 1937. 239 p. Illus., map. Bibliography: p. 207-215.
The best work available on the subject. Important for analysis of the background of Greece's involvement and the causes of her defeat.
Also important, because it is based upon Russian and other records, is Evgenii A. Adamow's *Die europäischen Mächte und Griechenland während des Weltkrieges* (Dresden, Reissner, 1932, 339 p.).
The best work in Greek, amply documented, though with a Venizelist slant, is Geōrgios Ventērēs' (Bentērēs) *Hē Hellas tou 1910-1920 (Greece of 1910-1920* (Athēnai, Aetos, 1931, 2 v.). The following two works attempt to refute Ventērēs' thesis: Prince Andrew of Greece's *Towards Disaster — The Greek Army in Asia Minor in 1921* (London, Murray, 1930), and Iōannēs Metaxas' *Historia tou ethnikou dichasmou kai tēs mikrasiatikēs katastrophēs* (History of the national split and the Asia Minor disaster) (Athēnai, 1935).

1112. Papadakēs, Vasileios Panagiōtou (Basilios Papadakis).   Diplōmatikē historia tou hellēnikou polemou, 1940-1945 (Diplomatic history of the Greek war, 1940-1945). Athēnai, 1957. 510 p.
A detailed account, based upon documents and supplemented by the personal memoirs of the author, who was minister of foreign affairs during the war.

Equally important is the broader work of a later foreign minister, Panagiotēs Pipinelēs, entitled *Historia tēs exōterikēs politikēs tēs Hellados, 1923-1941* (History of the foreign policy of Greece, 1923-1941) (Athēnai, Saliveros, 1948, 374 p.).

1113. Papadakēs, Vasileios Panagiōtou (Basile Papadakis).   Histoire diplomatique de la question Nord-Epirote 1912-1957. Athènes, J. Alevropoulos, Societé des études macédoniennes, 1958. 196 p. Maps. Bibliography: p. 178-182.

*See also* entry no. 1245.

Based upon documents, especially those of the Greek Foreign Ministry, this book clarifies Greece's claims in North Epirus and discusses the role of the Great Powers in the creation of the Albanian state.

A shorter account of the North Epirus Question is available in Panagiotēs Pipinelēs' *Europe and the Albanian Question*, 2d ed. (Chicago, Argonaut Press, 1963, 94 p.).

1114. Papagos, Alexandros.   Ho polemos tēs Hellados, 1940-1941 (The war of Greece, 1940-1941). Athēnai, Hoi Philoi tou Bibliou, 1945. 343 p.

An authentic account of military operations, written by the commander-in-chief of the Greek army. English, French, and Italian translations include only part of the book.

Also revealing is the work of an intelligence staff officer, Athanasios Korozēs, entitled *Hoi polemoi 1940-41: Epitychiai kai euthynai* (The wars of 1940-41: successes and responsibilities) (Athēnai, 1957, 4 v.). The two volumes published thus far take the narrative to the Italian attack on Greece (October 28, 1940).

1115. Pentzopoulos, Dimitri.   The Balkan Exchange of Minorities and Its Impact upon Greece. Paris, Mouton, 1962. 293 p. Illus. (Publications of the Social Sciences Center, Athens, 1)

*See also* entries no. 1043 *and* 1343.

Up-to-date, using all available material on the settlement of the refugees and the effect of the settlement on the Greeks of Greece.

Other works on the same subject are as follows: Henry Morgenthau's *I Was Sent to Athens* (Garden City, N.Y., Doubleday, 1929, 327 p.); Eliot G. Mears' *Greece Today: The Aftermath of the Refugee Impact* (Stanford, Stanford University Press, 1929, 336 p.); Charles B. Eddy's *Greece and the Greek Refugees* (London, Allen and Unwin, 1931, 274 p.); and Stephen P. Ladas' *The Exchange of Minorities: Bulgaria, Greece and Turkey* (New York, Macmillan, 1932, 849 p.).

1116. Stavrianos, L. S.   Greece: American Dilemma and Opportunity. Chicago, Regnery, 1952. 246 p.

*See also* entry no. 1193.

An analysis of the Greek political crisis during and after the

Second World War and the prospects of democratic solutions with American aid.

Other works, with divergent points of view are as follows: *Apple of Discord*, by Christopher M. Woodhouse (London, 1948); *The Greek Dilemma: War and Aftermath*, by William Hardy McNeill (Philadelphia, New York, 1947); *Report on the Greeks*, by Frank Smothers, William H. McNeill, and Elizabeth D. McNeill (New York, Twentieth Century Fund, 1948); and *The Price of Freedom: Greece in World Affairs, 1939-1953*, by Demetrius G. Kousoulas (Syracuse, 1953).

1117. Xydis, Stephen G.   Greece and the Great Powers, 1944-1947: Prelude to the Truman Doctrine. Thessaloniki, Institute for Balkan Studies, 1963. 758 p. Illus., maps. Bibliography: p. 721-738.

*See also* entries no. 182 *and* 1241.

Beginning with the establishment of the Greek government-in-exile, the author gives a detailed and documented survey of diplomatic events leading to the enunciation of the Truman Doctrine (March 1947), while the civil war in Greece was going through its most acute stage. This is by far the best work on the subject of the policies of the Great Powers in their relations with Greece in the last year of the war and immediately after.

Part of the subject — i.e., the relations of Greece with her northern neighbors — is described in a thorough and lucid way in Evangelos Kofos' *Nationalism and Communism in Macedonia* (Thessaloniki, Institute for Balkan Studies, 1964, 251 p.).

# 31

# the state

## A. LAW

*by Stephen G. Xydis*

### 1. The Constitutional System

1118. Alderfer, H.   Report on Greek Local Government. Athens, Civil Government Division, Mutual Security Agency, 1952. 49 p. (mimeographed).

A valuable study of the subject.

1119. Djiras, Alexandre C.   L'organisation politique de la Grèce d'après la constitution républicaine du 29 septembre 1925. Paris, Les Presses modernes, 1927. 176 p.

An analysis of the republican constitution of Greece.

1120. Kalodoukas, Dionysios.   To syntagma tou 1952 (The constitution of 1952). Athēnai, 1952. 203 p.

Includes an introduction on the constitutional history of modern Greece since 1864, an account of the revision work of 1946-1951, and comments on the new constitution as compared to that of 1864 (as revised in 1911).

1121. Kaltchas, Nicholas S.   Introduction to the Constitutional History of

Modern Greece. New York, Columbia University Press, 1940. 187 p. Bibliography: p. 173-176.

A brilliant study of the impact of international factors on Greek constitutional developments and Greek politics from the Greek War of Independence until the establishment of the Metaxas dictatorship in 1936.

1122. Kyriakopoulos, Ēlias K.    Ta syntagmata tēs Hellados (The constitutions of Greece). Athēnai, Ethnikon Typografeion, 1960. 895 p.

A collection of modern Greek constitutions that includes regional constitutions and those of the Ionian islands, Crete, and Samos, as well as a small number of constitutional projects such as that of Rhigas Pheraios of 1797. Introductory notes precede each text.

1123. Papadatos, St.    Hē politeiakē thesis tou Hagiou Orous (The political status of the Holy Mountain). Athēnai, 1965. 135 p.

A study of the autonomous régime of Mount Athos.

1124. Svōlos, Alexandros I., and G. Vlachos.    To syntagma tēs Hellados: Hermēneia, historia, synkritikon dikaion (The Constitution of Greece: interpretation, history, comparative law). Part I. Athēnai, 1954. 2 v. (364 p.)

This study — never completed — provides an analysis in depth of the first four articles of the constitution of 1952 (religion, relations between church and state, public law of the Hellenes, individual rights, the principle of equality before the law, individual freedoms).

## 2. Law Codes and Treatises

1125. Bouropoulos, Angelos.    Kōdix politikēs dikonomias (Code of civil procedure). Athēnai, N. Sakkoulas, 1951. 733 p.

Includes the author's annotations.

1126. Code civil héllénique.    Translated for the Institut héllénique de droit international et étranger by Pierre Mamopoulos. Introductory note by Petros Vallindas. Athènes, 1956. 411 p.

1127. Greece. Laws, statutes, etc.    Emporikos nomos, meta semeiōseōn, scholiōn, nomologias Arist. Ch. Tousē (Commercial law, with notes, comments, and judicial interpretations by A. C. Touses). 2d ed. Athēnai, Papazēsēs, 1958-1959. 2 v.

1128. Greece. Laws, statutes, etc.    Stratiōtikos poinikos kōdix. Synapheis eidikoi nomoi (Military penal code and related military laws). Compiled by Niketas P. Polychronopoulos. 2d ed. Athēnai, 1960. 495 p.

A comprehensive manual of Greek military law, prepared by a military judge. Useful as an aid to the study of politicomilitary events in modern Greek history.

1129. Hypallēlikos kōdix kai kōdix hypallēlon nomikōn prosōpōn dēmosiou dikaiou (nomos 1811 tou 1951). Me plērē hermēneutika scholia hypo M. D. Stasinopoulou (Employment code and code of employees of legal persons of public law [law 1811 of 1951], with complete interpretive comments by M. D. Stasinopoulos). Athēnai, Stegē tou Bibliou, 1951. 329 p.

1130. Kōdix poinikēs dikonomias (Code of criminal procedure). Athēnai, Zacharopoulos, 1946. 571 p.

1131. Panagiōtakos, Panagiōtēs.    Systēma tou ekklēsiastikou dikaiou kata tēn en Helladi ischyn autou (System of canon law in force in Greece). v. 3-4. Athēnai, 1957-1962. 768, 962 p.

1132. Papachadzēs, G.    Systēma tou en Helladi ischyontos dioikētikou dikaiou. Genikon meros (System of administrative law in force in Greece. General part). Athēnai, 1952. 405 p.

> The second part of this book deals particularly with the evolution of administrative law in Greece. The third part covers judicial regulation of the administrative machinery.

1133. Zepos, Panagiōtēs Iōannou.    Greek Law. Three Lectures Delivered at Cambridge and Oxford in 1946. Athens, 1949. 119 p.

> An excellent introduction to Greek law by an eminent Greek legal historian.

## B. POLITICS AND GOVERNMENT

*by Stephen G. Xydis*

### 1. Survey Studies

1134. Allied Mission to Observe the Greek Elections. Report of the Allied Mission to Observe the Greek Elections. Washington, D.C., U.S. Government Printing Office, 1946. 36 p. (U.S. Department of State. Publication 2522)

> An identical title was printed in 1946 in London by His Majesty's Stationery Office (Great Britain, Foreign Office. Greece no. 3, 1946. Great Britain, Parliament. Papers by Command. CMD. 6812).

1135. Burks, R. V.    The Dynamics of Communism in Eastern Europe. Princeton, Princeton University Press, 1961. 244 p. Maps, tables.

> Includes an interesting chapter on communism in Greece that is based on research and interrogations of communist detainees in Greek reform prisons.

1136. Daphnēs, Grēgorios.    Ta hellēnika politika kommata (1821-1961) (The Greek political parties [1821-1961]). Athēnai, 1961. 190 p.

> A useful survey of the numerous political parties that have appeared on the Greek political scene since the War for Independence.

1137. Daskalakēs, Geōrgios D.    To hellēnikon provlēma (The Greek problem). Athēnai, 1954. 83 p.

This and Daskalakēs' *Political Parties and Democracy* (*Politika kommata kai dēmokratia*, Athenai, 1958, 100 p.) are thoughtful functional essays about the realities of the power of bureaucracy as opposed to the norms of the essentially 19th century constitution of Greece and the role of political parties and parliamentarianism in Greek political life.

1138. EDA (Eniaia Dēmokratikē Aristera).    To eklogiko praxikopēma tēs 29ēs Oktōvriou 1961 (United Democratic Left; the electoral coup d'état of October 29, 1961). Athēnai, 1962. 600 p.

A "black book" of charges of widespread coercion and fraud during the 1961 elections. A similar book is Lefterēs Apostolou's *Hoi ekloges tēs 29ēs Oktōvriou 1961. Symperasmata kai didagmata* (The elections of October 29, 1961; conclusions and lessons) (Athēnai, 208 p.).

1139. Kofos, Evangelos.    Nationalism and Communism in Macedonia. Thessalonike, Institute for Balkan Studies, 1964. 251 p. Maps. Bibliography: p. 227-238.

*See also* entry no. 1340.

A thorough study of the problem seen from the Greek viewpoint.

1140. Korisis, Hariton.    Die politischen Parteien Griechenlands. Ein neuer Staat auf dem Weg sur Demokratie, 1821-1910. Hersbruck, Nürnberg, Pfeiffer, 1966. 260 p. Bibliography: p. 213-225.

*See also* entry no. 1104.

A pioneering effort in relating Greek political parties and political thoughts to the development of Greek society.

1141. Kousoulas, Dimitrios George.    Revolution and Defeat; the Story of the Greek Communist Party. London, Oxford University Press, 1965. 306 p. Maps. Bibliography: p. 292-295.

Likely to remain for a long time the standard book on this subject.

1142. Lamprinos, G.    Hē monarchia stēn Hellada (The monarchy in Greece). Budapest, 1965. 126 p.

A strongly anti-monarchist communist tract.

1143. Mathiopoulos, Basil P.    Die Geschichte der sozialen Frage und des Sozialismus in Griechenland (1821-1961). Hannover, Verlag für Literatur und Zeitgeschehen, 1961. 109 p. Bibliography: p. 171-180.

A detailed study of the development and character of the socialism of Greek workers and its social and political conditions.

1144. Meynaud, Jean.    Les forces politiques en Grèce. Montreal, 1965. 530 p. Maps. (Études de science politique, 10)

A behavioral and pressure group approach to Greek politics from 1945 to 1964 that is pervaded by left-wing propaganda. The response of the ERE (National Radical Party) to this book is found in Gerassimos Th. Lychnos' *La vérité sur les forces politiques en Grèce* (Athènes, 1966, 79 p.).

1145. Pipinelēs, Panagiotēs. To stemma eis to plaision tōn dēmokratikōn thesmōn (The Crown within the framework of democratic institutions). Athēnai, Vassileiou, 1960. 112 p.

The author, a staunch supporter of the monarchy, emphasizes the function of the Crown as a symbol of the continuity and unity of the state and the role of the king as a referee in the conflict of political parties and pressure groups.

1146. Vivliothēkē tēs Voulēs tōn Hellēnōn. Hai hellēnikai kyvernēseis kai ta proedreia voulēs kai gerousias 1926-1959 (Greek governments and presidencies of the Parliament and the Senate, 1926-1959). Athēnai, 1959. 288 p.

## 2. Political Personalities

1147. Alastos, Doros. Venizelos: Patriot, Statesman, Revolutionary. London, Lund Humphries, 1942. 304 p. Maps. Bibliography: p. 299-300.

A useful English-language biography of the eminent statesman.

1148. Arēs Velouhiotēs, ho prōtos tou agōna (1905-1945) (Aris Velouhiotis, first in the struggle [1905-1945]). Athēnai, Lagdas, 1964. 2 v.

A biography of the ELAS leader who was unwilling to comply with the terms of the Varkiza agreement of February 12, 1945, and was killed shortly thereafter.

1149. Gonatas, Stylianos. Apomnēmoneumata Stylianou Gonata (Memoirs of Stylianos Gonatas). Athēnai, 1958. 518 p. Illus., maps.

The prime minister of the revolutionary government (1922-1924) and subsequent holder of several ministerial posts gives a straightforward account of his life, which until 1924 was military and included participation in the Greek struggle in Macedonia and Thrace, the Balkan Wars, the First World War, and the expedition to the Ukraine and then to Asia Minor.

1150. Ioannidēs, Lakēs A. Cōnstantinos Karamanlēs. Thessalonikē, 1966. 196 p.

In the absence of any better study of the man who was prime minister of Greece for eight consecutive years (1955-1963), this short journalistic work of an admirer of the leader of ERE (National Radical Union) is helpful.

1151. Komnēnos, K. Geōrgios Papandreou. Athēnai, 1965. 638 p. Illus.

A useful biography of the leader of EK (Center Union) by a partisan.

1152. Mazarakēs-Ainian, Alexandros. Apomnēmoneumata (Memoirs). Athēnai, 1948. 698 p.

Memoirs of a cultured military man, one-time chief of staff and minister of war, who mixes history writing with copious quotations from his diary.

1153. Merkourēs, Stamatēs.  Georgiōs Kondylēs (George Kondylis). Athēnai, Mavridēs, 1954. 260 p.

The author, who at the time of his death in 1967 was a member of parliament cooperating with EDA (United Democratic Left), describes the astonishing military and political career of the man who in 1897 started out as a corporal in an evzone regiment and shortly before his death in 1936 briefly served as regent prior to the return of King George II to Athens.

1154. Metaxas, Iōannēs.  To prosōpiko hēmerologio (Personal diary). Athēnai, 1951-1960. 4 v. Illus., maps.

The diary of Metaxas starts in 1896 but has gaps from May 1903 to October 1910; from July 1912 to November 1918; and from June to December 1936. (The latter two gaps are the most regrettable.) Includes introductions, annotations, a biography, a chronology, several interesting documents, articles, and speeches, and the draft constitution Metaxas dictated shortly before his death. An indispensable source for understanding the man who was dictator of Greece in 1936-1941.

1155. Pangalos (Pankalos), Theodōros.  Ta apomnēmoneumata mou 1897-1947 (My memoirs, 1897-1947). Athēnai, 1950-1959. 2 v.

These memoirs, never finished because of the death of their author, dictator of Greece in 1925, include an analysis of the war of 1897, a detailed account of the military coup of 1909, a critique of the Balkan wars, and the familiar charges that during the First World War the Greek General Staff and Metaxas sought to undermine the position of Venizelos and prevent Greek participation in the Gallipoli campaign.

1156. Pipinelēs, Panagiotēs. Geōrgios B' (George II). Athēnai, 1951. 220 p.

The author, a staunch royalist who was for a while political adviser of King George II, paints an admiring portrait of the rather dour monarch, who was imbued by a strong desire to reestablish Greek political unity.

1157. Pournaras, Dēmētrios.   Eleutherios Venizelos. Athēnai, 1960. 518 p.

Presents Venizelos as a representative of the liberal bourgeoisie that had been struggling since 1821 for economic, social, and political progress against the rural lords and leading clans of Greece.

1158. Pyromaglou, Komnēnos.   Ho Geōrgios Kartalēs kai hē epochē tou 1934-1944 (George Kartalis and his times, 1934-1944). v. I. Athēnai, 1965. 680 p. Bibliography: p. 647-650.

A sympathetic biography of a politician who set up the Republican Party in the postwar period and died in 1957.

1159. Tsirimōkos, Ēlias.    Alexandros Svōlos. Athēnai, 1963. 144 p.
The socialist leader, who served as prime minister briefly in
1965, eulogizes a like-minded colleague, a distinguished professor of
constitutional law at the University of Athens.

1160. Tsolakoglou, Geōrgios.    Apomnēmoneumata mou (My memoirs).
Athēnai, 1959. 250 p.
An *apologia pro vita sua* of the general who capitulated in Epirus
on April 20, 1941, served as first puppet premier of Greece under
the occupation, and, after liberation, was tried and imprisoned.

1161. Venezēs, Ēlias.    Ho archiepiskopos Damaskēnos. Oi chronoi tēs
douleias (Archbishop Damaskinos; the years of slavery). Athēnai,
1952. 336 p.
Based on the Archbishop's personal papers and on interviews. Re-
counts the multifarious political, humanitarian, and religious activities in which the Archbishop of Athens, who was to serve as regent
from 1945 to 1946, was engaged during the occupation of Greece
(1941-1944).

1162. Vouros, Geōrgios.    Panagēs Tsaldarēs, 1867-1936. Athēnai, 1955.
568 p.
A somewhat plodding biography of the lackluster leader of the
Populist Party who became prime minister in the '30s and represented the conservative trend in Greek politics.

1163. Zalokōstas, Chrēstos P.    Alexandros A', Vasileus tōn Hellēnōn
(Alexander I, King of Greece). Athēnai, 1952. 222 p.
A biography by a friend of the short-lived king, who after his
father's deposition by allied intervention in 1917 vainly tried to play
the role of umpire between Venizelists and anti-Venizelists.

## 3. Political History

### a. General Studies

1164. Forster, Edward S.    A Short History of Modern Greece, 1821-1956.
Revised and enlarged by Douglas Dakin. New York, Praeger, 1957.
268 p. Illus.
See also entry no. 1051.
A concise survey work.

1165. Markezinēs, Spyridōn Vasileiou.    Politikē historia tēs neōteras Hellados, 1828-1964 (Political history of Modern Greece, 1828-1964).
Athēnai, 1966. 5 v.
Besides its importance as a historical text this work is perhaps
the finest illustrated history of Modern Greece ever published. Contains a remarkable collection of well-chosen and well-reproduced
illustrations and documents.

1166. Woodhouse, C. M.    Modern Greece. *In* Heurtley, W. A., *and others.*

A Short History of Greece From Early Times to 1964. Cambridge, the University Press, 1965. 202 p. Maps. Bibliography: p. 184-187.

1167. Markezinēs, Spyridōn Vasileiou.    Politikē historia tēs neōteras Hellados (Eisagōgika mathēmata) (The political history of Greece [introductory lessons]). Athēnai, 1962. 102 p.

### b. 1909-1940

1168. Benekos, G.    To kinēma tou 1935. (The sedition of 1935). Athēnai, 1965. 320 p.

An account of the unsuccessful effort of Venizelos to overthrow the government by force in March 1935.

1169. Daphnēs, Grēgorios.    Hē Hellas metaxy dyo polemōn, 1923-1940 (Greece between the two wars, 1923-1940). Athēnai, Ikaros, 1955. 2 v. Bibliography: v. 2, p. 477-479.

See also entries no. 1109 and 1210.

A first-class account, based on the personal papers of several leading Greek politicians of the interwar period.

1170. He dikē tōn Hex. Episēma Praktika. Prolegomena kai scholia St. Prōteou (The trial of the six; official proceedings; introduction and comments by St. Proteas). Athēnai, 1963. 824 p.

Important documentary source for understanding the political division in the Greek body politic from 1915 to 1947.

1171. Historia tou ethnikou dichasmou (1915-1935) hopōs tēn exethesan eis seiran arthrōn tōn ho Eleutherios Venizelos kai ho Ioannēs Metaxas (The history of the national division [1915-1935] as Eleutherios Venizelos and Ioannis Metaxas presented it in a series of articles). Athēnai, 1953. 284 p.

The two political leaders present their respective views on the causes of, responsibilities for, and meaning of the rupture in national unity that so gravely affected Greek politics from 1915 to 1947.

1172. Melas, Spyros.    Hē epanastasē tou 1909 (The revolution of 1909). Athēnai, Birēs, 1957. 384 p.

Melas emphasizes that this was the first military revolt not connected with a political party; its aim was not to set up a dictatorship but to open the way for a renaissance of the nation and of its ideals. Another view of the revolution is that of Tasos Vournas in *Goudi. To kinēma tou 1909* (Goudi: the coup of 1909) (Athēnai, 1957, 184 p.). He sees in the coup not only the expression of a general will to renovate the political institutions of Greece but also a refusal to embrace the social claims of the workers and peasants. Melas' work also evoked an attack by Th. Logothetēs in two books: *Ho akadēmaikos k. Spyros Melas plastographei tēn historian tou 1909* (The academician Mr. Spyros Melas falsifies the history of 1909) (Athēnai,

1957, 24 p.); and *Hē epanastasē tou 1909 kai oi kyrioi S. Melas, St. Stefanou, kai D. Pournaras* (The revolution of 1909 and Messrs. S. Melas, St. Stefanou, and D. Pournaras) (Athēnai, 1960, 24 p.).

1173. Waterlow, Sir Sidney.   Decline and Fall of Greek Democracy, 1933-1936. The Political Quarterly, v. 18, Apr. 1947: 95-106; July 1947: 205-219.

This former minister of Britain in Athens assays the causes and events that contributed to the overthrow of Greek parliamentary government on August 4, 1936, by John Metaxas' dictatorship.

#### c. Since 1940

1174. Argenti, Philip P.   The Occupation of Chios by the Germans and Their Administration of the Island. Cambridge, London, Cambridge University Press, 1966. 375 p. Illus., maps, facsims., tables.
*See also* entry no. 1299.

A very carefully researched study of the techniques and impact of the occupation on an insular community in the Aegean.

1175. Chandler, Geoffrey.   The Divided Land; an Anglo-Greek Tragedy. London, Macmillan; New York, St. Martins Press, 1959. 214 p. Illus.

Another book of experiences of a member of a British mission who parachuted into Greece during the occupation and remained there until 1946.

1176. Condit, D. M.   Case Study in Guerrilla War: Greece During World War II. Washington, D.C., Special Operations Research Office, The American University, 1961. 338 p. Illus., maps. Bibliography: p. 307-323.

A thorough study of Greek resistance movements during the Second World War. Useful as background for the postwar communist guerrilla warfare in Greece.

1177. Enepekidēs, Polychronēs K.   Hē Hellēnikē antistasis 1941-1944, hopōs apokalyptetai apo ta mystika archeia tēs Wehrmacht stēn Hellada (The Greek resistance of 1941-1944 as revealed in the secret archives of the Wehrmacht in Greece). Athēnai, 1964. 304 p.

Provides an interesting insight into Nazi German attitudes toward the resistance.

1178. Grēgoriadēs, Ph. N.   To antartiko ELAS-EDES-EKKA (The guerrilla movement, ELAS-EDES-EKKA). Athēnai, 1963. 2 v. (320, 316 p.).

This book emphasizes the EAM-ELAS and "Democratic Army" side of the picture, as does Grēgoriadēs' *Historia tou emphyliou polemou 1945-1949 (to deutero antartiko)* (History of the civil war, 1945-1949 [the second guerrilla movement]) (Athēnai, 1964-1965, 2 v.).

1179. Houtas, Stylianos.   Hē Ethnikē antistasē tōn Hellēnon 1941-1945

(The national resistance of the Greeks, 1941-1945). Athēnai, 1961. 635 p.

A leader of EDES (National Republican Greek League) and later a member of EK (Center Union Party) of George Papandreou dwells at length on his organization's underground activities and relations with other resistance groups and other political factions — Greek or British — active either in Greece itself or outside. Komnenos Pyromaglou writes in the same vein from a somewhat different angle in *Ho doureios hippos. Hē ethnikē kai politikē krisis kata tēn katochēn* (The Trojan Horse; the national and political crisis during the occupation) (Athēnai, 1958, 228 p.).

1180. Phos eis tēn politikēn krisin pou syneklonise tēn Hellada (Light on the political crisis that shook Greece). Athēnai, To Chrēmatisterion tou Vivliou, 1965. 112 p.

Documents on the crisis of July 15, 1965, that include the letters exchanged between King Constantine II and George Papandreou and the proceedings of the Crown Council of September 1 and 2, 1965.

1181. Kalantzēs, Kōstas.   Hē dekemvrianē epanastasē. To chroniko mias tetraetias 1941-1944 (The December revolution; the chronicle of the quadrennial, 1941-1944). Athēnai, Vassileiou, 1954. 240 p.

The author regards the December 1944 uprising as the climax of a process that began with the collapse of the Metaxas regime during the Second World War and featured the inertia of the old Greek political parties and communist leadership of the resistance movement.

1182. Kommounistikon Komma Hellados.   Pros tēn 3ē syndiaskepsē tou KKE (Toward the third conference of the Communist Party of Greece). Voukourestion, 1950.

Contains an account of the "three years' struggle of the Democratic Army of Greece" (1945-1949).

1183. Kōnstantopoulos, Savvas.   Ho phobos tēs diktatorias (The fear of dictatorship). Athēnai, 1966. 174 p. Bibliography: p. 165-174.

Analyzing the political situation, the editor of *Eleutheros Kosmos* charges George Papandreou with Bonapartist tendencies.

1184. Kotsaridas, Eleutherios I.   To chroniko tēs kriseos (Chronicle of the crisis). Athēnai, 1966. 57 p.

A journalist supporter of George Papandreou describes the crisis of July 15, 1965, and its background.

1185. McNeill, William H.   Greece: American Aid in Action, 1947-1956. New York, Twentieth Century Fund, 1957. 240 p. Illus., maps.
*See also* entries no. 1237, 1257, *and* 1308.

The author, who served in Greece as assistant military attaché in 1944-1946, surveys the decade of Greek political, economic, and social developments since the Truman Doctrine.

1186. McNeill, William H.   The Greek Dilemma: War and Aftermath. Philadelphia, New York, Lippincott, 1947. 291 p. Illus., maps.

A perceptive study of Greek society and politics from the Second World War until virtually the eve of the Truman Doctrine by a professional historian who served as assistant U.S. military attaché in Athens from November 1944 to June 1946.

1187. Marceau, Marc.   La Grèce des colonels. Parit, Laffont, 1967. 277 p. Plates.

An account of the military coup of April 21, 1967, its causes, and the events which led up to it, by the resident correspondent of *Le Monde*.

1188. Myers, Edmund C. W.   Greek Entanglement. London, Rupert Hart-Davis, 1955. 290 p.

Experiences of the leader of a British mission sent to Greece during the occupation.

1189. O'Ballance, Edgar.   The Greek Civil War, 1944-1949. New York, Praeger, 1966. 237 p. Maps. Bibliography: p. 225-227.
*See also* entry no. 1110.

The dates in the title notwithstanding, this book deals with the three successive rounds of communist-led guerrilla warfare since 1943 aimed at transforming Greece into a People's Republic. Reflecting the British tendency to downgrade the importance of resistance movements in occupied Europe, this study carefully analyzes the causes of the communist failure.

1190. Papakōnstantinou, Th. Ph.   Anatomia tēs epanastaseōs (Anatomy of revolution). Athēnai, 1952. 268 p.

A theoretical and historical analysis of communist dynamics and their application to Greece from 1941 to 1949.

1191. Rousseas, Stephen William.   The Death of a Democracy: Greece and the American Conscience. New York, Grove Press, 1967. 268 p. Bibliographical footnotes.

An analysis of the Greek military takeover of April 21, 1967, written from the point of view of Andreas Papandreou.

1192. Smothers, Frank, William H. McNeill, *and* Elizabeth D. McNeill. Report on the Greeks. New York, Twentieth Century Fund, 1948. 226 p. Illus., ports., maps.
*See also* entries no. 1262 *and* 1297.

Findings of a team which surveyed conditions in Greece in 1947.

1193. Stavrianos, L. S.   Greece: American Dilemma and Opportunity. Chicago, Regnery, 1952. 246 p.
*See also* entry no. 1116.

An American historian of Greek ancestry presents the left-wing viewpoint of Greek politics in the war and postwar periods.

1194. Sweet-Escott, Bickham.    Greece. A Political and Economic Survey, 1939-1953. London, New York, Royal Institute of International Affairs, 1954. 206 p. Maps, tables. Bibliography: p. 195-197.
   *See also* entries no. 1264 *and* 1298.
   Part 1 of this study provides a succinct account of Greek politics since the Second World War. The two appendixes deal with the problem of Cyprus and Greece's northern frontiers.

1195. Tsatsou, Iōanna.    Phylla katochēs (Pages about the occupation). Athēnai, 1965. 200 p.
   A sensitive diary selection concerning the period of the Axis occupation. Authored by the sister of Nobel prizewinner George Seferis.

1196. Andreadēs, K. G.    Hē Mousoulmanikē meionotēs tēs dytikēs Thrakēs (The Moslem minority of western Thrace). Thessalonikē, Hetairea Makedonikōn Spoudōn, 1956. 120 p. Illus.
   A rare Greek study on the Turkish minority. The author, a lieutenant colonel of the Greek gendarmerie, puts together evidence that shows the protection and care of the Moslem Greek nationals, many of whom he believes were originally Christians. Greece's concern for the Turkish minority is linked to the Greek minority remaining in Turkey. This problem is treated by P. Pipinelēs in his *Hē Hellēnotourkikē philia kai hē hellenikē meionotēs Konstantinoupoleōs* (The Greco-Turkish friendship and the Greek minority in Constantinople) (Athēnai, Kentron Kōnstantinoupolitōn, 1961, 30 p.). A French edition is also available.

1197. U.S. Library of Congress. *European Affairs Division.*    War and Postwar Greece: an Analysis Based on Greek Writings. Prepared by Floyd A. Spencer. Washington, D.C., 1952. 175 p. Bibliography: p. ix-xi.
   *See also* entry no. 1463.
   A basic bibliographic survey of the literature for the period 1940-1952. Attention is called to the materials listed therein; the compiler of the present chapter focuses chiefly on books which were published on this period after 1952.

1198. Woodhouse, Christopher M.    Apple of Discord; a Survey of Recent Greek Politics in Their International Setting. London, New York, Hutchinson, 1948. 320 p.
   *See also* entry no. 1240.
   A classic analysis of the complex and elusive play of internal and external political forces in wartime Greece by a British colonel who was on the spot most of the time and who was to become home secretary in the Conservative government of Lord Home.

1199. Zafeiropoulos, D.    Ho antisymmoriakos agōn 1945-1949 (The anti-guerrilla struggle, 1945-1949). Athēnai, A. Mavridēs, 1956. 288 p.

A thorough study of Greek Army counterinsurgency operations by a Greek officer. Based on numerous official documents (reports of the Chiefs of Staff and larger army units, commanders' accounts) as well as on the author's own experience. All aspects — military, political, and psychological — are covered. An interesting critique is made of the operations of the "Democratic Army."

1200. Zotos, Stephanos. Greece: The Struggle for Freedom. New York, Thomas Crowell, 1967. 194 p. Illus., maps. Bibliography: p. 187-188.

A lively though shallow journalistic account — personal impressions included — of the struggle of Greece against fascism, Nazism, and communism from October 1940 to August 1949.

## 4. Nationalities

### by Charilaos Lagoudakis

1201. Averōf, Evangelos D. Hē Politikē Pleura tou Koutsovlachikou zētēmatos (The political aspect of the Koutsovlach question). Athēnai, 1948. 218 p. Bibliography.

This is an authentic study of the Koutsovlachs in Greece, largely located in Epiros, Macedonia, and Thrace. The author, of Koutsovlach origin himself, is a prominent political leader who served as minister of foreign affairs from 1956 to 1963. The study reflects Greece's attitude toward the Koutsovlachs, who affected Greek relations with Italy prior to and during the Second World War. For an Italian analysis of the problem *see* Giovanni Amadori Virgiliz's *La Questione Rumeliote* (Bitono, Biblioteca Italiana di Politica Estera, no. 1, 1909).

1202. Ladas, Stephen P. The Exchange of Minorities: Bulgaria, Greece, and Turkey. New York, Macmillan, 1932. 849 p. Illus., maps. Bibliography: p. 831-832.

*See also* entries no. 223, 708, *and* 1341.

The book deals with the massive exchange of the ethnic minorities in Greece — Turks, Slavs, Albanians, and Vlachs — following the First World War. Also discussed is the international machinery used for the resettlement of emigrants and refugees. Related studies are those of Alexandre E. Devedji, *L'échange obligatoire des minorités grecques et turques en vertu de la Convention de Lausanne du 30 janvier, 1923* (Paris, P. Bossuet, 1929, 238 p.), and Charles Eddy, *Greece and the Greek Refugees* (London, G. Allen & Unwin, 1931, 280 p.).

1203. Papadakēs, Vasileios Panagiōtou (Basileios Papadakis). Hē prostasia tōn meionotētōn (The protection of the minorities). Athēnai, 1935.

Examines the protection of minorities, both on the basis of Greek laws and international agreements, and discusses the social and legal status of the native minorities in Greece.

## C. DIPLOMACY AND FOREIGN RELATIONS
## (INCLUDING MILITARY AFFAIRS)

*by Charilaos Lagoudakis*

### 1. General Works

1204. Balkan Studies. 1960– Thessalonikē. Semiannual.
*See also* entries no. 30 *and* 1004.

> Edited by Basil Laourdas, this publication of the Institute for Balkan Studies contains materials that present Greece's position in the Balkans. Its scope is primarily historical, but it also contains studies in English, German, and French dealing with Greece's contemporary relations with the Balkan and other countries.

1205. Diethnēs thesis tēs Hellados (The international position of Greece). *In* Megalē Hellēnikē enkyklopaideia (Great Greek encyclopedia). Volume entitled *Hellas*. Athēnai, Pyrsos, 1926-1934. p. 601-623.

> Treats Greece's international relations from 1821 to 1933 factually and chronologically. It covers relations with Turkey, Bulgaria, Yugoslavia, and Albania, the Balkan Pact of 1930, the League of Nations, and minorities. It contains a list of Greece's foreign treaties and a bibliography.

1206. Genikē Stratiōtikē Epitheōrēsis (General military review). 1950– Athēnai. Monthly.

> Contains articles by Greek army officers and many translations from foreign studies on contemporary military affairs. Also publishes materials on Greek military experience before and after the war of Greek independence in 1821. *See also* Gregorios Stephanou's compilation and evaluation of *The Military and Naval Press in Greece, 1835-1917*, Athens, 1917.

1207. International Relations.  A Quarterly Review of Signed Opinion. 1963-1964. Athens.

> A publication in Greek with an English edition. Contains for the most part articles on Greece's external policy and relations. The first four issues were published in 1963, and the last issue in 1964. Most of the contributors are Greeks with experience in foreign affairs, either as scholars or public figures. The publisher and editor was Vassos Vassiliou.

### 2. Histories of Foreign Relations

1208. Abbot, George F.  Greece and the Allies, 1914-1922. London, Methuen, 1922. 242 p.
*See also* entry no. 1108.

> This study treats the First World War as a landmark of Greek territorial expansion and as a national adventure which had significant impact on domestic politics and internal development. It reviews the Greek role in the war as a country divided between royalists

under King Constantine and republicans under Eleftherios Venizelos. The role of King Constantine in trying to maintain a pro-German neutrality is discussed by Paxton Hibben in his *Constantine I and the Greek People* (New York, Century, 1920, 592 p.). A critical study on the same theme is George M. Melas' *Ex-King Constantine and the War* (London, Hutchinson, 1920, 288 p.).

1209. Cervi, Mario. Storia della guerra di Grecia. Milano, Sugar Editore, 1966. 515 p.

This is one of the better accounts of the 1940 Greco-Italian war. The author regards Mussolini's attack on Greece as Ciano's war and the most inglorious military episode of the 20th century. His account, frank and dispassionate, is primarily based on Italian sources, but good use is also made of Greek, German, and British materials. The defeat of the Italian forces is significantly attributed to the toughness and tactical brilliance of the Greek resistance.

1210. Daphnēs, Grēgorios. Hē Hellas metaxy dyo polemōn, 1923-1940 (Greece between two wars, 1923-1940). Athēnai, Ikaros, 1955. 2 v. Bibliography: v. 2, p. 477-479.
See also entries no. 1109 and 1169.

A major study of the Greek national scene during the interwar period, dealing with both domestic and foreign policies. The author is a longtime diplomatic correspondent.

1211. Dontas, Domna. Greece and the Great Powers, 1863-1875. Thessalonikē, Institute for Balkan Studies, 1966. 223 p. Bibliography.
See also entry no. 1101.

The study traces the beginnings of an independent Greek foreign policy after 1863, when the Greeks overthrew King Otto and established a parliamentary government. Another useful reference for this period is Stamatios Theodōrou Laskaris' *La politique extérieure de la Grèce avant et après le Congrès de Berlin, 1875-1881* (Paris, Bessard, 1924, 223 p.).

1212. Dragoumēs, Nikolaos M. Historikes Anamnēseis (Historical memoirs). Athēnai, 1874.

These memoirs by King Otto's first foreign minister reflect the three-power conflicts over Greece during the period from 1833 to 1863. Subsequent editions were published in 1879 and 1925. Dragoumēs' views also appeared in *Le Spectateur de l'Orient* (Athènes, 1853-57, semimonthly), which he founded as a vehicle to enlighten Western opinion on the Greek position during the Crimean War.

1213. Driault, Édouard, and Michel Lhéritier. Histoire diplomatique de la Grèce de 1821 à nos jours. Paris, Les Presses Universitaires de France, 1925-26. 5 v. Maps, bibliographies.
See also entry no. 1049.

This study was based mainly on the archives of the Greek foreign

Office, which had not previously been open to scholars. Danish, Austrian, French, and British archives were also used.

1214. Greece. *Stratos. Genikon Epiteleion. Dieuthynsis Historias Stratou.* Ho Hellēnikos Stratos kata ton Prōton Pankosmion Polemon, 1914-1918. He ekstrateia eis tēn Mikran Asian, 1919-1922. Ho Hellēnikos Stratos kata ton Deuteron Pankosmion Polemon (The Greek Army during the First World War, 1914-1918. The Asia Minor campaign, 1919-1922. The Greek army during the Second World War). Athēnai, 1955-1966. 19 v.

This multivolume work, covering Greek military history from 1914 to 1941, was published by the General Staff of the Greek Army in the above-mentioned three monographic series.

1215. Grēgoropoulos, Theodōros. Apo tēn koryphē tou lophou (From the summit of the hill). Athēnai, 1966. 581 p. Illus., maps. Bibliography: p. 581.

These exceptional memoirs by General Gregoropoulos, once military representative to NATO in Washington and one of the foremost Greek experts on the Atlantic Alliance, cover the politico-military affairs of Greece during the past 50 years. *See also* the work of General Thrasyvoulos I. Tsakalōtos, entitled *Forty Years a Soldier of Greece* (Athens, Acropolis Press, 1960, 2 v.), in which he explains how and why Greece conducted a successful resistance to the fascist and communist aggressors from 1940 to 1949.

1216. Kavvadias, Epamēnontas P. Ho nautikos polemos tou 1940 hopōs ton ezēsa (The naval war of 1940 as I experienced it). Athēnai, 1950. 736 p. Illus., maps.

These memoirs of a Greek admiral cover the period from 1935 to 1943 and include an authentic account of the Greek naval operations during the Battle of Greece in 1940-41 and Greek participation in Allied naval operations. Another important source for the same period is Admiral Alexandros Sakellariou's *Hē thesis tēs Hellados eis ton Deuteron Pankosmion Polemon* (The position of Greece in the Second World War) (New York, Cosmos Greek-American Printing Company, 1944, 351 p.).

1217. Kōnstantopoulos, Savvas. Sovietikē Rōssia kai Hellas (Soviet Russia and Greece). Athēnai, Eleftheros Kosmos, 1968. 165 p.

The author, once a Marxist and now publisher of the ideological organ of the military régime in Greece, examines Greek-Soviet relations from 1920 to 1949. He reviews Moscow's attitude — toward the Greek expedition in Asia Minor, the Corfu incident with Italy, the questions of Macedonia and Thrace, the Axis attack on Greece in 1940, and the communist guerrilla war (1946-49) — and finds it consistently hostile to Greece.

1218. Lagoudakis, Charilaos G. Greece, 1946-1949. *In* Challenge and

Response in Internal Conflict. v. 2. Washington, D.C., Center for Research in Social Systems, 1967. p. 497-527.

A documented anatomy of the communist insurgency and counter-insurgency in Greece following the Second World War. It treats the international aspects of the insurgency as well as the administrative, social, geographic, political, and military factors that caused the disintegration of the Soviet-bloc–backed guerrilla movement. For an annotated bibliography by the same author on Greco-Soviet relations, see *Soviet Foreign Relations and World Communism*, edited by Thomas T. Hammond (Princeton, Princeton University Press, 1965), p. 482-497. Edgar O'Ballance in his notable book, *The Greek Civil War, 1944-1949* (New York, Praeger, 1966, 237 p.), perceptively discusses the inherent weaknesses of the Greek communists.

1219. Laskaris, Stamatios Theodōrou.   Diplomatikē historia tēs Hellados, 1821-1914 (Diplomatic history of Greece, 1821-1914). Athēnai, 1947. 267 p.

This is the second of three volumes in which the author traces the diplomatic history of Greece and Europe. The first, published in 1936, deals with the diplomatic history of Europe (1814-1914); the third is a supplement covering the period from 1914 to 1939 (Thessalonikē, Institute for Balkan Studies, 1954). It has two useful chapters on Greek relations with the Balkan countries from 1923-1930 and the Balkan Pact period from 1930 to 1939.

1220. Levandis, John A.   The Greek Foreign Debt and the Great Powers, 1821-1898. New York, Columbia University Press, 1944. 137 p. Bibliography: p. 117-129.

An outstanding Ph.D. thesis.

1221. Malainos, Epameinōndas I.   Historia tōn xenikōn epemvaseōn (History of foreign interventions). Athēnai, 1955–

The author examines foreign interventions in Greece as a factor in Greek foreign policy. He covers the period from the war of Greek independence in 1821 to the Treaty of Athens in 1913, which restored diplomatic relations with Turkey. Six volumes have been published thus far. A leftist Greek viewpoint on the subject is reflected in Giannēs Kōnstantinou Kordatos' *Hoi epemvaseis tōn Anglōn stēn Hellada* (The interventions of the British in Greece) (Athēnai, 1946, 57 p.).

1222. Mondini, Luigi.   Prologo del conflitto italo-greco. Roma, F. lli Treves Editori, 1945. 284 p.

Critical of Mussolini's attack on Greece, this Italian author reviews Greek relations with Italy, the great powers, the Balkan countries, and in particular with Albania. With reference to the Italian invasion of Greece in 1940, see also *The Ciano Diaries, 1939-1943* (Garden City, N.Y., Doubleday, 1946, 584 p.), and *The Greek White Book: Diplomatic Documents Relating to Italy's Aggression Against Greece* (London, Hutchinson, 1942, 121 p.). The

Italian attack on and occupation of the island of Corfu in 1923 were the prelude to Mussolini's invasion of Greece 17 years later. This incident and its international repercussions are explored by James Barros in his *The Corfu Incident of 1923* (Princeton, Princeton University Press, 1965, 339 p., bibliography, index). The author gives an excellent evaluation of the role the League of Nations played in helping to settle the dispute.

1223. Papagos, Alexandros. The Battle of Greece, 1940-1941. Translated by Patroclos Eliascos from the Greek version, published in 1945. Athens, The J. M. Scazikis "ALPHA" Editions, 1949. 406 p. Illus., maps.

The author headed the Greek counteroffensive against the Italian troops and the defense against the German forces in 1940-41. His account is an indispensable source. This first defeat of an Axis army was termed *The Greek Miracle*, which is the title of Stephen Lavra's account translated in English from the French by David Walker (New York, Hastings House, 1943, 144 p.). *See also* Papagos' *Ho Hellēnikos stratos kai hē pros polemon proparaskeuē tou* (The Greek army and its preparation for war) (Athēnai, 1945, 421 p.) and his biography by N. Theologos, *Alexandros Papagos* (Athēnai, 1946, 127 p.).

1224. Philaretos, G. Xenokratia kai Basileia en Helladi, 1821-1897 (Foreign rule and the kingdom in Greece, 1821-1897). Athēnai, 1935-1946. 3 v.

The author discusses the Greek monarchy as the product of foreign interests, particularly England, France, and Russia. Philaretos has been called the "father of Greek democracy." See also *Antagonismos tōn Megalōn dynameōn pros epikratēsin tēs politikēs tōn epiroēs en Helladi* (Conflict among the Great Powers for the supremacy of their political influence in Greece) by N. Levides, *Hellēnismos*, v. 15, 1912, p. 246-254, 309-315, and 427-432.

1225. Phōtiadēs, E. P., *and others, comps.* Stratiōtikē historia tēs Hellados (Military history of Greece). Athēnai, 1961. 854 p.

1226. Pipinelēs, Panagiotēs N. Historia tēs exōterikēs politikēs tēs Hellados, 1923-1941 (History of Greek foreign policy, 1923-1941). Athēnai, M. Saliveros, 1948. 374 p.

An authoritative study by one of Greece's foremost experts on foreign affairs. It covers the interwar period, during which Greece developed a policy aimed at preserving the status quo in the Balkans. Additional analyses of Greek foreign and domestic problems by Pipinelēs may be found in his bimonthly bulletin *Politika Phylla* (Political pages) (1953-1967).

1227. Politēs, Nikolaos. Les aspirations nationales de la Grèce. Paris, 1919.

By a distinguished professor of International Law at the Sorbonne and for many years the Greek Ambassador in Paris. Other informative studies of Greek national feeling are Edouard Driault's *La grande idée, la renaissance de l'hellénisme* (Paris, F. Alcan, 1920, 242 p.); Charles Vellay's *L'irrédentisme hellénique* (Paris, Perrin, 1913); and Eleutherios Venizelos' *Greece before the Peace Congress of 1919* (New York, 1919, 36 p.).

1228. Prevelakēs (Prevelakis), Eleutherios G.   British Policy toward the Change of Dynasty in Greece, 1862-1863. Athens, 1953. 194 p. Bibliography: p. 172-185.
       *See also* entry no. 1106.
       A scholarly study by a notable historian based on primary sources in the Greek and British Foreign Offices.

1229. Saraphēs, Stephanos.   Ho ELAS (The ELAS [Greek Popular Liberation Army]). Athēnai, Ta Nea Vivlia, 1946. 479 p. Abridged English edition: Greek Resistance Army; the Story of ELAS. London, Birch Books, 1951. 324 p. Illus.
       Seraphēs, commander of the communist-led resistance movement in occupied Greece during the Second World War, discusses in detail the activities of ELAS from 1943 to its dissolution in February 1945. On the nationalist resistance movement, see *Hē Ethnikē antistasis ton Hellēnōn* (The national resistance of the Greeks) by Stylianos Houtas (Athēnai, 1961, 634 p.).

1230. Streit, Geōrgios.   Der Lausanner Vertrag und der griechisch-türkische Bevölkerungsaustausch. Berlin, Stilke, 1929. 71 p. (Aus dem Institut für internationales Recht an der Universität Kiel. Reihe I/1o)
       A former Greek Minister of Foreign Affairs deals with the population exchange from the viewpoint of international law.

1231. Vakalopoulos (Bakalopoulos), Apostolos.   Ta Hellenika strateumata tou 1821: Organōsē, hēgesia, taktikē, ēthē, psychologia (The Greek military units of 1821: organization, leadership, tactics, customs, psychology). Thessalonikē, 1948. 304 p. Bibliography.
       A unique study of the Greek armed forces that fought for Greek independence in 1821. The author, a professor of history at the University of Thessalonikē, examines the Greeks who formed the revolutionary forces, the initial character and organization of the armed guerrillas, and their evolution from bands to a regular military establishment. See also Christos Byzantios' *Historia tōn kata tēn Hellēnikēn epanastasin ekstrateiōn kai mahōn kai meta tauta symvantōn, hōn symmeteschen ho taktikos stratos apo to 1821 mechri to 1833* (History of the expeditions and battles . . . during the Greek Revolution, 1821 to 1833) (Athēnai, 1901).

1232. Venizelos, Sophoklēs.   To Ēmerologion mou apo tēn mesēn Anatolēn (My journal from the Middle East). Athēnai, Hellenikē Hēmera, 1951.

Venizelos has played a crucial role in Greece's international affairs during and since the Second World War. His memoirs are an indispensable source for the period from 1941 to 1945. Of equal importance are the memoirs of Emmanouēl I. Tsouderos, *Hellēnikes anōmalies stē Mesē Anatolē* (Greek anomalies in the Middle East) (Athēnai, Aetos, 1945, 190 p.).

## 3. Survey Studies

1233. Couloumbis, Theodore A.    Greek Political Reaction to American and NATO Influences. New Haven, Yale University Press, 1966. 250 p.
    A well documented study which examines conservative, liberal, and communist attitudes in Greece toward NATO. Contains useful data on Greek politics and party platforms.

1234. Greece. The European Economic Community and a European Free Trade Area. Athens, Ministries of Coordination and Foreign Affairs of the Royal Hellenic Government, 1959. 204 p.
    A Greek "White Book" on EEC/FTA. It reproduces, in English, basic documents on the Greek position in the 1958-1959 negotiations for a free trade area within the OEEC area.

1235. Kalogeropoulos-Stratēs, Spyros.    La Grèce et les Nations Unies. New York, Manhattan Publishing Co., 1957. 190 p.
    The author examines the place of Greece within the U.N. structure. The book is reviewed by C. G. Lagoudakis in the October 1958 issue of The *American Journal of International Law*.

1236. Kyrou, Alexēs A.    Hellēnikē exōterikē politikē (Foreign policy of the Greeks). Athēnai, 1955. 459 p.
    This account by a distinguished Greek diplomat is a valuable contribution to understanding the motivations of Greek foreign policy.

1237. McNeill, William H.    Greece: American Aid in Action, 1947-1956. New York, Twentieth Century Fund, 1957. 240 p. Illus., maps.
    *See also* entries no. 1185, 1257, *and* 1308.
    An analysis of the socioeconomic problems of Greece with which American diplomacy had to deal in containing communism at the village, city, and national levels. *See also* P. Economou-Gouras' *To Dogma Trouman kai ē agōnia tēs Hellados* (The Truman Doctrine and the agony of Greece) (Athēnai, 1957, 236 p.) and Joseph Marion Jones' *The Fifteen Weeks: February 21 to June 5, 1947* (New York, Viking Press, 1955, 296 p.).

1238. Schramm v. Thadden, Ehrengard.    Griechenland und die Grossmächte 1913-1923. Göttingen, Vandenhoeck u. Ruprecht, 1933. 136 p. (Abhandlungen aus dem Seminar für Völkerrecht und Diplomatie an der Universität Göttingen, 8)

A well-balanced history of Greece during the First World War including the 1920 Greek expedition and defeat in Asia Minor.

1239. Schramm v. Thadden, Ehrengard. Griechenland und die Grossmächte im zweiten Weltkrieg. Wiesbaden, Steiner, 1955. 244 p. (Veröffentlichungen des Instituts für europäische Geschichte, Mainz, 9)

> Excellent diplomatic and political history of the Italian and German invasion of Greece in April 1939 and April 1941, respectively. For the war events *see* the following military study:
> Buchner, Alex. Der deutsche Griechenland-Feldzug. Operationen der 12. Armee 1941. Heidelberg, Vowinckel, 1957. 207 p. Maps.

1240. Woodhouse, Christopher M. Apple of Discord; a Survey of Recent Greek Politics in Their International Setting. London, New York, Hutchinson, 1948. 320 p.
> *See also* entry no. 1198.

> The author, commander of the Allied Mission to the Greek guerrillas during the Second World War, analyzes Greek resistance to the Italian, German, and Bulgarian troops within the framework of power politics. A supplementary study is William H. McNeill's *The Greek Dilemma: War and Aftermath* (Philadelphia, Lippincott, 1947, 291 p.). For a detached study on the resistance in occupied Greece *see* Doris M. Condit's *Case Study in Guerrilla War: Greece During World War II* (Washington, D.C., Special Warfare Research Division, American University, 1961, 338 p.).

1241. Xydis, Stephen G. Greece and the Great Powers, 1944-1947; Prelude to the Truman Doctrine. Thessalonikē, Institute for Balkan Studies, 1963. 758 p. Illus., maps. Bibliography: p. 721-738.
> *See also* entries no. 182 *and* 1117.

> A prelude to the Truman Doctrine. The author made a distinct contribution in sorting out the diplomatic background of the communist insurgency in Greece. The writings of two wartime prime ministers should also be consulted: George Papandreou's *The Liberation of Greece* (Athens, I. Skazikis, 1945, 252 p.); and Emmanouēl I. Tsouderos' *Ta Diplomatika paraskēnia, 1941-1944* (Diplomatic backstage, 1941-1944) (Athēnai, Aetos, 1950, 271 p.). The international aspects of Greece's problems during this period are perceptively discussed by Vaseilios Papadakēs in his *Diplomatikē historia tou Hellēnikou polemou, 1940-1945* (Diplomatic history of the Greek war, 1940-1945) (Athēnai, 1956), 512 p.).

## 4. Special Aspects

1242. Grivas, George. The Memoirs of General Grivas. Edited by Charles Foley. New York, Praeger, 1965. 226 p. Illus., map.
> Basic text for the study of the Greek involvement in Cyprus. Full original text: *Apomnēmonumata agōnos E.O.K.A. 1955-1959*

(Memoirs of the E.O.K.A. Struggle, 1955-1959) (Athēnai, 1961, 410, 72 p.)

*See also* Charles Foley's *Legacy of Strife: Cyprus from Rebellion to Civil War*, 2d ed. (Baltimore, Penguin Books, 1964, 187 p.).

1243. Kyrou, Alexēs A.   Hoi Balkanikoi geitones mas (Our Balkan neighbors). Athēnai, 1962. 246 p. Bibliography: p. 235-244.

A career diplomat, the author treats Greece's Balkan relations from professional experience. A brief survey of Greece's postwar Balkan relations is Harry N. Howard's "Greece and Its Balkan Neighbors (1948-1949)" in the semiannual *Balkan Studies*, v. 7, 1966: 1-26.

1244. Naltsas, Christophoros A.   To Makedonikon zētēma kai hē Sovietikē politikē (The Macedonian question and Soviet policy). Thessalonikē, Hetairia Makedonikōn Spoudōn, 1954. 544 p. Bibliography: p. 539-544.

The Macedonian controversy has been one of Greece's principal foreign problems before and after the Second World War. Naltsas, a Greek specialist on Balkan and Slavic affairs, develops the thesis that Russia has been the principal power manipulating the Macedonian questions. The study contains a good bibliography for Yugoslav, Bulgarian, and Greek sources. *See also* the study by General Dēmētrios Georgiou Zapheiropoulos: *To KKE kai hē Makedonia* (The Greek Communist Party and Macedonia) (Athēnai, 1948, 175 p.). For a recent study in English *see*:

Dakin, Douglas.   The Greek Struggle in Macedonia, 1897-1913. Thessalonikē, Institute for Balkan Studies, 1966. 538 p.

1245. Papadakēs, Vasileios Panagiōtou (Basile Papadakis).   Histoire diplomatique de la question Nord-Epirote, 1912-1957. Athènes, J. Alevropoulos, 1958. 195 p. Bibliography: p. 178-182.

*See also* entry no. 1113.

The history of the Greek claim to Northern Epiros, part of southern Albania, is outlined. For another authentic Greek viewpoint *see also* Panagiotēs Pipinelēs' *Europe and the Albanian Question*, 2d ed. (Chicago, Argonaut, 1963, 94 p.). Also noteworthy is Constantine Rentis' *To Voreioēpeirotikon zētēma* (The North Epirot question) (Athēnai, 1919).

1246. Papanastasiou, Alexandros P.   Meletes, Logoi, Arthra (Studies, lectures, and articles). Athēnai, 1957. 904 p.

Known in Greece as the father of the Balkan Union, Papanastasiou was one of the leaders of this movement that began in 1930 and was arrested by the Second World War. This volume contains his far-reaching work for Balkan unity.

1247. Xydis, Stephen G.   Cyprus: Conflict and Conciliation, 1954-1958. Columbus, Ohio State University Press, 1967. 792 p. Bibliography.

Focuses on the Cyprus crisis as a challenge for the United Nations when called upon to deal with colonial questions. The author, a professor of political science at Hunter College, concentrates on the diplomatic relations of Greece, Turkey, and the United Kingdom over Cyrus within the framework of the United Nations, and explores the degree to which this world organization can conciliate disputes among and between its member nations. The essence of the Cyprus problem is presented in a nutshell by Thomas Anthem in his brief *The Greeks Have a Word for It: Enosis* (London, St. Clements Press, 1954, 30 p.). The works of Doros Alastos, a Cypriot of long residence in England, cover the Greek position on Cyprus. *See* his *Cyprus: Past and Future* (London, Committee for Cyprus Affairs, 1944, 75 p.); and his *Cyprus Guerrilla: Grivas, Makarios, and the British* (London, Heinemann, 1960, 224 p.). Also valuable are the *Memoirs of General Grivas*, edited by Charles Foley (New York, Praeger, 1965, 226 p.). For an overall treatment of the Greek insurgency in Cyprus, *see* Charilaos G. Lagoudakis' "Cyprus, 1954-1958" in *Challenge and Response in Internal Conflict*, v. 2 (Washington, D.C., Center for Research in Social Systems, American University, 1967, p. 355-380).

## D. MASS MEDIA AND PUBLIC OPINION

### by Charilaos Lagoudakis

1248. Mager (Mayer), Kōstas. Historia tou Hellēnikou typou (History of the Greek press). Athēnai, A. Demopoulos, 1957-1960. 3 v.
    *See also* entry no. 958.
    This is the best and most complete account of the Greek press, covering the period from 1870 to 1959. The first volume deals with publications from 1870 to 1900; the second covers the provincial press during the same period; and the third reviews the whole press up to 1959. These volumes also include information on press associations and outstanding journalists and publishers. A good account of the Greek press in French is Apostolos Daskalakēs' *La Presse néo-hellénique*, edited by J. Gamber (Paris, Librairie Universitaire, 1930). Also useful is Dēmētrios Kalapothakēs' *A Short History of the Greek Press* (Athens, Ministry of Foreign Affairs, 1928, 16 p.). For a brief English-language survey consult:
    Olson, Kenneth E.   The Newspapers of Greece. *In his* The History Makers. Baton Rouge, Louisiana State University Press, 1966. p. 253-269.

1249. Radio-Programma (Radio program). 1962– Athēnai. Weekly.
    Contains program schedules of all radio stations in Greece. It includes book reviews and articles on music and the theater. Between 1947 and 1967 the Athens Institute for Communications Research published weekly surveys and public attitudes and media habits in Greece.

1250. Stergiopoulos, Charalambos B.   Ho Kinēmatographos kai hai epidraseis tou epi tōn paidōn kai ephēvōn (The cinema and its influence on children and adolescents). Thessalonikē, 1959. 47 p.
    Discusses the impact of motion pictures on Greek youth.

# 32

# the economy

*by Hourmouzis G. Georgiadis*
*(With the exception of section E)*

Surveys and General Studies 1251-1269
Agriculture 1270-1274
Industry 1275-1278
Money, Finance, Trade 1279-1284
Scientific Developments 1285-1286

## A. SURVEYS AND GENERAL STUDIES

1251. Agapitides, S.   The Development of the Local Economy in Greece. International Labor Review, v. 79, 1959: 79-90.
A survey of local development projects.

1252. Andreades, A. M., *and others*.   Les effets économiques et sociaux de la guerre en Grèce. New Haven, Yale University Press, 1929. 322 p. Maps, tables.
More philosophic than economic in its orientation, the book examines in a rather general way the impact of the First World War on the economy of Greece.

1253. Angelopoulos, A.   Prooptikes gia tēn Ellada tou 1970 (Greek prospects in 1970). Nea Oikonomia, Nov. 1965: 875-877.

1254. Arrow, Kenneth J.   Statistical Requirements for Greek Economic Planning. Athens, Center of Economic Research, 1965. 40 p. (Lecture Series, 18)

1255. Evelpides, C.   Some Economic and Social Problems in Greece. International Labour Review, v. 68, Aug. 1953: 151-165.
*See also* entry no. 1300.
The article demonstrates the extent of the heavy capital investment

which will be required if productivity is to be increased and living standards raised in the country.

1256. Gross, Hermann.   Südosteuropa. Bau und Entwicklung der Wirtschaft. Leipzig, Noske, 1937. 231 p. Maps, table, bibliography. (Beihefte zur Leipziger Vierteljahrsschrift für Südosteuropa, 1)

The best representation of the structure and trends of the Greek economy in the interwar period.

1257. McNeill, William H.   Greece: American Aid in Action, 1947-1956. New York, Twentieth Century Fund, 1957. 240 p. Illus., maps.
*See also* entries no. 1185, 1237, *and* 1308.

Based on a revisit to Greece eight years after the visit that produced the Twentieth Century Fund study published in 1948, this book deals with the impact of United States aid on Greece. Emphasis is placed on the effects of U.S. foreign economic policy on the villages and towns of the country.

1258. Nugent, Jeffrey B.   Programming the Optimal Development of the Greek Economy, 1954-1961. Athens, Center for Economic Research, 1966. 171 p.

The book includes a linear programming model for evaluating the Greek economy by sectors. It is a serious work and constitutes an outstanding contribution to the empirical writings concerning the Greek economy. (Appendix of statistical tables, consisting of 132 mimeographed pages, published separately.)

1259. Papandreou, Andreas G.   A Strategy for Greek Economic Development. Athens, Center of Economic Research, 1962. 179 p. (*Its* Research Monograph Series, 1)

In this book a general model of planning resource allocation for economic development is presented, and the feasibility of some alternative growth paths for the Greek economy in the decade 1963-1972 is explored. The book is an outstanding piece of work, of interest not only for its general methodological contribution, but also for its contribution to the problem of economic development in Greece.

1260. Pavlopoulos, P.   A Statistical Model for the Greek Economy, 1949-59. Amsterdam, North Holland Publishing Company, 1966. 337 p. Bibliography: p. 324-329. (Contributions to Economic Analysis, 44)

The book deals with the basic problem of quantifying economic relationships in a developing economy such as that of Greece and of using such relationships for policy purposes. A complete structural model is estimated for the period in question, and, on the basis of such a model, impact-multipliers and stability conditions are explored.

1261. Psomiades, H. J.   The Economic and Social Transformation of Modern Greece. Journal of International Affairs (New York), v. 19, Feb. 1965: 194-205.

*See also* entry no. 1312.

1262. Smothers, Frank, William H. McNeill, *and* Elizabeth D. McNeill. Report on the Greeks. New York, Twentieth Century Fund, 1948. 226 p. Illus., ports., maps.
*See also* entries no. 1192 *and* 1297.

An analysis of Greece as a critical area in developing world tension, by a Twentieth Century Fund team. The study was researched and written before the declaration of the Truman Doctrine and prior to Greece's entry into NATO. The economic aspect is one of several examined in the study.

1263. Suits, Daniel B.    An Econometric Model of the Greek Economy. Athens, Center of Economic Research, 1964. 131 p.

The study constitutes an attempt to construct a full-scale econometric model for the Greek economy. The author's main contribution is in demonstrating that such a model could in fact be estimated with the data which are available from statistical sources. The actual model, however, which the author does finally estimate is at best incomplete and sketchy.

1264. Sweet-Escott, Bickham.    Greece. A Political and Economic Survey, 1939-1953. London, New York, Royal Institute of International Affairs, 1954. 206 p. Maps, tables. Bibliography: p. 195-197.
*See also* entries no. 1194 *and* 1298.

A comprehensive survey of the main political and economic forces at work during the period in question. For an up-to-date treatment of post-World War II developments *see:*
Candilis, Wray O.    The Economy of Greece, 1944-1966. New York, Praeger, 1968. 250 p. Tables, charts, bibliography. An analytical study by a top economist with the American Bankers Association.

1265. Thomopoulos, P. A.    Diarthrōtikes metavoles stēn Hellēnikē Oikonomia (Structural changes in the Greek economy). Nea Oikonomia, Dec. 1965: 991-994.

1266. Tomazinis, A. R.    Recent Trends in the Economy of Greece. Land Economics, v. 35, Nov. 1959: 347-355.

1267. Triantis, Stephen G.    Common Market and Economic Development: The EEC and Greece. Athens, Center of Economic Research, 1965. 232 p. (*Its* Research Monograph Series, 14)

In this inadequate treatment of a crucial problem confronting the economy of Greece, the author attempts to examine the effect which the association of Greece with the Common Market is likely to produce on the country's overall rate of economic development. The analysis is very limited, and the arguments presented rarely, if ever, go beyond trivial and obvious points.

1268. Vouras, P. P.   The Changing Economy of Northern Greece Since World War II. Chicago, Argonaut, 1966. 227 p.

> A survey of the structural changes which have taken place in the economy of Northern Greece. An earlier edition was published by the Institute for Balkan Studies in 1962.

1269. Wapenhans, Willi.   Griechenland. Untersuchungen über die Wirtschaft eines kontinentaleuropäischen Entwicklungslandes. Giessen, Schmitz, 1960. 162 p. Tables. Bibliography: p. 148-152. (Osteuropastudien der Hochschulen des Landes Hessen. Reihe 1. Giessener Abhandlungen, 15)

> Study of the developmental stage of the Greek economy with regard to the possibility of joining the Common Market. In part one, the balance of payments problem is examined. The second part deals with the origin, distribution, and use of the national income.

## B. AGRICULTURE

1270. Food and Agriculture Organization of the United Nations.   Economic Survey of the Western Peloponnesus — Greece. Rome, 1965-1966. 6 v. Illus., maps.

1271. Kienitz, Friedrich.   Existenzfragen des griechischen Bauerntums. Agrarverfassung, Kreditversorgung und Genossenschaftswesen. Entwicklung und Gegenwartsprobleme. Berlin, Duncker und Humblot, 1960. 122 p. Illus.

> The book deals with the development of the present agrarian structure, agrarian credit, and the cooperative societies.

1272. McCorkle, C. O., Jr.   Fruit and Vegetable Marketing in the Economic Development of Greece. Athens, Center of Economic Research, 1962. 253 p. (*Its* Research Monograph Series, 3)

> After a limited attempt to demonstrate the techniques which are appropriate for market analysis in general, the author engages in a critical analysis of the organization and methods of marketing Greek fruits and vegetables. The study includes several useful suggestions for improving the marketing techniques of Greek fruits and other agricultural products.

1273. Panagou, S.   Ta agrotika mas proionta sta plaisia tes koinēs agoras (Our agricultural products in the Common Market). Nea Oikonomia, Mar. 1962: 193-199.

1274. Thompson, Kenneth.   Farm Fragmentation in Greece. Athens, Center of Economic Research, 1963. 263 p. Illus. (Research Monograph Series, 5) Bibliography: p. 261-263.

> *See also* entry no. 1047.

> In this study, the problem of fragmentation of Greek farms is

investigated in depth. The author examines the formidable waste of manpower, equipment, and land resulting from such fragmentation, and he concludes with a critical evaluation of the prevailing situation. A set of proposals for reform is also included.

## C. INDUSTRY

1275. Alexander, Alec. Greek Industrialists: an Economic and Social Analysis. Athens, Center of Economic Research, 1964. 182 p. (*Its* Research Monograph Series, 12)

The author makes the Greek industrial entrepreneur the focus of his inquiry, and he endeavors to list and analyze the incentives and disincentives imposed by the organization of the economic system of the country on industrial entrepreneurship. The analysis becomes often sociological rather than economic, frequently dealing with the position of the industrial entrepreneur in the Greek society and with the ordering of values in that society. The author argues that such ordering uniquely determines the relationship of the entrepreneur to his firm and his ability to influence his firm's economic progress.

1276. Association of Greek Industries. The State of Greek Industry in 1966. Athens, 1967. 117 p.

A survey of the performance of the industrial sector of the country during 1966, with additional information on the balance of payments status and on the overall level of national income. A useful publication, issued yearly, it contains summaries and discussions of the main economic developments that take place during each year. (The survey for 1966 also includes a summary of the main goals of the five-years development plan designed for the period 1966-70).

1277. Coutsoumaris, George. The Morphology of Greek Industry. Athens, Center of Economic Research, 1963. 430 p.

A haphazard reproduction of data from ready sources, lacking in orientation, purpose, and direction. The data are taken mostly from censuses of manufacturers conducted by the Greek government during various years. The only merit of the book is that it provides in a single source statistical material which could be obtained otherwise only by consulting several separate publications in Greek.

1278. Ellis, Howard S. Industrial Capital in Greek Development. Athens, Center of Economic Research, 1964. 335 p. (*Its* Research Monograph Series, 8)

The role played by the Greek capital market as a contributor to the economic development of the country is analyzed along with the concomitant problems of the financing of industry. After an examination of the "real factors" conditioning the country's rate of economic development, the author concludes with a set of proposals for policy formulation.

## D. MONEY, FINANCE, TRADE

1279. Abkommen zur Gründung einer Assoziation zwischen der Europäischen Wirtschaftsgemeinschaft und Griechenland und Anhänge [Brüssel], Veröffentlichungsstelle der Europäischen Gemeinschaft, 1962. 150 p.
Text of the agreement.

1280. Break, George.   Studies in Greek Taxation. Athens, Center of Economic Research, 1964. 250 p. (*Its* Research Monograph Series, 11)
The study is divided in two parts. The first part, which is purely descriptive, provides a review of the existing system of taxation in Greece and of its salient characteristics. The second part consists of a critical appraisal of the tax system in force and of its effects on resource allocation, administrative costs, and distribution of income. Such effects are found to be mostly adverse. The study concludes with a set of proposals for revising the prevailing system in a way which will render it more conducive to the economic development of the country.

1281. Damala, B.   Hai exōterikai synallagai kai hai nomismatikai exelixeis eis tēn chōran mas (Foreign exchange markets and monetary developments in our country). Nea Oikonomia, Nov. 1961: 761-770.

1282. Delivanis, D.   Die Probleme der Zahlungsbilanz und die aussenwirtschaftliche Integration Griechenlands. Wirtschaft und Gesellschaft Südosteuropas, 1961: 544-556.

1283. Ziegler, Gert.   Griechenland in der Europäischen Wirtschaftsgemeinschaft. München, Südosteuropa Verlagsgesellschaft, 1962. 110 p. Tables. (Südosteuropa-Studien, 4)
In the first part, the author offers an economic analysis of the agreement of July 9, 1961; in the second, he surveys the state of the Greek economy at the same time.
*See also* Ziegler's earlier study: *Der Osthandel Griechenlands in den Jahren 1956-1959* (Berlin, 1961, 28 p.).

1284. Zolotas, Xenophon.   Monetary Equilibrium and Economic Development. Princeton, Princeton University Press, 1965. 223 p. Illus.
A masterful analysis and evaluation of the economic policies pursued in Greece between 1960 and 1963, and an analysis of the structure of the economy as well. The book excels in theoretical rigor and statistical documentation. The last two chapters deal with the prospects of industrialization of the country and with the prospects and problems confronting the agricultural sector.
*See also* Zolotas' 1958 work of the same title, in which he provides a brief but concise discussion, using Greece as a case, of the problems confronting monetary authorities of developing countries in their efforts to secure a stable currency.

## E. SCIENTIFIC DEVELOPMENTS

*by Vladimir Slamecka*

1285. Haniotis, George V.   The Search for a National Scientific Policy in Greece. Minerva, 1965, no. 3: 312-320.

A brief history of the administration of scientific and technical research in Greece, with a discussion of the scale and patterns of the present scientific effort and the prospects and limitations of current and future policy.

1286. Organization for Economic Cooperation and Development. Greece. Paris, 1965. 71 p. Bibliography: p. 71. (*Its* Reviews of National Science Policy)

A study of the organization of science and the evolution and present status of national policy toward science in Greece. Part 1 is a review of the situation by outside experts; part 2, a discussion of problems and policies with a Greek delegation; and part 3, a statement of national resources, organizations involved in science policy and scientific research, and a statistical account of their activities. *See also* Angelos N. Kalogeras' *Hē organōsis tēs epistēmonikēs ereunēs en Helladi* (Organization of scientific and technical research in Greece) (Athēnai, Hellenikon Kentron Paragōgikokētos, 1963, 163 p.). A summary in English is included.

# 33

# the society

*by Constantine A. Yeracaris*

## A. BIBLIOGRAPHIC MATERIALS

1287. Holloway, C. W.   Greece: a Selected Bibliography. Air University Libraries, Maxwell Air Force Base, Alabama, 1950. 6 p. (Mimeographed)

1288. Kerner, Robert J.   Social Sciences in the Balkans and in Turkey; a Survey of Resources for Study and Research in These Fields of Knowledge. Berkeley, University of California Press, 1930. 137 p.
   *See also* entry no. 257.
      Greece is covered on pages 110-113. Periodicals published in Greek devoted to the social sciences are listed on pages 112-113.

1289. U.S. *Library of Congress. Division of Bibliography.*   Greece: A Selected List of References. Compiled by Ann Duncan Brown and Helen Dudenbostel Jones. Washington, D.C., 1943. 101 p.
   *See also* entry no. 960.

1290. Vagiakakos (Bagiakakos), Dikaios V.   Schediasma peri tōn toponymikōn kai anthrōpologikōn spoudōn en Helladi, 1833-1962 (Essay on toponymic and anthropological studies in Greece, 1833-1962). Athēna (Athens), v. 66, 1962: 300-424; and v. 67, 1963-1966: 145-369.

General annotated bibliography of anthropological and ethnographic studies, in Greek and French.

For an annotated bibliography listing 738 books, articles, and periodicals see *Modern Greek Society: Continuity and Change* by Evan Vlachos (Fort Collins, Col., Colorado State University, Dept. of Sociology and Anthropology, 1969, 177 p.).

## B. SURVEY STUDIES

1291. McLellan, Grant S., *ed.* Greek Social Characteristics. Cambridge, Mass., Associates for International Research, Inc., 1956. 149 p. (mimeographed) Bibliography: 7 leaves at end.

Compilation of papers by social scientists. A good profile serving as a useful introduction to modern Greece from historical, political, and sociological points of view, with some rural bias since most studies reported were conducted on small communities. Includes reports on social and political values, some of which lack insight on minority problems and the role of the military in politics.

1292. Marketos, Babēs I., *ed.* A Proverb for It; 1510 Greek Sayings. Translated by Ann Arpajoglou. New York, New World Publishers, 1945. 191 p. Illus.

Compilation of modern and ancient proverbs as expressions of folk literature and folk social criticism.

1293. Mead, Margaret, *ed.* Cultural Patterns and Technical Change. New York, New American Library, 1955. 352 p. Diagr. (A Mentor Book, MD 134)

The section on Greece (p. 57-96) attempts to portray the whole culture of Greece on the basis of selective literature and impressions. Although limited in scope and speculative, it does give some insights (with a rural bias).

1294. Pepelasis, Adamandios A. Image of the Past and Economic Backwardness. Human Organization (Lexington), v. 17, Winter 1959: 19-27.

The author explores the thesis that the romantic penchant of contemporary Greeks for revering their country's glorious past actually is a retarding factor in economic growth. Includes some hasty generalizations (political, social, and legal) which are unfounded, but presents a useful account of current educational and legal practices in Greece.

1295. Sanders, Irwin T. Rainbow in the Rock; the People of Rural Greece Cambridge, Mass., Harvard University Press, 1962. 363 p. Illus.

*See also* entries no. 992, 1046, *and* 1460.

The author attempts to define personality types of the Greek people and to analyze those traits which explain their social and cultural survival. Based on case studies of a number of communities in various parts of Greece, it includes data on all major social institutions.

1296. Scholte, Henrik.    Griekenland; land, volk, cultuur. Baarn, Het Wereldvenster, 1963. 286 p. Illus.

A brief history of Greece, its people and culture.

1297. Smothers, Frank A., William H. McNeill, *and* Elizabeth D. McNeill. Report on the Greeks. New York, Twentieth Century Fund, 1948. 226 p. Illus., ports., maps.

*See also* entries no. 1192 *and* 1262.

By a journalist, a military attaché, and a writer. Emphasis on political developments during and after the Second World War. Rather impressionistic.

1298. Sweet-Escott, Bickham.    Greece. A Political and Economic Survey, 1939-1953. London, New York, Royal Institute of International Affairs, 1954. 206 p. Maps, tables. Bibliography: p. 195-197.

*See also* entries no. 1194 *and* 1264.

A succinct and well-documented account.

## C. SOCIAL ORGANIZATION, SOCIAL PROBLEMS, AND SOCIAL CHANGE

1299. Argenti, Philip P.    The Occupation of Chios by the Germans and Their Administration of the Island. Cambridge, London, Cambridge University Press, 1966. 375 p. Illus., maps, facsims., tables.

*See also* entry no. 1174.

An excellent monograph, with ample documentation, portraying aspects of life during the period 1941-1944.

1300. Evelpides, C.    Some Economic and Social Problems in Greece. International Labour Review (Geneva), v. 68, Aug. 1953: 151-165.

*See also* entry no. 1255.

Primarily a survey of economic problems in modern Greece. Provides an analysis of statistical data and explores some of their social aspects.

1301. Friedl, Ernestine.    Lagging Emulation in Post-Peasant Society. American Anthropologist (Menasha,Wis.), v. 66, 1964: 569-586.

A penetrating study of "orderly" changes through the mechanism of "lagging emulation" of urban values by rural communities in Modern Greece.

1302. Friedl, Ernestine.    Role of Kinship in the Transmission of National

Culture to Rural Villages in Modern Greece. American Anthropologist (Menasha, Wis.), v. 61, 1959: 30-38.

A study of the role of kinship in providing continuity in a changing Greek society.

1303. Greece (Kingdom of).   Statistikē tēs dikaiosynēs (politikēs dikaiōsynēs, englēmatologikēs kai sophrōnistikēs) etous 1964; H: 15 Dikaiosynē (Legal statistics for civil and criminal law, and correctional statistics, for the year 1964. H: 15 Justice). Athēnai, Ethnikē Statistikē Ypēresia tēs Hellados, 1966. 107 p.

The first part includes cases handled by civil courts and public notaries; the second, criminal statistics; and the third, correctional statistics.

1304. Jecchinis, Christos.   Trade Unionism in Greece. A Study in Political Paternalism. Chicago, Roosevelt University, 1967. 205 p.

An excellent monograph on Greek trade-unionism, a subject which has not received adequate scholarly attention.

1305. Kousoulas, Dimitrios George.   Revolution and Defeat; the Story of the Greek Communist Party. London, New York, Oxford University Press, 1965. 306 p. Maps. Bibliography: p. 292-295.

See also entry no. 1141.

A historical treatise on the communist social movement in Greece from 1920 through 1950. Valuable for understanding modern Greek society. Good coverage of anti-movement tactics, especially as implemented by the Metaxas dictatorship (1936-1941).

1306. Lambiri, Jane (Ioanna).   Social Change in a Greek Country Town. The Impact of Factory Work on the Position of Women. Athens, Center of Planning and Economic Research, 1965. 163 p. (Research Monograph Series, 13)

See also entry no. 1037.

A study of the impact of industrialization in a town in modern Greece, with special emphasis on the status of women.

1307. Langsford, Georges.   Reorganization of Public Administration in Greece. Paris, Organization for Economic Cooperation and Development, 1965. 111 p.

A report on central public administration authorities in Greece. Includes an examination of educational problems and plans for reorganization.

1308. McNeill, William H.   Greece: American Aid in Action, 1947-1956. New York, Twentieth Century Fund, 1957. 240 p. Illus., maps.

See also entries no. 1185, 1237, and 1257.

The treatment of political and economic conditions from 1947 through 1949 as related to the American Aid Program is rather superficial. Contains some interesting accounts of life in the villages.

1309. Munkman, C. A.   American Aid to Greece: a Report on the First Ten Years. New York, Frederick A. Praeger, 1958. 306 p.
>Based on about 100 reports by the U.S. Economic Mission to Greece. Economic, health, and social problems such as housing and public administration are discussed.

1310. Organization for Economic Cooperation and Development. *Mediterranean Regional Project*. Country Reports: Greece. Paris, 1965. 195 p. Illus.
>*See also* entry no. 1042.
>Study by a team of economists and statisticians on the educational needs of Greece and the existing potentialities. Includes proposals for future planning.

1311. Pepelasis, Adamandios A.   Legal System and Economic Development of Greece. Journal of Economic History (New York), v. 19, 1959: 173-198.
>A historical study of the relationship between the legal system in Greece and economic development since the 18th century.

1312. Psomiades, H. J.   The Economic and Social Transformation of Modern Greece. Journal of International Affairs (New York), v. 19, Feb. 1965: 194-205.
>*See also* entry no. 1261.
>A summary of basic changes since the War of Independence (1821-1829), with useful material on the period since the Second World War.

1313. Sanders, Irwin T.   Nomadic Peoples of Northern Greece: Ethnic Puzzle and Cultural Survival. Social Forces (Chapel Hill, N.C.), v. 33, Dec. 1955: 122-129.
>Insightful account of the nomadic shepherds.

1314. Sanders, Irwin T.   Village Social Organization in Greece. Rural Sociology (Baton Rouge, La.), v. 18, 1953: 366-375.
>A summary of the findings of studies on 13 villages in central and northern Greece. Includes information on family, church, school, community, and political organization.

1315. Stycos, J. Mayone.   Patterns of Communication in a Rural Greek Village. The Public Opinion Quarterly (Princeton, N.J.), v. 16, 1952: 59-70.
>A study of village opinion, with empirical data.

1316. Tsouderos, John E.   Hoi geōrgikoi synetairismoi en tō plaisiō tēs Hellēnikes koinōnikēs diarthrōseōs (The agricultural cooperatives within the framework of the structure of Greek society). Athēnai, Hesteia, 1960. 193 p.

Includes data on the history and locations of agricultural co-operatives in Greece since 1915.

## D. MIGRATION AND URBANIZATION

1317. Kayser, Bernard, *and* Kenneth Thompson.  Economic and Social Atlas of Greece. Athens, National Statistical Service of Greece, 1964. 1 v. (unpaged). Illus., maps, diagrs.

*See also entry* no. 1036.

Complete data and analysis for the period 1956-1960, covering geology, migration, urbanization, population composition, labor force, vital statistics. In Greek, English, and French.

1318. Greece. *Genikē Statistikē Hypēresia.*    Ekthesis dokimastikēs ereunis epi tōn kinētrōn kai tōn synthēkōn metanasteuseōs tou plēthysmou tōn agrotikon periochon (Report on the exploratory survey into moti-vations and circumstances of rural migration). A: 4 Population, Athēnai, 1962. 46 p.

The analysis, in Greek and English, covers four villages (in different regions), on the basis of extensive data from questionnaires.

1319. Kayser, Bernard.    Géographie humaine de la Grèce; éléments pour l'étude de l'urbanisation. Paris, Presses Universitaires de France, 1964. 147 p. Tables, maps, bibliography.

*See also* entry no. 1035.

Detailed analysis of population redistribution and emigration in Greece between 1928 and 1961. Data on urbanization, mortality, fertility, and age composition are extensively utilized. Indispensable reference work for the study of modern Greek society.

1320. Moustaka, Calliope.    The Internal Migrant; a Comparative Study in Urbanization. Athens, Center of Social Sciences, 1964. 105 p. Illus., forms, maps, bibliographies.

Reports a sample survey of the social characteristics of 840 in-ternal migrants from Zagori (Epirus) and Paros Island (Aegean Sea). Useful data, but few analytical insights.

1321. Settas, Nikolaos Chr.    Ta aitia tēs astyphilias kai tēs metanasteuseōs tōn agrotōn tes Euvoias (Factors in urbanization and emigration of the farmers in Euboea). Athēnai, Anōtatē Geōponikē Scholē, 1965. 173 p.

This doctoral dissertation examines the internal and external mi-gration of residents of six communities of the Isle of Euboea during a period of 30 years.

1322. Ward, Benjamin.    Greek Regional Development. Athens, Center of Economic Research, 1965. 159 p. (Research Monograph Series, 4)

Chapter four presents a succinct analysis of urban growth in Greece since 1848 as related to economic growth and development.

## E. THE FAMILY; WOMEN; CHILDREN

1323. Campbell, John K.   Honour, Family, and Patronage; a Study of
Institutions and Moral Values in a Greek Mountain Community.
Oxford, Clarendon Press, 1964. 393 p. Map, plates. Bibliography:
p. 365.
*See also* entry no. 1389.
A penetrating study of a nomadic community. An excellent chapter (7) on the complementarity and reciprocity of husband-wife relations within a male-dominated family system is equally applicable to
sedentary rural communities.

1324. Lambiri, Jane (Ionna).   Impact of Industrial Employment on the
Position of Women in a Greek Country Town. British Journal of
Sociology (London), v. 14, 1963: 240-247.
Explores the gradual readjustment of cultural values and prac-
tices. Interview and observational data.

1325. Pitt-Rivers, Julian, *ed.*   Mediterranean Countrymen; Essays in the
Social Anthropology of the Mediterranean. The Hague, Mouton,
1963. 236 p.
Included are three essays on Greece: J. K. Campbell, "The Kindred
in Greek Mountain Communities," concerning role of the kinship
systems in the persistence of traditional social structures among
shepherds; E. Friedl, "Some Aspects of Dowry and Inheritance in
Boeotia," on kinship and dowry systems in a modern Greek village;
H. Levy, "Inheritance and Dowry in Classical Greece," with emphasis on the continuity of the tradition of dowry from ancient Greece
to modern society.

1326. Safilios-Rothschild, Constantina.   A Comparison of Power Structure
and Marital Satisfaction in Urban Greek and French Families. The
Journal of Marriage and the Family (Menasha, Wis.), v. 39, May
1964: 345-352.
Relates the husband's authority and marital satisfaction to the number of children, wife's employment, education of spouses, occupational status, and income.

1327. Safilios-Rothschild, Constantina.   Morality, Courtship, and Love in
Greek Folklore. Southern Folklore Quarterly (Jacksonville, Fla.),
v. 19, 1965: 295-308.
A cursory examination of morality and heterosexual love in Greek
culture, based on folklore accounts.

1328. Safilios-Rothschild, Constantina.   Some Aspects of Fertility in Urban Greece. *In* World Population Conference, 2d, Belgrade, 1965.
v. 11. New York, United Nations, 1967. p. 228.
Based on data from 400 couples. An analysis of rationality in family
planning.

1329. Valaoras, Vassilios G., Antonia Polychronopoulou, *and* Dimitri Trichopoulos. Control of Family Size in Greece. Population Studies; a Quarterly Journal of Demography (Cambridge, Eng.), v. 18, 1965: 265-278.

> Findings of a 1962 field survey of over 3,800 mothers. Analysis of family planning by age and area.

1330. Vlachos, Evangelos Constantine. An Annotated Bibliography on Greek Migration. Athens, Social Sciences Center, 1966. 127 p.

> A research monograph covering an important Greek social problem.

## F. HEALTH

1331. Blum, Richard H., *and* Eva Blum. Health and Healing in Rural Greece; a Study of Three Communities. Stanford, California, Stanford University Press, 1965. 269 p. General Bibliography: p. 257-262; References Cited: p. 253-256.

> A valuable analysis, based on informal contacts with various members of the communities, observation during medical examinations, responses to standardized questionnaires, and references to secondary sources. Includes data on birth, abortion, death, health practices, and attitudes toward various illnesses. *See also* Ernestine Friedl's "Hospital Care in Provincial Greece," in *Human Organization* (Lexington), v. 16, Winter 1958: 24-27, a case study on the relationship between social prestige and acceptance of hospital care.

1332. McDougall, J. B. Tuberculosis in Greece; an Experiment in the Relief and Rehabilitation of a Country. Bulletin of the World Health Organization (Geneva), v. 1, 1947-48: 103.

> A report on tuberculosis morbidity and mortality statistics for the period 1934-1946. Survey of available services and results of the UNRRA program to combat the disease.

1333. Zavitsianos, Theodosios X. Ta iatrika-psychologika kai koinōnika provlēmata tēs ephēvikēs ēlikias en Helladi. Hē ephēvikē thnēsimotēs (1921-1961) kai nosērotēs (1960-61). Koinōnikē sēmasia. Dēmopathologikai synepeiai kai tropos antimetōpiseōs toutōn (Medical-psychological and social problems of puberty in Greece. Puberty mortality [1921-1961] and morbidity [1960-61]. Social importance. Demopathological consequences and means to face them). Athēnai, 1966.

> Paper read at the 21st Panhellenic meeting of the Medical and Surgical Association of Athens. Based on case studies compiled by the author and the School of Public Health.

## G. REGIONAL STUDIES

1334. Abbott, George F. Macedonian Folklore. Cambridge, The University Press, 1903. 372 p.

Report on research in the folklore of Greek-speaking parts of Macedonia.

1335. Allbaugh, Leland G.    Crete; a Case Study of an Underdeveloped Area. Princeton, Princeton University Press, 1953. 572 p. Illus., maps. Bibliography: p. 455-460.

A sociological and economic survey reporting the findings of a Rockefeller Foundation mission during 1948 and 1949. Data derived through multipurpose survey sampling and secondary sources. Covers family, health, food and nutrition, community facilities, government, organization, and social problems.

1336. Argenti, Philip P., *and* H. J. Rose.    The Folk-Lore of Chios. Cambridge, University Press, 1949. 2 v.

A definitive ethnographic study.

1337. Friedl, Ernestine.    Vasilika; a Village in Modern Greece. New York, Holt, Rinehart and Winston, 1962. 110 p. Illus.

A case study which offers insights into village life, family division of labor, and political institutions.

## H. MINORITIES

1338. Allen, Harold B.    Come Over into Macedonia; the Story of a Ten-Year Adventure in Uplifting a War-torn People. New Brunswick, N.J., Rutgers University Press, 1943. 313 p. Plates, ports. Map on lining-papers.

An account by the director of the Near East Foundation's program for the settlement of Greek refugees from Asia Minor in Macedonia after the Greek disaster in 1922.

1339. Delivanis, D.    Achievements in the North of Greece (1912-1962). Balkan Studies (Thessalonikē), v. 3, 1962: 257-266.

A brief account of minority problems and progress toward their solution.

1340. Kōfos, Evangelos.    Nationalism and Communism in Macedonia. Thessalonikē, Institute for Balkan Studies, 1964. 251 p. Maps. Bibliography: p. 227-238.

See also entry no. 1139.

A definitive study on the "Macedonian Question."

1341. Ladas, S. P.    The Exchange of Minorities: Bulgaria, Greece, and Turkey. New York, Macmillan, 1932. 849 p. Illus., maps. Bibliography: p. 831-832.

See also entries no. 223, 708, *and* 1202.

An account of the historical, political, and social origins of minorities in modern Greece after the First World War. Invaluable for understanding some of the present minority problems in Greece.

1342. Morgenthau, Henry.    I Was Sent to Athens. Garden City, N.Y., Doubleday, Doran and Compay, Inc., 1929. 327 p. Plates, maps.

An account by the man responsible for the program of settlement of Greek refugees from Asia Minor following the First World War.

1343. Pentzopoulos, Dēmētrēs.    The Balkan Exchange of Minorities and Its Impact upon Greece. Paris, Mouton, 1962. 293 p. Illus. (Publications of the Social Sciences Center, Athens, 1)

*See also* entries no. 1043 *and* 1115.

Deals primarily with the integration of Greek refugees from Asia Minor. Explores the value of the "exchange" of populations as a method of solving problems of minorities.

# 34

# Intellectual and Cultural Life*

* Since the principal focus of this bibliographic area guide is on more recent times, the coverage of Ancient and Hellenistic Greece, notwithstanding its clear impact on Modern Greece, could not be included.

General Theater 1511-1514
Greek Theater from 1790 to the Present 1515-1518
The Shadow Theater of Karagiozes 1519-1520
The Greek Cinema 1521-1522

## A. LANGUAGE

*by Constantine A. Trypanis*

### 1. Modern Greek

1344. Chatzidakēs, Geōrgios N.   Mesaiōnika kai nea hellēnika (Medieval and Modern Greek). Athēnai, 1907. 2 v.

> The basic work on the Medieval and Modern Greek languages. *See also* his *Syntomos historia tēs hellēnikēs glōssēs* (Survey of the history of the Greek language) (Athēnai, Bibliopōleion I. N. Siderē, 1915, 144 p.).

1345. Du Cange, Charles du Fresne.   Glossarium ad scriptores mediae et infimae graecitatis. Lugduni, Apud Anissonios, J. Posuel et C. Rigaud, 1688. 2 v. Illus. Reprinted Graz, Akademische Druck- und Verlagsanstalt, 1958. 2 v.

> Still the most important dictionary of Medieval Greek.

1346. Kapsomenos, S. G.   Die griechische Sprache zwischen Koiné und Neugriechisch. *In*: Congrès international des études byzantines. *11th, Munich, 1958.* Berichte zum XI. Internationalen Byzantinisten-Kongress, München, 1958. München, In Kommission bei Beck, 1958. p. 1-39.

> A survey of the Greek language between the conquests of Alexander and the emergence of Modern Greek. Includes a good bibliography. *See also*:
>
> Wolf, K.   Studien zur Sprache des Malalas. München, 1911-1912. 2 v.
>
> Psaltes, Stamatios B.   Grammatik der byzantinischen Chroniken. Göttingen, Vandenhoeck und Ruprecht, 1913. 394 p. (Forschungen zur griechischen und lateinischen Grammatik, 2. Hft.)

1347. Koraēs, Adamantios.   Atakta; ēgoun pantopaon eis tēn archaian kai nean Hellēnikēn glōssan (Miscellany; i.e. various observations on Ancient and Modern Greek). Paris, F. Didot, père et fils, 1828-1835. 5 v.

> The collected glossological writings of the great Greek philologist. *See also*:
>
> Psichari, Jean.   Études de philologie néo-grecque; recherches sur le développement historique du grec. Paris, É. Bouillon, 1892. 377 p.

(Bibliothèque de l'École des hautes études . . . Sciences philologiques et historiques, 92. fasc.) Includes a very full bibliography.

1348. Lampe, Geoffry W. H.   A Patristic Greek Lexicon. Oxford, Clarendon Press, 1961–

An important recent addition to the lexicography of Patristic Greek.

1349. Sophocles, Evangelinus A.   Greek Lexicon of the Roman and Byzantine Periods (from B.C. 146 to A.D. 1100). New York, F. Ungar, 1957. 2 v.

Important but incomplete dictionary of Greek in the Later Roman Empire. Previous editions appeared in 1870 and 1914.

## 2. Serials on Modern Greek

1350. Athēna; syngramma periodikon. Tēs en Athēnais Epistēmonikēs Hetaireias (Athena; a journal of the Athenian Society of Scholars). v. 1– 1889– Illus., plates, port., maps, plans, facsims., tables.

Glotta; Zeitschrift für griechische und lateinische Sprache. Göttingen, Vandenhoeck und Ruprecht. 1907–

Volumes 1-30 (1889-1919) of *Athēna* issued in four parts annually; volume 31– (1920–) isssued in one volume annually.

## 3. Grammar and Syntax

1351. Chatzidakēs, Georgios N.   Einleitung in die neugriechische Grammatik. Leipzig, Breitkopf und Härtel, 1892. 464 p. (Bibliothek indogermanischer Grammatik, Bd. 5)

An important introduction to Modern Greek grammar on an historical basis. *See also*:
Triantaphyllidēs, Manolēs A.   Neoellēnikē grammatikē; historikē eisagogē (Modern Greek grammar; historical introduction). Athēnai, 1938. 667 p. Triantaphyllidēs' writings on the language problem are also to be found in volume six of his *Hapanta* (Complete works) (Thessalonike, 1963). *See also*:
Kantos, Konstantinos S.   Glōssikai paratēreseis . . . (Linguistic observations . . . ). Athēnai, 1882. 593 p.

1352. Thumb, Albert.   Handbuch der neugriechischen Volkssprache. Grammatik, Texte, Glossar. 2., verb. und erweiterte Aufl. Strassburg, K. J. Trübner, 1910. 359 p.

An excellent survey of Modern Greek grammar accompanied by illustrative texts. An English translation appeared as *Handbook of the Modern Greek Vernacular* (Edinburg, T. and T. Clark, 1912, 371 p.; reprinted: Chicago, Argonaut, 1964, 370 p.). *See also*:
Pernot, Hubert Octave.   Grammaire du grec moderne. Paris, Garnier Frères, 1921-1930. 2 v. (Collection de manuels pour l'étude du grec moderne, no. 1, 3)

Bachtin, Nicholas.   Introduction to the Study of Modern Greek. Cambridge, England, Printed at the Press of F. Juckes, Birmingham, 1935. 86 p.

1353. Tzartzanos, Achilleus A.   Neoellēnikē syntaxis tēs koinēs dēmotikēs (Syntax of the common spoken Modern Greek idiom). 2d ed. Athēnai, 1948-1953.

The best book on Modern Greek syntax.

## 4. Historical Surveys of the Language Problem

1354. Megas, A. E.   Historia tou glōssikou zētēmatos (History of the language question). Athēnai, I. Kollaros, 1925-1927. 2 v.

An up-to-date survey of the language problem in modern Greek life and letters. *See also*:

Krumbacher, Karl.   Das Problem der neugriechischen Schriftsprache. München, K. B. Akademie in Kommission des G. Franzschen Verlags (J. Roth), 1902. 226 p. Translated into Greek, with a reply by Chatzidakis in *To provlēma tēs neōteras graphomenēs Hellēnikēs hypo k. Krumbacher, kai apantēsis eis auton hypo G. N. Chatzidaki* (Athenai, 1905).

Bernardakis, D.   Pseudattikismou Elenchos (An examination of false Atticism). Trieste, 1884.

Rhoidēs, Emmanuēl D.   Peri tēs sēmerinēs Hellēnikēs glōssēs (On contemporary modern Greek). Hestia, 1885. p. 275 ff.

## 5. Dictionaries

1355. Akadēmia Athēnon.   Lexikon, tēs hellēnikēs glōssēs (Dictionary of the Greek language). Athēnai, 1933–

The great historical dictionary of Greek undertaken by the Academy of Athens and still in process of publication. *See also*:

Lexikographikon archeion tēs mesēs kai neas hellēnikēs (Lexicographical archive of Medieval and Modern Greek). Athēnai, Typois P. Sakellariou, 1915-1923. 7 v.

Akadēmia Athēnon.   Lexikographikon deltion (Lexicographical journal). Athēnai, 1939–

1356. Andriōtēs, Nikolaos P.   Etymologiko lexiko tēs koinēs Neoellēnikēs (Etymological dictionary of Modern Greek). Athēnai, 1951. 312 p. (Collection de l'Institut français d'Athènes, 24)

A good short etymological dictionary of Modern Greek, tracing the sources of the demotic vocabulary.

1357. Dēmētrakou mega lexikon tēs Hellēnikēs glōssēs (Dēmētrakos' great dictionary of Modern Greek). Athēnai, Dēmētrakou, 1936-1950. 9 v.

The fullest dictionary of Greek of all periods.

1358. Pring, Julian T., *comp.*   The Oxford Dictionary of Modern Greek (Greek-English). Oxford, Clarendon Press, 1965. 219 p.

A most useful short dictionary which includes a large proportion of the words of the spoken idiom.

1359. "Prōias" lexikon tēs neas Hellēnikēs glōssēs ("Proias" dictionary of Modern Greek). 2d ed. Athēnai, Ekdotikos oikos S. P. Dēmētrakou, 196?. 2 v.
    A comprehensive lexicon of Modern Greek as spoken and read.

## B. LITERATURE

### by Constantine A. Trypanis

#### 1. Byzantine and Medieval Greece

1360. Bardenhewer, Otto.    Geschichte der altkirchlichen Literatur. Freiburg im Breisgau, St. Louis, Mo., Herder, 1912-1932. 5 v.
    This is the basic work on early Christian writings.

1361. Beck, Hans G.    Kirche und theologische Literatur im Byzantinischen Reich. München, Beck, 1959. 835 p. (Handbuch der Altertumswissenschaft, 12. Abt.: Byzantinisches Handbuch 2. T., 1. Bd.)
    The religious literature of Byzantium from the Cappadocian Fathers to the Heyschats and Uniats of the 14th and 15th centuries is discussed here. The work brings up to date Ehrhard's edition of Krumbacher's work (see entry no. 1367). For hagiography, see:
    Bibliotheca hagiographica graeca. 3d ed. Bruxelles, Société des Bollandistes, 1957. 3 v.

1362. Cantarella, Raffaele.    Poeti bizantini. Milano, Vita e pensiero, 1948. 2 v. (Edizioni dell'Università cattolica del Sacro Cuore. Serie "Corsi universitari," v. 21-22)
    An anthology with useful bibliography and notes.

1363. Christ, Wilhelm von, ed.    Anthologia graeca carminum christianorum. Lipsiae, B. G. Teubner, 1871. 268 p. Facsim.
    Still the best anthology of Greek Christian hymns. The useful introduction (in Latin) discusses the different types of hymns and their authors. On music and meter it is less reliable.

1364. Dieterich, Karl.    Geschichte der byzantinischen und neugriechischen Litteratur. Leipzig, C. F. Annelangs Verlag, 1902. 242 p. (Die Litteraturen des Ostens in Einzeldarstellungen, Bd. 4)
    A summary of literature in Greek from the foundation of the Byzantine Empire to the end of the 19th century. Dieterich is much concerned with Eastern and Western influence on Greek writing.

1365. Dölger, Franz.    Die byzantinische Dichtung in der Reinsprache; ein Abriss. Berlin, Wissenschaftliche Editionsgesellschaft, 1948. 46 p.
    Dölger's short introduction to Byzantine poetry in the "pure" language includes remarks on meter and an analysis on the forms employed by Byzantine poets as well as recent bibliography.

1366. Impellizzeri, Salvatore.   La letteratura bizantina da Costantino agli iconoclasti. Bari, Dedalo libri, 1965. 315 p. (Università degli studi di Bari. Istituto di storia medievale e moderna. Saggi. 5)

> The most recent general account of the earlier half of Byzantine literature. One may also refer to Dölger's contribution to the *Cambridge Medieval History*, 2d ed., v. 4: "The Byzantine Empire" (Cambridge, The University Press, 1966), pt. 2, 207-263.

1367. Krumbacher, Karl.   Geschichte der byzantinischen Litteratur, von Justinian bis zum Ende des Oströmischen Reiches, 527-1453. 2d ed. Edited by A. Ehrhard and H. Gelzer. München, C. H. Beck, 1897. 1197 p. Reprinted New York, B. Franklin, 1958. 2 v. (Burt Franklin Bibliographical Series, 13)

> Krumbacher's history of Byzantine literature marks the beginning of systematic study of this subject. His sound judgments and extensive bibliographies of texts, studies, and manuscripts are still the basis for research into this field.

1368. Trypanis, Constantine A. (Kōnstantinos A. Trypanēs), *comp.* Medieval and Modern Greek Poetry; an Anthology. Oxford, Clarendon Press, 1951. 285 p. 2d rev. ed. Oxford, Clarendon Press, 1964.

> Selection of Katharevousa and Demotic poetry from the fourth century to Elytes. Useful introduction and notes. *See also*:
>
> Soyter, Gustav, *ed.*   Byzantinische Dichtung; eine Auswahl aus gelehrter und volkstümlicher Dichtung vom 4. bis 15. Jahrhundert, griechisch und deutsch im Versmass der Urtexte. Athens, Verlag der "Byzantinisch-neugriechische Jahrbücher," 1938. 111 p. (Texte und Forschungen zur byzantinisch-neugriechischen Philologie . . . Nr. 28)

1369. Editions of Byzantine Greek texts.

> The most complete series of texts remains:
>
> Migne, Jacques P., *ed.*   Patrologia cursus completus . . . Series graeca . . . Lutetiae Parisiorum, 1857-1866. 161 in 166 v. The historical texts can be found in:
>
> Corpus scriptorium historiae byzantinae. Edited by B. G. Niebuhr. Bonnae, Imprensis E. Weberi, 1828-1897. 50 v.
>
> Both these collections include the Greek text and a Latin translation. Some of the religious texts have been brought up to date in the series *Sources chretiennes* (Paris, 1956-). *See also* the Teubner and Budé series.

1370. Editions of medieval Greek texts.

> In addition to those found in *Patrologia graeca* (see entry 1369), one may consult:
>
> Legrand, Émile L. J., *ed.*   Bibliothèque grecque vulgaire. Paris, 1880-1913. 10 v.
>
> Wagner, Wilhelm, *ed.*   Carmina graeca medii aevi edidit Gulielmus Wagner. Lipsiae, In aedibus B. G. Teubneri, 1874. 382 p.
>
> Particularly good editions of individual works include:

The Chronicle of Morea. To khronikon tou Moreōs. A History in Political Verse . . . with introduction, critical notes, and indices by John Schmitt . . . London, Methuen, 1904. 640 p. Front. (map).

Machairas, Leontios. Recital Concerning the Sweet Land of Cyprus, Entitled "Chronicle." Edited with a translation and notes by R. M. Dawkins. Oxford, The Clarendon Press, 1932. 2 v. Fold. map, fold. geneal. table.

## 2. Modern Greece

### a. Surveys

1371. Apostolakēs, Giannēs M.   Ta dēmotika tragoudia (The folk songs). Athēnai, A. M. Kontomaris, 1929. 332 p.

————. To klephtiko tragoudi (The songs of the Klephts). Athēnai, Bibliopōleion tēs "Hestias," 1950. 179 p.

Pioneer studies of the Greek folk songs. Other editions of Greek folk songs, both in the original and in translation, include:

Fauriel, Claude C., *ed and tr.* Chants populaires de la Grèce moderne. Paris, Dondey-Dupré, père et fils, 1824-1825. 2 v.

Passow, Arnold, *ed.* Carmina popularia graeciae recentioris. Lipsiae, 1860. 650 p.

Politēs, Nikolaos G. Eklogai apo ta tragoudia tou Hellēnikou laou (An anthology of Modern Greek folk songs). Athēnai, Typois P. Leonē, 1932. 326 p.

Petropoulos, D. Hellēnika dēmotika tragoudia (Modern Greek folk songs). Athēnai, 1956. 2 v. (Vasikē vivliothēkē, 46-47)

Akadēmia Athēnōn. Hellēnika demotika tragoudia (Modern Greek folk songs). Athēnai, 1962. 516 p.

1372. Boutieridēs, Ēlias P. Historia tēs Neoellēnikēs logotechnias (History of modern Greek literature). Athēnai, 1924-1927. 454 p.

A good survey of the subject. Another version, with additions by Dēmētrēs Giakos covering the period 1931-1965 was published as *Syntomē historia tēs neoellēnikēs logotechnias, 1000-1930* (Abridged history of Modern Greek literature, 1000-1930) (Athēnai, Bibliopōleion D. N. Papadēma, 1966, 426 p.).

1373. Dēmaras, Kōnstantinos Th. (C. Th. Dimaras). Historia tēs neoellēnikēs logotechnias (History of modern Greek literature). Athēnai, Ikaros, 1948-1949. 2 v. 2d ed.: Athēnai, 1955. 478 p. 3d ed.: Athēnai, Ikaros, 1964. 16, 642 p.

*See also* entry no. 984.

The best history of the subject in Modern Greek. It has been published in French under the title *Histoire de la Littérature néohellénique* (Athènes, Collection de l'Institut français d'Athènes, n.d.).

1374. Jenkins, Romilly J. T. Dionysius Solomós. Cambridge, The University Press, 1940. 224 p. Front (port.), map.

A general study of one of the greatest modern Greek poets.

1375. Karantōnēs, Andreas.   Ho poiētēs Geōrgios Sepherēs (The poet George Seferis). Athēnai, Bibliopōleion tēs "Hestias," 1957. 207 p.
    A study of Greece's greatest living poet. *See also*:
    Gia ton Spherē (Essays in honor of Seferis). Athēnai, 1961. 496 p.

1376. Katsimbalēs, Geōrgios K.    Vivliographia Giōrgou Sephere (Bibliography of George Seferis). Athēnai, 1961. 67 p.

————.   Vivliographia I. Makrygiannē (Bibliography of John Makriyiannis). Athēnai, Typographeio Sergiadē, 1957. 15 p.

————.   Vivliographia Kōstē Palama, 1943-1953 (Bibliography of Kostis Palamas, 1943-1953). Athēnai, Typographeio Sergiadē, 1953. 86 p.

————.   Vivliographia Lamprou Porphyra (Bibliography of Lampros Porphyras). Athēnai, Typographeio Sergiadē, 1956. 24 p.

————.   Vivliographia N. Kazantzakē (Bibliography of N. Kazantzakis). Athēnai, 1958–

————.   Vivliographia Theophilou Chatzēmichaēl (Bibliography of Theophilos Chatzamichael). Athēnai, Typographeio Sergiadē, 1957. 19 p.

————.   Vivliographia Kosta Krystallē (Bibliography of Kostas Krystallis). Athēnai, 1957.

————.   Symplēroma vivliographias K. Krystallē (Supplement to the bibliography of Kostas Krystallis). Athēnai, 1943.

1377. Kazantzakēs, Nikos.   The Odyssey: A Modern Sequel. Translation into English verse, introduction, synopsis, and notes by Kimon Friar. Illustrated by Ghike. New York, Simon and Schuster, 1958. 824 p.
    Kazantzakis' major work in a masterful translation. Several of his other writings are available in Western languages. For a biography of the writer by his widow Helen Kazantzakis who draws extensively on his letters to her, see: *Nikos Kazantzakis* (New York, Simon and Schuster, 1968, 589 p.).

1378. Keeley, Edmund, *ed. and tr.*   Six Poets of Modern Greece. Chosen, translated and introduced by Edmund Keeley and Philip Sherrard. London, Thames and Hudson, 1960. 192 p.

1379. Knös, Börje.   L'historie de la littérature néo-grecque; la période jusqu'en 1821. Stockholm, Almquist och Wiksell, 1962. 690 p. (Acta Universitatis Upsaliensis. Studia graeca Upsaliensia, 1)
    Particularly valuable for the study of Greek literature during the period of the Turkish occupation. *See also*:
    Sathas, Kōnstantinos N.   Neoellēnikē philologia. Viographia tōn en tois grammasi dialampsantōn Hellēnōn 1453-1821 (Modern Greek literature. Biographies of distinguished Greek literary figures, 1453-1821). Athēnai, 1868. 761 p.

1380. Kyriakidēs, Stilpōn P.  Hai historikai archai tēs dēmōdous neoellēnikēs poiēseōs (The historical beginnings of popular Greek poetry).
Thessalonikē, 1934. 30 p. Reprinted, with additions: Thessalonikē,
1954. 46 p.
> A short study in Greek.

1381. Manousakas, M.  Krētikē logotechnia (Cretan literature). Thessalonikē, 1965. 63 p.
> An excellent outline of the literature that flourished in Venetian-
> occupied Crete after the fall of Constantinople. *See also*:
> Xanthoudidēs, S. A., *ed.*  Erōtokritos. Hērakleion, 1915. The
> classic edition of the Cretan romantic epic.
> Chortatzēs, Georgios.  Krētikon theatron. Erophile tragōdia Geōr-
> giou Chortatzē (1600) (The Cretan theater. Erophile, a tragedy by
> Georgios Chortatzes [1600]). Edited and with introduction and glos-
> sary by Steph. Xanthoudides. Athen, P. D. Sakellarios, 1928. 166 p.
> (Texte und Forschungen zur byzantinisch-neugriechischen Philolo-
> gie . . . Nr. 9)
> Megas, Geōrgios A., *ed.*  Thysia tou Avraam (The sacrifice of
> Abraham). 2d ed. Athēnai, 1954. 256 p.

1382. Sachinēs, Apostolos.  He synchronē pezographia mas (Our contemporary prose writers). Athēnai, Ikaros, 1951. 176 p.

———.  To historiko mythistorēma (The historical novel). Athēnai,
Diphros, 1957. 172 p.

———.  To neoellēniko mythistorēma (The modern Greek novel).
Athēnai, 1958. 316 p.
> Three books by one of Greece's leading literary critics on aspects
> of modern Greek prose.

1383. Sepheriadēs, Geōrgios.  On the Greek Style; Selected Essays in
Poetry and Hellenism. Translated by Rex Warner and Th. D. Fran-
gopoulos. Boston, Little, Brown, 1966. 196 p.
> Essays on contemporary Greek culture, by one of the greatest
> modern poets, who is also a Nobel prize winner.

1384. Valsa, M.  Le théâtre grec moderne de 1453 à 1900. Berlin, Akademie-Verlag, 1960. 384 p. (Berliner byzantinische Arbeiten, Bd. 18)
*See also* entry no. 1514.
> A detailed account of the history of modern Greek theater.

**b. Anthologies of Modern Greek Prose and Poetry**

1385. Valetas, Geōrgios.  Anthologia tēs dēmotikēs pezographias (Anthology of prose in the colloquial language). Athēnai, P. Panos, 1947.
3 v.

Politēs, Linos. Poiētikē anthologia (Anthology of Poetry [12th-20th
century]). Athēnai, Ekdóseis Galaxia, 1963-1967. 7 v.

Apostolidēs, Paulos. Anthologia, 1708-1952 (Anthology, 1708-1952). Athēnai, 1954. 2 v.

Additional texts will be found in the *Vasikē vivliothēkē* series (*see* entry 1371), which offers material from the Byzantine, Medieval and Modern periods.

### c. Modern Greek Periodicals

1386. The Charioteer. 1960– New York, Parnassos. Irregular.

Nea Hestia (New hearth). 1927– Athēnai. Semimonthly.

To nea grammata (New letters). 1935-1944. Athēnai. Semimonthly.

Anglohellēnikē epitheōrēsis (Anglohellenic review). 1945-1950. Athēnai. Monthly.

The *Charioteer* is a good collection of modern Greek literature in English translation. Numbers seven and eight for 1965, published as a cumulated 192-page issue, is perhaps the only available anthology of Cypriot literature in English translation (reprinted: New York, October House, 1966).

## C. FOLKLORE

### by Constantine A. Trypanis

1387. Akadēmia Athēnōn. *Laographikon Archeion.* Epetēris (Journal of the Folklore Archive). 1– 1939– Athēnai. Illus. Annual (irregular).

*See also* the journal *Laographia* (Folklore) founded by N. G. Politēs (entry 1391).

1388. Baud-Bovy, Samuel, *ed.* Chansons du Dodecanèse. Athènes, J. N. Sideris, 1935– La chanson populaire grecque du Dodecanèse. Paris, Société d'édition "Les Belles Lettres," 1936. 1 v. (Collection de l'Institut néo-hellènique de l'université de Paris. 2 sér. t. III)

An account of the music of Greek folksongs with particular reference to those of the Dodecanese.

1389. Campbell, John K. Honour, Family, and Patronage; a Study of Institutions and Moral Values in a Greek Mountain Community. Oxford, Clarendon Press, 1964. 393 p. Map, plates. Bibliography: p. 365.

*See also* entry no. 1323.

A detailed account of the life of the Sarakatsanoi, a mountain community in Central Greece.

1390. Dawkins, Richard M., *ed. and tr.* Forty-five Stories from the Dodekanese. Cambridge, University Press, 1950. 559 p.

———. Modern Greek Folktales. Oxford, Clarendon Press, 1953. 491 p.

————. More Greek Folktales. Oxford, Clarendon Press, 1955. 178 p.

These tales, chosen, translated, and edited by the most distinguished British scholar in the field, give a good picture of the outlook and character of Greek folklore.

1391. Frazer, *Sir* James G.   The Golden Bough; a Study in Comparative Religion. New York, London, Macmillan, 1894. 2 v.

Frequently reprinted in both complete and abridged editions, Frazer's book, despite its age, is still indispensable for the study of Greek folklore.

1392. Kyriakidēs, Stilpōn P.   Hellenikē laographia (Greek folklore). Athēnai, 1922. 1 v.

A good survey of some of the themes encountered in Greek folklore. A more recent edition appeared in 1965 (Akadēmia Athēnōn. Dēmosieumata tou Laographikou Archeiou, ar. 8). *See also*:

Swanson, Donald C. E.   Modern Greek Studies in the West; a Critical Bibliography of Studies on Modern Greek Linguistics, Philology and Folklore in Languages other than Greek. New York, New York Public Library, 1960. 93 p.

1393. Lawson, John C.   Modern Greek Folklore and Ancient Greek Religion; a Study in Survivals. Cambridge, England, University Press, 1910. 620 p.

An interesting account of the synthesis of Christian and pagan beliefs and motifs in modern Greek folklore. Detailed but not fully reliable.

1394. Megas, Geōrgios A.   Hellēnikai heortai kai ethima tēs laikēs latreias (Greek festivals and customs of popular worship). Athēnai, 1956. 252 p. Illus.

————. Greek Calendar Customs. Athens, 1958. 159 p. Illus.

These two books deal with the Christian and pagan festivals observed by the modern Greek people. One may also refer to Bernhard Schmidt's *Das Volksleben der Neugriechen und das hellenische Alterthum* (Leipzig, B. G. Teubner, 1871, 251 p.).

1395. Merlier, Melpo.   Essai d'un tableau du folklore musical grec. Le syllogue pour l'enregistrement des chansons populaires. Athènes, J. N. Sideris, 1935. 64 p. Illus., fold. map.

A pioneer, yet all-embracing work on modern Greek folk music and song. One may also refer to Georges Lambalet's *La musique populaire grecque; chants et danses. Étude critique, transcription et harmonisation* (Athènes, 1934, 195 p.).

1396. Nilsson, Martin P.   Geschichte der griechischen Religion. 2d rev. and enl. ed. München, Beck, 1955-1961. 2 v. Illus. (Handbuch der Altertumswissenschaft, 5. Abt., 2 T.)

The basic work on the history of ancient Greek religion.

1397. Politēs, Nikolaos G.   Neoellēnikē mythologia (Modern Greek mythology). Athēnai, 1871-1874. 2 v. (Meletē epi tou viou tou neōterou Hellēnikou laou, v. 1, pt. 1-2)

————.   Meletai peri tou viou kai tes glōssēs tou Hellēnikou laou (Studies on the life and language of the Greek people). Athēnai, 1899-1904. 6 v.

————.   Leographika symmeikta (Various folklore studies). Athēnai, 1920-1931. 3 v. Illus., plates.

Politēs was the founder of folklore studies in modern Greece. In these volumes he relates folktales and traditions to classical and literary originals. *See also* the editions of folksongs listed under "Literature" above as well as Politēs' own folklore serial *Laographia* (Folklore) (Athēnai, 1909–, irregular).

1398. Preller, Ludwig.   Griechische Mythologie. 4. Aufl., bearb. von Carl Robert. Berlin, Weidmann, 1887-1926. 2 v. in 3.

A basic work on ancient Greek mythology and as such important for the study of modern Greek folklore.

1399. Rōmaios, K.   Konta stis rizes (Near the roots). Athēnai, 1959. 485 p. Bibliography: p. 467-470.

This excellent volume traces a number of modern Greek folklore customs to their origins.

1400. Spatalas, G.   Hē stichourgia tōn Hellēnikōn dēmotikōn tragoudiōn (The meters of the Greek folksongs). Athēnai, 1960. 40 p.

A reliable account of the meter of Greek folksong. Reprinted from *Kainouria Epochē* (New epoch), no. 1, 1960.

# D. HISTORY OF THOUGHT AND CULTURE

*by Constantine A. Trypanis*

## 1. Byzantium and Medieval Greece

### a. Monographic Studies

1401. Baynes, Norman H.   Byzantium; an Introduction to East Roman Civilization. Oxford, Clarendon Press, 1948. 436 p. Plates, fold. maps.

A collection of essays offering a good introduction to Byzantine civilization. It sketches the history and deals with the cultural phenomena of the Later Roman Empire. Particularly valuable are the introduction and the contribution by H. Gregoire. *See also*:

Mathew, Gervase.   Byzantine Aesthetics. London, J. Murray, 1963. 189 p. Illus., maps.

Wellesz, Egon.   A History of Byzantine Music and Hymnography. 2d rev. and enl. ed. Oxford, Clarendon Press, 1961. 461 p. Plates, music.

1402. Bréhier, Louis.   Le monde byzantin. Paris, A. Michel, 1947-1950.
3 v. Plates, fold. maps. (L'évolution de l'humanité, synthèse collective, 2. sect., 32)

These three volumes present a well-documented account of the history, administration, and culture of the Byzantine empire. *See also*:

Diehl, Charles.   Figures byzantines. Paris, A. Colin, 1924-1925.
2 v. Translated into English as *Byzantine Portraits* (New York, A. A. Knopf, 1927, 342 p.).

Tatakis, Basile.   La philosophie byzantine. *In*: Bréhier, Émile.
Histoire de la philosophie. Fascicule supplémentaire, No. 2. Paris, Presses universitaires de France, 1949. 323 p.

1403. Hunger, Herbert.   Byzantinische Geisteswelt, von Konstantin dem Grossen bis zum Fall Konstantinopels. Baden-Baden, Holle, 1958. 335 p.

The most recent independent work on Byzantine cultural history. *See also*:

Rice, David T.   The Byzantines. New York, Praeger, 1962. 224 p.
Illus. (Ancient Peoples and Places, 27)

Runciman, Sir Steven.   Byzantine Civilization. New York, Green; London, E. Arnold, 1933. 320 p.

1404. Hussey, Joan M., *ed.*   The Byzantine Empire. *In*: The Cambridge Medieval History, 2d ed. 4 v. Cambridge, England, University Press, 1966. 1 v. in 2.

In this, the most recent general publication on Byzantine studies, many aspects of Byzantine cultural life are examined. Particularly useful are the chapters on literature and the numerous bibliographies.

1405. Koukoules, Phaidōn I.   Vyzantinōn vios kai politismos (Life and culture of the Byzantines). Athēnai, 1948-? Plates, plan. (Collection de l'Institut français d'Athènes, 10-13, 43, 73, 76, 90, . . .).

A basic work on Byzantine culture and behavior. Equally valuable for modern Greek folklore studies. It may be compared with Franz Dölger's *Paraspora. 30 Aufsätze zur Geschichte, Kultur und Sprache des byzantinischen Reiches* (Ettal, Buch-Kunst-Verlag, 1961, 447 p., illus.).

1406. Miller, William.   The Latins in the Levant; a History of Frankish Greece (1204-1566). London, J. Murray, 1908. 675 p. Maps. Reprinted: Cambridge, Speculum Historiale; New York, Barnes and Noble, 1964. 675 p.

Miller's analysis of Frankish elements in Greece from the time of the Fourth Crusade is still the standard work on the period. Using a large number of sources he examines the effects on Greek and Frank of the cultural and political contacts to which both sides were exposed. One may also refer to the author's *Essays on the Latin Orient* (Cambridge, The University Press, 1921, 582 p., illus., plates). An earlier period is the subject of:

Dölger, Franz.   Byzanz und daes Abendland vor den Kreuzzügen. *In*: International Congress of Historical Sciences, Rome, 1955. Atti del X Congresso internazionale, Roma 4-11 settembre 1955. Roma, 1957. p. 67-112.

### b. Serials

1407.  Serials devoted to Byzantine topics:

Byzantinisch-neugriechische Jahrbücher; internationales wissenschaftliches Organ . . . 1920-1925, Berlin; 1926–, Athens. Irregular.
*See also* entry no. 1005.

Byzantinische Zeitschrift. 1892– Leipzig, B. G. Teubner. Quarterly.

Byzantion; revue internationale des études byzantines. t. 1– 1924– Paris, E. Champion; Liege, Vaillant-Carmanne, 1924– Semiannual.

Congrès international des études byzantines. *1st, Bucharest, 1924–* Comptes- rendus. 1925–

Epetēris hetairias Vyzantinōn Spoudōn (Yearbook of the Society for Byzantine Studies). 1924– Athēnai. Annual.

Dumbarton Oaks Papers. 1941– Washington, D.C. Annual. The leading Byzantine journal in the United States featuring articles on Byzantine history, letters, art.

Greek, Roman and Byzantine Studies. 1958– Durham, N.C., Duke University. Quarterly. Contains articles on the Byzantine and early post-Byzantine period.

Jahrbuch der Österreichischen Byzantinischen Gesellschaft. Wien-Graz, Köln, 1951–

Studi bizantini e neoellenici . . . v. 1– Napoli, R. Ricciardi, 1924– Illus., plates, plans, facsims.

Theologische Literaturzeitung. 1– 8 Jan. 1876– Leipzig, J. C. Hinrichs. Biweekly, 1876-1938; monthly, 1939– (1945, 1946 suspended).

Vizantiiskii vremennik. Leningrad, 1894-1927; Moskva, 1947– Irregular.

Zeitschrift für die neutestamentliche Wissenschaft und die Kunde des Urchristentums . . . 1900-1942, 1949- Giessen, J. Ricker. Irregular.

## 2. Modern Greece

### a. Monographic Studies

1408.  Finlay, George.   A History of Greece from Its Conquest by the Romans to the Present Time, B.C. 146 to A.D 1864. Rev. and enl. ed. Oxford, Clarendon Press, 1877. 7 v.
*See also* entry no. 1050.

This pioneering work was among the first of the histories which tried to establish a continuity of Greek life from the Roman occupation through the Byzantine Empire to the foundation of the modern state. It should be read in conjunction with the more recent work of Vakalopoulos (*see* entry 1411).

1409. Meyendorff, Jean.   St. Grégoire Palamas et la mystique orthdoxe. Paris, Éditions du Seuil, 1959. 187 p. (Collections Microcosme. Maîtres spirituels, 20)

Excellent introduction to Greek Orthodox spirituality.

1410. Paparrēgopoulos, Kōnstantinos.   Historia tou hellenikou ethnous (History of the Greek people). 6th ed., rev. by Paulos Karolides. Athēnai, Eleutheroudakēs, 1932. 8 v. Illus., maps, tables, bibliography.

*See also* entries no. 986 *and* 1062.

To this day the most important history of the Greek people in Greek. It is of special significance for the period from 1453 to the Liberation. An abstract of this work appeared as *Ta didaktikōtera Porismata tēs Historias tou Hellēnikou Ethnous* (Athēnai, 1930, 1 v.). First published in 1860-1872.

1411. Vakalopoulos (Bakalopoulos), Apostolos E.   Historia tou neou Hellēnismou (History of modern Greece). v. 1– Thessalonikē, 1961– Illus., maps.

*See also* entry no. 1063.

This is the most recent study of the emergence of modern Greece. The author, using a large number of sources, traces the growth of "Hellenism" from the time of the Byzantine Empire. *See also*:

Geanakoplos, Deno John.   Greek Scholars in Venice. Cambridge, Mass., Harvard University Press, 1962. 348 p. Illus., ports., map. Bibliography: p. 305-337. Greek edition: *Hellēnes logioi eis tēn Venetian* (Athēnai, Phexēs, 1965, 294 p.). A valuable work for the study of the survival and dissemination of Greek culture after 1453. *See also* his collection of essays, *Byzantine East and Latin West: Two Worlds of Christendom in the Middle Ages and Renaissance; Studies in Ecclesiastical and Cultural History* (Oxford, Blackwell, 1966, 206 p., illus., bibliog.).

1412. Papadopoulos, Chrysostomos.   Historia tēs ekklēsias tēs Hellados (History of the Greek Church). Athēnai, 1920. 1 v.

*See also*:

Ware, Timothy.   The Orthodox Church. Baltimore, Penguin Books, 1963. 352 p. (A Pelican Original, A592)

Zananiri, Gaston.   Histoire de l'Église byzantine. Paris, Nouvelles Éditions latines, 1954. 316 p.

On the Greek Church, the reader may also refer to the articles on "Orthodoxy" and "The Greek Church" in the following religious encyclopedias:

Die Religion in Geschichte und Gegenwart; Handwörterbuch für Theologie und Religionswissenschaft. 3., völlig neu bearbeitete Aufl., in Gemeinschaft mit Hans Frhr. v. Campenhausen, hrsg. von Kurt Galling. Tübingen, Mohr, 1957-1965. 7 v. Maps (part col.), plates.

Oxford Dictionary of the Christian Church. Edited by F. L. Cross. London, New York, Oxford University Press, 1957. 1492 p.

Cabrol, Fernard. Dictionnaire d'archéologie chrétienne et de liturgie. Paris, Letouzey et Ané, 1907-1953? 14? v. Illus., plates (part col., part fold.), fold. plans, facsims. (part fold.).

New Catholic Encyclopedia. New York, McGraw-Hill, 1967. 15 v. Illus. (part col.), facsims., maps, ports. (part col.).

Thrēskeutikē kai ēthikē enkyklopaideia (Encyclopedia of religion and morals). Athēnai, 1961–

1413. Voumvlinopoulos, G. E. Bibliographie critique de la philosophie grecque depuis la chute de Constantinople à nos jours, 1453-1953. Athènes, Presses de l'Institut Français d'Athènes, 1966. 236 p.

Writings by and about Greek philosophers over the past 500 years. Chronological arrangement within century subdivisions at the end of which there are summaries of the philosophical trends. A bibliography of bibliographies, and an index of names are provided.

### 3. Periodicals

1414. Ho Eranistēs (Collections). 1963– Athēnai. Bimonthly.

Published by the Group for the Study of the Greek Enlightenment, it is essentially the voice of the Center for Neohellenic Studies under K. Th. Dēmaras, the well-known historian of Modern Greek culture. This is in many ways a scholarly avant-garde publication containing articles in Greek and the major European languages. Annual cumulative index.

1415. Athene; the American Magazine of Hellenic Thought. 1940– Chicago. Quarterly.

Published by the poet, D. A. Michalaros, until his death in 1967. Very valuable for the study of the cultural life of the Greek-American community.

1416. Greek Heritage. 1963-1965. Chicago, Athenian Corp. Quarterly.

A very ambitious publication covering the whole span of Greek culture. Contains numerous articles from internationally established scholars.

### E. RELIGION

*by Demetrios J. Constantelos*

1417. Alivisatos, Hamilcar. Hē Hellēnikē Orthodoxos Ekklēsia (The Greek Orthodox Church). Athēnai, 1955. 206 p.

A series of important lectures by a leading Greek Orthodox theologian on the Greek Orthodox Church from the historical, theological, canonical, and ecumenical viewpoints. Authoritative and objective.

1418. Alivisatos, Hamilcar, *ed.* Procès-verbaux du Premier congrès de théologie orthodoxe à Athènes, 29 novembre-6 décembre 1936. Athēnai, Pyrsos, 1939. 540 p.

Includes several important communications bearing on the history, theology, polity, and ecumenical position of the Orthodox Church, written by eminent theologians of all Orthodox jurisdictions.

1419. Alivisatos, Hamilcar, *ed.*   Saint Paul's Mission to Greece; Nineteenth Centenary. Athens, 1953. 645 p.

An important volume of communications, studies, and chronicles of the Greek Church. Includes materials in languages other than Greek.

1420. Andrew, Timothy.   The Eastern Orthodox Church; a Bibliography. 2d ed. Brookline, Mass., 1957. 79 p.

A careful cataloging of theological and religious books dealing with the history, theology, worship, and ethos of the Greek Church. Should be supplemented by Iōannēs N. Karmirēs's *Hē Ellēnikē Theologikē Vivliographia tēs teleutaias dekaetias, 1945-1955* (Greek theological bibliography of the last decade, 1945-1955) (Istanbul, 1957, 20 p.) and Vasileios Th. Stauridēs's *Hē Orthodoxos Hellēnikē Vivliographia epi tēs Oikoumenikēs kinēseōs* (Orthodox Greek bibliography on the ecumenical movement) (Athēnai, 1960, 20 p.).

1421. Bratsiōtēs (Mpratsiōtēs), Panagiōtēs I.   Hē Ellēnikē Theologia kata tēn teleutaian Pentēkontaetian (Greek theology in the last fifty years). Athēnai, 1948. 48 p.

First published in the theological journal *Theologia*, volume 19 (1941-1948). An authoritative bibliographic account of theological and religious studies in 20th century Greece.

1422. Bratsiōtēs (Mpratsiōtēs), Panagiōtēs I.   Von der griechischen Orthodoxie. Christliche Konfessionen in Selbstdarstellungen. Edited by Günter Stachel. Würzburg, Echter Verlag, 1966. 156 p.

A contribution to one of four volumes on Christian creeds and the churches. Gives a clear picture of the Church of Greece, its fundamental beliefs, practices, ethos, relations with the World Council of Churches, church-state relations, and other important aspects. The author is a leading authority on theology, religion, and the Church of Greece.

1423. Callinicos, Constantine.   A Brief Sketch of Greek Church History. Translated by Katherine Natzio. London, The Faith Press, 1931. 159 p.

A short history of the evolution of the Orthodox Church which emphasizes the more recent period, written by the then Vicar of the Greek Church in Manchester.

1424. Constantelos, Demetrios J.   The Greek Orthodox Church: Faith, History and Practice. New York, Seabury Press, 1967. 127 p.

"It is elucidating and authoritative in its correct interpretation of the spirit, dogma, traditions, and practices . . . may be used both as a primer for those previously unacquainted with Orthodoxy, and as instructive source of information and food for thought by the practitioners . . . encompasses much interpretative material that may be of no little value to theologians, even to those well-versed in Orthodoxy." (From the foreword by Archbishop Iakovos.)

1425. Ekklēsia (Church). 1923– Athēnai. Biweekly.
    Official publication of, and an important source of information on, the Church of Greece. Includes theological studies, critical comments, current events, chronicles, and book reviews.

1426. Etteldorf, Raymon.    The Soul of Greece. Westminster, Md., Newman Press, 1963. 235 p. Illus. Bibliography: p. 225-228.
    A good popular account of the present state of the Greek Church. Gives historical background and offers insights into the faith, worship, and practice of the church from a Roman Catholic viewpoint.

1427. Gavin, Frank S. B.    Some Aspects of Contemporary Greek Orthodox Thought. Milwaukee, Morehouse Publishing Co., 1923. 430 p.
    A penetrating analysis of Greek Orthodox theological teachings as expressed in the writings of Greek theologians of the 1920s. The author is grounded in the Anglican tradition and often treats his subject in terms of Latin and Anglo-Catholic precepts.

1428. The Greek Orthodox Theological Review. v. 1– 1954– Brookline, Mass. Semiannual.
    A scholarly periodical, official publication of the Holy Cross Greek Orthodox Theological School, Brookline, Mass., under the auspices of the Greek Archdiocese of North and South America. Includes studies, articles, critical reviews, and book notes by leading theologians, historians, and classical philologists of the Greek Church of Greece proper and the diaspora, as well as of other Orthodox and non-Orthodox jurisdictions.

1429. Grēgorios ho Palamas (Gregory Palamas). 1917– Thessalonikē. Monthly.
    Official publication of the Diocese of Thessalonike, in collaboration with the Theological Faculty of the University of Thessalonike. Has included many important studies, articles, and reviews. An excellent mirror of the religious life and theological work of northern Greece.

1430. Hammond, Peter.    The Waters of Marah; the Present State of the Greek Church. London, Rockliff, 1956. 186 p. Illus.
    See also entry no. 989.
    Brief but excellent treatment of the Greek Church since 1945. Objective and perhaps the best work by a non-Orthodox writer.

1431. Karmirēs, Ioannēs N.    Ta Dogmatika kai Symvolika Mnēmeia tēs

Orthodoxou Katholikēs Ekklēsias (The doctrinal and symbolic books of the Orthodox Catholic Church). Athenai, 1952-1953. 2 v. (1067 p.).

An indispensable work for the theology of the Greek Church. Both volumes include the sources from which the Greek Church draws its theology.

1432. Kephala, Euphrosyne. The Church of the Greek People Past and Present. London, Williams and Norgate, 1930. 128 p.

A short but perceptive book on the history, nature, characteristics, ritual, and theologians of the 1930s. An excellent introduction to the study of the Greek Church.

1433. Konidarēs, Gerasimos I. Ekklēsiastikē Historia tēs Ellados (Ecclesiastical history of Greece). Athēnai, 1954-1960. 543 p.

The best history of the Church of Greece proper from the first century to 733, by the Church historian at the University of Athens. A second volume is expected to cover the period from 733 to the present.

1434. Konidarēs, Gerasimos I. Hē Hellēnikē Ekklēsia hōs politistikē dynamis en tē historia tēs Chersonēsou tou Aimou (The Greek Church and its influence upon the civilization of the Balkans). Athēnai, 1948. 209 p.

Presents the Greek Church as an important factor not only in the Greek nation but also for the civilization of Bulgarians, Romanians, Serbians, and Albanians.

1435. Mouratidēs, Kōnstantinos D. Schesis Ekklēsias kai Politeias (Church and state relations). Athenai, 1965. 216 p.

The author, a professor of canon law at the School of Theology of the University of Athens, treats his subjects from an Orthodox point of view on the basis of current thought in ecclesiology and the science of government. A second volume is to follow.

1436. Die Orthodoxe Kirche in griechischer Sicht. Edited by Panagiōtes Bratsiōtēs. Stuttgart, Evangelisches Verlagswerk, 1959-1960. 2 v. Bibliographies. (Die Kirchen der Welt, Bd. 1)

Studies and essays by the foremost theologians of modern Greece. An indispensable work for the student of Greek Orthodox theology, history, canon law, and mysticism.

1437. Papadopoullos (Papadopoulos), Theodore H. Studies and Documents Relating to the History of the Greek Church and People under Turkish Domination. Brussels, 1952. 507 p. Facsims. (Bibliotheca Graeca aevi posterioris, 1) Bibliography: p. xi-xxiv.

See also entry no. 1070.

An indispensable tool for the study of the Greek Church and the Greeks during the Ottoman period. The author has compiled important materials objectively and with a critical sense.

1438. Poulitsas, Panagiōtēs E. Schesis Politeias kai Ekklēsias (State and church relations). Athēnai, 1946. 389 p.

One of the most important contributions on this subject. Submitted to the Greek government on the occasion of a canonical problem which disturbed the Greek Church in 1935. The author presents an objective and well documented survey of church-state relations from the early Christian period to the present.

1439. Stauridēs, Vasileios. Historia tēs Oikoumenikēs Kinēseos (History of the ecumenical movement). Athēnai, 1964. 159 p.

A comprehensive and straightforward treatment, with emphasis on the role played by the Orthodox Church in the movement.

1440. Theologia (Theology). 1923– Athēnai. Quarterly.

The most important theological journal in the Greek language. The chief organ of the theological faculties of the University of Athens and the University of Thessalonike. Usually contains technical theological studies and critical reviews.

1441. Thrēskeutikē kai ēthikē enkyklopaideia (Religious and moral encyclopedia). Edited by A. Martinos. Athēnai. 1962-1968. 12 v. Illus., maps. Includes bibliographies.

A landmark in modern Greek Orthodox theology, Church history, and religion in general. Contributors include outstanding theologians, historians, and social scientists of Greece and of other Orthodox jurisdictions. Entries cover all fields of theology — doctrinal, historical, practical, ethical, and social. Encompasses contemporary trends and events and presents the life of the church today. *See also* *Thrēskeutikē kai Christianikē Enkyklopaideia* (Religious and Christian encyclopedia) (Athēnai, 1936-1940), of which only three volumes appeared.

1442. Trempelas, Panagiōtēs N. Dogmatikē tēs Orthodoxou Katholikēs Ekklēsias (Dogmatics of the Orthodox Catholic Church). Athēnai, 1959-1961. 3 v.

The most thorough presentation available by a leading Greek theologian. A must for every student of the Greek Church. The first volume was published in French as *Dogmatique de Église Orthodoxe Catholique*. Traduction française par l'archimandrite Pierre Dumont O.S.B. Tome I. (Bruges, Editions de Chevetogne et Desclee de Brouwer, 1966, 646 p.).

1443. Tsirintanēs, Alexandros N. Towards a Christian Civilization; a Draft Issued by the Christian Union of Professional Men of Greece. Athens, 1950. 270 p.

A Greek Orthodox manifesto, reflecting the thought, anxieties, and yearnings of the religious intelligentsia of postwar Greece. The author is a layman of the Greek Church and a professor of law at the University of Athens.

1444. Ware, Timothy.   The Orthodox Church. Baltimore, Penguin Books, 1963. 352 p. Bibliography: p. 335-340.

> A very good account of Greek Orthodoxy as a part of worldwide Orthodoxy in general. The author, a convert to the Orthodox Church, often expresses his personal insights and interpretations.

1445. Zōē, *Athens*.   Theologia Alētheia kai Zōē (Theology: truth and life). Athēnai, 1962. 237 p.

> Essays by the younger theologians of Greece and other Orthodox jurisdictions on the future of religious thought and its place in the life of modern man.

## F. EDUCATION

### by Demetrios J. Constantelos

1446. Dendrinou Antonakaki, Kalliniki.   Greek Education: Reorganization of the Administrative Structure. New York, Columbia University Press, 1955. 274 p.

> An important study of trends in Greek society as they affect education. The author emphasizes the need for changes based on traditional Greek philosophy, the principles of democracy, and contemporary educational developments.

1447. Euangelidēs, Tryhōn.   Hē Paideia epi Tourkokratias (Education under the Turkish domination). Athēnai, 1936. 2 v.

> A unique work, covering the period from the 15th to the 20th century. Presents a wealth of information (often uncritically, however), with footnotes but no bibliography.

1448. Exarchopoulos, Nikolaos I.   Genikē didaktikē (General didactics). Athēnai, 1961. 2 v.

> The standard work in Greek, by an acknowledged authority on education. The language is purist but the treatment of the subject is thorough and scholarly.

1449. Geōrgoulēs, Konstantinos G.   Hē Hellēnikē ekpaideusis (Greek Education). *In* Neōteron enkyklopaidikon lexikon. v. 7. Athēnai, "Hēlios," [1949?]. p. 1551-1558.

> An important and authoritative survey of the organization and development of primary, secondary, and higher education from 1828 through 1950. Includes statistics. The author was formerly secretary general of the Ministry of Education.

1450. Geōrgoutzos, P. N., *and others*.   Ekpaideusis (Education). *In* Megalē hellēnikē enkyklopaideia. Supplement, v. 10. Athēnai, Ho Phoinix, 1932. p. 628-645.

> The most important survey of primary, secondary, technical, and higher education in Greece after the War of Independence. Scholarly, authoritative, and comprehensive. Extensive bibliography. *See also*

the articles by C. Lephas in the original volume 10 of the same encyclopedia (Athēnai, 1932), p. 313-334.

1451. Glēnos, D. A.    Enas ataphos nekros (An unburied corpse). Athēnai, 1925. 320 p.

The Greek educational system of 1925 is described. The author proposes radical changes, including the introduction of the demotic language as the language of instruction. A controversial book which became the starting point for a new study of Greek education in the 1930s.

1452. Haralambides, Theodor.    Die Schulpolitik Griechenlands; Studie zur Kulturgeschichte Neugriechenlands, 1821-1935. Berlin, Junker u. Dünnhaupt, 1935. 207 p. (Neue deutsche Forschungen. 50. Abt. Pädagogik. 2)

A dissertation on education policy during the 19th century and the reforms introduced in 1929. Includes proposals for further improvements.

1453. He Hellēnike paideia (Greek education). Athēnai, Hetairia Hellēnikōn Spoudōn, 1957. 152 p.

A very important symposium of papers by leading Greek educators such as E. Papanoutsos, H. Alivizatos, and others. Both liberal and conservative views are presented.

1454. Hellēnochristianikē agōgē (Hellenic-Christian education). 1947– Athēnai.

Official monthly publication of the Christian Union of Educators. Studies and articles cover all aspects of education. Includes comments, critical reviews, and educational news.

1455. Isegonēs, Antōnios M.    Historia tēs paideias (History of education). Rodos, 1958. 352 p. Bibliography: p. 336-345.

A work directed primarily to teachers and students of education. Well written and erudite.

1456. Lephas, Christos, ed.    Paideia. To Nomothetikon ergon tou Hypourgeiou Paideias kai Thrēskeumatōn: 1930-32. Hypourgia G. Papandreou (Education. The legislative work of the Ministry of Education and Religion: 1930-1932. Ministry of G. Papandreou). Athēnai, 1932. 714 p.

A very important collection of laws, recommendations, and constitutional reforms enacted while George Papandreou served as Minister of Education. An indispensable source book.

1457. Papanoutsos, E. P.    Agōnes kai agōnia gia tēn paideia (Struggles and agony for education). Athēnai, 1965. 379 p.

A collection of articles originally published in leading newspapers and journals in Greece. A controversial but most important evaluation and critique of education in Greece today. The author proposes drastic measures for the restoration and reorientation of Greek education.

1458. Porismata Epitropēs Paideias (Conclusions of the Commission on Education). Athēnai. Ethnikon Typographeion, 1958. 218 p.

Presents the views, critiques, and recommendations of a committee which studied the problems of education between June 24, 1957 and January 10, 1958.

1459. Psychologia kai zōē (Psychology and life). Edited by Aristos A. Aspiōtēs. 1951– Athēnai.

An important series of monographs, written by or under the direction of a psychiatrist, on such subjects as adolescence, child psychology, crisis in the age of puberty, youth and society, the child and sex, and youth and education. The series is in progress.

1460. Sanders, Irwin T. Rainbow in the Rock; The People of Rural Greece. Cambridge, Harvard University Press, 1962. 363 p. Illus. *See also* entries no. 992, 1046, *and* 1295.

An excellent anthropological study of the Greek people. Includes an important chapter on education in the village school (p. 241-257).

1461. Skouteropoulos, Iōannēs N. Ho Skopos tēs Agōgēs tōn Ellēnopaidōn (The aim of education of Greek youth). Athēnai, 1929. 215 p.

Although some of the material is outdated, many of the philosophical principles are under discussion today. The emphasis is on Graeco-Christian humanism as the foundation of education.

1462. Skouteropoulos, Iōannēs N. Ta Scholeia, ētoi Ennoia skopos kai organōsis autōn (The schools, their meaning, aim, and their organization). Athēnai, 1947. 216 p.

The author discusses the purpose of the schools in general, educational materials, and the foundations of education in Greece, and proposes measures for the organization of public, primary, and secondary schools.

1463. U.S. Library of Congress. *European Affairs Division.* War and Postwar Greece: An Analysis Based on Greek Writings. Prepared by Floyd A. Spencer. Washington, D.C., 1952. 175 p. Bibliography: p. ix-xi.

*See also* entry no. 1197.

An excellent treatment of, inter alia, educational problems in modern Greece.

1464. Vourverēs, K. Hellēnikos anthrōpismos (Hellenic humanism). *In* Neōteron enkyklopaidikon lexikon Hēlios. v. 7. Athēnai, "Hēlios," [1949?]. p. 725-739.

The classical conception of humanism and its importance in education are discussed by a leading classical scholar.

## G. FINE ARTS

*by Manolis Chatzidakis*

### 1. Byzantine Art

#### a. Monumental Art

1465. Bouras, Charalambos.   Vyzantina staurotholia me neurōseis (Byzantine cross-vaults with ribs). Athēnai, 1965. 82 p. Illus.

An interesting monograph on the problem of the origin and appearance of cross-vaults with ribs in the Byzantine architecture. Includes an architectural analysis of the different forms of cross-vaults. Summary in French.

1466. Chatzidakis, Manolis (Manōlēs Chatzēdakēs), *and* André Grabar. Byzantine and Early-Mediaeval Painting. London, 1965. 28 p. Illus.

A history of Byzantine painting, introducing in some parts a new point of view. The following books and articles treat Byzantine painting of different Greek provinces: M. Chatzidakis' *Byzantine Monuments in Attica and Boeotia; Architecture — Mosaics — Wall Paintings* (Athens, Athens Editions, 1956, 28 p.); Andreas Ioannou's *Byzantine Frescoes of Euboea in the Thirteenth and Fourteenth Centuries* (Athens, Zygos, 1959, 24 p.); Manolis Chatzidakis' "Mediaeval Painting in Southern Greece; Some Examples Published for the First Time," *The Connoisseur*, no. 603, 1962: 29-33; and N. Drandakis' *Byzantinai toichographiai tēs Mesa Manēs* (Byzantine wall paintings of Mesa Manē) (Athēnai, 1964, 139 p.).

1467. Chatzidakis, Manolis, *and* André Grabar.   Greece. Byzantine Mosaics. New York, New York Graphic Society, 1959. 25 p. Illus. Bibliography: p. 22. (UNESCO World Art Series, no. 13)

Chatzidakis analyzes the great mosaic ensembles of the 11th to the 14th centuries, outlining the main features of the monumental art of Byzantium.

*See also* A. Orlandos' *Hē Parēgorētisa tēs Artās* (The church of Paregoretissa at Arta) (Athēnai, Archaeological Society of Athens, 183 p.).

1468. Michelēs, Panagiōtēs. An Aesthetic Approach to Byzantine Art. London, 1955. 184 p.

A systematic study of the aesthetic principles of Byzantine artistic creation. A Greek edition was published in 1947.

1469. Orlandos, Anastasios.   Hē xylostegos palaiochristianikē vasilikē tēs Mesogeiakēs Lekanēs (The early Christian wood-roofed Basilica of the Mediterranean area). Athēnai, Archaeological Society of Athens, 1952-57. 2 v. with index. Bibliography, illus.

A systematic study of the origin and appearance of the basilica, its architectural forms, and its decorations. *See also* the study of G. and M. Sōtēriou, entitled *Hē Vasilikē tou Hagiou Dēmētriou Thes-*

*salonikēs* (The Basilica of Saint Demetrios of Thessalonica) (Athēnai, Archeological Society of Athens, 1952, 2 v.). Also very useful is the work of St. Pelekanidis, *Gli affreschi paleochristiani et i più antici mosaici parietale di Salonico* (Ravenna, Studi Università degli studi di Bologna, Instituto di Antichita Ravennati e Bizantine, 1963, 60 p.).

1470. Orlandos, Anastasios. Monastēriakē architektonikē (Monastic architecture). 2d ed. Athēnai, 1958. 180 p. Illus.

A detailed monograph on the architecture of Byzantine and post-Byzantine monasteries, especially of the Greek area. *See also* articles on the same subject in *Archeion Vyzantinōn Mnēmeiōn tēs Hellados* (Archive of the Byzantine monuments of Greece), v. 1-10, 1935-1964.

1471. Pallas, Demetrios. Passion und Bestattung Christi. München, 1965. 339 p. (Miscellanea Byzantina Monacensia, 2)

A study of the ritual, iconographical, and archaeological problems of icons of the cycle of the Passion of Christ.

1472. Pelekanidēs, Stylianos M. Kastoria. I. Vyzantinai toichographiai (Kastoria. I. Byzantine wall paintings). Thessalonikē, Society of Macedonian Studies, 1953. 60 p. Illus. (*Its* Macedonian Library, no. 17)

A detailed album of the Byzantine and post-Byzantine wall paintings of Kastoria, a provincial art center.

*See also* A. Orlandos' "The Byzantine Monuments of Kastoria," *Archeion Vyzantinōn mnēmeiōn tēs Hellados*, v. 4, 1938: 1-215; N. Moutsopoulos' *The Monastery of the Virgin Mary Mavriotissa at Castoria* (Athens, 1967, 94 p.); and St. Pelekanidēs *Vyzantina kai Metavyzantina mnēmeia tēs Prespas* (Byzantine and post-Byzantine monuments of Prespa) (Society of Macedonian Studies, no. 35, 116 p.).

1473. Xyngopoulos, André. Thessalonique et la peinture macedonienne. Athènes, Society of Macedonian Studies, 1955. 93 p. Illus.

A study of the original and the center of the so-called Macedonian school of painting of the 13th and 14th centuries.

For a more complete account of the artistic activity of Thessalonica, *see* A. Xyngopoulos' *Hē psēphidōtē diakosmēsis tou naou tōn Hagiōn Apostolōn Thessalonikēs* (The mosaic wall decoration of the Church of the Holy Apostles in Thessalonica) (Thessalonikē, 1956, 72 p.); Manolis Chatzidakis' "Rapports entre la peinture de la Macedoine et de la Crète au XIV<sup>e</sup> siecle," *Proceedings* of the Ninth International Congress of Byzantine Studies, Athens, v. 2, 1955, p. 136-149; A. Xyngopoulos' *Manouēl Panselinos* (Athēnai, 1956, 28 p.); A. Xyngopoulos' *Hoi toichographies tou Hagiou Nikolaou Orphanou Thessalonikēs* (The wall paintings of the Church of Saint Nicholas Orphanos in Thessalonica) (Athēnai, 1964, 35 p.).

1474. Xyngopoulos, Andreas. Schediasma Historias tēs thrēskeutikēs zōgraphikēs meta tēn halōsin (An outline of the history of religious painting after the fall of Constantinople). Athēnai, Archaiologikē hetairia, 1957. 419 p. Illus., bibliography.

A fundamental study on the post-Byzantine painting in the Greek area.

*See also* Manolis Chatzidakis' *Contribution à l'étude de la peinture post-byzantine, Hellénisme Contemporain (à l'occasion des 500 années de la Prise de Constantinople)* (Athènes, 1953, 32 p.); A. Orlandos' *L'architecture religieuse en Grèce pendant la domination turque, Hellénisme Contemporain (à l'occasion des 500 anées de la Prise de Constantinople)* (Athènes, 1953, 12 p.); and A. Hadjēmichalē's *La sculpture sur bois. Hellénisme Contemporain* (Athènes, 1950, 50 p.).

### b. Catalogs, Guides, Bibliographies, and Periodicals

1475. Bibliographie de l'Art Byzantin et Post-Byzantin.    Athènes, National Greek Committee of the International Association of Southeast European Studies, 1966. 70 p.

This is a bibliography of 939 Greek scholarly works; it covers the years 1950-1965.

1476. Byzantine Art — An European Art; 9th Exhibition of the Council of Europe. Athens, 1964. 614 p. Illus., bibliography.

This catalog contains introductory articles on architecture, painting, and minor arts written by well known Byzantinologists, and detailed descriptions of the exhibited objects. Greek and French editions are also available. The lectures given on the occasion of the exhibition are published under the title *Byzantine Art — An European Art; Lectures* (Athens, 1966, 177 p.).

1477. Collection Hélène Stathatos.    Les Objets Byzantins et Post-Byzantins. Limoges, 1957. 119 p. Illus.

The precious objects of the collection — bijoux, bronzes, icons, embroideries, and woodcarvings — are described by Mrs. Stathatos, E. Coche de la Ferté, P. J. Croquison, A. Xyngopoulos, and M. Chatzidakis.

1478. Chatzēdakē-Beē (Chatzidaki-Bees), Eugenia.    Mouseion Benakē. Ekklēsiastika kentēmata (Benaki Museum; ecclesiastical embroideries). Athēnai, 1954. 110 p. Illus.

A detailed catalog of the embroideries of the Museum, mostly post-Byzantine, with useful general remarks on their art and workmanship.

For the workmanship of other embroideries, *see also* A. Hadjēmichalē's "Ta chrysoklavarika syrmateina-syrmatesika kentēmata" (Gold-filled embroideries), *Mélanges offerts à Octave et Melpo Merlier*, v. 2 (Athènes, 1956), p. 447-449.

1479. Chatzidakis, Manolis (Manōlēs Chatzēdakēs).    Mystras — Historia, mnēmia, technē (Mystras—history, monuments, art). 2d ed. Athēnai, 1956. 112 p. Illus.

An exemplary guide with an analysis of the schools of wall painting of the Palaeologian era represented in the churches of Mystras.

1480. Chatzidakis, Manolis (Manōlēs Chatzēdakēs). Icônes de Saint-Georges des Grecs et de la collection de l'Institut hellenique de Venise. Venise, Bibliothèque de l'Institut Hellēnique d'Etudes Byzantines et Post-Byzantines de Venise, 1962. 222 p. Illus.

A systematic catalog of the Byzantine and post-Byzantine icons of the collection with detailed iconographic and aesthetic remarks. An important contribution to the study of the post-Byzantine paintings.

*See also* N. Drandakēs' *Hō Emmanuēl Tzane Bounialēs theōroumenos ex eikonōn tou sōzomenōn kyriōs en Venetiai* (Emmanuel Tzane Bouniales, considered mainly by his icons preserved in Venice) (Athēnai, 1962, 189 p.) and M. Chatzēdakēs' "Ho Zōgraphos Euphrosynos" (The painter Euphrosynos), *Krētika chronika*, v. 10, 1956: 273-291.

1481. Dēltion tēs Christianikēs Archaeologikēs Hetaireias (Bulletin of the Christian Archaeological Society). 1959-1965. Athēnai.

With many contributions by Greek and non-Greek scholars on early Christian and Byzantine art and archaeology.

1482. Lazarev, Viktor Nikitich. Feofan Grek i ego shkola (Theofanes the Greek and his school). Moskva, Iskusstvo, 1961. 1932 p. Plates.

An interesting work by the well-known Russian historian of Byzantine art on the Greek who became the Russian El Greco in the late 14th and early 15th centuries. Contains important material relative to the formative Greek influence on the development of Russian art.

*See also* Lazarev's *Istoriia vizantiiskoi zhivopisi* (History of Byzantine painting) (Moskva, Iskusstvo, 1947-1948, 2 v.); and Igor E. Grabar's *Istoriia russkago iskusstva* (History of Russian Art) (Moskva, I. Knebel', 1910-1914, 6 v.).

1483. Sōtēriou, George, *and* Mary Sōtēriou. Eikones tēs Monēs Sina (Icons of the Sinai Monastery. Athēnai, 1956-1958. 2 v. Illus.

With this book one is introduced for the first time in a scientific way to the great number of first-class icons assembled in the monastery from the 5th to the 15th centuries. Of great importance is the discovery of icons painted in the encaustic manner dating from the 5th to the 7th centuries.

For the Byzantine icon in general *see* M. Chatzidakis' *L'icône byzantine* (Venezia, 1959, 40 p.). For the Byzantine icons of Greece, *see* M. Chatzidakis' contribution in the work by K. Weitzann, M. Chatzidakis, S. Radojčic, and K. Miatev, *Frühe Ikonen* (Wien, München, 1965), p. 37-96. A French edition of the last work was published in Paris in 1966; a Bulgarian edition, in Sofia the same year; and an English and Spanish one in 1969.

## 2. Folk Art

1484. Athens. Benaki Museum.    Greek National Costumes. Athens, 1948-1954. 2 v. Illus.
      A unique album with a detailed description and illustrations in color. The text is in English, Greek, and French.

1485. Hadjēmichalē, Anghelikē.    Sarakatsanoi. Athēnai, 1957. 2 v. Illus., maps, bibliography.
      A detailed study of the life, customs, activities, and art of the Sarakatsans, the nomads of Greece.

1486. Hellēnika laika kai metabyzantina xyloglypta (Greek folk and post-Byzantine woodcarvings). Athēnai, 1962. 32 p. Illus.

1487. Kyriakidēs-Nestor, Alkis.    To hyphanta tēs Makedonias kai tēs Thrakēs (Textiles of Macedonia and Thrace). Athēnai, 1965. 124 p. Illus.
      The study considers the subject from the technical, economical, historical, and aesthetic viewpoints and proceeds to interpretations within the framework of Modern Greek folk-life and tradition. Summary in English.

1488. Megas, Gēorgios A.    Hē hellēnikē oikia (The Greek house). Athēnai, 1949. 134 p. Illus.
      A study on the forms and development of the Greek peasant house.

## 3. Modern Art

1489. Calligas, Marinos.    Modern Art in Greece and Some Contemporary Greek Painters. The Connoisseur, no. 603, 1962: 39-43.

1490. Chatzidakis, Manolis.    Some Aspects of Modern Greek Art. Atlantic Monthly. June 1955: 127-138.

1491. Greek Painters of the Nineteenth Century. Athens, 1957. 26 p. Illus.
      Contains notes on 26 painters and reproductions of their characteristic works.

## H. MUSIC

### by Miloš Velimirović

### 1. Reference Aids and Serials

1492. Kösemihal, Mahmut R.    Balkanlarda musikî hareketleri (Music developments in the Balkans). Istanbul, Nümune matbaasi, 1937. 387 p. Illus., bibliographies.
      The first survey of recent (19th and early 20th century) developments in the music of Greece, Bulgaria, Yugoslavia, and Rumania. Greek music is discussed on pages 7-122. The coverage is uneven,

apparently depending on the type of information available to the author from the respective countries.

1493. Michaēlidēs, Solōn M.    Greek Music (Modern). *In* Grove, Sir George. Dictionary of Music and Musicians. 5th ed., edited by Eric Blom. v. 3. London, Macmillan; New York, St. Martin's Press, 1954. p. 781-782.

The only survey of the history of music in Greece during the last century that is available in English in an easily accessible reference volume. Includes a good bibliography. Far too few works have been published in Greece on the recent history of Greek music. Most frequently a general history of music by a Western writer is translated into Greek, with the translator then appending a chapter on music in Greece. This is the case with Spanoudis' translation of Landormy's book (Athens, 1931), with Sklavos' translation of Riemann's book (Athens, 1933), with Skiadaresēs' translation of Dufourcq's book (Athens, 1947) and most recently with Foibos Anōgeianakēs' translation of Karl Nef's book (Athens, 1960). The latter has the merit, at least, of being more extensive than such previous addenda (p. 546-611 in the Greek edition of Nef's book), and it has the largest bibliography on this subject.

1494. Motsenigos, Spyros G.    Neoellēnikē mousikē (Neohellenic music). Athēnai, 1958. 462 p. Illus., facsims, ports. Bibliography: p. 453-456.

In sheer size the "thickest" history of music in modern Greece. The author is apparently extremely concerned with the development of military bands and begins and ends the volume with a discussion of such bands all over Greece. Some attention is also paid to the 19th century "Ionian culture" and musical developments, especially on the island of Corfu. More concerned with the role of music than with evaluating musical styles and compositions.

1495. Mousikē kinēsis (Developments in music). 1949-1956. Athēnai. Monthly.

The last recorded music periodical in Greece. Publication irregular, 1949-1951. Music periodicals have had a very hard time establishing themselves in Greece. The only known bibliography of such periodicals is James B. Coover's list of only six periodicals published in 1901 in *Grove's Dictionary of Music and Musicians*, 5th ed., edited by E. Blom (v. 6, 1954, p. 656). To this list two more periodicals should be added: *Mousikē epitheōrēsis* (Music review), edited by N. G. Papas (nine issues between October 1921 and June 1922), and *Mousikos kosmos* (The world of music), edited by Th. Thoridēs (six issues in 1929).

1496. Vetter, Walther, Max Wegner, *and* Minos E. Dounias.    Griechenland. *In* Musik in Geschichte und Gegenwart; allgemeine Enzyklopädie der Musik. v. 5. Kassel, Bärenreiter-Verlag, 1956. cols. 840-896.

A comprehensive survey of data on music in Greece, divided into three sections: A. "Antike Musik," by W. Vetter (cols. 840-865; exhaustive bibliography); B. "Griechische Instrumente und Musik-bräuche," by M. Wegner (cols. 865-881, with selective bibliography and references to standard works for additional information); and C. "Volksmusik und neuere Musik," by Minos E. Dounias (cols. 882-896; folk music discussed in cols. 882-892, which include a list of the most significant editions and a bibliography; "new music," i.e., that composed during the last hundred years, is covered in cols. 892-896; bibliography is meager through no fault of the author's, since so little has been written on this period). A more recent although brief survey of music in Greece is F. Bussi's "Grecia; eta moderna," in *Enciclopedia della musica*, v. 2 (Milano, Ricordi, 1964), p. 354-356.

## 2. History

1497. Dragoumis, Markos Ph.   The Survival of Byzantine Chant in the Monophonic Music of the Modern Greek Church. *In* Velimirović, Miloš, *ed.*   Studies in Eastern Chant, v. 1. London, Oxford University Press, 1966. p. 9-36. Bibliography: p. xiii-xvi.

One of the finest studies so far on the structure and tradition in Greek church music with regard to its presents forms and its roots in the Byzantine Chant. The volume contains a comprehensive bibliography of the writings of Egon Wellesz and H. J. W. Tillyard, the two "founders of Byzantine musicology," which may serve as a guide to studies in Byzantine music of the Middle Ages.

1498. Hadzēapostolos, Ant.   Historia tou hellēnikou melodramatos (History of Greek opera). Athēnai, 1949. 176 p.

Cited in *Bulletin analytique de bibliographie hellénique* (Athènes), 11, 1950 (published in 1951): item no. 853, with the comment that the study is detailed for the period between 1887 and 1900, but rather brief for the period between 1900 and 1943. This appears to be the only volume dedicated entirely to the history of opera in Greece until 1943.

1499. Henderson, Isobel.   Ancient Greek Music. *In* Wellesz, Egon, *ed.* Ancient and Oriental Music. London, Oxford University Press, 1957. p. 336-403. Bibliography: p. 495-498. (New Oxford History of Music, v. 1)

Still the most easily accessible authoritative and reliable study of the subject. Extensive bibliography of sources and modern literature. An excellent pictorial supplement, with reproductions of representations of musical instruments in Ancient Greece, is Max Wegner's *Griechenland; Musikgeschichte in Bildern* (Leipzig, Deutscher Verlag für Musik, 1963, 141 p., illus., facsim., map. Bibliography: p. 133-136. [Musikgeschichte in Bildern, Bd. 2, Lfg. 4]).

1500. Papadopoulos, Geōrgios I.   Symbolai eis tēn historian tēs par ēmin ekklēsiastikēs mousikēs (Contributions to the history of our church music). Athēnai, Kousoulinos & Athanasiadēs, 1890. 592 p.

Not only a survey of the development of church music as viewed by the Greeks, but also a biographical dictionary of all known medieval and more recent church musicians, composers, and singers. Unfortunately, the data for the medieval period are almost totally unusable, owing to the reliance on tradition rather than on written sources. Data about the composers and singers of the last three or four centuries are much more useful and on the whole reliable. Another attempt at a bio-bibliographical dictionary of medieval Byzantine musicians was published in installments by Dom Casimir Éméreau in *Échos d'Orient* (v. 21, 1922 to v. 25, 1926), yet this project remained unfinished. *See also* M. Velimirović's "Byzantine Composers in MS Athens 2406," in *Essays Presented to Egon Wellesz*, edited by J. Westrup (London, Oxford University Press, 1966), p. 7-18.

1501. Papaioannou, John G.    Nikos Skalkottas.    *In* Hartog, Howard, *ed.* European Music in the Twentieth Century. London, Routledge & Paul, 1957. p. 336-345.

Also published (in 1961) as a Pelican Book (A514) with unchanged pagination. The only monograph published to date on a single Greek composer of modern times. The author is the founder of a Skalkottas Museum in Greece and is the outstanding Greek authority on modern trends among the Greek composers. Papaioannou's collection of contemporary music manuscripts is unmatched in Greece. He is both a patron and apostle of modern music in present-day Greece.

1502. Philoxenēs, Kyriakos.    Lexikon tēs hellēnikēs ekklēsiastikēs mousikēs (Dictionary of Greek Church music). Constantinople, 1868-1869.

Only two volumes published, covering letters A-M. A great bibliographic rarity, unavailable for inspection. It is presumed to be the most elaborate official statement on Greek church music as performed in modern times. At present, the work of Western scholars on the history of Greek church music in the Middle Ages (known as Byzantine music) is purposely ignored and the official Greek attitude is to refer to the present-day chanting as "Byzantine" and to reiterate the pronouncements of Konstantinos Psahos (Psachos), enunciated in his *Hē parasēmantikē tēs byzantinēs mousikēs.* (The notations of Byzantine Music) (Athēnai, P. D. Sakellariou, 1917, 94 p.), concerning the "unchangeable" music in use in the Greek church.

1503. Slonimsky, Nicolas.    New Music in Greece. Musical Quarterly (New York). v. 51, 1965: 225-235.

An informative, if incomplete, survey of the strivings of the younger generation of composers in contemporary Greece. Since 1966 this youngest group has succeeded in establishing itself and organizing an annual "Hellenic Week of Contemporary Music," during which many first performances are staged. For this occasion a special program in booklet form is issued; those for 1966 (April 14-21) and 1967 (March 29-April 5) contain extensive biographical data on the composers. The booklets are published in Greek and English and also contain full programs, photographs of composers, and samples of scores. These programs are among the most important sources of "up-to-date" information on contemporary composers.

1504. Velimirović, Miloš. Study of Byzantine Music in the West. Balkan Studies, (Thessalonikē), v. 5, 1964: 63-76.

Survey of the work of Western European and American scholars in the field of Byzantine (medieval Greek) music.

## I. MODERN GREEK THEATER AND CINEMA

### by Andonis G. M. Decavalles

### 1. General Reference Works

1505. Grecia: Età moderna. In Enciclopedia dello spettacolo. v. 7. Roma, Casa Editrice Le Maschere, 1962. col. 1687-1702.

This article contains sections on (1) dramatic theater (col. 1688-1698) by Giannēs Siderēs; (2) musical theater (col. 1698-1700) by Fivos Anoianakis; (3) ballet (col. 1700-1701) by Costas Nicols; and (4) the cinema (col. 1701-1702) by F. Iliadēs. Except for the section on ballet, each section contains a bibliography.

1506. Megalē hellēnikē enkyklopaideia. Ekdosis deutera, enēmerōmenē dia symplērōmatōn (Great Greek encyclopedia. 2d ed., updated by supplements). Athēnai, Ekdotikos organismos "Ho Phoinix," 1956-1965. 24 v.

————. Symplērōma (Supplement). Athēnai, Ekdotikos organismos "Ho Phoinix." 1957-1963. 4 v.

See also entry no. 965.

Volume 10 of the encyclopedia contains the following articles on Greek theater: (1) "Vyzantinon theatron" (Byzantine theater) and "Krētikon theatron" (Cretan theater) by S. Antoniades, p. 410-412 (with bibliography); (2) "Neoellēnikon theatron" (Modern Greek theater) by N. I. Laskarēs, p. 412-416 (with extensive bibliography by Laskarēs and P. N. Papas); (3) "Operetta" by N. I. Laskarēs, p. 416; (4) "Melodrama" (Opera) by D. Lavrankas, p. 471-472; and (5) "Kinēmatographos (Cinema) by D. A. Gaziadēs, p. 477 and A. Sakellarios, p. 477-478.

1507. Theatro; dimēnē theatrikē epitheōrēsē (Theater; a bimonthly theatrical review). Athēnai. 1961–

Studies, articles, research, and reports on the theater in Greece and abroad and on records and films. Includes texts of Greek plays and non-Greek plays in Greek translation.

1508. Theatro (The theater). Athēnai. 1957– Annual.

Covering theater, music, dance, and cinema, this annual is a large-format luxury publication giving an illustrated chronicle of the theatrical and other artistic events of the year, as well as full texts of Greek plays and foreign plays in Greek translation.

## 2. Byzantine and Cretan Theater

1509. Cottas, Vénétia.   Le théâtre à Byzance. Paris, Librairie Orientaliste Paul Geuthner, 1931. 290 p. Bibliography: p. 265-277.

A well documented scholarly study tracing the growth of the modern Greek theater from the Byzantine hippodrome to the church drama. *See also*:

Mavrogordato, John.   The Cretan Drama. Journal of Hellenic Studies, v. 48, 1928: 75-96, 243-246.

Vogt, Albert.   Études sur le théâtre byzantin. Byzantion, t. VI, 1931: 37-74.

Bréhier, Louis.   Le théâtre religieux à Byzance. Journal des Savants, Aug. 1913: 357-361; Sept. 1913: 395-404.

La Piana, George.   Le rappresentazioni Sacre nella letteratura bizantina dalle origini al sec. IX. Grottaferratta, S. Nilo, 1912. 344 p.

1510. Sathas, Kōnstantinos N.   Historikon dokimion peri tou theatrou kai tēs mousikēs tōn vyzantinōn, ētoi eisagōgē eis to krētikon theatron (Historical essay on the theater and music of the Byzantines; i.e., an introduction to the Cretan theater). En Venetia, 1878. 420 p.

An early scholarly text of high historical importance, this book serves as an introduction to a second volume by Sathas entitled *Krētikon theatron: Syllogē anekdotōn kai agnōstōn dramatōn* (Cretan theater; collection of unpublished and unknown dramas) (En Venetia, 1879, 467 p.). The second volume contains the plays "Zēnōn," "Stathēs," "Gyparēs," and "Erōphilē."

## 3. General Theater

1511. Gidel, Charles A.   Le théâtre chez les Grecs modernes. *In his*: Nouvelles études sur la littérature grecque moderne. Paris, Maisonneuve, 1878. p. 569-600.

An account of the early Greek plays. For further information on the early developments *see also*:

Andreades, A. M.   Le théâtre grec contemporain. Geneva, 1927. 24 p.

————.   Les théâtres à Vienne. Brussels, Van Sulper, 1929. 122 p.

Bourdon, G.   La resurrection d'un art. Le théâtre grec moderne. Paris, 1892. 123 p.

1512. Laskarēs, Nikolaos I.   Historia tou neohellēnikou theatrou (History of the Neo-Hellenic theater). Athēnai, M. Vasileiou, 1938-39. 2 v. (333, 420 p.)

Perhaps the most thorough, detailed, well-informed, and well-documented study of the topic written by its foremost historian. It traces the development of modern Greek theater from the Byzantine times to 1938. Laskarēs' numerous and extensive articles and contributions to Greek encyclopedias, newspapers, and periodicals of his time cover most aspects, stages, and significant people in Greek theatrical life. He contributed to such publications as *Olympia* (1896), *Panathēnaia* (1900 and on), *Hestia* (1904), *Proodos* (1917), *Paraskēnia* (1924), *Hellēnike Epitheōrēsis* (1928), and *Enkyklopaidikon Lexikon Eleutheroudakē* (v. 5, 1929).

1513. Siderēs, Giannēs. The Modern Greek Theatre: a Concise History. Translated from the Greek by Lucille Vassardaki. Athens, Diphros, 1957. 67 p. Bibliography, illus.

This book, by the foremost living historian of modern Greek theater and the director of the Theatrical Museum in Athens, is a survey leading up to about 1957. It is a shorter simplified version of his two volume: *Historia tou neou hellēnikou theatrou* (History of the new Hellenic theater) (Athēnai, 1951-52). In the introduction, Emil Hourmouzios deals with "The Ancient Drama in Our Time," and Linos Politēs writes on "The Theater in Crete During the Time of the Renaissance." *See also* Guglielmo Chillemi's *Il dramma antico nella Grecia moderna* (Bologna, Capella editore, 1963, 146 p.), an account of the development of modern Greek theater, especially the modern productions of classical drama.

1514. Valsa, M. Le théâtre grec moderne de 1453 à 1900. Berlin, Akademie-Verlag, 1960. 384 p. (Berliner byzantinische Arbeiten, Bd. 18) *See also* entry no. 1384.

A well-informed and well-documented study of the plays, playwrights, and theaters in historical perspective. Valsa also wrote *Le théâtre crétois au XVIII⁰ siècle* (Paris, 1931).

## 4. Greek Theater from 1790 to the Present

1515. Melas, Spyros. Penēnta chronia theatro (Fifty years in the theater). Athēnai, Fexē, 1960. 429 p. Illus., ports.

An autobiographical account by a distinguished Greek novelist, playwright, journalist, member of the Academy of Athens, as well as co-founder and former director of the Nea Skenē theater in Athens, giving a vivid picture of theatrical developments from 1910 to 1960.

Most significant additional sources of information are the theatrical reviews and critiques regularly contributed by Alkēs Thrylos (Mrs. Ouranēs) to the now semimonthly *Nea Hestia* (the most important modern Greek literary magazine since its foundation in 1927) and also the articles contributed by Aimilios Chourmouzios (Emil Hourmouzios) to the Athenian daily *Kathēmerinē*.

1516. Rodas, Michaēl. Morphes tou theatrou (Faces of the theater). v. 1. Athēnai, Pēgasos, 1944. 109 p.

A very valuable book for its excellently drawn literary protraits of significant people in the development of the Greek theater from

1900 to 1944. Written by a man who knew these people very closely. Subjective approach.

1517. Siderēs, Giannēs, *ed.*    Neoellēniko theatro (1795-1929) (Neo-Hellenic theater [1795-1929]). Athēnai, Zacharopoulos, 1952. 385 p. Bibliography. (Vasikē vibliothēkē, 40)

A collection of the 16 most significant Greek plays produced from 1790 to 1952, containing an introduction by the editor and short biographical notes. *See also* F. M. Pontani's *Teatro neoellenico* (Milano, 1962, 276 p.), an anthology of modern Greek drama with an introduction by Bruno Lavagnini.

1518. Thespis: a Quarterly Bulletin. Athens. 1959–

In issues no. 2 and 3, 1959, Giannēs Siderēs wrote a 34-page survey of the development of modern Greek theater. Other issues deal with ancient drama in modern times, with relevant articles by leading scholars and many illustrations of world productions.

## 5. The Shadow Theater of Karagiozes

1519. Caïmi, Giulio.    Karaghiozi; ou la comédie grecque dans l'âme du théâtre d'ombres. Athènes, Hellēnikēs Technes, 1935. 144 p. Illus., bibliography.

An excellently illustrated book on the Greek shadow theater of Karagiozēs.

1520. Spatharēs, Sōtērēs.    Apomnēmoneumata S. Spatharē kai hē technē tou Karagiozē (Memoirs of S. Spatharēs and the art of Karagiozēs). Athēnai, Pergamos, 1960. 227 p.

Among the best available accounts of the shadow theater in Greece.

## 6. The Greek Cinema

1521. Bessy, Maurice, *and* Jean-Louis Chardans.    Grec (cinéma). *In their* Dictionnaire du cinéma et de la télévision. v. 2. Paris, Jean Jacques Pavert, 1966. p. 456-459.

A short but very informative article on the development of the Greek cinema from 1906 to the present. It also provides abridged filmography.

Additional useful data on the subject can be found in specialized periodicals such as *Bianco e Nero* (Roma) for 1955, *Cinema* (Roma) for 1956, *International Motion Picture Almanac* for 1956, and others.

1522. Eliadēs, Ph.    Ho hellēnikos kinēmatographos, 1906-1960 (The Hellenic cinema, 1906-1960). Athēnai, Ekdotes "Phantasia," 1960. 168 p. Illus. Bibliography: p. 172-173.

A survey, mostly through illustrations and photographs, of the development of the Hellenic cinema. Includes a chronological list of films produced to 1960, a list of producers, and a list of cinema magazines.

# PART FIVE

# ROMANIA

# 35

# GENERAL
# REFERENCE AIDS
# and
# BIBLIOGRAPHIES

*by Robert G. Carlton*

## A. BIBLIOGRAPHIES

### 1. Bibliographies of Bibliographies

1523. Cardaş, Gh.   Bibliografia bibliografiilor româneşti (Bibliography of Romanian bibliographies). *In his* Tratat de bibliografie (Treatise on bibliography). Bucureşti, Tip. "Bucovina," 1931. p. 279-380.

Probably the most complete list of Romanian bibliographies ever published, this bibliography is invaluable for the specialist. Includes descriptions of 506 general and specialized bibliographies.

*See also* Ioachim Craciun's "Bibliografia la Români" (Bibliography among Romanians) in *Anuarul Institutului de Istorie Naţională*, v. 4, 1926/27, p. 483-513.

1524. Romania. Romanian Literature. *In* Besterman, Theodore. A World Bibliography of Bibliographies . . . 4th ed., v. 4. Lausanne, Societas Bibliographica, 1966. col. 5442-5446.

Lists 39 general and specialized bibliographies relating to Romania and the Romanian language. Another short bibliography of bibliographies is:

Lambrino, Alexandre. "Roumanie." *In* Malclès, Louise N. Les sources du travail bibliographique. v. 2. Genève, Lille, 1952. p. 783-794. Covers basically the fields of language, literature, and history.

1525. Tomescu, Mircea.   Rumänien. *In* Die Bibliographie in den europäischen Ländern der Volksdemokratie. Leipzig, Verlag für Buch- und Bibliothekswesen, 1960. p. 69-88. (Bibliothekswissenschaftliche Arbeiten aus der Sowjetunion und den Ländern der Volksdemokratie in deutscher Übersetzung, Reihe B, Bd. 3)

A brief historical sketch of bibliographical work prior to the Second World War, with a more detailed outline of postwar developments. A list of the most important bibliographic publications in various fields is appended.

A more extensive treatment of the history of bibliography in Romania is B. Theodorescu's *Istoria bibliografiei romîne* (History of Romanian bibliography) (Bucuresti, Fundația culturala, 1945, 272 p.), which has not been reported among the holdings of any major U.S. library.

## 2. General Bibliographies

1526. Academia română, *Bucharest*.   Catalogul publicațiunilor Academiei Române, 1867-1923 (A catalog of the publications of the Romanian Academy, 1867-1923). București, Cultura Națională, 1924. 69 p.

A useful guide to the publications of the Romanian Academy in its early years. The bibliographical data are not as complete as could be desired (e.g., pagination is not supplied), but the chronological and alphabetical listings should provide the necessary access. Undated supplements were issued for 1924-1926 (4 p.), 1926-1928 (4 p.), and 1929-1930 (4 p.).

The Academy's publications for a later period are listed in *Editura Academiei Republicii Populare Romîne; catalog general, 1948-1954* (The publishing house of the Academy of the Romanian People's Republic; general catalog, 1948-1954) (București, 1956, 719 p.), which records periodicals, monographs, and translations.

1527. Bianu, Ioan, *and* Nerva Hodoş.   Bibliografia românéasca veche, 1508-1830 (Old Romanian bibliography, 1508-1830). Edițiunea Academiei Române. București, Atelierele Socec, 1903-1912. 3 v. Illus., facsims.

Invaluable for the study of early bibliography, publishing, and typography. Includes bibliographic descriptions; original texts of prefaces, dedications, and epilogs (along with Romanian translations for those in foreign languages); and specimens of pages when they are of special interest from the point of view of typography. Volume 4, addenda and corrigenda, published in 1944.

1528. Breslau. Osteuropa-Institut.    Osteuropäische Bibliographie. v. 1-4, 1920-1923. Breslau, Priebatschs Buchhandlung, 1921-1928. Annual. *See also* entry no. 21.

Contains Romanian material in volumes 1-3 only. Volumes 1 and 2 are arranged by subject with subdivision by country, volume 3 by country with subdivision by subject. The section for Romania in volume 3 covers 32 pages with listings of scholarly monographs and articles in Romanian and in West European languages. Author index.

1529. Bucharest. Biblioteca Centrală de Stat.    Anuarul cărţii din Republica Populară Romînă, 1952-1954 (The book annual for the Romanian People's Republic, 1952-1954). Bucureşti, Editura Ştiinţifică, 1957. 410 p.

Apparently not continued. Preface contains a short history of efforts to establish a national bibliography in Romania. Conventional subject arrangement, with periodicals excluded. Alphabetical index of authors and of title entries.

1530. Bucharest. Biblioteca Centrală de Stat. Bibliografia Republicii Socialiste România; cărţi, albume, hărţi, note muzicale (The bibliography of the Socialist Republic of Romania; books, albums, maps, music scores). 1951– Bucureşti. Semimonthly.

The Romanian national bibliography. Generally published with a delay of several months. Subject classification is according to Marxist methodology. Each issue contains a name index, but no cumulative indexes are published. Known earlier as *Buletinul bibliografic al cărţii* (Bibliographic bulletin for books) (1951-1954), *Buletinul bibliografic. Seria A* (Bibliographic bulletin. Series A) (1954-1957), and *Bibliografia Republicii Populare Romîne; cărţi, albume, hărţi, note muzicale* (Bibliography of the Romanian People's Republic; books, albums, maps, music scores) (1958-1965).

1531. Buescu, Victor, *and* Émile Turdeanu.    Les études roumaines à l'étranger, de 1947 à 1951. Revue des études roumaines (Paris), v. 1, 1953: 223-240.

Continuations were published in the same journal as follows: For 1952-1953, v. 2, 1954: 235-241. For 1954-1955, v. 3/4, 1955/1956: 239-265. For 1956-1958, v. 5/6, 1957/1958: 282-331. For 1959-1962, v. 9/10, 1965: 189-257. Valuable listings of Romanian studies abroad.

1532. Crăciun, Ioachim.    Bibliographie de la Transylvanie roumaine, 1916-1936. Cluj, 1937. 366 p. (Revue de Transylvanie, t. 3, no. 4)

Contains 4,056 items published during the period 1916-1936 and related to Romanian Transylvania, "all the Romanian territory detached from Hungary." The starting point of 1916 was chosen because that was the year "when free Romania entered the war alongside the great western powers for the deliverance of the Romanians of Transylvania." Titles are given in original languages and — except when they are in German, English, Spanish, French, or Italian — are followed by French translations. Coverage: history; agrarian affairs; the church; military affairs; economic conditions; law; ethnography; geography and demography; literature, philology, and linguistics; medicine; folklore; the press; and theater and music.

1533. Fischer-Galati, Stephen A.    Rumania, a Bibliographic Guide. Washington, D.C., U.S. Government Printing Office, 1963. New York, Arno Press, 1968. 75 p.

The first in a series of bibliographical area guides issued by the Slavic and Central European Division of the Library of Congress. Consists of an extensive bibliographical essay followed by an alphabetical listing of the 748 publications mentioned in the essay. Medicine, the natural sciences, and technology are excluded. Library of Congress call numbers and/or location symbols for other holding libraries are supplied.

1534. Novaia literatura po Rumynii (Recent literature about Romania). 1960– Moskva. Monthly.

Issued jointly by a series of Soviet libraries, this useful bulletin is not limited to Soviet writings. The majority of the material listed consists of articles from Romanian journals, but items from French, German, and Soviet sources are also included. The convenient subject arrangement offsets in large part the lack of indexes. Mimeographed.

1535. Păduraru, Octav.    Anglo-Roumanian and Roumanian-English Bibliography. Bucureşti, Monitorul Oficial şi Imprimeriile Statului, Impr. Naţională, 1946. 244 p.

An extremely valuable and a unique list. Notwithstanding the title and declared scope, however, this bibliography of over 9,000 entries includes many items not in English and not by British or American authors. In his commendable effort to be as comprehensive as possible, the compiler introduced a great deal of material that is of marginal value, or related to Romania only very tenuously. Arranged alphabetically by subject, with a name index included. Coverage is from the earliest times to May 1945. The chief merit of this bibliography lies in the inclusion of much periodical literature from journals not devoted specifically to area studies.

1536. Rally, Alexandre, *and* Getta H. Rally.    Bibliographie franco-roumaine. Paris, Leroux, 1930. 2 v.

A meticulously prepared bibliography which, unfortunately, provides coverage only through 1929. The first volume lists works in

French by Romanian authors, arranged alphabetically by name, and includes a supplement showing French-language journals published in Romania. The second volume, devoted to French works pertaining to Romania, is arranged by broad subject categories, and provides a bibliography, a name index, and a subject index.

1537. Romanian Books; a Quarterly Bulletin. 195?– Bucharest, Central Office of the Romanian Publishing Houses and Bookselling.

A descriptive bulletin listing new books both in Romanian and in other languages. English translations are given for non-English titles, and bibliographical data and annotations are also in English. Averages about 80-90 pages per issue, and a few short articles with news in the publishing world are usually included.

Other sources of data on new Romanian publications are the monthly Romanian pre-publication list *Cărți noi* (New books) and the regular and special catalogs of the West German bookseller Kubon & Sagner.

1538. Ruffini, Mario. Introduzione bibliografica allo studio della Romania. L'Europa orientale (Roma), v. 15, 1935: 236–289.

Limited generally to publications still in print at the time of issuance, this guide tends to stress Romanian and Italian works. The descriptions supplied are usually quite brief, frequently to the point that they are virtually useless. Although now somewhat dated, this guide retains some value, especially for those interested in building collections within the following categories into which the material is arranged: language, history of literature, cultural history, history, geography, folklore and ethnography, art, and the economy.

1539. Savadjian, Léon. Bibliographie balkanique, 1920-1939. Paris, Société générale d'imprimerie et d'édition, 1931-1939. 8 v.

A series of annual lists, except for volume 1, which is for 1920-1930, and volume 2, for 1931-1932. Covers books published after 1920 in French, English, Italian, and German. Each list includes sections on Romania and on the Balkans as a whole. "Principal articles" published in periodicals are also covered, and biographical data are supplied for some authors. Author indexes.

1540. Südosteuropa-Bibliographie. Bd. 1– 1945/50– München, R. Oldenbourg.

*See also* entries no. 13 *and* 482.

Relevant items:

Popinceanu, Ion, *and* Constantin Sporea. Rumänische Bibliographie 1945-1950. Bd. 1, 1. Teil (1956), p. 31-56. 515 items.

Rumänische Bibliographie 1951-1955. Bd. 2, 2. Teil (1962), p. 495-576. 1,319 items.

Sporea, Constantin, *and* Gertrud Krallert-Sattler. Rumänische Bibliographie 1956-1960. Bd. 3, 1. Teil (1964), p. 289ff. 3,025 items.

A selective bibliography of high quality compiled by the Südost-Institut München. Arranged along conventional lines with the following principal categories: general works, the land, history and politics, language and literature, religion and the church, state and law, economic and social affairs, and spiritual and cultural life. Includes both monographic and periodical literature, in Romanian and in West European languages. Few annotations are provided, but German translations are supplied for items not in West European languages. Author indexes.

1541. U.S. *Library of Congress. Division of Bibliography.* The Balkans: IV. Rumania. Washington, D.C., 1943. 70 p.

Designed to be used in conjunction with part 1 of the same five-part bibliographical series on the Balkans, which covers the area as a whole, and with the occasional references to Romania in the other three volumes. Arranged by broad subject categories, some of them further subdivided chronologically. Use is hampered somewhat by the fact that long monographs are mixed in indiscriminately with short articles. Few annotations provided. English titles for the period from the Versailles Treaty to 1943 are emphasized.

1542. Veress, Endre (Andrei), *ed.* Bibliografia română-ungară (Romanian-Hungarian bibliography). Bucureşti, Cartea Românească, 1931-1935. 3 v.

This list concerning Romanians in Hungarian literature and Hungarians in Romanian literature is subdivided chronologically as follows: v. 1, 1473-1780; v. 2, 1781-1838, and v. 3, 1839-1878.

The scope is somewhat broader than suggested by 'the title, including, for example, a number of German, English, and other works. Locations are shown in most instances. Contains general indexes, author indexes, and indexes of publishers and printers.

For a recent list of material pertaining to the Hungarians in Romania, see *Hungarians in Rumania and Transylvania; a Bibliographical List of Publications in Hungarian and West European Languages Compiled From the Holdings of the Library of Congress,* by Elemer Bako and William Sólyom-Fekete (Washington, D. C., 1969, 192 p.).

## 3. Bibliographies of Serials

1543. Hodoş, N., *and* A. S. Ionescu (A. Sadi-Ionescu). Publicaţiunile periodicii româneşti (Ziare, gazete, reviste). Descriere bibliografică . . . cu o intr. de I. Bianu. Tom I. Catalog alfabetic, 1820-1906 (Romanian serial publications [newspapers, journals, magazines]. Bibliographical description . . . with an introduction by I. Bianu. Volume 1. Alphabetical catalogue, 1820-1906). Bucureşti, Librările Socec & Sfetea, 1918. 811 p.

Only one volume published. Lists newspapers and journals in Romanian regardless of place of publication; serial publications issued in Romania regardless of language; and serials about Romania independently of place of publication or language. About 5,000 entries.

1544. Newspapers and Periodicals from Romania. 195?– Bucharest, Cartimex. Annual.

> A subscription list published in recent years by the Romanian publications export agency and including all serials available by purchase, but excluding many materials normally obtainable through exchange agreements only. Separate listings are provided for scientific and popular newspapers and periodicals in foreign languages, and for publications in the languages of the national minorities. Brief annotations in English, French, and German are supplied. Information on frequency and price is given in a price list annex.

1545. Rumania. *In* List of the Serial Publications of Foreign Governments, 1815-1931. Edited by Winifred Gregory. New York, H. W. Wilson, 1932. p. 498-502.

> Apparently the only list of its kind in existence, this roster of several hundred Romanian official publications shows holdings by major U.S. libraries.
>
> The *Union List of Serials*, 3d ed. (New York, H. W. Wilson, 1965), may also be consulted for North American holdings of Romanian serials, though official publications are excluded.

1546. U.S. *Bureau of the Census.* Bibliography of Social Science Periodicals and Monograph Series: Rumania, 1947-1960. Washington, D.C., 1961. 27 p. (Foreign Social Science Bibliographies, Series P-92, no. 1)
*See also* entry no. 25.

> Lists Romanian periodicals and monograph series in the social sciences for the period 1947-1960, but only if available in the Library of Congress. The unorthodox and somewhat confusing system used for entries detracts from its usefulness, but subject and issuing-agency indexes are helpful, as is the practice of supplying Library of Congress call numbers.

1547. U.S. *Library of Congress. Slavic and Central European Division.* Newspapers of East Central and Southeastern Europe in the Library of Congress. Edited by Robert G. Carlton. Washington, D.C., 1965. 204 p.
*See also* entry no. 28.

> Shows holdings of 94 post-World War I newspapers in the Library of Congress published in Romania, with indication of the titles being currently received.

## B. ENCYCLOPEDIAS AND BIOGRAPHIC MATERIALS

1548. Dicţionar enciclopedic ilustrat "Cartea Românească" (The "Cartea Românească" illustrated encyclopedic dictionary). Bucureşti, Editura Cartea Românească, 1931. 1948 p. Illus., plates, maps, diagrs.

> A handy, one-volume encyclopedia which retains its value. Consists of two parts: (1) a historical and current dictionary of the

Romanian language, and (2) a universal historical and geographical dictionary.

1549. Dicţionar enciclopedic romîn (Romanian encyclopedic dictionary). Bucureşti, Editura Politică, 1962-1966. 4 v. Illus., plates, maps.

The first general encyclopedia published in post-World War II Romania. Sponsored by the Romanian Academy and edited by a committee of distinguished scholars and academicians headed by Athanase Joja. Contains about 46,000 entries.

Although the lack of bibliographical information and suggestions for further reading is a drawback, still a great deal of fairly up-to-date information may be gleaned from its pages.

1550. Directory of Rumanian Officials. (n.p.) 1966. 206 p.

Issued by an unidentified source, this directory is based on data received through June 1966. Contains sections for government; party; mass organizations; institutions concerned with international and foreign relations; educational, cultural, and religious institutions; economic institutions; and mass information media. Only positions, names, and dates of tenure are shown. Includes some blanks where no information was available. Name index.

1551. Enciclopedia României (The encyclopedia of Romania). Bucureşti, Imprimeria Naţională, 1936-1941. 4 v. Illus., ports., maps.

The essential encyclopedia for pre-World War II Romania, this presentation is arranged topically rather than alphabetically: volume 1, The State; volume 2, The Land; and volumes 3 and 4, The Economy. The unpublished volumes 5 and 6 were to have dealt with culture. Volumes 1, 3, and 4 have author and subject indexes, and volume 2 contains a geographical index of localities in Romania.

1552. Who's Who in Central and East-Europe, 1933/34-1935/36. Edited by Stephen Taylor. Zurich, Central European Times Publishing Co., 1935-1937. 2 v.

A useful guide to prominent Romanians of the mid-1930s, containing biographic and bibliographic sketches of some 1,500 Romanians (905 in volume 2). The criteria for inclusion included official position and "special prominence in creditable lines of effort."

Other sources of biographic information are Who's Who in Eastern Europe (n.d., n.p.), published in the early 1960s, which supplies data on 21 prominent persons, largely politicians; and Andrew G. Caranfil's Biographical Information of Members of the Rumanian Grand National Assembly (New York, U.S. Joint Publications Research Service, 1957, 103 1.).

## C. HANDBOOKS, SURVEYS, GUIDEBOOKS, AND DIRECTORIES

1553. Bucureşti; ghid (Bucharest; a guidebook). Bucureşti, Editura Meridiane, 1963. 342 p. Illus., maps.

Far more detailed than the sections on the capital city included in guidebooks covering the country as a whole. Consists of three major sections: geographic, demographic, and historical data; political and social organizations; and useful locations and addresses. An annex contains a guide to Bucharest streets and a detailed map of the city.

1554. Clark, Charles U.    United Roumania. New York, Dodd, Mead, 1932. 418 p. Illus., maps. Bibliography: p. 377-396.

Based largely on the author's earlier (1922) *Greater Roumania*, but substantially rewritten, this survey by a sympathetic observer is a combination of scholarly research and personal impressions. Economic conditions are discussed only in passing, with the emphasis on recent history, folk art, and peasant customs. Constitutes to a certain extent an apologia for anti-Semitism in Romania and for the country's conduct during the First World War and the subsequent Hungarian campaign.

1555. Cretzianu, Alexandre, *ed.*    Captive Rumania; a Decade of Soviet Rule. New York, Praeger, 1956. 424 p.

A handbook containing contributions related to the various facets of Romanian life, chiefly during the period from 1945 to 1955. Written mostly by émigrés. Very skimpy in historical background and perspective, and heavy on postwar political events, of which most of the authors had direct knowledge and experience. Stresses the loss of religious and other personal freedoms and the subjugation of the economy and political line to Soviet dictates. More typical of the situation during the mid-1950s than of that today.

1556. Fischer-Galati, Stephen A., *ed.*    Romania. Published for the Mid-European Studies Center of the Free Europe Committee, Inc. New York, Praeger, 1956. 399 p. Bibliography: p. 369-382. (East Central Europe under the Communists)

Described as "a sincere attempt to present an objective picture of Romanian developments since 1945," this survey presents a great deal of useful information in easily readable fashion. Well organized by broad subject categories, it is especially strong on the economic situation during the late 1940s and early 1950s. Individual contributions were written by the editor and by Serge H. Aronovici, George H. Bossy, Randolph Braham, Andrew G. Caranfil, Abraham Melezin, Fred S. Pisky, and Nicolas Spulber.

A competent survey of more recent conditions in Romania is Heinz Siegert's *Rumänien heute* (Wien, Düsseldorf, Econ-Verlag, 1966, 282 p.).

1557. Flegon, Alec.    Rumania Trade Directory. London, Flegon Press, 1962. 51 p.

Although organized in a somewhat confusing fashion, this guide is of some use to businessmen and others interested in the Romanian economy and in commercial relations. Features data on Romanian foreign trade, a list of foreign trade and other government agencies, a roster of manufacturing establishments, and a "Who's Who in Rumanian Industry."

*Hints to Business Men Visiting the Socialist Republic of Rumania* (London, Board of Trade, 1965, 32 p.) is one of a series of British guides aimed principally toward the commercial traveler.

1558. Great Britain. *Foreign Office. Historical Section.* Rumania. London, H.M. Stationery Office, 1920. 144 p. (Handbooks . . . , no. 23)

Intended for the use of the British delegation to the Paris Peace Conference, this handbook deals with pre-World War I Romania only. The major subdivisions include geography, political history, social and political conditions, and economic conditions. Useful for the study of the Romanian situation just prior to the creation of Greater Romania.

1559. Hoffmann, Walter. Rumänien von heute; ein Querschnitt durch Politik, Kultur und Wirtschaft. Bucureşti, Verlag Cugetarea, 1941. 230 p. Plates, maps.

Published after Romanian adherence to the Three Power Pact and association with the German attack on the Soviet Union, this book reflects the Nazi viewpoint. The author repeatedly implies that the rump Romania left from the Vienna Award is temporary only, and that "the Romania of tomorrow will have a completely different appearance." Stresses the contributions of the "Volksdeutschen" to Romanian evolution and German-Romanian relations.

1560. Romania; a Guidebook. By Şerban Cioculescu, Ion Marin Sadoveanu, and others. Bucharest, Meridiane, 1967. 491 p. Illus.

An up-to-date guidebook in English, containing a wealth of the kind of information wanted by a casual or holiday traveler. Includes an extensive chapter (p. 389-456) on the "Museums of Romania."

Other recent and competent guidebooks are Ted Appleton's *Your Guide to Romania* (London, Alvin Redman, 1965, 223 p.), May Mackintosh's *Rumania* (London, Robert Hale, 1963, 191 p.), *Rumania* by Nagel Publishers (Geneva, Paris, 1967, 368 p.), and Peter Latham's *Romania: A Complete Guide* (London, Garnstone Press, 1967, 245 p.).

1561. Rouček, Joseph S. Contemporary Roumania and Her Problems; a Study in Modern Nationalism. Stanford, Stanford University Press, 1932. 422 p. Bibliography: p. 383-411.

Written by a self-admitted "critical friend" of Romania, the four chief sections of this survey deal with historical development, political life, the constitutional and administrative system, and economic affairs. A fifth concluding section stresses that the greatest need of the country in the 1930s was to improve the economic situation, through foreign exploitation and emphasis of agriculture rather than industrialization. The extensive bibliography is among its best features.

1562. Rumania. *Camera de Comerț a Republicii Populare Romîne.* Commercial Guide to Rumania. 4th ed. Bucharest, Chamber of Commerce of the Rumanian People's Republic, 1964. 203 p.

The most detailed commercial guide available in English, although somewhat dated by now. Includes data on the banking and exchange system and regulations, customs regulations, insurance, shipping, postal rates, commercial representation abroad, and export-import companies.

1563. Rumania. Bucharest, Foreign Languages Pub. House, 1959. 861 p. Illus.

A handbook written by a team of scholars and writers, including Constantin Daicoviciu, George Oprescu, Ion Marin Sadoveanu, Demostene Botez, and others. A curious combination of useful information on physical geography and tourism together with tiresome propaganda extolling economic developments, culture, and history.

More recent, but sketchier, official treatments are *Rumania in Brief* (Bucharest, Meridiane, 1962, 116 p.), and *Romania; Geography, History, Economy, Culture* (Bucharest, Meridiane, 1966, 202 p.).

## D. TRANSLATIONS, ABSTRACTS, AND INDEXES

1564. Academia Republicii Populare Romîne. *Biblioteca.* Indexul lucrărilor științific publicate în periodicele și culegerile editate de Academia R. P. Romîne, 1948-1954. Index des travaux scientifiques publiés dans les périodiques et les recueils, édités par l'Académie de la R.P. Roumaine, 1948-1954. București, Editura Academiei Republicii Populare Romîne, 1957. 590 p.

Reliable guide to the contents of Romanian scholarly journals of the early postwar period. Embraces the social sciences and humanities as well as the pure and applied sciences.

1565. Bucharest. Biblioteca Centrală de Stat. Bibliografia periodicelor din Republica Socialiste Română (Bibliography of periodicals in the Socialist Republic of Romania). 1953– Bucharest. Semimonthly.

A guide to the contents of Romanian periodicals. Up to 1957 called *Buletinul bibliografic. Seria B. Articole și recenzi din presa* (Bibliographic bulletin. Series B. Articles and reviews in the press). Neither cumulative indexes nor indexes for individual issues are published.

For a guide to the contents of earlier Romanian periodicals, see *Bibliografia analitică a periodicelor românesti, 1790-1850* (Analytical bibliography of Romanian periodicals, 1790-1850) (București, 1966-1967, 3 pts.).

1566. East European Accessions Index. v. 1-11, 1951-1961. Washington, D.C., Library of Congress. Monthly.

*See also* entries no. 14 *and* 36.

This accessions index recorded receipts by the Library of Congress and other participating North American libraries of monographic and periodical materials published in Romania and in Romanian. Coverage includes monographs published after 1944, and periodicals issued after 1950. Titles of monographs and of periodicals are given in the original language and in English translation. Tables of contents are shown in English for selected periodicals.

A subject index is included with each issue, and the December issue for each year contains an annual cumulation of periodical and newspaper receipts for the year.

1567. Kyriak, Theodore E. East Europe; Bibliography Index to U.S. JPRS Research Translations. 1962– Washington, D.C., Research Microfilms. Monthly.

Formerly issued in a somewhat haphazard arrangement, this publication has been improved greatly within recent years. The sections of relevance here are a bibliography of all U.S. Joint Publications Research Service social science series, including report numbers and tables of contents; a list of ad hoc releases in the social sciences; and a subject index for publications in the social sciences. A recent issue listed 115 references to Romania in the subject index. This is a unique guide to a body of elusive and important material.

JPRS publications are also listed in the *Monthly Catalog of U.S. Government Publications*, issued by the Superintendent of Documents, U.S. Government Printing Office.

1568. Radio Free Europe. Situation Report: Rumania. New York. Irregular.

Valuable analyses in mimeographed form by experienced observers of the current scene in Romania.

Additional timely information from Romania can be found in the *Rumanian Press Survey*, also published irregularly by Radio Free Europe.

1569. Rumanian Press Review. 1946– Bucharest. Daily (irregular).

*See also* entry no. 60.

Published jointly by the U.S. and British diplomatic missions in Romania, this summary of the daily press is invaluable for persons who do not read Romanian. Special supplements are sometimes published.

The provincial press is covered by *Summary of the Rumanian Provincial Press*, published, usually weekly, by the U.S. Joint Publications Research Service since 1958.

1570. Romanian Scientific Abstracts. Social Sciences. 1964– Bucharest. Monthly.

*See also* entry no. 1910.

Abstracts of Romanian material published in scholarly journals. Embraces law and the humanities as well as the social sciences.

A list of Western-language periodicals dealing with Romania is contained in *The USSR and Eastern Europe: Periodicals in Western Languages* (Washington, U.S. Government Printing Office, 1967, 89 p.), prepared by Paul L. Horecky and Robert G. Carlton.

## E. DICTIONARIES (BILINGUAL)

1571. Dicţionar de buzunar romîn-francez (Romanian-French pocket dictionary). Compiled by Irina Eliade, Jana Gheorghiu, and Liliana Popovici-Pamfil. Bucureşti, Editura Ştiinţifică, 1961. 278 p.

To be used in the absence of a recent, comprehensive Romanian-French dictionary. An older but still serviceable dictionary is Frédéric Damé's *Nouveau dictionnaire roumain-français* (Bucarest, Impr. de l'État, 1893-1895, 4 v.).

1572. Dicţionar romîn-german (Romanian-German dictionary). By Mariana Şora and others. Edited by Mihai Isbăşescu. Bucureşti, Editura Ştiinţifică, 1963. 733 p.

The German-Romanian counterpart is *Dicţionar german-român* published by Academia Republicii Socialiste România (Bucuresti, 1966, 1172 p.). Among older, but still useful dictionaries, the following may be cited:

Tiktin, Hariton.   Rumänisch-deutsches Wörterbuch. Bukarest, Staatsdruckerei, 1903-1925. 3 v.

Schroff, Maximilian.   Rumänisch-deutsches Wörterbuch. Bukarest, Socec, 1925. 626 p.

1573. Dicţionar tehnic poliglot (Polyglot technical dictionary). Bucureşti, Editura Tehnică, 1963. 1235 p.

An extremely useful polyglot technical dictionary listing terms in Romanian, Russian, English, German, French, and Hungarian. The principal listing is of Romanian expressions, with the equivalents in other languages shown. Separate indexes are provided for terms in the other languages. Contains some 23,000 items.

1574. Leviţchi, Leon.   Dicţionar român-englez (Romanian-English dictionary). 2d rev. and enl. ed. Bucureşti, Editura Ştiinţifică, 1965. 600 p.

The most recent, best, and most complete Romanian-English dictionary available. Both this second edition and the first (Bucuresti, Editura Ştiinţifică, 1960, 1170 p.) are far superior to other bilingual dictionaries.

The comparable English-Romanian tool is *Dicţionar englez-român* (English-Romanian dictionary) (Bucureşti, Editura Ştiinţifică, 1965, 604 p.).

## F. LIBRARIES

1575. Bucharest. Biblioteca Centrală de Stat.   Ghidul bibliotecilor din R.P.R. (Guide to libraries in the Romanian People's Republic). Bucureşti, Editura de Stat Didactică şi Pedagogică, 1958. 250 p.

The most complete guide available to Romanian libraries. Contains a section on historical development, descriptions of 584 libraries, an alphabetical index of libraries, and an index of subject matter indicating the libraries with collections in specialized fields.

1576. Kellogg, Frederick.   Historical Research Materials in Rumania. Journal of Central European Affairs, v. 23, Jan. 1964: 485-494.

While written by a scholar interested primarily in historical source materials, this article is a convenient survey of and guide to Romanian libraries and archives in general. Covers state, academy and university libraries, specialized institutes, and both state and regional archival collections.

1577. Pihuljak, Irene.   Das rumänische Bibliothekswesen; eine Skizze seiner Geschichte. Wien, Österreichische Nationalbibliothek, 1961. 37 p. (Biblos-Schriften, Band 32)

Reprint of a two-part article in the Austrian library journal *Biblos* (v. 8, 1959, p. 60-74 and 150-165). Devoted chiefly to the establishment and history of libraries in Romania. Also contains a brief sketch on the locations and collections of libraries in post-World War II Romania. Includes a unique bibliography of 33 items related to the history of Romanian libraries.

*See also* "Rumänien," in *Handbuch der Bibliothekswissenschaft*, 3. Band, 2 Hälfte, *Geschichte der Bibliotheken* (Wiesbaden, Otto Harrassowitz, 1957), p. 534-535.

1578. Studii şi cercetari de documentare şi bibliologie (Studies and research in documentation and bibliology). 1959– Bucureşti. Quarterly (irregular).

Useful not only for the fields indicated in the title, but also for information from the Romanian library world in general. Volume 9, 1967, no. 2/3 contained a series of articles dealing with the history and collections of the largest Romanian library — that of the Academy.

Current developments in Romanian librarianship can also be followed in the monthly *Revista bibliotecilor* (Library journal) (1948–, Bucureşti), formerly called *Călăuza bibliotecarului* (Librarian's guide).

## G. MISCELLANEOUS REFERENCE AIDS

1579. Academia Republicii Socialiste România.   Academy of the Socialist Republic of Romania; Organization, Research. Bucharest, Editura Academiei, 1966. 318 p.

*See also* entry no. 1875.

A guide to the structural organization of the Academy and to the research work carried out by it. For a brief history of the Academy, see *Académie de la République Socialiste de Roumanie, bref historique* (Bucarest, Editura Academiei, 1968, 151 p.).

1580. Delegation of U.S. Book Publishers Visiting Rumania. Book Publishing and Distribution in Rumania; Report of the Delegation of U.S. Book Publishers Visiting Rumania, October 1-10, 1965. New York, American Book Publishers Council, American Textbook Publishers Institute, 1966. 60 p.

*See also* entry no. 63.

The only recent and fairly comprehensive survey in English of publishing in Romania. Presents statistics, organizational aspects, data on copyright and translation rights, etc., along with the routine features of book manufacturing, distribution, and registration. An appendix lists the principal publishers with information on the types of books each publishes.

1581. Rumania. *Direcţiunea Centrală de Statistică.* Anuarul statistic al R.S.R. (Statistical annual for the Socialist Republic of Romania). 1904– Bucureşti.

The basic source for statistical data on Romania, this yearbook suffers from a defect common in the East European countries — the use of relative rather than absolute figures.

The same agency issues a less detailed *Rumanian Statistical Pocket Book*, which is also published in French, Spanish, and Russian editions.

1582. U.S. *Office of Geography.* Rumania; Official Standard Names Approved by the United States Board on Geographic Names. Washington, D.C., U.S. Government Printing Office, 1960. 450 p. (U.S. Board on Geographic Names. Gazetteer no. 48)

Contains approximately 36,500 entries for Romanian localities and geographic features. Unapproved spellings provide references to the officially accepted form. Data supplied include latitude and longitude, and references to standard Army Map Service and Romanian maps on which the entries can be located. Spellings are based on 1954 orthography, which has since been "reformed."

For similar data on pre-World War II Romania, *see* George I. Lahavari's *Marele dicţionar geografic al Romîniei* (Large Romanian geographic dictionary) (Bucureşti, Stab. Grafic J. V. Socecu, 1898-1902, 5 v.).

# 36

# the land

*by George W. Hoffman*

Bibliographies and Survey Studies 1583-1598

Serials 1599-1601

Regional Studies and Special Aspects 1602-1611

## A. BIBLIOGRAPHIES AND SURVEY STUDIES

1583. Academia Republicii Populare Romîne. *Institutul de Geologie şi Geografie.* Monografia geografică a Republicii Populare Romîne (Geographic monograph of the People's Republic of Romania). Edited by I. P. Gherasimov and others. Bucureşti, Editura Academiei Republicii Populare Romîne, 1960–. Illus., maps, diagrs., profiles, tables, atlases. Includes bibliographies.

    Standard survey of the physical and economic geography of Romania. For a French treatment of the subject, under the same sponsorship, see: *Recueil d'études géographiques concernant le territoire de la République populaire roumaine, publiées à l'occasion du XIX<sup>e</sup> Congrès international de géographie, Stockholm, 1960* (Bucarest, Éditions de l'Académie de la République populaire roumaine, 1960, 178 p., illus., maps, bibliogr.).

1584. Armand, David L'vovich. Rumyniia; fiziko-geograficheskoe opisanie (Romania; physical-geographic description). Moskva, Izd-vo Akademii nauk SSSR, 1946. 257 p. Illus., maps. Bibliography: p. 249-256.

    A brief but valuable physical geography.

1585. Călinescu, Raul, *and others.* Geografie fizică a R.P.R. (Physical geography of the Romanian People's Republic). Bucureşti, Litografia Invăţămîntului, 1955. 774 p. Illus., maps.

    The outstanding physical geography of Romania. Includes bibliographies.

1586. Cucu, Vasile, *and* Alexandru Roşu. Bibliografie geografică, 1944–

1964, Romînia (Bibliography of geography, 1944-1964, Romania). Bucureşti, Editura de Stat pentru Imprimate şi Publicaţii, 1964. 154 p. (Biblioteca geografului, no. 1)

The same authors also prepared *The Physical and Economic Maps of the Socialist Republic of Romania* (Bucharest, Meridiane Pub. House, 1966, 26 p.).

1587. Enciclopedia României (An encyclopedia of Romania). v. 2. Bucureşti, Imprimeria Naţională, 1938. Illus., ports., maps.

Excellent geographic descriptions.

1588. Fichuez, Robert. Rumania. *In* Deffontaines, Pierre, *ed*. Larousse Encyclopedia of Geography. 1. Europe. New York, Prometheus Press, 1961. p. 283-294.

Survey of the regional geography of Romania.

1589. Haşeganu, Mihail. Geografie economică a R.P.R. (Economic geography of the Romanian People's Republic). Bucureşti, Editura Ştiinţifică, 1957. 534 p. Illus., maps, diagrs. Bibliography: p. 527-530.

1590. Haşeganu, Mihail, *and others*. Wirtschaftsgeographie der Rumänischen Volksrepublik. Berlin, Verlag Die Wirtschaft, 1962. 192 p. Illus., maps, diagrs.

Survey of the economic geography of Romania. Romanian edition published by Editura Meridiane (Bucureşti, 1962).

1591. Helin, Ronald A. The Volatile Administrative Map of Rumania. *In*: Association of American Geographers. Annals, v. 57, Sept. 1967: 481-502.

A series of maps indicating the political objectives of reforms in Romania's administrative boundaries since the end of the First World War.

1592. Martonne, Emmanuel de. La Roumanie. *In* Martonne, Emmanuel de, *ed*. Géographie universelle. v. 4. Paris, Armand Colin, 1931. p. 699-810.

Survey of the regional geography of Romania.

1593. Mehedinţa, Simeon. Rumania and Her People, an Essay in Physical and Human Geography. Bucharest, 1939. 111 p. Illus. (maps), plates, bibliographical footnotes. (Romanian Academy. Romanian Studies, 1)

1594. Mihăilescu, Vintilă. România, geografie fizică (Physical geography of Romania). Bucureşti, Atelierele Grafice Socec, 1936. 278 p. Illus., maps. Bibliography: p. 251-273.

A classic study of the subject.

1595. Morariu, Tiberiu, *and others*.  Nouă geografie a patriei (New geography of the homeland). Bucureşti, Editura Ştiinţifică, 1964. 354 p. Maps, illus.
General geography of Romania.

1596. Morariu, Tiberiu, *and others*.  The Geography of Romania. Bucharest, Meridiane, 1966. 133 p. Illus., 6 fold. maps (2 col.)
Valuable physical and economic geography of the country.

1597. Sandru, Ion, *and* Vasile Cucu.  Some Considerations on the Development of Geography in the Socialist Republic of Rumania. The Professional Geographer, v. 18, July 1966: 219-223.
Valuable summary of the development of Romanian geography.

1598. Tufescu, Victor.  Atlas geografic: Republica Socialistă România (Geographic atlas: Socialist Republic of Romania). Bucureşti, Editura Didactică şi Pedagogică, 1965. 110, 34 p. Chiefly illus., col. maps.
Contains large- and small-scale maps on the physical, economic, and political geography of the country.

# B. SERIALS

1599. Revue roumaine de géologie, géophysique, et géographie. Série de géographie. v. 1–, 1957– Bucarest, Éditions de l'Académie de la République populaire roumaine. Annual.
Separate subseries for geography began with volume 8 (1964). Title varies: 1957/1963, *Revue de géologie et de géographie*. Two numbers a year, 1958-1963; annual, 1957, 1964–. Articles are reprints or translations of studies published in other Romanian geographical journals. Since volume 8, in English or French.

1600. Societatea de Ştiinţe Naturale şi Geografie din Republica Populară Romînă. Comunicări de geografie (Transactions in geography). 1962– Bucureşti. Annual.
Successor to *Comunicări de geologie-geografie*. In Romanian, with supplementary tables of contents and summaries in English and Russian. Specializes in physical and economic geography of Romania.

1601. Studii şi cercetări de geologie, geofizica si geografie. Seria geografie (Studies and research in geology, geophysics, and geography. Geography series). 1964– Bucureşti, Editura Academiei Republicii Populare Romîne. Annual.
Studies, proceedings, and notes on all aspects of the economic and physical geography of Romania. Successor to *Probleme de geografie* (v. 1-10, 1954-1963). Supplementary tables of contents and abstracts in English and Russian.

## C. REGIONAL STUDIES AND SPECIAL ASPECTS

1602. Blanc, André. Problèmes de géographie urbaine en Roumanie. Revue géographique de l'Est (Nancy), v. 3, July-Sept. 1963: 307-331.
Critical evaluation of urban revolution in major Romanian cities.

1603. Iordan, Iorgu. Toponimia romînească (Romanian toponomy). Bucureşti, Editura Academiei Republicii Populare Romîne, 1963. 581 p. Fold. map. Bibliography: p. xii-xxv.

1604. Kundig-Steiner, Werner. Nord-Dobrudscha. Zürich, Aschmann und Schiller, 1946. 332 p. Illus., maps (Istanbuler Schriften, no. 15)
Discussion of the relationship between nature and human activity in North Drobruja during the 19th and 20th centuries.

1605. Martonne, Emmanuel de. The Carpathians: Physiographic Features Controlling Human Geography. Geographical Review, v. 3, June 1917: 417-427.
Geographic description with emphasis on physical geography.

1606. Mihăilescu, Vintilă. Carpaţii sud-estici de pe teritoriul R.P. Romîne; studiu de geografie fizică cu privire specială la relief. (The Southeast Carpathians in the territory of Romania; study of the physical geography with special emphasis on the relief). Bucureşti, Editura Ştiinţifică, 1963. 373 p. Illus., maps (part fold., 1 col.), profiles. Bibliography: p. 365-372.
A detailed regional geography.

1607. Mihăilescu, Vintilă. Dealurile şi cîmpiile României; studiu de geografia a reliefului (The hills and plains of Romania; study of geographic relief). Bucureşti, Editura Ştiinţifică, 1966. 351 p. Illus., maps.
Detailed analytical study of the relief of large geographical units.

1608. Morariu, Tiberiu, *and others.* Contributions by Rumanian Geographers. Revue roumaine de géologie, géophysique et géographie. Serie de géographie (Bucharest), v. 8, 1964: 266 p.
Numerous articles in important fields of geographic research prepared in connection with the XXth International Geographical Congress (London, 1964).

1609. Sandru, Ion, *and others.* Contribution géographique à la classification des villes de la Republique Populaire Roumaine. Annales de géographie (Paris), v. 72, Mar.-Apr. 1963: 162-185.
Distribution and classification of major Romanian cities.

1610. Sandru, Ion. Vergleichende Betrachtung der rumänischen Städte. Geographische Berichte (Berlin), v. 5, 1960: 29-39.
Changes in the locational pattern and functions of Romanian cities are discussed.

1611. Traeger, Paul. Die Deutschen in der Dobrudscha; zugleich ein Beitrag zur Geschichte der deutschen Wanderung in Osteuropa. Stuttgart, Verlagsaktiengesellschaft, 1922. 222 p. Illus., plates, map. (Schriften des Deutschen Ausland-Instituts, Stuttgart. A. Kulturhistorische Reihe, Bd. 6)

History and description of the German minority in the Dobruja, who were transferred to Germany during the Second World War.

# 37

# the people

*by Stephen Fischer-Galati*

Ethnology 1612-1634
Demography 1635-1643

## A. ETHNOLOGY

### 1. General Works and Journals

1612. Agrarian Reform in Roumania and the Case of the Hungarian Optants in Translyvania before the League of Nations. Paris, Imprimerie du Palais, 1927. 320 p.

> Contains valuable data on the population problems of Transylvania.

1613. Clark, Charles U. Racial Aspects of Romania's Case. New York, Caxton Press, 1941. 50 p. Tables, maps.

> Succinct, if somewhat biased, survey of ethnographic problems in Transylvania.

1614. Dragomir, Silviu. The Ethnical Minorities in Transylvania. Geneva, Sonor, 1927. 129 p. Map.

> *See also* entry no. 1758.

> Brief but intelligent and objective discussion of the subject.

1615. Fischer, Emil. Die Herkunft der Rumänen; eine historisch-linguistisch-ethnographische Studie. Bamberg, Handels-Druckerei, 1904. 303 p. Plates, map. Bibliography: p. 211-216.

> Another scholarly inquiry into the origins and survival of the Romanians.

1616. Hall, Donald J. Rumanian Furrow. London, Methuen, 1933. 224 p. Illus., plates.

> Journalistic but with much insight into Romanian population and related political problems.

351

1617. Manuila, Alexandre.   Recherches sérologiques et anthropologiques chez les populations de la Roumanie et des régions voisines. Zürich, Arts Graphiques Orell Füssli, 1957. 357 p.
Emphasizes Romanian problems.

1618. Manuila, Sabin.   Ethnographic Atlas of Rumania, 1930. Atlas ethnographique de la Roumanie, 1930. Bucarest, State Print. Off., 1943. 1 v. Maps.
Excellent atlas. The maps, on the scale of 1:300,000, locate the population graphically by size and ethnic group.

1619. Manuila, Sabin.   La population de la Dobroudja. Bucarest, Institut Central de Statistique, 1939. 156 p. Maps, diagrs.
Basic study on the subject.

1620. Manuila, Sabin.   Studiu etnografic asupra populatiei României. (Ethnographic study on the population of Romania). Bucureşti, Editura Institutului Central de Statistică, 1940. 107 p. Maps, diagrs. Statistical tables: p. 53-103.
Brief but sound ethnographic study.

1621. Nicoresco, Paul.   La Roumanie nouvelle. Bucarest, Globus, 1924. 164 p. Map. Bibliography: p. 159-160.
Contains interesting data on the population of Greater Romania.

1622. Papahagi, Tache.   Images d'éthnographie roumaine, dacoroumaine et aroumaine. v. 2. Bucureşti, 1930. 227 p. Illus.
Important comparative survey.

1623. Revista de etnografie şi folclor (Review of ethnography and folklore). Anul 1–, 1956– Bucureşti, Editura Academiei Republicii Socialiste România. Bimonthly.
Excellent journal, strong on folklore. Contains illustrations, music, portraits.

1624. Ruffini, Mario.   Storia dei Romeni di Transilvania. Torino, La Stampa, 1942. 279 p.
Valuable for the study of the Romanian population of Transylvania.

1625. Vulpesco, Michel.   Les coutumes roumaines périodiques; études descriptives et comparées . . . Suivies d'une bibliographie générale de folklore roumain. Paris, Larose, 1927. 303 p. Illus., plates, music. Bibliography: p. 259-303.
Outstanding contribution on Romanian mores and traditions.

## 2. Specific Ethnic Groups

1626. Berkowitz, Joseph.   La question des Israélites en Roumanie. Étude de son histoire et de divers problèmes de droit qu'elle soulève. Paris, Jouve, 1923. 795 p. Bibliography: p. 9-18.

*See also* entry no. 110.

The most comprehensive monograph on the Jewish question in Romania.

1627. Constante, C. *and* Anton Golopenția, *eds.* Românii din Timoc; culegere de izvoare (The Romanians of Timoc; a collection of sources). București, Tipografia Bucovina, I. E. Torouțiu, 1943-1944. 3 v. in 2. Illus., maps, tables.

Valuable contribution on the problems of the Romanians of the Timoc region in the Banat.

1628. Hâciu, Anastase N. Aromânii. (The Aromunes). Focșani, 1936. 616 p.

Important, if not always scholarly, contributions to the history and civilization of the Aromunes.

1629. Nistor, Ion I. Românii și Rutenii în Bucovina; studiu istoric și statistic. (Romanians and Ruthenians in Bukovina; historical and statistical study). București, Socec și C. Sfetea, 1915. 209 p. Bibliography: p. xiii-xx.

*See also* entry no. 1772.

Basic study of population problems in the Bukovina.

1630. Popa-Lisseanu, Gheorghe. Sicules et Roumains; un procès de dénationalisation. Bucarest, Socec, 1933. 80 p. Maps.

Important contribution on the Szekler minority in Romania.

1631. Potra, George. Contribuțiuni la istoricul țiganilor din România. (Contributions to the history of the Gypsies in Romania). București, Fundația Regele Carol I, 1939. 376 p. Plates. Bibliography: p. 332-343.

The only important study on the Gypsies in Romania.

1632. Teutsch, Friedrich. Die Siebenbürger Sachsen in Vergangenheit und Gegenwart. 2d enl. ed. Hermannstadt, W. Krafft, 1924. 367 p. Bibliography: p. 361-365.

The best contribution on the history and civilization of the Transylvanian Saxons.

1633. Wlislocki, Heinrich von. Volksglaube und Volksbrauch der Siebenbürger Sachsen. Berlin, E. Felber, 1893. 212 p. Bibliography: p. xi-xiii. (Beiträge zur Volks- und Völkerkunde, 1)

Dated but important work on the Transylvanian Saxons.

1634. Zaharieff, Malomir. Les minorités bulgares en Roumanie. (Conditions d'une entente bulgaro-roumaine). Paris, Domat-Montchrestien, 1940. 99 p.

Superficial but the only study on the Bulgarian minorities in Romania.

## B. DEMOGRAPHY

### 1. Basic Sources, Methodology, General and Special Aspects

1635. Buletinul demografic al României (Romanian demographic bulletin). 1932– Bucureşti, Institutul Central de Statistică. Monthly. Illus. (maps), tables, diagrs.
> Contains invaluable demographic data.

1636. Manuila, Sabin, *and* D. C. Georgescu.   Populaţia României. Cu o anexă cuprinzând populaţia capitalei după datele recensământului general al populaţiei din 29 Decembrie 1930 (The population of Romania. With an appendix comprising the population of the capital according to the data of the general census of population of December 29, 1930). Bucureşti, Imprimeria Naţională, 1938. 311 p. Illus., maps, diagrs.
> Excellent demographic study.

1637. Murgoci, G.   La population de la Bessarabie; étude démographique. . . . Paris, 1920. 80 p. Maps, tables, diagrs.
> Primarily a demographic survey.

1638. Rumania. *Direcţia Centrală de Statistică.*   Recensămîntul populaţiei din 21 Februarie 1956 (Population census of 21 February 1956). Bucureşti, 1959-1961. 3 v. Maps, diagrs.
> *See also* entry no. 1845.
> Essential compilation of statistical data.

1639. Rumania. *Institutul Central de Statistică*   Anuarul demografic; mişcarea populaţiei României (Demographic yearbook; the movement of Romanian population). 1871– Bucureşti. Annual.
> Basic annual compilation.

1640. Rumania. *Institutul Central de Statistică.*   Recensământul general al populaţiei României din 29 Decemvrie 1930 (The general population census of Romania of 29 December 1930). Edited by Sabin Manuila. Bucureşti, Editura Institutului Central de Statistică, 1938-1941. 10 v. Maps, diagrs.
> The fundamental work on the Romanian population in the interwar period.

1641. Rumania. *Institutul Central de Statistică.*   Recensământul general al României din 1941, 6 Aprilie, date sumare provizorii (The general census of Romania of 1941, 6 April; provisional summary data). Bucureşti, 1944. 300 p.
> Only of statistical value.

## 2. Census Interpretations and Analyses

1642. Colescu, Leonida.   Analiza rezultatelor recensământului general al populaţiei României de la 1899 (Analysis of the results of the general census of the Romanian population of 1899). Bucureşti, Institutul Central de Statistică, 1944. 141 p. Port., fold. col. maps, diagr., forms. (Rumania. Institutul Central de Statistică. Retipăriri, 1)

   Valuable demographic analysis.

1643. Rumania. *Direcţia Centrală de Statistică.*   Recensămîntul populaţiei din 21 Februarie 1956; structura social-economică a populaţiei: populaţia activă, populaţia pasivă; grupe sociale; ramuri, subramuri de activitate (Population census of 21 February 1956; socioeconomic structure of the population: active population, passive population, social groups; branches and sub-branches of activity). Bucureşti, 1960. 1021 p.

   *See also* entry no. 1887.

   Exhaustive compilation of statistical data.

# 38

# hIStORY

by Stephen Fischer-Galati

Bibliography and Historiography 1644-1646
General Surveys 1647-1655
Special Questions 1656-1659
Origins through 1848 1660-1670
1848-1917 1671-1676
Since 1918 1677-1683

## A. BIBLIOGRAPHY AND HISTORIOGRAPHY

1644. Cernovodeanu, P., *and* P. Simionescu. Essai de bibliographie selective concernant l'histoire de Roumanie. Revue roumaine d'histoire, 1965, no. 3: 641-664; 1966, no. 3: 547-572.

1645. Henry, Paul. Histoire roumaine. Revue historique (Paris), v. 175, Nov.-Dec. 1935: 486-537; v. 194, Jan.-Mar. 1944: 42-65; v. 194, Apr.-June 1944: 132-150; v. 194, July-Sept. 1944: 233-252.
Comprehensive, annotated survey of modern Romanian historiography.

1646. Cercetarea istoriei Romîniei în anii puterii populare (1947-1962) (Research in Romanian history during the years of the people's regime, 1947-1962). Studii; revista de istorie, v. 15, 1962, no. 6: 1355-1778.
Critical annotated review of the principal publications on Romanian history during the period 1947-1962.

## B. GENERAL SURVEYS

1647. Academie Republicii Populare Romîne. Istoria Romîniei (The history of Romania). Bucureşti, Editura Academiei, 1960-1964. 4 v. Illus., plates, maps, diagrs., facsims., plans, tables, bibliographies.
The fundamental Marxist work on the history of Romania.

1648. Din istoria Transilvaniei (From the history of Transylvania). 2d ed. Bucureşti, Editura Academiei Republicii Populare Romîne, 1961. 2 v. Illus., col. plates, ports., maps, facsims., bibliographical footnotes.
A noteworthy Marxist history of Transylvania, written by Constantin C. Daicoviciu and others. The first volume of a third edition was issued by the same publisher in 1963.

1649. Giurescu, Constantin C.    Istoria Românilor (History of the Romanians). Bucureşti, Fundaţia Regală pentru Literatură şi Artă, 1940-1944. 4 v. Illus., ports., maps, facsims.
The best multivolume history of the Romanians through the 18th century. The treatment of the 19th and 20th centuries is perfunctory.

1650. Giurescu, Constantin C.    Istoria Românilor din cele mai vechi timpuri până la moartea regelui Ferdinand (History of the Romanians from the oldest times to the death of King Ferdinand). 2d ed. Bucureşti, Cugetarea-Georgescu Delafras S. A., 1944. 543 p.
An excellent brief history of the Romanians.

1651. Iorga, Nicolae.    Geschichte des rumänisches Volkes im Rahmen seiner Staatsbildungen. Gotha, F. A. Perthes, 1905. 2 v.
The standard account of Romanian history in German. Excellent early Iorga.

1652. Iorga, Nicolae.    Histoire des Roumains et de la romanité orientale. Bucarest, 1937-1944. 9 v. Plates, ports., map, plans, facsims.
Iorga's *chef d'œuvre*, reflecting his historic genius and prejudices.

1653. Makkai, Laszlo.    Histoire de Transylvanie. Paris, Presses universitaires de France, 1946. 382 p. Plates, ports., maps.
Intelligent survey of the history of Transylvania.

1654. Seton-Watson, Robert W.    A History of the Roumanians; from Roman Times to the Completion of Unity. Cambridge, England, Cambridge University Press, 1934. 596 p. Ports., map.
The basic history of the Romanians in English. The account of the history of the Romanians in Transylvania is particularly valuable.

1655. Xenopol, Alexandru D.    Istoria Romînilor din Dacia Traiană. (History of the Romanians from Trajan's Dacia). Iaşi, Fraţii Şaraga, 1896. 12 v. in 3. Port.
The first "modern" history of the Romanians by the founder of "modern" Romanian historiography.

## C. SPECIAL QUESTIONS

1656. Bezviconi, Gheorghe G.    Boierimea Moldovei dintre Prut şi Nistru

(The boyars of Moldavia between the Prut and the Dniester). Bucureşti, Fundaţia Regele Carol I, 1940-1943. 2 v.
Valuable contribution to the social history of Moldavia.

1657. Brătianu, George I.   Une enigme et un miracle historique: le peuple roumain. 2d ed. Bucarest, 1942. 226 p. Plates, map.
One of the basic studies of the problem of the "disappearance" of the Romanians.

1658. Daicoviciu, Constantin.   Problema continuităţii în Dacia (The problem of continuity in Dacia). Cluj, 1940. 72 p.
Learned account of a controversial subject.

1659. Prokopowitsch, Erich.   Die rumänische Nationalbewegung in der Bukowina und der Dako-Romanismus. Graz, Köln, Böhlau, 1965. 192 p. Bibliography: p. 171-175. (Studien zur Geschichte der österreichisch-ungarischen Monarchie, Bd. 3)
See also entry no. 1773.
Systematic study of the nationality problems of Bukovina, based largely on secondary sources.

## D. ORIGINS THROUGH 1848

1660. Academia Republicii Populare Romîne. *Institutul de Istorie.*   Studii cu privire la Ştefan cel Mare (Studies concerning Stephen the Great). Bucureşti, Editura Academiei, 1956. 241 p.
Collection of essays stressing socioeconomic and political forces affecting the course of Romanian history in the 15th century.

1661. Andreescu, Constantin I., *and* Constantin A. Stoide.   Ştefăniţă Lupu, domn al Moldovei (1659-1661) (Ştefăniţă Lupu, Ruler of Moldavia [1659-1661]). Bucureşti, Fundaţia Regele Carol I, 1938. 198 p.
A basic work on medieval Romania.

1662. Berza, M., *ed.*   Cultura moldovenească in timpul lui Ştefan cel Mare; culegere de studii (Moldavian culture in the time of Stephen the Great; collection of studies). Bucureşti, Editura Academiei, 1964. 682 p. Bibliography: p. 641-675.
See also entry no. 1966.
Distinguished collection of essays on the culture of Moldavia in the 15th century.

1663. Ciorănescu, Alexandre.   Domnia lui Mihnea III [Mihail Radu] 1658-1659 (The rule of Mihnea III [Mihail Radu] 1658-1659). Bucureşti, 1936. 181 p.
Outstanding contribution to medieval Romanian history.

1664. Filitti, Ioan (Jean) C.   Les Principautés roumaines sous l'occupation russe (1828-1834): Le règlement organique; étude de droit public et

d'histoire diplomatique. Bucarest, Imprimerie de l'Indépendance Roumaine, 1904. 285 p.
> Detailed study of the period 1828-1834 with special emphasis on the "constitutional experiment."

1665. Oţetea, Andrei.   Tudor Vladimirescu şi mişcarea eteristă în Ţările Româneşti, 1821-1822 (Tudor Vladimirescu and the Hetairist movement in the Romanian Provinces, 1821-1822). Bucureşti, 1945. 411 p. Illus., ports. (Institutul de Studii şi Cercetări Balcanice. Seria istorică, nr. 5)
> Distinguished analysis of the revolt of 1821 emphasizing, rightly, the socioeconomic aspects of Vladimirescu's movement and actions.

1666. Panaitescu, P. P.   Dimitrie Cantemir, viaţa şi opera (Dimitrie Cantemir, life and work). Bucureşti, Editura Academiei Republicii Populare Romîne, 1958. 265 p. Port., illus. (Biblioteca istorică, 3)
> Excellent monographic study of the rule of Dimitrie Cantemir and his relations with Russia.

1667. Panaitescu, P. P.   Mihai Viteazul (Michael the Brave). Bucureşti, Fundaţia Regele Carol I, 1936. 269 p. Map.
> Brilliant analysis of the character of the rule of Michael the Brave and European diplomacy at the turn of the 17th century.

1668. Pârvan, Vasile.   Dacia; an Outline of the Early Civilizations of the Carpatho-Danubian Countries. Cambridge, The University Press, 1928. 216 p. Plates, map.
> Classic study of the subject by the leading student of early Romanian history.

1669. Sârbu, Ion.   Mateiu-Vodă Băsărabas auswärtige Beziehungen 1632-1654. Leipzig, Friedrich, 1899. 356 p.
> Distinguished study on Romanian diplomatic relations during the Thirty Years' War. A major contribution to the diplomatic history of Europe in the 17th century.

1670. Ursu, Ion.   Ştefan cel Mare, domn al Moldovei dela 12 Aprilie 1457 până la 2 Iulie 1504 (Stephen the Great, Ruler of Moldavia from 12 April 1457 to 2 July 1504). Bucureşti, Institutul de Arte Grafice Antonescu, 1925. 461 p. Illus. (Biblioteca istorică, 2)
> The standard biography of Stephen the Great and his times.

## E. 1848-1917

1671. Henry, Paul.   L'abdication du prince Cuza et l'avènement de la dynastie de Hohenzollern au trône de la Roumanie; documents diplomatiques. Paris, Alcan, 1930. 485 p. Bibliographical footnotes.
> Excellent collection of primary sources; admirable historical in-

troduction to the problems connected with Cuza's replacement by Carol of Hohenzollern.

1672. Iorga, Nicolae.   Războiul pentru Independența României; acțiuni diplomatice și stări de spirit (The War for Romanian Independence; diplomatic actions and frames of mind). București, Cultura Națională, 1927. 242 p. Plates, port.

Best account, à faute de mieux, of the Romanian War for Independence, 1877-1878.

1673. Oțetea, Andrei, and others.   Studii privind Unirea Principatelor (Studies concerning the unification of the Principalities). București, Editura Academiei Republicii Populare Romîne, 1960. 542 p. Map, coats of arms, tables, bibliographical footnotes.

A critical Marxist review of the problems related to the union of Moldavia and Wallachia.

1674. Pătrășcanu, Lucrețiu D.   Un veac de frământări sociale, 1821-1907 (A century of social unrest, 1821-1907). București, Editura "Cartea Rusă," 1945. 295 p. Illus., ports., facsims.

See also entry no. 1718.

Brilliant interpretation of the sociopolitical problems of 19th century Romania by a leading Marxist intellectual.

1675. Riker, Thad W.   The Making of Roumania; a Study of an International Problem, 1856-1866. London, Oxford University Press, 1931. 592 p. Illus., map. Bibliography: p. 567-572.

See also entry no. 1719.

The classic study of the subject.

1676. Sturdza, Dimitrie A., ed.   Charles Ier, roi de Roumanie; chroniques, actes, documents. Bucarest, C. Göbl, 1899-1904. 2 v. Port., facsim.

Essential data for the study of the rule of Carol I.

## F. SINCE 1918

1677. Fischer-Galati, Stephen.   The New Rumania: From People's Democracy to Socialist Republic. Cambridge, M.I.T. Press, 1967. 126 p. (Studies in International Communism, 10)

See also entry no. 1806.

Basic study of the political evolution of Romania since 1944. See also the same author's The Socialist Republic of Rumania (Baltimore, Johns Hopkins Press, 1969, 113 p.).

1678. Hillgruber, Andreas.   Hitler, König Carol und Marschall Antonescu; die deutsch-rumänischen Beziehungen, 1938-1944. Wiesbaden, F. Steiner, 1954. 382 p. Ports., map. Bibliography: p. 357-366. (Veröffentlichungen des Instituts für europäische Geschichte, Mainz, Bd. 5)

*See also* entry no. 1790.
Illuminating synthesis of German-Roumanian relations based primarily on original German sources.

1679. Liveanu, V.    1918 (i.e., O mie nouă sute optsprezece); din istoria luptelor revoluționare din Romînia (1918; from the history of revolutionary struggles in Romania). București, Editura Politică, 1960. 678 p.
Detailed account of the sociopolitical unrest generated in Romania by the Bolshevik Revolution in 1918.

1680. Mitrany, David.    The Land and the Peasant in Rumania; the War and Agrarian Reform (1917-1921). London, H. Milford, Oxford University Press; New Haven, Yale University Press, 1930. New York, Greenwood Press, 1968. 627 p. Maps, diagrs. Bibliography: p. 594-611.
*See also* entries no. 1835 *and* 1895.
Exhaustive study of the problems of the peasant and of agricultural Romania by a distinguished student of Romanian society and politics.

1681. Partidul Muncitoresc Romîn. *Comitetul Central. Institutul de Istorie a Partidului.*    Contribuții la studiul influenței Marii Revoluții Socialiste din Octombrie în Romînia (Contributions to the study of the influence of the Great October Socialist Revolution in Romania). București, Editura de Stat pentru Literatură Politică, 1957. 366 p. Tables, bibliographical footnotes.
Standard late-Stalinist interpretation of the impact of the Bolshevik revolution in Romania. Interesting in terms of more recent accounts of Russo-Romanian relations.

1682. Pătrășcanu, Lucrețiu D.    Sous trois dictatures. Paris, J. Vitiano, 1946. 326 p.
Penetrating analysis of Romanian politics and power elite primarily during the interwar years. A translation of *Sub trei dictaturi* (București, Forum, 1945, 256 p.).

1683. Roberts, Henry L.    Rumania; Political Problems of an Agrarian State. New Haven, Yale University Press, 1951. Hamden, Conn., Archon Books, 1969. 414 p. Map. Bibliography: p. 381-399.
*See also* entries no. 1747, 1856, 1896, *and* 1990.
Excellent account of Romanian political and socioeconomic developments in the 20th century.

# 39

# the state

## A. LAW

### 1. Legal History*

*by Keith Hitchins*

1684. Adunarea izvoarelor vechiului drept romînesc scris (The collection of sources for Old Romanian written law). Bucureşti, 1957–

A series of critical editions which are indispensable for the study of Romanian society and institutions before 1865. Each volume is provided with an introductory essay and the necessary scholarly apparatus. The volumes which have appeared so far are:

Legiuirea Caragea (The law code of Caragea). Bucureşti, Editura Academiei Republicii Populare Romîne, 1955. 336 p. A general law code for Wallachia, promulgated in 1818.

* The most recent editions are listed here because they are more readily available.

362

Pravilniceasca condică, 1780 (The code of laws, 1780). Bucureşti, Editura Academiei Republicii Populare Romîne, 1957. 268 p. Dispositions relating to legal procedures and the organization of courts in Wallachia.

Sobornicescul hrisov, 1785, 1835, 1839 (The charter of the Council, 1785, 1835, 1839). Bucureşti, Editura Academiei Republicii Populare Romîne, 1958. 110 p. One of the most important pieces of legislation in the 18th century, concerned with the sale, donation, and inheritance of land in Moldavia.

Codul Calimah (The Calimah code). Bucureşti, Editura Academiei Republicii Populare Romîne, 1958. 1016 p. Promulgated in 1817 in Moldavia and dealing primarily with questions of civil law.

Manualul juridic al lui Andronachi Donici (The juridical manual of Andronachi Donici). Bucureşti, Editura Academiei Republicii Populare Romîne, 1959. 183 p. A handbook for jurists rather than an official code and widely used in Moldavia between 1814 and 1865.

Cartea romînească de învăţătura, 1646 (The Romanian book of instructions, 1646). Bucureşti, Editura Academiei Republicii Populare Romîne, 1961. 431 p. The first known Romanian lay code of laws.

Îndreptarea legii, 1652 (The guide to the law, 1652). Bucureşti, Editura Academiei Republicii Populare Romîne, 1962. 1013 p. The first printed lay code of laws in Wallachia.

1685. **Alexandrescu, Dimitri,** *ed.*    Explicaţiunea teoretică şi practică a dreptului civil român în comparaţiune cu legile vechi şi cu principalele legislaţiuni streine (A theoretical and practical interpretation of Romanian civil law in comparison with old laws and the principal foreign legislation). Iaşi, 1886-1915. 11 v.

A systematic and exhaustive commentary on the Romanian civil code of 1866. Especially useful to the historian of Romanian institutions.

1686. **Arion, Dinu C.**    Le "Nomos Georgikós" et la régime de la terre dans l'ancien droit roumain jusqu'à la réforme de Constantin Mavrocordat (1733-1769). Paris, Librairie de Recueil Sirey, 1929. 210 p. Bibliography: p. 205-208.

A concise exposition of the influence of Byzantine agrarian law on Romanian legislation up to the middle of the 18th century.

1687. **Berechet, Ştefan.**    Legătura dintre dreptul bizantin şi românesc (The relation between Byzantine and Romanian law). v. 1, part 1, Izvoarele (Texts). Vaslui, 1937. 376 p.

A useful introduction to one of the fundamental problems of medieval Romanian law. For a more recent discussion *see*: Gheorghe Cronţ, "Dreptul bizantin în ţările romîne. Pravila Moldovei din 1646" (Byzantine law in the Romanian lands. The law code of Moldavia of 1646) in *Studii; revista de istorie*, v. 11, 1958, no. 5: 33-59.

1688. Lévy-Ullmann, Henri, *and* Boris Mirkine-Guetzévitch, *eds.*    La vie juridique des peuples. Tome 4. Roumanie. Paris, Librairie Delagrave, 1933. 452 p.

> A valuable series of articles surveying Romanian public and private law between the two world wars written by Romanian specialists.

1689. Peretz, Ion.    Curs de istoria dreptului român (A course in the history of Romanian law). Bucureşti, 1926-1931. 4 v. in 5.

> The best general survey for the period before the introduction of the Civil Code of 1866. Equally useful is Stefan Berechet's *Istoria vechiului drept românesc* (A history of Old Romanian law), v. 1 (Iasi, 1934, 622 p.).

1690. Rumania. *Laws, statutes, etc.*    Acte şi legiuiri privitoare la chestia ţărănească (Acts and legislation concerning the peasant question). Bucureşti, Atelierele grafice Socec, 1907-1908. 12 v.

> A monumental collection of laws, proposals and debates from the earliest times to the beginning of the 20th century. Series two covers the reign of Carol I and is indispensable for any investigation of the agrarian problem in modern Romania.

1691. Rumania. *Laws, statutes, etc.*    Codul general al României (Codurile, legile, şi regulamentele uzuale în vigoare) 1856-1943 (The general code of Romania [codes, laws, and ordinary statutes in force] 1856-1943). Bucureşti, Impr. Centralâ, 1907-1944. 30 v.

> The most complete collection for the period covered.

1692. Şotropa, Valeriu.    Introducere şi bibliografie la istoria dreptului român (An introduction to and a bibliography for the history of Romanian law). Cluj, 1937. 232 p.

> An indispensable tool, systematically arranged and annotated.

## 2. The Legal System

*by Virgiliu Stoicoiu*

### a. Bibliographies and Periodicals

1693. Revista română de drept (Romanian law review). 1945– Bucureşti. Monthly.

> Title varies: 1945-1966, *Justiţia nouă*. Published by the Association of Jurists of the Socialist Republic of Romania. Includes articles, digested and annotated court decisions, and tables of contents in Romanian, Russian, and French.

1694. Revue roumaine des sciences sociales. Série de sciences juridiques. 1957– Bucarest. Semiannual.

> Published under the auspices of the Academy of the Socialist Republic of Romania. Includes articles and annotated court deci-

sions (usually the work of members of the Institute for Legal Research), as well as book reviews and current bibliography.

1695. Stoicoiu, Virgiliu. Legal Sources and Bibliography of Romania. New York, F. A. Praeger, 1964. 237 p. (Praeger Publications in Russian History and World Communism, no. 24)

A selective legal bibliography chiefly of Romanian publications (with English translations) on general and special topics. Coverage from the 17th century up to 1964. Books and articles in English, French, German, Italian, Russian, and Spanish are also listed. A list of laws in force on January 1, 1963, and indexes of authors, titles, and subjects (before and after 1948) are also included.

1696. Studii și cercetări juridice (Studies and legal research). 1956– București. Quarterly.

Published under the auspices of the Academy of the Socialist Republic of Romania. Includes articles and annotated court decisions (usually the work of members of the Institute for Legal Research), as well as book reviews and current bibliography.

#### b. Primary Sources of Law

1697. Buletinul oficial al Republicii Socialiste România (Official gazette of the Socialist Republic of Romania). 1949– București.

Published in three parts: I. Decrees, laws, resolutions, ordinances; II. Parliamentary records; III. Official communiqués and private legal announcements. Title varies: 1949-1956, *Buletinul oficial al Republicii Populare Române*; 1956-1965, *Buletinul oficial al marii adunări naționale a Republicii Populare Romîne*.

See also: *Colecție de legi, decrete, hotărîri și alte acte normative* (Collection of laws, decrees, resolutions and other regulations) (1949–, București, bimonthly), published by the Ministry of Justice, and *Colecție de hotarîri și dispoziții ale Consiliului de Miniștrii al Republicii Populare Romîne* (Collection of the resolutions of the Council of Ministers of the Romanian People's Republic) (1951–, București, weekly).

1698. Culegere de decizii ale Tribunalului Suprem (Collection of the decisions of the Supreme Court). 1954– București. Annual.

Contains rulings and selected cases and decisions of the Supreme Tribunal since August 1, 1952, arranged according to comprehensive topics. See also: *Repertoriu de practică judiciară* (Summary of leading court decisions), compiled by Camil Gall and Nicolae Hogas (București, Editura Științifică, 1963, 595 p.), for digested court decisions in alphabetical order from November 1, 1957 to April 1, 1962 and notes on "wrong" decisions; and *Repertoriu alfabetic de practică judiciară* (Summary of leading court decisions arranged in alphabetical order), compiled by Adrian D. Dimitriu and Camil Gall (București, Editura Științifică, 1958, 400 p.), for digested decisions formerly published in *Culegere de decizii ale plenului și colegiilor Tribunalului Suprem* (August 1, 1952 to December 31,

1954) and in the periodicals *Legalitatea populară* and *Justiţa nouă* (1945 to 1957).

### c. Codes and Textbooks

1699. Codul civil; text oficial cu modificările pînă la data de 15 Iulie 1958 (Civil code; official text with all amendments up to July 15, 1958). Bucureşti, Editura Ştiinţifică, 1958. 510 p.

The 1958 version of the Civil Code of December 1, 1865. Based on volume 1 of *Legislaţia civilă uzuală* (Civil legislation in every-day use) (Bucureşti, Editura Ştiinţifică, 1956, 405 p.), published by the Ministry of Justice. Old provisions should be considered abrogated when in conflict with the new legislation. Explanatory footnotes on the amended provisions are included.

*See also* Francisc Deak's *Drept civil; teoria contractelor speciale* (Civil law; the theory on special contracts) (Bucureşti, Editura Didactică şi Pedagogică, 1963, 311 p.), published under the auspices of the Ministry of Education, a study on the new concept of contracts supported by up-to-date court decisions and legal writings; and Scarlet Şerbănescu's *Codul familiei adnotat* (Family code annotated) (Bucureşti, Editura Ştiinţifică, 1963, 413 p.), with comments and pertinent court decisions on each article. English edition: *The Family Code in the Rumanian People's Republic* (Bucharest, Foreign Languages Publishing House, 1958, 106 p.).

1700. Codul de procedură civilă; text oficial cu modificările pînă la data de 1 Iunie 1958, urmat de o anexă de acte legislative (Code of civil procedure; official text with all amendments up to June 1, 1958, followed by an annex with legal enactments). Bucureşti, Editura Ştiinţifică, 1958. 349 p.

The 1958 version of the Code of Civil Procedure of 1948, published by the Ministry of Justice. See also *Codul de procedură civilă adnotat* (The code of civil procedure annotated), edited by Graţian Porumb (Bucureşti, Editura Ştiinţifică, 1960-1962, 2 v.), for comments on each individual article; Ilie Stoenescu and Arthur Hilsenrad's *Procesul civil în R.P.R.* (Civil proceedings in the Romanian People's Republic) (Bucureşti, 1966, 496 p.), a textbook on the most important court procedures in civil matters; and A. Hilsenrad, D. Rizeanu, and C. Zirra's *Notariatul de stat* (State notary) (Bucureşti, Editura Stiinţifică, 1964, 307 p.), a study on special notarial procedures (civil execution, inheritance matters, notarizing documents).

1701. Codul muncii; text oficial cu modificările pînă la data de 1 Aprilie 1961 (Labor code; official text with all amendments up to April 1, 1961). Bucureşti, Editura Ştiinţifică, 1961. 59 p.

The 1961 version of the Labor Code of 1950. See also *Legislaţia uzuală a muncii* (Labor legislation in every-day use), compiled by L. Miller (Bucureşti, Editura Ştiinţifică, 1961, 685 p., illus., forms), for labor legislation and rulings of the Supreme Tribunal concerning various problems in labor law.

1702. Codul penal; text oficial cu modificările pînă la data de 1 Decembrie 1960, urmat de o anexă de legi penale speciale (Criminal code; official text with all amendments up to December 1, 1960, followed by an annex including some special criminal legislation). Bucureşti, Editura Ştiinţifică, 1961. 427 p.

> The 1960 version of the Criminal Code of February 27, 1948. All abrogated provisions are given in footnotes. *See also* Ion Oancea's *Drept penal; partea generală* (The criminal law; general part) (Bucureşti, Editura Didactică şi Pedagogică, 1965, 403 p.), a study on general principles of criminal law with reference to particular decisions of the Supreme Tribunal; *Infracţiuni contra avutului obştesc* (Crimes against socialist property) by Vintila Dongoroz and others, published under the auspices of the Institute for Legal Research of the Academy of the Romanian People's Republic (Bucuresti, Editura Academiei R.P.R., 1963, 481 p., bibliographical footnotes), for the interpretation of criminal provisions dealing with the protection of socialist property (particularly useful because it interprets the new crimes introduced by the communist régime and takes issue with opposing views); and *Codul de procedură penală; text oficial cu modificarile până la data de 1 Decembrie 1960 urmat de o anexă de acte legislative* (Code of criminal procedure; official text with all amendments up to December 1, 1960, followed by an annex including various laws) (Bucureşti, Editura Ştiinţifică, 1960, 374 p.), the 1960 version of the 1948 Code of Criminal Procedure.

1703. Cosma, Doru. Dreptul de folosinţă asupra locuinţelor (Statutory limits upon the use of houses). Bucureşti, Editura Ştiinţifică, 1963. 349 p. Bibliographical footnotes.

> A study on special legislation dealing with limitations in the allotment of living space to each person in the Romanian People's Republic, as enforced by the courts. See also *Legislaţia locativă adnotată* (Housing legislation annotated), compiled by Vasile Patulea (Bucureşti, Editura Ştiinţifică, 1963, 166 p.), for court decisions, notes, and bibliography on each article of Decree No. 78 of 1952, dealing with limitations on living space.

1704. Ionescu, Dionisie, *and others*. Dezvoltarea constituţională a Statului Român (The constitutional development of the Romanian state). Bucureşti, Editura Ştiinţifică, 1957. 597 p. Bibliography: p. 566-593. *See also* entry no. 1739.

> A study of the constitutions and the economic, legal, social, and political order, from the time of the Romanian Principalities up to and including the period of the Romanian People's Republic. Includes an extensive bibliography in Romanian and other languages.
>
> See also: *Constituţia Republicii Populare Române* (Constitution of the Romanian People's Republic) (Bucureşti, 1948, 24 p.) for the text of the 1948 constitution; *Konstitutsiia Rumynskoi Narodnoi Respubliki* (Constitution of the Romanian People's Republic) (Moskva, Gosudarstvennoe izdatel'stvo iuridicheskoi literatury, 1952, 35 p.) for the Russian translation of the 1948 constitution;

*Constitution of the Rumanian People's Republic as Amended up to March 10, 1958* (Bucharest, Foreign Languages Publishing House, 1958, 78 p.) for the English translation of the 1952 constitution; *Verfassung der Rumänischen Volksrepublik. Stand vom 31. März 1960* (Berlin, VEB Deutscher Zentralverlag, 1960, 46 p.) for the German translation of the 1952 constitution as in force as of March 31, 1960. An English publication of the 1965 constitution is available in *Constitutions of the Communist Party-States* by Jan F. Triska (Stanford, The Hoover Institution, 1968, p. 378-394).

1705. Principii de drept (Principles of law). Bucureşti, Editura Ştiinţifică, 1959. 980 p.

> Published by the Ministry of Justice. A compendium by various legal writers explaining the new principles and procedures as found in the laws, regulations and decisions of the Supreme Tribunals of the Romanian People's Republic and the USSR. See also *Studii juridice* (Legal studies) (Bucureşti, Editura Academiei R.P.R., 1960, 587 p., bibliographical footnotes), published by the Institute for Legal Research of the Academy of the Romanian People's Republic, for various aspects of administrative law, criminal law, inheritance law, government contracts, and social security.

1706. Rumania. *Ministerul Justiţiei.* Legislaţia gospodăriilor agricole colective şi a întovărăşirilor agricole (Legislation concerning collective farms and peasant household associations). Bucureşti, Editura de Stat pentru Literatură Economică şi Juridică, 1956. 559 p.

> Collection of laws and regulations dealing with the organization and management of the collective farms since the land reform of 1945.

1707. Stănescu, V. Manual de drept financiar (Manual of financial law). Bucureşti, Editura Didactică şi Pedagogică, 1963. 2 v.

> A study of the control of the socialist economic system, the State budget and financial institutions and their functioning in the Romanian People's Republic. Published under the auspices of the Ministry of Education and the University of Bucharest.
>
> See also: *Legislaţia financiară a R.P.R. Textele oficiale cu modificarile până la data de 1 Septembrie 1957* (The financial legislation of the Romanian People's Republic. Official texts with amendments up to September 1, 1957), published by the Ministry of Justice (Bucureşti, Editura Ştiinţifică, 1957, 599 p.); *Călăuza economică şi financiară. Legi, regulamente, hotărâri ale Consiliului de Miniştrii, decizii, instrucţiuni, normative, circulări* (Economic and financial guide. Laws, regulations, resolutions of the Council of Ministers, ordinances, instructions, norms, circulars) (Bucureşti, Editura de Stat, 1948–).

1708. Vîntu, I., *and others.* Sfaturile populare, organe locale ale puterii de stat în R.P.R. (People's councils, the local agencies of state power

in the Romanian People's Republic). Bucureşti, Editura Academiei R.P.R., 1964. 450 p. Bibliographical footnotes.
*See also* entry no. 1756.
   Published under the auspices of the Institute for Legal Research of the Academy of the Romanian People's Republic. An analytical presentation of the establishment, jurisdiction, and power of the local soviets.

## B. GOVERNMENT AND POLITICS

*by Keith Hitchins*

### 1. Up to 1821

1709. Buzescu, Alexandru Al.   Domina în Ţările Române până la 1866 (The office of Prince in the Romanian lands up to 1866). Bucureşti, Tiparul "Cartea Românească," 1943. 333 p.
   Traces the political and legal significance of the prince in the history of Moldavia and Wallachia. An important synthesis, since the prince was a major force in Romanian constitutional development.

1710. Costăchel, V., P. P. Panaitescu, *and* A. Cazacu. Viaţa feudală în Ţara Romînească şi Moldova (sec. XV-XVII) (Feudal life in Wallachia and Moldavia, 15th to 17th century). Bucureşti, Editura Ştiinţifică, 1957. 559 p. Bibliography: p. 547-556.
   A comprehensive survey. Valuable chapters on the prince, the feudal domain, and the administration of justice.

1711. Crestomaţie pentru studiul istoriei statului şi dreptului R.P.R. (A chrestomathy for the study of the history of the state and law of the Romanian People's Republic). Bucureşti, Editura de Stat pentru Literatura Economică şi Juridică, 1955-1963. 3 v.
   An extensive collection of sources from ancient times to 1848. A topical arrangement facilitates the study of the evolution of administrative and juridical institutions. Carefully prepared indices permit the fullest use of this material.

1712. Giurescu, Constantin C.   Contribuţiuni la studiul marilor dregătorii în secolele XIV şi XV (Contributions to the study of high offices in the 14th and 15th centuries). *In*: Rumania. Comisia Istorică. Buletinul (Bucureşti), v. 5, 1927: 1-176.
   A detailed study of public administration in Moldavia and Wallachia in the early feudal period.

1713. Ştefănescu, Ştefan.   Bănia în Ţara Românească (The office of Ban in Wallachia). Bucureşti, Editura Ştiinţifică, 1965. 246 p.
   Based on a vast bibliography of printed sources and secondary works, it examines the origins and development of this institution in

the 15th and 16th centuries. It is useful for the general study of administrative and military history, since the Ban was a combination of provincial governor and general.

1714. Vîrtosu, Emil.   Titulatura domnilor și asocierea la domnie în Țara Romînească și Moldova (pînă în secolul al XVI-lea) (The titles of the princes and the practice of association in ruling in Wallachia and Moldavia through the 16th century). București, Editura Academiei Republicii Populare Romîne, 1960. 314 p. (Biblioteca istorică, 9)

Much broader in scope than the title suggests, it treats in detail the attributes of princely power, the laws of succession, and the principles of feudal sovereignty.

## 2. 1821-1866

1715. East, William G.   The Union of Moldavia and Wallachia — 1859. Cambridge, The University Press, 1929. 220 p. Bibliography: p. 205-211.

A concise, scholarly account. It may be supplemented by a valuable collection of sources, *Documente privind Unirea Principatelor* (Documents relating to the union of the Principalities), edited by Andrei Oțetea (București, Editura Academiei Republicii Populare Romîne, 1959-1963, 3 v.). The introductions to volumes 1 and 2 by Dan Berindei and to volume 3 by Cornelia C. Bodea describe in detail the internal political situation in both principalities between 1854 and 1859. Russia's role in the union of the Principalities is described by V. N. Vinogradov, *Rossiia i ob"edinenie rumynskikh kniazhestv* (Russia and the union of the Rumanian Principalities) (Moscow, Izd-vo Akademii nauk SSSR, 1961, 329 p. Bibliography: p. 317-326); and by Barbara Jelavich, *Russia and the Rumanian National Cause, 1858-1859* (Bloomington, Ind., 1959, 169 p. Indiana University Publications, Slavic and East European Series, v. 17. Bibliography: p. 160-162). Vinogradov, on the basis of Russian archive material and printed sources, argues that Russia's contribution to the union was paramount. Jelavich suggests that the Russians were less than enthusiastic about it.

1716. Filitti, Ioan C.   Frământările politice și sociale în principatele române de la 1821 la 1828 (Political and social unrest in the Romanian Principalities from 1821 to 1828). București, Cartea Românească, 1932. 192 p.

The most detailed treatment of internal political conditions for the period. The same author's *Principatele române de la 1828 la 1834* (The Romanian Principalities from 1828 to 1834) (București, Inst. de Arte Grafice "Bucovina," 1934, 385 p.), and *Domniile române sub Regulamentul Organic, 1834-1848* (The Romanian Princedoms under the Organic Statutes, 1834-1848) (București, Socec, 1915, 688 p.), analyze in considerable detail the constitutional and administrative innovations introduced by the Russians during their protectorate over the Principalities. They are basic works for the period. *See also* V. Ia. Grosul's *Reformy v dunaiskikh kniazhestvakh i Rossiia, 20-30 gody XIX veka* (Reforms in the Danubian Principalities and Russia; the 1820s and 1830s) (Moskva, Izd-vo Nauka, 1966, 408 p.; bibliography: p. 388-401).

1717. Giurescu, Constantin C.   Viaţa şi opera lui Cuza Vodă (The life and work of Prince Cuza). Bucureşti, Editura Ştiinţifică, 1966. 476 p.

The most comprehensive biography to date, based upon an extensive use of primary and secondary materials. *See also* Andrei Rădulescu, *Organizarea statului în timpul domniei lui Cuza-Vodă* (The organization of the state during the reign of Prince Cuza) (Bucureşti, Cartea Românească, 1932, 45 p.). A concise account by one of contemporary Romania's most distinguished legal scholars. Cuza's fall is described at length in Paul Henry, *L'abdication du Prince Cuza et l'avènement de la dynastie de Hohenzollern au trône de la Roumanie, documents diplomatiques* (Paris, Felix Alcan, 1930, 485 p.). It contains a precious annex of documents dealing with the change of dynasty and the installation of a new liberal regime.

1718. Pătrăşcanu, Lucreţiu D.   Un veac de frământări sociale, 1821-1907 (A century of social unrest, 1821-1907). Bucureşti, Editura "Cartea Rusă," 1945. 295 p. Illus., ports., facsims.

*See also* entry no. 1674.

Pătrăşcanu was a leading communist intellectual of the 1930s and minister of justice from 1945 until 1948, when he was purged. This work emphasizes the importance of economic factors in determining the political and social development of the country and is useful because it deals with questions frequently neglected by non-Marxist historians.

1719. Riker, Thad W.   The Making of Roumania; a Study of an International Problem, 1856-1866. London, Oxford University Press, 1931. 592 p. Illus., map. Bibliography: p. 567-572.

*See also* entry no. 1675.

A splendid monograph based on an exhaustive investigation of English, French, and German archives. It deals primarily with the negotiations of the Great Powers over the future form of government of the Romanian Principalities.

### 3. 1866-1918

1720. Brătianu, Ioan I. C.   Discursuri (Speeches). Bucureşti, Cartea Românească, 1933-1940. 4 v.

By the leader of the Romanian Liberal Party during and after the First World War until his death in 1927. Useful for the politics and policies of the Liberals, especially during the war.

1721. Dobrogeanu-Gherea, Constantin.   Neoiobăgia; studiu economico-sociologic al problemei noastre agrare (Neo-serfdom; an economic-

sociological study of our agrarian problem). Bucureşti, Socec, 1910. 494 p.
*See also* entry no. 1877.

A study of the impact of modern, Western-style capitalism on an agrarian and underdeveloped Romania by that country's most important Marxist theorist.

1722. Gane, C.    P. P. Carp şi locul său în istoria politică a Ţării (P. P. Carp and his place in the political history of the country). Bucureşti, Editura ziarului "Universul," 1936. 2 v.

A massive, scholarly study of a conservative leader who favored close political and economic ties with Germany. Extremely useful for the political history of Romania from the last quarter of the 19th century until the end of the First World War. It may be supplemented by P. P. Carp, *Discursuri* (Speeches), v. 1, 1868-1888 (Bucureşti, Socec, 1907, 482 p.).

1723. Ionescu, Virgil.    Mihail Kogălniceanu; contribuţii la cunoaşterea vieţii activităţii şi concepţiilor sale (Mihail Kogălniceanu; contributions to an understanding of his life, activity, and ideas). Bucureşti, Editura Ştiinţifică, 1963. 379 p.

The most recent biography of one of Romania's outstanding public figures in the 19th century. A thorough study which treats Kogălniceanu as a historian, man of letters, humanitarian, and political leader. Still useful is Nicolae Iorga, *Mihail Kogălniceanu; scriitorul, omul politic şi Românul* (Mihail Kogălniceanu; the writer, the politician, and the Romanian) (Bucureşti, Socec, 1921, 212 p.). It consists of three separate essays, the most original of which treats Kogălniceanu as a politician. For his views on a variety of subjects *see*: Mihail Kogălniceanu, *Discursuri parlamentare din epoca Unirii* (Parliamentary speeches during the era of the Union), edited by Vladimir Diculescu (Bucureşti, Editura Ştiinţifică, 1959, 422 p.).

1724. Maiorescu, Titu.    Discursuri parlamentare cu priviri asupra desvoltării politice a României sub domnia lui Carol I (Parliamentary speeches concerning the political development of Romania during the reign of Carol I). Bucureşti, Socec, Minerva, 1897-1915. 5 v.

A useful collection by a conservative and an outstanding philosopher and literary critic who played a major role in the development of modern Romanian literature.

1725. Marghiloman, Alexandru.    Note politice, 1897-1924 (Political notes, 1897-1924). Bucureşti, Institutul de Arte Grafice "Eminescu," 1927. 5 v.

The memoirs of the pro-German conservative who headed the Romanian government for a short time after its capitulation to Germany in March 1918. Particularly useful for the war period and the peace negotiations in 1919.

1726. Partidul Muncitoresc Romîn. *Comitetul Central. Institutul de Istorie a Partidului.* Mişcarea muncitorească din România, 1893-1900 (The labor movement in Romania, 1893-1900). Bucureşti, Editura Politică, 1965. 454 p.

A useful collection of twelve articles dealing with various aspects of the labor movement and the activities of the Social Democratic Workers Party of Romania. It may be used in conjunction with *Documente din mişcarea muncitorească, 1872-1916* (Documents from the labor movement, 1872-1916), edited by Mihail Roller, 2d ed. (Bucureşti, Editura C.G.M., 1947, 667 p.). In spite of many omissions and the absence of archive material, this volume remains the best collection for the period.

1727. Partidul Muncitoresc Romîn. *Comitetul Central. Institutul de Istorie a Partidului.* Presa muncitorească şi socialistă din România (The labor and socialist press in Romania). Bucureşti, Editura Politică, 1964–

*See also* entry no. 1827.

An invaluable anthology for the study of the socialist movement. A concise introductory essay precedes each excerpt. Two volumes issued so far: v. 1, 1865-1900; v. 2, 1900-1921.

1728. Petrescu, Constantin T.    Socialismul în România (Socialism in Romania). Bucureşti, 1945. 441 p.

*See also* entry no. 1902.

By the former president of the Romanian Socialist Party, this is the only general history of the socialist movement in Romania. Most of the book deals with the period before 1919 and is more of a chronicle than an attempt at synthesis.

1729. Răutu, Constantin.    Ion C. Brătianu. Omul — Timpurile — Opera (1821-1891) (Ion C. Brătianu. The man, the times, and the accomplishments [1821-1891]). Turnu-Severin, Datina, 1940. 249 p.

The most recent biography of Romania's prime minister from 1876 to 1888 and one of Carol I's closest advisers. Although laudatory, it provides a good general account of Brătianu's varied activities. Two sizable collections of Brătianu's speeches and papers have been published which are indispensable for the internal history of Romania in the second half of the 19th century: Ion C. Brătianu, *Discursuri, scrieri, acte şi documente* (Speeches, writings, acts and documents) Bucureşti, Independenţa, 1912, 3 v.), and Ion C. Brătianu, *Acte şi cuvântari* (Acts and speeches) (Bucureşti, Cartea Românească, 1930-1939, 9 v.).

1730. Stere, Constantin.    Socialdemocratism sau poporanism (Social Democracy or populism). Viaţa românească (Iaşi), Aug. 1907: 170-193; Sept. 1907: 313-341; Oct. 1907: 15-48; Nov. 1907: 173-208; Jan. 1908: 49-75; Apr. 1908: 59-80.

*See also* entry no. 1881.

Perhaps the best account of the Romanian Populists. Stere argues that full-scale industrial development for Romania is impossible and that agriculture will continue to be the main determinant of its social and political development. It may be contrasted with H. Sanie-levici, *Poporanismul reacționar* (Reactionary Populism) (București, Socec, 1921, 441 p.), a collection of essays highly critical of populist doctrine.

1731. Sturdza, Dimitrie A., *ed.* Domnia Regelui Carol I. Fapte — Cuvân-tări — Documente (The reign of King Carol I. Facts, speeches, docu-ments). v. 1 (1866-1876). București, Carol Göbl, 1906. 872 p.

There is no satisfactory history of Carol I's reign. The above work, containing much valuable source material, is the most com-plete study of the first ten years of his reign. A massive eyewitness account is *Aus dem Leben König Karls von Rumänien; Aufzeich-nungen eines Augenzeugen* (Stuttgart, Cotta'sche Buchhandlung, 1894-1900, 4 v.). It is important for both Carol's internal and for-eign policies. Of value also is *Cuvântarile Regelui Carol I* (The speeches of King Carol I), edited by Constantin C. Giurescu (Bu-curești, Fundația pentru Literatură și Artă Regele Carol II, 1939, 2 v.).

1732. Xeni, C. Take Ionescu. 3d ed. București, Universul, 1933. 456 p.

The best biography of one of Romania's major political figures. A leader of the Conservative Democrats at the outbreak of the First World War, he advocated an alliance with the Allies as the best means of completing the union of all Romanians. *See also*: Take Ionescu, *Discursuri politice (1886-1900)* (Political speeches [1886-1900]) (București, 1897-1901, 5 v.).

1733. Xenopol, Alexandru D. Istoria partidelor politice în România (The history of political parties in Romania). v. 1. București, Albert Baer, 1910. 626 p.

The only such history to date, by one of Romania's most distin-guished historians. Thorough and judicious, it deals primarily with the 19th century through the accession of Carol I and the adoption of the constitution of 1866.

### 4. 1918-1944

1734. Carp, Matatias. Cartea neagră; suferințele evreilor din România, 1940-1944 (The black book; the sufferings of the Jews of Ro-mania, 1940-1944). București, Socec, 1945-1948. 3 v. Illus., facsims. *See also* entry no. 111.

The most comprehensive history of Romanian Jewry during the Second World War. A detailed account of German influence on the policy of the Romanian government toward the Jews between 1940 and 1944 is Martin Broszat, "Das Dritte Reich und die rumänische Judenpolitik," in: *Gutachten des Instituts für Zeitgeschichte* (Mün-chen, Selbstverlag des Instituts für Zeitgeschichte, 1958), p. 102-183. It is thorough and based chiefly on German documents.

1735. Codreanu, Corneliu Zelea. Eiserne Garde. 3d ed. Berlin, Brunnen-Verlag/W. Bischoff, 1942. 439 p.

The memoirs of the leader of the Iron Guard movement. A somewhat expanded version of the Romanian original, *Pentru legionari*
(For the Legionaries) (3d ed., Bucureşti, Editura Mişcării Legionare,
1940, 1 v.). Of use also for an understanding of Codreanu's attitudes on various political and social problems is the collection of
his notes to legionary officials and public pronouncements published
by I. Georgescu Delatopoloveni, *Circulările Căpitanului, 1934-
1937* (The circular letters of the Captain, 1934-1937) (n.p., 1937,
175 p.). In spite of its laudatory tone, Ion Banea's biography of
Codreanu, *Căpitanul* (The Captain), 2d ed. (Sibiu, Editura "Totul
pentru Ţara," 1937, 143 p.), is a useful chronicle of the Legionary
movement.

1736. Georgescu, Titu.   De la greva generală la crearea P.C.R. (From the
general strike to the creation of the Communist Party of Romania).
Bucureşti, Editura Ştiinţifică, 1962. 208 p.

A useful narrative account, which may be compared with Vasile
Liveanu, "Date privind pregătirea şi desafăşurarea Congresului I
al Partidului Comunist din Romînia" (Data concerning the preparation and work of the first congress of the Communist Party of Romania), in *Studii şi materiale de istorie contemporană*, v. 2 (Bucureşti, 1962), p. 129-199. An excellent collection of material dealing
with the early history of the party is *Documente din istoria mişcării
muncitoreşti din România, 1916-1921* (Documents from the history
of the labor movement in Romania) (Bucureşti, Editura politică,
1966, 791 p.).

1737. Georgescu, Titu, *and* Mircea Ioanid.   Presa P.C.R. şi a organizaţiilor
sale de masă, 1921-1944 (The press of the Communist Party of
Romania and of its mass organizations, 1921-1944). Bucureşti, Editura Ştiinţifică, 1963. 384 p.

An extremely useful and thorough annotated bibliography covering the Romanian, Hungarian, and German language press.

1738. Institutul Social Român, *Bucureşti*.   Doctrinele partidelor politice
(The doctrines of the political parties). Bucureşti, Cultura Naţională,
n.d. 304 p.

A series of lectures on contemporary political doctrines and
parties given in the early 1920s. Among the most significant are those
on nationalism by Nicolae Iorga, conservatism by Alexandru Marghiloman, socialism by Şerban Voinea, peasantism by Virgil Madgearu, and liberalism by I. G. Duca.

1739. Ionescu, Dionisie, *and others*.   Dezvoltarea constituţională a Statului
Român (The constitutional development of the Romanian State). Bu-
cureşti, Editura Ştiinţifică, 1957. 597 p. Bibliography: p. 566-593.
*See also* entry no. 1704.

An interesting survey of the 19th and 20th centuries with some
harsh judgments on political life between the two world wars.

1740. Iorga, Nicolae.    Supt trei regi (Under three kings). Bucureşti, 1932. 462 p.

An account of parties and politicians between 1904 and 1930 with strong personal opinions of men and events by Professor Iorga, who was much more than a detached observer. In *Doi ani de restauraţie* (Two years of restoration) (Vălenii-de-munte, Datina Românească, 1932, 126 p.), he describes the serious economic and political crisis of the early '30s and his own brief tenure as prime minister. His account of the events in the summer of 1932 immediately following his resignation is entitled *Isprava* (Success) (Vălenii-de-munte, Datina Românească, 1932, 72 p.).

1741. Madgearu, Virgil N.    Evoluţia economiei româneşti după razboiul mondial (Romanian economic evolution since the World War). Bucureşti, Independenţa economică, 1940. 403 p. Biblioteca economică, studii şi cercetări, 1)

*See also* entry no. 1884.

An analysis of the bases of Romanian economic life and the government's industrial, agricultural, and financial policies in the 1920s and 1930s. An essential work by an outstanding economist and a National Peasant theorist who sets forth the doctrines of liberal capitalism.

1742. Manoilescu, Mihail.    Rostul şi destinul burgheziei româneşti (The role and the destiny of the Romanian bourgeoisie). Bucureşti, Cugetarea, 1942. 444 p.

A searching analysis of the origins, attributes, and mission of the Romanian middle class by a one-time liberal and later corporatist.

1743. Partidul Muncitoresc Romîn. *Comitetul Central. Institutul de Istorie a Partidului.*    Documente din istoria P.C.R. (Documents from the history of the Communist Party of Romania). Bucureşti, Editura pentru Literatură Politică, 1953-1957. 4 v.

The most complete collection of documents on the Romanian Communist Party so far published. Material is especially abundant on the foundation of the party, the various party congresses and meetings, the party's activities in labor unions and youth groups, and its position on major political, economic, and social questions.

1744. Pătrăşcanu, Lucreţiu.    Sub trei dictaturi (Under three dictatorships). Bucureşti, Forum, 1945. 256 p.

*See also* entry no. 1870.

A Marxist analysis of Romanian political life between the two World Wars. The three dictatorships are those of King Carol II, the Iron Guard, and Marshal Ion Antonescu. A French edition is entitled *Sous trois dictatures* (Paris, J. Vitiano, 1946, 326 p.). A companion work, *Problemele de bază ale României* (The fundamental problems of Romania), 3d ed. (Bucureşti, Editura de Stat, 1946, 337 p.), deals at length with the agrarian problem. His analysis is incisive and generally sound, but he neglects a number of noneconomic factors which would help to account for the crisis on the land.

1745. Pe marginea prăpastiei, 21-23 ianuarie 1941 (On the brink of the abyss, January 21-23, 1941). Bucureşti, 1942. 2 v.

Published by the Antonescu regime to prove the treacherous and chaotic nature of the Iron Guard after its abortive uprising in January 1941. Although biased, it is valuable for the organization and activities of the Guard during its uneasy association in government with Antonescu from September 1940 to January 1941.

1746. Rădulescu-Motru, Constantin. Ţărănismul, un suflet şi o politică (Peasantism, a soul and a policy). Bucureşti, Cultura Naţională, 1924.

An attempt to formulate a doctrine of conservative populism and to demonstrate the benefits of a patriarchal, mystical peasant society as opposed to the world of money and machines of the bourgeoisie and its state.

1747. Roberts, Henry L. Rumania; Political Problems of an Agrarian State. New Haven, Yale University Press, 1951; Hamden, Conn., Archon Books, 1969. 414 p. Map. Bibliography: p. 381-399.

See also entries no. 1683, 1856, 1896, and 1990.

An excellent, detailed analysis of Romania's political and economic development from the end of the First World War to the early years of the communist regime.

1748. Zeletin, Ştefan. Burghezia română, originea şi rolul ei istoric (The Romanian bourgeoisie; its origin and historical role). Bucureşti, Cultura Naţională, 1925. 393 p.

See also entry no. 1905.

An important analysis of the middle class as the driving force in Romania's development and of its modern instrument, the Liberal Party. The author argues that it is the destiny of the Liberals to perfect an industrial and financial system capable of satisfying the needs of all. In Neoliberalismul (Neoliberalism) (Bucureşti, Ed. revistei "Pagini agrare şi sociale," 1927, 278 p.), he modified his views to include the social organization of production and state intervention in economic life.

## 5. Since 1945

1749. Floyd, David. Rumania, Russia's Dissident Ally. New Yo~~ ger, 1965. 144 p. (Praeger Publications in Russian ^ World Communism, no. 160)

See also entry no. 1807.

A journalistic account of Russo-Romanian re^ ments within Romania which led to her asser pendence from the Soviet Union.

1750. Gheorghiu-Dej, Gheorghe. Articole și cuvîntări (Articles and speeches). București, Editura Politică, 1956-1962. 4 v.

Useful collections of public acts of the leader of the Romanian Communist Party from 1952 until his death in 1965.

1751. Ionescu, Ghiță. Communism in Rumania, 1944-1962. London, New York, Oxford University Press, 1964. 378 p. Bibliography: p. 358-367.

See also entries no. 1868 and 1989.

The fullest account available in English.

1752. Lebedev, Nikolai I. Padenie diktatury Antonesku (The fall of the Antonescu dictatorship). Moscow, Mezhdunarodnye otnosheniia, 1966. 479 p. Bibliography: p. 472-477.

A Soviet view of events in Romania between 1940 and the assumption of power by the National Democratic Front in 1945. Based on the extensive use of published primary and secondary sources and some Russian archive material.

1753. Markham, Reuben H. Rumania under the Soviet Yoke. Boston, Meador, 1949. 601 p. Maps.

The author, a journalist, displays an intimate knowledge of conditions in Romania immediately after the Second World War. His intense anticommunism sometimes detracts from an otherwise able account.

1754. Partidul Muncitoresc Romîn. Comitetul Central. Rezoluții și hotărîri ale Comitetului Central al Partidului Muncitoresc Român (Resolutions and decisions of the Central Committee of the Romanian Workers Party). București, Editura pentru Literatură Politică, 1952-1954. 2 v.

A valuable collection concerning such major problems as party membership and organization, the first five-year plan, and the collectivization of agriculture.

1755. Partidul Muncitoresc Romîn. Congres. Congresul al II-lea al Partidului Muncitoresc Romîn, 23-28 decembrie 1955 (The Second Congress of the Romanian Workers Party, December 23-28, 1955). București, Editura Politică, 1956. 908 p.

Together with the works mentioned below, one of the best sources for the domestic and foreign policies of the present Romanian government. See also: Congresul al III-lea al Partidului Muncitoresc Romîn, 20-25 iunie 1960 (The Third Congress of the R.W.P., June 20-25, 1960) (București, Editura Politică, 1960, 760 p.); and Congresul al IX-lea al Partidului Comunist Român, 15-24 iulie 1965 (The Ninth Congress of the Romanian Communist Party, July 15-24, 1965) (București, Editura Politică, 1965, 864 p.).

1756. Vîntu, I., and others. Sfaturile populare, organe locale ale puterii de stat în R.P.R. (People's councils, the local organs of state power

1750. Gheorghiu-Dej, Gheorghe.    Articole şi cuvîntări (Articles and speeches). Bucureşti, Editura Politică, 1956-1962. 4 v.
>Useful collections of public acts of the leader of the Romanian Communist Party from 1952 until his death in 1965.

1751. Ionescu, Ghiţă.    Communism in Rumania, 1944-1962. London, New York, Oxford University Press, 1964. 378 p. Bibliography: p. 358-367.
>*See also* entries no. 1868 *and* 1989.
>The fullest account available in English.

1752. Lebedev, Nikolai I.    Padenie diktatury Antonesku (The fall of the Antonescu dictatorship). Moscow, Mezhdunarodnye otnosheniia, 1966. 479 p. Bibliography: p. 472-477.
>A Soviet view of events in Romania between 1940 and the assumption of power by the National Democratic Front in 1945. Based on the extensive use of published primary and secondary sources and some Russian archive material.

1753. Markham, Reuben H.    Rumania under the Soviet Yoke. Boston, Meador, 1949. 601 p. Maps.
>The author, a journalist, displays an intimate knowledge of conditions in Romania immediately after the Second World War. His intense anticommunism sometimes detracts from an otherwise able account.

1754. Partidul Muncitoresc Romîn. *Comitetul Central.*    Rezoluţii şi hotărîri ale Comitetului Central al Partidului Muncitoresc Român (Resolutions and decisions of the Central Committee of the Romanian Workers Party). Bucureşti, Editura pentru Literatură Politică, 1952-1954. 2 v.
>A valuable collection concerning such major problems as party membership and organization, the first five-year plan, and the collectivization of agriculture.

1755. Partidul Muncitoresc Romîn. *Congres.*    Congresul al II-lea al Partidului Muncitoresc Romîn, 23-28 decembrie 1955 (The Second Congress of the Romanian Workers Party, December 23-28, 1955). Bucureşti, Editura Politică, 1956. 908 p.
>Together with the works mentioned below, one of the best sources for the domestic and foreign policies of the present Romanian government. See also: *Congresul al III-lea al Partidului Muncitoresc Romîn, 20-25 iunie 1960* (The Third Congress of the R.W.P., June 20-25, 1960) (Bucureşti, Editura Politică, 1960, 760 p.); and *Congresul al IX-lea al Partidului Comunist Român, 15-24 iulie 1965* (The Ninth Congress of the Romanian Communist Party, July 15-24, 1965) (Bucureşti, Editura Politică, 1965, 864 p.).

1756. Vîntu, I., *and others.*    Sfaturile populare, organe locale ale puterii de stat în R.P.R. (People's councils, the local organs of state power sis is incisive and generally sound, but he neglects a number of noneconomic factors which would help to account for the crisis on the land.

1745. Pe marginea prăpastiei, 21-23 ianuarie 1941 (On the brink of the abyss, January 21-23, 1941). Bucureşti, 1942. 2 v.

Published by the Antonescu regime to prove the treacherous and chaotic nature of the Iron Guard after its abortive uprising in January 1941. Although biased, it is valuable for the organization and activities of the Guard during its uneasy association in government with Antonescu from September 1940 to January 1941.

1746. Rădulescu-Motru, Constantin.  Ţărănismul, un suflet şi o politică (Peasantism, a soul and a policy). Bucureşti, Cultura Naţională, 1924.

An attempt to formulate a doctrine of conservative populism and to demonstrate the benefits of a patriarchal, mystical peasant society as opposed to the world of money and machines of the bourgeoisie and its state.

1747. Roberts, Henry L. Rumania; Political Problems of an Agrarian State. New Haven, Yale University Press, 1951; Hamden, Conn., Archon Books, 1969. 414 p. Map. Bibliography: p. 381-399.

See also entries no. 1683, 1856, 1896, and 1990.

An excellent, detailed analysis of Romania's political and economic development from the end of the First World War to the early years of the communist regime.

1748. Zeletin, Ştefan.  Burghezia română, originea şi rolul ei istoric (The Romanian bourgeoisie; its origin and historical role). Bucureşti, Cultura Naţională, 1925. 393 p.

See also entry no. 1905.

An important analysis of the middle class as the driving force in Romania's development and of its modern instrument, the Liberal Party. The author argues that it is the destiny of the Liberals to perfect an industrial and financial system capable of satisfying the needs of all. In Neoliberalismul (Neoliberalism) (Bucureşti, Ed. reviste "Pagini agrare şi sociale," 1927, 278 p.), he modified his views to include the social organization of production and state intervention in economic life.

## 5. Since 1945

1749. Floyd, David.  Rumania, Russia's Dissident Ally. New York, Praeger, 1965. 144 p. (Praeger Publications in Russian History and World Communism, no. 160)

See also entry no. 1807.

A journalistic account of Russo-Romanian relations and developments within Romania which led to her assertion of greater independence from the Soviet Union.

in the Romanian People's Republic). Bucureşti, Editura Academiei
R.P.R., 1964. 450 p. Bibliographical footnotes.
*See also* entry no. 1708.

An excellent detailed study of the origins, organization and functioning of these organs of local authority, published under the auspices of the Institute for Legal Research of the Romanian Academy.
*See also* Ioan Ceterchi's *The State System of the Socialist Republic
of Romania* (Bucharest, Meridiane, 1967, 130 p.).

## C. THE NATIONALITY PROBLEM
### *by Keith Hitchins*
#### 1. Transylvania

1757. Chereşteşiu, Victor.   Adunarea naţională de la Blaj, 3-5 (15-17)
mai 1848; începuturile şi alcătuirea programului revoluţiei din 1848
din Transilvania (The National Assembly of Blaj, 3-5 [15-17] May
1848; the beginnings and the drawing up of the revolutionary program of 1848 in Transylvania). Bucureşti, Editura Politică, 1966.
671 p.

A detailed history of the Romanian national movement in Transylvania in the spring of 1848. Based on extensive published and
archival material.

1758. Dragomir, Silviu.   The Ethnical Minorities in Transylvania. Geneva,
Sonor, 1927. 129 p. Map.
*See also* entry no. 1614.

A defense of Romanian nationality policies. *See also* the same
author's *La Transylvanie avant et après l'arbitrage de Vienne* (Sibiu,
Centrul de Studii şi Cercetări privitoare la Transilvania, 1943, 52 p.).
Dragomir demonstrates the ethnic predominance of the Romanians
in Transylvania and the importance of that province to Romania's
economic and geographical unity, and brands the Vienna Award
of 1940 both unjust and impractical.

1759. Dragomir, Silviu.   Studii şi documente privitoare la revoluţia Românilor din Transilvania în anii 1848-49 (Studies and documents
concerning the revolution of the Romanians of Transylvania in
1848-49). Sibiu-Cluj, Cartea Românească, 1944-1946. 4 v. (numbered 1-3 and 5).

The first three volumes contain indispensable archive material
concerning Romanian national aspirations and Magyar-Romanian
relations in 1848. Volume 5 and the same author's *Avram Iancu*
(Bucureşti, Editura Ştiinţifică, 1965, 304 p.), the biography of the
outstanding Romanian military hero of the revolution, together form
a judicious survey of the revolution and are important as a background to the nationality problem in Transylvania throughout the
19th century.

1760. Hitchins, Keith.   The Rumanian National Movement in Transylvania, 1780-1849. Cambridge, Mass., Harvard University Press, 1969. 320 p.

A study of the Romanian struggle for cultural identity and the growth of national consciousness. For a biography of one of the leading figures in Romanian public life in Transylvania and Hungary for over four decades before his death in 1918 *see*:

Georgescu, Ioan. George Pop de Băsești. Oradea, Astra, 1935. 432 p.

1761. Kemény, Gábor. Iratok a nemzetiségi kérdés történetéhez Magyarországon a dualizmus korában, 1867-1918 (Documents concerning the history of the nationality question in Hungary during the era of Dualism, 1867-1918). Budapest, Tankönyvkiadó, 1952-1966. 4 v.

A rich collection with much hitherto unpublished material on the Romanians from the Hungarian National Archives. The volumes which have appeared so far bring the collection down to 1906.

1762. Miko, Imre. Nemzetiségi jog és nemzetiségi politika; tanulmány a magyar közjog és politikai történet köréböl (Nationality law and nationality policy; a study of Hungarian constitutional law and political history). Kolozsvár, Minerva, 1944. 551 p.

An exhaustive analysis of the legal position of the non-Magyar nationalities, particularly the Romanians, in Hungary between the end of the eighteenth century and the beginning of the Second World War. A useful supplementary bibliography by the same author is *La question de Transylvanie devant l'opinion européenne, 1865-1920* (Lugos, Husvéth és Hoffer, 1936, 47 p.).

1763. Nagy, Lajos. A kisebbségek alkotmányjogi helyzete nagyrományiában (The constitutional position of the minorities in Greater Romania). Kolozsvár, Minerva, 1944. 300 p.

A scholarly treatment and the only comprehensive study of the problem for the period 1918-1940. One may compare it with Imre Mikó, *Huszonkét év, 1918-1940* (Twenty-two years, 1918-1940) (Budapest, Studium, 1940, 326 p.), which deals with the political and economic conditions of the Magyars of Greater Romania. The author is critical of the Romanian agrarian reform and administration generally.

The pertinent non-Romanian literature is listed in:

Bako, Elemer, *and* William Sólyom-Fekete, *comps.* Hungarians in Rumania and Transylvania. A Bibliographical List of Publications in Hungarian and West European Languages. Washington, D.C., Library of Congress, 1969. 192 p.

1764. Netea, Vasile. George Barițiu. Viața și activitatea sa (George Barițiu; his life and activity). București, Editura Științifică, 1966. 365 p.

The most extensive biography of the leading figure in the Romanian national movement in Transylvania in the second half of the 19th century. A useful anthology of his writings, which reveal the many-sided character of the nationality problem is George Bariţiu, *Scrieri social-politice* (Socio-political writings), edited with an introductory essay by Victor Chereşteşiu, Camil Muresan, and George Em. Marica (Bucureşti, Editura Politică, 1962, 431 p.).

1765. Netea, Vasile. Istoria Memorandului Românilor din Transilvania şi Banat (The history of the Memorandum of the Romanians of Transylvania and the Banat). Bucureşti, Fundaţia Regele Mihai I, 1947. 482 p.

The most detailed account of the celebrated trial in the 1890s of Romanian political leaders who bypassed the Hungarian government to lay their grievances directly before Emperor Francis Joseph. The conflicting goals of Romanian and Hungarian nationalism are also graphically revealed in the records of the trial published by I. P. Papp, *Procesul Memorandului Românilor din Transilvania* (The Trial in the Case of the Memorandum of the Romanians of Transylvania) (Cluj, Editura Bulletinului Justiţiei, 1933-1934, 2 v.).

1766. Păcăţianu, Teodor V. Cartea de aur sau luptele politice-naţionale ale Românilor de sub coroana ungară (The golden book, or the national-political struggles of the Romanians under the Hungarian Crown). Sibiu, Tipografia arhidiecezană, 1904-1915. 8 v.

The most extensive collection of materials on the Romanian national movement in Transylvania and Hungary in the 19th century and the beginning of the 20th. Most of the selections are taken from newspapers and other published collections.

1767. Popovici, D. La littérature roumaine à l'époque des lumières. Sibiu, Centrul de Studii şi Cercetări privitoare la Transilvania, 1945. 516 p. (Bibliotheca Rerum Transilvaniae, XII)

*See also* entry no. 1940.

An excellent account of the intellectual origins of the Romanian national movement and the influence of the French and German Enlightenments. An interesting interpretation of the same subject by one of Romania's greatest poets is Lucian Blaga, *Gîndirea românească în Transilvania în secolul al XVIII-lea* (Romanian thought in Transylvania in the 18th century) (Bucureşti, Editura Ştiinţifică, 1966, 230 p.).

1768. Prodan, David. Supplex Libellus Valachorum. Cluj, Editura Universităţii "Victor Babeş," 1948. 301 p.

A masterly study of the first truly national manifestation of the Romanians of Transylvania — the drawing up of a lengthy petition to the Emperor Leopold II in 1791 setting forth their demands for equality with the other nations of Transylvania. The Romanian movement in general in the 18th century is treated as a part of the evolution of political and social thought in Central Europe rather than as an isolated phenomenon.

1769. Tóth, Zoltán.   Az erdélyi román nacionalizmus első százada, 1697-1792. (The first century of Transylvanian Romanian nationalism, 1697-1792). Budapest, Athenaeum, 1946. 412 p.
   A thoroughly scholarly study based on the extensive use of archive material by a leading Hungarian specialist on the nationality problems of his country.

## 2. Bukovina

1770. Balan, Teodor.   Suprimarea mişcărilor naţionale din Bucovina pe timpul războiului mondial, 1914-1918 (The suppression of national movements in Bukovina during the World War, 1914-1918). Cernăuţi, Editura autorului, 1923. 216 p.
   The activities of Romanian nationalists and Austrian countermeasures.

1771. Beck, Erich.   Bibliographie zur Landeskunde der Bukowina. Literatur bis zum Jahre 1965. München, Verlag des Südostdeutschen Kulturwerks, 1966. 378 p. (Veröffentlichungen des Südostdeutschen Kulturwerks. Reihe B. 19)
   Lists 7,371 items available in German and Austrian libraries on a variety of subjects.

1772. Nistor, Ion I.   Românii şi Rutenii în Bucovina; studiu istoric şi statistic (Romanians and Ruthenians in Bukovina; a historical and statistical study). Bucureşti, Socec şi C. Sfetea, 1915. 209 p. Bibliography: p. xiii-xx.
   See also entry no. 1629.
   The relations between the two nationalities from the 17th century to 1910. Emphasis on the efforts of the Romanians to overcome the consequences of massive Ruthenian immigration in the 18th and 19th centuries.

1773. Prokopowitsch, Erich.   Die rumänische Nationalbewegung in der Bukowina und der Dako-Romanismus. Graz, Köln, Böhlau, 1965. 192 p. Bibliography: p. 171-175. (Studien zur Geschichte der österreichisch-ungarischen Monarchie, Bd. 3)
   See also entry no. 1659.
   A thorough and carefully documented study of the period from the end of the 18th century through the First World War. The author devotes special attention to the evolution of the Daco-Roman Idea, a body of doctrine designed to foster the union of all Romanians into a Greater Romania.

## 3. Bessarabia

1774. Arbore, Zamfir C.   Basarabia în secolul XIX (Bessarabia in the 19th century). Bucureşti, Carol Göbl, 1898. 790 p.

The most comprehensive account available with an annex of Russian legislation specifically concerning Bessarabia.

1775. Cazacu, P.   Moldova dintre Prut şi Nistru, 1812-1918 (Moldavia between the Prut and the Dniester, 1812-1918). Iaşi, Viaţa Romînească, n.d. 345 p.

An useful survey. The second and most valuable part of the work deals with the period between the Russian revolution of February 1917 and the union of Bessarabia with Romania in 1918. For the Soviet point of view, see S. Ia. Afteniuk's *Revoliutsionnoe dvizhenie v 1917 godu i ustanovlenie sovetskoi vlasti v Moldavii* (The revolutionary movement in 1917 and the establishment of Soviet power in Moldavia) (Kishinev, Kartia moldoveniaske, 1964, 632 p.).

1776. Diaconescu, Emil.   Românii din răsărit — Transnistria (The Romanians of the East — Transnistria). Iaşi, Ath. Gheorghiu, 1942. 240 p.

A general survey of Romanian settlements in the area between the Dniester and the Bug rivers to 1940. Based on an extensive bibliography of printed Russian and Romanian sources, it attempts to justify Romania's claim to this territory.

1777. Erbiceanu, Vespasian.   Naţionalizarea justiţiei şi unificarea legislativă în Basarabia (The nationalization of justice and legislative unification in Bessarabia). Bucureşti, Imprimeria naţională, 1934. 215 p. (Academia Română. Studii şi cercetări, 23)

An important essay on the introduction of Russian law into Bessarabia after its annexation by Russia in 1812 followed by a detailed study of the integration of Bessarabia into the Romanian constitutional framework after 1918.

1778. Nistor, Ion I.   Istoria Basarabiei (The history of Bessarabia). Cernăuţi, "Glasul Bucovinei," 1923. 455 p. (Biblioteca Aşezământului I. C. Brătianu, no. 1)

A general survey, social and cultural as well as political, from ancient times to 1918. The status of Bessarabia as an historical Romanian land is stressed. This interpretation may be compared with a recent Soviet work covering the same period published by Akademiia nauk Moldavskoi SSR, Institut istorii, *Istoriia Moldavskoi SSR* (The history of the Moldavian SSR) (v. 1, Kishinev, Kartia moldoveniaske, 1965, 659 p., illus., maps, ports.).

## D. DIPLOMACY AND FOREIGN RELATIONS

*by Ghiţă Ionescu*

### 1. Prior to 1945

1779. Bălteanu, Boris.   Relaţiile Guvernului Statelor Unite Americei cu regimul fascist din România (septembrie 1940-junie 1942) (The re-

lations of the U.S. Government with the fascist regime in Romania
[September 1940-June 1942]). Studii, revistă de istorie, no. 11,
1958: 77-99.

Biased account of diplomatic exchanges between the U.S. Embassy in Bucharest and the Antonescu government. Based on unpublished Romanian documents.

1780. Boldur, Alexandru V.  La Bessarabie et les relations russo-
roumaines. Paris, J. Gamber, 1927. 410 p.

The classical Romanian viewpoint on this question and its impact
on the relations between the two countries.

1781. Campus, Eliza.  Trativele diplomatice in preajma dictatului dela
Viena (Aprilie-August 1940) (Diplomatic negotiations on the eve
of the Vienna-Diktat [April-August 1940]). Studii, v. 10, 1957,
no. 3: 167-195.

The author uses for her critical views of the precommunist regime
some new sources found in the archives.

1782. Cândea, Virgil, Dinu Giurescu, and Mircea Malița.  Pagini din
trecutul diplomatiei românești (Texts from Romania's diplomatic
past). București, Editura Politică, 1966. 253 p.

A biased but useful collection of Romanian diplomatic documents. See also:

Reprezentanțele diplomatice ale Românei (The diplomatic missions of Romania). v. 1, 1859-1917. București, Editura Politică,
1967. 420 p. Covers the period from the establishment of the first
Romanian diplomatic mission (in Belgrade) to 1917. Another volume for the post-1917 period is to follow.

1783. Cretzianu, Alexandre.  The Lost Opportunity. London, J. Cape,
1957. 188 p.

A personal account, based on the author's knowledge of Romania's diplomatic history, of the negotiations between King Michael
and the Allies at the end of the Second World War to extricate Romania from the war with Germany and to prevent her from falling
into the exclusive orbit of Soviet Russia.

1784. Cretzianu, Alexandre.  La politique de paix de la Roumanie a
l'égard de l'Union soviétique. Paris, Institut universitaire roumain
Charles 1er, 1954. 16 p.

Sketchy account of USSR-Romanian relations over some thirty
years.

1785. Duroselle, Jean-Baptiste, ed.  Les frontières européenes de l'URSS,
1917-1941. Paris, A. Colin, 1957. 354 p. Maps. (Cahiers de la Fondation nationale des sciences politiques, 85. Relations internationales)

Useful material on the Romanian frontiers.

1786. Gafencu, Grigore.   Derniers jours de l'Europe: un voyage diplomatique en 1939. Paris, L.U.F., 1946. 252 p.

Personal recollections of King Carol's Foreign Secretary. Also published as *Last Days of Europe; a Diplomatic Journey in 1939* (New Haven, Yale University Press, 1948, 239 p.).

1787. Gafencu, Grigore.   Les préliminaires de la guerre à l'est. Fribourg, 1946. 412 p.

English version published as *Prelude to the Russian Campaign, from the Moscow Pact (August 21st, 1939) to the Opening of Hostilities in Russia (June 22nd, 1941)* (London, F. Muller, 1945, 348 p.).

This narration, by the former Romanian foreign secretary and ambassador to Moscow, of the outbreak of the war between Russia and Nazi Germany provides an excellent description of Romania's diplomatic importance in Europe, as well as a *pro-domo* explanation of King Carol II's policy of "neutrality" (1936-1940), of which the author was one of the architects.

1788. Gheorghe, Ion.   Rumäniens Weg zum Satellitenstaat. Heidelberg, Vowinckel, 1952. 444 p.

Polemical account of the prewar and war years by a former Romanian military attaché and ambassador in Hitler's Germany.

1789. Hague. International Court of Justice.   Interpretation of Peace Treaties with Bulgaria, Hungary, and Romania; Advisory Opinions of March 30th and July 18th, 1950. Hague, 1950. 453 p.

1790. Hillgruber, Andreas.   Hitler, König Carol und Marschall Antonescu; die deutsch-rumänischen Beziehungen, 1938-1944. Wiesbaden, F. Steiner, 1954. 382 p. Ports., map. Bibliography: p. 357-366. (Veröffentlichungen des Instituts für Europäische Geschichte, Mainz, Bd. 5)

*See also* entry no. 1678.

This account, based on published German documents as well as some unpublished dispatches and memoranda of the German Ambassador in Romania during the period of the collapse of King Carol II's policy of neutrality and Hitler's outright domination of Romania's foreign policy, is indispensable to the student of the period.

1791. Ionescu, Ghiţă.   Les états danubiens, les états balkaniques et l'Europe. *In* Beloff, Max, *and others, eds.* L'Europe du XIXe du XXe siècle (1914– aujourd'hui). Milano, Marzorati, 1964. p. 1126-1178.

Contains implicitly a diplomatic history of Romania from 1919 to 1953.

1792. Machray, Robert.   The Little Entente. London, Allen and Unwin, 1929. 394 p. Map, ports.

A useful history of the loose diplomatic organization, under

France's auspices, linking Czechoslovakia, Romania, and Yugoslavia. This organization gradually dissolved in the 1930s.

1793. Manuila, Sabin.    The Vienna Award and Its Demographical Consequences. Bucharest, National History Institute, 1945. 56 p.

1794. Nano, F. C.    The First Soviet Double Cross; a Chapter in the Secret History of World War II. Journal of Central European Affairs, v. 12, 1952/53: 236-258.

> The author, a former Romanian Ambassador in Stockholm, tells how the Soviet government tried through its embassy in Stockholm to cut short the diplomatic negotiations with the Allies in Cairo in 1944 and to open direct negotiations with the Antonescu government.

1795. Petresco-Comnène, Nicolas M.    Preludi del grande dramma; ricordi e documenti di un diplomatico. Roma, Edizioni Leonardo, 1947. 507 p. Maps. (Documenti e testimonianze, 11)

> A firsthand, if not too sagacious, account by a former Romanian foreign secretary and ambassador to Berlin from the period 1936-1941.

1796. Seton-Watson, Robert W.    Treaty Revision and the Hungarian Frontiers. London, Eyre and Spottiswoode, 1934. 75 p. Illus., map.

> An objective view of the Transylvania problem after the 1919 peace treaties.

1797. Sofronie, Georges.    La position internationale de la Roumanie; étude juridique et diplomatique de ses engagements internationaux. Bucarest, Centre de hautes études internationales, 1938. 162 p. (Brochure d'information, no. 1)

> A scholarly description of Romania's international position, rights and commitments, as derived from the peace treaties of Versailles, Trianon, and St. Germain-en-Laye, in a Europe still under the auspices of the League of Nations.

1798. Spector, Sherman D.    Rumania at the Paris Peace Conference; a Study of the Diplomacy of Ion C. Bratianu. New York, Bookman Associates, 1962. 368 p. Illus.

> A useful book on the subject, based on a Ph.D. dissertation.

1799. Szaz, Zoltan.    The Transylvania Question; Romania and the Belligerents: July-Oct. 1914. Journal of Central European Affairs, v. 13, 1953/54: 338-351.

> Scholarly, but not impartial.

1800. Titulescu, N.    Discursuri (Speeches). Bucureşti, Editura Ştiinţifică, 1967. 623 p.

————.    Two Neighbours of Russia and Their Policies: Roumania and Bessarabia. Nineteenth Century and After, June 1924: 791-803.

The first is a collection of speeches delivered in the 1920s and 1930s by Romania's most famous diplomat, selected and edited by a commission of Romanian officials in the 1960s. The second is one of the few works which authoritatively defines Romania's rights to Bessarabia.

## 2. After the Second World War

1801. Brown, James F.   Rumänien — der unbotmässige Verbündete. Die rumänische Aussenpolitik im Jahre 1967. Europa-Archiv, v. 22, no. 24, Dec. 25, 1967: 875-885.

Brief, but serious, survey of Romania's foreign policy in 1967 by Radio Free Europe's chief political analyst.

1802. Burks, R. V.   The Rumanian National Deviation: an Accounting. *In* Eastern Europe in Transition, edited by Kurt London. Baltimore, Johns Hopkins Press, 1966. p. 93-117.

1803. Campbell, J. C.   The European Territorial Settlement. Foreign Affairs, Oct. 1947: 196-218.

————. Diplomacy on the Danube. Foreign Affairs, Jan. 1949: 315-327.

Two firsthand accounts by an American expert, who is also one of the keenest observers of Romania's recent diplomatic history.

1804. Ceauşescu, Nicolae.   Speech Concerning the Foreign Policy of the Communist Party and of the Romanian Government, Delivered at the Grand National Assembly Session on July 24, 1967. Bucharest, Romanian News Agency, 1967. 64 p.

A propagandist description, by the new leader of the Romanian Socialist Republic, of a socialist foreign policy based on the idea of national sovereignty. See also *Basic Principles of Romania's Foreign Policy* (Bucharest, Meridiane, 1968, 99 p.).

1805. Ciurea, Emile C.   Le traité de paix avec la Roumanie du 10 février 1947. Paris, Éditions A. Pedone, 1954. 284 p.

The most complete and scholarly account of the negotiations preceding the conclusion of the Treaty and an intepretation of its provisions and significance.

1806. Fischer-Galati, Stephen.   The New Rumania: From People's Democracy to Socialist Republic. Cambridge, Mass., M.I.T. Press, 1967. 126 p. (Studies in International Communism, 10)

*See also* entry no. 1677.

Contains an account of the loosening of Soviet-Romanian relations after 1958, with some personal interpretations. *See also* the same author's *The Socialist Republic of Rumania* (Baltimore, Johns Hopkins Press, 1969, 113 p.).

1807. Floyd, David.   Rumania, Russia's Dissident Ally. New York, Prae-

ger, 1965. 144 p. (Praeger Publications in Russian History and World Communism, no. 160)
*See also* entry no. 1749.
An informative work.

1808. Ionescu, Ghiţă. Communist Rumania and Nonalignment (April 1964-March 1965). Slavic Review, v. 24, no. 2, June 1965: 241-258.

1809. Ionescu, Ghiţă. The Reluctant Ally; a Study of Communist Neo-Colonialism. London, Ampersand Books, Allen and Unwin, 1965. 133 p.

> This short work, the subject of which is the change in relations between Romania and Soviet Russia during and after the COMECON crisis of 1962-1963, also contains a description of the reorientation of Romanian diplomacy after these events.

1810. Lumea (The world). 1964– Bucureşti. Weekly.

> Publishes articles on international affairs as well as a weekly selection of articles or extracts from articles published in the world press and specially selected for Romanian readers.

1811. Paris Conference to Consider the Draft Treaties of Peace with Italy, Rumania, Bulgaria, Hungary, and Finland, 1946. Selected Documents. Washington, D.C., U.S. Government Printing Office, 1947. 1442 p.

> Contains a complete set of documents on Romania's diplomatic position before and after the conference.

## E. MILITARY AFFAIRS

### *by Ghiţă Ionescu*

1812. Anescu, Vasile, Eugen Banat, *and* Ion Cupşa.    Participation of the Romanian Army in the Anti-Hitlerite War. Bucharest, Military Publishing House, 1966. 108 p.

1813. Carp, Mircea, *and* Basil Ratziu.    The Armed Forces. *In* Cretzianu, Alexandre, *ed.* Captive Rumania; a Decade of Soviet Rule. New York, Praeger, 1956. p. 355-374.

> Describes the internal and external organization of the Romanian Armed Forces during the Stalinist years.

1814. Cretzianu, Alexandre.    The Soviet Ultimatum to Rumania (26 June 1940). Journal of Central European Affairs, v. 9, no. 4, Jan. 1950: 396-403.

———.    The Rumanian Armistice Negotiations: Cairo 1944. Journal of Central European Affairs, v. 11, no. 3, Oct. 1951: 243-258.

1815. Cupşa, Ion, *ed.*    Contribuţia României la razboiul anti-hitlerist (23 August 1944-9 Mai 1945) (The Romanian contribution to the anti-Hitler war [23 August 1944-9 May 1945]). Bucuresti, Editura Militară a Ministerului Forţelor Armate ale Republicii Populare Române, 1958. 572 p. Illus., facsims., maps, ports.

An official account of Romania's military effort after the conclusion of the armistice with the Allies.

1816. Friessner, Hans.   Verratene Schlachten: die Tragödie der deutschen Wehrmacht in Rumänien und Ungarn. Hamburg, Holsten-Verlag, 1956. 267 p. Illus.

Describes from the German point of view the dramatic end of the Romanian-German military collaboration.

1817. Hillgruber, Andreas.   Die letzen Monate der deutsche-rumänischen Waffenbruderschaft (1944).   Wehrwissenschaftliche Rundschau. 1960: 377-397.

This eminent historian adds to his book an epilogue on the purely military aspects of the end of the German-Romanian collaboration Based on firsthand sources.

1818. Kiritescu, Constantin.   La Roumanie dans la guerre mondiale (1916-1919). Paris, Payot, 1934. 496 p.

A translation of the most complete history of Romania's participation in the First World War. *See also* Pamfil Seicaru's *La Roumanie dans la Grande guerre* (Paris, Minard, 1968, 461 p.).

1819. Rumania. *Ministerul Afacerilor Straine*.   Memorandum on the Military and Economic Contribution of Romania to the War against Germany and Hungary. Bucharest, State Printing Office, 1946. 26 p. Maps.

1820. Soare, Corneliu.   Cu privire la izvoarele tăriei forţelor armate (On the sources of strength of the armed forces). Bucureşti, Editura Militară, 1967. 191 p.

A work in which communism and nationalism merge into a general explanation of the high morale and modern equipment of the Romanian Army today.

1821. U.S. *Dept. of State*.   Armistice Agreement between the U.S.A. and the U.S.S.R. and the U.K. and Rumania. Annex and Protocol Signed in Moscow, September 12, 1944. Washington, D.C., 1946. 17 p. (U.S. Dept of State, Publication 2847)

1822. Viaţa militară (Military life).   196– Bucureşti. Monthly.

A publication of the Armed Forces in Romania.

## F. MASS MEDIA

*by Ghiţă Ionescu*

1823. Boilă, Romulus.   Press and Radio. *In* Cretzianu, Alexandre, *ed.*

Captive Rumania; a Decade of Soviet Rule. New York, Praeger, 1956. p. 257-284.

Although now out of date, this article gives an accurate description of how communist censorship of the press was instituted in Romania.

1824. Bratu, Savin, *and* Zoe Dumitrescu. Contemporanul şi vremea lui ("The Contemporary" and its times). Bucureşti, Editura de Stat pentru Literatură şi Artă, 1959. 335 p.

A biased but massive history of the most important left-wing periodical.

1825. Busek, Antony. How the Communist Press Works. New York. Praeger, 1964. 287 p. (Praeger Publications in Russian History and World Communism, no. 147)

In addition to a very useful description of the press system in communist countries, this book also contains ample, if scattered, material on the press in Romania. Consult also the following articles:

Olson, Kenneth E. The Press of Rumania. *In his* The History Makers. Baton Rouge, Louisiana State University Press, 1966. p. 400-413.

Fein, Leonard J., *and* Victoria E. Bonnell. Press and Radio in Rumania: Some Recent Developments. Journalism Quarterly, v. 42, Summer 1965: 443-449.

1826. 25 de ani dela apariţia ziarului Scînteia, organul C. C. al P. C. R. (The 25th anniversary of the appearance of the newspaper *Scînteia*, the organ of the C.C. of the C.P.R.). *In* Partidul Muncitoresc Romîn. Institutul de Istorie a Partidului. Analele, v. 2, 1956, no. 4.

An official study published on the occasion of the 25th anniversary of the official newspaper of the Romanian Communist Party.

1827. Partidul Muncitoresc Romîn. *Comitetul Central. Institut de Istorie a Partidului.* Presa muncitorească şi socialistă din România (The labor and socialist press in Romania). Bucureşti, Editura Politică, 1964–

*See also* entry no. 1727.

A complete history of the workers' and socialist press in Romania, written by communist historians. Two volumes issued so far: v. 1, 1865-1900; v. 2, 1900-1921.

1828. Presa noastră (Our press). 1955– Bucureşti. Monthly.

This official publication of the Union of Journalists of Romania contains articles of professional interest as well as lists of the newspapers.

1829. Romania. *In* UNESCO. World Radio and Television. Paris, UNESCO, 1967. p. 136-137.

Up-to-date information on radio and television in the Socialist Republic of Romania.

1830. Telecomunicații (Telecommunications). 1957– București. Monthly. Illus.

    Bimonthly — May/June 1964; monthly — July 1964–. A publication specializing in information on radio and television in Romania, accenting the technical aspects.

# 40

# the economy

*by John M. Montias*

Economic History 1831-1836

Survey Studies and General Data on the Economy 1837-1847

Agriculture, Industry, Finance, Living Conditions,
Foreign Trade 1848-1860

Serials 1861-1864

## A. ECONOMIC HISTORY

1831. Academia Republicii Populare Romîne. *Institutul de Cercetări Economice.* Dezvoltarea economiei RPR pe drumul socialismului, 1948-1957 (The economic development of the Romanian People's Republic on the way to socialism, 1948-1957). Bucureşti, Editura Academiei R.P.R., 1958. 426 p. Plates, map, diagrs., tables. Bibliographical footnotes.

> Russian translation: *Razvitie ekonomiki Rumynskoi narodnoi respubliki po puti sotsializma, 1948-1957* (Moskva, Inostrannaia literatura, 1958). First of a series of reports on the Romanian economy prepared by the Institute for Economic Research. Valuable particularly for the early postwar period and for the years of the New Course (1953-1955). On the early postwar period, *see also* V. A. Karra's *Stroitel'stvo sotsialisticheskoi ekonomiki v Rumynskoi narodnoi respubliki* (The construction of the socialist economy in the Romanian People's Republic) (Moskva, Akademiia nauk SSSR, 1953, 214 p.).

1832. Cioriceanu, Georges D.  La Roumanie économique et ses rapports avec l'étranger de 1860 à 1915. Paris, Marcel Giard, 1928. 443 p. Plates, maps, tables. Bibliography: p. 429-435.

> Little analysis but a mass of facts on the history of Romanian

agriculture, industry, and foreign trade. Another useful source dealing with the history of fiscal and commercial policy, as well as with industry and agriculture, is N. Resmeritza's *Essai d'économie roumaine moderne, 1831-1931* (Paris, Université de Paris, 1931, 411 p.; "Bibliographie": p. 401-408). This source is authoritative only on the period prior to the First World War.

1833. Enciclopedia României (The encyclopedia of Romania). v. 4. Bucureşti, Imprimeria Naţională, 1943. 1081 p. Illus., ports., maps.

An indispensable reference work for the prewar Romanian economy containing, inter alia, the only published national-income estimates for 1937 and 1938 based on Western methodology and a sector-by-sector description of manufacturing activity.

1834. Madgearu, Virgil N.    Rumania's New Economic Policy. London, P. S. King and Son, 1930. 63 p.

An important statement by one of Romania's outstanding economists and statesmen. Represents the National Peasant point of view on industrialization policy. For a more detailed presentation of Madgearu's views against the background of Romanian economic history in the prewar period, see *Evoluţia economiei româneşti după Razboiul mondial* (Romanian economic evolution since the world war) (Bucureşti, Independenţa Economică, 1940, 403 p., bibliographical footnotes).

1835. Mitrany, David.    The Land and the Peasant in Rumania; the War and Agrarian Reform (1917-1921). London, H. Milford, Oxford University Press; New Haven, Yale University Press, 1930. New York, Greenwood Press, 1968. 627 p. Maps, diagrs. Bibliography: p. 594-611.

See also entries no. 1680 *and* 1895.

Classic study of Romanian agrarian relations, especially valuable for its analysis of the land reform after the First World War.

1836. Zagoroff, S. D.    Agriculture and Food in Rumania during World War II. *In* Zagoroff, S. D., Jenö Vegh, and Alexander D. Bilimovich. The Agricultural Economy of the Danubian Countries, 1935-1945. Stanford, Stanford University Press, 1955. 478 p. Illus., maps.

A meticulous survey of Romanian agriculture by a qualified agricultural expert. Virtually the only reliable source on Romania's food output and consumption for the wartime period. On Romania's grain output, marketings, and exports before the Second World War, *see* Michael Rothmann's *Die Getreidewirtschaft Rumäniens* (Berlin, Reichsnährstand Verlag-Ges., 1940, 196 p., maps, tables). For a more recent, highly critical view of Romania's prewar agriculture, *see* O. Parpală's *Aspecte din agricultura Romaniei Burghezo-moşiereşti in perioada dintre cele două razboaie mondiale* (Aspects of the agriculture of bourgeois-landowners' Romania between the two world wars) (Bucureşti, Editura Academiei Republicii Socialiste România, 1966, 219 p.).

# B. SURVEY STUDIES AND GENERAL DATA ON THE ECONOMY

1837. Academia Republicii Populare Romîne. *Institutul de Cercetări Economice.* Dezvoltarea economică a Romîniei, 1944-1964 (Economic development of Romania, 1944-1964). Bucureşti, Editura Academiei R.P.R., 1964. 787 p. Illus., maps (part fold.). Bibliographical footnotes.

>   A comprehensive volume of essays on the Romanian economy, arranged by topics rather than by economic sectors. Chapters on prewar and early postwar economic development in Romania, demography and labor force, the organization of planning, the regional growth of industry, economic links between town and country, foreign trade, and living standards. For a German-language survey, *see* Gerhard Huber's *Die ökonomische Entwicklung der Rümanischen Volksrepublik* (Berlin, Deutsche Akademie der Wissenschaften, 1962, 164 p.).

1838. Academia Republicii Populare Romîne. *Institutul de Cercetări Economice.* Economia Romîniei între anii 1944-1959 (The Romanian economy during the peroid 1944-1959). Bucureşti, Editura Academiei R.P.R., 1959. 648 p. Maps, diagrs. Bibliographical footnotes.

>   The most informative of the volumes on the national economy prepared by the Institute for Economic Research. Covers all basic economic sectors, national income, foreign trade, etc.

1839. Academia Republicii Populare Romîne. *Institutul de Cercetări Economice.* Studii de economie socialistă (Studies on the socialist economy). Bucureşti, Editura Academiei R.P.R., 1961. 330 p. Diagrs. Bibliographical footnotes.

>   Essays on economic planning, wage policy, depreciation, and other aspects of the role of the "law of value" in Romanian economic development.

1840. Kaser, Michael C.   An Estimate of the National Accounts of Rumania Following Both Eastern and Western Definitions. Soviet Studies (Glasgow), v. 18, July 1966: 86-90.

>   An ingenious attempt to reconstruct the unpublished estimates of Romanian national income prepared by Romania's Central Statistical Office. For additional useful data, *see* Dan Grindea's *Venitul naţional în Republica Socialistă România* (National income in the Romanian Socialist Republic) (Bucureşti, Editura Ştiinţifică, 1967. 551 p.).

1841. Moldovan, Roman, *and others.*   Valorificarea superioară a resurselor naturale (The process of increasing the value added to natural resources). Bucureşti, Editura Politică, 1965. 277 p.

>   Articles in support of the government policy of processing natural resources through various industrial stages with a view to increasing the value of exports (by adding as much value from domestic labor

and other factors of production as possible to the original resources). The viewpoint of the authors is mercantilistic and ignores traditional comparative-advantage arguments.

1842. Montias, John M.   Economic Development in Communist Rumania. Cambridge, Mass., M.I.T. Press, 1967. 327 p. Illus. Bibliography: p. 307-310. (Studies in International Communism, 11)
   Contains: (1) a detailed account of postwar industrialization based in part on an independent measure of industrial output; (2) a survey of Romanian agriculture focused on the effects of collectivization on output and efficiency; (3) an analysis of postwar foreign-trade patterns; and (4) an account of Romania's troubled relations with COMECON since the early 1950s. Appendices on the petroleum and gas industry, national income, and the relation between the import and export of staple products and domestic production round out the discussion of the text. On Romania's relations with CEMA, see also Jean Paul-Saltiel's L'attitude de la Roumanie vis-à-vis d'une planification supranationale (Cahiers de l'ISEA, December 1965. Série economie planifiée, G. 22, No. 168, 3-120), a reconstruction of the background of Romania's dispute with COMECON, together with an analysis of Romania's economic structure. Contains an aggregated input-output table based on structural coefficients estimated from the input-output tables of Hungary and other CEMA countries.

1843. Răvar, I., and others.   Dezvoltarea complexă şi echilibrată a economiei naţionale (The complex and balanced development of the national economy). Bucureşti, Editura Politică, 1965. 307 p.
   A collection of essays on current topics by various economists and statisticians. The authors enthusiastically support the government policy of balanced development (between agriculture and industry, accumulation and consumption, foreign trade and the domestic economy, and among regions).

1844. Rumania. Direcţia Centrală de Statistică.   Anuarul statistic al R.P.R., 1966 (Statistical annual of the Socialist Republic of Romania, 1966). Bucureşti, Direcţia Centrală de Statistică, 1966. 709 p.
   The ninth statistical yearbook since 1957. Each edition contains a few new series, but no basic data have been added since the publication of the foreign trade breakdowns by commodity groups in 1965. A summary of the yearbook containing the most important statistics for recent years is to be found in the yearly Rumanian Statistical Pocket Book (Bucharest, Central Statistical Office, annual, illus.), published in English and other languages.

1845. Rumania. Direcţia Centrală de Statistică.   Recensămîntul populaţiei din 21 Februarie 1956 (Population census of 21 February 1956).
   Volume 1. Rezultate generale (General results). Bucureşti, Direcţia Centrală de Statistică, 1959. 1081 p. Maps, diagrs.

Volume 2. Structura social-economică a populaţiei: populaţia activă, populaţia pasivă; grupe sociale; ramuri; subramuri de activitate (Socioeconomic structure of the population: active population, passive population; social groups; branches, subbranches of activity). Bucureşti, Direcţia Centrală de Statistică, 1960. 1021 p.

Volume 3. Structura social-economică a populaţiei: ocupaţii (Socioeconomic structure of the population: occupations). Bucureşti, Direcţia Centrală de Statistică, 1961. 1469 p. *See also* entry no. 1638.

Essential reference work for demographic analysis. Numerous, well-presented maps, tables, comparisons with 1930 census. Prewar population data are all recalculated for present territory of Romania. *See also*: Rumania. *Direcţia Centrală de Statistică.* Labour Force in the Socialist Republic of Rumania. Bucharest, Central Statistical Board, 1968. 118 p.

1846. Rumania. *Direcţia Centrală de Statistică.* Studii de statistică; Lucrările consfătuiri ştiinţifice de statistică, 27-29 Noiembriie 1961 (Studies in statistics; proceedings of the Scientific Conference on Statistics, November 27-29, 1961). Bucureşti, Editura Ştiinţifică, 1962. 696 p.

Papers on mathematical statistics and economics and on highly technical aspects of Romanian statistics and planning. This and two subsequent volumes — Proceedings of the Second Conference on Statistics of 29 November–1 December 1962, published in 1963, and of the Third Conference of 5-7 December 1963, published in 1964 — provide details on the statistical methods in use in Romania not to be found elsewhere. Some overlap with articles published in *Revista de statistică* (Bucureşti, frequency varies).

1847. United Nations. *Economic Commission for Europe.* Economic Development in Rumania. Economic Bulletin for Europe (Geneva), v. 13, no. 2, Jan. 1961: 55-107.

An objective and well-balanced survey of postwar economic growth, based exclusively on official statistics. For a less analytical but more detailed account, *see* Otto Liess's "Planwirtschaft und Sozialismus in Rumänien" in *Die Wirtschaftssystem der Staaten Osteuropas und der Volksrepublik China; Untersuchungen der Entstehung, Entfaltung und Wandlung sozialistischer Wirtschaftssysteme*, v. 2, edited by Georg John (Berlin, Duncker und Humblot, 1962, 510 p.).

## C. AGRICULTURE, INDUSTRY, FINANCE, LIVING CONDITIONS, FOREIGN TRADE

1848. Academia Republicii Populare Romîne. *Institutul de Cercetări Economice.* Probleme ale creării şi dezvoltării bazei tehnice-materiale a socialismului în R.P.R. (Problems of the creation and development of the material-technical basis of socialism in the Romanian People's Republic). Bucureşti, Editura Academiei R.P.R., 1963. 390 p.

Essays on the resource base of Romanian industrialization, including capital formation, labor force, natural resources, and financial accumulation.

1849. Constantinescu, Olga, *and* N. N. Constantinescu. Cu privire la problema revoluţiei industriale în Romînia (On the problem of the industrial revolution in Romania). Bucureşti, Editura Ştiinţifică, 1957. 205 p.

Dense with facts and data on Romanian industry since the 1860s. Subject to the limitations of its national-communist point of view, one of the best documented books on modern Romanian economic history. *See also* the following prewar studies: Aurelian Z. Strat's *Des possibilités de développement industriel de la Roumanie* (Paris, Les Presses universitaires de France, 1932, 261 p., tables); Carol G. Rommenhöller's *Gross-Rumänien, seine ökonomische, soziale, finanzielle und politische Struktur, speziell seine Reichtümer* (Berlin, Puttkammer und Muhlbrecht, 1926, 735 p.); and N. P. Arcadian's *Industrializarea României* (The industrialization of Romania) (2d ed., Bucureşti, Imprimeria naţională, 1936, 372 p., tables).

1850. Florescu, Mihail, *and others.* Dezvoltarea industriei socialiste în RPR (The development of socialist industry in the Romanian People's Republic). Bucureşti, Editura Ştiinţifică, 1959. 597 p. Illus., diagrs., tables. Bibliographical footnotes.

The most comprehensive survey available of the development of Romania's individual industries, with emphasis on the branches of heavy industry. One of the few postwar books to mention problems and obstacles along with achievements.

1851. Kariagin, I. D. Neftianaia promyshlennost' Rumynii i ekonomicheskie problemy ee razvitiia v usloviiakh narodno-demokraticheskogo stroia (The petroleum industry of Romania and the economic problems of its development under the conditions of the people's-democratic order). Moskva, Gosudarstvennoe nauchnotekhnicheskoe izdatel'stvo neftianoi i gornotoplivnoi literatury, 1958. 345 p. Map, diagrs., Bibliography: p. 341-343.

The best available survey of Romania's oil industry during the period of its most rapid postwar expansion. Essential for an understanding of the subsequent stagnation of petroleum output. For a recent English-language treatment, see *The Oil and Gas Industry in Romania*, by T. Hanciulescu and T. Tanasescu (Bucharest, Meridiane, 1967, 105 p.).

1852. Levente, Mihai, E. Barat, *and* M. Bulgaru, *eds.* Analiza statistico-economică a agriculturii (A statistical-economic analysis of agriculture). Bucureşti, Editura Ştiinţifică, 1961. 339 p.

Contains a succinct but useful statistical survey of Romanian agriculture, including indices of peasant consumption not found in any statistical compendia, and a systematic description of the forms used by the Romanian Statistical Office in collecting and analyzing agricultural statistics. For a fuller description of Romanian agriculture, stressing technical rather than economic problems, see *Agricultura Romîniei, 1944-1964* (The agriculture of Romania, 1944-1964) edited by Nicolae Giosan, B. Şchiopu, and D. Davidescu (Bucureşti, Editura Agro-Silvică, 1964, 389 p., illus. [part col.], fold. col. map). A reasonably objective description of Romanian agriculture prior to full-scale collectivization, including detailed statistical information on state farms, may also be found in:

Rumania. *Ministerul Agriculturii şi Silviculturii.* Dezvoltarea agriculturii în Republica Populară Romînă (Agricultural development in the Romanian People's Republic). Bucureşti, Editura Agro-Silvică de Stat, 1958. 226 p. Illus., diagrs., tables. Bibliographical footnotes.

1853. Malinschi, Vasile, Roman Moldovan, *and* Vasile Rausser, *eds.* Industria Romîniei, 1944-1964 (Romanian industry, 1944-1964). Bucureşti, Editura Academiei R.P.R., 1964. 803 p. Illus., maps (part fold.). Bibliographical footnotes.

Essays in support of the industrialization policy of the Romanian Communist Party and government. Contains descriptions by specialists of the expansion of various branches of Romanian industry, including a valuable survey of petroleum mining and refining.

1854. Manoilescu, Mihail. The Theory of Protection and International Trade. London, P. S. King and Son, 1931. 262 p. Diagrs. Bibliography: p. 260-262.

A sophisticated plea for a protectionist commercial policy designed to promote rapid industrialization. Contains the original version of the argument that comparative costs are not a proper guide to trade policy when labor is in surplus, since, in this case, relative money costs, which reflect actual wages paid out, will tend to diverge from real costs.

1855. Oleinik, Ivan P. Razvitie promyshlennosti Rumynii v usloviiakh narodno-demokraticheskogo stroia (The industrial development of Romania under the conditions of the people's-democratic order). Moskva, Proizvodstvenno-izdatel'skii kombinat VINITI, 1959. 441 p. Bibliography: p. 431-438.

Romanian translation: *Dezvoltarea industriei Rominiei în anii regimului democrat popular* (Bucureşti, Editura Politică, 1960, 422 p.).

The most comprehensive Soviet work on Romanian industry, prior to the great expansion of 1958-1965. Contains information unavailable in Romanian sources, especially on Soviet-Romanian economic relations.

1856. Roberts, Henry L.   Rumania; Political Problems of an Agrarian State. New Haven, Yale University Press, 1951. Hamden, Conn., Archon Books, 1969. 414 p. Map. Bibliography: p. 381-399.
*See also* entries no. 1683, 1747, 1896, *and* 1990.

A classic study on the political-economic problems of Romania between the First World War and the aftermath of the Second World War. Contains a useful statistical appendix for the prewar period and an annotated bibliography.

1857. Rumania. *Direcţia Centrală de Statistică.*   Dezvoltarea agriculturii Republicii Populare Române; culegere de date statistice (The development of agriculture in the Romanian People's Republic; a collection of statistical data). Bucureşti, 1961– 601 p. Illus. (part col.), maps (part col.).
*See also* entry no. 1897.

A detailed compilation of agricultural statistics complementing the statistical yearbooks. Provides comprehensive coverage of physical input and output data, but supplies very little information on prices, costs, and sales. An index of the real incomes of peasants and other data for the early 1950s not contained in the above compilation may be found in an earlier volume published by the Direcţia Centrală de Statistică: *Dezvoltarea agriculturii Republicii Populare Romîne* (The development of the agriculture of the Romanian People's Republic) (Bucureşti, Direcţia Centrală de Statistică, 1961, 418 p., maps [part col.], diagrs. [part col.], tables).

1858. Rumania. *Direcţia Centrală de Statistică.*   Dezvoltarea industriei Republicii Populare Romîne; culegere de date statistice (The development of the industry of the Romanian People's Republic; compilation of statistical data). Bucureşti, 1964. 415 p. Illus. (part col.).
*See also* entry no. 1903.

Supplies more detailed breakdowns of industrial output, of the labor force, and of the capital stock employed in industry than the statistical yearbooks. Virtually no information on current costs, sales, and profits.

1859. Ţaigar, Simion.   Veniturile populaţiei şi nivelul de trai în R.P.R. (The income of the population and the standard of living in the Romanian People's Republic). Bucureşti, Editura Politică, 1964. 295 p. Illus. Bibliographical footnotes.

In spite of its apologetic character, this is the best available survey of postwar developments in the field of wages, social benefits, consumption, and levels of living.

1860. Vacarel, Iulian.   Finanţele Republicii Populare Romîne (The finances of the Romanian People's Republic). Bucureşti, Editura Didactică şi Pedagogică, 1964. 310 p. Bibliographical footnotes.

Chiefly devoted to the state budget, but also includes chapters on the finances of state enterprises and insurance. Very few financial statistics, but still somewhat more informative than Mihail Popovici's *Sistemul bugetar al R.P.R.* (The budget system of the Romanian People's Republic) (București, Editura Științifică, 1964, 270 p.). Some useful data for the period 1950 to 1956 may be found in Alexander Șesan's *Aspecte din istoria aparatului financiar din R.P.R.* (Aspects of the history of the financial apparatus in the Romanian People's Republic) (București, Editura Științifică, 1958, 225 p., illus.).

## D. SERIALS

1861. Probleme economice (Problems of economics). 1949– București. Monthly.
*See also* entry no. 1873.
Published by the Institute for Economic Research of the Academy of Sciences and by the Society for Economic Science of the Romanian Socialist Republic. An indispensable source of information on Romanian economic theory and practice.

1862. Revista de statistică (Statistics journal). 1956– București. Frequency varies.
Publication of the Central Direction of Statistics, specializing in statistical problems and containing occasional articles on mathematical economics. Supplies few statistical data not published in systematic statistical compilations. Particularly useful for the detailed study of the methods used by statisticians in collecting their data and in constructing their aggregates.

1863. Revue roumaine des sciences sociales. Série de sciences économiques. 1957?– Bucarest, Éditions de l'Académie de la République Socialiste Roumaine. Semiannual.
Good selection of articles in French, English, and Russian on various aspects of the Romanian economy.

1864. Viața economică (Economic life). 1963– București. Weekly.
Published by the Society for Economic Science of the Romanian Socialist Republic. Features topical articles on the economy of Romania, past and present. Each number contains detailed and objective information on foreign (including capitalist) economies.

# 41

# the society

*by Ghiţă Ionescu*
*(With the exception of section H)*

General Works and Surveys 1865-1871
Periodicals 1872-1874
Sociological Thought and Research 1875-1881
The Socioeconomic Structure 1882-1887
Women, Youth, Social Welfare 1888-1891
Agriculture 1892-1898
Industry, Labor, Social Strata 1899-1905
Psychology 1906-1911

## A. GENERAL WORKS AND SURVEYS

1865. Academia Republicii Populare Romîne. L'homme et la société contemporaine. Bucarest, Éditions de l'Académie de la République populaire roumaine, 1963. 391 p.

A symposium of essays inquiring into a wide range of problems concerning the relationship between man and society.

1866. Chetaru, Ovidiu, *and* Al. Tănase. Dezvoltarea suprastructurii socialiste in România: Aspecte sociologice (The development of the socialist superstructure in Romania: sociological aspects). Bucureşti, Editura Politică, 1966. 398 p.

Orthodox Marxist-Leninist interpretation of the building of the "socialist superstructure" in Romania since 1947, but with a dash of the Romanian doctrine of sovereignty and nationalism.

1867. Constantinescu, Miron, *ed.* Cercetări sociologice contemporane (Contemporary sociological research). Bucureşti, Editura Ştiinţifică, 1966. 394 p.

Edited by the holder of the recently reopened chair of sociology at Bucharest University, this work contains several studies on minor sociological problems of contemporary Romania.

1868. Ionescu, Ghiță.   Communism in Rumania, 1944-1962. London, New York, Oxford University Press, 1964. 378 p. Bibliography: p. 358-367.
See also entries no. 1751 and 1989.

————.   The Politics of the European Communist States. New York, Praeger, 1967. 302 p. Bibliography: p. 291-296.
See also entry no. 149.
The first contains an analysis of the evolution of Romanian society in the eighteen years. The second deals with the relations between state and society in Romania and the other East European states.

1869. Lepădătescu, Mircea.   Sistemul organelor statului în Republica Socialistă România (The system of state organs in the Socialist Republic of Romania). București, Editura Ştiinţifică, 1966. 411 p.
Useful as a general Marxist-Leninist study of the relations between state and society in the Socialist Republic of Romania.

1870. Pătrăşcanu, Lucreţiu.   Sub trei dictaturi (Under three dictatorships). București, Forum, 1945. 256 p.
See also entry no. 1744.
French edition published as Sous trois dictatures (Paris, J. Vitiano, 1946, 326 p.). This book, mainly political, is also a significant interpretation by a Romanian Marxist-Leninist of the socioeconomic evolution of Romania between the two world wars.

1871. Rumania. Direcţia Centrală de Statistică.   Population Census of February 21st, 1956; General Results. Bucharest, 1959. 74 p.

## B. PERIODICALS

1872. Analele Institutului de studii istorice şi social-politice de pe lângă C.C. al P.C.R. (Annals of the Institute of Historical and Sociopolitical Studies attached to the Central Committee of the Romanian Communist Party). 1955– Bucureşti.
Although concerned primarily with historical problems, this publication contains numerous studies of social history.

1873. Probleme economice (Problems of economics). 1949– Bucureşti. Monthly.
See also entry no. 1861.
The principal journal of economics in Romania since 1949. Frequently publishes studies on, or related to, social problems.

1874. Revue roumaine des sciences sociales. 1956– Bucarest. Quarterly.

Roumanian Journal of Sociology. 1962– Bucharest. Irregular.

Two periodicals designed to inform the foreign public of the work of the Romanian school of sociology. Contain translations of some studies and research in the field. The English edition is a selective anthology; the French edition is divided into several series (economic, juridic, philosophic, etc.).

## C. SOCIOLOGICAL THOUGHT AND RESEARCH

1875. Academia Republicii Socialiste România. Academy of the Socialist Republic of Romania; Organization, Research. Bucharest, Editura Academiei, 1966. 318 p.
*See also* entry no. 1579.
Apart from providing the English-speaking reader with a general view of the work and organization of the most august learned body of the Socialist Republic of Romania, it also contains useful references to social research now underway in Romania.

1876. Bădină, Ovidiu.   Cercetarea sociologică concretă; tradiții românești (Specific sociological research; the Romanian tradition). București, Editura Politică, 1966. 189 p.
An attempt made by a young Romanian sociologist to show the continuity between the old Romanian school of sociology, criticized by the communist theoreticians, and the new "empirical" research undertaken in the 1960s in some Romanian universities. Also contains a useful bibliography.

1877. Dobrogeanu-Gherea, Constantin.   Neoiobăgia; studiu economico-sociologic al problemei noastre agrare (Neo-serfdom; an economic-sociological study of our agrarian problem). București, Socec, 1910. 494 p.
*See also* entry no. 1721.
The principal work of the founder of Romanian socialist doctrine and the theory of "neo-serfdom."

1878. Gusti, Dimitrie.   Sociologia militans; introducere in sociologia politică (Militant sociology; an introduction to political sociology). București, Institutul Social Român, 1935. 614 p.
The main theoretical work of the leading Romanian sociologist. Extracts have been published in his *Pagini alese* (Selected writings) (București, Editura Științifică, 1965, 405 p.).

1879. Mosely, Philip E.   The Sociological School of Dimitrie Gusti. Sociological Review, v. 28, no. 2, Apr. 1936: 165.

1880. Pătrășcanu, Lucrețiu D.   Problemele de bază ale României (The basic problems of Romania). 3d ed. București, Editura de Stat, 1946. 337 p. Bibliographical notes: p. 329-337.
An uncertain and involved attempt by the author to reconcile

his genuinely scholarly queries with the propaganda line of the Romanian Communist Party to which he still belonged.

1881. Stere, Constantin.   Socialdemocratism sau poporanism (Social democracy or populism). Viaţa românească (Iaşi), Aug. 1907: 170-193; Sept. 1907: 313-341; Oct. 1907: 15-48; Nov. 1907: 173-208; Jan. 1908: 49-75; Apr. 1908: 59-80.
See also entry no. 1730.
A series of articles rightly recognized as the basic text of Romanian populism.

## D. THE SOCIOECONOMIC STRUCTURE

1882. Grindea, Dan.   Venitul naţional în Republica Socialistă România (The national income of the Socialist Republic of Romania). Bucureşti, Editura Ştiinţifică, 1966. 521 p.
Marxist theoretical analysis of the national income, containing a substantial amount of special statistics.

1883. Iordan, D. I.   Venitul naţional al României (The national income of Romania). Bucureşti, Cartea Românească, 1929. 284 p.
A scholarly work on the national income in the 1920s. Somewhat hampered by a paucity of statistics.

1884. Madgearu, Virgil N.   Evoluţia economiei româneşti după războiul mondial (Romanian economic evolution since the World War). Bucureşti, Independenţa Economică, 1940. 403 p. (Biblioteca economică, studii şi cercetări, 1)
See also entry no. 1741.
This classic work on the Romanian economy contains a most important analysis of the basic social problems of the country.

1885. Manuilă, Sabin.   Demografia rurală a României (The rural demography of Romania). Bucureşti, Institutul Central de Statistică, 1940. 30 p. Illus., charts, tables.

————.   Structure et développement du peuple roumain. Paris, 1940.
The most scholarly works on the subject by Romania's foremost statistician.

1886. Rădulescu, I., and M. Dulea. Structura economică şi de clasă a Republicii Populare Române (The economic and class structure of the Romanian People's Republic). Bucureşti, Editura Politică, 1960. 100 p.
An orthodox Marxist-Leninist précis on the class structure of the Romanian People's Republic.

1887. Rumania. Direcţia Centrală de Statistică.   Recensămîntul popu-

lației din 21 februarie 1956; structura social-economică a populației (The population census of February 21st, 1956; the socioeconomic structure of the population). București, 1960-1961. 2 v.
*See also* entry no. 1643.
A useful reference work.

## E. WOMEN, YOUTH, SOCIAL WELFARE

1888. Asigurările sociale de stat în Republica Socialistă România (State social security in the Socialist Republic of Romania). București, Editura Politică, 1968. 208 p.
Collection of official texts and legislation on the present system of social security in Romania.

1889. Boiangiu, Constantin, Mircea Epureanu, *and* Mihail Rob. Protecția muncii în Republica Socialistă România (Labor protection in the Socialist Republic of Romania). București, Editura Politică, 1966. 127 p.
Description of the social legislation in the Romanian Socialist Republic.

1890. Conferința națională a femeilor din Republica Socialistă România (National conference of women of the Socialist Republic of Romania). București, Editura Politică, 1966. 91 p.
Account of the national conference of Romanian women held in 1966, which discussed the role of women in the Socialist Republic of Romania.

1891. Statutul unităților și detașamentelor de pionieri din Republica Socialistă România (The statutes of the Pioneer units and detachments in the Socialist Republic of Romania). București, Editura Politică, 1967. 47 p.
Statutes of the "Pioneers," an official organization for children between the ages of nine and fourteen in the Socialist Republic of Romania.

## F. AGRICULTURE

1892. Gormsen, Marius. Short Introduction to the Principal Structural Problems of Agriculture in Rumania. Bucharest, Cartea Româneasca, 1945. 77 p.
This excellent report by a Danish expert on Romania's agricultural problems also makes important comments on the Romanian peasant class.

1893. Gusti, Dimitrie, *ed.* 60 sate românești (60 Romanian villages). București, Institutul de Științe Sociale al României, 1941-1943. 5 v. (1 unpublished).
A survey of village life and communities undertaken in 1938 by

teams of students under the supervision of Professor Gusti. An invaluable source.

1894. Hall, Donald J.    Romanian Furrow. London, Methuen, 1933. 224 p. Front., plates, ports.

Impressionistic, but very penetrating account of the life and condition of the Romanian peasant between the two world wars.

1895. Mitrany, David.    The Land and the Peasant in Rumania; the War and Agrarian Reform (1917-1921). London, H. Milford, Oxford University Press; New Haven, Yale University Press, 1930. New York, Greenwood Press, 1968. 627 p. Maps, diagrs. Bibliography: p. 594-611.

*See also* entries no. 1680 *and* 1835.

A massive and by now classic work on the subject.

1896. Roberts, Henry L.    Rumania; Political Problems of an Agrarian State. New Haven, Yale University Press, 1951. Hamden, Conn., Archon Books, 1969. 414 p. Map. Bibliography: p. 381-399.

*See also* entries no. 1683, 1747, 1856, *and* 1990.

This work has now become indispensable for the student of Romanian society, before and after the Second World War, as well as for all those interested in the special problems of an agrarian state.

1897. Rumania. *Direcţia Centrală de Statistică.*    Dezvoltarea agriculturii Republicii Populare Române; culegere de date statistice (The development of agriculture in the Romanian People's Republic; a collection of statistical data). Bucureşti, 1961– Illus. (part col.), maps (part col.).

*See also* entry no. 1857.

Although, or perhaps because, it stops before the "achievement of collectivization," this chronological collection of agricultural statistics is useful for tracing the ups and downs of Romanian agriculture under communism.

1898. Stahl, Henri H., *ed.*    Nerej, un village d'une région archaïque; monographie sociologique. Bucarest, Institut de sciences sociales de Roumanie, 1939. 3 v. Illus., maps, plates, tables. (Bibliothèque de sociologie, ethique et politique: Sociologie de la Roumanie 1)

Sociological research in depth, even if now outdated.

## G. INDUSTRY, LABOR, SOCIAL STRATA

1899. Ionescu, Constantin.    Forţa de muncă în Republica Socialistă România. Din recensămîntele anilor 1952, 1955, 1961 şi 1964 (The labor force in the Socialist Republic of Romania; from the censuses of 1952, 1955, 1961, and 1964). Bucureşti, Direcţia Centrală de Statistică, 1967. 448 p.

Based on not entirely reliable official statistical findings, this book attempts to describe the growth of industrial manpower in Romania after the nationalization of industry and the first two five-year plans for industrialization.

1900.   Labor. *In* Cretzianu, Alexandre, *ed.* Captive Rumania: a Decade of Soviet Rule. New York, Praeger, 1956. p. 374-389.

Useful only as an outraged description of how the Romanian communist government destroyed in 1945-1947 the independence of the trade unions and transformed them into "transmission belts" of its dictatorship. Written by "a former member of the Bucharest bar."

1901.   Mircea, Biji, G. Belu, *and others.*   Resursele de muncă și utilizarea lor in economia națională (Labor resources and their utilization in the national economy). *In* Dezvoltarea economică a României, 1944-1964. București, Editura Academiei, 1964. p. 184-237.

Collective research on the growth of industrial manpower during the first twenty years of communist administration.

1902.   Petrescu. Constantin T.   Socialismul în România (Socialism in Romania). București, 1945. 441 p.

*See also* entry no. 1728.

This attempt to trace the history of the socialist movement in Romania by the leader of the Romanian Socialist Party who died in a communist prison, is indispensable as a contribution to the history of the workers' class and of the trade unions in Romania.

1903.   Rumania. *Direcția Centrală de Statistică.*   Dezvoltarea industriei Republicii Populare Române; culegere de date statistice (The development of industry in the Romanian People's Republic; a collection of statistical data). București, 1964. 415 p. Illus. (part col.).

*See also* entry no. 1858.

English version published as *The Growth of Industry in the Rumanian People's Republic; Compendium of Statistics* (Bucharest, 1964, 134 p.).

1904.   Voinea, Șerban.   Marxism oligarhic; contribuție la problema dezvoltării capitaliste a României (Oligarchic Marxism; a contribution to the problem of capitalist development in Romania). București, Editura I. Brănișteanu, 1926. 251 p.

Originally conceived as an answer to Zeletin's book on the Romanian bourgeoisie, this work by one of the most serious Romanian Marxists is an important contribution to the study of Romanian society after the First World War.

1905.   Zeletin, Ștefan.   Burghezia română, originea și rolul ei istoric (The Romanian bourgeoisie; its origin and historical role). București, Cultura Națională, 1925. 393 p.

*See also* entry no. 1748.

An ingenious rather than scholarly essay on the role of the middle classes in Romanian society, before and after the First World War.

## H. PSYCHOLOGY

### by Josef Brožek

1906. Fischbein, E.    Conceptele figurale (Spatial concepts). Bucureşti, Editura Academiei Republicii Populare Romîne, 1963. 473 p.

The subtitle specifies the content. It reads as follows: "Theoretical and experimental investigations on the nature of geometrical concepts and their development during ontogenesis." Summaries in Russian and in French (p. 457-473).

1907. Popescu-Neveanu, Paul.    Tipurile de activitate nervoasă superioară la om (Types of higher nervous activity in man). Bucureşti, Editura Academiei Republicii Populare Romîne, 1961. 445 p.

Based on the study of the literature of the subject and on the author's investigative work. Contains an extensive list of references, principally to Russian publications (p. 383-420), and summaries in Russian and in English (p. 433-442).

1908. Revue roumaine des sciences sociales. Série de psychologie. 1964– Bucarest, Académie de la République Socialiste Roumaine. Semi-annual.

Publishes in the major languages original papers, reviews, bibliographies, and notes on current developments in the field. This journal is the principal source of information on Romanian psychology for readers not familiar with the Romanian language.

1909. Roşca, Alexandru, ed.    Tratat de psihologie experimentală (Experimental psychology). Bucureşti, Editura Academiei Republicii Populare Romîne, 1963. 650 p. Illus.

This university textbook of general experimental psychology is the result of cooperative endeavor involving seven authors. Ample references to world literature, chiefly to Soviet publications, are appended to each chapter. This is probably the best source of information on the work of Romanian psychologists. Extensive summaries in Russian, French, and English.

1910. Romanian Scientific Abstracts. Social Sciences.    1964– Bucharest. Monthly.

See also entry no. 1570.

Includes abstracts of Romanian writings on psychology.

1911. Şchiopu, Ursula.    Curs de psihologia copilului (Textbook of child psychology). Bucureşti, Editura Didactică şi Pedagogică, 1963. 464 p.

Discusses the history and general aspects of child psychology and considers the psychological characteristics of children from infancy to adolescence. The references, appended to each of the 10 chapters, are limited almost solely to Russian and Romanian literature.

# 42

# ıntellectual and
# cultural lıfe

## A. LANGUAGE

*by Emanuel Turczynski*

### 1. Reference and Survey Works, Serials

1912. Academia Republicii Populare Romîne. *Filiala Cluj. Institutul de Lingvistică.* Atlasul lingvistic romîn; seria nouă (Linguistic atlas of Romania; new series). Bucureşti, Editura Academiei Republicii Populare Romîne, 1956-1965. 4 v. Illus., col. maps.

1913. Densuşianu, Ovid. Histoire de la langue roumaine. Paris, E. Leroux, 1901-1938. 2 v.

An excellent linguistic history. A new Romanian edition was recently published as *Istoria limbii romîne* (Bucureşti, Editura Ştiinţifică, 1961).

1914. Leipzig. Universität. *Institut für rumänische Sprache.* Jahresbericht. Leipzig, J. A. Barth, 1894-1921. 29 v.
Includes numerous studies on Romanian linguistics. Continued since 1925 as *Balkan-Archiv*.

1915. Limba română (The Romanian language). 1952– Bucureşti, Editura Academiei. Bimonthly.
Includes articles on linguistics, the literary language, history of Romanian linguistics, philology, grammar, and vocabulary. See also *Studii şi cercetări lingvistice* (Linguistic studies and research) (Bucureşti, Editura Academiei, 1950– quarterly).

1916. Puşcariu, Sextil I.   Die rumänische Sprache, ihr Wesen und ihre volkliche Prägung. Translated by Heinrich Kuen. Leipzig, Harrassowitz, 1943. 612 p. 35 maps (Rumänische Bibliothek, 1)
Originally published as *Limba română, volumul I. Privire generală* (The Romanian language, v. 1. General survey) (Bucureşti, Fundaţia pentru Literatură şi Artă "Regele Carol II," 1940).

1917. Rosetti, Alexandru.   Istoria limbii romîne (A history of the Romanian language). Bucureşti, Editura Ştiinţifică, 1964-1966. 6 v. Maps.
A basic study of the origins and development of the Romanian language. Includes a bibliography and index of authors.

1918. Ruffini, Mario.   La scuola latinista romena, 1780-1871; studio storico-filologico. Roma, Angelo Signorelli, 1941. 192 p. (Piccola biblioteca Romena, 8)

1919. Schroeder, Klaus-Henning.   Einführung in das Studium des Rumänischen. Sprachwissenschaft und Literaturgeschichte. Berlin, Erich-Schmidt, 1967. 159 p.
*See also* Wolfgang Rothe's *Einführung in die historische Laut und Formenlehre des Rumänischen* (Halle/Saale, Niemeyer, 1957, 133 p., bibliographical references).

## 2. Grammar, Pronunciation

1920. Lombard, Alf.   Le verbe roumain; étude morphologique. Lund, C. W. K. Gleerup, 1954-1955. 2 v. Bibliography: v. 2, p. 1132-1141.
*See also*:
Academia Republicii Populare Romîne. *Institutul de Lingvistică.* Gramatica limbii romîne (A grammar of the Romanian language). Bucureşti, Editura Academiei, 1963, 2 v.

1921. Nandriş, Grigore.   Colloquial Roumanian: Grammar, Exercises,

Reader, Vocabulary. London, Kegan Paul, Trench, Trubner, 1945. 340 p. Illus. (map). 4th rev. impression: London, Routledge and Paul; New York, Dover Publications, 1966. 252 p.

A good textbook of the Romanian language. *See also* Ana Cartianu, Leon Leviţchi, and Virgil Stefănescu-Drăgăneşti's *A Course in Modern Rumanian* (v. 1) and *An Advanced Course in Modern Rumanian* (2d ed.) (Bucharest, Publishing House for Scientific Books, 1964). Still one of the best descriptive grammars of Romanian is Carlo Tagliavini's *Rumänische Konversations-Grammatik*, 5th ed. (Heidelberg, Julius Groos Verlag, 1938, 452 p.).

1922. Nandriş, Octave.   Phonétique historique du roumain. Paris, C. Klincksieck, 1963. 321 p. (Bibliothèque française et romane. Ser. A: Manuels et études linguistiques, 5)

A synoptical presentation of the Latin elements in the Romanian language. *See also* Anton Balotă's *La nasalisation et le rhotacisme dans les langues roumaine et albanaise* (Bucarest, 1926). For pre-Ottoman elements in Romanian *see* Heinz F. Wendt's *Die türkischen Elemente im Rumänischen* (Berlin, Akademie-Verlag, 1960, 188 p.), reviewed in *Zeitschrift für romanische Philologie* (Tübingen), v. 77, 1961: 434-436.

1923. Sandfeld, Kristian, *and* Hedvig Olsen.   Syntaxe roumaine. Paris, Droz; Copenhague, Munksgard, 1936-1962. 3 v.

A work of basic research, indispensable for the study of the structure of the Romanian language.

### 3. Monolingual Dictionaries

1924. Dicţionarul limbii romîne literare contemporane (A dictionary of the contemporary Romanian literary language). Bucureşti, Editura Academiei Republicii Populare Romîne, 1955-1957. 4 v.

The standard dictionary of modern Romanian.

1925. Dicţionarul limbii romîne moderne (A dictionary of the modern Romanian language). Bucureşti, Editura Academiei Republicii Populare Romîne, 1958. 961 p. Illus., col. plates, col. maps.

A basic encyclopedic dictionary, containing more than 50,000 entries. May be supplemented by *Dicţionarul limbii române* (Bucureşti, Editura Academiei Republicii Populare Romîne, 1913–), four volumes of which have been published to date (A-M).

1926. Meyer-Lübke, Wilhelm.   Romanisches etymologisches Wörterbuch. 3d rev. ed. Heidelberg, C. Winter, 1935. 1204 p. (Sammlung romanischer Elementar- und Handbücher, III. Reihe: Wörterbücher, 3)

Originally published in 1911. Essential for Latin elements in the Romanian language. *See also* Sextil Puşcariu's *Etymologisches Wörterbuch der rumänischen Sprache*, v. 1 (Heidelberg, C. Winter, 1905, 235 p. [Sammlung romanischer Elementarbücher, III. Reihe: Wörterbücher, 1]).

## 4. Dialectology

1927. Klein, Karl K., *and* Ludwig E. Schmitt, *eds.* Siebenbürgisch-deutscher Sprachatlas. v. 1. Marburg, N. G. Elwert, 1961. 21 p. Fold. col. maps (Deutscher Sprachatlas; Regionale Sprachatlanten, 1)

A basic work. *See also* the following dialect studies: *Siebenbürgische Mundarten. Beiträge*, by Karl Klein, Helmut Protze, and Hellmut Klima (Berlin, Akademie-Verlag, 1959, 143 p.); *Wörterbuch der nordsiebenbürgischen Handwerkssprache*, by Friedrich Krauss (Siegburg, F. Schmitt, 1957, 1199 p.); *Die Mundart von Burgberg. Laut- und Formenlehre eines Siebenbürgisch-sächsischen Dorfes*, by Artur Maurer (Marburg, N. G. Elwert, 1959, 153 p., tables); *Die Mundart der siebenbürgischen Landler; eine bairische Siedlermundart des 18. Jahrhunderts*, by Alfred Obernberger (Marburg, N. G. Elwert, 1964, 170 p., 8 maps); and *Die Landler in Siebenbürgen; Geschichte und Mundart*, by Bernhard Capesius (Bukarest, Akademie der Rumänischen Volksrepublik, 1962, 190 p., map.).

1928. Papahagi, Tache. Dicţionarul dialectului aromîn, general şi etimologic. Dictionnaire aroumain (macédo-roumain) générale et étymologique. Bucureşti, Editura Academiei Republicii Populare Romîne, 1963. 1264 p. Illus.

A basic work, on the vocabulary of the Macedo-Romanian language spoken by the Vlach people. Especially important for Balkanologists and Romanists who deal with East-Roman languages. *See also* Grigore Nandriş's "The Arumanian or Macedo-Rumanian Element in the Oxford Heptaglott Lexicon," *Slavonic and East European Review*, no. 35, 1956/57: 345-359.

## B. LITERATURE

*by Emanuel Turczynski*

### 1. Serials and Bibliography

1929. Academia Republicii Populare Romîne. *Biblioteca.* Bibliografia literaturii romîne, 1948-1960 (Bibliography of Romanian literature, 1948-1960). Chief editor: Tudor Vianu. Bucureşti, Editura Academiei Republicii Populare Romîne, 1965. 1123 p.

A systematic bibliography.

1930. Revue des études roumaines. v. 1– 1953– Paris. Annual.

Contributions by émigré Romanian writers and scholars in the fields of literary history and folklore.

1931. Romanian Review. v. 1– 1946– Bucharest. Frequency varies.

A literary review, also published in German, French, and Russian editions.

1932. Studii şi cercetări de istorie literară şi folclor (Studies and research on the history of literature and folklore). 1952– Bucureşti. Quarterly.

1933. Viaţa românească (Romanian life). 1906-1916, 1920-1940, 1944– Bucureşti. Monthly.
>   A leading literary periodical which has published many important original works.

## 2. Histories of Literature and Anthologies

1934. Cartojan, Nicolae.   Cărţile populare în literatura românească (Popular prose romances in Romanian literature). Bucureşti, Editura Casei Şcoalelor, Fundaţia pentru Literatură şi Artă Regele Carol II, 1929-1938. 2 v.
>   May be supplemented by the more recent *Cărţile populare în literatura romînească*, by Ion Chiţimia and Dan Simionescu (Bucureşti, Editura pentru Literatură, 1963, 2 v.).

1935. Dumitriu, Petru.   Gescheiterte Koexistenz; Skizze einer Literaturgeschichte Rumäniens im letzten Jahrzehnt. Osteuropa (Stuttgart), v. 11, 1961: 783-795.
>   *See also* Dumitru Micu's *Literatura romînă la începutul secolului al XX-lea, 1900-1916; publicaţii, grupări, curente* (Romanian literature from the beginning of the 20th century, 1900-1916; publications, groupings, tendencies) (Bucureşti, Editura pentru Literatură, 1964, 344 p.).

1936. Dumitriu, Petru, *ed.*   Rumänien erzählt. Frankfurt am Main, Hamburg, Fischer, 1967. 175 p.
>   Twelve Romanian short stories in German translation. *See also* Romul Munteanu's *Rumänische Anthologie* (Halle/Salle, Niemeyer, 1962, 134 p.), and Nicolae Iorga's *Anthologie de la littérature roumaine des origines au XX^e siècle* (Paris, Delagrave, 1920).

1937. Lupi, Gino.   Storia della letteratura romena. Firenze, G. C. Sansoni, 1955. 431 p. Illus., 32 plates, ports., facsims.
>   Contains a detailed bibliography of the important Romanian literature prior to the Second World War. The author is well acquainted with both the literature and the country.

1938. Munteano, Basil.   Modern Roumanian Literature. Bucharest, Editura Cuvântul, 1943. 322 p.
>   Translated by Cargi Sprietsma. Originally published as *Littérature roumaine (Panorama de la littérature roumaine contemporaine)* (Paris, Sagittaire, 1938, 332 p.).

1939. Panaitescu, Petre P.   Die Anfänge des Schrifttums in rumänischer Sprache. Südostforschungen (München), v. 11, 1952: 3-33.

1940. Popovici, D.   La littérature roumaine à l'époque des lumières. Sibiu,

Centrul de Studii şi Cercetări privitoare la Transilvania, 1945. 516 p. (Bibliotheca Rerum Transilvaniae, XII)
*See also* entry no. 1767.
A basic work on Romanian literature of the Age of Reason. Includes ample bibliographic data.

1941. Rosetti, Alexandru, *and others.*   Istoria literaturii romîne (A history of Romanian literature). Bucureşti, Editura Academiei Republicii Populare Romîne, 1964– Illus., facsims., ports.
Includes excerpts, social and critical commentary, a bibliography, and indices. Published volumes:
1. Folclorul. Literatura romînă în perioada feudală, 1400-1780 (Folklore. Romanian literature in the feudal period, 1400-1780). 1964, 807 p.
2. De la şcoala ardeleană la junimea (From the Transylvanian school to the Junimea group). 1968, 840 p.

1942. Steinberg, Jacob, *ed.*   Introduction to Rumanian Literature. New York, Twayne Publishers, 1966. 441 p.
" . . . contains sketches, short stories, and excerpts from novels written in the span of less than a century, ranging from Creanga's 'Recollections from Childhood' and including the works of the youngest prose writers of our days."

1943. Tappe, Eric D., *comp.*   Rumanian Prose and Verse. London, University of London, 1956. 193 p.

### 3. Leading Writers and Poets

1944. Creangă, Ion.   Opere (Works). Revised edition, with a glossary by G. T. Kirileanu. Bucureşti, Editura pentru Literatură, 1957. 351 p.

———.   Contes populaires de Roumanie (Poveşti). Translated and annotated by Stoian Stanciu. Introduction by N. Iorga. Paris, Maisonneuve, 1931. 245 p.
The first is a collection of Creangă's tales, with a glossary of his idiomatic expressions. The second includes the best tales by the popular Romanian writer. *See also* George Călinescu's *Ion Creangă; viaţa şi opera* (Ion Creangă; life and work) (Bucureşti, Editura pentru Literatură, 1964, 405 p.), and Jean Boutière's *La vie et l'œuvre de Ion Creangă, 1837-1889* (Paris, 1930, 254 p.).

1945. Eminescu, Mihail.   Opere (Works). Critical edition, revised by Perpessicius. Bucureşti, Fundaţia pentru Literatură şi Artă "Regele Carol II," 1939-1963. 6 v. Port., facsims.

———.   Der Abendstern. Gedichte. Berlin-Weimar, Aufbau-Verlag, 1964.
*See also* Eminescu's *Opere alese* (Selected works) (Bucureşti, Editura pentru Literatură, 1964, 1965, 3 v.), published by the same

editor. The six-volume edition contains a thoroughly annotated and nearly complete collection of Eminescu's works.

*Der Abendstern* is a verse translation of Eminescu's best-known poems, with a commentary by Werner Bahner. *See also* Rosa del Conte's *Mihai Eminescu o dell'Assoluto* (Modena, Societa tipografica editrice modenese, 1962, 482 p.); Alain Guillermon's *La genèse intérieure des poésies d'Eminescu* (Paris, Didier, 1963, 470 p.); László Gáldi's *Stilul poetic al lui Mihai Eminescu* (The poetic style of Mihai Eminescu) (Bucureşti, Editura Academiei, 1964, 472 p.); and Alfred Noyer-Wiedner's "Die Einheit des Mannigfaltigen in Eminescus Somnoroase păsărele" in *Romanische Forschungen* (Frankfurt am Main), v. 77, 1965: 259-280.

1946. Sadoveanu, Mihail.    Opere (Works). Bucureşti, Editura pentru Literatură şi Artă, 1948–
    *See also* the following English translations of Sadoveanu's works: *The Hatchet*, translated from the Romanian by Eugenia Farca (London, Allen and Unwin, 1965, 162 p.); *Evening Tales*, translated from the Romanian by E. Farca and others (Bucharest, Foreign Languages Publishing House, 1958, 443 p.); *Tales of War* (Bucharest, "The Book" Publishing House, 1954, 199 p.); and *Ancuţa's Inn* (Bucharest, "The Book" Publishing House, 1954, 175 p.).

### 4. Foreign Literary Influences

1947. Duţu, Alexandru.    Shakespeare in Rumania; a Bibliographical Essay. Bucharest, Meridiane, 1964. 239 p. Illus., facsims., ports.
    *See also* entry no. 2067.
    A review of translations and performances of Shakespeare's plays in Romania. See also *Istoria Teatrului în România* (A history of the theater in Romania), v. 1, edited by G. Oprescu (Bucureşti, Editura Academiei, 1965, 379 p., illus.).

1948. Klein, Karl K.    Rumänisch-deutsche Literaturbeziehungen; Zwei Studien aus dem Aufgabenkreis der Deutschforschung an den rumänischen Universitäten. Heidelberg, C. Winter, 1929. 150 p.
    *See also* the periodicals *Forschungen zur Volks- und Landeskunde* (Sibiu, Verlag der Akademie der Rumänischen Volksrepublik, 1959–) and *Südostdeutsche Vierteljahresblätter* (München, Südostdeutsches Kulturwerk, 1958–).

### C. FOLKLORE

#### by Emanuel Turczynski

#### 1. Surveys and Reference Works

1949. Block, Martin.    Rumänien. *In* Kultur der romanischen Völker. Potsdam, Akademische Verlagsgesellschaft Athenaion, 1939. p. 347-367. (Handbuch der Kulturgeschichte, Abt. 2, Bd. 3)
    A good survey of Romanian folklore.

1950. Bachelin, Léo, *ed.*    Sept contes roumains. Avec une introduction générale et un commentaire folkloriste. Translated by Jules Brun. Paris, Firmin-Didot, 1894. 343 p.

> An informative introduction to Romanian folklore, with seven well-chosen examples of Romanian folk tales.

1951. Schullerus, Adolf.    Verzeichnis der rumänischen Märchen und Märchenvarianten, nach dem System der Märchentypen Antti Aarnes zusammengestellt. Helsinki, Acad. Scient. Fennica, 1928. 99 p. (F F Communications no. 78)

> Of great value for research on Romania's folklore. *See also* Ovidiu Bîrlea's *Antologie de proză populară epică* (Anthologies of popular epic prose) (Bucureşti, Editura pentru Literatură, 1966, 3 v.).

## 2. Anthologies and Collections

1952. Cortés y Vázquez, Luis L.    Antología de la poesía popular rumana. Edición bilingüe con un estudio preliminar y notas. Salamanca, Consejo Superior de Investigaciones Científicas, Colegio Trilingüe, Universidad de Salamanca, 1955. 326 p. Illus. (Tesis y estudios Salamantinos, 8)

> An extensive collection of Romanian popular poems.

1953. Creangă, Ion.    Folk Tales from Roumania. Translated from the Romanian by Mabel Nandris. London, Routledge & Paul, 1952. 170 p.

> A good selection of tales by the great Romanian writer.

1954. Dima, Alexander, *ed.*    Rumänische Märchen. Leipzig, Harrassowitz, 1944. 264 p. (Rumänische Bibliothek 2)

> A small but representative selection. For Transylvania *see also* Josef Haltrich's *Deutsche Volksmärchen aus dem Sachsenlande in Siebenbürgen* (München, Hans Meschendörfer, 1956, 260 p.).

1955. Diplich, Hans, *tr.*    Rumänische Lieder. München, Südostdeutsche Kulturwerk, 1953-1963. 2 v.

> A representative selection of Romanian folk songs, excellently translated into the corresponding German poetical form.

1956. Friedwagner, Matthias.    Rumänische Volkslieder aus der Bukowina. v. 1. Liebeslieder. Würzburg, K. Triltsch, 1940. 595 p. Illus., maps. (Literaturhistorische-musikwissenschaftliche Abhandlungen, v. 5)

> Cultural and literary relations between Romania and Germany in the area are discussed in *Buchenland. Hundertfünfzig Jahre Deutschtum in der Bukowina*, edited by Franz Lang (München, Verlag des Südostdeutschen Kulturwerks, 1961, 527 p., illus., maps, diagrs., plan, tables).

1957. Löpelmann, Martin.    Aus der Volksdichtung der macedonischen Rumänen. Leipzig, Armanen-Verlag, 1934. 132 p.

> *See also* Mihail Obedenaru-Georgiade's *Texte macedo-române, basme și poesii poporale de la Crusova; publicate după manuscrisele originale de I. Bianu* (Macedo-Romanian texts, folk tales and poems from Crusova; published from original manuscripts of I. Bianu) (București, Sito-Tipografia C. Göbl, 1891, 380 p.).

1958. Rudow, Carl F.    Rumänische Volkslieder. Translated with an introduction: Der rumänische Volksgeist nach seinen dichterischen Erzeugnissen. 2d ed. Leipzig, H. Barsdorf, 1888. 112 p.

## 3. Special Studies

1959. Beza, Marcu. Paganism in Roumanian Folklore. London and Toronto, 1928. 161 p. Illus., front., plates.

> A useful synopsis.

1960. Irimie, Cornel.    Das Hirtenwesen der Rumänen; Forschungen in der Marginimea Sibiului bei Hermannstadt/Sibiu. München, Südosteuropa-Verlagsgesellschaft, 1965. 60 p. (Südosteuropa-Studien, 7)

1961. Popinceanu, Ion.    Religion, Glaube und Aberglaube in der rumänischen Sprache. Nürnberg, H. Carl, 1964. 312 p. Bibliography: p. 267-275. (Erlanger Beiträge zur Sprach-und Kunstwissenschaft, Bd. 19)

> Linguistic-folkloristic study of the ecclesiastical and liturgical language and of the vocabulary of cult and profane language. Reviewed in *Südost-Forschungen* (München), v. 4, 1965: 324-325.

1962. Schullerus, Adolf.    Siebenbürgisch-sächsische Volkskunde im Umriss. Leipzig, Quelle und Meyer, 1926. 179 p. Illus.

> *See also* Tancred Bănățeanu, Gheorghe Focșa, and Emilia Ionescu's *Arta populara în Republica Populara Romîne; Port, țesături, cusaturi* (Popular art in the Romanian People's Republic; costumes, textiles, embroideries) (București, Editura de Stat pentru Literatură și artă, 1958, 421 p., 56 col. plates).

1963. Weigand, Gustav L.    Die Aromunen; ethnographisch-philologisch-historische Untersuchungen über das Volk der sogenannten Makedo-Romanen oder Zinzaren. Leipzig, J. A. Barth, 1894-1895. 2 v.

> Collection of various kinds of folk poetry. Reviewed in *Zeitschrift für romanische Philologie*, v. 20, 1896: 88-100.

1964. Wlislocki, Heinrich von.    Volksdichtungen der siebenbürgischen und südungarischen Zigeuner. Wien, C. Graeser, 1890. 431 p. Illus.

> See also *Zigeunermärchen*, edited by Walter Aichele and Martin Block (Düsseldorf-Köln, Diederich, 1962, 392 p.).

## D. HISTORY OF THOUGHT

*by Radu R. Florescu*

### 1. Intellectual and Cultural Life in General

1965. Antip, C.   Contribuţii la istoria presei române (Contributions to the history of the Romanian press). Bucureşti, Uniunea Ziariştilor din Republica Populară Romînă, 1964. 216 p.

Although Marxist in viewpoint and heavily centered upon the labor press, this is a scholarly work which traces the evolution of the newspaper in Romania, on the basis of the most recent research, from the foundation of Eliade's *Curierul românesc* (Romanian Courier) in the 1830s to the publication for the first time of the current communist dailies. A specific contribution to the history of the working class press is *Presa muncitorească şi socialistă din România* (The Romanian labor and socialist press) (Bucureşti, Editura Politică, 1964–). Based upon a study of one hundred newspapers, the two volumes published so far cover the evolution of the socialist movement from 1865 to 1921 as reflected in the leftist press and centering upon the newspaper *Contemporanul*, edited by Dobrogeanu-Gherea, father of Romanian socialism. An older general work, still of some value, is Nicolae Iorga's *Istoria presei româneşti de la primele începuturi până la 1916* (A history of the Romanian press from its first beginnings until 1916) (Bucureşti, Adevărul, 1922, 315 p.). Although outdated, Iorga's is undoubtedly the best comprehensive survey of the Romanian press. It is very useful for the revolutionary literature of 1848.

1966. Berza, M., *ed.*   Cultura moldovenească în timpul lui Ştefan cel Mare; culegere de studii (Moldavian culture at the time of Stephen the Great; collection of studies). Bucureşti, Editura Academiei, 1964. 682 p. Bibliography: p. 641-675.
*See also* entry no. 1622.

An impressive commemorative volume on various aspects of Moldavian culture during one of its greatest periods. It includes broad analytical essays on written culture (E. Stănescu), urban culture (R. Manolescu), relations with Byzantium (A. Elian), art (C. Nicolescu), etc. Working with an impressive new documentation, this team of historians has succeeded in reformulating many of the old questions and has established a good case for an elaborate program for further research. The bibliography by Şerban Papacostea is one of the most comprehensive for the cultural history of the period and, in particular, for the reign of Stephen the Great. At the end of the volume there is a convenient summary, in French, of each individual study.

1967. Călinescu, G.   Istoria literaturii române (The history of Romanian literatur). Bucureşti, Editura pentru Literatură, 1968. 429 p.

An abridged version of Calinescu's large-scale history of Romanian literature, which remains the most profound synthesis of Romanian culture from its origins to 1946. The present compendium is of great value to the nonspecialist interested in gaining a general impression of Romania's cultural progress through the ages. A full-scale re-edition of this work is to be published in the near future.

1968. Cartea în Republica Populară Română (The book in the Romanian People's Republic). Bucureşti, Scînteia, 1959. 156 p.

A convenient guide to the history of the book in the Romanian Socialist Republic, though overstating the qualitative and quantitative changes which have occurred in all forms of writing since 1948. For a richly illustrated historical survey see Émile Turdeanu's *Le livre roumain à travers les siècles. Exposition présentée dans le cadre de la journée roumaine 24-26 janvier, Paris 1956* (Paris, Institut Universitaire Charles I, 1956, 55 p., plates).

1969. Constantinescu-Iaşi, Petre.    Relaţiile culturale romîno-ruse din trecut (Romanian-Russian cultural relations of the past). Bucureşti, Editura Academiei Republicii Populare Romîne, 1954. 228 p. Bibliography: p. 225-228.

Professor Constantinescu-Iaşi traces the fruitful bilateral cultural contacts between the Romanian lands and Russia to the medieval period. The role of Russian teachers, printers, artists, and ecclesiastics in promoting a cultural Renaissance in Moldavia is emphasized as much as that of Moldavians (Peter Movilă, D. Cantemir, etc.) who played a significant role in Russia's cultural past.

1970. Curticăpeanu, Vasile.    Die rumänische Kulturbewegung in der österreichisch-ungarischen Monarchie. Bukarest, Editura Academiei Republicii Socialiste România, 1966. 149 p. Bibliography: p. 143-150. (Bibliotheca historica Romaniae, Studien, 10)

The most recent Marxist evaluation of cultural nationalism in Transylvania during the struggle for political emancipation. Basing his findings on a variety of new documentary sources, the author traces the development of Transylvania schools, reading societies, and printing presses, and studies their interaction with similar institutions in the Old Kingdom and their role in promoting Transylvanian irredentism.

1971. Eliade, Pompiliu.    De l'influence française sur l'esprit public en Roumanie. Les origines; étude sur l'état de la société roumaine a l'époque des règnes phanariotes. Paris, E. Leroux, 1898. 436 p. Bibliography: p. 405-422.

Eliade's work is tidy, well written and very readable, but too imaginative and partisan in spirit. In spite of its date, the work is still of some value as a study in the 18th century cultural history.

1972. Ionniţiu, Nicolae.    Despre carte şi slujitorii ei (About the book and its servants). Bucureşti, Cartea Românească, 1942. 400 p.

The most scholarly history of the Romanian book and of the printing press from the beginning of the 16th century to the outbreak of the Second World War, written by the director of one of the largest publishers during the interwar period.

1973. Lovinescu, Eugen.   Istoria civilizaţiei române moderne (A history of modern Romanian civilization). Bucureşti, Ancora, 1924-1925. 3 v.

A classic liberal interpretation of the cultural forces which contributed to the formation of a distinctively modern Romanian civilization, and an assessment of its contributions to the culture of the West. For a more specialized work highlighting Western and particularly Italian cultural influences, *see* Nicolae Iorga's *Études roumaines. 1. Influences étrangères sur la nation roumaine* (Paris, Gamber, 1923, 91 p.).

1974. Momente ale revoluţiei culturale din România (Moments in the Romanian cultural revolution). Bucureşti, Editura Ştiinţifică, 1966. 373 p.

Eight studies by members of the Academy of the Romanian Socialist Republic which provide a synopsis of various aspects of the Marxist cultural revolution achieved by the current regime since 1948. A convenient analysis of the new approach is provided by Ioan Moraru's chapter on culture in general. For a briefer version in English one may consult *The Upsurge of Culture in the Rumanian People's Republic* (Bucharest, Institute for Cultural Relations with Foreign Countries, 1954, 205 p.).

1975. Săvulescu, Trăian.   Quatre-vingt dix années de vie académique en Roumanie. Bucarest, Editura Academiei Republicii Populare Romîne, 1956. 76 p.

A brief history of the Romanian Academy (now the Academy of the Romanian Socialist Republic), by a former president. The Academy began as a society for the compilation of a Romanian dictionary in 1866; today it embraces virtually all fields of intellectual endeavor in the sciences and the humanities, monopolizing the academic life of the nation and publishing the more distinguished works. Although tending to spotlight academic achievement since the reform of 1948, the author stresses continuity and recognizes the contributions of the past. The role of distinguished members of the Romanian Academy is briefly evoked in the Romanian version of this work, *90 ani de viaţa academică în ţara noastră* (Bucureşti, Editura Academiei Republicii Populare Romîne, 1956, 177 p.).

1976. Zamfirescu, Dan.   Studii şi articole de literatură Română veche (Studies and articles in ancient Romanian literature). Bucureşti, Editura pentru Literatură, 1967. 321 p.

A brilliant series of studies and essays relating to Romanian literature from the 15th to the 18th century, stressing the essential unity and continuity of Romanian culture in all the three principalities. *See also* the author's study "Expresie genială a vechii civilizaţiei românești" (A genial expression of the old Romanian civilization) in *Argos*, no. 8, 1967.

## 2. Philosophy

1977. Bădărău, Dan. Filozofia lui Dimitrie Cantemir (The philosophy of Dimitrie Cantemir). București, Editura Academiei Republicii Populare Romîne, 1964. 412 p.

> The first comprehensive Marxist account of the philosophical aspect of Cantemir's thought, based on some previously unpublished manuscripts. This work represents Cantemir not only as a traditional humanist but also as a profound philosopher of history who gave a dynamic cyclical explanation of the historical process. Includes a summary in French (p. 394).

1978. Bădărău, Dan. Un système matérialiste métaphysique au 19ᵉ siècle: La philosophie de Basile Conta 1846-1882. Paris, Les Presses universitaires de France, 1924. 304 p.

> The only scholarly work in a Western language attempting to evaluate the importance of Vasile Conta, a Romanian adherent of the 19th century materialist school.

1979. Bagdasar, N. Istoria filozofiei romînești (A history of Romanian philosophy). București, 1940. 438 p.

> The best prewar history of Romanian philosophy. This work centers upon the thought of the 17th and 18th century chroniclers, the "National School" founded by G. Lazar at the beginning of the 19th century, and the idealistic bourgeois tradition established by Vasile Conta and Titu Maiorescu. For an older history which is still of some use, *see* Marin Stefănescu's *Filozofia românească* (Romanian philosophy) (București, Răsăritul, 1922, 328 p.).

1980. Buhociu, Octavian. La philosophie de l'histoire d'A.D. Xenopol; l'évolution, la guerre, la série historique, la logique de la succession. Paris, Facultés des Lettres, Université de Paris, 1957. 189 p. Bibliography: p. 178-189.

> A doctoral dissertation with a brilliant analysis of A. D. Xenopol's *Principes fondamentaux de l'histoire* (Paris, E. Leroux, 1899, 348 p.), a work which made a good deal more impact in the West than it did in his native Romania.

1981. Gulian, C. I., *ed.* Istoria gîndirii sociale si filozofice în Romînia (The history of social and philosophic thought in Romania). București, Editura Academiei Republicii Populare Romîne, 1964. 623 p. Bibliographical footnotes.

> The most recent general synthesis of the history of Romanian philosophy (15th to 20th century), based on Marxist-Leninist premises and written by a committee of scholars from the Philosophy Institute of the University of Bucharest and Cluj. This textbook concentrates upon neglected progressive thinkers, ties philo-

sophical problems to the material life of society, looks upon philosophy as a weapon in the class struggle, and downgrades the idealist tradition of the past. One of the chief problems facing the Western reader is the Marxist chronology. This work supersedes C. I. Gulian's *Din istoria filozofiei în Romînia* (Concerning the history of Romanian philosophy) (București, Editura Academiei Republicii Populare Romîne, 1955-1960, 3 v.). For a study on the penetration of Marxist ideology to 1917 *see* Radu Pantazi's *Filozofia marxistă în Romînia* (Marxist philosophy in Romania) (București, Editura Politică, 1963, 224 p.).

1982. Iorga, Nicolae.   Cugetări (Reflections). București, Editura Tineretului, 1968. 304 p.

First published in 1911. Although containing but a small fragment of Iorga's philosophic thought, this work comes closer to a philosophy of history than any other work published by the great historian. The preface is written by Barbu Theodorescu, author of *Nicolae Iorga, viața și opera* (Nicolae Iorga, life and work), a two-volume biobibliography on Iorga (București, Cartea Românească, 1931-1935). Another work of some philosophical significance which remained unfinished in Iorga's lifetime, has been prepared for publication in 1969 by his daughter Liliana and his son-in-law Professor Pippide under the title *Materiale pentru o istorie umană* (Materials for a history of humanity) (București, Editura Academiei Republicii Socialiste Roînânia).

1983. Marxism-Leninism și gîndirea științifică romînească (Marxism-Leninism and Romanian scientific thought). București, Editura Academiei Republicii Populare Romîne, 1964. 340 p.

A number of studies in Marxist interpretations ranging from philosophy to fine arts. Of particular interest are "The Victory of Marxist-Leninist Ideology in Romania" by A. Joja; "The Marxist Interpretation of the History of our Country" by A. Oțetea; and "The Opposition between Marxism-Leninism and Contemporary Bourgeois Philosophy" by M. Ralea. See also *Dezvoltarea conștiinței socialiste în Republica Populară Română: contribuție la cercetarea problemei* (The development of a socialist conscience in the Romanian People's Republic: a contribution to research on the problem) (București, Editura Academiei Republicii Populare Romîne, 1961, 516 p., bibliography), a study of the role of the Communist Party in developing a "socialist conscience" among all segments of society on a wide variety of subjects.

1984. Philosophes roumains contemporains. București, Editura Academiei Republicii Populare Romîne, 1958. 307 p.

Fourteen studies reflecting the interests of contemporary philosophers· in a variety of problems. Among the more vital are "The Marxist-Leninist Dialectic as a Foundation of Methodology for Science" by A. Joja; "Marxism and Idealism in the History and Theory of Culture" by C. I. Gulian; "On the Philosophy of the Absurd" by N. Florian; "The Influence of Historical Forces on Perception" by M. Ralea; "The Double Negative and Current Language" by Dan Bădărău; "Ontology and Logic in Dialectical Materialism" by H. Wald; "Liberty and Logic" by Al. Tănase; "The Syllogism" by F. Tuțugan; "Unity of Logic in the History of Philosophy" by I. Banu; "Scientific Idea" by M. Breazu; and "Hegel's Concept" by D. D. Rosaca. Brief summaries appear in English and French at the end. *See also* Mihail Ralea's *Studii de psihologie și filozofie* (Studies in psychology and philosophy) (București, Editura Republicii Populare Romîne, 1955, 152 p.).

## 3. Social and Political Thought

1985. Bădină, Ovidiu.   Dimitrie Gusti; contribuție la cunoașterea operei și activității sale (Dimitrie Gusti; a contribution to the knowledge of his work and activity). București, Editura Științifică, 1965. 206 p.

The most recent Marxist evaluation of Professor Gusti's monographic sociological school which supports a gradual shift toward Marxist ideas. *See also* Erno Gall's *Sociologia burgheză din România; studii critice* (Bourgeois sociology in Romania; critical studies) (2 ed., București, Editura Politică, 1963, 279 p.), a generous assessment of Gusti's monographic school and a Marxist indictment of prewar sociological trends (such as S. Zeletin's liberal and C. Rădulescu-Motru's peasantist solutions). For a non-Marxist interpretation, *see* P. E. Mosely's "The Sociological School of Dimitrie Gusti," *Sociological Review*, v. 28, Apr. 1936: 149-165. Professor Gusti's complete works (*Opere*) are now being republished. The first volume, edited by O. Bădină and O. Neamțu, has thus far come out (București, Editura Științifică, 1968, 562 p.).

1986. Blaga, Lucian.   Gîndirea românească în Transilvania în secolul al XVIII-lea (18th century Romanian thinking in Transylvania). București, Editura Științifică, 1966. 230 p.

A posthumous study by a leading Romanian philosopher who views the ideology of the Romanian Transylvanian School as an expression of internal social and political needs. An excellent interpretation of Transylvanian Latinism by a Western scholar is Keith Hitchins' "Samuel Clain and the Rumanian Enlightenment in Transylvania," *Slavic Review*, v. 23, Dec. 1964: 660-675. *See also* Hitchins' *The Rumanian National Movement in Transylvania, 1780-1849* (Cambridge, Mass., Harvard University Press, 1969, 320 p.).

1987. Campbell, John C.   French Influence and the Rise of Rumanian Nationalism. The Generation of 1848. Cambridge, Mass., Unpublished doctoral dissertation, Harvard University, 1940. 463 p. Bibliography: p. 440-463.

Although unpublished, this is by far the most thorough and comprehensive study of the elements responsible for the formation of a Romanian national consciousness during the so-called era of national regeneration.

1988. Dobrogeanu-Gherea, Constantin.  Scrieri social-politice (Sociopolitical writings). Bucureşti, 1966. 425 p.

A selection of the writings of the leading exponent of Marxism in Romania, including excerpts from his famous work *Neoiobăgia: studiu economico-sociologic al problemei noastre agrare* (Neo-serfdom: an economic-sociological study of our agrarian problem) (Bucureşti, Socec, 1910, 496 p.). The standard work on Romanian socialism is Constantin T. Petrescu's *Socialismul în România* (Socialism in Romania) (Bucureşti, 1945, 441 p.). Over three-quarters of this book is devoted to the years preceding 1919. An interesting essay which focuses attention on the chief issues between Marxism and Populism in Romania is that of David Mitrany entitled "Marx against the Peasant," which appears in *London Essays in Economics: in Honor of Edwin Cannan*, edited by Theodor E. G. Gregory and Hugh Dalton (London, Routledge, 1927), p. 319-376. See also *Texte privind dezvoltarea gândirii social politice în România* (Texts concerning the development of social political thinking in Romania) (Bucureşti, Editura Academiei Republicii Populare Romîne, 1954, 412 p.). It is essentially a series of excerpts maintaining the continuity of progressive thinking from the 16th century chroniclers to the late 19th century.

1989. Ionescu, Ghiţă.  Communism in Rumania, 1944-1962. London, New York, Oxford University Press, 1964. 378 p. Bibliography: p. 358-367.

*See also* entries no. 1751 *and* 1868.

Published under the auspices of the Royal Institute of International Affairs. Essentially a political history of Romania under the current regime, from the viewpoint of a Western scholar. The bibliography is useful. The communist position is best expressed in G. Gheorghiu-Dej's *Artikel und Reden; Auswahl aus den Jahren 1945-52* (Berlin, Dietz, 1955, 396 p., illus.) and *Artikel und Reden, Dezember 1955-Juli 1959* (Bukarest, Politischer Verlag, 1959, 812 p.). The most recent such work is Nicolae Ceauşescu's *The Romanian Communist Party, Continuer of the Romanian People's Revolutionary and Democratic Struggle of the Traditions of the Working Class and Socialist Movement in Romania* (Bucharest, Agerpress, 1966, 101 p.). For the political thinking underlining Romania's recent administrative reforms *see also* Nicolae Ceauşescu's *Expunere cu privire la îmbunătăţirea organizării administrative a teritoriului Republicii Socialiste România* (An exposition on the improvement of the administrative organization of the territory of the Romanian Socialist Republic) (Bucureşti, Editura Politică, 1968, 40 p.).

1990. Roberts, Henry L.  Rumania; Political Problems of an Agrarian State. New Haven, Yale University Press, 1951. Hamden, Conn., Archon Books, 1969. 414 p. Map. Bibliography: p. 381-399.

*See also* entries no. 1683, 1747, 1856, *and* 1896.

A penetrating treatment of the ideology of Romania's prewar political parties from 1907 to the period of communist control. His analysis of the political philosophy of the liberal, national peasant,

Iron Guard, and Carlist movements during the interwar period is particularly perceptive. The bibliography is invaluable, though outdated. Another symposium of useful lectures on the political theories prevalent during this same period was sponsored by the Romanian Social Institute: *Doctrinele partidelor politice* (The doctrines of the political parties) (Bucureşti, n.d., 1 v.). This includes studies on nationalism ((by N. Iorga); peasantism (by V. Madgearu); liberalism (by I. G. Duca); conservatism (by N. Marghiloman); neoliberalism (by M. Manoilescu); and socialism (by Ş. Voinea). The collection reflects the desire of the Romanians to relate their political parties to their Western counterparts.

1991. Rogger, Hans, *and* Eugen Weber, *eds.*   The European Right. A Historical Profile. Berkeley and Los Angeles, The University of California Press, 1965. 589 p.

Weber's chapter on Romania (p. 501-574) is a sympathetic and yet objective treatment of the history of the Iron Guard movement (the only scholarly account in the English language). The work is weak on sources and the bibliography only adequate for works in foreign languages (p. 573-574).

## 4. Scientific Thought

1992. Andonie, G. S.   Istoria matematicii din România (A history of mathematics in Romania). Bucureşti, Editura Ştiinţifică, 1966. 2 v.

The most ambitious history to date on the development of mathematical thought in Romania. This work contains a wealth of new biographic and monographic material on the founders of the Romanian mathematical school and includes an extensive bibliography at the end of each chapter. A third volume, to be published shortly, will treat the period from 1944 to the present.

1993. Din istoria medicinei româneşti şi universale (Concerning the history of Romanian and world medicine). Bucureşti, Editura Academiei Republicii Populare Romîne, 1962. 524 p.

A recent survey of Romanian medical achievement viewed within the context of medical progress in other lands. By far the most interesting study is that of Valeriu L. Bologa, a leading Romanian historian of medicine. In N. Vătămanu's *De la începuturile medicinei româneşti* (The beginnings of Romanian medicine) (Bucureşti, Editura Ştiinţifică, 1967, 300 p.), a leading expert traces the origins of Romanian medicine to the 14th century leprosariums, 16th century dispensaries, and prominent 17th century medical practitioners in Transylvania. For medical achievements in Transylvania, *see* Valeriu L. Bologa's *Contribuţiuni la istoria medicinei din Ardeal* (Contributions to the history of medicine in Transylvania) (Bucureşti, Cartea Românească, 1927, 104 p.). *See also* Victor Gomoiu's "Contributions de quelques medécins roumains aux progrès des sciences" in *Archives internationales d'histoire des sciences*, v. 1 (Lausanne, 1948), p. 291, a report presented to the 5th International Congress on the History of Science, held at Lausanne in 1948.

1994. Inaintaşi de seamă ai ştiinţei româneşti (Notable precursors of Romanian science). Bucureşti, 1961. 228 p.

A series of biographical essays of uneven merit, based on Marxist-Leninist premises and dealing with 19th century Romanian scientists.

1995. La vie scientifique en Roumanie: Sciences pures. v. 1. Bucarest, Academia Română, 1936. 371 p.

The most ambitious prewar monograph on the totality of scientific life in Romania, containing a series of unequal studies on the development of mathematics, physics, chemistry, etc. By far the most interesting study is that of Petre Sergescu, "Le développement des sciences mathématiques en Roumanie," essentially a historical sketch of the development of Romanian science from the 16th century to the 20th. The emphasis throughout is on the close relationship between Romanian and Western (especially French) scientific currents of thought. For the applied sciences, see *La vie scientifique en Roumanie; sciences appliqués*, v. 2 (Bucarest, Academia Română, 1937, 247 p.), which contains articles on civil engineering, agriculture, mining, industry, medicine, and veterinary medicine. The study on medicine by Professor George Marinescu has an excellent description of the progress of Romanian medicine until 1937. It also contains a list of the more interesting medical papers presented to international medical congresses during the interwar period. One flaw is a tendency to eulogize Romanian achievements.

1996. La science dans la République Populaire Roumaine. Bucureşti, Editura Academiei Republicii Populare Romîne, 1953. 201 p.

A slightly uncritical description of recent scientific accomplishments in the Romanian Socialist Republic. Another source of information on the progress of the various scientific disciplines are the proceedings of the yearly scientific congresses and the numerous scientific journals (about 130 in all), which include *Gazeta de matematică şi fizică* (Journal of mathematics and physics), a monthly published by the Society of Mathematical Sciences and offering a wide choice of theoretical studies; *Revista de fizică şi chimie* (Review of physics and chemistry), a monthly published by the Society of Physics and Chemistry; the *Romanian Medical Review*, etc.

## E. RELIGION (OTHER THAN JUDAISM)

### by Radu R. Florescu

1997. Beza, Marcu. The Rumanian Church. London, Society for Promoting Christian Knowledge, 1943. 64 p. Illus., plates, bibliography.

A brief but convenient historical sketch of the Romanian Orthodox Church by a leading Romanian Byzantinist. The book stresses ecumenism, the strong cultural ties with Byzantium, and the preeminent role of Orthodoxy in preserving national culture during the Middle Ages. The bibliography on page 60 is inadequate.

1998. Biserica Română Unită. Două sute cinci zeci de ani de istorie. (The

Uniate Church. Two hundred and fifty years of history). Madrid, Rivadenyra, 1952. 411 p.

The only recent general study of the Uniate Church of Transylvania, by a very unequal and somewhat prejudiced group of Uniate priests and scholars. This is certainly no definitive history (the authors readily admit the imperfections); the tone is apologetic, and the fact that this work was published four years after the forced reunion between the Uniate Church and Orthodoxy must be borne in mind. The only archives which have been consulted in depth are the Vatican sources. The study nevertheless contains a wealth of information and places in true focus the significant role played by the Uniate Church in Romania's national life. Of the individual studies, Mons. Octavian Bârlea's on the Uniate Church between the wars and P. Carnaţiu's on the union of the Translvanian Church with Rome are the most scholarly. This work can be looked upon as the basis for a vast program of future research. The bibliography at the end of each of the seven main sections is fairly comprehensive.

1999. Cândea, Romulus.  Der Katholizismus in den Donaufürstentümern; sein Verhältnis zum Staat und zur Gesellschaft. Leipzig, R. Voigtländer, 1916. 139 p. (Beiträge zur Kultur- und Universalgeschichte, Heft 36. Heft 10 der neuen Folge)

A scholarly work, initially published as a doctoral dissertation at the University of Leipzig, on the relationship of the Catholic Church to the Romanian state and society.

2000. Cultele în România (Religious rites in Romania). *In* Enciclopedia României. v. 1. Bucureşti, Imprimeria Naţională, 1936. p. 417-422.

Although issued under the auspices of the government of King Carol II, the section on the religious denominations in Romania is a fair and critical essay on the parallel historical development of all religious denominations in the Romanian lands, with particular emphasis on the interwar period. There is a short but useful bibliography on page 442.

2001. Gherman, *Rev.* Pierre.  L'Ame roumaine écartelée; faits et documents. Paris, Editions du Cèdre, 1955. 258 p. Illus., ports., maps.

An overdramatized and not too scholarly account of church-state relations in Romania, with some insight into the pre-Khrushchev era. The author's viewpoint is determined by the fact that he is a priest of the Uniate Church, disestablished by the communists and forcibly reunited with Orthodoxy in 1948. In view of the more recent conciliatory attitude toward the Church, the pessimistic predictions of Rev. Gherman do not seem to have been fulfilled. A condensed English version of the book is *Ten Years Ago; the Story of the Persecution of the Catholic Church of Byzantine Rite in Romania* (Youngstown, Ohio, Gaspan Printing Company, 1958, 43 p.). *See also* Nicolae Pop's *Kirche unter Hammer und Sichel; die Kirchen*

*Verfolgung in Rumänien, 1945-1951* (Berlin, Morus-Verlag, 1953, 146 p., illus., ports., maps).

2002. Iorga, Nicolae.    Istoria Bisericii româneşti şi a vieţii religioase a Românilor (History of the Romanian Church and the religious life of the Romanians). Vălenii-de-Munte, Neamul Românese, 1908-1909. 2 v.

Although outdated, these two volumes, written under government assignment, still represent the most comprehensive study of the history of religious life in all three Romanian provinces from the early beginnings of Christian life to the end of the 19th century. This is by no means one of Iorga's best works, but it is based on a rich collection of primary sources collected from the archives of bishoprics and monasteries, often the result of personal investigations. The organization is confusing because of dissimilar conditions of religious experience in the older principalities of Moldavia and Wallachia and Transylvania. Main themes are often lost in a superfluity of historical minutiae. The close association between Orthodoxy and Romanian national life is overemphasized to the detrmient of the Uniate experience in Transylvania. Contains no bibliography, only incidental footnotes and a useful appendix containing the names of the various ecclesiastical leaders in all three provinces. A second, revised edition was published in 1928-1930.

2003. Istoria bisericii Romîne, manual pentru institutele teologice (The history of the Romanian church; a manual for theological institutes). Bucureşti, Editura Institutului Biblic şi de Misiune Ortodoxă, 1957-1958. 2 v.

The only exhaustive study of the Romanian Orthodox Church published since 1948. Written by a collaborative team of priests (G. I. Moisescu, Şt. Lupas, A. Filipaşcu) under the auspices of the patriarchy, the book reflects official thinking and deals with such sensitive questions as relations between church and state and the reunion between the Uniate Church and Orthodoxy in 1948.

2004. Lupas, Ioan.    Ursprung und Entwicklung der bedeutendsten confessionellen Minderheiten in Rumänien. Vertrag gehalten im Aulagebäude der Friedrich-Wilhelms Universität in Berlin am 11 Mai 1934. Jena, J. W. Gronau, 1936. 23 p. Bibliographical footnotes. (Vom Leben und Wirken der Romänen, 11, Rumänische Reihe, Heft 8)

2005. Mateiu, Ion.    Contribuţiuni la istoria dreptului bisericesc (Contributions to the history of ecclesiastical law). v. 1. Bucureşti, Tipăritura Cărţilor Bisericeşti, 1922. 404 p. Bibliography: p. 399-404.

A study of church-state relations, with an excellent though outdated bibliography. An earlier and briefer analysis of the same subject which is still of some value is Alexandru Georgescu's *Beiträge zum Verhältnis zwischen Staat und Kirche in Rumänien* (Bukarest, Minerva, 1913, 71 p.; bibliography: p. 3-5).

2006. Meteş, Stefan. Istoria bisericii şi a vieţii religioase a românilor din Transilvania şi Ungaria (History of the Church and the religious life of the Romanians from Transylvania and Hungary). Sibiu, Cartea Românească, 1936. 596 p.

The most comprehensive and scholarly history of the Catholic, Lutheran, Calvinist, and Orthodox Churches of Transylvania and Hungary. The first volume unfortunately goes only to 1698, and the work was never completed.

2007. Popan, Flaviu, *and* Čedomir Drašković. Orthodoxie heute in Rumänien und Jugoslawien. Wien, Herder, 1966. 190 p.
See also entry no. 2933.

An instructive study on the organization and the present state of the Romanian Orthodox Church and of its relations with the communist state.

2008. Puşcariu, Ilarion. Metropolia Românilor ortodocşi din Ungaria şi Transilvania. Studiu istoric despre reînfiinţarea metropoliei dimpreună cu o colecţiune de acte (The Archbishopric of the Romanian Orthodox Church of Hungary and Transylvania. A historical study concerning the reestablishment of the archbishopric together with a collection of documents). Sibiu, 1900. 434 p.

An outdated though useful study of the struggle of the Orthodox Church of Transylvania from the time of its forceful incorporation into the Serbian bishopric of Carlowitz (1783) through the establishment of an autonomous archbishopric (1864). The latter half of the book, by far the more interesting, consists of documents in Latin, German, and Romanian reproduced from the archives of the archbishopric of Sibiu. These are particularly valuable for the period of Bishop Andrei Şaguna.

2009. Roth, Erich. Die Geschichte des Gottesdienstes der Siebenbürger Sachsen. Göttingen, Vandenhoeck und Ruprecht, 1954. 281 p. (Forschungen zur Kirchen- und Dogmengeschichte, Bd. 3)

The most recent and scholarly study of the Lutheran Saxon Church of Transylvania. *See also* Bishop Friedrich Teutsch's *Geschichte der Evangelischen Kirche in Siebenbürgen* (Hermannstadt, W. Kraft, 1921-1922, 2 v., map), which includes an excellent though outdated bibliography (v. 2, p. 619-624); and *Kirche und Schule der Siebenbürger Sachsen in Vergangenheit und Gegenwart* (Hermannstadt, W. Kraft, 1924, 367 p.).

2010. Roth, Erich. Die Reformation in Siebenbürgen. Ihr Verhältnis zu Wittenberg und der Schweiz. Graz-Köln, Böhlau, 1962-1964. 2 v. (Siebenbürgisches Archiv, 3. Folge)
A basic work, richly documented and containing a bibliography.

2011. Wilbur, Earl M. History of Unitarianism in Transylvania, England, and America. Cambridge, Mass., Harvard University Press, 1952. 518 p.

The only study in English on the history and development of unitarianism in Transylvania.

2012. Wirth, Guenter.   Christliches Leben im neuen Rumänien; Reportagen und Betrachtungen. Berlin, Union Verlag, 1954. 55 p.

An East German reporter's somewhat superficial glance at religious life in Romania, suggesting perfect coexistence between the state and the so-called minority churches (Protestant and Roman Catholic), thus contesting the view of the Reverend Gherman and others writing abroad. For fuller information on the life of the Orthodox Church in present-day Romania and the views of its clergy *see* the following reviews: *Biserica Orthodoxă Română* (The Romanian Orthodox Church) (Bucureşti, 1951–, monthly), the official organ of the Holy Synod, publishing primarily correspondence between the Romanian and other Orthodox Churches; and *Orthodoxia* (Orthodoxy) (Bucureşti, 1951–, quarterly), published by the Biblical Institute. Some idea of the religious life of minority churches can be gained from *Revista Cultului Mozaic din R.P.R.* (Review of the Jewish cult of the R.P.R.) (Bucureşti, 1956–); *Indrumătorul Creştin Baptist* (The Baptist Christian guidepost) (Bucuresti, 1957–, monthly); and *Curierul Adventist* (The Adventist courier) (Bucureşti, 1958–, bimonthly).

2013. Zeiller, Jacques.   Les origines chrétiennes dans les provinces danubiennes de l'Empire romain. Paris, E. de Boccard, 1918. 667 p. Bibliography: p. 603-630.

This work focuses on the study of Christian origins in all Roman Danubian lands (including Moesia and Illiricum). Chapter 2 (p. 27-52) represents one of the most scholarly accounts of the beginnings of Christian life in the Roman province of Dacia until the reign of Emperor Justinian. Another work, now outdated, which sets out to prove the Latin origins of the first Christian establishments in the Romanian lands is G. M. Ionescu's *Istoria bisericii Românilor din Dacia Trajană* (History of the Romanian Church of Trajan's Dacia), v. 1 (Bucureşti, Stabiliment de Arte Grafice Universală, 1905, 678 p.).

## F. Education

### by Radu R. Florescu

2014. Bîrsănescu, Ştefan.   Academia domnească din Iaşi 1714-1821 (The Princely Academy of Jassy, 1714-1821). Bucureşti, Editura de Stat Didactică şi Pedagogică, 1962. 204 p. Illus. Bibliography: p. 200-204.

A Marxist interpretation of the 107-year history of the first institution of higher learning in Moldavia, based upon rich new primary documentation drawn from the archives of this school. The Academy's organization and curriculum is set within the context of the socioeconomic needs of the period. There is a useful critique of prewar historiography on the subject, an interesting comparative note on similar institutions of higher learning functioning in the West during that time, and a wealth of information on student life, teaching standards, and curriculum. French and German summaries are included at the end. The bibliography is excellent, both for the pre-1948 and post-1948 periods.

2015. Braham, Randolph L.   Education in the Rumanian People's Republic. Washington, D.C., U.S. Government Printing Office, 1963. 229 p. Bibliography: p. 224-229 (U.S. Office of Education, Bulletin no. 1, 1964)

Written under government contract and published by the U.S. Office of Education. It is certainly the best analysis available in English of the prewar and communist period. This work is obviously directed to the professional educator and is at times exceedingly technical. Most of the conclusions point to the progress achieved since the Second World War in eradicating illiteracy and in creating the "socialist man." The prophecies, however, concerning the elimination of the lingering remains of nationalism seem unwarranted. There is a useful list of textbooks used in the various elementary and secondary schools and a fair bibliography (p. 224-229). See also *Education in Rumania (Rumanian People's Republic)*, by Herta Hasse and Seymour M. Rosen (Washington, D.C., U.S. Department of Health, Education, and Welfare, Office of Education, 1960, 26 p.). Two less satisfactory studies of education during the interwar years are Ely Palmer's *Education in Rumania* (Washington, D.C., Department of State, 1928, 31 p.), and Gaston Richard's "L'Education nationale dans l'état roumain contemporain, ses conditions ethniques et sociales," *Revue Internationale de Sociologie* (Paris), v. 42, no. 1/2, Jan.-Feb. 1934: 29-53.

2016. Bucharest University, 1864-1964. Edited by Alexandru Balaci and Ion Ionaşcu, with the cooperation of A. Halanay and others. Bucharest, Graphic Arts Printing Press, 1964. 84 p.

A compendium of unequal studies, edited on the occasion of the centenary of the University of Bucharest by a committee of scholars from the Academy. There is a good study of the first institution of higher learning in Wallachia (The Academy of St. Sava), which preceded the foundation of the University proper. With respect to the University, emphasis is placed on the period after 1948 when the whole structure was remodeled, though the essential continuity of academic life from 1864 onwards is not overlooked. There is an equally well-balanced companion volume available in English on the history of the Alexander Cuza University of Jassy: *The A. I. Cuza University of Jassy, 1860-1960* (Bucharest, Scientific Publishing House, 1960, 148 p.). *See also* C. Ionescu-Bujor's *Higher Education in Rumania* (Bucharest, Meridiane, 1964, 55 p.), which is little more than a guidebook on the philosophy and organization of higher learning in the Romanian People's Republic from 1944 to 1964. Most of the statistics are presented comparatively to underscore the achievements of the present régime. For recent innovations and experimentation, see also *Revista învăţământului superior* (1962–, monthly), published by the Ministry of Education.

2017. Le développement de l'enseignement de la République populaire roumaine. Bucarest, Meridian Publishing House, 1959–.

A series of reports presented to the International Conferences on Public Education, published in both English and French. It is the best means of keeping up to date with the various facets and recent changes of the educational movement in the Romanian Socialist Republic. For a very brief summary of the post-1948 approach, see *L'enseignement à la portée de tous dans la République populaire roumaine* (Bucarest, Éditions en langues étrangères, 1956, 55 p.). In addition see *Revista de pedagogie* (Pedagogical review) (1952–, monthly 1956-1958, bimonthly 1959–), the journal of the Institute of Pedagogical Science; and *Gazeta învăţământului* (The Education Gazette) (1949–, weekly, the official Journal of the Ministry of Education. Recent legal provisions on education are contained in *The Education Law of the Socialist Republic of Romania* (Bucharest, Didactical and Pedagogical Pub. House, 1968, 61 p.).

2018. Gabrea, I. Şcoala românească: structura şi politica ei (The Romanian school: its structure and policy). Bucureşti, Cartea Românescă, 1933. 342 p.

An adequate survey, outlining theories of education during the interwar years. See also *Organizarea învăţământului* (The organization of teaching), by G. C. Antonescu and Iosif I. Gabrea (Bucuresti, Cartea Românesca, 1933, 290 p.). A brief digest of 19th and 20th century legislation for primary education is contained in C. Angelescu's *Loi de l'enseignement primaire de l'état et de l'enseignement normal primaire* (Bucarest, Cartea Românească, 1925, 241 p., tables, diagr.). Reliable for prewar educational code is *Codul învăţământului primar, secundar, superior* (The primary, secondary, and higher education code), by Paul Negulescu, Ion Dumitrescu, George Alexianu, Titus Dragoş, and D. C. Demetrescu (Bucureşti, Editura librăriei Pavel Suru, 1929, 856 p.).

2019. Iorga, Nicolae. Istoria învăţământului românesc (The history of Romanian education). Bucureşti, Casa Şcoalelor, 1928. 350 p.

Translated into French by Alexandrine Dumitrescu as *Histoire de l'enseignement en pays roumain* (Bucarest, Édition de la Caisse des Écoles, 1932, 316 p.). Still the chief prewar synthesis covering the history of education in all Romanian lands from the close of the 15th century to the middle of the 19th. Written with Iorga's usual acumen, extraordinary erudition, and concern for detail, this book sets out to prove the popular prewar thesis of the beneficial effects that have resulted from cultural contacts with the Western world. Education contacts with Russia are deemphasized and scant attention is paid to the efforts of the Latinist School of Transylvania. One serious flaw is the organization of the book, always difficult when dealing with the history of all three provinces. There are innumerable small inaccuracies and imprecise citations in footnotes, index, and bibliography. A less brilliant but better-organized prewar synthesis is *Istoria pedagogiei românești* (History of Romanian pedagogy), by G. Tăbăcaru and C. Moscu (București, Tipografia Națională, 1929, 434 p.). *See also* P. Răscanu's *Istoria învățământului secundar* (History of secondary education) (Iași, Tipografia Nățională, 1906, 240 p.).

2020.  Potra, George.   Petrache Poenaru, ctitor al învățământului în țara noastră 1799-1875 (Petrache Poenaru, founder of education in our country, 1799-1875). București, Editura Științifică, 1963. 392 p. Bibliography: p. 287-392.

This work is based largely on new unpublished material and gives much fresh information about the educational philosophy of Petrache Poenaru, a pioneer in the organization of the Romanian educational system (he was director of Wallachian schools from 1832 until 1848). The bibliography is excellent.

2021.  Rura, Michael J.   Reinterpretation of History as a Method of Furthering Communism in Rumania: A Study in Comparative Historiography. Washington, D.C., Georgetown University Press, 1961. 123 p. Bibliography: p. 117-123.

A sound critique of communist indoctrination in the schools during the Stalinist period. It seems rather weak on the analysis of the teaching of history in prewar schools. For further information, on an anticommunist theme, see *The Perversion of Education in Rumania* (Washington, D.C., Rumanian National Committee, 1950, 96 p.). Essentially a detailed analysis of the educational reform of 1948, it is written by a group of exiled politicians with a definite bias. Its charge that the structure and content of education in Rumania was effectively Russified is relevant only for the 1948 to 1956 period. This study is now completely outdated.

2022.  Stanciu, Stoian, *ed.*   Din istoria pedagogiei românești: culegere de studii (Concerning the history of Romanian education: Collection of Studies). București, Editura de Stat Didactică și Pedagogică, 1965-1967. 3 v.

Revised and enlarged edition of the earlier *Din istoria pedagogiei românești* (București, 1957, 479 p.). The standard Marxist account, by a number of educators from the Academy of the Romanian Socialist Republic, tracing the development of Romanian education from its earliest beginning up to and including the socialist period. Great emphasis here has been placed upon the continuity of Romanian schooling and the contribution of the bourgeois educators of the past. A good deal of attention is given to Spiru Haret, the founder of the modern educational system in Romania.

2023.  Urechiă, Vasile A.   Istoria scólelor de la 1800-1864 cu o scurtă întroducere coprinḑend note din istoria culturei naționale anterioare secolului al 19-lea și cu numeróse fac-simile de documente, semnături autografe, etc. (The history of schools from 1800 through 1864, with a short introduction, including notes concerning the history of national culture preceding the 19th century, etc.). v. 1. Bucureşti, Imprimeria Statului, 1892. 404 p.

A classic honored by the Romanian Academy, and the first scientific investigation by a well-known historian on the beginnings of a national Romanian educational system. Should serve the reader as a primary source and reference because of its wealth of documentary material drawn from the archives of the Moldavian and Wallachian departments of education, from monasteries, bishoprics, educational institutions, and student diaries and notebooks.

## G. THE FINE ARTS

### by Radu R. Florescu

2024. Balş, G.    Bisericile şi mănăstirile moldoveneşti din veacul al 16-$^{lea}$ (Moldavian churches and monasteries of the 16th century). Bucureşti, Comisia Monumentelor Istorice, 1928. 397 p. Bibliography: p. 384.

A sequel to a study on Moldavian churches and monasteries at the time of Stephen the Great, tracing the development of ecclesiastical art from the reign of Prince Peter Rareş to Peter the Lame.

2025. Beza, Marcu.    Byzantine Art in Roumania. London, B. T. Batsford, 1940. 104 p.

Includes 47 color and black-and-white reproductions. A study of Moldavian and Wallachian artistic treasures which the author located in various Eastern churches and monasteries, particularly on Mt. Athos. These consist mostly of icons, holy-water vessels, caskets, embroideries, Gospel books, etc. The wealth of this legacy bears out the author's contention that the princes in both provinces considered themselves true patrons of Eastern Orthodoxy.

2026. Comărnescu, Petru.    Ion Ţuculescu. Bucharest, Meridiane, 1967. 77 p.

A challenging interpretation in English of the works of one of the most original of Romania's contemporary artists, by an unorthodox yet most stimulating art historian. For a more classical approach focusing on a more classical contemporary artist see Barbu Brezianu's study on Tonitza (Bucureşti, Editura Academiei Republicii Socialiste România, 1967, 217 p.). Mr. Brezianu is one of the most brilliant of Professor G. Oprescu's research assistants, and is at present working on a definitive biography of Brancusi.

2027. Dunăre, N., and L. Ghergariu, eds.    Arta populară din Valea Jiului regiunea Hunedoara (Popular art in the valley of the Jiu, the Hunedoara region). Bucureşti, Editura Academiei Republicii Populare Romîne, 1966. 581 p. Illus., maps. Bibliography: p. 523-533. (Studii de etnografie, 2)

The first large-scale regional study of folk art for the Hunedoara region. The authors look upon art from a strictly Marxist standpoint and with an eye to the peasants' needs to provide for their daily existence. They also react against the geographic determinist approach of the prewar school. Includes summaries in Russian and French.

2028. Geist, Sidney.   Brancusi: A Study of the Sculpture. New York, Grossman, 1968. 247 p.

Although hardly a definitive study this work is the first to relate Brancusi the man to the artist, with emphasis on the developmental sequence of the artist's work. Much of the research on Brancusi's pre-1914 work is owed to Mr. Barbu Brezianu of the History of Art Institute, Bucharest.

2029. Ionescu, Grigore.   Istoria arhitecturii în România (The history of architecture in Romania). Bucureşti, Editura Academiei Republicii Populare Romîne, 1962-1963. 2 v. Illus., maps, plans. Bibliography: v. 1, p. 509-513.

The most distinguished history of Romanian architecture, by the leading prewar specialist. The first volume covers the feudal period to the end of the sixteenth century; the second takes up the history of Romanian architecture from 1500 to 1944. A third is planned to describe recent developments. Though paying lip service to Marxist terminology, the work is conceived in traditional terms. The author emphasizes the impact of the Italian Renaissance in Moldavia and Transylvania and that of Byzantium in Wallachia. Stress is placed on the importance of folk architecture in determining style and on the impact of the rural over the urban areas. Thus, despite its eclectic nature, a basic unity of style is preserved throughout the ages. There is an excellent last chapter in the second volume dealing with the development of Romanian architecture between the two World Wars. For Ionescu's pre-Marxist views see *Istoria arhitecturii românesti din cele mai vechi timpuri până în 1900* (History of Romanian architecture from the earliest times up to 1900) (Bucureşti, Cartea Românească, 1937, 482 p.; French summary: p. 429-482). *See also* the studies by N. Ghika-Budeşti: "Evoluţia arhitecturii în Muntenia şi Oltenia, partea întâia: originile şi înrăuririle străine până la Neagoe Basarab" ("The evolution of architecture in Wallachia and Oltenia; Part one: the origins and foreign influences up to Neagoe Basarab"), *Buletinul Comisiei Monumentelor Istorice*, 20, 1927, p. 121-158; and "Partea doua: Vechiul stil românesc din veacul al 16$^{lea}$" (Part 2: the old Romanian style of the 16th century), *Buletinul Comisiei Monumentelor Istorice*, 23, 1930, p. 1-63. A convenient guide, existing in English translation, is *Arhitectura în Republica Populara Română* (Architecture in the Romanian People's Republic) (Bucureşti, Editura pentru Literatură şi Artă, 1952, 142 p.). Another summary in French is G. Gusti, I. Baroi, M. Cafee, and A. Moisescu's *L'Architecture en Roumanie* (Bucarest, Meridiane, 1965, 239 p.).

2030. Iorga, Nicolae.   L'art populaire en Roumanie, son caractère, ses rapports et son origine. Paris, Gamber, 1923. 135 p.

Studies the unitary character of Romanian popular art, preserved despite diverse manifestations in the three provinces. Iorga also stresses influences stemming from Serbia, Bulgaria, Greece, and even Albania, and relies upon ethnography to prove the common origins of popular art in Eastern Europe. On the same theme, *see* Tancred Bănățeanu's *Studii și cercetari de etnografie și arta populară* (Studies and research of ethnography and popular art) (București, Caiete de arta populară, 1960, 380 p.).

2031. Iorga, Nicolae.   Istoria artei medievale și moderne în legătură cu dezvoltarea societății (A history of medieval and modern art in connection with the development of society). București, P. Suru, 1923. 198 p.

An interesting endeavor to explain artistic history in terms of the development of society, written with Iorga's usual flair but poorly organized. In essence it presents his course at the University of Bucharest.

2032. Iorga, Nicolae, *and* G. Balș.   Histoire de l'art roumain ancien: l'art roumain du 14ième siècle au 19ième siècle; description et documentation historique. Paris, E. de Boccard, 1922. 412 p. Illus., plates, plans. Bibliography: p. 401.

A classic synthesis describing the development of a "Romanian" style of artistic endeavor. Iorga traces the medieval origins of Romanian art back to 15th century Moldavia, much influenced by Western modes of artistic expression. In contrast, Wallachian art developed later and bore the stamp of Byzantium. Through reciprocal influences a genuine national style emerged in the 17th century. Balș's contribution to the history of Moldavian architecture is truly outstanding. The bibliography is outdated.

2033. Muzicescu, M. A., *and* M. Berza.   Mănăstirea Sucevita (The monastery of Sucevita). București, Editura Academiei Republicii Populare Romîne, 1958. 196 p. Illus. Bibliography: p. 195-196. (Monografii de monumente, 1)

A scholarly assessment of the artistic significance of one of the last great monastic foundations of the 16th century, which combines classical with post-classical architectural elements and marks a period in the evolution of religious art at the time of Stephen the Great. The Meridiane Publishing House has an interesting popularized series in English and the other Western languages on the main monastic foundation.

2034. Old Rumanian Art. București, Meridiane, 1965. 1 v.

A recent guide to the Old Romanian section of the Art Museum of the Romanian Socialist Republic. Contains 164 reproductions illustrating a wide variety of Moldavian, Wallachian, and Transylvanian artistic forms, including embroidery, sculpture, ornaments, ceramics, religious manuscripts, miniatures, icons, mural paintings, etc. The introductory study stresses the native element, particularly in the decorative arts and in craftsmanship, and notes the gradual secularization of artistic endeavor at the close of the Middle Ages.

2035. Oprescu, George.    N. Grigorescu, 2d ed. Bucureşti, Meridiane, 1963. 181 p.

Translations in English, French, German, Spanish, and Russian. Part of the *Masters of Rumanian Painting* series, each volume of which includes a short introductory study, a brief biographical sketch, and reproductions of the most representative works. Among the studies that have appeared to date are B. Moisescu-Măciucă's *T. Aman* (Bucureşti, Meridiane, 1962, 1 v.), M. Benedict's *St. Luchian* (Bucureşti, Meridiane, 1962, 1 v.), M. Popescu's *Grigorescu* (Bucureşti, Meridiane, 1963, 181 p.), and T. Vianu's *Corneliu Baba* (Bucureşti, Meridiane, 1964, 182 p.).

2036. Oprescu, George.    Peasant Art in Roumania. London, The Studio, 1929. 182 p. Bibliography: p. xv.

Essentially a simplified English version of a far more basic Romanian work by the same author, *Arta ţărănească la români* (Bucuresti, Cultura Naţională, 1922, 74 p.). Intended for the British public, it appeared initially in a special issue of the journal *The Studio*.

2037. Oprescu, George.    Roumanian Art from 1800 to our Own Days. Malmo, Ljustrycksanstalt Kroon, 1935. 192 p. Plates, ports.

Not one of Oprescu's outstanding works. Includes a 62-page introduction, the remainder of the book being reproductions of the most noted works of nineteenth century sculptors and artists. On the basis of vigor and frankness of style, Oprescu rates the lesser-known painters Andreescu and Luchian above the more internationally respected Grigorescu.

2038. Oprescu, George.    Sculptura românească (Romanian sculpture). Bucureşti, Meridiane, 1965. 1 v.

A reprint of a work published in 1955. The author traces the evolution of Romanian sculpture from feudal times to the current period. There are over 120 reproductions of outstanding works by both native sculptors and foreign artists (G. Asachi, K. Storck, F. Storck, P. Paciurea, C. Brancusi, I. Jalea, C. Melea, C. Baraschi, G. Anghel, S. Ionescu, V. Hegel, etc.). Brief biographical comments and a critique of each artists's work are included. A comparable work is available in English: D. Dancu, A. Diaconu, and C. D. Constantinescu's *Rumanian Sculpture* (Bucureşti, 1957, 156 p.).

2039. Oprescu, George.    Scurtă istorie a artelor plastice în Republica Populară Romînă (A short history of plastic arts in the Romanian People's Republic). Bucureşti, Editura Academiei Republicii Populare Romîne, 1957-1958. 2 v. Bibliography: v. 1, p. 301-302; v. 2, p. 245-248.

Volume 1 is subtitled *Arta românească în epoca feudală* (Rumanian art in the feudal period), and volume 2, *Secolul al 19-lea* (The 19th century). The most significant work on the subject to date, edited by Academician G. Oprescu with the help of a team from the Academy of the Romanian Socialist Republic. The new sources clarify many of the problems raised by Iorga and others in previous monographs. In accordance with recent trends, the sources of artistic inspiration emphasize native rather than foreign influences. The chapters by R. Bogdan on Romanian painters of the 19th century and that by R. Niculescu on sculpture are particularly impressive.

2040. Oprescu, George, *and* M. Popescu, *eds.* Artele plastice în România după 23 August 1944 (The plastic arts in Romania after August 23, 1944). Bucureşti, Editura Academiei Republicii Populare Romîne, 1959. 186 p. Illus., bibliography.

Also published in an abridged English version: *The Plastic Arts in Rumania after 23 August 1944* (Bucharest, Meridiane, 1961, 46 p.). An essential companion volume to Oprescu's more ambitious work (*see* entry no. 2039), this provides a study of the revolt of contemporary Romanian painters and graphic artists against the conventional foreign inspired themes of the preceding generation. The emphasis nevertheless centers on the essential continuity of artistic endeavor. There is a useful list of international art festivals where Romanian artists have exhibited their work (p. 163-168). For recent reproductions of the new art see *Contemporary Rumanian Painting* (Bucharest, Meridiane, 1956, 148 p.). This work contains 56 color reproductions of the works of some relatively obscure contemporary Romanian artists who demonstrate a wide range of versatility and great creative talent. The introductory chapter is written by Academician G. Oprescu. In addition to the classi cal painters, the Meridiane Publishing House also has a recent series of monographs, published in all Western languages, on contemporary Romanian artists.

2041. Oreste, Tafrali. Le trésor byzantin et roumain du monastère de Putna. Paris, Paul Geuthner, 1931. 352 p. Bibliography: p. 81-83.

In spite of the frequent destructions caused by war and the very dubious reconstructions, the author has nevertheless succeeded in demonstrating the authentic Byzantine origins of the famous monastery of Stephen the Great. Quite a remarkable work by the well-known professor at the University of Jassy. The bibliography is outdated.

2042. Réau, Louis. L'art roumain. Paris, Librairie Larousse, 1946. 105 p. Bibliography: p. 102-105.

Based on a series of lectures given at the Institute of Romanian Studies at the Sorbonne. Written by a leading Western scholar in the history of art, this is one of the most perceptive and best written general accounts of Romanian architecture, painting, sculpture, iconography, and popular art. Suitable for both layman and scholar, the work contains brief biographical sketches of leading Romanian artists.

2043. Rumanian Architecture.   Bucharest, Rumanian Institute for Cultural Relations with Foreign Countries, 1953. 142 p.

A brief account of recent changes in architectural styling during the Stalinist and post-Stalinist period, as reflected in a number of public buildings (e.g., the Scînteia House), theaters (e.g., the Bălcescu open air theater), etc. *See also* Jean Monda's *Arhitectura nouă în Republica Populară Română* (The new architecture in the Romanian People's Republic) (Bucureşti, Editura Ştiinţifică, 1965, 100 p.).

2044. Sebestyen, G., *and* V. Sebestyen.   Arhitectura renaşterii în Transilvania (Renaissance architecture in Transylvania). Bucureşti, Editura Academiei Republicii Populare Romîne, 1962. 252 p. Illus., maps. Bibliography: p. 239-242.

A comprehensive Marxist account of the social and technological circumstances accounting for the emergence of an 18th century renaissance in Transylvanian architecture, as reflected in the styles of patrician houses, public buildings, military constructions, churches, and fortresses — both in the towns and in the rural districts. An interesting concluding chapter establishes the close relationship between the Transylvanian and Moldo-Wallachian architectural developments.

2045. Stănciulescu, F., A. Gheorghiu, P. Stahl, *and* P. Petraşcu.   Arhitectura populară românească regiunea Bucureşti (Popular Romanian architecture of the Bucharest region). Bucureşti, Editura Ştiinţifică, 1958. 136 p. Illus., maps. Bibliography: p. 137.

An interesting new series of regional architectural studies, with particular emphasis on peasant styling. A simliar monograph by the same authors has appeared on peasant architecture for the Ploeşti region, and a third for Dobrogea.

2046. Ştefănescu, I. D.   L'évolution de la peinture religieuse en Bukovine et en Moldavie depuis les origines jusqu'au 19ième siècle. Paris, Geuthner, 1928. 2 v. Illus.

Together with *L'évolution de la peinture religieuse en Bukovine et en Moldavie, nouvelles recherches d'études iconographiques* (Paris, Geuthner, 1929, 1 v., plates), represents Professor Ştefănescu's masterly synthesis on religious painting in Bukovină and Moldavia; these studies deserve to be ranked as classics, in spite of some of the problems which have not been completely resolved, even in the more specialized revised study on iconography.

2047. Ştefănescu, I. D.   La peinture religieuse en Vallachie et en Transylvanie depuis les origines jusqu'au 19e siècle. Paris, Geuthner, 1932. 439 p. Illus., map, portfolio of 100 plates. Bibliography: p. 383-386.

An extension of Professor Ştefănescu's brilliant analysis to Wallachian and Transylvanian mural paintings and icons. This study was greatly hampered by frequent destructions and by some very careless reconstructions which occurred in many of the Wallachian monasteries (even at the famed church of Curtea de Argeş). The author argues that Byzantine, Serbian, and Moldavian influences are clearly perceptible in Wallachian religious architecture and iconography. *See also* I. D. Stefănescu's *L'art byzantin et l'art lombard en Transylvanie; peintures murales de Valachie et de Moldavie* (Paris, Geuthner, 1938, 163 p., illus., plates, map; bibliography: p. 145), the last volume in the same series, which concentrates on Lombard, Saxon, and Szekler churches of Transylvania.

2048. Vătăşianu, Virgil.  Istoria artei feudale în ţările Romîne. Arta în perioada de dezvoltare a feudalismului (A history of feudal art in the Romanian lands. Art during the period of feudal development). v. 1. Bucureşti, Editura Academiei Republicii Populare Romîne, 1959. 1018 p. Illus., maps, plans. Bibliography: p. 947-964.

A definitive history of feudal art in all Romanian provinces to the 17th century, which outdates the Iorga-Balş interpretation (*see* entry no. 2032), completes it, and solves a variety of problems previously ignored. It is written by a committee of experts from the Art Institute of the Academy of the Romanian Socialist Republic, under the direction of one of the leading scholars in the history of art. Its Marxist viewpoint tends to deemphasize the impact from abroad and takes the local social and economic milieu more into account. It also includes a study of the artistic creations of all minorities on Romanian soil (German, Hungarian, etc.), which have been ignored in the past. The bibliography is excellent. Volume 2 has not appeared to date. On a more limited theme *see* Virgil Vătăşianu's *Pictura murală românească în veacul XIV-XVI* (Romanian mural painting in the 14th-16th century) (Bucureşti, Editura de Stat Didactică şi Pedagogică, 1965, 40 p.). Essentially a series of lectures given at the summer school of the University of Bucharest. See also *Istoria artei româneşti* (The history of Rumanian art) (Bucureşti, Meridiane, 1967, 1 v.). The survey, which ends with the 17th century, is designed for the general reading public.

2049. Zderciuc, B., P. Petraşcu, *and* I. Bănăţeanu.   Folk Art in Rumania. Bucharest, Meridiane, 1964. 60 p.

An abridged edition of *Istoria artei populare româneşti* (A history of popular art in Romania) (Bucureşti, Meridiane, 1964, 180 p.). Representative selections of varied types of peasant art (furniture, embroidery, earthenware, ceramics, wooden engravings, stained glass, village architecture, etc.), with brief explanatory comments by a team of experts from the Folk Art Museum of Bucharest. For costume embroidery in the Old Kingdom, *see* T. Bănăţeanu's *Portul popular românesc* (The Romanian folk costume) (Bucureşti, Editura de Stat Didactică şi Pedagogică, 1965, 107 p.); for the Transylvanian costume, *see* P. Petrescu's *Costumal popular românesc din Transilvania* (The Romanian folk costume of Transylvania) (Bucureşti,

Editura de Stat Didactică și Pedagogică, 1959, 144 p., illus., plates, maps).

# H. MUSIC

## by Miloš Velimirović

### 1. Reference Aids and Serials

2050. Cosma, Viorel, ed.   Compozitori și muzicologi români; mic lexicon (Romanian composers and musicologists; a small lexicon). București, Editura Muzicală a Uniunii Compozitorilor din R.S.R., 1965. 386 p. Ports., bibliographies.

> Perhaps the most comprehensive biographical dictionary of Romanian composers, folk music collectors, and musicologists. Includes selective lists of works.

2051. Coover, James B.   A Bibliography of East European Music Periodicals. IX. Rumania. In Fontes Artis Musicae, v. 7. Kassel, Bärenreiter-Verlag, 1960. p. 69-70.

> A listing of music periodicals which have been published in Romania (15 titles).

2052. Muzica (Music). 1950– București. Monthly. Illus., ports., facsims., music.

> Articles on musical life in Romania and abroad. Edited by A. Tudor from 1950 to 1952, by V. Tomescu in 1953, by Z. Vancea from 1954 to 1964, and again by V. Tomescu since 1964. From about 1954, scholarly studies included as monthly supplements. From 1955 until 1958, at least nine numbered special supplements entitled Studii muzicologice were published.

2053. Studii de muzicologie (Studies in musicology). v. 1– 1965– București. Annual.

> The 1965 volume contains 14 studies, of which those by George Breazul on the pentatonic scale and the pre-pentatonic stage of development of music, by I. D. Petrescu on some aspects of Byzantine music, and by G. Ciobanu on some musical elements common to the folk music of Romania and of Bulgaria are especially interesting. The 1966 volume contains eleven studies, three of which deal with the works of Enescu. Of interest also is the study on organ music in Romania by V. Bickerich.

### 2. Surveys

2054. Breazul, George.   La musique roumaine. In Encyclopédie de la musique. v. 3. Paris, Fasquelle, 1961. p. 977-980.

> Brief yet useful survey of the history of music in Romania. A similar article is Zeno Vancea's "Romania" in Enciclopedia della musica, v. 4 (Milano, Ricordi, 1964), p. 42-44. An article on Romanian music is in preparation for inclusion in the supplement to

the German encyclopedia *Die Musik in Geschichte und Gegenwart; allgemeine Enzyklopädie der Musik*, edited by Friedrich Blume (Kassel, Bärenreiter-Verlag, 1949-1968, 14 v., illus., ports., facsims., music).

2055. Brîncuş, P., *and* N. Călinoiu. Muzica în Romînia după 23 August 1944 (Music in Romania since 23 August 1944). Bucureşti, Editura Muzicală a Uniunii Compozitorilor din R.S.R., 1965. 365 p. Illus., facsims., music, ports. Bibliography: p. 363-365.

A richly illustrated survey of musical life in Romania since the end of the Second World War. A separate chapter is dedicated to each of the main genres of musical composition. Includes an alphabetical listing of composers and their compositions during this period (p. 325-355), as well as a selective listing of musicologists and their main publications (p. 355-359), unfortunately without the usually cited bibliographical data.

2056. Cassini, Leonard. Music in Rumania. London, Fore Publications, 1954. 72 p. Illus., music.

The only such publication in English in book form. For more recent developments consult Nicolas Slonimsky's "Modern Composition in Rumania," *Musical Quarterly*, v. 51, 1965: 236-243, and Irving Lowens' insightful report on a music festival in 1964, published in the same volume (p. 413-418).

2057. Ciobanu, Gheorghe. La culture musicale byzantine sur le territoire de la Roumanie jusq'au XVIIIᵉ siècle. *In* Lissa, Zofia, *ed.* Musica Antiqua Europae Orientalis; Acta scientifica congressus, Bydgoszcz, Polska, 1966. Warszawa, Państwowe Wydawn. Naukowe, 1966. p. 419-430.

The most significant of the three studies presented in the section on Romanian music at the congress. The two other studies are Viorel Cosma's "Aspects de la culture musicale sur le territoire de la Roumanie entre le XIVᵉ et le XVIIIᵉ siècle" (p. 403-418) and Romeo Ghircoiaşiu's "Les mélodies roumaines du XVIᵉ-XVIIIᵉ siècles" (p. 431-452).

2058. Ghircoiaşiu, Romeo. Contribuţii la istoria muzicii romîneşti (Contributions to the history of Romanian music). v. 1. Bucureşti, Editura Muzicală, 1963. 250 p. Illus., music. Bibliography: p. 241-248.

A fine survey of all data pertinent to the history of the development of musical life in Romania until the beginning of the 19th century. Cristian C. Ghenea's *Din trecutul culturii muzicale româneşti* (From the past of Romanian musical culture) (Bucureşti, Editura Muzicală, 1965, 203 p., illus., facsims., ports.) may be used as a complementary volume; the author takes a "sociological" approach to the same period and includes a different set of illustrations and a discussion of "songs of protest and revolutionary songs."

2059. Posluşnicu, Mihail Gr. Istoria musicei la Români, de la Renaştere până'n epoca de consolidare a culturii artistice (History of Romanian music from the Renaissance up to the age of the consolidation of artistic culture). Bucureşti, Cartea Românească, 1928. 632 p. Illus., ports, facsims., music, bibliographical footnotes.

This work and P. Niţulescu's *Muzica românească de azi* (Contemporary Romanian music) (Bucureşti, 1939, 1102 p.) are the most detailed prewar publications on the history of music in Romania. Both are evaluated as "superior" by Stephen A. Fischer-Galati in his *Rumania, a Bibliographic Guide* (Washington, D.C. U.S. Library of Congress, 1963), p. 29.

### 3. Special Aspects, Personalia

2060. Breazul, George.   Gavriil Musicescu; schiţă monografică (Gavriil Musicescu; a monographic sketch). Bucureşti, Editura Muzicală, 1962. 223 p. Facsims., music, port., bibliographical footnotes.

Breazul (1887-1961), one of the finest Romanian musicologists, writes on the romantic composer of songs and organizer of musical life in the second half of the 19th century. Another worthwhile biographical study is Viorel Cosma's *Ciprian Porumbescu; monografie* (Bucureşti, Editura de Stat pentru Imprimate şi Publicaţii, 1957, 76 [35] p., illus., ports., facsims., music; bibliography: p. 74-77). Porumbescu, another promising composer of songs, died in his 30th year in 1883.

2061. Cosma, Octavian L.   Opera romînească; privire istorică asupra creaţiei lirico-dramatice (The Romanian opera; a historical examination of lyrical-dramatic creation). Bucureşti, Editura Muzicală, 1962. 2 v. Illus.

The only specialized study dealing with the history of opera in Romania. Volume 1 covers the period until the Second World War. The second volume covers the postwar period. In addition, there is an alphabetic listing of all Romanian composers and their dramatic works (p. 267-275), and a chronological catalogue of all stage performances in Bucharest and the provinces from 1772 through 1921 (p. 276-290).

2062. Dumitrescu, Ion.   Muzica în Bucureştiul de ieri şi de azi (Music in Bucharest in the past and in the present). Bucureşti, Editura Muzicală, 1959. 68 p. Illus.

2063. Tudor, Andrei.   Enescu. Bucureşti, Editura Muzicală, 1958. 123 p.

A thorough biography of George Enescu, the best-known Romanian violinist and composer. Contains a detailed chronology of his life (p. 99-118) and a catalogue of his compositions (p. 119-121). English, Russian, French, German, and Hungarian translations were published by the Union of Romanian Composers between 1957 and 1963. A more recent study is George Bălan's *George Enescu, mesajul-estetica* (George Enescu; the message and the aesthetics) (Bucureşti, Editura Muzicală, 1962, 316 p., illus., facsims., music, ports.).

## I. THEATER AND CINEMA

*by Radu R. Florescu*

### 1. Theater

2064. Alterescu, Simion, *ed.* Istoria teatrului în România (History of the theater in Romania). v. 1. Bucureşti, Editura Academiei Republicii Populare Romîne, 1965. 380 p. Bibliography: p. 345-357.

Planned as a five-volume history. Written by a committee of scholars from the Academy of the Romanian Socialist Republic under the direction of Professor Alterescu and projected on a far more ambitious scale than Massoff's three-volume history of the theater. This volume traces the history of the Romanian theater from the ancient rites performed at the courts of boyars and princes during the Middle Ages up to the formation of a native theatrical school in the first half of the 19th century. The authors study the totality of the theatrical phenomenon as a reflection of the social and economic circumstances of each period and emphasize the peasant traditions rather than foreign influences. The bibliography is excellent.

2065. Caragiale, Ion Luca. Opere (Works). Bucureşti, Editura de Stat pentru Literatură şi Artă, 1959-1962. 3 v.

————. Oeuvres. Bucarest, Meridiens-Editions, 1962. 780 p.

Caragiale sur les scènes roumaines et étrangères. Bucarest, Commission nationale de la République populaire roumaine pour l'UNESCO, 1962. 121 p. Illus.

Writings by the noted Romanian playwright and on the stage performances of his works.

2066. Cluceru, Sonia. Figuri de seamă ale teatrului romînesc (Significant figures in the Romanian theater). Bucureşti, Meridiane, 1963. 68 p.

A series of monographs and biographical sketches dedicated to the most eminent theatrical figures (playwrights, stage designers, directors, actors, etc.) in the Romanian theater. Individual biographies of prominent Romanian actors are eventually planned by the Meridiane Publishing House.

2067. Duţu, Alexandru. Shakespeare in Rumania; a Bibliographical Essay. Bucharest, Meridiane, 1965. 239 p. Illus., facsims., ports.

*See also* entry no. 1947.

Translated into French, Russian, and Spanish. An account of Shakespearean theatrical productions in Romania, based primarily on records of the plays themselves. There is an interesting critique of the quality of Shakespearean theatrical performances. The preface is written by Mihnea Gheorghiu, a well-known translator of Shakespearean plays. The volume is richly illustrated with reproductions of scenery and photographs of famous Romanian Shakespearean actors from a wide diversity of plays.

2068. Eliade, Pompiliu.   Teatrul naţional din Bucureşti în 1908-9 (The National Theater of Bucharest, 1908-9). Bucureşti, Tipografia "Vointa Naţională," 1909. 122 p.

A well-known historian, minister of public instruction, and director general of the Bucharest Theater stresses the importance of that theater as a school for patriotism. He includes a subtle analysis of the shortcomings and inadequacies of the theatrical companies, the management, and the performers, while pleading for reform and particularly for financial independence. For an earlier period, *see* S. Alterescu and I. Tornea's *Teatrul naţional I. L. Caragiale 1852-1952* (The I. L. Caragiale National Theater, 1852-1952 (Bucureşti, Meridiane, 1952, 250 p.), published on the occasion of the centenary of the Caragiale Theater.

2069. Massoff, Ion.   Eminescu şi teatrul (Eminescu and the theater). Bucureşti, Editura pentru Literatură, 1964. 228 p. Illus.

The most recent work highlighting Eminescu's theatrical activities with various companies and describing his career as a theater critic for the daily *Timpul*.

2070. Massoff, Ion.   Teatrul Romînesc; privire istorică (The Romanian theater; a historical view). Bucureşti, Editura pentru Literatură, 1961-1966. 2 v. Bibliography.

Two volumes of a planned three-volume work, by one of the leading experts in the history of the Romanian theater. The first is a history of the Romanian theater from its early folkloric origins until 1860. The second, by far the more interesting, covers the period of formation of a national theater and dramatic school in all three Romanian provinces, extending to 1916. A third volume, to be published shortly, will presumably include the current, socialist phase. Professor Massoff's book, in spite of its Marxist-Leninist terminology, represents one of the most scholarly, best-documented, and most detailed studies available to date. A good deal of new data emerges in his detailed analysis of the main theatrical companies and his biographical sketches of the most outstanding Romanian actors. The bibliography is quite comprehensive.

2071. Massoff, Ion, *and* Radu Tănase.   C. Tănase. Bucureşti, Meridiane, 1964. 284 p.

An interesting biography of the life and times of one of the great Romanian actors, who played a significant role in the history of the Romanian theater.

2072. Oprescu, George, *ed.*   Teatrul în Romania după 23 August 1944 (The theater in Romania after August 23, 1944). Bucureşti, Editura Academiei Republicii Populare Romîne, 1959. 394 p. Illus., ports. Bibliography: p. 379-383.

An adequate though somewhat uncritical account of the contemporary Romanian theater, by the leading prewar expert in the history of art. This is by no means one of Oprescu's more distinguished efforts. For a shorter, popular account see *The Theater in the Rumanian People's Republic* (Bucharest, Meridiane, 1961, 80 p.). See also *Les instituts de théatres en Roumanie* (Bucarest, Meridiane, 1961, 32 p.) and *Theatre, Opera, Ballet in Rumania* (Bucharest, Foreign Language Publishing House, 1957, 1 v.).

2073. Prodan, Paul.   Teatrul românesc contemporan, 1920-1927 (The contemporary Romanian theater, 1920-1927). Bucureşti, Fundaţia Culturală Principele Carol, 1927. 335 p.

A lively account of the high artistic standards achieved by the Romanian theater in the early 20th century, stressing its close contacts with the French theatrical world.

2074. Schileru, Eugen.   Scenografia românească (Romanian stage design). Bucureşti, Meridiane, 1965. 232 p.

Translated into English, French, German, and Spanish. Includes 434 black-and-white and color reproductions. The reproductions and interpretations stress the imaginative talent of some 46 contemporary Romanian stage designers with a wide diversity of solutions for complicated problems in staging. Their repertoire includes both classical and modern plays, the legitimate theater, opera, and ballet. An introductory study by critic E. Schileru traces the history of Romanian stage design in the last 120 years.

2075. Sturdza, Petre.   Amintiri: 40 ani de teatru (Reminiscences: Forty years of theater). Bucureşti, Meridiane, 1966. 350 p.

The personal recollections of Petre Sturdza (1869-1933), which throw a good deal of light not only upon the activities of the Romanian theater but also on its relationship to the Western theatrical world, with which Sturdza was intimately connected.

2076. Vasiliu, Mihai.   Alexandru Davila. Bucureşti, Meridiane, 1965. 214 p.

An excellent study of a great playwright, actor, and director of the National Theater of Bucharest at the turn of the 20th century, who was responsible for a definite "moment" in its history by raising the prestige of the theater, improving conditions for actors, and creating a dramatic company which bore his name.

## 2. Cinema

2077. Cantacuzino, Ion.   Momente din trecutul filmului românesc (Landmarks in the history of Romanian film-making). Bucureşti, Meridiane, 1966. 91 p. Bibliography: p. 59-64.

The first attempt to record in one volume the history of film-making in Romania. The author describes the first films made in Romania (1891) and the making of the first Romanian film ("The

War of Independence"), and covers the period of sound motion pictures up to 1948. The bibliography is the most comprehensive on the subject.

2078. Catalogues des films de courts métrages. Bucarest, RomFilm, 1964. 122 p.

Brief technical comments and summaries on recent scientific, cultural, geographical, and educational films, including those which have won recognition at international film festivals. RomFilm has a similar volume listing long feature films with brief summaries and names of directors, writers, actors, technicians, etc. See also *Catalogue of Rumanian Documentary Films* (Bucharest, RomFilm, 1966, 1 v.), with brief summaries of 124 recent Romanian documentaries on industry, agriculture, science, plastic arts, ethnography, tourism, education, and other cultural subjects, and *Catalogue de films de l'archive roumaine* (Bucarest, RomFilm, 1959, 75 p.). Current achievements in the Romanian film industry are covered in the review *Le film roumain* (Bucharest, 1958–), published by the Center for Film Distribution of Bucharest.

2079. Constantinescu, M., V. Dascălu, *and* Dumitru.   Munca de masă în filme la sate (Mass work in films for rural use). Bucureşti, Direcţia Reţelei Cinematrografice şi de Difuzare a Filmului, 1960. 64 p.

Some figures on the extensive efforts made to use cinematography as a means of educating the masses in the rural areas. For the use of the film for communist indoctrination, see *Catalog de filme în sprijinul educaţiei comuniste a tineretului* (Catalogue of films in support of the communist education of youth) (Bucureşti, Direcţia Reţelei Cinematografice şi de Difuzare a Filmului, 1964, 1 v.). Also consult the journal *Film* (Bucureşti, 1958–), published by the Cinematographic Section of the Ministry of Public Instruction.

# PART SIX

# yugoslavia

# 43

# GENERAL
# REFERENCE AIDS
# AND
# BIBLIOGRAPHIES

*by Paul L. Horecky*

## A. BIBLIOGRAPHIES

### 1. Bibliography of Bibliographies

2080. Savez društava bibliotekara FNRJ. Bibliografija jugoslovenskih bibliografija, 1945-1955 (Bibliography of Yugoslav bibliographies, 1945-1955). Beograd, Bibliografski institut FNRJ, 1958. 270 p. (*Its* Izdanja, 2)

> The first attempt at such a compilation in Yugoslavia. The 1,141 entries include references to books, parts of books, and periodical articles. There is an author index. For a listing of major bibliographies see the article "Bibliografija" in *Enciklopedija Jugoslavije*

451

(Encyclopedia of Yugoslavia), v. 1 (Zagreb, Izd. Leksikografskog zavoda FNRJ, 1955), p. 504-519.

## 2. National Bibliography

2081. Bibliografija Jugoslavije; članci i književni prilozi u časopisima (Bibliography of Yugoslavia; articles and literary contributions in periodicals). v. 1– 1950– Beograd, Bibliografski institut FNRJ. Quarterly.

> Since 1952, this section of the Yugoslav national bibliography has been issued in three series: A. Društvene nauke (Social sciences); B. Prirodne i primenjene nauke (Natural and applied sciences); and C. Filologija, umetnost, šport, književnost, muzikalije (Philology, art, sport, literature, musical scores). Arrangement within each series is by decimal classification. There is an annual supplement with author and subject indexes.

2082. Bibliografija Jugoslavije; knjige, brošure i muzikalije (The Bibliography of Yugoslavia; books, pamphlets, and music). v. 1– 1950– Beograd, Bibliografski institut FNRJ. Semimonthly.

> The Yugoslav national bibliography, listing monographs currently published in the territory of Yugoslavia; arranged by decimal classification. Cumulated author and subject indexes are published annually. For the period 1945-1949, see *Jugoslovenska bibliografija* (Yugoslav bibliography) (Beograd, Direkcija za informacije Vlade FNRJ, 1949-1950, 5 v.).
>
> For the years before the Second World War, only fragmentary coverage is available: *Popis Knjiga, koje izlaze u Kraljevini Jugoslaviji* (List of books published in the Kingdom of Yugoslavia) (v. 1; Jan./Feb. 1941, Zagreb, Hrvatsko bibliotekarsko društvo); *Prilog jugoslovenskoj bibliografiji za 1938* (Supplement to the Yugoslav bibliography for 1938) (Beograd, 1939), by Boško Veljković; *Jugoslovenska bibliografija; bibliographie Yougoslave* (v. 1-2, no. 7/9; Jan./Feb. 1934-July/Sept. 1935, Beograd, Savez knjižarskih organizacija Kraljevine Jugoslavije, 2 v. in 1); *Jugoslovenski bibliografski godišnjak za 1933 god.* (Yugoslav bibliographic annual for the year 1933), issued by Narodna biblioteka (Beograd, Štamparija Drag. Popovića, 1935); and *Bibliograf; popis novih knjiga i periodičnih publikacija u Kraljevini Srba, Hrvata, i Slovenaca* (The bibliographer; description of new books and periodical publications in the Kingdom of the Serbs, Croats, and Slovenes) (v. 1; Jan.-Dec. 1926, Beograd, monthly [irregular]).

2083. Bibliografija jugoslovenske periodike (Bibliography of Yugoslav serials). 1956– Beograd, Bibliografski institut FNRJ. Quarterly.

> Title varies: Jan.-Dec. 1956, *Spisak časopisa i novina štampanih na teritoriji FNRJ* (List of periodicals and newspapers printed in the territory of the FPRY); Jan. 1957-Dec. 1958, *Spisak listova i časopisa štampanih na teritoriji FNRJ* (List of papers and periodicals printed in the territory of the FPRY).

An alphabetical listing, with bibliographic data, of periodicals and newspapers published in Yugoslavia, apparently based on the receipts of serials by legal deposit at the Bibliographic Institute.

## 3. Bibliographies Covering All or Several of Yugoslavia's Lands

2084. Badalić, Josip. Jugoslavica usque ad annum MDC. Bibliographie der südslawischen Frühdrucke. 2d improved ed. Baden-Baden, Heitz, 1966. 132 p. Illus. Bibliography: p. 131-133 (Bibliotheca bibliographica Aureliana, 2)

> The standard bibliography of incunabula and 16th century publications by Yugoslav authors. Chronological arrangement with an author index and many facsimiles of title pages.

2085. Belgrade. Vojnoistorijski institut. Bibliografija izdanja u Narodno-oslobodilačkom ratu, 1941-1945 (Bibliography of publications issued during the national liberation struggle, 1941-1945). Compiled by Vinko Branica and others. Beograd, 1964. 815 p. Fascisms., map, *See also* entry no. 1441.

> A comprehensive bibliography of books, pamphlets, and periodicals published during the Second World War in Yugoslavia, with 9,103 entries and indexes of places, issuing bodies, authors, and editors. Includes only publications supporting Tito's resistance movement. Preface also in Russian, French, and English.

2086. Jovanović, Vojislav M. Engleska bibliografija o istočnom pitanju u Evropi (An English bibliography on the Eastern question in Europe). Beograd, Državna štamparija kraljevine Srbije, 1908. 111 p. (Srpska kraljevska akademija. Spomenik, 48. Drugi razred, 40)

> An important tool for historical research; covers the period 1481-1906 and contains 1,521 entries.
>
> Special attention is called to the up-to-date *Bibliography of English Language Sources on Yugoslavia* by Joel M. Halpern (2d ed., Amherst, University of Massachusetts, Department of Anthropology, 1969, 134 p.). Eighteen major subject categories are covered, with emphasis on socioeconomic matters.
>
> French-language writings are covered by the following: *Ogled francuske bibliografije o Srbima i Hrvatima, 1544-1900. Essai de bibliographie française sur les Serbes et les Croates*, by Nikola S. Petrović (Beograd, Drž. štamparija, 1900, 314 p.); and *Essai de bibliographie française sur les Serbes, Croates et Slovènes depuis le commencement de la guerre actuelle*, by Rista J. Odavić (Paris, Chez l'auteur, 1918, 160 p.), which includes references to books and periodical articles published during the First World War.
>
> For a bibliography of Czech and Slovak books and articles, including translations from the languages of Yugoslavia, on a variety of topics relating to that country, see *Jugoslavie; soupis literatury o současné Jugoslavii a doporučující bibliografie překladů z let 1945-1956* (Yugoslavia; a list of writings about contemporary Yugoslavia and a recommending bibliography of translations from the years

1945-1956), prepared by Oton Berkopec and published by the Library of the Charles University) (Praha, 1956, 34 p.).

For a German bibliography covering selected books and articles in various languages relating to Yugoslavia, see *Die westlichen Länder des europäischen Südostens, 1937/41*, edited by Heinrich Jilek and issued by the Deutsches auslandswissenschaftliches Institut Berlin (Leipzig, O. Harrassowitz, 1942, 159 p.).

A bibliography of writings on relations between Norway and Yugoslavia is offered by Arne Gallis and Slobodan Komadinić in their *Jugoslavia-Norge: en bibliografi* (Yugoslavia-Norway; a bibliography) (Oslo, 1953, 70 p.).

2087. Jugoslovenska književnost u inostranstvu; bibliografija (Yugoslav literature in foreign countries; a bibliography). 1– 1959– Beograd, Jugoslovenska autorska agencija. Irregular.

Lists Yugoslav writings published in foreign translations. Foreign writings published in translation in Yugoslavia are recorded in *Bibliografija prevoda objavljenih u Jugoslaviji, 1944-1959* (A bibliography of translations published in Yugoslavia, 1944-1959) (Beograd, 1963. 2 v.), Issued by Savez književnih prevodilaca Jugoslavije, this compilation includes about 11,000 entries arranged by subject. Soviet writings translated into the languages of Yugoslavia are listed in *Bibliografija prevoda sa jezika naroda SSSR, 1941-1948* (A bibliography of translations from languages of the peoples of the USSR, 1941-1948) (Beograd, 1950, 318 p.), which contains 6,217 entries arranged by decimal classification.

2088. Leskovsek, Valentin. Yugoslavia; a Selected Bibliography with a Brief Historical Survey. Washington, D.C., Catholic University of America, 1958. 137 l. Map.

A basic survey of books about Yugoslavia, prepared as a master's thesis in library science. Arranged by subjects and by regions, with an author index.

2089. Udruženje univerzitetski obrazovanih žena u Jugoslaviji. Bibliografija knjiga ženskih pisaca u Jugoslaviji (A bibliography of books by women authors in Yugoslavia). Beograd, 1938. 3 v. in 1.

Title, introductions, and tables of contents also in French. The first volume lists works published in Voivodina, Serbia, Macedonia, and Montenegro; the second, Slovenia; and the third, Croatia, Slavonia, Dalmatia, and Bosnia and Hercegovina.

2090. Zagreb. Jugoslavenski leksikografski zavod. Bibliografija rasprava, članaka i književnih radova (Bibliography of essays, articles, and literary works). Chief editor, Mate Ujević. v. 1– Zagreb, 1956–
*See also* entry no. 2761.

An ambitious attempt to produce a bibliographic record of the contents of the Yugoslav press. Arrangement is by subject. The seven volumes (of a projected 25) published so far cover literature in general, the theory of literature, comparative literature, the history of Yugoslav literatures, the history of foreign literatures, literary periodicals and societies, history in general with its auxiliary sciences, sources of history, and a retrospective bibliography of materials published in Yugoslav periodicals from the 18th century to 1945.

2091. Zagreb. Jugoslavenski bibliografski zavod. Grada za bibliografiju jugoslavenske periodike (Sources for the bibliography of Yugoslav periodicals). Edited by Mate Ujević. Zagreb, 1955. 440 p. (Anali Leksikografskog zavoda FNRJ, sv. 2)

The most extensive listing of Yugoslav periodicals in a single volume. For earlier bibliographic coverage of Yugoslav periodicals, the following works should be consulted: *Bibliografija jugoslovenskih listova i časopisa* (Bibliography of Yugoslav newspapers and periodicals) (Beograd, Izd. Jugoslovenske knjige, 1950, 99 p.); *Bibliografija južnoslovenske povremene štampe do kraja 1934 godine* (Bibliography of the Yugoslav periodical press to the end of 1934) (Beograd, A. M. Popović, 1935); *Spisak najnovijih listova u Kraljevini Srba, Hrvata i Slovenaca* (A list of the newest newspapers in the Kingdom of the Serbs, Croats, and Slovenes) (Beograd, 1927); and *Jugoslovenska štampa; referati i bibliografija* (The Yugoslav press; reports and bibliography) (Beograd, Štampano u Državnoj štampariji, 1911, 292 p.), issued by the Serbian Journalistic Association.

### 4. Bosnia and Hercegovina

2092. Bejtić, Alija. Bibliografija štampanih radova o Sarajevu do kraja 1954 godine (A bibliography of printed works about Sarajevo to the end of 1954). Sarajevo, Muzej grada Sarajeva, 1964. 452 p.

Contains 3,835 entries for books and articles about the capital of Bosnia.

2093. Sarajevo. Narodna biblioteka NR Bosne i Hercegovine. Bosansko-hercegovačka bibliografija knjiga i brošura, 1945-1951 (Bosnian-Hercegovinian bibliography of books and pamphlets, 1945-1951). By Đorđe Pejanović. Sarajevo, Svjetlost, 1953. 271 p.

Arranged by subject. Continued by *Bosansko-hercegovačka bibliografija knjiga za 1952 godinu* (Bosnian-Hercegovinian bibliography of books for the year 1952) (Sarajevo, Svjetlost, 1954, 110 p.), also prepared by Pejanović and issued by Narodna biblioteka Narodne Republike Bosne i Hercegovine. Newspapers and periodicals are described in Pejanović's *Bibliografija štampe Bosne i Hercegovine, 1850-1941* (Bibliography of the press of Bosnia and Hercegovina, 1850-1941) (Sarajevo, Izdavačko preduzeće "Veselin Masleša," 1961, 222 p.). Another regional bibliography is *Bibliografija knjiga i periodičnih izdanja štampanih u Hercegovini, 1873-1941* (A bibliography of books and periodical publications printed in Hercegovina, 1873-1941) (Mostar, Izdanje Savjeta za kulturu Narodnog odbora Sreza Mostar, 1958, 132 p.), by Lina Štitić and Hamid Dizdar.

## 5. Croatia

2094. Bibliografija rasprava, članaka i književnih radova u časopisima Narodne Republike Hrvatske (Bibliography of essays, articles, and literary works in periodicals published in the People's Republic of Croatia). 1945/46– Zagreb, Jugoslavenska akademija znanosti i umjetnosti. Annual.

> An index to periodicals published in Croatia; arranged by subject. For foreign Croatica see *The Croatian Publications Abroad after 1939; a Bibliography* by George J. Prpic (Cleveland, John Caroll University, 1969, 66 p.).

2095. Combi, Carlo A.    Saggio di bibliografia istriana. Capodistria, G. Tondelli, 1864. 484 p.

> A bibliography of the Croatian and Slovenian part of Istria, with 3,060 entries for monographs and periodical articles, and name and subject indexes.
>
> For a bibliography of Slavic writings published in Rijeka, see *Fluminensia Croatica; bibliografija knjiga, časopisa i novina izdanih na hrvatskom ili srpskom jeziku na Rijeci* (Fluminensia Croatica; a bibliography of books, periodicals, and newspapers published in Rijeka in Croatian or Serbian) (Zagreb, Jugoslavenska akademija znanosti i umjetnosti, 1953, 172 p.) by Tatjana Blažeković. It covers books for the period 1530-1952 in 503 entries, and periodicals for 1858-1952 in 48 entries; indexed.
>
> A similar bibliography for the city of Zadar in Dalmatia is *Jadertina Croatica; bibliografija knjiga, časopisa i novina izdanih na hrvatskom ili srpskom jeziku u Zadru* (Jadertina Croatica; a bibliography of books, periodicals, and newspapers published in Zadar in Croatian or Serbian) (Zagreb, Jugoslavenska akademija znanosti i umjetnosti, 1949-1954, 2 v.), by Vjekoslav Mastrović. For books, it covers the period 1789-1949 in 1,803 entries, and for periodicals, the period 1806-1953 in 112 entries. A third part of the bibliography is a classified index to 17 periodicals.

2096. Hrvatska bibliografija (Croatian bibliography). v. 1-4; 1941-1944. Zagreb, Hrvatska državna tiskara. Monthly (irregular).

> Covers publications issued in the wartime Croatian "state." Only the first four issues of the fourth volume were published. For the period immediately following the Second World War, see *Bibliografija knjiga tiskanih u Narodnoj Republici Hrvatskoj* (Bibliography of books printed in the People's Republic of Croatia), of which five volumes covering the years 1945-1950 were published (Zagreb, Jugoslavenska akademija znanosti i umjetnosti, 1948-1956, 5 v.).

2097. Kukuljević-Sakcinski, Ivan.    Bibliografija hrvatska. Dio prvi. Tiskane knjige (Croatian bibliography. First Part. Printed books). Zagreb, Brzotiskom D. Albrechta, 1860. 233 p.

———. Dodatak k prvomu dielu. Tiskane knjige (Supplement to

the first part. Printed books). Zagreb, Tiskom i nakladom A. Jakića, 1863. 31 p.

The first Croatian bibliography, covering books from the 15th century to 1860. In three sections, according to alphabet (Glagolitic, Cyrillic, and Roman), each alphabetically arranged. Continued by Vatroslav Jagić in "Hrvatsko-srbski knjigopis za god. 1864," published in *Književnik* (Booklover), v. 2, 1865; and by D. Jagić in "Hrvatsko-srbski knjigopis za god. 1865," published in the same journal in the following year. Coverage from 1877 to 1881 is provided by *Slovanský katalog bibliografický. Catalogue slave bibliographique* (v. 1-5; 1877-1881, Praha, Tiskem dra. E. Grégra, 1878-1883, 5 v.). For subsequent years coverage is fragmentary and must be pieced together from the following sources: 1906, in *Glas Matice hrvatske* (Voice of Matica hrvatska); 1907-1908, in Strossmayer's *Koledar* (Calendar); and 1908-1909, in *Glas Matice hrvatske*.

2098. Valentinelli, Giuseppe.   Bibliografia della Dalmazia e del Montenegro; saggio. Zagabria, Coi tipi del L. Gaj, 1855. 339 p.

————. Supplementi al saggio bibliografico della Dalmazia e del Montenegro. Zagabria, 1862. 132 p.

An annotated bibliography, arranged by subject, with name and subject indexes; published for the Società slavo-meridionale. The same author prepared a bibliography of manuscripts relating to Dalmatia in the Biblioteca Nazionale Marciana: *Bibliografia dalmata tratta da' codici della Marciana di Venezia* (Venezia, Tip. Cecchini e Naratovich, 1845, 45 p.).

## 6. Macedonia

2099. Andonov-Poljanski, Hristo.   Britanska bibliografija za Makedonija. British Bibliography on Macedonia. Skopje, Arhiv na Socialistička Republika Makedonija, 1966. 512 p.

A comprehensive, well-arranged, annotated bibliography of over 4,000 entries for books, articles, and maps published in Great Britain which relate to Macedonia from the dawn of history until the present. There is an index of authors, but no subject index.

2100. Dimiǩ, Netalija.   Bibliografija na statii i knigi za N.O.B. vo Makedonija (A bibliography of articles and books on the national liberation struggle in Macedonia). Skopje, Institut za nacionalna istorija, 1953. 152 p.

Covers events of the Second World War in Macedonia as reported through 1951 in Yugoslav books and periodicals.

Bulgarian materials on the history of Macedonia are listed in "Bŭlgarskiiat periodichen pechat na Makedoniia" (Bulgarian periodical literature on Macedonia), by Stoian Simeonov, in *Sbornik Solun-Sofiia* (1934).

A bibliography of the capital of Macedonia is *Prilog bibliografiji Skoplja* (A contribution to the bibliography of Skopje) (Skopje, 1935-1940, 4 v.), compiled by Haralampie Polenakoviǩ.

2101.  Skopje, Yugoslavia. Narodna i univerzitetska biblioteka. Makedonska bibliografija (Macedonian bibliography). 1944/49– Skopje.

> Published annually with some years cumulated, this bibliography is divided into two parts: (1) books, pamphlets, and music, and (2) periodical articles. See also *Bibliografija na doktorskite disertacii na Univerzitetot vo Skopje* (Bibliography of doctoral dissertations defended at Skopje University) (Skopje, Univerzitet, 1969, 28 p.).

## 7. Montenegro

2102.  Odbor za proslavu četiristošezdesetogodišnjice Obodske štamparije. Pregled štamparsko izdavačke djelatnosti u Crnoj Gori, 1494-1954 (Survey of printing and publishing activities in Montenegro, 1494-1954). Cetinje, 1955. 307 1.

> A comprehensive bibliography with 3,580 entries for monographs and periodicals published in Montenegro; chronological arrangement. To be supplemented by *Razvitak štampe i štamparstva u Crnoj Gori, 1493-1945* (The development of the press and printing in Montenegro, 1493-1945) (Beograd, Jugoslovenski institut za novinarstvo, 1965, 262 p., illus., facsims., bibliography), by Niko S. Martinović.
>
> For an earlier bibliography of periodicals, see *Pregled štampe u Crnoj Gori, 1834-1934* (A survey of the press in Montenegro, 1834-1934) (Cetinje, Izdala Banovinska štamparija "Obod," 1934, 173 p.), by Dušan D. Vuksan.

2103.  Šoć, Pero Đ.   Ogled bibliografije o Crnoj Gori na stranim jezicima (A survey of the bibliography about Montenegro in foreign languages). Beograd, 1948. 531 p. (Srpska akademija nauka. Posebna izdanja, knj. 144)

> A comprehensive work based on the holdings of many libraries, chiefly in France and Italy; includes author and subject index.
>
> For 19th century sources of information, see *Pokušaj za bibliografiju o Crnoj Gori* (A tentative bibliography on Montenegro) (Cetinje, Državna štamparija, 1892, 62 p.), by Marko Dragović, which lists 460 entries; 200 are in non-Yugoslav languages.

## 8. Serbia

2104.  Belgrade. Matična biblioteka "Đorđe Jovanović" opštine Stari grad. Prilog bibliografiji Beograda (Contribution to a bibliography of Belgrade). Beograd, 1964. 32 p.

> For other regional bibliographies, see *Vranje, okolina i ljudi; bibliografija objavljenih članaka i knjiga* (Vranje, land and people; bibliography of published articles and books) (Vranje, Državni arhiv, 1964, 70 p.), by Rista Simonović; and *Bibliografia o Limskoj dolini, 1. dio* (Bibliography of the Lim Valley, part 1) (Ivangrad, Izdanje autora, 1964, 115 p.), by Svetozar Popović.

2105.  Belgrade. *Univerzitet.*   Bibliografija doktorskih disertacija, 1951-1963 (A bibliography of doctoral dissertations, 1951-1963). Beograd, Publikacija Rektorata Univerziteta, Odsek za nastavu i naučni rad, 1964. 109 p.

An earlier bibliography of doctoral dissertations at the same university is *Doktorske disertacije na beogradskom univerzitetu, 1905-1950* (Doctoral dissertations at the University of Belgrade, 1905-1950) (Beograd, Naučna knjiga, 1951, 21 p.).

2106. Dragović, Vuk.    Srpska štampa između dva rata. 1. Osnova za bibliografiju srpske periodike 1915-1945 (The Serbian press between the two wars. 1. Foundation for a bibliography of Serbian periodicals, 1915-1945). Beograd, 1956. 422 p. (Srpska akademija nauka. Građa, knj. 11; Istoriski institut, knj. 8)

For books published just after the Second World War, see *Bibliografija Srbije* (1947-1948, Beograd, Izd. Ureda za informacije pri Pretsedništvu vlade Narodne Republike Srbije, 1948-1949), arranged by subject.

2107. Kon, Geca, *firm, Belgrade*.    Katalog izdanja, 1901-1935 (Catalog of publications, 1901-1935). Beograd, 1935. 363 p.

A trade catalog issued by the former leading publishing house of Yugoslavia; a useful source in the absence of consecutive bibliographic coverage for the period. For an earlier trade catalog, see *Glavni katalog celokupne srpske književnosti* (General catalog of the entire Serbian literature), 4th ed. (Beograd, 1912, 507 p.), issued by the bookseller Mita Stajić.

2108. Mihailović, Georgije.    Srpska bibliografija XVIII veka (Serbian bibliography of the 18th century). Beograd, 1964. 383 p. Facsims., maps.

*See also* entry no. 2822.

A reliable, scholarly work and the standard bibliography for the period; summaries in Russian, English, and French. Serbian 18th century imprints in the library of Matica srpska in Novi Sad and the Serbian National Library in Belgrade are listed in *Srpska štampana knjiga 18. veka; katalog* (The Serbian printed book in the 18th century; a catalog) (Novi Sad, Matica srpska, 1963, 201 p.).

2109. Novaković, Stojan.    Srpska bibliografija za noviju književnost, 1741-1867 (Serbian bibliography of the more recent literature, 1741-1867). Beograd, Državna štamparija, 1869. 644 p.

The first Serbian bibliography compiled by an outstanding man of letters; issued by the Serbian Learned Society. A basic work of continuing value for the study of Serbian culture, it contains 3,291 entries chronologically arranged. Continued by the same author for the years 1868-1876 in issues of *Glasnik Srpskog učenog društva* (Bulletin of the Serbian Learned Society) for 1869-1872, 1874-1875, and 1877-1878. Similar bibliographies for some subsequent years (1877-1878, 1883, and 1884) by Dragutin Posniković, appeared in the *Glasnik Srpskog učenog društva* (Bulletin of the Serbian Learned

Society) for 1886, 1884, and 1885 respectively. A bibliography for 1893 compiled by Danilo A. Živaljević was separately published by the Serbian Royal Academy as number 27 in its Spomenik series: *Srpska i hrvatska bibliografija za 1893 godinu* (Serbian and Croatian bibliography for the year 1893 (Beograd, Drž. štamparija kraljevine Srbije, 1895, 82 p.).

2110. Pogodin, Aleksandr L'vovich. Rusko-srpska bibliografija 1800-1925 (Russian-Serbian bibliography, 1800-1925). Beograd, Štamparija "Mlada Srbija," 1932-36. 2 v. (Srpska kraljevska akademija. Posebna izdanja, knj. 92, 110. Filozofski i filološki spisi, knj. 22, 29)

One of the first Serbian bibliographies of this type. The first part lists Serbian translations of Russian writings published separately or in periodicals; the second part, translations published in newspapers and almanacs.

# 9. Slovenia

2111. Plesničar, Pavel. Narod naš dokaze hrani; bibliografski pregled slovenskega tiska na Primorskem do konca l. 1918 (Our nation preserves the evidence; a bibliographic survey of Slovenian imprints in the Coastland through 1918). Ljubljana, 1940. 128 p.

A detailed bibliography of Slovenian monographs and periodicals published in the territory annexed by Italy in 1920.

2112. Simonič, Franc. Slovenska bibliografija. 1. del. Knjige, 1500-1900 (Slovenian bibliography. Part 1. Books, 1500-1900). Ljubljana, Slovenska matica, 1903-05. 627 p.

Covers monographs in Slovenian and by Slovenian authors in any language from the beginning of Slovenian publishing to 1900. A remarkable work by the outstanding Slovenian bibliographer. Continued by Karol Glaser for 1901 and by Janko Šlebinger for the period 1902-1906 in *Zbornik Matice slovenske* (Miscellany of the Matica slovenska), 1902-1906. The bibliography for 1907-1912 appeared as a monograph: *Slovenska bibliografija za l. 1907-1912* (Slovenian bibliography for the years 1907-1912), by Janko Šlebinger (Ljubljana, Slovenska matica, 1913, 336 p.). A bibliography limited to linguistics, literature, and history compiled by Šlebinger appeared in *Časopis za slovenski jezik, književnost in zgodovino* (Journal for the Slovenian language, literature, and history), 1921-1928; a bibliography for 1929 and part of 1930, also from his pen, appeared in the periodical *Slovenski tisk* (Slovenian press), 1929-1930, and for the year 1929 as a monograph: *Slovenska bibliografija za leto 1929* (Slovenian bibliography for the year 1929), by Janko Šlebinger (Ljubljana, Slovenska matica, 1930, 85 p.). Bibliographic information about Slovenian monographs is available also in the trade catalog *Slovenska knjiga; seznam po stanju v prodaji dne 30. junija 1939* (The Slovenian book; a list of books available in the book trade on June 30, 1939), by Niko Kuret (Ljubljana, Organizacija knjigarjev Dravske banovine, 1939, 392 p.).

2113. Šlebinger, Janko.    Slovenski časniki in časopisi; bibliografski pregled od 1797-1936 (Slovenian newspapers and periodicals; a bibliographic survey from 1797 to 1936). Ljubljana, 1937. 175 p.

A comprehensive bibliography of Slovenian periodicals which is still the best source of bibliographic information for the years covered. Arranged by the beginning year of publication with alphabetical indexes of titles, subjects, and places of publication. For Slovenian periodicals published between 1849 and 1959 in the Coastland region, *see* Miša Šalamun's "Slovensko primorsko časopisje; zgodovinski pregled in bibliografski opis" (Slovenian Coastland periodicals; a historical survey and bibliographic description) in Srečko Vilhar's *Prerez zgodovine slovenskih knjižnic in knjižničarstva na Primorskem* (Survey of the history of Slovenian libraries and librarianship in the Coastland) (Koper, Študijska knjižnica, 1961, 111 p.). For Slovenian periodicals in the city of Trieste, see *Giornali e periodici di Trieste 1781-1946* (Trieste, Associazione della stampa giuliana, 1947, 20 p.). A bibliography of Slovenian periodicals in the United States, compiled by Ivan Molek, appeared under the title "Slovenski časniki in revije v Ameriki" (Slovenian newspapers and periodicals in America) in *Ameriški družinski koledar* (American family almanac), v. 27, 1941 (Chicago, Yugoslav Workmen's Pub. Co.), p. 118-122.

Recently, a survey of Slovenian periodicals in the U.S. was compiled by Jože Bajec: *Petinsedemdeset let slovenskega časnikarstva v ZDA* (Seventy-five years of Slovenian journalism in the U.S.A.) (Ljubljana, Slovenska izseljenska matica, 1966, 52 p.).

2114. Slovenska bibliografija (Slovenian bibliography). 1– 1945/47– Ljubljana, Narodna in univerzitetna knjižnica.

An annual bibliography of Slovenian monographs and periodicals, with complete coverage of Slovenian-language imprints in Yugoslavia and partial coverage of Slovenian imprints outside Yugoslavia. The first volume covers the period May 9, 1945, to the end of 1947. Beginning with volume five, 1951, it includes analytical coverage of articles and literary contributions from periodicals. An analytical bibliography of articles covering the period from May 9, 1945, to the end of 1950 was published separately: *Slovenska bibliografija; članki in leposlovje v časopisih in zbornikih, 1945-1950* (Slovenian bibliography; articles and literary contributions in periodicals and collections, 1945-1950) (Ljubljana, Slovenska akademija znanosti in umetnosti, 1963, 561 p.). Current Slovenian publications are listed in the periodical *Knjiga; glasilo slovenskih založb* (The book; organ of Slovenian publishers) (1–, 1953–, Ljubljana). An annual bibliography of monographs in the Slovenian language published outside Yugoslavia has been published since 1956 in *Zbornik Svobodne Slovenije* (Almanac of Free Slovenia) (Buenos Aires).

2115. Truber, Primus.    Register und summarischer Innhalt, aller der Windischen Bücher, die von Primo Trubero, biss auff diess 1561 Jar in Truck geben seind. Tübingen, Ulrich Morharts Wittib., 1561. 12 p.

The first Slovenian bibliography of books by Primož Trubar (Primus Truber) compiled by the author himself and dedicated to Hans Ungnad, the patron of the Slavic printing office in Urach, Germany. Another bibliography of Trubar's writings is Friedrich Ahn's *Bibliographische Seltenheiten der Truberliteratur* (Leipzig, O. Harrassowitz, 1894, 48 p.). For a bibliography of early Slovenian books printed in Ljubljana see *Die slovenischen Erstlingsdrucke der Stadt Laibach 1575-1580* (Graz, Leuschner & Lubensky, 1896, 21 p.), also by Friedrich Ahn.

## B. ENCYCLOPEDIAS*

2116. Enciklopedija Jugoslavije (Encyclopedia of Yugoslavia). Chief editor, Miroslav Krleža. Zagreb, Izd. Leksikografskog zavoda FNRJ, 1955– Illus., col. plates, ports., maps.

A massive and impressive work of lexicography — to comprise eight volumes, when completed — which records the accomplishments of the South Slavs in all fields of human endeavor as viewed and interpreted by a large team of contemporary Yugoslav scholars and experts. A mine of information and an indispensable aid for the study of Yugoslavia. Excellent in format and technical production. The chief editor is the greatest living Croat writer. Under his general direction, the Yugoslav Lexicographic Institute in Zagreb has been engaged in the preparation of a series of topical encyclopedias, which, though international in coverage, are invaluable for the study of Yugoslavia:

Enciklopedija Leksikografskog zavoda (Encyclopedia of the Lexicographic Institute). Chief editors, Marko Kostrenčić and Miroslav Krleža. Zagreb, Izd. Leksikografskog zavoda FNRJ, 1955-1964. 7 v. Illus., col. plates, ports., maps. A general encyclopedia with many items of relevance to Yugoslavia.

Enciklopedija likovnih umjetnosti (Encyclopedia of fine arts). Chief editor, Andre Mohorovičić. Zagreb, Izd. Leksikografskog zavoda FNRJ, 1959– Illus., col. plates, ports. Pictorial materials of high technical perfection.

Medicinska enciklopedija (Encyclopedia of medicine). Zagreb, Izd. Leksikografskog zavoda FNRJ, 1957-1965. 10 v. Illus.

Muzička enciklopedija (Encyclopedia of music). Chief editor, Josip Andreis. Zagreb, Izd. Leksikografskog zavoda FNRJ, 1958-1963. 2 v. Illus. Substantial coverage of music in Yugoslavia.

Pomorska enciklopedija (Maritime encyclopedia). Chief editors, Miroslav Krleža and Mate Ujević. Zagreb, Izd. i naklada Leksikografskog zavoda FNRJ, 1956-1964. 8 v. Illus., maps, ports. A rather unusual encyclopedic undertaking in this field, with profuse illustrations and much information on Yugoslavia as a country bordering the sea.

* Entries are listed in reverse chronological order by period treated.

Šumarska enciklopedija (Encyclopedia of forestry). Chief editors, Aleksandar Ugrenović and Zvonimir Potočić. Zagreb, Izd. Leksikografskog zavoda, 1949-1953. 2 v. Illus. One of the few encyclopedias on this subject, with many useful data of local significance.

2117. Jugoslavija (Yugoslavia). Edited by Ljubica D. Trajković. Beograd, Turistička štampa, 1958. 2 v. Illus., maps.

A convenient guide with detailed information on Yugoslavia's geography, climatic conditions, natural resources, cultural memorabilia, and tourist attractions.

Several other encyclopedias, though general in scope, are of special interest because of the corpus of data supplied on the Yugoslav scene:

Mala politička enciklopedija (Small encyclopedia of politics). Edited by Iso Baruh. Beograd, Savremena administracija, 1966. 1531 p.

Mala enciklopedija Prosveta; opšta enciklopedija (Small Prosveta encyclopedia; a general encyclopedia). 2d ed. Beograd, Prosveta, 1968. 2 v. Illus., ports., maps.

Međunarodni politički leksikon (Lexicon of international politics). Edited by Marijan Hubeny, Branko Kojić, and Bogdan Križman. Zagreb, Novinsko izdavačko poduzeče, 1960. 592 p. The first lexicon of its kind in Yugoslavia, under the editorship of noted experts. Covers the legal and economic aspects of international relations with detailed attention to Yugoslav institutions and concepts.

Pravni leksikon (Lexicon of law). Edited by Borislav Blagojević. Beograd, Savremena administracija, 1964. 1107 p. Prepared under the direction of a leading Yugoslav jurist, it has substantial coverage of Yugoslavia's legal system.

Privredni leksikon (Lexicon of economics). Edited by Martin Dobrinčić and others. Zagreb, Informator, 1961. 787 p.

Vojna enciklopedija (Military encyclopedia). Edited by Boško Šilgejović. Beograd, Redakcija Vojne enciklopedije, 1958– Eight volumes so far published. Much space is devoted to Yugoslav conditions.

2118. Hrvatska enciklopedija (Croatian encyclopedia). Chief editor, Mate Ujević. Zagreb, Konzorcija Hrvatske enciklopedije, 1941-1945. 5 v. Illus., plates, ports., maps.

A remarkable work compiled under the direction of an eminent scholar, lexicographer, and bibliographer, now deceased. Only five volumes were published, covering A to Elektrika.

For Slovenia see Krajevni leksikon Slovenije (Regional lexicon of Slovenia), a publication now in progress (Ljubljana, Državna založba Slovenije, 1968–)

2119. Stanojević, Stanoje. Narodna enciklopedija srpsko-hrvatsko-slovenačka (National encyclopedia of Serbian, Croatian, and Slovenian affairs). Zagreb, Bibliografski zavod d.a., 1925-1929. 4 v.

The first national encyclopedia of Yugoslavia, reflecting the state of affairs after the First World War. Indispensable for research on that period. Separate editions were published in the Cyrillic and the Roman alphabets.

## C. BIOGRAPHIES*

### 1. Yugoslavia as a Whole

2120. Biografija (Biography). *In* Enciklopedija Jugoslavije. v. 1. p. 570-575. *See* entry no. 2116.

An informative and detailed survey article on biographic materials concerning noteworthy representatives of the peoples of Yugoslavia.

2121. Ko je ko u Jugoslaviji; biografski podaci o jugoslovenskim savreme-nicima (Who's who in Yugoslavia; biographic information on Yugoslav contemporaries). Edited by Slavko Janković and Mihajlo Milanović. Beograd, Sedma sila, 1957. 810 p.

The most recent Who's Who in Yugoslavia, containing some 6,000 biographic entries. An earlier publication with the same title (Beograd, Jugoslovenski godišnjak, 1928, 168 p.) offers biographies of leading Yugoslavs as of 1928.

For biographic data on members of Yugoslavia's legislative bodies, *see*:

Sedma sila, Novinsko-izdavačko preduzeče, *Belgrade*. Savezna i republičke skupštine (Federal and republic legislative assemblies). Beograd, 1964. 311 p.

A similar source of biographic information for the mid-thirties is *Biografski leksikon. Narodno predstavništvo: Senat* (Biographic lexicon. The National Assembly: the Senate) (Beograd, 1935? 352 p.), prepared by Čedomil Mitrinović. It also contains data on the organizational structure of these assemblies as well as statistical tables on their composition by sex, age, and occupation.

Biographic sketches of 1,307 members of the partisan movement in the Second World War, who were subsequently awarded the medal of National Hero of Yugoslavia, are listed in Slobodan Petrović's *Zbornik narodnih heroja Jugoslavije* (Collection of national heroes of Yugoslavia) (Beograd, Omladina, 1957, 1003 p.).

As this guide goes to print, the imminent publication has been announced of a new current biographic dictionary, *Ko je ko u Jugoslaviji* (Who's who in Yugoslavia). (Beograd, Hronometar, ca. 800 p.).

2122. Ko je ko u Jugoslaviji. 1. Lekari (Who's who in Yugoslavia. v. 1: Physicians). Chief editors: Dragan Marković and Miloš Mimica. Beograd, Izdanje Saveza lekarskih društava Jugoslavije i NIP Export Press, 1968– Illus.

This 768-page volume appears to be the first in an intended series of biographic directories for various professions.

* Entries are listed in reverse chronological order by period treated.

2123. Radonić, Jovan.    Slike iz istorije i književnosti (Sketches from history and literature). Beograd, Državna štamparija, 1938. 533 p.

A collection of biographic essays on personalities of Yugoslavia's recent and remote past, written by a noted historian over a period of 45 years. Analogous in coverage is Hermann Wendel's *Südslawische Silhouetten* (Frankfurt am Main, Frankfurter Societäts-Druckerei, 1924, 219 p.); the first part describes the lives and works of "Fighters" (from Zaharija Orfelin to Jovan Skerlić) and the second, those of "Poets" (from France Prešeren to Aleksandar Šantić).

2124. Znameniti i zaslužni Hrvati te pomena vrijedna lica u hrvatskoj povijesti od 925-1925 (Prominent and meritorious Croats and noteworthy personalities in Croatian history from 925 to 1925). Zagreb, Hrvatski štamparski zavod, 1925. 126, 297 p. Illus., plates.

Published on the occasion of "the millennium of the Croatian Kingdom," this commemorative album consists of two parts: the first (p. 3-126) presents surveys of the history of Croatia, Bosnia, and Istria, of Croatian letters, of the development of the Croatian language, and of the lives of Croatian rulers, dukes, bans, and bishops; the second (p. 3-297) lists biographies. Copiously illustrated.

Ten biographic essays on Croatian personalities from the fifteenth to the nineteenth century are the subject of Ivan Kukuljević-Sakcinski's *Glasoviti Hrvati prošlih vjekova* (Renowned Croats of times past) (Zagreb, Matica hrvatska, 1886, 268 p.).

2125. Zorzut, Miloš, *ed.*    Suvremeni pisci Jugoslavije (Contemporary writers of Yugoslavia). Zagreb, Stvarnost, 1966. 397 p. Ports.

A biographic directory in alphabetic arrangement containing detailed biobibliographic data on the writers listed.

## 2. Bosnia-Hercegovina

2126. Jelenić, Julijan.    Biobibliografija franjevaca Bosne Srebrenićke (Biobibliography of the Franciscans from the Srebenica Monastery in Bosnia). Zagreb, 1925. 44 p.

Only one volume (Ančić-Josić) was published.

## 3. Croatia

2127. Grlović, Milan. Album zaslužnih Hrvata XIX stoljeća (Album of meritorious Croats of the 19th century). Zagreb, Nakl. Matičevog litografskog zavoda, 1898-1900. 2 v. Illus.

The first volume presents biographies, and the second, pictorial material. Illustrated by Stjepan Kovačević.

2128. Ljubić (Gliubich), Šime.    Dizionario biografico degli uomini illustri della Dalmazia. Vienna, Rod. Lechner, 1856. 80, 325 p.

A biographic dictionary of distinguished Dalmatians, to be supplemented by Giuseppe Ferrari-Cupilli's *Biografie e necrologie d'il-*

*lustri e benemeriti Dalmati* (Zara, 1874, 325 p.). A corresponding biographic work on Istria is provided by Pietro Stancovich's *Biografia degli uomini distinti dell' Istria*, 2d ed. (Capodistria, C. Priora, 1888, 460 p.). In *Znameniti Hrvati Bošnjaci i Hercegovci u turskoj carevini* (Croats of Bosnia and Hercegovina famous in the Ottoman Empire) (Zagreb, Štamparija Grafika, 1931, 79 p.), the author, Safvet Bašagić, addresses himself to a special stratum of Croats and provides a useful glossary of Turkish terms.

2129. Duišin, Viktor A., *conte.*   Heraldički zbornik (Armorial). Zagreb, 1938-1939. 2 v. in 3.

One of the few Yugoslav publications on heraldry. Only the first volume, consisting of two parts, and the first part of the second volume (together covering the letters A-J) were published. An indispensable source for heraldic study relative to the lands of Yugoslavia formerly under the Austro-Hungarian Monarchy is *Biographisches Lexikon des Kaiserthums Österreich*, by Constantin Wurzbach, Ritter von Tannenberg (Wien, K. K. Hof- und Staatsdruckerei, 1856-1891, 60 v.).

## 4. Serbia

2130. Gavrilović, Andra, *ed.*   Znameniti Srbi XIX veka (Prominent Serbs of the 19th century). Srpska štamparija, 1901-1904. 3 v. Ports.

A basic work.

2131. Milićević, Milan Đuro.   Pomenik znamenitih ljudi u srpskog naroda novijega doba (Commemorative album of prominent people of the Serbian nation in recent times). Beograd, Srpska Kraljevska štamparija, 1888. 874 p.

A standard work for historical biographic research, which was updated through 1900 by a supplement, *Dodatak pomeniku od 1888* (Beograd, Srpska Kraljevska štamparija, 1901, 198 p.).

2132. Matica srpska, *Novi Sad. Galerija.*   Portreti Srba XVIII veka (Portraits of Serbs in the 18th century). Novi Sad, 1965. 161 p. Illus.

An exhibit catalog with a German summary. Contains reproductions of portraits as well as brief biographic data.

## 5. Slovenia

2133. Slovenski biografski leksikon (Slovenian biographic lexicon). Ljubljana, 1925–

A massive work on the lives and accomplishments of notable Slovenians, indispensable for orientation in the history and culture of the Slovenian people. Begun under the editorship of Izidor Cankar (with the collaboration of Joža Glonar, France Kidrič, and Janko Šlebinger), continued by France K. Lukman and France Kidrič, and more recently under the direction of Alfonz Gspan. Ten fascicles, covering A-Steklasa, have been published so far.

## D. REFERENCE AND RESEARCH AIDS

2134. Imenik mesta u Jugoslaviji sa poštama i teritorijalno nadležnim sudovima i javnim tužilaštvima (Directory of localities with listings of post offices, courts, and offices of public prosecutors). Beograd, Službeni list FNRJ, 1965. 471 p.

A gazetteer of localities within the administrative-territorial structure as of November 1965. Lists localities both alphabetically and under the republic, province, and district in which they are located; also lists districts by republics. For the official U.S. gazetteer of Yugoslavia, see *Yugoslavia; Official Standard Names Approved by the United States Board on Geographic Names* (Washington, D.C., U.S. Office of Geography, 1961, 495 p., Gazetteer no. 55).

2135. Plamenatz, Ilija P., *comp.*    Yugoslav Abbreviations; a Selective List. 2d ed. Washington, D.C., Slavic and Central European Division, Library of Congress, 1959. 185 p.

Lists 3,000 abbreviations, especially for names of government institutions and official bodies, industrial and trade establishments, and the more important newspapers and periodicals. Each abbreviation is followed by its expansion and its translation in English.

2136. Privredni adresar SFRJ 1966 (Trade directory of the Socialist Federal Republic of Yugoslavia for 1966). Beograd, Privredni pregled, 1966. 1274 p.

A serviceable directory, now published biannually, offering a wealth of information on Yugoslavia's economic institutions and enterprises in all branches of the economy. Tables of contents in English and other major languages.

2137. Statistički godišnjak SFRJ (Statistical yearbook of the Socialist Federal Republic of Yugoslavia). 1954– Beograd, Savezni zavod za statistiku. Annual.

A basic source of statistical information. Those unfamiliar with the languages of Yugoslavia can conveniently use an English-language key, published annually since 1954 by the Yugoslav Statistical Office under the title *Statistical Yearbook of the Socialist Federal Republic of Yugoslavia* and offering English translations of the table of contents and of the textual parts in the corresponding statistical tables of the original.

Other useful sources of current or retrospective statistical data are:

Yugoslavia. *Savezni zavod za statistiku*. Statistical Pocket-Book of Yugoslavia. 1955– Beograd. Annual. A condensed version of the Serbo-Croatian statistical yearbook giving "the most essential in·formation on the social and economic structure of Yugoslavia." Also published in French, German, and Russian.

Jugoslavija, 1945-1964, (Yugoslavia, 1945-1964). Beograd, 1965. 373 p. A statistical conspectus for the period indicated.

Yugoslavia. *Opšta državna statistika.* Statistički godišnjak. Annuaire statistique. kn. 1-9; 1929-1939. Beograd. Annual.

Great Britain. *Dept. of Overseas Trade.* Report of the Economic and Industrial Conditions of the Serb-Croat-Slovene Kingdom. 1921-1938. London.

Serbia. *Uprava državne statistike.* Statistika Kraljevine Srbije. Statistique du Royaume de Serbie. kn. 1-32; 1892-1913. Beograd.

2138. Yugoslav Scientific Directory 1964. Belgrade, Nolit, 1964. 590 p.

A most useful compendium — in the vein of the *World of Learning* — abounding with information on a multitude of institutional intellectual activities in Yugoslavia. The directory provides data on the organizational structure, programs, and staffs of academies of sciences, universities, learned societies, professional organizations, libraries, museums, and archives. Indexes of scientific institutions (by disciplines, types, and location) and of names are appended, along with texts of pertinent legislation and a roster of legal enactments. Published for the U.S. National Library of Medicine, the directory is available from the Office of Technical Services, U.S. Department of Commerce, Washington, D.C., 20235.

2139. Yugoslav Survey. 1960– Belgrade, Federal Secretariat of Information. Quarterly.

Carries current information on political, economic, social and cultural developments in Yugoslavia, based on official sources and prepared by specialists. A Serbo-Croatian edition has been published monthly since 1957 under the title *Pregled* (Survey).

## E. DICTIONARIES (BILINGUAL AND MULTILINGUAL)

2140. English:

Drvodelić, Milan.   Hrvatskosrpsko-engleski rječnik (Croato-Serbian–English dictionary). Zagreb, Školska knj., 1961. 912 p.

Relatively the most detailed though by no means entirely satisfactory dictionary from Serbo-Croatian into English.

Enciklopediski englesko-srpskohrvatski rečnik (Encyclopedic English–Serbo-Croatian dictionary). Prepared by Svetomir Ristić, Živojin Simić, and Vladeta Popović. Beograd, Prosveta; London, Cambridge University Press, 1963. 2 v.

The largest and most complete dictionary for the combined Serbo-Croatian terminology, compiled by leading Anglicists.

The best dictionary for Croatian equivalents of English terms is *Englesko-hrvatski rječnik* (English-Croatian dictionary), 3d ed. (Zagreb, Zora, 1963, 1464 p.), prepared under the direction of Rudolf Filipović, noted expert in English linguistics at the University of Zagreb, with a team of collaborators.

Two smaller all-purpose dictionaries were compiled by Svetislav Marić under the titles *Englesko-srpskohrvatski rečnik* (English-Serbocroatian dictionary) and *Srpskohrvatski-engleski rečnik* (Serbocroatian-English dictionary) (Novi Sad, Matice srpska, 1968, 2 v.).

Kotnik, Janko.   Slovene-English dictionary.  6th rev. and enl. ed. Ljubljana, Državna založba Slovenije, 1967. 831 p.

Grad, Anton, *and others*.  English-Slovene dictionary.  Angleško-slovenski slovar. Ljubljana, Državna založba Slovenije, 1967. 1120 p.

Gruik̂, (Grujić), Branislav, *and* Dušan Crvenkovski.  Mal anglisko-makedonski rečnik.  A pocket English-Macedonian dictionary. Skopje, Prosvetno delo; Cetinje, Obod, 1961? 307 p.

2141. French:

Hrvatskosrpsko-francuski rječnik (Croato-Serbian–French dictionary). Compiled by Jean Dayre and others. 2d ed. Zagreb, Novinarsko izdavačko poduzeće, 1960. 960 p.

Medić, Filip, *and* Etienne Laurent.   Francusko-srpski rečnik (French-Serbian dictionary). Beograd, Knjižarnica Rajkovića i Čukovića, 1930. 1256 p.

Miličević, Nika.   Francusko-srpski rečnik (French-Serbian dictionary). Beograd, Kreditna i pripomoćna zadruga Profesorskog društva, 1942. 714 p.

Putanec, Valentin.   Francusko-hrvatskosrpski rječnik (French–Croato-Serbian dictionary). Zagreb, Školska knjiga, 1957. 959 p.

Kotnik, Janko.   Slovensko-francoski slovar (Slovenian-French dictionary). Ljubljana, Jugoslovanska knjigarna, 1937. 458 p.

Pretnar, Janko.   Francosko-slovenski slovar (French-Slovenian dictionary). 3d ed. Ljubljana, Jugoslovanska knjigarna, 1941. 623 p.

Kitanovski, Dano.   Francusko-makedonski rečnik. Dictionnaire français-macédonien. Skopje, Prosvetno delo, 1967. 548 p.

2142. German:

Enciklopedijski nemačko-srpskohrvatski rečnik (German–Serbo-Croatian encyclopedic dictionary). Prepared by Svetomir Ristić and Jovan Kangrga. 2d ed. Beograd, 1963. 2 v.

Ristić, Svetomir, *and* Jovan Kangrga.  Rečnik srpskohrvatskog i nemačkog jezika (Dictionary of the Serbo-Croatian and German languages). Beograd, Knjižarnica Rajkovića i Čukovića, 1928. 1263 p.

Tomšič, France.  Nemško-slovenski slovar (German-Slovenian dictionary). 5th ed. Ljubljana, Državna založba Slovenije, 1964. 989 p.

————.   Slovensko-nemški slovar (Slovenian-German dictionary). Ljubljana, Državna založba Slovenije, 1966. 768 p.

Aleksovska, Margarita, *and others*.   Makedonsko-germanski rečnik. Makedonisch-deutsches Wörterbuch. Skopje, Prosvetno delo; Cetinje, Obod, 1966. 400 p.

2143. Italian:

Deanović, Mirko, and J. Jernej.   Hrvatskosrpsko-talijanski rječnik (Croato-Serbian–Italian dictionary). 2d enl. ed. Zagreb, Školska knjiga, 1963. 1191 p.

————.   Talijansko-hrvatskosrpski rječnik (Italian–Croato-Serbian dictionary). 3d enl. ed. Zagreb, Školska knjiga, 1960. 914 p.

Bajec, Anton.   Italijansko-slovenski slovar (Italian-Slovenian dictionary). 2d ed. Ljubljana, Državna založba Slovenije, 1960. 798 p.

Nurigiani, Giorgio.   Rečnik na italijanskiot i makedonskiot jazik. Prv del: Italijansko-makedonski. Vocabolario delle lingue italiana e macedone. Prima parte: Italiano-macedone. Rome, Teleuropa, 1967. 751 p.

2144. Russian:

Moskovljević, Miloš S.   Rečnik ruskog i srpskohrvatskog jezika (Russian–Serbo-Croatian dictionary). Beograd, Naučna knjiga, 1963. 750 p.
   Consists of two parts, Russian–Serbo-Croatian, and Serbo-Croatian–Russian.

Kotnik, Janko.   Slovensko-ruski slovar (Slovenian-Russian dictionary). Ljubljana, Državna založba Slovenije, 1950. 735 p.

Pretnar, Janko.   Rusko-slovenski slovar (Russian-Slovenian dictionary). 2d ed. Ljubljana, Državna založba Slovenije, 1964. 995 p.

Gruiḱ (Grujić) Branislav, and Ksenija Gavriš. Mal rusko-makedonski rečnik. Karmannyĭ russko-makedonskiĭ slovar'. Skopje, Prosvetno delo; Cetinje, Obod, 1966. 401 p.

2145. Multilingual:

Pavlica, Josip.   Frazeološki slovar v petih jezikih; rječnik slovenačkih, hrvatsko-srpskih, latinskih, njemačkih, francuskih i engleskih fraza (A dictionary of phrases in five languages; dictionary of Slovenian, Croato-Serbian, Latin, German, French, and English phrases). Ljubljana, Državna založba Slovenije, 1960. 686 p.

# F. ACADEMIES AND LEARNED SOCIETIES

2146. Jugoslavenska akademija znanosti i umjetnosti.   Popis izdanja, 1867-1950 (List of publications, 1867-1950). Prepared by Antun Ðamić and Ilka Verona under the editorship of Josip Badalić. Zagreb, 1951. 521 p.
   A bibliographic record of the Academy's publishing activities in many fields of learning. The first part lists books and periodicals chronologically, within major publications series, and the second contains an alphabetical listing of authors of individual writings. Continued and updated by Popis izdanja Jugoslavenske akademije znanosti i umjetnosti u Zagrebu, 1945-1965) (Zagreb, Jugoslavenska akademija znanosti i umjetnosti, 1966, 292 p.
   A brief history of the Academy accompanied by lists of its present members, institutes, and publications is offered in L'Académie yougoslave des sciences et des arts, 1866-1966 (Zagreb, Jugoslavenska akademija znanosti i umjetnosti, 1966, 94 p., illus.).

2147. Matica hrvatska, *Zagreb*. Matica hrvatska, 1842-1962. Povijest Matice hrvatske. Bibliografija izdanja Matice (The Croatian Cultural Society, 1842-1962. History of the Matica hrvatska. Bibliography of the Matica hrvatska). Prepared by Jakša Ravlić and Marin Somborac. Zagreb, 1963. 434 p. Illus., Bibliography.

*See also* entry no. 2914.

A history of the society, with a chronologically arranged bibliography of 1,385 publications issued under its sponsorship.

2148. Milisavac, Živan. Matica srpska (The Serbian Cultural Society). Novi Sad, Matica srpska, 1965. 311 p. Illus.

A comprehensive history of this venerable Serbian cultural institution, spanning almost 140 years of activity. Divided into two parts: 1826-1944 and 1945-1964, respectively. Appendixes: lists of publications; founders, patrons, and officers; and prize-winning publications.

Its publishing activities until 1949 are recorded in *Bibliografija izdanja Matice srpske* (Bibliography of publications of Matica srpska) (Novi Sad, 1950, 157 p.), which lists in chronological order 881 items — monographs and serials — issued by the Society or published elsewhere with its financial support. A title-author-subject index and a statistical table on the Society's publishing programs are appended.

For an informative survey article on the Society, *see* Robert F. Price's article, "The Matica Srpska and Serbian Cultural Development," published in *The Quarterly Journal of the Library of Congress*, v. 22, July 1965, p. 259-264.

2149. Slovenska matica v Ljubljani. Slovenska matica, 1864-1964 (The Slovenian Cultural Society, 1864-1964). Edited by France Bernik. Ljubljana, 1964. 446 p. Facsims., ports.

A commemorative symposium reviewing 100 years of study and research. For a listing of publications sponsored by the Slovenian Academy of Arts and Sciences, *see* Primož Ramovž' *Biblioteka in publikacije Slovenske akademije znanosti in umetnosti v letih 1938-1951* (The library and publications of the Slovene Academy of Arts and Sciences during the years 1938-1951) (Ljubljana, Slovenska akademija znanosti in umetnosti, 1952, 139 p.). Current developments are reported in the Academy's Letopis (Annals).

2150. Srpska akademija nauka i umetnosti, *Belgrade*. Pregled izdanja, 1847-1959 (List of publications, 1847-1959). Beograd, 1961. 273 p.

Covers a wide spectrum of knowledge as reflected in the substantial body of published research of the foremost Serbian cultural institution. Books and serials are recorded, the latter with the tables of contents of individual issues. It is the first consolidated record of the Academy's publications over a period of 112 years. Author index. For a recent supplement *see*:

Srpska akademija nauka i umetnosti. Pregled izdanja, 1965-1966

(List of publications of the Serbian Academy of Arts and Sciences, 1965-1966). Beograd, Naučno delo, 1967. 158 p.

2151. Živanović, Milan Ž. Bibliografija srpske književne zadruge 1892-1967 (Bibliography of the Serbian Cooperative Book Society). Beograd, Srpska književna zadruga, 1967. 443 p. Illus., ports., facsims.

## G. LIBRARY INSTITUTIONS, ARCHIVES AND MUSEUMS, PRINTING AND PUBLISHING

### 1. Library Institutions

2152. *Belgrade.* Jugoslovenski bibliografski institut. Bibliografski zbornik 1968 (Bibliographic almanac 1968). Beograd, 1968. 172 p.

Focuses on the functions, activities, and publications of the Bibliographic Institute, which is the center for the bibliographic registration of all Yugoslav publications and for the exchange of official publications with foreign countries.

2153. Savez društava bibliotekara FNRJ. Biblioteke u Jugoslaviji (Libraries in Yugoslavia). Edited by Nikola Justinijanović and others. Beograd, 1962. 404 p.

A directory of almost all types of libraries in Yugoslavia, arranged by republics and autonomous provinces. Size of collections is given. The same organization sponsored and published under the editorship of Matko Rojnić *Yugoslav Libraries* and *Les bibliothèques yougoslaves* (both Zagreb, 1954, 61 p.).

For an informed and well-documented survey study of Yugoslavia's research and university libraries, one should consult *Die Entwicklung der wissenschaftlichen Bibliotheken Jugoslawiens seit 1945* (Köln, Greven, 1958, 176 p., Arbeiten aus dem Bibliothekar Lehrinstitut des Landes Nordrhein-Westfalen, Heft 14) by Klaus D. Grothusen. Useful statistical data on library developments between 1956 and 1964 can be found in:

Lakočević, Ljubomir. Libraries. Yugoslav Survey, no. 26, 1966: 3825-3836.

Enciklopedijski leksikon bibliotekarstva (Encyclopedic lexicon of librarianship) by Kosta Grubačić (Sarajevo, Zavod za izdavanje udžbenika, 1964, 336 p.) is interesting for its emphasis on Yugoslav library affairs.

The official organ of the Association of Librarians of the People's Republic of Serbia is the bimonthly *Bibliotekar* (The librarian) (Beograd, Društvo bibliotekara NR Srbije, 1948–), devoted to theory and practice of librarianship, the history of libraries, and current publishing in the field.

For histories and descriptions of major libraries, *see*:

Čulić, Branko, *and* Kosta Grubačić. Narodna biblioteka NR Bosne i Hercegovine, 1945-1965 (The National Library of the People's Republic of Bosnia and Hercegovina, 1945-1965). Sarajevo, Narodna biblioteka, 1965. 146 p.

Društvo bibliotekarjev Slovenije.    Slovenske knjižnice. Pregled ob štiristoletnici slovenske knjige (Slovenian libraries. A Survey of 400 years of the Slovenian book). Ljubljana, 1951. 219 p.

Durković-Jakašić, Ljubomir.    Istorija srpskih biblioteka, 1801-1850 (History of Serbian libraries, 1801-1850). Beograd, Zavod za izdavanje udžbenika Socijalističke Republike Srbije, 1963. 211 p. Illus., facsims.

Kićović, Miraš.    Istorija Narodne biblioteke u Beogradu (History of the National Library in Belgrade). Beograd, Narodna biblioteka, 1960. 214 p.

Matica srpska. *Biblioteka.*    Građa za istoriju Biblioteke Matice srpske (Materials for a history of the library of the Matica srpska). Chief editor, Pavle Maletin. Novi Sad, 1965-1966. 3 v. (v. 1: 1864-1892; v. 2: 1892-1899; v. 3: 1899-1918). See also *Biblioteka Matice srpske* (The Library of the Matica srpska) by the same sponsor (Novi Sad, 1964, 68 p.).

Pejanović, Đorđe.    Istorija biblioteka u Bosni i Hercegovini od početka do danas (History of libraries in Bosnia and Hercegovina from the beginnings until today). Sarajevo, Izdavačko preduzeće Veselina Masleša, 1960. 104 p.

## 2. Archives and Museums

2154. Savez društava arhivskih radnika FNRJ.    Les Archives de Yougoslavie. Belgrade, 1956. 33 p.

A concise introduction to Yugoslavia's major archives. For a guide to the Serbian Government Archives, *see*:

Serbia. *Državna arhiva.*    Državna arhiva NR Srbije (The State Archives of the People's Republic of Serbia). Compiled by Milorad Soškić. Beograd, 1951. 227 p.

Slovenian archives are the subject of *Vodnik po arhivih Slovenije* (Guide to Slovenia's archives) (Ljubljana, Društvo arhivarjev Slovenija, 1965, 615 p.)

Among the more important professional journals on archives are:

Arhivski pregled (Archival survey). v. 1– 1955– Beograd, Društvo arhivskih radnika i arhiva SR Srbije. Semiannual.

Arhivski vjesnik (Archival bulletin). 1960– Zagreb, Državni arhiv u Zagrebu. Irregular.

2155. Savez muzejskih društava Jugoslavije.    Muzeji Jugoslavije (Yugoslavia's museums). Chief editor, Dragoljub S. Janković. Beograd, 1962. 176 p. Illus.

## 3. Printing and Publishing

2156. Delegation of U.S. Book Publishers Visiting Yugoslavia.    The Book Industry in Yugoslavia. New York, American Book Publishers Council and American Textbook Publishers Institute, 1964. 41 p. *See also* entry no. 63.

A concise and informative report on the major aspects of book publishing, supported by statistical tables.

2157. Plavšić, Lazar.  Srpske štamparije od kraja XV do sredine XIX veka (Serbian printing houses from the end of the 15th to the middle of the 19th century). Beograd, 1959. 334 p.

Includes three categories: (1) establishments which were Serbian by virtue of their being located on Serbian or Montenegrin soil and owned by Serbs; (2) establishments in non-Serbian lands but owned by Serbs; and (3) foreign establishments owned by non-Serbs but which actively printed Serbian works. This is a real contribution to Serbian cultural and intellectual history.

2158. Skerlić, Jovan.  Istorijski pregled srpske štampe, 1791-1911 (Historical survey of the Serbian press, 1791-1911). Beograd, Izd. Srpskog novinačkog udruženja, 1911. 81 p.

The author was a prominent Serbian literary critic and writer.

2159. Vuković, Milan T.   Mali knjižarski leksikon (Small lexicon of bibliophily). Beograd, 1959. 791 p.

Of special interest are the following features relevant to the Yugoslave scene: a brief directory of writers; an alphabetic listing of collected and selected works, and of monographic series; a roster of Yugoslav publishing houses, before and after 1948; and a selective bibliography of Yugoslav bibliographies and catalogs.

## H. YUGOSLAVS IN THE UNITED STATES

2160. Govorchin, Gerald Gilbert.   Americans from Yugoslavia. Gainesville, University of Florida, 1961. 352 p.

The first attempt to deal with the immigration in toto from Yugoslavia. The causes of emigration, statistics, organizational activities, and Yugoslav contributions to the U.S. are described.

There are two directories of societies and important individuals of Yugoslav descent in the U.S.: J. Poljak's *Almanak i statistika Južnih Slavena u Sjedinjenim Državama Sjeverne Amerike* (Almanac and statistics of the Southern Slavs in the U.S.) (Chicago, Yugoslav Directory & Almanac Publishing Co., 1926, 288 p.) and Ivan Mladineo's *Narodni adresar Hrvata-Slovenaca-Srba. The National Directory of the Croat-Slovene-Serb Organizations, Institutions, Business, Professional and Social Leaders in the United States and Canada* (New York, 1937, 1244 p.).

Shorter studies are Milivoy Stoyan Stanoyevich's *The Yugoslavs in the United States of America* (New York, Yugoslav Section of America's Making, Inc., 1921, 30 p.) and Eleanor E. Ledbetter's *The Yugoslavs of Cleveland, With a Brief Sketch of Their Historical and Political Backgrounds* (Cleveland, Mayor's Advisory War Committee, 1918, 30 p.).

Additional data on Yugoslavs in the U.S. can be found in:

Croatian Fraternal Union of America.   Kratki pregled povijesti Hrvatske bratske zajednice, 1894-1949 (Short survey of the history of the Croatian Fraternal Union, 1894-1949). Pittsburgh, 1949. 254 p.

Slepčević, Petar.   Srbi u Americi; beleške o njihovu stanju, radu i nacionalnoj vrednosti (Serbs in America; notes about their situation, work, and national importance). Geneva, Štamparija Ujedinjenja, 1917. 99 p.

Trunk, Jurij M.   Amerika in Amerikanci (America and the Americans). Celovec, Samozaložba, 1912. 606 p.

Zavertnik, Jože.   Ameriški Slovenci; pregled splošne zgodovine Združenih držav, slovenskega naseljevanja in naselbin in Slovenske Narodne Podporne Jednote (American Slovenes; a survey of the history of the U.S. Slovenian immigration and settlements and the Slovenian National Benefit Society). Chicago, Slovenska narodna podporna jednota, 1925, 632 p.

Arnez, John. Slovenci v New Yorku (Slovenians in New York). New York, Studia Slovenica, 1966. 268 p.

# 44

# GENERAL AND
# DESCRIPTIVE WORKS

*by Vladimir N. Pregelj*

2161. Aldiss, Brian Wilson.   Cities and Stones; a Traveller's Yugoslavia. London, Faber and Faber, 1966. 291 p. Illus., maps.

> Two Britons, one Land-Rover, six months in Yugoslavia. A lively and interesting travel account with a strong emphasis on the present and just enough history to make the present understandable.

2162. Auty, Phyllis.   Yugoslavia. New York, Walker, 1965. 251 p. Illus., maps, ports. Bibliography: p. 226-228.

> A concise yet fairly comprehensive recent view of Yugoslavia, with adequate emphasis on historical background and development, but with primary interest in the postwar period. A serious general work, which includes a Who's Who of the more prominent personalities mentioned in the text (p. 229-240).
>
> General descriptive works on some of the individual republics include:
>
> Čuješ, Rudolf, *ed*.   This is Slovenia; a Glance at the Land and Its People. Toronto, Slovenian National Federation of Canada, 1958. 221 p. Illus., ports., map. Bibliography: p. 210 (Research Center for Slovenian Culture, Willowdale, Ont., Publication no. 1)
>
> Eterovich, Francis H., and Christopher Spalatin, *eds*.   Croatia: Land, People, Culture. Toronto, University of Toronto Press, 1964– Illus., maps, ports., bibliographies. Contains a foreword by Ivan Meštrović. Only v. 1 (408 p.) published so far.

2163. Bihalji-Merin, Oto, and Lise Bihalji-Merin.   Jugoslawien; Kleines Land zwischen den Welten. 2d ed. Stuttgart, Kohlhammer, 1966. 310 p. Illus.

> Experiences and reflections brought back from a leisurely trip through Macedonia, Montenegro, Bosnia, and Hercegovina, and up the Adriatic coast. This is the "second, reworked and expanded" edition of a book first published in Serbo-Croatian, *Mala zemlja*

476

*između svetova; kontemplativna putovanja* (Beograd, Prosveta, 1954, 421 p.), and then in German (Stuttgart, Kohlhammer, 1955; Zürich, Europa, 1955, 358 p.).

2164. Boulanger, Robert.    Yougoslavie. 3d ed. Paris, Hachette, 1966. 627 p. Maps. Bibliography: p. 69-71. (Les Guides bleus)

A very good, very detailed, almost pedantic guide, designed primarily for the tourist interested mainly in the history and art of the country. In addition to 54 detailed itineraries by road, it contains sketchy itineraries by every Yugoslav railroad line. Three adequate road maps (Yugoslavia, coastal region, Belgrade) and several city plans are included. Sections on geography and art by Paul Fénelon and Louis Réau respectively. Another useful, if somewhat abbreviated, guide in French is:

Maury, Paul. Vacances en Yougoslavie. Verviers, Gérard, 1963. 154 p. Illus., maps. (Marabout-Flash, 130) Arranged by subject rather than geography. One of its particularly useful features is a list of suggested itineraries for tourists with limited funds or time. A good complement to a more comprehensive guide.

2165. Byrnes, Robert F., ed.    Yugoslavia. New York, Praeger, 1957. 488 p. Maps, tables. Bibliography: p. 447-469. (East Central Europe under the Communists. Praeger Publications in Russian History and World Communism, no. 23)

*See also* entries no. 2485 *and* 2599.

A collection of scholarly studies on Yugoslavia. Places primary emphasis on the postwar period and contains a wealth of factual information on the country's development during its first postwar decade. Sponsored by the Free Europe Committee.

2166. Cuddon, John A.    The Companion Guide to Yugoslavia. London, Collins, 1968. 480 p. Illus., maps.

A guide to a well-planned trip by car through Yugoslavia, touching virtually everything worth seeing, with plenty of background information, occasionally erroneous, in an easily readable style.

2167. Čulić, Dmitar J.    Urlaub in Jugoslawien; ein Reiseführer für Menschen von heute. Gütersloh, Bertelsmann, 1966. 190 p. Illus., maps. (Bertelsmann Reiseführer)

An adequate and well-arranged guide, translated from Serbo-Croatian by Marija Uroić.

2168. Fodor, Eugene, *ed*.    Yugoslavia 1968. New York, McKay, 1968. 314 p. Illus., maps.

An excellent guide to Yugoslavia; revised annually, but in places still somewhat less than up to date. Less detailed than *Guides bleus*, but with a somewhat broader scope (includes comparatively more information on what to do as against what to see than the French guide; pointers to entertainment, good eating, sports), and less formal in style. It is designed primarily for the driving tourist; has good

sectional road maps and indicates the location of motels and garages.
Other comprehensive guide books to Yugoslavia include:

Baedekers Autoführer-Verlag, *Stuttgart.* Jugoslawien und Griechenland. 4th ed. Stuttgart, Baedeker, 1966. 368 p. Illus., maps. (Baedekers Autoführer)

————. Yugoslavia. New York, Macmillan, 1964. 179 p. Illus., maps. (Baedeker's Autoguides)

Gracalic, Ladislav. Yugoslavia. 2d ed. New York, McGraw-Hill, 1966. 575 p. Maps. (The Nagel Travel Guide Series)

Grieben, *firm, publishers.* Jugoslawische Adriaküste. New ed. München, K. Thiemig, 1966. 222 p. Maps. (Grieben-Reiseführer, 282)

————. Jugoslawisches Binnenland. München, K. Thiemig, 1965. 226 p. Maps. (Grieben-Reiseführer, 283)

Jugoslavija; turistička enciklopedija (Yugoslavia; an encyclopedia of tourism). Beograd, Kultura, 1958. 2 v.

2169. Gesemann, Gerhard, *and others.* Das Königreich Südslawien. Leipzig, Noske, 1935. 262 p. Illus.

Reference book on Yugoslavia in the interwar period.

2170. Hielscher, Kurt. Picturesque Yugo-Slavia; Slavonia [i.e., Slovenia], Croatia, Dalmatia, Montenegro, Herzegovina, Bosnia, and Serbia; Landscape, Architecture, Life of the People. New York, Brentano, 1926. Plates, map.

A well-selected and representative collection of photographs of Yugoslav countryside and people. Captions in German, English, and French. Also published in a British edition by "The Studio," London.

2171. Johnson, Stowers. Yugoslav Summer. London, Hale, 1967. 208 p. Plates, map.

An account of a recent trip through Yugoslavia from north to south, with glimpses into the history of the land. Somewhat unreliable in spelling of Yugoslav proper names.

2172. Jugoslawien; Leben, Kunst, Landschaft. München, Gräfe und Unzer, 1966. 97 p. Plates, map. (Reihe "Farbige Welt")

A fine selection of photographs (some in color) of unusual scenery and people.

2173. Jugoslavensko Novinarsko Udruženje. Kraljevina Srba, Hrvata i Slovenaca (Kingdom of the Serbs, Croats, and Slovenes). Ljubljana, Jugoslovensko Novinarsko Udruženje, 1927. 2 v. in 1. Illus., plates, ports., maps.

A pictorial and narrative portrait of early Yugoslavia edited by Krešimir Kovačić and others. Interesting and useful for historical comparisons. Part 1: pictorial; part 2: articles on a variety of topics of interest, each in a different language (Serbo-Croatian, Slovene, German, French, English). Captions to pictures in Serbo-Croatian or Slovene, English, French, and German. Book was republished in 1929 in a bound edition with the English title *Kingdom of Yugoslavia* on front cover and spine.

2174. Kanitz, Felix P.   Das Königreich Serbien und das Serbenvolk von der Römerzeit bis Gegenwart. Leipzig, Meyer, 1904-1914. 3 v.

Standard work on land and people (ethnography and folklore), history and state, economy and cultural life, with emphasis on the 19th century.

2175. Kerner, Robert Joseph, *ed.*   Yugoslavia. Berkeley, University of California Press, 1949. 558 p. Illus., ports., maps. Bibliography: p. 529-544.

A collection of scholarly studies on Yugoslavia's past and present (up to 1948). One of the most comprehensive works on Yugoslavia. Somewhat one-sided on a few aspects of wartime events and developments. A historical chronology (p. 441-481) is included.

2176. Markert, Werner, *ed.*   Jugoslawien. Köln, Böhlau, 1954. 400 p. Maps. Bibliography: p. 353-372. (Osteuropa-Handbuch, 1)
*See also* entry no. 51.

An overall excellent collection of painstakingly researched studies by Austrian and German scholars. Factual, objective, and balanced, if somewhat dated. Especially good on wartime developments, weak on literature. A documentary part (p. 303-400) includes a historical chronology, 1917-1953 (p. 309-332) and a gazetteer of local names mentioned in the text, in their former and current forms (p. 375-383). For recently published surveys of Yugoslavia, see *Yugoslavia*, with an introduction by Fitzroy Maclean (New York, Viking Press, 1969, 296 p., illus.) and *A Handbook of Yugoslavia* (Belgrade, 1969, 265 p., illus.). The latter attempts to provide an account of the history of the peoples of Yugoslavia and "of all aspects of their lives."

2177. Neumayr, Ernst.   Zwischen Adria und Karawanken; Reisen durch Jugoslawien. Stuttgart, Goverts, 1964. 181 p. Illus., map.

A cross between a travel account and an expanded essay on Yugoslavia, this book makes for pleasant and informative reading. It has insight, concise relevance, and whimsy, including a final chapter containing a clever "Vocabularium balkanicum." Illustrations are mostly people-centered and not of the run-of-the-mill category.

2178. Normand, Suzanne, *and* Jean Acker.   Yugoslavia. London, N. Kaye, 1956. 144 p. Plates, map.

A richly illustrated travelogue, translated from the French by Jean Penfold, occasionally off the beaten path, which could double as a tourist guide. Originally published in French as *La Yougoslavie* (Paris, Arthaud, 1954, 139 p.).

2179. Pillement, Georges.   La Yougoslavie inconnue; itinéraires archéologiques. Paris, B. Grasset, 1967. 317 p. Plates, maps.

Eleven itineraries by land and a cruise along the Adriatic coast, designed specifically for the lover of antiquities and art. Includes total distance and a detailed map for each itinerary. Some unusual photography by the author.

2180. Ribnikar, Jara. Yugoslavia— One Long Summer. New York, McGraw-Hill, 1964. 96 p. of illus.

A collection of mostly well-selected views of Yugoslavia (some in color) with a brief introduction into the natural beauties and historical treasures of the land. Captions to pictures on a foldout sheet at the end of the book. Published also in a German edition, *Jugoslawien — ein langer Sommer* (Beograd, Jugoslavija, 1963).

2181. St. John, Robert. The Silent People Speak. Garden City, N.Y., Doubleday, 1948. 397 p. Maps.

Yugoslavia of the early postwar years is shown, somewhat admiringly, through the author's experiences and mostly through his conversations with the little people. A sequel to the author's *From the Land of Silent People* (Garden City, N.Y., Doubleday, 1942, 353 p.), a narrative of his experiences in wartime (1941) Yugoslavia.

2182. Sidgwick, Christopher. A Fortnight in Yugoslavia. 5th ed. London, P. Marshall, 1965. 118 p. Illus.

A brief but pleasant tourist guide in the form of a narrative based on personal experience. Geared primarily for use by Britons.

2183. Stojković, Živorad, *ed.* A Look at Yugoslavia. Belgrade, Yugoslavia, 1960. 101 plates, map.

One hundred well-selected views of Yugoslavia, with a map showing the location of each view. Photos by Tošo Dabac and others. Captions to illustrations are somewhat expanded and give additional background information; unfortunately, they do not accompany the plates, but are collected at the end of the book. The book has also been published in Serbo-Croatian as *Jugoslavija; zemlja i oblici* (Yugoslavia; land and forms), and in German as *Jugoslawien in Form und Gestaltung.*

A look at Yugoslavia through a graphic artist's eyes is offered by:
Ivanović, Ljubomir. Crteži; Jugoslovenski predeli (Drawings; Yugoslav landscapes). Beograd, Državna Štamparija, 1937. 9 p. 52 plates (pencil drawings). Foreword and captions in Serbo-Croatian, French, and German.

Lavrin, Nora (Fry). Jugoslav Scenes. London, S. Nott, 1935. 45 p. 18 plates (dry-point).

2184. Tornquist, David. Look East, Look West; the Socialist Adventure in Yugoslavia. New York, Macmillan, 1966. 310 p. Illus., map.
*See also* entry no. 2662.

An interesting firsthand report on a two-year stay in Yugoslavia in the mid-1960s. Less encyclopedic and history-minded than Rebecca West's classic, but showing a great deal of insight into the conditions and especially the people of present-day Yugoslavia. The illustrations are few, poorly selected, and largely irrelevant.

2185. West, Rebecca.   Black Lamb and Grey Falcon; a Journey through Yugoslavia. New York, Viking Press, 1941. 2 v. Plates, ports., maps. Bibliography: p. 1151-1158.

*See also* entry no. 2663.

A book which expands the author's 1937 inquisitive and perceptive trip through most of the country (Slovenia was skipped) into a subjective encyclopedic essay on prewar Yugoslavia. Obviously somewhat dated, but within that limitation still a useful, comprehensive source.

# 45

# the lano

*by George W. Hoffman*

Bibliographies, Atlases, Survey Studies 2186-2198
Regional Studies and Special Aspects 2199-2230
Periodicals 2231-2237

## A. BIBLIOGRAPHIES, ATLASES, SURVEY STUDIES

2186. Blanc, André. La Yougoslavie. Paris, Librairie Armand Colin, 1967. 228 p. Illus. (Collection Armand Colin, no. 398)
A brief regional survey.

2187. Blanc, André. Yugoslavia. *In* Larousse Encyclopedia of Geography. v. 1. Europe. New York, Prometheus Press, 1961. p. 301-318.
Survey of the regional geography of Yugoslavia.

2188. Blašković, Vladimir. Ekonomska geografija Jugoslavije (Economic geography of Yugoslavia). Zagreb, Birotehnički izdavački zavod, 1962. 282 p. Maps, illus.

2189. Chataigneau, Y., *and* Jules Sion. La Yougoslavie. *In* Chataigneau, Y., and Jules Sion, *eds*. Géographie universelle. v. 7, part 2. Paris, Armand Colin, 1934. p. 410-476.
Survey of the regional geography of Yugoslavia.

2190. Hoffman, George W., *and* Fred W. Neal. Yugoslavia and the New Communism. New York, Twentieth Century Fund, 1962. 546 p. Maps, tables. Bibliography: p. 511-527.
*See also* entries no. 2490, 2577, *and* 2604.
Survey of Tito's communist system in its historical, geographic, and cultural setting.

2191. Kongres geografa Jugoslavije. Zbornik (Proceedings of Congresses of Yugoslav Geographers and Yugoslav Geographical Societies).
Each volume contains detailed proceedings, papers presented, and

discussions. Important source of information on the status of geographical research in the country as a whole and in the individual republics. Congresses have been held in Zagreb, 1950; Skopje, 1952; Sarajevo, 1954; Belgrade, 1956; Cetinje, 1959; Ljubljana, 1962; and Zagreb, 1964.

2192. Mardešić, Petar, *and* Zvonimir Dugački. Geografski atlas Jugoslavije (Geographical Atlas of Yugoslavia). Zagreb, Znanje, 1961. 256 p. Illus., maps, tables.

2193. Marković, Jovan. Fizička geografija Jugoslavije (Physical geography of Yugoslavia). 2d ed. Beograd, 1968. 188 p. Maps.
First edition published in 1963.

2194. Melik, Anton. Jugoslavija; zemljepisni pregled (Yugoslavia; geographical survey). 3d ed. Ljubljana, Državna založba Slovenije, 1958. 675 p. Maps, illus. Bibliography: p. 654-665.
First edition published in 1949. Topical regional description of the economic geography of Yugoslavia.

2195. Milojević, Borivoje Ž. Geography of Yugoslavia; a Selective Bibliography. Washington, D.C., Library of Congress, Reference Dept., Slavic and East European Division, 1955. 79 p.
A useful bibliography of 830 items, prepared by the well-known Yugoslav geographer.

2196. Milojević, Borinoje Ž. Yugoslavia; Geographical Survey. Belgrade, Committee for Cultural Relations with Foreign Countries, 1958. 111 p. Illus.
General geographical description of Yugoslavia, including brief coverage of the major regions.

2197. Milošević, Miodrag. Geografija Jugoslavije (Geography of Yugoslavia) 3d ed. Beograd, "Naučna knjiga," 1967. 250 p. Illus.
A recent physical geography.

2198. Rogić, Veljko, *and* Stanko Žujić. Geografija Jugoslavije (Geography of Yugoslavia). Zagreb, Školska knjiga, 1960. 242 p. Maps, illus.
A valuable survey, written for the 14-17 age group but of interest to more sophisticated readers. English translation prepared by the Joint Publications Research Service (JPRS: 11327, December 4, 1961, 375 p.).

## B. REGIONAL STUDIES AND SPECIAL ASPECTS

2199. Adria, Reiseführer und Atlas. Zagreb, Jugoslovenski leksikografski zavod, 1965. 148 p. Maps, illus.
A valuable reference work, with brief geographical and historical descriptions of important places.

2200. American-Yugoslav Project in Regional and Urban Planning Studies. Selected Bibliography of Planning Studies in S.R. of Slovenia. Ljubljana, Urbanistični institut SR Slovenije, 1967. 56 p.
A valuable and detailed bibliography.

2201. Roglić, Josip. Die wirtschaftsgeographischen Beziehungen des jugoslawischen Küstenlandes mit den östlichen Bundesländern Österreichs. Österreichische Osthefte, March 1962: 111-112.
A study of the economic relationship between Yugoslavia's Adriatic littoral and the eastern provinces of Austria.

2202. Blanc, André. La Croatie occidentale: Étude de géographie humaine. Paris, Institut d'études slaves de l'Université de Paris, 1957. 498 p. Illus., maps. (Travaux publiés par l'Institut d'études slaves, 25)
See also entry no. 2533.
Imprint of traditional economies on the landscape of Croatia.

2203. Blanc, André. Problèmes d'habitat rural en Croatie occidentale. Annales de géographie (Paris), v. 62, Mar.-Apr. 1953: 108-117.
Discussion of habitat, types of settlement, and problems of dispersion.

2204. Cornish, Vaughn. Bosnia, the Borderland of Serb and Croat. Geography, v. 20, Dec. 1935: 260-270.
Geographical description of the historical changes.

2205. Cvijić, Jovan. Grundlinien der Geographie und Geologie von Mazedonien und Altserbien nebst Beobachtungen in Thrazien, Thessalien, Epirus und Nordalbanien. Gotha, J. Perthes, 1908. 392 p. Illus., plates, fold. maps. (Petermanns geographische Mitteilungen [Gotha], Ergänzungsheft Nr. 162)
Geographic description of areas in southeast Europe by an authority on Serbian geography.

2206. Eterovich, Francis H., and Christopher Spalatin, eds. Croatia: Land, People, Culture. v. 1. Toronto, University of Toronto Press, 1964. 408 p. Illus., maps, ports., bibliographies.
See also entry no. 2506.
Covers geographic and demographic statistics of Croatia and Bosnia-Hercegovina, archaeology, political history up to 1526, military history, economic development, ethical heritage, folk arts and handicrafts, literature, music, architecture, sculpture, and painting.

2207. Fisher, Jack C. Yugoslavia, a Multinational State; Regional Difference and Administrative Response. San Francisco, Chandler Publishing Co., 1966. 244 p. Illus., maps. Bibliography: p. 223-231.
See also entries no. 2488, 2525, and 2619.

2208. Günther, Horst.    Die Verstädterung in Jugoslawien. Darstellung und Probleme. Wiesbaden, Harrassowitz, 1966. 224 p. Maps. Bibliography: p. 220-224.
*See also* entry no. 2678.
Discussion of special features of urbanization in Yugoslavia, with emphasis on demographic, economic, social, and cultural consequences. A typology of Yugoslav towns with respect to their functional differentiation is given.

2209. Hoffman, George W.    Changes in the Agricultural Geography of Yugoslavia. In Pounds, Norman J. G., *ed*. Geographical Essays on Eastern Europe. Bloomington, Indiana University, 1961. p. 101-140. (Indiana University Publications, Russian and East European Series, v. 24)
Changes in organization, land use, and production since the Second World War.

2210. Hoffman, George W.    Yugoslavia: Changing Character of Rural Life and Rural Economy. American Slavic and East European Review, Oct. 1956: 294-315.
Discusses the changes in rural life and economy and especially their impact on the people.

2211. Ilešič, Svetozar.    Die Flurformen Sloweniens im Lichte der europäischen Flurforschung. Münchener geographische Hefte 16, 1959. 132 p. Maps.
Originally published in Slovenian as *Sistemi poljske razdelitve na Slovenskem* (Academia Scientiarum et Artium Slovenica, Institutum Geographicum, Opera 2, 1950). Structure, types, and geographic distribution of fields in Slovenia.

2212. Johnson, W. B., *and* I. Crkvencic.    Examples of Changing Peasant Agriculture in Croatia, Yugoslavia. Economic Geography (Worcester), v. 33, Jan. 1957: 50-71.
Microgeographic study emphasizing changing peasant agriculture.

2213. Krager, Adolf.    Die Entwicklung der Siedlungen im westlichen Slawonien. Kölner geographische Arbeiten, Heft 15, 1963. 119 p. Maps, illus.
Contribution to the cultural geography of the Sava-Drava lands.

2214. Lichtenberger, Elisabeth, *and* Hans Bobek.    Zur kulturgeographischen Gliederung Jugoslawiens. Geographischer Jahresbericht aus Österreich (Wien), v. 26, 1955-56: 78-154.
An analysis of cultural influences, based on a study trip during the summer of 1955.

2215. Marković, Jovan Đ.    Geografske oblasti Socijalističke Federativne Republike Jugoslavije (Geographic regions of the Socialist Federative

Republic of Yugoslavia). Beograd. Zavod za izdavanje udžbenika Socialističke Republike Srbije, 1967. 823 p. Illus., maps. Bibliography: p. 822-824.

A textbook sponsored by Belgrade University.

2216. Melik, Anton.   Slovenija; geografski opis (Slovenian geography). Ljubljana, Slovenska matica, 1935-1960. 2 v. in 5. Maps, illus., charts. Bibliography: v. 1: p. 598-603.

Published in five sections: volume 1, Splošni del (General part) (new edition, 1963); volume 2, Opis Slovenskih prokrajin (Description of Slovenian regions): I. zvezek: Slovenski alpski svet (The Slovenian Alps; II. zvezek: Štajerska s Prekmurjem in Mežiško dolino (Styria and the Trans-Mura region and Meža Valley); III. zvezek, Posavska Slovenija (Sava valley Slovenia); IV. zvezek, Slovensko Primorje (The Slovenian Littoral). Detailed description of the regional geography of Slovenia.

2217. Milojević, Borivoje Ž.   Les vallées principales de la Yougoslavie. 1958. 160 p. Maps. (Srpsko geografsko društvo. Mémoires, v. 9)

Primarily a physical geographic analysis.

2218. Milojević, Borivoje Ž.   Littoral et îles dinariques dans le royaume de Yougoslavie. Beograd, Impr. nationale du royaume de Yougoslavie, 1933. 226 p. Illus., maps. (Srpsko geografsko društvo. Mémoires, v. 2)

Includes seven articles published in 1927, together with some later material; largely physical geographic description.

2219. Moodie, Arthur E.   The Italo-Yugoslav Boundary, a Study in Political Geography. London, George Philip & Son, 1945. 241 p. Illus., maps, diagrs. Bibliography: p. 233-238.

See also entries no. 2520 and 2552.

Study of a frontier problem in the Julian region.

2220. Ogilvie, Alan G.   A Contribution to the Geography of Macedonia. Geographical Journal (London), v. 55, Jan. 1920: 1-34.

Geographical description of Macedonia, with emphasis on the physical geography.

2221. Roglić, Josip.   The Geographical Setting of Medieval Dubrovnik. In Pounds, Norman J. G., ed. Geographical Essays on Eastern Europe. Bloomington, Indiana University, 1961. p. 141-158. (Indiana University Publications. Russian and East European Series, v. 24)

Historical-geographic analysis of the significance of Dubrovnik.

2222. Roglić, Josip.   Prilog regionalnoj podjeli Jugoslavije (Contribution to the knowledge of the regional geography of Yugoslavia). Geografski glasnik (Zagreb), v. 16/17, 1954/55: 9-22.

A discussion of the regional divisions of Yugoslavia and their impact on national unity.

2223. Roglić, Josip.   Yugoslav Littoral. *In* Houston, James M. The Western Mediterranean World; an Introduction to Its Regional Landscapes. London, Longmans, 1964. p. 546-579.
Regional geography of the Adriatic Littoral of Yugoslavia.

2224. Rubić, Ivo.   Naši otoci na Jadranu (Our islands in the Adriatic). Split, Izdanje Odbora za Proslavu, 1952. 167 p. Illus., bibliography.
A physical and cultural description of Yugoslavia's Adriatic islands.

2225. Rungaldier, Randolf.   Natur- und Kulturlandschaft zwischen Donau und Theiss. Beiträge zu einer Landeskunde. Wien, Franz Deuticke, 1943. 127 p. Illus., maps, profiles. (Abhandlungen der Geographischen Gesellschaft in Wien. 14. Band, Heft 4)
Physical and cultural geography of the region between Danube and Tisa.

2226. Schultze, Leonhard S. Makedonien, Landschafts- und Kulturbilder. Jena, G. Fischer, 1927. 250 p. Illus.
A detailed geographical discussion.

2227. Taylor, Griffith.   The Geographical Scene. *In* Kerner, Robert J., *ed*. Yugoslavia. Berkeley, University of California Press, 1949. p. 3-23.
Regional geography of Yugoslavia.

2228. Wilkinson, Henry R.   Jugoslav Kosmet: The Evolution of a Frontier Province and Its Landscape. *In* Institute of British Geographers. Transactions and Papers, no. 21, 1955: 171-193.
Discussion of the contrast between *planina* (mountains) and *pays* (plains), in terms of pastoral economy and crops.

2229. Wilkinson, Henry R.   Maps and Politics; a Review of the Ethnographic Cartography of Macedonia. Liverpool, University Press, 1951. 366 p. Illus., maps. Bibliography: p. 333-349.
*See also* entries no. 713 *and* 2522.
Detailed analysis of the ethnic geography of Macedonia, with emphasis on map presentation.

2230. Zagreb. Jugoslavenski leksikografski zavod. The Yugoslav Coast. Guide and Atlas. Zagreb, 1966. 117, 31 p. Illus., maps.
Valuable reference book–atlas with brief geographical and historical descriptions of all important places. Original edition: *Jadran; vodič i atlas*. German edition: *Adria. Reiseführer und Atlas* (1965).

## C. PERIODICALS

2231. Geografski glasnik. Bulletin de géographie. 1929– Zagreb. Annual.
Publication suspended, 1940-1948. Issued by the Geographical
Society of Croatia. In Croatian, with abstracts in French, German,
or English.

2232. Geografski horizont (Geographical horizon). 1955– Zagreb. Quarterly.
Issued by the Geographical Society of Croatia. Especially oriented
toward secondary school teachers. In Croatian or Serbian.

2233. Geografski pregled.    Revue de géographie. 1957– Sarajevo. Annual.
Issued by the Geographical Society of Bosnia and Hercegovina.
In Serbian or Croatian, with summaries in English, French, or other
languages.

2234. Geografski vestnik.    Bulletin de la Société de géographie de Ljubljana, časopis za geografijo in sorodne vede . . . 1925– Ljubljana.
Annual.
Issued by the Geographical Society in Ljubljana. In Slovenian,
with abstracts in English or French.

2235. Geografski zbornik. Acta geographica. 1952– Ljubljana. Annual.
Issued by the Geographical Institute of the Slovenian Academy of
Sciences. In Slovenian, with summaries in English or French.

2236. Geografsko društvo na N.R. Makedonija.    Geografski razgledi.
Revue géographique. 1962– Spokje. Annual.
In Macedonian, with French or German summaries.

2237. Srpsko geografsko društvo.    Glasnik. Bulletin. 1912– Beograd.
In Serbian and French, with summaries in English, French, and
German. Volumes 5-27 (1921-1947) issued by the society under its
variant name, *Geografsko društvo*.

# 46

# the people

*by Andrew Elias*

## A. DEMOGRAPHY

### 1. Population Theory

2238. Belgrade. Institut društvenih nauka. *Centar za demografska istraživanja.* Stanovništvo (Population). 1963– Beograd. Quarterly.

> A scholarly journal treating the analysis of demographic changes and the socioeconomic development of the population in Yugoslavia and, occasionally, elsewhere.

2239. Yugoslavia. *Savezni zavod za statistiku.* II demografski seminar (Second seminar in demography). Beograd, 1957. 250 p. Maps, tables.

> A collection of papers presented at a 1956 symposium of Yugoslav demographers (the first one was held in 1954). It contains some of the best methodological and conceptual information pertaining to the demographic statistics of Yugoslavia.

### 2. Size, Composition, and Distribution of the Population

2240. Belgrade. Institut društvenih nauka. *Centar za demografska istraživanja.* Šema stalnih rejona za demografska istraživanja (A structure of permanent regions for demographic research). Beograd, 1963. 132 p. Illus., maps.

A study of the population of Yugoslavia, divided into 79 first-degree regions with an average population of 234,000 and 20 second-degree regions with an average population of 931,000. The criteria for setting up the regions are listed. Statistical data are taken primarily from the last two censuses.

2241. Belgrade. Institut društvenih nauka. *Centar za demografska istraživanja.* Smrtnost odojčadi u Jugoslaviji (Infant mortality in Yugoslavia). Beograd, 1966. 288 p.

A detailed and analytical study into the causes of the relatively high infant mortality rate in Yugoslavia. Summaries in French and English are provided.

2242. Croatia-Slavonia. *Zemaljski statistički ured.*    Statistički atlas Kraljevine Hrvatske i Slavonije, 1875-1915 (Statistical atlas, Kingdom of Croatia and Slavonia, 1875-1915). Prepared by R. Signjar. Zagreb, 1915. 12 p. 61 fold. 1, of maps, diagrs. (*Its* Publikacije, 67)

A collection of 108 maps and graphs on demographic, economic, and social statistics, pertaining to this area and period.

2243. Đorđević, Vera, *and* Dragomir Popović, *comps.*    Demografska bibliografija (Demographic bibliography). Beograd, Institut društvenih nauka, 1963. 163 p.

A compilation of 949 sources, both Yugoslav and foreign, published between 1945 and 1961. More current bibliographic material on the subject is regularly listed in the periodical *Stanovništvo* (Population).

2244. Kesić, Branko. Vitalna statistika (Vital statistics). Zagreb, Institut za higijenu rada Jugoslavenske akademije znanosti i umjetnosti, 1957. 100 p. Illus., bibliography.

A short account of population change in Yugoslavia. Interregional as well as international comparisons refer primarily to the period since the Second World War.

2245. Macura, Miloš.    Stanovništvo i radna snaga kao činioci privrednog razvoja Jugoslavije (Population and labor as factors in Yugoslavia's economic development). Beograd, Nolit, 1958. 373 p.

*See also* entry no. 2606.

A first-rate study of the trends in the age, sex, and employment structure of the population of Yugoslavia, essentially during the post-war years. It also includes chapters on the qualification and training of the labor force. A summary in English is provided.

2246. Marković, Petar J.    Strukturne promene na selu kao rezultat ekonomskog razvitka, 1900-1960 (Structural changes in the village as a result of economic development, 1900-1960). Beograd, Zadružna

knjiga, 1963. 164 p. Illus. Bibliography: p. 153-155.
*See also* entry no. 2671.

A revised doctoral dissertation dealing with the demographic and economic changes of the rural population in Yugoslavia between 1900 and 1960, with emphasis on the period since the Second World War.

2247. Myers, Paul F., *and* Arthur A. Campbell.   The Population of Yugoslavia. Washington, D.C., U.S. Government Printing Office, 1954. 161 p. (U.S. Bureau of the Census. International Population Statistics Reports. Series P-90, no. 5)

A comprehensive study of the recent changes in population structure and distribution in Yugoslavia. It also includes a discussion of educational and employment trends. The text is supplemented by six appendixes with valuable conceptual and methodological background information.

2248. Simeunović, Vladimir.   Stanovništvo Jugoslavije i socijalističkih republika 1921-1961 (Population of Yugoslavia and of the socialist republics, 1921-1961). Beograd, Savezni zavod za statistiku, 1964. 135 p.

A very useful study on the structural changes in the population of Yugoslavia as a whole and in its individual republics. Based on the results of all five censuses, taken in 1921, 1931, 1948, 1953, and 1961.

2249. Vasović, Milorad.   Najnovije naseljavanje Crnogoraca u nekim Bačkim selima (The latest Montenegrin settlements in some Bačka villages). Novi Sad, Matica srpska, 1959. 169 p. Illus., maps. Bibliography: p. 163-164.

A study of the ethnic and socioeconomic structure of the population in central Bačka (Vojvodina) based on an analysis of data for five towns. Special emphasis is given to the migrants from Montenegro to Bačka. Other similar volumes stress the migrants from other constituent republics.

2250. Yugoslavia. *Savezni zavod za statistiku.*   Jugoslavija, 1945-1964; statistički pregled (Yugoslavia 1945-1964; a statistical survey). Beograd, 1965. 373 p. Illus., map.
*See also* entry no. 2626.

A survey of Yugoslavia's socioeconomic growth, especially during the first two decades after the Second World War. There are chapters on population change and on the growth of the labor force.

2251. Yugoslavia. *Savezni zavod za statistiku.*   Tablice mortaliteta 1952-1954 (Mortality tables for 1952-1954). Beograd, 1960. 77 p. Diagrs., tables.

Mortality tables of the population of Yugoslavia as a whole and of its individual republics.

2252. Zwitter, Fran.    Prebivalstvo na Slovenskem od XVIII. stoletja do današnjih dni (The population of Slovenia from the 18th century to our time). Ljubljana, Znanstveno društvo, 1936. 112 p. (Znanstveno društvo v Ljubljani. Razprave, 14. Historični odsek, 5)

A detailed study of the population movement in the Slovenian regions, with a summary in German.

## 3. Sources of Population Data

2253. Serbia. *Zavod za statistiku.*    Stanovništvo Narodne republike Srbije od 1834-1953 (Population of the People's Republic of Serbia from 1834 to 1953). v. 1. Beograd, 1953– Maps, diagrs. (*Its* Izdanja, serija B, sveska 1)

A collection of selected data from various censuses. Very useful for comparing changes in administrative boundaries. Includes a detailed bibliography.

2254. Statistička revija (Statistical review). 1951– Beograd. Quarterly.

A journal of the Yugoslav Statistical Society containing scholarly contributions on population subjects. Each issue contains an extensive bibliography of the latest local and foreign publications of interest to statisticians. Tables of contents and summaries in French and English.

2255. Yugoslavia. *Opšta državna statistika.*    Definitivni rezultati popisa stanovništva od 31 januara 1921 godine (Definitive results of the population census of January 31, 1921). Sarajevo, Državna štamparija, 1932. 467 p. Tables.

Data on the first population census in Yugoslavia. The results of the second census, taken in 1931, were published in four volumes under an analogous title in 1937 and 1938. The results of the first post-World War II census were published between 1951 and 1956 in ten volumes under the general title *Konačni rezultati popisa stanovništva od 15 marta 1948 godine* (Final results of the population census of March 15, 1948). The results of the following census were published in great detail in 17 volumes with the general title *Popis stanovništva 1953* (Population census of 1953). For the latest census, taken on March 31, 1961, 16 large volumes of *Popis stanovništva 1961* (Population census of 1961) have been published thus far. All census publications for the post–World War II period have been issued by Savezni zavod za statistiku (Federal Statistical Office). The prewar and postwar issues of *Statistički godišnjak* (Statistical yearbook) present summary data on the various censuses.

2256. Yugoslavia. *Savezni zavod za statistiku.*    Demografska statistika 1963 (Demographic statistics, 1963). Beograd, 1965. 263 p.

A comprehensive compilation of demographic data for recent years, published annually since 1956. From 1950 to 1955, it was published under the title *Vitalna statistika* (Vital statistics).

## B. ETHNOLOGY AND RELATED FIELDS*

### by Joel Halpern

### 1. Bibliographies

2257. Arheologija. *In* Enciklopedija Jugoslavije. v. 1. Zagreb, Leksikografski zavod FNRJ, 1958. p. 170-183.

> By republics, surveys of the history of archaeology and presents bibliographic reviews, followed by a survey of sites by various contributors.

2258. Filipović, Milenko S.  Bibliografija radova Dr. Milenka Filipovića (Bibliography of publications of Dr. Milenko Filipović). Zbornik Matice srpske za društvene nauke (Novi Sad), v. 28, 1960: 159-170.

> Lists of 280 items published from 1924 to 1960 by the outstanding Serb ethnographer. See also Manojlo Gluščević's *Život i rad Profesora Dr. Milenka S. Filipovića* (Life and works of Professor Milenko Filipović), Geografski pregled, v. 6, 1962, p. 13-24, for a critical assessment of his writings.

2259. Halpern, Joel M.  Bibliography of English Language Sources on Yugoslavia. 2d ed. Edited by Stanley Radosh and assisted by Mira Nikolic. Amherst, University of Massachusetts, Dept. of Anthropology, 1969. 134 p.

> Reprinted in *Sociologija sela*, v. 4, Apr.-June 1965: 87-92. Lists chiefly anthropological and sociological sources.

2260. Kolinin, Nađa.  Etnološka bibliografija Jugoslavije za 1957-1959 (Ethnological bibliography of Yugoslavia for 1957-1959). Etnološki pregled, v. 4, 1962: 169-200.

> Lists approximately 1,000 Serbo-Croat references.

2261. Pleše, Branko.  Bibliografija radova Profesora Milovana Gavazzi-a (Bibliography of the works of Professor Milovan Gavazzi). Etnološki pregled, v. 6/7, 1965: 125-136.

> A list of the publications of the outstanding Croat ethnologist, with a brief review of his scholarly contributions in the same issue (p. 3-6).

2262. Pogačnik, Anton, *and* Vida Brodar, *comps.* Antropološka bibliografija o Jugoslaviji (Bibliography of works on physical anthropology in Yugoslavia). Beograd, 1963. 51 p. (Antropološko društvo Jugoslavije, Posebna izdanja, sv. 1)

> Lists sources on physical anthropology.

2263. Thompson, Charles T.  Yugoslavia. *In* Sweet, Louise, *ed.* Introductory Bibliographies on Circum-Mediterranean Peasantry, II. Behavior Science Notes, v. 2, 1967, no. 2: 124-142.

* See also chapter 50.

Lists mainly English and Serbo-Croat titles, with some French and German ones.

## 2. General Survey Works

2264. Bidwell, Charles E.    Language, Dialect, and Nationality in Yugoslavia. Human Relations Notes, v. 15, 1962, no. 3, Aug.: 217-225. *See also* entry no. 2503.

Maintains that the individual tends to equate language or dialect difference with ethnic, class, religious, or regional difference, and that typically language as an index of such difference comes to have a high affective value.

2265. Bogišić, Valtazar.    Zbornik sadašnjih pravnih običaja u Južnih Slavena (Collection of contemporary legal customs among the South Slavs). Zagreb, Jugoslavenska akademija znanosti i umjetnosti, 1874. 714 p.

A pioneering survey of folk practices, based on questionnaires. A valuable historical commentary on Bogišić's work, comparing his findings to data from India, is found in the work of the social theorist H. S. Maine, "South Slavonians and Rajpoots," in *The Nineteenth Century*, v. 2, no. 10, Dec. 1877: 796-819. For an evaluation of his work and bibliography see Marko Kostrenčić's "Valtazar Bogišić," in *Enciklopedija Jugoslavije*, v. 1 (Zagreb, Leksikografski zavod FNRJ, 1955), p. 635-636.

2266. Cvijić, Jovan.    La péninsule balkanique. Paris, A. Colin, 1918. 528 p. Illus., maps.

*See also* entries no. 77 *and* 219.

The classic work in Serb ethnography; deals with settlement patterns, origins and migrations of populations, and psychological characteristics of the South Slavs. Some of these concepts are summarized in Cvijić's articles in the *Geographical Review* (v. 5, 1918): "Geographical Distribution of the Balkan Peoples" (p. 345-361), and "The Zones of Civilization of the Balkan Peninsula" (p. 470-482). The regional monographs series "Naselja i poreklo stanovništva" (Settlements and origins of population) issued by the ethnographic division of the Serbian Academy of Sciences, which by 1965 had reached 35 volumes, attempts to document general patterns set forth in Cvijić's major work.

For evaluations of his work, *see* Vojin Milić's "Sociološka koncepcija Jovana Cvijiča" (Sociological concepts of Jovan Cvijić), in *Književnost*, v. 2, Sept. 1956: 161-179; Oct. 1956: 313-335; and Nov./Dec. 1956: 457-468; Vojislav Radovanović's *Jovan Cvijić* (Beograd, Nolit, 1958, 223 p.); *Jovan Cvijić: autobiografija i drugi spisi* (Jovan Cvijić, autobiography and other writings), edited by V. Stojanović (Beograd, Srpska književna zadruga, 1965, 374 p.); and Petar Jovanović's article in *Enciklopedija Jugoslavije*, v. 2 (Zagreb, Leksikografski zavod FNRJ), p. 510-511.

2267. Dvorniković, Vladimir. Karakterologija Jugoslavena (Yugoslav character). Beograd, Geca Kon, 1939. 1060 p. Illus.
See also entry no. 2504.
Synthesizes ethnic, geographic, historic, and artistic factors to present a picture of Yugoslav character. This unique effort is also concerned with the role of state and moral values. 1,282 footnotes, many with multiple citations.

2268. Etnografija. In Enciklopedija Jugoslavije. v. 3. Zagreb, Leksikografski zavod FNRJ, 1958. p. 271-279.
Each of the six republics is treated separately in bibliographic essays by different authors.

2269. Lockwood, William G., ed. Essays in Balkan Ethnology. v. 1. Berkeley, Kroeber Anthropological Society, 1967. 126 p.
Special publication, mainly on Yugoslavia, with articles by E. Hammel on Serb attitudes toward food and sex, by L. Bresloff on a Bosnian village, and by A. Simic on the blood feud in Montenegro.

2270. Markotić, Vladimir. Archaeology. In Eterovich, Francis H., and Christopher Spalatin, eds. Croatia: Land, People, Culture. Toronto, University of Toronto Press, 1964. p. 20-72. Bibliography.
A good background summary from the viewpoint of an anthropological archaeologist.

2271. Nedeljković, Dušan, and others. Narodi Jugoslavije (Peoples of Yugoslavia). Beograd, 1965. 238 p. (Srpska akademija nauka. Posebna izdanja, v. 385; Etnografski institut, v. 13)
The Serbo-Croat version of the Ethnographic Institute of the Soviet Academy of Science's unit on Yugoslavia, in their "Narody mira" (Peoples of the World) series. Brief summary data are presented on the various Yugoslav nationalities, with emphasis on material culture and folk tradition. Another general survey is Borivoje Drobnjaković's Etnologija naroda Jugoslavije, I (Ethnology of the peoples of Yugoslavia, I) (Beograd, Naučna knjiga, 1960, 261 p.). It treats the material more topically, with attention to historical origins and with emphasis on Serbia.

2272. Radić, Antun. Osnova za sabiranje i proučavanje građe o narodnom životu (A basis for gathering and studying materials on folk life). 2d ed. Zagreb, Jugoslavenska akademija znanosti i umjetnosti, 1929. 112 p.
An early field manual for ethnologists and others, by one of the leaders of the Croatian Peasant Party. Similar guides appeared in Serbia as early as 1896, e.g., Jovan Cvijić's Upustva za proučavanje sela u Srbiji i ostalim srpskim zemljama (Guide for the study of villages in Serbia and other Serbian areas) (Beograd, Srpska državna štamparija, 24 p.). Subsequent editions have been issued by the Ethnographic Institute of the Serbian Academy of Sciences.

2273. Škerlj, Božo.  Yugoslavia, an Anthropological Review for 1952-
54. *In* Thomas, William L., Jr., *ed.* Yearbook of Anthropology,
1955. New York, Wenner-Gren Foundation for Anthropological
Research, 1955. 836 p. Bibliography.

> A survey of the status of archaeology, ethnology, and physical
> anthropology, with a detailed bibliography including a list of per-
> tinent periodicals.

## 3. Regional Studies and Special Aspects

2274. Balikçi, Asen.  Quarrels in a Balkan Village. American Anthropologist, v. 67. Dec. 1965: 1456-1469.

> Explores conflict in dyadic relationships in a Yugoslav Mace-
> donian village.

2275. Benac, Alojz.  Studije o kamenom i bakarnom dobu u sjeveroza-
padnom Balkanu (Studies of the Stone and Copper Ages in the
Northwest Balkans). Sarajevo, Veselin Masleša, 1964. 176 p.

> Bosnia, Montenegro, and Dalmatia are the geographic areas cov-
> ered, with emphasis on the rich neolithic sites.

2276. Cary, Joyce.  Memoir of the Bobotes. Austin, University of Texas
Press, 1960. 154 p. (Texas Quarterly, v. 3, no. 1: Supplement)

> An interesting account by the English novelist of his experiences
> in Montenegro during the Balkan War of 1912.

2277. Crocetti, Guido, *and others.*  Selected Aspects of the Epidemiology
of Schizophrenia in Croatia. Milbank Memorial Fund Quarterly,
v. 42, Apr. 1964: 9-37.

> Findings lead to the tentative conclusion that Dalmatia and Istria
> produce more psychotic persons than comparable populations else-
> where in Yugoslavia.

2278. Đorđević, Tihomir.  Naš narodni život (Our folk life). Beograd,
Geca Kon, 1930-1934. 10 v. Bibliography.

> A collection of writings on folk practices among Serbs. Volumes
> 2 to 4 deal with marriage and the family; volumes 6 through 9 con-
> tain data on Gypsies. An earlier survey by the same author contains
> as well a useful bibliography of French and German sources on
> Yugoslav ethnology, "Serbian Habits and Customs," Folklore, v. 28,
> 1917: 36-51. *See also* Đorđević's *Zle oči u verovanju Južnih Slovena*
> (The evil eye in South Slav beliefs) (Beograd, 1938, 347 p.).

2279. Đurić, Vladimir R.  Changes in Settlements in Yugoslavia. Washington, D.C., U.S. Joint Publications Research Service, 1961. 302 p.
(JPRS Report no. 11536)

> Translation of an article in *Srpski etnografski zbornik* (v. 74, 1960:
> 245-397). A general survey integrating geographical, historical, and
> cultural factors.

2280. Durham, Mary E. Some Tribal Origins, Laws, and Customs of the Balkans. London, Allen and Unwin, 1928. 318 p.

A classic work focusing on the tribal groups in Montenegro and Albania.

2281. Ehrich, Robert W. Some Comments on the Racial History of Montenegro, in the Light of Archeological, Historical, Ethnographic, and Anthropometric Data. *In* International Congress of Prehistoric and Protohistoric Sciences. 6th, Rome, 1965. Communications, v. 2 (Sessions 1-6), 1965: 105-108.

Suggests Illyrians, Romans, and Slavs as three major influxes of population elements. *See also* Ehrich's "Some Doubts about the Validity of the Dinaric Racial Classification, a Preliminary Report," in *American Journal of Physical Anthropology*, v. 5, 1947: 322-336.

2282. Erdeljanović, Jovan. Život i običaji plemena Kuča (Life and customs of the Kuča tribe). Beograd, Akademija nauka i umetnosti, 1931. 596 p. (Srpski etnografski zbornik, v. 48)

Information on social structure, traditional economy, and folk beliefs of one Montenegrin lineage. For anthropogeographical data on the same group see the author's *Kuči, pleme u Crnoj Gori* (The Kučas, a tribe in Montenegro) (Beograd, 1907, 345 p.). For a historical study, see his *Stara Crna Gora, etnička prošlosti i formiranje crnogorskih plemena* (Old Montenegro, her ethnic past and the formation of Montenegrin tribes) (Beograd, 1926, 891 p.). For more data on Montenegrin social structure see also Milovan Đilas' novel *Montenegro* (New York, Harcourt, Brace and World, 1963, 367 p.); his autobiographical account *Land without Justice* (New York, Harcourt, Brace and World, 1958, 365 p.); and his study *Njegoš: Poet, Prince, Bishop* (New York, Harcourt, Brace and World, 1966, 498 p.).

2283. Filipović, Milenko S. Folk Religion among the Orthodox Population in Eastern Yugoslavia. *In* Harvard Slavic Studies, v. 2. Cambridge, Harvard University Press, 1954. p. 359-374.

Focuses on pre-Slavic elements.

2284. Filipović, Milenko S., *ed.* Banatske Here (The Hera of Banat). Novi Sad, Vojvodjanski Muzej, 1958. 426 p. (Vojvodjanski muzej. Posebna izdanja, 1)

A cooperative effort of 13 ethnologists, dealing with the settlement patterns, traditional economy, and social life of a small ethnic group of Dinaric origin living in Banat (Vojvodina).

2285. Gavazzi, Milovan. Godina dana hrvatskih narodnih običaja (The yearly cycle of Croat folk customs). Zagreb, Matica Hrvatska, 1939. 2 v.

Easter and Christmas customs receive most attention in this review of Catholic folk practices.

2286. Gavazzi, Milovan.   Pregled etnografije Hrvata (Review of Croatian ethnography). Zagreb, Kluba ABC, 1940. 80 p.

Devoted mainly to material culture, especially village architecture and implements associated with the traditional peasant economy. *See also* the author's "Etnografiji sastav" (Ethnographic composition) in *Zemljopis Hrvatske* (Geography of Croatia), edited by Z. Dugački (Zagreb, Matica Hrvatska, 1942, 673 p.). This is chiefly an analysis of the historical origins of various elements in Croat peasant culture.

2287. Halpern, Joel M.   A Serbian Village. New York, Harper & Row Colophon Books, 1967. 358 p.

An anthropological community study of a village in Šumadija (central Serbia), based on research done in 1953-1954, with revisions and additions based on 1966 field work. A monograph on the same area in the period before the First World War is Jeremije M. Pavlović's *Život i običaji narodni u Kragujevačkoj Jasenici u Šumadiji* (Peasant life and customs in the Jasenica region of the Kragujevac District in Šumadija) (Beograd, 1921, 271 p.; Srpski etnografski zbornik, 22).

2288. Karadžić, Vuk S.   Život i običaji naroda srpskoga (Life and customs of the Serbian people). Beograd, Srpska književna zadruga, 1957. 337 p.

A catalog of customs, including definitions of folk terms, by the pioneer Serb ethnologist. For a biography, see Miodrag Popović's *Vuk Stef. Karadžić, 1787-1864* (Beograd, Nolit, 1964, 479 p.). *See also Vukov zbornik* (A Vuk collection), edited by V. Novak (Beograd, Akademija nauka, 1966, 716 p.), especially the article by Radomir Lukić on "Vuk i naša sociologija (Vuk and our sociology), which treats his impact on ethnology and the other social sciences as well, particularly as they relate to peasant society.

2289. Kemp, P.   Healing Ritual; Studies in the Technique and Tradition of the Southern Slavs. London, Faber and Faber, 1935. 335 p.

A study of folk medicine and folk psychology, based in part on the author's field observations.

2290. Krasnići, M.   Šiptarska porodična zadruga u Kosovsko-Metohijskoj oblasti (Albanian family zadruga in Kosovo-Metohija). Glasnik muzeja Kosovo-Metohija, v. 4/5, 1959/60: 131-171.

A field study in the Kosmet region, where the zadruga structure is best preserved.

2291. Mirković, Mijo, ed.   Otok Sušak: zemlja, voda, ljudi, gospodarstvo, društveni razvitak, govor, nošnja, građevine, pjesma i zdravlje (The Island of Sušak: land, water, people, economy, social development, speech, costume, architecture, songs, and health). Zagreb, 1957. 586 p. (Jugoslavenska akademija znanosti i umjetnosti, Djela, v. 49)

A complex investigation, with various contributors in the natural and social sciences and with emphasis on demography, physical anthropology, and medicine. A similar study of karst villages near the coast is B. Kesić's *Dabri i susjedna sela srednjeg Velebita* (Dabri and neighboring villages in the central Velebit area) (Zagreb, Institut za medicinska istraživanja, 1959, 133 p.).

2292. Mosely, Philip E.    Adaptation for Survival: The Varžić Zadruga. Slavonic and East European Review, v. 31, 1943: 147-173.

An excellent case study of a zadruga in Slavonia.

2293. Narodopisje Slovencev (Ethnography of the Slovenes). Edited by Rajko Ložar. Ljubljana, 1944-1952. 2 v. Illus.

*See also* entry no. 2864.

The standard reference work on Slovene ethnography, with extensive references.

2294. Nimac, Franjo, *and others*.    Seljačke obiteljske zadruge (Peasant family zadrugas). Zagreb, Filozofski fakultet, Sveučilište u Zagrebu, 1960. 45 p.

A collection of case studies from the 19th and 20th centuries, with an English summary. A related study is "Zadruga Domladovac" (The Domladovac zadruga) by Drzislav Švab and Franko Petrić in *Zbornik za narodni život i običaje južnih Slovena*, v. 27, 1929: 92-110.

2295. Novak, Vilko.    Slovenska ljudska kultura (Slovenian folk culture). Ljubljana, Oris, 1960. 261 p.

A general survey stressing material culture and folk traditions.

2296. Stead, Alfred, *ed.*    Servia by the Servians. London, William Heinemann, 1909. 377 p. Map.

Contains useful chapters by Tichomir Georgevitch (Tihomir Đorđević) on superstitions and traditions; Sima Troyanovitch, on manners and customs; C. Koumanoudi, on local administration; and M. Avramovitch, on rural cooperation.

2297. Thurnher, Majda.    A Survey of Balkan Houses and Farm Buildings. *In* Kroeber Anthropological Society. Papers, no. 14, Spring 1956: 19-22.

An analysis of settlement patterns, house and outbuilding construction, and courtyards in Balkan peasant communities.

2298. Tomić, Persida, *ed.*    Jadar: Vukov zavičaj (Jadar: Vuk's [Karadžić] native region). Beograd, 1964. 502 p. (Etnografski muzej, Glasnik, v. 27)

Contains 22 articles on this region in southwest Serbia dealing with various ethnographic subspecialities including both historical and contemporary data. A similar approach to a region in eastern Bosnia is *Etnološko folklorističa istraživanja u Žepi* (Ethnological and folkloristic research in Žepa), edited by Z. Čulić (Sarajevo,

Zemaljski muzej u Sarajevu, 1964, 312 p.). Similiar studies of other regions appear in earlier issues of the *Glasnik*, i.e., on Livanjsko Polje, v. 15/16, and on Imljani, v. 17.

2299. Trifunoski, Jovan.    Makedonska gradska naselja (Macedonian urban settlements). Beograd, Davidović, 1947. 60 p.

One of the few attempts by geographers or ethnologists to deal with urban populations. Uses census data.

# 47

# history

by *Charles and Barbara Jelavich*

## A. BIBLIOGRAPHY AND HISTORIOGRAPHY

2300. Kos, Milko.   Pregled slovenske historiografije (Survey of Slovene historiography). Jugoslovenski istoriski časopis (Ljubljana), v. 1/2, 1935: 8-21.
    A brief survey of Slovene historiography by an excellent historian.

2301. Petrovich, Michael B.   Dalmatian Historiography in the Age of Humanism. Medievalia et Humanistica (Boulder), v. 12, 1958: 84-103.
    Describes the origins of scientific historical writing among the Yugoslavs.

2302. Petrovich, Michael B.   The Rise of Modern Serbian Historiography. Journal of Central European Affairs (Boulder), v. 16, 1957: 1-24.
    An informative and interesting account of the early Serbian historians.

2303. Petrovich, Michael B.   The Rise of Modern Slovenian Historiography. Journal of Central European Affairs (Boulder), v. 22, 1963, no. 4: 440-467.
    Excellent basic study.

2304. Rojnić, Matko, *and others*.   Bibliografija (Bibliography). *In* Enciklopedija Jugoslavije. v. 1. Zagreb, Leksikografski zavod FNRJ, 1955. p. 504-519.

In this general article on bibliographies in Yugoslavia, there are sections in which bibliographies on history are listed. Many of these refer to articles or to sections on history within general bibliographies. This reference, together with the two volumes on Yugoslav historiography edited by Tadić (*see entries* 2305 and 2307), are indispensable references for scholars and librarians.

2305. Savez društava istoričara Jugoslavije. Historiographie yougoslave, 1955-1965. Edited by Jorjo Tadić. Belgrade, 1965. 525 p.

This volume was presented to the XII International Historical Congress in Vienna. All aspects of historical research — books, articles, research organizations, etc. — are discussed and cited. Indispensable. Chapters are written in French.

2306. Šišić, Ferdinand. Hrvatska historiografija od XVI do XX stoljeća (Croatian historiography from the 16th to the 20th centuries). Jugoslovenski istoriski časopis (Ljubljana), v. 1, 1935, no. 1/2: 22-51; v. 2, 1936, no. 1/4: 16-48.

Perhaps the greatest Croatian historian discusses the evolution of Croatian historical writing. Indispensable aid on this subject.

2307. Yugoslav National Committee for Historical Studies. Dix années d'historiographie yougoslave 1945-1955. Edited by Jorjo Tadić. Beograd, "Jugoslavija," 1955. 685 p.

An indispensable volume prepared by the Yugoslav historians for the Tenth International Congress of Historians held in Rome. The volume begins with studies on historiography and then proceeds to individual topics, concluding with the histories of the individual peoples of Yugoslavia. The chapters are written in French or English. All the books and articles on Yugoslav history published in these years are discussed. Basic for any scholar or library interested in developing a collection on Yugoslav history.

## B. JOURNALS

2308. Arhiv za povestnicu jugoslavensku (Archive for Yugoslav history). 1851-1875. Edited by Ivan Kukuljević-Sakcinski. Zagreb, Gaja. 12 v. Illus.

An important 19th century publication of sources for Yugoslav history.

2309. Godišnjica Nikole Čupića (Yearbook of Nikola Čupić). 1877-1914; 1921-1941. Beograd, Izdanje Čupićeve zadužbine. 50 v.

Although it includes other subjects, this is one of the most important sources for Serbian history.

2310. Historijski pregled (Historical survey). 1954- Zagreb. Quarterly.

The organ of the Association of Historical Societies of Yugoslavia. In addition to scholarly articles, the review prints the proceedings, actions, etc. of professional meetings.

2311. Historijski zbornik (Historical review). 1948– Zagreb, Povijesno društvo Hrvatske. Annual.

A review which has published many major articles revising previous interpretations of Croatian history. The basic journal for Croatia.

2312. Istoriski časopis (Historical journal). 1948– Beograd.

The standard postwar Serbian historical journal. Organ of the Historical Institute of the Serbian Academy of Sciences.

2313. Jugoslovenski istoriski časopis (Yugoslav historical review). 1962– Beograd. Quarterly.

An attempt to carry on in the Yugoslav tradition of its interwar predecessor (*see entry* 2314). A basic journal. Organ of the Savez društava istoričara Jugoslavije.

2314. Jugoslovenski istoriski časopis (Yugoslav historical journal). 1935-1938. Ljubljana, Jugoslovensko istorisko društvo. 5 v. in 6.

A shortlived but first-rate journal conceived of and edited in the Yugoslav spirit. Contains articles on historiography, periodization, etc. Basic for any scholar or library.

2315. Zgodovinski časopis (Historical journal). 1948– Ljubljana. Quarterly.

The standard journal for Slovenian history.

## C. SERBIAN, MACEDONIAN, AND MONTENEGRIN HISTORY*

2316. Stanojević, Stanoje.   Istorija srpskoga naroda (History of the Serbian people). 3d rev. ed. Beograd, Izdavačka knjižarnica Napredak, 1926. 431 p. Illus., ports., maps, facsim.

A useful synthesis of Serbian history by one of the best Serbian scholars of the 20th century.

2317. Jireček, Josef K. Istorija Srba (History of the Serbs). 2d rev. and enl. ed. Translated by Jovan Radonić. Beograd, Naučna knjiga, 1952. 2 v.

Originally published as *Geschichte der Serben* (Gotha, Friedrich Andreas Perthes, 1911), this revised and enlarged edition of Jiriček's well-known work remains the best general survey of meedieval Serbian history. The author was fully acquainted with the sources, and he had a feeling for Serbian history.

2318. Zlatarski, Vasil N.   Istoriia na bŭlgarskata dŭrzhava priez sriednitie

* The arrangement in this and following sections of this chapter follows a chronological pattern.

viekove (History of the Bulgarian state during the Middle Ages). Sofiia, 1918-1940. 3 v. in 4.
See also entry no. 572.
Basic work on Macedonia by a great scholar.

2319. Dušanov zakonik.    Zakonik cara Stefana Dušana 1349 i 1354 (The law code of Tsar Stefan Dušan of 1349 and 1354). Edited by Nikola Radojčić. Beograd, Naučno delo, 1960. 176 p.
Basic for this major document.

2320. Novaković, Stojan.    Srbi i Turci XIV i XV veka (The Serbs and Turks in the 14th and 15th centuries). Beograd, 1960. 487 p. (Srpska književna zadruga, kolo 53, knj.: 356-357)
A well-known work by an early Serbian scholar, which is still valuable for the end of the Serbian medieval empire.

2321. Popović, Dušan J.    Srbi u Vojvodini (The Serbs in the Vojvodina). Novi Sad, Matica srpska, 1957-1963. 3 v. Illus., facsims., maps, ports.
Covers the history of the Serbs from the earliest times to 1861. A work of real scholarship by an outstanding scholar.

2322. Kostić, Mita.    Dositej Obradović u istorijskoj perspektivi XVIII i XIX veka (Dositej Obradović in the historical perspective of the 18th and 19th centuries). Beograd, Srpska akademija nauka, 1952. 304 p. (Srpska akademija nauka. Posebna izdanja, knj. 190. Istoriski institut, knj. 2)
The best study of a famous Serbian intellectual of the Enlightenment.

2323. Srpski narod u XIX veku (The Serbian people in the 19th century). Edited by Stanoje Stanojević. Beograd, G. Kon, 1934-1941. 14 v. (v. 1-10, 15-16, 18-19)
Although only 14 of the projected 20 volumes in this major series were completed, it nevertheless is basic for 19th century Serbian history. Semi-popular in character, but written by distinguished scholars, these volumes discuss political, military, constitutional, and regional history.

2324. Čubrilović, Vaso.    Istorija političke misli u Srbiji XIX veka (The history of political ideas in Serbia in the 19th century). Beograd, Prosveta, 1958. 578 p. (Istoriska biblioteka, 1 kolo, 1 knj.)
The best synthesis of Serbian political thought. Describes Garašanin's Načertanije as a Greater Serbian program. Critical of the Serbian ruling circles. Author was one of Princip's fellow conspirators.

2325. Prodanović, Jaša M.    Istorija političkih stranaka i struja u Srbiji (History of political parties and currents in Serbia). Beograd, Prosveta, 1947. 526 p.

A good general discussion of political parties from Karađorđe through Milan Obrenović by a respected scholar.

2326. Đorđević, Miroslav.    Politička istorija Srbije XIX i XX veka. v. 1: 1804-1813 (The political history of Serbia in the 19th and 20th centuries. v. 1: 1804-1813). Beograd, Prosveta, 1956. 354 p.

The only successful postwar attempt to analyze the political aspects of the Serbian revolution.

2327. Jakšić, Grgur.    Evropa i vaskrs Srbije, 1804-1834 (Europe and the resurrection of Serbia, 1804-1834). 4th enl. ed. Beograd, Narodna štamparija, 1933. 434 p.

Originally written as a doctoral dissertation in French, *L'Europe et la résurrection de la Serbie (1804-1834)*, this work remains valuable for the formative years of the young Serbian nation.

2328. Pavlowitch, Stevan K.    Anglo-Russian Rivalry in Serbia, 1837-1839; the Mission of Colonel Hodges. Paris, Mouton, 1961. 207 p. Bibliography: p. 197-202. (Études sur l'économie et la sociologie des pays slaves, 5)

A good scholarly monograph on a limited topic based on extensive unpublished materials.

2329. Ranke, Leopold von.    The History of Servia and the Servian Revolution, with a Sketch of the Insurrection in Bosnia. Translated from the German by Mrs. Alexander Kerr. London, Bohn, 1853. 520 p.

Written by one of the greatest historians, it should be consulted for an understanding of the knowledge about Serbia in the first half of the 19th century.

2330. Stojančević, Vladimir.    Miloš Obrenović i njegovo doba (Miloš Obrenović and his times). Beograd, Prosveta, 1966. 487 p. (Istorijska biblioteka, 2. kolo, 2. knj.)

The author concludes that Miloš was "the greatest figure of Serbian history in the nineteenth century." A much needed biography of Karađorđe's successor.

2331. Stoianovich, Traian.    The Pattern of Serbian Intellectual Evolution, 1830-1880. Comparative Studies in Society and History (The Hague), v. 1, 1959, no. 3: 242-272.

A thoughtful essay on a vital problem.

2332. Jovanović, Slobodan.    Sabrana dela (Collected works). Beograd, G. Kon, 1932-1940. 17 v.

Monumental works of Serbia's greatest historian. Whereas most of the volumes deal with Serbian history from 1838 to 1903, essays on Edmund Burke, the French Revolution, etc. are also included. Written in a beautiful literary style. A tribute to scholarship in the Balkans.

2333. Jakšić, Grgur, *and* Vojislav Vučković. Spoljna politika Srbije za vlade Kneza Mihaila; prvi balkanski savez (The foreign policy of Serbia during the reign of Prince Michael; the first Balkan alliance). Beograd, 1963. 576 p.

Two well-known scholars carefully analyze a crucial period in Serbian and Balkan history. Based on extensive domestic and foreign unpublished archival material.

2334. McClellan, Woodford D. Svetozar Marković and the Origins of Balkan Socialism. Princeton, N.J., Princeton University Press, 1964. 308 p. Bibliography: p. 275-296.

*See also* entry no. 2911.

An excellent book combining Serbian and Russian archival materials, this study reveals the plight of socialism in a backward, rural civilization.

2335. MacKenzie, David. The Serbs and Russian Pan-Slavism, 1875-1878. Ithaca, N.Y., Cornell University Press, 1967. 365 p.

A well-documented work based upon unpublished and published Russian and Serbian sources as well as the available materials in other languages.

2336. Živanović, Živan. Politička istorija Srbije u drugoj polovini devetnaestog veka (Political history of Serbia in the second half of the 19th century). Beograd, G. Kon, 1923-1925. 4 v.

A major work on the last two decades of the 19th century. More detailed than the volumes by Slobodan Jovanović, but lacking the literary qualities of the latter. Nevertheless, important for Serbian history.

2337. Ćorović, Vladimir. Odnosi između Srbije i Austro-Ugarske u XX veku (The relations between Serbia and Austria-Hungary in the 20th century). Beograd, Državna štamparija, 1936. 779 p.

A valuable work, suppressed by the Yugoslav government when published, on the Austro-Serbian background to the First World War. Good documentation, including unpublished Serbian archival material.

2338. Vucinich, Wayne S. Serbia between East and West; the Events of 1903-1908. Stanford, Stanford University Press, 1954. 304 p. Bibliography: p. 269-283. (Stanford University Publications. University Series. History, Economics, and Political Science. v. 9)

*See also* entry no. 2517.

A detailed, careful discussion of the political, diplomatic, and economic events leading up to the Balkan crisis.

2339. Đorđević, Dimitrije. Carinski rat Austro-Ugarske i Srbije 1906-1911 (The customs war of Austria-Hungary and Serbia, 1906-1911). Edited by Jorjo Tadić. Beograd, 1962. 733 p. Bibliography: p. 682-

690. (Istorijski institut. Jugoslovenske zemlje u XX veku. Knjiga 1)
    Supplements volume by Vucinich. Uses Serbian, French, Austrian,
    and Russian archival materials. Sheds new light on Serbia's role
    in the Zagreb and Friedjung trials.

2340. Übersberger, Hans.   Österreich zwischen Russland und Serbien. Zur
    südslawischen Frage und der Entstehung des ersten Weltkrieges.
    Köln-Graz, Böhlau, 1958. 332 p. Illus., bibliography.
    The author is a well-known Austrian scholar, who edited the
    Austro-Hungarian documents on the origins of the First World
    War. He personally knew many of the individuals involved in this
    period.

2341. Aleksić-Pejković, Ljiljana.   Odnosi Srbije sa francuskom i engle-
    skom, 1903-1914 (The relations of Serbia with France and England,
    1903-1914). Beograd, Izdanje istorijskog instituta, 1965. 961 p.
    (Istorijski institut u Beogradu. Jugoslovenske zemlje u XX veku, 3)
    A major contribution to the study of the origins of the war. The
    author has used unpublished Yugoslav, Austrian, British, and French
    sources. A good example of recent Yugoslav scholarship.

2342. Jovanović, Jagoš.   Stvaranje crnogorske države i razvoj crnogorske
    nacionalnosti; istorija Crne Gore od početka VIII vijeka do 1918
    godine (The formation of the Montenegrin state and the develop-
    ment of Montenegrin nationality; the history of Montenegro from
    the beginning of the 8th century to 1918). Cetinje, Obod, 1947.
    445 p.
    A good general survey.

## D. CROATIAN AND DALMATIAN HISTORY

2343. Šišić, Ferdinand.   Pregled povijesti hrvatskoga naroda (Survey of
    the history of the Croatian people). 3d ed. Zagreb, Matica hrvatska,
    1962. 550 p. Illus., facsims., maps.
    Šišić was one of Croatia's greatest historians and Jaroslav Šidak,
    who edited this volume, one of his best students. The republication
    of this volume, which first appeared in 1916, with Šidak's corrections
    and revisions, to include the period to 1918, is a tribute to Šišić's
    scholarship. It is the best one-volume history of Croatia available.
    It contains an up-to-date bibliography for each chapter and a com-
    plete bibliography of Šišić's works.

2344. Šišić, Ferdinand.   Hrvatska povijest (Croatian history). Zagreb,
    Matica hrvatska, 1906-1913. 3 v. (Mala knjižnica Matice hrvatske,
    sv. 1, 5, 7)
    Šišić's major general study of Croatian history. Third volume
    ends in 1847.

2345. Guldescu, Stanko.   History of Medieval Croatia. The Hague, Mouton, 1964. 351 p. (Studies in European History, 1)
> Discusses sympathetically the different theories concerning the origins of the Croats and their history to the Battle of Mohacs in 1526.

2346. Klaić, Vjekoslav.   Povjest Hrvata od najstarijih vremena do svršetka XIX stoljeća (History of the Croats from the earliest times to the end of the 19th century). Zagreb, Knjižara L. Hartmana, 1899-1911. 3 v. in 5. Illus., facsims.
> The standard work on medieval Croatia by a great historian. Completed only through the 16th century.

2347. Lucio, Giovanni (Johannes Lucius, Ivan Lučić). De Regno Dalmatiae et Croatiae libri sex. Amstelodami, I. Blaeu, 1668. 474 p. Fold. maps, geneal. tables.
> The first scholarly history by a South Slav historian.

2348. Smičiklas, Tade.   Povijest hrvatska (Croatian history). Zagreb, Naklada Matice hrvatske, 1879-1882. 2 v. (Poučna knjižnica Matice hrvatske, knj. 4-5)
> A good general survey to 1848 by one of the early distinguished Croatian historians.

2349. Horvat, Josip.   Kultura Hrvata kroz 1000 godina (The culture of the Croats during 1000 years). Zagreb, A. Velzek, 1939-1942. 2 v. Illus., plates, ports.
> See also entry no. 2907.
> A sweeping synthesis of Croatian cultural achievements by a gifted writer and patriot. Richly illustrated, including reproductions of major historical documents.

2350. Črnja, Zvane.   Kulturna historija Hrvatske (Cultural history of Croatia). Zagreb, Epoha, 1964. 748 p. Illus. Bibliography: p. 661-701.
> See also entry no. 2906.
> A postwar author gives a socialist interpretation to Croatia's cultural achievements. He criticizes some of Croatia's 19th century "heroes."

2351. Rothenburg, Gunther E.   The Austrian Military Border in Croatia: 1522-1747. Urbana, Ill., University of Illinois Press, 1960. 156 p.
> A basic work on a fascinating institution, which played a vital role in Croatian and Serbian history as well as Habsburg and Ottoman. Continued by the author's The Military Border in Croatia, 1740-1881; A Study of an Imperial Institution (Chicago, University of Chicago Press, 1966, 224 p.)

2352. Šidak, Jaroslav.   Hrvatsko pitanje u Habsburškoj monarhiji (The

Croatian question in the Habsburg Monarchy). Historijski pregled (Zagreb), v. 9, 1963: 101-121, 175-194.

An excellent interpretation of this complex problem by the best present-day historian in Croatia.

2353. Polić, Martin. Parlementarna povijest Kraljevine Hrvatske, Slavonije i Dalmacije sa bilježkama iz političkoga, kulturnoga i društvenoga života (The parliamentary history of the kingdom of Croatia, Slavonia and Dalmatia with notes from political, cultural, and social life). Zagreb, Knjižara Franje Suppana, 1899-1900. 2 v.

An indispensable work for the study of political conflicts and developments in Croatia in the second half of the 19th century.

2354. Rački, Franjo. Korespondencija Rački-Strossmayer (The Rački-Strossmayer correspondence). Edited by Ferdinand Šišić. Zagreb, Jugoslavenska akademija znanosti i umjetnosti, 1928-1931. 4 v.

The most important published source for the views of the two men most responsible for the development of the Yugoslav idea, the advocacy of South Slav cooperation, and the formation of the Yugoslav Academy. *See also*:

Rački, Franjo. Franjo Rački u govorima i raspravama (Franjo Rački in speeches and essays). Edited by Viktor Novak. Zagreb, 1925. 262 p. Perhaps the best brief interpretation of the views and beliefs of Rački, a co-founder of the Yugoslav Academy, as reflected through his own pronouncements.

2355. Šidak, Jaroslav, *and others*. Povijest hravatskoga naroda g. 1860-1914 (History of the Croatian people 1860-1914), Zagreb, Školska knjiga, 1968. 352 p. Bibliography: p. 333-352.

A critical account of Croatian history written in the best scholarly tradition by four gifted historians — Šidak, Mirjana Gross, Igor Karaman, and Dragovan Šepić. It is the most objective interpretation available of this period of Croatian history.

2356. Horvat, Josip. Ante Starčević; kulturno-povjesna slika (Ante Starčević; a cultural-historical portrait). Zagreb, A. Velzek, 1940. 398 p. Bibliography: p. 391-393.

A popular biography of the founder of the ultranationalist Croatian Party of the Right.

2357. Gross, Mirjana. Vladavina hrvatsko-srpske koalicije, 1906-1907 (The rule of the Croatian-Serbian coalition, 1906-1907). Beograd, 1960. 248 p. (Institut društvenih nauka. Odeljenje za istoriske nauke. Serija I. Monografije)

An outstanding book concerning the coalition which helped resolve the frictions of the eighties and nineties between Croats and Serbs and which laid the basic groundwork for the emergence of the Yugoslav state.

2358. Marjanović, Milan. Savremena Hrvatska (Contemporary Croatia).

Beograd, Nova štamparija "Davidović," 1913. 360 p. (Srpska književna zadruga. Kolo 22, br. 153)

A political and philosophical interpretation of Croatian history, stressing the historical factors which produced the conditions in Croatia at the beginning of this century. A good account of the evolution of Yugoslavism.

2359. Bogdanov, Vaso. Historija političkih stranaka u Hrvatskoj od prvih stranačkih grupiranja do 1918 (The history of political parties in Croatia from the first political groupings to 1918). Zagreb, Novinarsko izdavačko poduzeće, 1958. 794 p.

Prepared by a Marxist historian, this volume begins with the activities of the Freemasons in the era of Joseph II and continues through Starčević's Party of the Right, but not up to 1918. It contains valuable quotations and documents. The author's views have been criticized in Yugoslavia.

2360. Smith Pavelić, Ante. Dr. Ante Trumbić; problemi hrvatsko-srpskih odnosa (Dr. Ante Trumbić; problems of Croatian-Serbian relations). München, Knjižnica Hrvatske revije, 1959. 333 p. Ports., illus. Bibliography: p. 317-320. (Knjižnica Hrvatske revije, knj. 3)

See also entry no. 2555.

Trumbić was the most important Croatian politician advocating the formation of a Yugoslav state. He was the head of the Yugoslav Committee during the war and subsequently Yugoslav foreign minister. This book is a judicious attempt to explain Trumbić's beliefs, goals, and activities.

2361. Šepić, Dragovan. Supilo Diplomat: Rad Frana Supila u emigraciji 1914-1917 godine (Supilo the Diplomat: the work of Frano Supilo in emigration 1914-1917). Zagreb, Naprijed, 1961. 274 p.

An excellent monograph on one of the most influential Croats advocating Yugoslavism.

2362. Novak, Grga. Prošlost Dalmacije (The past of Dalmatia). Zagreb, Izdanje Hrvatskog izdavalačkog bibliografskog zavoda, 1944. 2 v. Illus., ports., maps. Bibliography: p. 499-475. (Zemlje i narodi, sv. 4-5)

Although a general work, it is written by a scholar who has devoted his life to the study of Dalmatia and who is now president of the Yugoslav Academy. Covers the period from earliest times to the end of the First World War.

## E. SLOVENE HISTORY

2363. Grafenauer, Bogo. Zgodovina slovenskega naroda (History of the Slovene people). 2d rev. and enl. ed. Ljubljana, Državna založba Slovenije, 1964-1965. 2 v. Illus., maps.

The most recent general interpretation by an excellent scholar.

This revised, enlarged edition only covers the period through the 15th century.

2364. Gruden, Josip. Zgodovina slovenskega naroda (History of the Slovene people). Celje, Družba sv. Mohorja, 1910. 1088 p. Illus., ports., map.

Although over a half century old, this is still a valuable general survey of Slovene history from the earliest times to the French Revolution.

2365. Kos, Milko. Zgodovina Slovencev od naselitve do petnajstega stoletja (History of the Slovenes from their settlement to the 15th century). Ljubljana, Slovenska matica, 1955. 426 p. Bibliography: p. 357-383.

Basic work by a distinguished scholar. Also published in Serbian as *Istorija Slovenaca od doseljenja do petnaestog veka* (Belgrade, Prosveta, 1960, 409 p.).

2366. Mal, Josip. Zgodovina slovenskega naroda: najnovejša doba (History of the Slovenian people, most recent era). Celje, Družba sv. Mohorja, 1928 (i.e. 1929-1939). 1213 p. Issued in parts. Illus., ports., map. Bibliography: p. 1209-1213. (Redna knjiga za člane Družbe sv. Mohorja, zv. 8, 11, 14-16)

A detailed survey of Slovenian history in the 19th century. A basic work.

2367. Prijatelj, Ivan. Slovenska kulturnopolitična in slovstvena zgodovina 1848-1895 (Slovene cultural, political and literary history, 1848-1895). Ljubljana, Državna založba Slovenije, 1955-1961. 4 v. Ports., facsims.

A major work by an excellent literary historian.

## F. BOSNIAN HISTORY

2368. Ćirković, Sima M. Istorija srednjevekovne bosanske države (History of the medieval Bosnian state). Beograd, Srpska književna zadruga, 1964. 415 p. Illus., facsims., tables, plates.

A scholarly work by a very able Byzantinist on a fascinating and important aspect of South Slav and even Balkan history. Good illustrations.

2369. Ekmečić, Milorad. Ustanak u Bosni, 1875-1878 (The uprising in Bosnia, 1875-1878). Sarajevo, "Veselin Masleša," 1960. 391 p.

Of the many books on this topic, this is the best.

2370. Sugar, Peter F. Industrialization of Bosnia-Hercegovina, 1878-1918. Seattle, University of Washington Press, 1963. 275 p. Maps, tables. Bibliography: p. 247-257.

*See also* entry no. 2593.

The standard work on a basic subject which affected the future
of the Habsburg empire and the formation of the Yugoslav state.

2371. Ninčić, Momčilo.   La crise bosniaque (1908-1909) et les puis-
sances européenes. Paris, A. Costes, 1937. 2 v. "References aux
sources documentaires et bibliographiques": v. 1, p. 391-416; v. 2,
p. 383-409.

Painstaking research, based upon Serbian sources, by a onetime
Yugoslav foreign minister. Essential for a study of the Serbian
attitude during the Bosnian crisis.

2372. Dedijer, Vladimir.   The Road to Sarajevo. New York, Simon and
Schuster, 1966. 550 p. Illus., map, ports. Bibliography: p. 517-529.
See also entry no. 2519.

A provocative book, challenging previous interpretations on the
assassination at Sarajevo. The author believes that the assassins
acted on their own initiative, motivated by political, economic and
social conditions in Bosnia, and not on directions and inspiration
from Belgrade. Although based on extensive research, the book is
more political than historical in character. Strongly anti-Habsburg
and anti-German.

## G. YUGOSLAV HISTORY

2373. Historija naroda Jugoslavije (History of the nations of Yugoslavia).
Edited by Anto Babić and others. Zagreb, Školska knjiga, 1953-
1959. 2 v. Illus., ports., maps.

The first two volumes of the five volume history of the South
Slavs. These two volumes (over 2300 pages) cover the period through
the 18th century. Individual chapters are written by recognized
specialists. Excellent bibliographies included. The first volume reflects the political trends of the immediate postwar years, but this
is not so evident in the second. This is a comprehensive work covering politics, economics, literature, social structure, military affairs,
etc. A basic reference for Yugoslav history.

2374. Ćorović, Vladimir.   Istorija Jugoslavije (History of Yugoslavia).
Beograd, Narodno delo, 1933. 613 p. Plates, facsims.

The only succesful scholarly attempt in Serbo-Croatian to present
a survey of Yugoslav history in the interwar period.

2375. Maur, Gilbert in der.   Die Jugoslawen einst und jetzt. Leipzig-
Wien, Günther, 1936-1938. 3 v. Maps.
See also entry no. 2561.

Extensive treatment of the 19th and 20th centuries, especially
of the foreign and domestic policies between 1918 and 1938.

2376. Haumant, Émile.   La formation de la Yougoslavie (XV°-XX°
siècles). Paris, Éditions Bossard, 1930. 752 p. Illus., maps. (Institut

d'études slaves de l'Université de Paris. Collection historique, 5)
*See also* entry no. 2510.

The best one-volume survey of Yugoslav history in a western
language. Sympathetic to the Yugoslav idea.

2377. Clissold, Stephen, *ed.*   A Short History of Yugoslavia: From Early
Times to 1966. Cambridge, The University Press, 1966. 280 p.
Maps. Bibliography: p. 265-266.

A concise survey largely based on material originally published
in a Handbook on Yugoslavia by the Naval Intelligence Division of
the British Admiralty and now updated by a few new chapters.

2378. Akademiia nauk SSSR. *Institut slavianovedeniia.*   Istoriia Iugoslavii
(History of Yugoslavia). Edited by Iu. V. Bromlei and others.
Moskva, Izd-vo Akademii nauk SSSR, 1963. 2 v. Illus., facsims.,
maps, ports., bibliographies.
*See also* entry no. 2556.

Companion volumes to the histories of Bulgaria, Czechoslovakia,
Poland, etc. previously written by Soviet scholars. Contains contributions by respected Soviet historians, as, for example, Bromlei,
Nikitin, and Pisarev. The sections on the 19th century are better
than those on the interwar years. Does not go beyond 1945. Some of
the interpretations have been challenged by Yugoslav scholars.

2379. Matl, Josef.   Südslawische Studien. München, Oldenbourg, 1965.
598 p. (Südost-Institut München. Südosteuropäische Arbeiten, 63)

A major reference work for the study of the South Slavs, covering both books and periodicals. A perceptive discussion by a distinguished scholar of South Slavic matters.

2380. Novak, Viktor, *comp.*   Antologija jugoslavenske misli i narodnog
jedinstva 1390-1930 (Anthology of the Yugoslav idea and of national
unity, 1390-1930). Beograd, 1930. 931 p.
*See also* entry no. 2511.

Basic reference for the study of the "Yugoslav" movement. The
author begins by citing King Tvrtko's title which named most of
the South Slav lands. Well documented with easy cross references.

2381. Wendel, Hermann.   Der Kampf der Südslawen um Freiheit und
Einheit. Frankfurt am Main, Frankfurter Societäts-Druckerei, 1925.
798 p.

The author was a German socialist who was very sympathetic to
the Yugoslav cause. This book is one of the best accounts of Yugoslav history in a western language.

2382. Ostrogorski, Georgije.   Pronija. Prilog istoriji feudalizma u Vizan-
tiji i u južnoslovenskim zemljama (Pronija; a contribution to the history of feudalism in Byzantium and in the Yugoslav lands). Beograd, Naučna knjiga, 1951. 200 p. (Srpska akademija nauka. Posebna izdanja, knj. 176)

A major work on Balkan feudalism by the greatest living Byzantinist.

2383. Radonić, Jovan. Rimska kurija i južnoslavenske zemlje od XVI do XIX veka (The Roman Curia and the South Slavic lands from the 16th to the 19th century). Beograd, Srpska akademija nauka, 1950. 746 p. (Srpska akademija nauka. Posebna izdanja, knj. 155.)
See also entry no. 2935.

Although written in the immediate postwar years with the aim of discrediting the Catholic church, this work nevertheless has much valuable information on a major problem of South Slav history.

2384. Seton-Watson, Robert W. The Southern Slav Question and the Habsburg Monarchy. London, Constable, 1911. 463 p. Map. Bibliography: p. 445-452.
See also entry no. 2515.

Although somewhat outdated, this volume remains valuable for certain subjects in the 19th century. It contains much information on the Zagreb and Friedjung trials. It also reproduces the Strossmayer-Gladstone correspondence.

2385. Zwitter, Fran, Jaroslav Šidak, and Vaso Bogdanov. Les problèmes nationaux dans la monarchie des Habsbourg. Beograd, 1960. 148 p.

Three distinguished Yugoslav scholars interpret the 19th century problems of the Dual Monarchy. This work was presented to the International Historical Congress in Stockholm, 1960.

2386. Pisarev, Iurii A. Osvoboditel'noe dvizhenie iugoslavianskikh narodov Avstro-Vengrii 1905-1914 (The liberation movement of the Yugoslav peoples of Austria-Hungary 1905-1914). Moskva, Izdatel'stvo Akademii nauk SSSR, 1962. 419 p. Bibliography: p. 388-404.

An interesting work by an able young Soviet scholar. His interpretation varies in many respects from that of his Yugoslav colleagues.

2387. Šišić, Ferdinand. Jugoslovenska misao; istorija ideje Jugoslovenskog narodnog ujedinjenja i oslobođenja od 1790-1918 (The Yugoslav idea; the history of the idea of Yugoslav national unification and liberation from 1790 to 1918). Beograd, Balkanski institut, 1937. 280 p. (Biblioteka "Balkan i balkanci," br. 3-4)

A great scholar, a strong supporter of South Slav unity, interprets the Yugoslav movement somewhat idealistically at a time when the Yugoslav state was on the verge of internal disintegration.

2388. Marjanović, Milan. Londonski ugovor iz godine 1915 (The London Pact of 1915). Zagreb, Jugoslavenska akademija znanosti i umjetnosti, 1960. 469 p. Bibliography: p. 467-469. (Prilozi novijoj jugoslovenskoj historiji, knj. 3)

This book, published posthumously, is the culmination of the work of a man who devoted his entire life to the cause of Yugoslav unity. A detailed study with important documents.

2389. Tomasevich, Jozo.   Peasants, Politics, and Economic Change in Yugoslavia. Stanford, Stanford University Press, 1955. 743 p. Maps, tables. Bibliography: p. 703-726.
*See also* entries no. 2436, 2543, *and* 2638.
Although this excellent book is intended primarily as an economic history, it is, nevertheless, the best history of Yugoslavia in English. It stresses political and economic development and not cultural and religious. It covers the period to 1941.

2390. Janković, Dragoslav, *and* Bogdan Krizman, *eds.*   Građa o stvaranju Jugoslovenske države (Sources for the formation of the Yugoslav state). Beograd, Kultura, 1964. 2 v. (Institut društvenih nauka. Odeljenje za istorijske nauke. Serija III. Građa)
This two-volume collection of Yugoslav sources is absolutely essential for the study of the formation of the new state. Expertly edited and presented.

2391. Lederer, Ivo J.   Yugoslavia at the Paris Peace Conference; a Study in Frontier Making. New Haven, Yale University Press, 1963. 351 p. Ports., maps. Bibliography: p. 317-329.
*See also* entries no. 2429, 2516, *and* 2551.
The standard work on the difficult problems which the new state had to face and solve in view of the various political commitments made by the Allies during the war.

2392. Pribićević, Svetozar.   Diktatura Kralja Aleksandra (The dictatorship of King Alexander). 2d ed. Beograd, Prosveta, 1953. 304 p.
This is the best account of the reign of King Alexander even though it is written by one of his political adversaries.

2393. Čulinović, Ferdo.   Jugoslavija između dva rata (Yugoslavia between two wars). Zagreb, Jugoslavenska akademija znanosti i umjetnosti, 1961. 2 v. Illus., ports., maps. (Izdanja Historijskog instituta Jugoslavenske akademije znanosti i umjetnosti u Zagrebu, knj. 1-2)
*See also* entry no. 2423.
A well-known Croatian scholar seeks to analyze a period of Yugoslav history now generally ignored by contemporary historians. Describes the internal conflicts and external pressures. It is critical of both Serbs and Croats.

2394. Hoptner, Jacob B.   Yugoslavia in Crisis, 1934-1941. New York, Columbia University Press, 1962. 328 p. Bibliography: p. 308-313.
*See also* entries no. 2425 *and* 2560.
Using unpublished sources, the author describes the last years of the interwar Yugoslav state.

# 48

# the state

## A. LAW

### by Alexander Adamovitch

### 1. Reference Works

2395. Gsovski, Vladimir, *and* Kazimierz Grzybowski, *eds.* Government, Law, and Courts in the Soviet Union and Eastern Europe. London, Stevens; New York, Praeger, 1959. 2 v. Bibliography: p. 1945-2009. *See also* entries no. 146 *and* 629.

  A comprehensive symposium on the political, economic, and legal development in the Soviet Union and the Eastern European Communist countries, covering the origin of the regimes, private and criminal law, judicial procedure, administration of justice, land and peasant, and worker and factory. Contributors for Yugoslavia are K. Jaszenko, B. Maksimovich, Fr. Gjupanovich, and A. Adamovitch. *See also* Branko M. Pešelj's "The Socialist Character of Yugoslav Law," in *Review* (London), published by the Studies Centre for

Yugoslav Affairs, v. 2, 1961, no. 2: 94-132. The author attempts a synthetic approach to the Yugoslav version of the concept of "rule of law."

2396. Pravni leksikon (Law encyclopedia). Chief editor. Borislav Blagojević. Beograd, Savremena administracija, 1964. 1107 p.
A general encyclopedia of law which pays particular attention to Yugoslav conditions. *See also*:
Horvat, Marijan, *and others.* Rječnik historije države i prava (Dictionary of the history of government and law). Zagreb, Informator, 1968. 927 p.

## 2. International Law

2397. Popović, Đura D.   Klasici međunarodno-pravne doktrine (Classic international law doctrines). Beograd, Rajković, 1933. 122 p.

2398. Pržić, Ilija A.   Novo međunarodno pravo; rasprave i članci (New international law; cases and articles). Beograd, G. Kon, 1934. 290 p.

2399. Schweissguth, Edmund.   Jugoslawien. *In* Fragen des mitteleuropäischen Minderheitsrechts. Herrenhalb, Erdmann, 1967. p. 33-84. (Studien des Instituts für Ostrecht, München, Bd. 18)
A study on the status of the minorities in Yugoslavia.

2400. Šišić, Ferdo (Ferdinand), *comp.*   Dokumenti o postanku Kraljevine Srba, Hrvata i Slovenaca, 1914-1919 (Documents concerning the creation of the Kingdom of the Serbs, Croats, and Slovenes, 1914-1919). Zagreb, Naklada Matice hrvatske, 1920. 329 p.
Collection of historical documents connected with the struggle for and completion of the union of the South Slavs. Chronologically arranged.

2401. Sprudzs, Adolf, *ed.*   Legal Aspects of Yugoslav Foreign Trade. A Selected Bibliography. Chicago, 1968. 26 p. (The University of Chicago Law School Library Publications. Bibliographies and Guides to Research, no. 3)
Lists books and articles in English, French, German, and Serbo-Croatian.

2402. Zimmermann, Werner G.   Valtazar Bogišić, 1834-1908. Ein Beitrag zur südslawischen Geistes- und Rechtsgeschichte im 19. Jahrhundert. Wiesbaden, Steiner, 1962. 530 p. (Veröffentlichungen des Instituts für europäische Geschichte, Mainz, 22)
*See also* entry no. 235.
An excellent study of the lifework of Valtazar Bogišić, eminent social philosopher and jurist, presented against the backdrop of legal developments among the South Slavs in the second half and at the turn of the 19th century.

## 3. Constitutional Law

2403. Đorđević, Jovan. Novi ustavni sistem (The new constitutional system). Beograd, 1964. 1046 p.

A monumental study of the Yugoslav constitutional system discussing every feature of it in detail. The author is Yugoslavia's leading constitutional lawyer. *See also* his earlier work: *Ustavno pravo FNRJ* (Constitutional law of the Federal People's Republic of Yugoslavia) (Beograd, Arhiv za pravne i društvene nauke, 1953, 436 p.). For Western-language publications on the subject consult:

Schweissguth, Edmund. Die Enwicklung des Bundesverfassungsrechts der Föderativen Volksrepublik Jugoslawien. Frankfurt, West Berlin, Verlag für internationalen Kulturaustausch, 1960. 307 p. (Studien des Instituts für Ostrecht, München, 9)

Strasbourg. Université. *Centre de Recherche sur l'URSS et les Pays de l'Est*. Travaux. Le fédéralisme yougoslave. Études coordonnées par l'Institut de droit comparé de Belgrade. Paris, Dalloz, 1966. 247 p. (Annales de la faculté de droit et des sciences politiques et économiques de Strasbourg, 19)

2404. Jovanović, Slobodan. O državi; osnovi jedne pravne teorije (The state; foundations of a legal theory). 3d rev. and enl. ed. Beograd, Geca Kon, 1922. 448 p. Bibliographies.
*See also* entry no. 2512.

First edition published in 1906 under the title *Osnovi pravne teorije o državi. See also* the author's *Ustavno pravo Kraljevine Srba, Hrvata i Slovenaca* (Constitutional law of the Kingdom of the Serbs, Croats, and Slovenes) (Beograd, 1924, 472 p.), and *Naše ustavno pitanje u XIX veku* (Our constitutional problem in the 19th century) (Beograd, 1908).

2405. Tasić, Đorđe. Jedan pokušaj podele državnih funkcija u formalnom i materjalnom smislu (An attempt to separate the governmental functions, formally and substantively). Ljubljana, 1926. 82 p.

2406. Vilfan, Sergij. Rechtsgeschichte der Slowenen bis zum Jahre 1941. Graz, Leykam, 1968. 242 p.

Translation of *Pravna zgodovina Slovencev* . . . (Ljubljana, Slovenska matica, 1961, 567 p.).

## 4. Administrative Law

2407. Yugoslavia. *Laws, statutes, etc.* Komentar zakona o opštem upravnom postupku (Commentary on the law on general administrative procedure). 5th ed. Edited by Bogdan Majstrović. Beograd, Izd. Službenog lista SFRJ, 1966. 457 p. Bibliographical footnotes.

*See also* Alexander Adamovitch's "Judicial Control of Administrative Acts," in *Highlights of Current Legislation and Activities in Mid-Europe*, v. 6, no. 5, July-Aug. 1958, p. 289-298, a special study on the Yugoslav *contentieux administratif* (judicial review of administrative acts).

## 5. Economic Law

2408. Geršković, Leon.   Društveno upravljanje u Jugoslaviji (Corporate management in Yugoslavia). 2d ed. Beograd, Savremena administracija, 1959. 230 p. (Priručna biblioteka za pravna i društvena pitanja, 18, 1959 godine)

> A study on the workers' management system in Yugoslavia. *See also* the author's "Osnovni principi novih privrednih propisa" (Basic principles of the new economic regulations) in *Arhiv za pravne i društvene nauke*, v. 67, 1952, no. 3, p. 267-295, an analytical study of the principles governing the contemporary Yugoslav economic organization.

2409. Sirotković, Jakov.   Problemi privrednog planiranja u Jugoslaviji (Problems of economic planning in Yugoslavia). Zagreb, Naprijed, 1961. 436 p. Bibliography: p. 431-434.

> A comprehensive study on the principles of economic planning in the Yugoslav People's Democracy.

## 6. Private Law and Procedure

2410. Adamovitch, Alexander.   Yugoslavia. *In* Szirmai, Z., *ed.* Law of Inheritance in Eastern Europe and in the People's Republic of China. Leyden, A. W. Sijthoff, 1961. p. 247-270. (Law in Eastern Europe, v. 5)

> A condensed analysis of the new inheritance code in Yugoslavia, with an introduction covering the previous inheritance rules and regulations effective in the various jurisdictional territories of the country.

2411. Begović, Mehmed Đ.   Porodično pravo (Domestic relations). Beograd, Naučna knjiga, 1961. 230 p.

> A comprehensive study on family law, covering marriage, husband and wife relations, and filiation. *See also* Ana Prokop's *Usvojenje po zakonodavstvu FNRJ* (Adoption under the law of the Federal People's Republic of Yugoslavia) (Zagreb, Nakladni zavod Hrvatske, 1948, 123 p.), and *The Family Law* (Belgrade, Institute of Comparative Law, 1962, 61 p.).

2412. Legradić, Rudolf.   Teorija stvarnog prava i stvarno pravo FNRJ (Theory of property rights and property law of the Federal People's Republic of Yugoslavia). Skopje, 1957. 258 p.

> A standard book on property and its theoretical foundations in the Yugoslav Republic. *See also* Andrija Gams' "O diskusiji o socijalističkoj svojini" (Discussion on socialist ownership). *In* Belgrade. Univerzitet. Pravni fakultet. Anali, v. 3, 1955, no. 4: 414-426.

2413. Zuglia, Srećko.   Građanski parnični postupak FNRJ (Civil pro-

cedure of the Federal People's Republic of Yugoslavia). Zagreb,
Školska knjiga, 1957. 655 p. (Udžbenici Zagrebačkog sveučilišta)
Standard commentary on the Code of Civil Procedure.

## 7. Criminal Law and Procedure

2414. Srzentić, Nikola, *and* Aleksandar Stajić.   Krivično pravo FNRJ.
Opšti deo (Criminal law of the Federal People's Republic of Yugoslavia. General part). Beograd, 1961. 431 p.
A standard commentary on the provisions governing the general
principles of the new Criminal Code. May be supplemented by:
Tahović, Janko.   Komentar krivičnog zakonika (Commentary on
the Criminal Code). Beograd, 1956. 695 p.
Yugoslavia. *Laws, statutes, etc.*   Criminal Code. Belgrade, Institute of Comparative Law, 1964. 163 p.

2415. Yugoslavia. *Laws, statutes, etc.*   Komentar zakonika o krivičnom
postupku (Commentary on the code of criminal procedure). Edited
by Tihomir A. Vasiljević. Beograd, Savremena administracija, 1957.
488 p.

## 8. Patents, Trademarks, Copyright

2416. Bogdanović, Andrija.   Zaštita prava industrijske svojine (Protection of patents and trademarks). Beograd, 1956. 51 p.

2417. Štempihar, Jurij.   Avtorsko pravo (Copyright). Ljubljana, Gospo-
darski vestnik, 1960. 217 p.

## 9. Taxation

2418. Yugoslavia. *Laws, statutes, etc.*   Zbirka propisa o doprinosima i
porezima građana, sa objašnjenjima i dodatkom (Collection of regulations on duties and taxes, with explanations and supplement).
Edited by Mihailo V. Šćekić. Beograd, Savremena administracija,
1966. 708 p. Forms.

## B. POLITICS AND GOVERNMENT

*by Wayne S. Vucinich*

### 1. Before the Second World War

2419. Beard, Charles A., *and* George Radin.   The Balkan Pivot: Yugoslavia; a Study in Government and Administration. New York, Macmillan, 1929. 325 p.
A discussion of Yugoslav political problems in the years immediately following the First World War. Antiquated but still useful.

2420. Belgrade. Institut za izučavanje radničkog pokreta. *Odelenje za*

*istoriju jugoslovenskog radničkog pokreta.* Istorija radničkog pokreta; zbornik radova (History of the labor movement; collection
of works). Beograd, 1965–
  A collection of articles reflecting the views and interpretations of
  present-day Yugoslav historians.

2421. Biber, Dušan.  Nacizem in Nemci v Jugoslaviji, 1933-1941 (National Socialism and Germans in Yugoslavia, 1933-1941). Ljubljana,
Cankarjeva založba, 1966. 480 p.
  A study of Nazi activities among the Germans in Yugoslavia and
  of governmental policy on this subject. For a German treatment of
  German-Yugoslav relations from 1933 to 1945 see *Jugoslawien
  und das Dritte Reich* by Johann Wuescht (Stuttgart, Seewald, 1969,
  359 p., bibliography).

2422. Boban, Ljubo.  Sporazum Cvetković-Maček (The Cvetković-Maček
agreement). Beograd, 1965. 435 p. (Institut društvenih nauka.
Odeljenje za istorijske nauke. Serija I.: Monografije, 5)
  A critical analysis, based on archival sources, of an attempt at
  solving the Croatian question on the eve of the Second World War.

2423. Čulinović, Ferdo.  Jugoslavija između dva rata (Yugoslavia between two wars). Zagreb, Jugoslavenska akademija znanosti i u-
mjetnosti, 1961. 2 v. Illus., ports., maps. (Izdanja Historijskog instituta Jugoslavenske akademije znanosti i umjetnosti u Zagrebu, knj.
1-2)
  *See also* entry no. 2393.
  A useful survey of the history of the major political developments
  in interwar Yugoslavia. Although hastily put together, the book is
  nonetheless the most comprehensive study of the subject.

2424. Horvat, Josip.  Politička povijest Hrvatske, 1918-1929 (Political
history of Croatia, 1918-1929). Zagreb, 1938. 452 p. Illus., ports.
Bibliography: p. 453.
  An appraisal by a well known Croatian historian of political developments affecting Croatia.

2425. Hoptner, Jacob B.  Yugoslavia in Crisis, 1934-1941. New York,
Columbia University Press, 1962. 328 p. Bibliography: p. 308-313.
  *See also* entries no. 2394 *and* 2560.
  A well documented study of Yugoslavia's international relations
  on the eve of the Second World War.

2426. Istorija XX (i.e., dvadesetog) veka; zbornik radova (History of the
20th century; a collection of writings). Beograd, 1959–
  Issued by the Section of Historical Sciences of the Institute of
  Social Sciences in Belgrade. Essays on various aspects of Yugoslav
  politics and government as viewed by contemporary Yugoslav historians.

2427. Istorijski arhiv Komunističke Partije Jugoslavije (Historical archive of the Communist Party of Yugoslavia). Beograd, 1949-1951. 7 v. in 8. Facsims.

A collection of documentary materials on the history of the Yugoslav Communist Party, issued under the auspices of the Historical Section of the Party's Central Committee. See also *Pedeset godina Saveza komunista Jugoslavije. 1919-1969.* (Fifty years of the League of Communists of Yugoslavia. 1919-1969), prepared under the chief editorship of Miodrag Živković (Beograd, Privredni pregled, 1969, 389 p., illus.).

2428. Krizman, Bogdan, *ed.*   Zapisnici sa sednica delegacije Kraljevine SHS na Mirovnoj konferenciji u Parizu, 1919-1920 (Minutes of the meetings of the delegation of the Kingdom of Serbs, Croats, and Slovenes at the Peace Conference in Paris, 1919-1920). Beograd, Kultura, 1960. 427 p. (Institut društvenih nauka. Odeljenje za istorijske nauke. Serija III. Građa)

2429. Lederer, Ivo J.   Yugoslavia at the Paris Peace Conference; a Study in Frontier Making. New Haven, Yale University Press, 1963. 351 p. Ports., maps. Bibliography: p. 317-329.

*See also* entries no. 2391, 2516, *and* 2551.

The definitive study of the formation of Yugoslavia in 1918, including a treatment of political, ethnic, and border questions.

2430. Maček, Vladko.   In the Struggle for Freedom. Translated by Elizabeth and Stjepan Gazi. New York, R. Speller, 1957. 280 p. Illus.

A Croatian national leader and head of the Croatian Peasant Party discusses his political and other activities in Yugoslavia before and during the Second World War.

2431. Marković, Lazar.   Jugoslovenska država i Hrvatsko pitanje, 1914-1929 (The Yugoslav state and the Croatian question, 1914-1929). Beograd, Izdavačko i knjižarsko preduzeće G. Kon, a. d., 1935. 372 p.

A discussion of the constitutional struggle and of the first Yugoslav constitution of the interwar period as it related to the organization of the state and the status of the Croats.

2432. Meštrović, Ivan.   Uspomene na političke ljude i događaje (Memoirs of politicians and events). Buenos Aires, 1961. 417 p. (Knjižnica Hrvatske revije, knj. 5)

Memoirs of the late internationally recognized Croatian sculptor, describing his personal reminiscences and experience in interwar Yugoslavia and in the Croatian wartime puppet state.

2433. Pribićević, Svetozar.   La dictature du roi Alexandre; contribution à l'étude de la démocratie. Paris, P. Bossuet, 1933. 324 p.

A prominent Serbian politician discusses the political conditions under the regime of King Alexander. A Serbian translation appeared as *Diktatura Kralja Aleksandra* (Beograd, Prosveta, 1953, 304 p.).

2434. Ribar, Ivan.    Politički zapisi (Political notes). Beograd, Prosvjeta, 1948-1952. 4 v.

Writings of a well-known Croatian political figure who joined Tito's Partisans during the Second World War. The book is chiefly concerned with Yugoslavia in the interwar period.

2435. Stojadinović, Milan.    Ni rat ni pakt; Jugoslavija između dva rata (Neither war nor the pact; Yugoslavia between the two wars). Buenos Aires, 1963. 760 p.

Memoirs by the former prime minister, elaborating on the policies of his government vis-à-vis the Axis powers and its conflict with the Regent, Prince Paul. *See also*:

Ristić, Dragiša N.    Yugoslavia's Revolution of 1941. University Park, Pennsylvania State University Press, 1966. 175 p. Bibliography: p. 161-163. A documented study by an associate of General Simović.

2436. Tomasevich, Jozo.    Peasants, Politics, and Economic Change in Yugoslavia. Stanford, Stanford University Press, 1955. 743 p. Maps, tables. Bibliography: p. 703-726.

*See also* entries no. 2389, 2543, *and* 2638.

A most valuable work on Yugoslav political and economic problems during the interwar period. Still the standard reference work.

2437. Yugoslavia. *Constitution*.    Ustav Kraljevine Jugoslavije od 3. septembra 1931 (Constitution of the Kingdom of Yugoslavia of September 3, 1931). Beograd, Geca Kon, 1937. 63 p.

For the earlier constitutional texts of Yugoslavia *see*:

Yugoslavia. *Constitution*.    Ustav Kraljevine Srba, Hrvata i Slovenaca (Constitution of the Kingdom of the Srebs, Croats, and Slovenes). Beograd, Državna štamparija Kraljevine Srba, Hrvata i Slovenaca, 1921. 48 p. A text of the much criticized and widely discussed Vidovdan Constitution of 1921.

Yugoslavia. *Constitution*.    Nacrt ustava po predlogu Stojana Protića . . . Definitivni tekst, posle diskusije sa Komisijom (Draft of a constitution in accordance with the proposal of Stojan Protić . . . Definitive text, after discussion in the Commission). Beograd, Geca Kon, 1920. 127 p. (Građa za ustav i osnovne zakone, 1). One of the principal critics of the government's proposed constitution was the Serbian leader Stojan Protić. His proposal would have provided a certain degree of local autonomy.

2438. Yugoslavia. *Narodna Skupština*.    Stenografske beleške (Stenographic notes). Beograd, 1922-1939. 70 v.

The record of parliamentary proceedings, speeches, and legislation.

2439. Serials.

A serious student of interwar Yugoslavia will find official and unofficial periodicals and journals of great value. For the interwar period, the official journal, *Službene Novine* (Official gazette) (Beograd, 1918–) published laws, decrees, and regulations and is an indispensable source of information on the state and institutional systems. A number of daily newspapers are likewise valuable: *Politika* (Politics) (Beograd, 1904–) was an independent newspaper with a liberal political tendency; *Pravda* (Truth) (Beograd, 1904–) supported the government after 1929; *Novosti* (News) (Zagreb, 1907-1941) endorsed the Yugoslav government's policies, while *Hrvatski dnevnik* (Croatian daily) (Zagreb, 1936-1941) expressed the views of the Croatian Peasant Party. *Vreme* (The Times) (Beograd, 1921–), the second largest Yugoslav paper, supported the government. *Obzor* (Survey) (Zagreb, 1906-1941), reflected the views of a certain group of liberal Croatian intelligentsia. *Jutarnji list* (Morning journal) (Zagreb, 1911–), a popular journal, was associated with the Croatian Peasant Party. *Slovenec* (The Slovenian) (Ljubljana, 1873-1945) was the leading Slovene paper, essentially conservative in its treatment of political affairs, and was under the strong influence of Slovene clerics. *Jutro* (Morning) (Ljubljana, 1919-1945) was the organ of the liberals.

An informative periodical on the political and economic affairs of interwar Yugoslavia was *Arhiv za pravne i društvene nauke* (Archive of legal and social sciences) (Beograd, 1906–). Since 1948 it has appeared as the organ of the Union of Lawyers of Yugoslavia. *Narodno blagostanje* (Public welfare) (Beograd, 1929–) published articles on Yugoslav economic and political developments. *Nova Evropa* (New Europe) (Zagreb, 1920-1941, monthly) was also an important and useful publication.

## 2. The Second World War*

2440. Antifašističko veće narodnog oslobođenja Jugoslavije. *Zasjedanje.* Prvo i drugo zasjedanje AVNOJ-a (The first and second sessions of the Anti-fascist Council for National Liberation of Yugoslavia). Zagreb, 1963. 372 p.

The proceedings of the revolutionary parliaments held by the communists during the Second World War, and their analyses.

2441. Belgrade. Vojnoistorijski institut.    Bibliografija izdanja o Narodno oslobodilačkom ratu, 1941-1945 (Bibliography of publications on the national liberation war, 1941-1945). Compiled by Vinko Branica and others. Beograd, 1964. 815 p. Facsims., map, ports.

*See also* entry no. 2085.

To be used in conjunction with the following reference aid:

Hronologija oslobodilačke borbe naroda Jugoslavije, 1941-1945 (Chronology of the national liberation struggle of the peoples of Yugoslavia, 1941-1945). Prepared by Milan Andrić and others. Beograd, Vojnoistorijski institut, 1964. 1265 p. Illus., map, ports.

* Consult also memoirs listed in Section 3.

2442. Belgrade. Vojnoistorijski institut.    Oslobodilački rat naroda Jugoslavije, 1941-1945 (The war for liberation of the peoples of Yugoslavia, 1941-1945). 2d rev. and enl. ed. Edited by Velimir Terzić and others. Beograd, 1963-1965. 2 v.

Official standard work on the history of the war. A first edition in two volumes appeared in 1957-1958. Documentary materials on the war may be found in:

Zbornik dokumenata i podataka o narodno-oslobodilačkom ratu jugoslovenskih naroda (Collection of documents and materials on the National Liberation War on the Yugoslav peoples). Beograd, 1949-1965. 9 v. Illus., maps, facsims.

Ustanak naroda Jugoslavije, 1941. Zbornik (The uprising of the peoples of Yugoslavia in 1941. A collection). Chief editor: Milinko Đurović. Beograd, Vojno delo, 1964-1966. 6 v. Illus.

Material on the situation in separate regions of Yugoslavia in this period may be found in the following:

Antifašističko sobranie na narodnoto osloboduvanje na Makedonija. Zbornik na dokumenti ot Antifašističkoto sobranie na narodnoto osloboduvanje na Makedonija (ASNOM) (Collection of documents of the Anti-Fascist Council for the National Liberation of Macedonia [ASNOM]). Skopje, Institut za nacionalna istorija, 1964. 722 p. Covers the period from August 2, 1943 to December 30, 1944.

Gizdić, Drago.    Dalmacija, 1942 (Dalmatia, 1942). Zagreb, Glavni odbor Saveza boraca Hrvatske, 1959. 827 p. (*His* Dalmacija; prilozi historiji narodnooslobodilačke borbe, knj. 2) A valuable source on the activities, military and political, of the communist forces in Dalmatia during the year 1942.

Humo, Avdo, *ed.*    Hercegovina u NOB (Hercegovina in the National Liberation War). Beograd, Vojnoizdavački zavod JNA "Vojno delo," 1691. 973 p. A collection of articles by participants in the partisan struggle in Hercegovina. While not a scholarly work, it provides useful information on political and military organization and strategy.

Jovanović, Batrić.    Crna Gora u narodnooslobodilačkom ratu i socijalističkoj revoluciji (Montenegro in the National Liberation War and the socialist revolution). Beograd, Vojno delo, 1960– Illus., ports., fold. maps. (Iz ratne prošlosti naših naroda, knj. 26-. Redovna izdanja, knj. 21–). A monumental study, intended to be complete in two volumes, of communist resistance in Montenegro. The first volume was criticized for its "mistaken" interpretations.

Mikuž, Metod.    Pregled zgodovine narodnoosvobodilne borbe Slovenije (A survey of the history of the liberation struggle in Slovenije). Ljubljana, Cankarjeva založba, 1960-1961. 2 v. A documented study of the subject up to the capitulation of Italy.

Zemaljsko antifašističko vijeće narodnog oslobođenja Hrvatske. Zbornik dokumenata, 1943 (Collection of documents, 1943). Chief editor: Hodimir Sirotković. Zagreb, Institut za historiju radničkog pokreta, 1964. 723 p.

Extensive materials on major battles in the Yugoslav struggle are provided by:

Perović, Milislav, ed.    Sutjeska; zbornik radova (Sutjeska; a collection of essays). Beograd, Vojnoizdavački zavod JNA, Vojno delo, 1960-1961. 5 v. Materials on the Battle of Sutjeska, considered to be one of the most decisive contests between Tito's National Liberation Movement and his various opponents.

Savković, Svetislav, ed.    Neretva; zbornik radova (Neretva; a collection of articles). Beograd, Vojnoizdavački zavod JNA, 1965. 3 v. Studies of a major battle in which Tito's followers annihilated Mihailović's Chetniks.

2443. Čolaković, Rodoljub.    Zapisi iz oslobodilačkog rata (Notes from the War of Liberation). Zagreb, Naprijed, 1946-1949. 3 v. Illus., port., map.

Notes on the communist military and political struggle during the Second World War. The author is one of the leading communist organizers and writers. Index to all three volumes in volume 3.

2444. Croatia (*Kingdom and Republic, 1941-1945*). *Laws, statutes, etc.* Zbornik zakona i naredaba Nezavisne Države Hrvatske (Collection of laws and decrees of the Independent State of Croatia). Zagreb, 1941-1945. 5 v. in 4.

An important collection for the study of the Ustaša regime.

2445. Croatia (*Kingdom and Republic, 1941-1945*). *Sabor.* Brzopisni zapisnici Prvog zasjedanja Hrvatskog državnog sabora u Nezavisnoj Državi Hrvatskoj godine 1942 (Stenographic notes on the first session of the Croatian State Assembly in the Independent State of Croatia in 1942). Zagreb, 1942.

An official statement of Ustaša organization and objectives and a report on those who, with Axis aid, established the Croatian state.

2446. Čulinović, Ferdo.    Dvadeset sedmi mart (The twenty-seventh of March). Zagreb, Jugoslavenska akademija znanosti i umjetnosti, 1965. 372 p. Illus., bibliographical notes. (Izdanja Historijskog instituta Jugoslavenske akademije znanosti i umjetnosti u Zagrebu, knj. 2)

The most extensive study of the Yugoslav coup d'état of March 1941, providing an interpretation which is much like that of the communist historians.

2447. Dedijer, Vladimir.    Dnevnik (Diary). 2d ed. Beograd, Jugoslovenska knjiga, 1951. 871 p. Illus., plates, ports., maps, facsims.

A comprehensive diary reporting the activities of Tito's followers during the Second World War as seen by a leading figure in the partisan movement. A considerably condensed English translation by Alec Brown is available in *With Tito through the War; Partisan Diary 1941-1944* (London, A. Hamilton, 1951, 403 p.).

2448. Đilas, Milovan.    Članci, 1941-1946 (Articles, 1941-1946). Beograd, Kultura, 1947. 368 p. Illus.

Articles on a variety of themes concerning the Yugoslav communist movement during and immediately after the Second World War.

2449. Đonlagić, Ahmet, *and others.*    Yugoslavia in the Second World War. Belgrade, Međunarodna štampa, 1967. 244 p. Maps.

A substantially shortened translation of the original *Jugoslavija u drugom svetskom ratu*, representing a concise political and military history in the perspective of Yugoslav historians.

2450. Fotitch, Constantin.    The War We Lost; Yugoslavia's Tragedy and the Failure of the West. New York, Viking Press, 1948. 344 p.

*See also* entry no. 2567.

A pro-Mihailović account of the Yugoslav civil war, 1941-1944, by the Yugoslav ambassador to Washington.

2451. Hory, Ladislaus, *and* Martin Broszat.    Der kroatische Ustascha-Staat, 1941-45. Stuttgart, Deutsche Verlags-Anstalt, 1964. 183 p. Map, bibliographical footnotes. (Schriftenreihe der Vierteljahrshefte für Zeitgeschichte, Nr. 8)

A worthwhile study of the Croatian Ustaša state during the Second World War.

2452. International Conference on the History of the Resistance Movements. *3rd, Karlovy Vary, 1963.*    Les systèmes d'occupation en Yougoslavie, 1941-1945. Edited by Petar Brajović, Jovan Marjanović, and Franjo Tudman. Belgrade, Institut pour le mouvement ouvrier, 1963. 564 p. Maps, bibliogr. references.

Conference reports in French, English, or Russian.

2453. Jovićević, Niko.    Od pete ofanzive do slobode (From the fifth offensive to liberation). Beograd, Vojno delo, 1955. 746 p.

A lengthy study of the National Liberation Movement and Tito's partisans in the final stages of the Second World War.

2454. Kocbek, Edvard.    Listina. Dnevniški zapiski od 3. maja do 2. decembra 1943 (A document; diary entries from May 3 to December 2, 1943). Ljubljana, Slovenska matica, 1967. 548 p. (Spomini in srečanja, 2)

Revealing memories by a Slovenian Christian Socialist who came to play a prominent role in the wartime Liberation Front. For other of his personal accounts *see*:

Tovarišija. Dnevniški zapiski od 17. maja 1942 do 1. maja 1943 (Camaraderie; diary entries from May 17, 1942 to May 1, 1943). Maribor, Založba "Obzorja," 1967. 421 p.

Slovensko poslanstvo. Dnevnik s poti v Jajce, 1943 (Slovenian mission. Diary from the travel to Jajce, 1943). Celje, Mohorjeva družba, 1964. 215 p. Illus., plates, ports.

2455. Kardelj, Edvard.    Put nove Jugoslavije; članci i govori iz narodnooslobodilačke borbe, 1941-1945 (The path of new Yugoslavia; articles and speeches from the national liberation struggle, 1941-1945). 2d ed. Beograd, Kultura, 1949. 580 p. Port.

Views of a number of problems of the Yugoslav resistance movement.

2456. Knežević, Radoje L.   Knjiga o Draži (A book about Draža). Windsor, Canada, Srpska narodna odbrana, 1956. 2 v.

Reminiscences, documents, and other materials about Draža Mihailović.

2457. Ljotić, Dimitrije V.   Iz moga života (From my life). München, 1952. 229 p.

The Serbian fascist leader's views of Yugoslav politics. A collection of essays and articles.

2458. Maclean, *Sir* Fitzroy.   Eastern Approaches. London, Cape, 1966. 543 p. Plates.

Eyewitness account by the chief of the British Mission to Tito's forces. For other personal narratives *see*:

British:
Clissold, Stephen.   Whirlwind. London, Cresset; New York, Philosophical Library, 1949. 245 p. Maps.

Lawrence, Christie N.   Irregular Adventure. London, Faber & Faber, 1947. 276 p. Maps.

American:
St. John, Robert.   From the Land of Silent People. Garden City, N.Y., Doubleday, 1942. 353 p.

German:
Neubacher, Hermann.   Sonderauftrag Südost 1940-1945. 2d ed. Göttingen Musterschmidt-Verlag, 1957. 215 p. Illus.

Russian:
Biriuzov, Sergei S.   Sovetskii soldat na Balkanakh (A Soviet soldier in the Balkans). Moska, Voen. izd-vo, 1963. 334 p. Illus., plans, ports.

2459. Marjanović, Jovan, *and* Pero Morača.   Narodnooslobodilački rat — narodna revolucija u Jugoslaviji, 1941-1945; kratki pregled (The national liberation war — the people's revolution in Yugoslavia, 1941-1945; a short survey). 7th ed. Beograd, Kultura, 1961. 141 p. Illus.

A short history by two prominent military historians. *See also*:
Čubelić, Tomo.   Pregled historije narodnooslobodilačkog rata i revolucije Jugoslavije (Historical survey of the national liberation war and the revolution in Yugoslavia). 11th enl. ed. Zagreb, Matica hrvatska, 1968. 200 p.

2460. Martin, David.   Ally Betrayed; the Uncensored Story of Tito and

Mihailovich. New York, Prentice-Hall, 1946. 372 p. Illus., map, plates, ports. Bibliography: p. 359-360.

A presentation of Mihailović's side of the Yugoslav civil war. A popular rather than scholarly work.

2461. Mihailović, Draža, *defendant*. The Trial of Dragoljub-Draža Mihailović, Stenographic Record and Documents. Belgrade, Union of the Journalists' Associations of the Federative People's Republic of Yugoslavia, 1946. 552 p. Illus., ports., facsims.

A report of the trial, including documents on the basis of which Mihailović was convicted.

2462. Petranović, Branko. Političke i pravne prilike za vreme privremene vlade DFJ (Political and legal conditions during the period of the Provisional Government of Democratic Federal Yugoslavia). Beograd, 1964. 232 p. Bibliography: p. 223-227. (Institut društvenih nauka. Odeljenje za istorijske nauke. Serija I: Monografije, 4)

An account of the organization of the Tito government and of the securing of international recognition.

2463. Plenča, Dušan. Međunarodni odnosi Jugoslavije u toku drugog svjetskog rata (International relations of Yugoslavia during the Second World War). Beograd, Institut društvenih nauka, 1962. 425 p. Bibliographic footnotes.

*See also* entry no. 2569.

A well documented study of the relations between the government of Marshal Tito and the royal government-in-exile and of the means whereby the former won international recognition.

2464. Simović, Vojislav. AVNOJ, pravno politička studija (Anti-fascist Council for the Liberation of Yugoslavia; a legal and political study). Beograd, Kultura, 1958. 191 p.

A study of the organization, function, and legal status of the Council, which acted as a revolutionary parliament during the Second World War.

2465. Tuđman, Franjo. Okupacija i revolucija; dvije rasprave (Occupation and revolution; two studies). Zagreb, 1963. 316 p. Bibliography: p. 249-265.

A discussion of the collapse of Yugoslavia in April 1941, the enemy occupation, and the beginnings and development of the communist revolution. May be supplemented by the author's *Stvaranje socijalističke Jugoslavije; historijska studija i pregled razvoja socijalističke revolucije i oslobodilačkog rata jugoslavenskih naroda* (The formation of socialist Yugoslavia; a historical study and survey of the development of the socialist revolution and the war for liberation of the Yugoslav peoples) (Zagreb, Naprijed, 1960, 337 p.).

2466. Serials.

During the war, the Yugoslav government-in-exile continued to publish its official gazette *Službene novine* (Official gazette), while in the occupied areas of the country various newspapers appeared under the control of the occupying powers or their satellite governments. Of these, the most important were *Novo vreme* (New times) (Beograd, 1941-1944); *Hrvatski narod* (The Croatian people) (Zagreb, 1939-1944); *Nezavisna Hrvatska* (Independent Croatia) (Zagreb, 1941-1944); *Glas Crnogoraca* (Voice of the Montenegrins) (Cetinje, 1941-1943). Official publications of the German authorities in Belgrade included the monthly *Amtsblatt der Serbischen Ministerien* (Belgrade, Staatsdruckerei, 1941-1943) and *List uredaba Vojnog Zapovednika u Srbiji. Verordnungsblatt des Militärbefehlshabers in Serbien* (Beograd, Državna štamparija, 1941-1944).

The Communist Party's principal organ was *Borba* (The struggle) (Beograd, 1922-), which was founded in Zagreb in 1922, appeared subsequently in various forms and other names during the period of the Communist Party's prohibition, and was issued more or less regularly by Tito's followers from 1941 to 1944. Since 1944 it has been issued in Belgrade as a daily. Newspapers appearing in the chief cities of the republics of the Yugoslav federation also were issued during the war under clandestine circumstances and are important sources of information. They include *Vijesnik* (The messenger) (Zagreb, 1940); *Slovenski poročevalec* (Slovenian reporter) (Ljubljana, 1941-); *Nova Makedonija* (New Macedonia) (Skopje, 1944-); *Slobodna Dalmacija* (Free Dalmatia) (Split, 1943-); and *Oslobođenje* (Liberation) (Sarajevo, 1943-).

## 3. Since the Second World War

### a. Constitution and Government*

2467. Kardelj, Edvard.  O ustavnom sistemu Socijalističke Federativne Republike Jugoslavije (About the constitutional system of the Socialist Federal Republic of Yugoslavia). Beograd, Komunist, 1963. 113 p.

A Marxist analysis of the Yugoslav constitutional system, explaining innovations in the constitutional structure of the state.

2468. Yugoslavia. *Constitution.*  Ustav Socijalističke Federativne Republike Jugoslavije sa ustavima socijalističkih republika i statutima autonomnih pokrajina (Constitution of the Socialist Federal Republic of Yugoslavia with the constitutions of the socialist republics and statutes of autonomous provinces). Beograd, Novinska ustanova Službeni List SFRJ, 1963. 662 p. (Zbirka saveznih propisa, br. 2)

The third postwar constitution of Yugoslavia, and constitutions of its individual republics and provinces, marking a number of departures from the communist systems of the East European countries. Available in English as *Constitution of the Socialist Federal Republic of Yugoslavia*, edited by Borislav Blagojević (Belgrade, Sekretarijat saveznog izvršnog veća za informacije, 1963, 191 p.;

* *See also* Section A of this chapter.

Collection of Yugoslav Laws, v. 7). The report on the new constitution given to the Federal Assembly by Edvard Kardelj, with excerpts from treatises on the subject by Edvard Kardelj, Milentije Popović, Veljko Vlahović, and Petar Stambolić are brought together in *The Constitutional System of the Socialist Federative Republic of Yugoslavia* (Belgrade, Review of International Affairs, 1963, 63 p.). The two preceding constitutions of the Yugoslav republic are available in English as:

Yugoslavia. *Constitution.* Constitution of the Federative People's Republic of Yugoslavia, 1946. Belgrade, Official Gazette of the Federative People's Republic of Yugoslavia, 1946. 48 p. The first postwar constitution which follows the Soviet model in many of its provisions.

Yugoslavia. *Constitution.* Fundamental Law Pertaining to the Bases of the Social and Political Organization of the Federal People's Republic of Yugoslavia and of the Federal Organs of State Authority. Beograd, Union of Jurists' Associations of Yugoslavia, 1953. 99 p. The fundamental law of 1953 marks a departure from the Soviet constitutional model, providing for a certain decentralization of economic management and devolution of power. The introduction is written by Edvard Kardelj, one of Yugoslavia's leading theoreticians.

2469. Yugoslavia; Constitutional Judicature. Translated by Borivoje P. Ljotić. Edited by Borislav Blagojević. Belgrade, Institute of Comparative Law, 1965. 70 p.

### b. Source Materials

2470. The Soviet-Yugoslav Dispute; Text of the Published Correspondence. London, New York, Royal Institute of International Affairs, 1948. 79 p.

*See also* entry no. 2583.

Letters exchanged between the Yugoslav and Soviet communist leaders on the dispute which led to Yugoslavia's expulsion from the Cominform and the break in relations between Yugoslavia and the Soviet Union. Also available as:

Savez komunista Jugoslavije. *Centralni komitet.* Pisma CK Komunističke partije Jugoslavije i pisma CK SKP (b) (Letters of the Central Committee of the Communist Party of Yugoslavia and letters of the Central Committee of the VKP [b]). Beograd, 1948. 54 p.

2471. Yugoslavia. *Savezna Narodna Skupština.* Stenografske beleške. Redovno zasedanje (Stenographic notes; regular session). Beograd, 1946–

————. Stenografske beleške. Vanredno zasedanje (Stenographic notes; special session). Beograd, 1946–

The minutes of the Federal Assembly. Similar records are published for the legislative assemblies of the republics.

2472. Yugoslavia. *Treaties, etc. (1945–).* Međunarodni ugovori FNRJ

(International agreements of the Federal People's Republic of Yugoslavia). Beograd, Ministarstvo inostranih poslova, 1945–
    A collection of treaties and agreements concluded between Yugoslavia and foreign countries.

2473. Yugoslavia. *Laws, statutes, etc.* Zbirka zakona FNRJ (Collection of laws of the Federal People's Republic of Yugoslavia). Beograd, Izdanje Službenog lista FNRJ, 1944–

### c. Writings and Accounts by Political Leaders

2474. Dedijer, Vladimir. Tito. New York, Simon and Schuster, 1953. 443 p.
    *See also* entry no. 2575
    The best and most authoritative biography of the Yugoslav leader by Tito's erstwhile friend and comrade in arms. The author has also written on other topics relating to Yugoslav politics, including a study of Yugoslav-Albanian relations, *Jugoslavensko-albanski odnosi, 1939-1948* (Yugoslav-Albanian relations) (Zagreb, Borba, 1949, 225 p.), and an account of the Paris Conference of 1947, *Pariska konferencija* (Paris conference) (Beograd, Trideset dana, 1947, 470 p.).

2475. Đilas, Milovan. Anatomy of a Moral; the Political Essays of Milovan Djilas. Edited by Abraham Rothberg, with an introduction by Paul Willen. New York, Praeger, 1959. 181 p. (Praeger Publications in Russian History and World Communism, no. 84)
    A criticism of the Yugoslav social order by one who helped establish it. Đilas' writings also include his widely publicized *The New Class; an Analysis of the Communist System* (New York, Praeger, 1957, 214 p.), the autobiographical *Land without Justice* (New York, Harcourt, Brace, 1958, 358 p.), and *Članci, 1941-1946* (Articles, 1941-1946) (Beograd, Kultura, 1947, 368 p.).

2476. Kardelj, Edvard. Beleške o našoj društvenoj kritici (Notes on our social criticism). Beograd, Kultura, 1966. 197 p.
    The leading Yugoslav communist theorist complains of the survival of Stalinist type dogmatism state-capitalist concepts of social relations and nationalistic egotism and comments on what he believes to be constructive and destructive criticism. This may be compared with the author's *O osnovama društvenog i političkog uređenja FNRJ* (On the foundations of the social and political order of the People's Republic of Yugoslavia) (Beograd, Kultura, 1953, 172 p.), and with his *Problemi naše socialističke izgradnje* (Problems of our socialist development) (Beograd, Kultura, 1960-1965, 5 v.), a collection of speeches and writings.

2477. Kidrič, Boris. Zbrano delo; članki in razprave (Collected works; articles and essays). Ljubljana, Cankarjeva založba, 1958-1962. 3 v.
    A leading communist organizer deals with a variety of aspects of

Yugoslav political and economic life before, during and after the Second World War, with special attention to Slovenia.

2478. Pijade, Moša S.    Izbrani spisi (Selected writings). Beograd, Institut za izučavanje radničkog pokreta, 1964– Illus., facsims., ports., bibliography.

Writings by one of the leading Yugoslav communist theorists on a variety of political questions. Thus far five books, forming volume 1, have been published.

2479. Ranković, Aleksandar.    Izbrani govori i članci, 1941-1951 (Selected speeches and articles, 1941-1951). Zagreb, Kultura, 1951. 430 p.

Materials of one of Tito's wartime lieutenants.

2480. Tito, Josip Broz.    Govori i članci (Speeches and articles). Zagreb, Naprijed, 1959–

The 16 volumes already published cover writings and speeches from 1941 to 1961. Volume 12 contains a subject index to the preceding 11 volumes. *See also* his *Selected Speeches and Articles, 1941-1961* (Zagreb, Naprijed, 1963, 459 p.). Tito's views on military affairs are contained in his *Vojna djela* (Military affairs) (Beograd, Vojnoizdavački zavod JNA "Vojno delo," 1961, 3 v.).

2481. Ziherl, Boris.    Članci i rasprave; od početka 1945 godine naovamo (Articles and studies; from the beginning of 1945 to the present). Beograd, Kultura, 1948. 464 p.

Because of the author's position, his articles and comments are valuable for students of Yugoslav political developments before the break with Stalin.

#### d. Surveys, Studies of Special Aspects, and Serials

2482. Avakumović, Ivan.    History of the Communist Party of Yugoslavia. v. 1– Aberdeen, Aberdeen University Press, 1964– Bibliographies. *See also* entry no. 2557.

The only work of its kind in English. This first volume (207 p.) covers the history of the Communist Party of Yugoslavia from 1918 to 1941.

2483. Bošković, Mirko.    Društveno-politički sistem Jugoslavije (The sociopolitical system of Yugoslavia). Zagreb, Naprijed, 1963. 364 p.

A detailed and authoritative analysis of the Yugoslav social and political system.

2484. Belgrade. Institut za izučavanje radničkog pokreta.    Pregled istorije Saveza komunista Jugoslavije (Survey of the history of the Union of Communists of Yugoslavia). Edited by Rodoljub Čolaković and others. Beograd, 1963. 570 p.

The most authoritative short history of the Yugoslav Communist Party from its inception to 1958. For a recent party history *see*:

Morača, Pero. Istorija Saveza komunista Jugoslavija (History of the League of Communists of Yugoslavia). Beograd, Rad, 1966. 246 p.

2485. Byrnes, Robert F., ed. Yugoslavia. New York, Praeger, 1957. 488 p. Maps, tables. Bibliography: p. 447-469. (East Central Europe Under the Communists. Praeger Publications in Russian History and World Communism, no. 23)
See also entries no. 2165 and 2599.
Handbook of factual and statistical information on nearly every aspect of Yugoslav life in the period 1945-1957. Sponsored by the Free Europe Committee.

2486. Čulinović, Ferdo. Državnopravni razvitak Jugoslavije (State and legal development of Yugoslavia). Zagreb, Školska knjiga, 1963. 375 p. Bibliography.
One section discusses the legal development of Yugoslavia by provinces. The second treats Yugoslavia as a whole in the years 1918-1963. A wider period is covered in the author's *Državnopravna historija jugoslavenskih zemalja XIX i XX vijeka* (State and legal history of the Yugoslav lands in the 19th and 20th centuries) (Zagreb, Školska knjiga, 1953-1954, 2 v.).

2487. Đorđević, Jovan. La Yougoslavie. Paris, Librairie générale de droit et de jurisprudence, 1967. 483 p. (Comment ils sont gouvernés, t. 15)
A survey by a prominent Yugoslav lawyer and political scientist.

2488. Fisher, Jack C. Yugoslavia, a Multinational State; Regional Difference and Administrative Response. San Francisco, Chandler Publishing Co., 1966. 244 p. Illus., map. Bibliography: p. 223-231.
See also entries no. 2207, 2525, and 2619.
An analysis of the Yugoslav administrative system and a discussion of the country's urban development.

2489. Geršković, Leon. Historija narodne vlasti (History of popular rule). Beograd, Savremena administracija, 1957. 299 p.
A textbook for law students. Discusses the emergence of the Yugoslav communist state during the Second World War and since.

2490. Hoffman, George W., and Fred W. Neal. Yugoslavia and the New Communism. New York, Twentieth Century Fund, 1962. 546 p. Maps, tables. Bibliography: p. 511-527.
See also entries no. 2190, 2577, and 2604.
The best survey of postwar political, social, and economic developments in Yugoslavia. For an up-to-date analysis of Yugoslavia's independent domestic developments *see*:
Petrovich, Michael B. Significance of the Yugoslav "Heresy." *In* Burks, R. V., ed. The Future of Communism in Europe. Detroit, Wayne State University Press, 1968. p. 69-102.

2491. Jončić, Koča.   Nacionalne manjine u Jugoslaviji (National minorities in Yugoslavia). Beograd, Savremena administracija, 1962. 179 p. Tables. (Priručna biblioteka za pravna i društvena pitanja, 26)
Statistics on the Yugoslav minorities and a discussion of their participation in Yugoslav political, economic, and cultural affairs. Contains texts of legislation concerning the minorities. An English-language translation of a more recent book by the same author was published as *The Relations between Nationalities in Yugoslavia* (Belgrade, Međunarodna štampa-Interpress, 1967, 76 p.).

2492. Jovanović, Aleksandar.   Društveno-političko uređenje FNRJ (Social and political organization of the Federal People's Republic of Yugoslavia). Beograd, Rad, 1958. 333 p. Bibliography.
For a special aspect of sociopolitical organization *see*:
Društveno-političke zajednice (Sociopolitical units).   Editor: Dragoljub Đurović.   Beograd, Međunarodna štampa-Interpress, 1968– Illus., ports. Two volumes published so far, the first of which contains a biography of leading officials.

2493. Mala politička enciklopedija (Small political encyclopedia). Editor in chief, Jovan Đorđević. Beograd, Savremena administracija, 1966. 1531 p.
Though general in scope, this work is a useful source of information on Yugoslav affairs.

2494. Milatović, Mile.   Slučaj Andrije Hebranga (The case of Andrija Hebrang). Beograd, Kultura, 1952. 265 p. Illus.
A statement of the charges which brought about the liquidation of the erstwhile minister for industry.

2495. Pejanović, Dušan.   The Yugoslav People's Army in the Reconstruction and Development of the Country (1945-1967). Belgrade, Vojnoizdavački zavod, 1967. 141 p. Illus., ports.
Translation of *Jugoslovenska narodna armija u izgradnji zemlje.*

2496. Ulam, Adam B.   Titoism and the Cominform. Cambridge, Mass., Harvard University Press, 1952. 243 p. Bibliography: p. 235-236. (Russian Research Center Studies, 5)
*See also* entry no. 2584.
An analysis of Yugoslav-Soviet relations and the events that led to the expulsion of Yugoslavia from the Cominform.

2497. Yugoslavia. *Laws, statutes, etc.*   The Local Government. Beograd, 1962. 124 p. (Institute of Comparative Law. Collection of Yugoslav Laws, v. 2)

2498. Zagreb. Univerzitet. *Institut za historiju države i prava.*   Nova Jugoslavija; pregled državnopravnog razvitka povodom desetgodišnjice drugog zasjedanja AVNOJ-a (New Yugoslavia; survey of state and legal development on the occasion of the tenth anniversary of the second session of the Antifascist Council for National Liberation). Edited by Konstantin Bastaić and others. Zagreb, 1954. 420 p.

Fourteen essays treating different aspects of state and legal development.

2499. Zalar, Charles. Yugoslav Communism; a Critical Study. Washington, D.C., U.S. Government Printing Office, 1961. 387 p. Bibliography: p. 307-358.

See also entry no. 2586.

2500. Živančević. Mihailo M.   Jugoslavija i federacija (Yugoslavia and federation). Beograd, 1938. 423 p.

One of the principal political problems in interwar Yugoslavia was the constitution and the organization of the state. There was a sharp conflict between exponents of a centralized and unitary state and those who advocated large-scale ethnic autonomy and federalism. This study touches on some of these problems.

2501. Serials.

Postwar Yugoslavia has witnessed a proliferation of journals and periodicals, with publications appearing devoted to nearly every aspect of state and society. The official gazette of the federal government is its Službeni list (Official gazette) (Beograd, Narodna skupština, 1945–), and similar organs are issued by each of the republics of the federation. Borba (The struggle), until 1953 the organ of the League of Communists and since then sponsored by the Socialist Alliance of Working People of Yugoslavia, is an indispensable source of information on government and politics, continuing its history which began in 1922 (see entry no. 2466). The major newspapers of the republics, which began publication in the clandestine conditions of wartime (see entry no. 2466) continue to appear as the principal local newspapers of the country. Of other contemporary Yugoslav journals, Politika (Politics) (Beograd, 1904–) is among the best. In the prewar period it was an independent journal, and since 1945 it has become a semi-official organ.

The Communist Party theoretical journals are likewise of great importance. The leading ones are Komunist (The Communist) (Beograd, 1943–), now a weekly, the organ of the Central Committee of the League of Communists of Yugoslavia, and the quarterly Socijalizam (Socialism) (Beograd, 1958–). Students of Yugoslav affairs will likewise find Naša stvarnost (Our reality) ( Beograd, 1936-1939, 1953–), a theoretical Marxist journal edited by Milentije Popović, to be of value. In the postwar period publication was resumed of the Arhiv za pravne i društvene nauke (Archive for legal and social sciences). Other journals of interest include Gledišta (Viewpoints) (Beograd, 1960–, monthly); Naši razgledi (Our views) (Ljubljana, 1952–, biweekly); and Praxis (Zagreb, 1964–, bimonthly).

Journals in English include Review of International Affairs (Beograd, 1949–, weekly) and Socialist Thought and Practice (Beograd, 1965–, quarterly).

## C. THE NATIONAL QUESTION*

*by Traian Stoianovich*

### 1. Language, Culture, and National Character

2502. Matl, Josef.  Südslawische Studien. München, Oldenbourg, 1965. 598 p. (Südost-Institut München. Südosteuropäische Arbeiten, 63)

Articles on history, religion, anthropology, and literature. Major contribution on "The Problem of Eurasian Cultural Fluctuation in Slavic, and Especially South Slavic, Territory" (p. 147-158). Rejects both "European" and "dualist" interpretations of Slavic evolution, neither accepting the view that Slavic history duplicates European patterns, with time gap and geographic difference, nor the view that the Slavic world in general and South Slavs in particular are sharply divisible into two separate entities: Roman-Germanic, Catholic, and Protestant in the West and Byzantine-Orthodox in the East. Posits thesis of continual interweaving, syncretism, and fusion of western and eastern cultural traits ever since the early Middle Ages and among all Slavs, with variations in the degree and manner of cultural interpenetration and with fluctuations in the relative importance of the processes of Westernization and Easternization.

2503. Bidwell, Charles E.   Language, Dialect, and Nationality in Yugoslavia. Human Relations Notes (London), v. 15, no. 3, Aug. 1962: 217-225.

*See also* entry no. 2264.

Describes dialect differences — *kaj-, ča-, što-*dialects, variations in the accent system, varieties of reflex of Common Slavic îe (ъ), and absence or presence of rising and falling intonation — and the formation of South Slavic nationalities. Patterns of word borrowing from other languages as a further criterion of linguistic nationality are also examined (e.g., *Vizantija* in Serbian and *Bizant* in Croatian for Byzantium), as are the migrations of the Ottoman era and confusion of dialects. See also *Die serbokroatischen Dialekte: ihre Struktur und Entwicklung* by Pavle Ivić ('s-Gravenhage, Mouton, 1958, 325 p.); *Geschichte der serbokroatischen Sprache* by Ivan Popović (Wiesbaden, Otto Harrassowitz, 1960, 687 p.).

2504. Dvorniković, Vladimir.   Karakterologija Jugoslovena (Characterology of the Yugoslavs). Beograd, Geca Kon, 1939. 1060 p. Illus. (Čovečanstvo: Zbornik za kulturnu i političku istoriju, knj. 2)

*See also* entry no. 2267.

Geography itself has been unfavorable to the political synthesis of the Yugoslavs. Their history has been one of uninterrupted struggle to change from people dominated by space (*Raumvolk* or *narod prostora*) into historical people with a sense of time (*Zeitvolk* or *narod vremena*). Slavic aversion to discipline takes the form of religious heresy (Bogomilism), peasant rebellions, and resistance against bureaucracy and political centralization. The author probes

* The arrangement is by topical affinity.

into all aspects, all *patterns*, of Yugoslav culture: artifacts, art, music, rural and urban society, psychology, ideology, geography, race, and history. Influenced by Jovan Cvijić, he goes much beyond Cvijić to Wundt, to Freud, and to *Gestalt* psychology.

2505. Gesemann, Gerhard. Heroische Lebensform: Zur Literatur und Wesenskunde der balkanischen Patriarchalität. Berlin, Wiking Verlag, 1943. 371 p.

Gesemann's inaugural address — *Der montenegrinische Mensch* — in 1933-1934 as rector of Charles University (Prague), with chapters on Scot, Mainot, and Corsican highlanders. As it extends southwestward from Šumadija to Kopaonik, Stari Vlah, and Hercegovina, and southward from Bosnia Krajina to Lika, Senj, Kotari, Dalmatian Zagora, and Boka, the mountain cult of heroism reaches its peaks in Montenegro and northern Albania. For typology of South Slavic culture and psychology, with emphasis on the idea that Serbia (Šumadija and Morava region), by its cultural plurality and central geography, is predestined to unite the Dinaric with the Carpatho-Balkan, Rhodope, and Pannonian regions, *see* Jovan Cvijić: *La Péninsule balkanique* (Paris, A. Colin, 1918, 528 p.); "The Zones of Civilization of the Balkan Peninsula," *Geographical Review*, v. 5, 1918: 470-482; and his *Govori i članci* (Speeches and articles) (Beograd, "Napredak," 1921, 2 v.).

2506. Eterovich, Francis H., *and* Christopher Spalatin, *eds.* Croatia: Land, People, Culture. v. 1. Toronto, University of Toronto Press, 1964. 408 p. Illus., maps, ports., bibliographies.
*See also* entry no. 2206.

Croatian nationality in terms of geography, history, economy, ethics, folk arts, literature, music, and art. For the thesis of the "impossible existence of any Yugoslavia," see: *The Croatian Nation in Its Struggle for Freedom and Independence: A Symposium by Seventeen Croatian Writers*, edited by Antun F. Bonifačić and Clement S. Mihanovich (Chicago, "Croatia" Cultural Publishing Center, 1955, 441 p.). One contributor, Stephen K. Sakač, emphasizes the "Iranian" origin of the Croats, while Vatro Murvar contends that the Vlach element in Serbian and other Balkan nationalities made for their violence, authoritarianism, and migratory habits, a thesis present also in L. von Südland's (pseudonym of Ivo Pilar), *Die südslawische Frage und der Weltkrieg* (Wien, Manz, 1918, 796 p.). A second edition of the last appeared in Croatia in 1944.

2507. Tomašić, Dinko A. The New Class and Nationalism. Journal of Croatian Studies (New York), v. 1, 1960: 53-74.

Top Yugoslav political and military leaders in communist as in precommunist Yugoslavia are largely of Orthodox background and "Dinaric" culture, to which the author attributes qualities of violence, ruthlessness, power-seeking, and political orientation toward Belgrade. The "new class" of communist Yugoslavia uses "national communism" as a means of protection against the "new class" of the

Soviet Union. More on Tomasic's dubious conception of a Serbian culture of predatory herdsmen and brigands and a Croatian culture of peaceful and democratic agriculturalists in his *Personality and Culture in Eastern European Politics* (New York, George W. Stewart, 1948, 249 p., map). For the view that Russia is "the originator of national Communism," *see* "The Origins of National Communism," *Virginia Quarterly Review* (Charlottesville), v. 34, no. 2, Spring 1958: 277-291; and "Nationalism and National Minorities in Eastern Europe," *Journal of International Affairs* (New York), v. 20, no. 1, 1966: 9-31, both by Thomas T. Hammond.

## 2. Class and Nationality

2508. Bogdanov, Vaso.  Historijska uloga društvenih klasa u rješavanju južnoslovenskog nacionalnog pitanja (Historical role of social classes in the solution of the South Slavic national question). Sarajevo, Izdavačko preduzeće "Veselin Masleša," 1956. 172 p.

The struggle for national liberation as the battle of a "nation" of peasants and urban "bourgeois" youth aligned against foreign "feudal" states and lords (Turks, Germans, Magyars) and against the "estates" conception of society (1789-1848) receives new form between 1849 and 1918. Bourgeois political clubs and parties, now partially admitted into the administrative apparatus of the post-1848 states, henceforth embrace in part the view that autonomy can be won by legal means on the basis of historical rights. As failure of the bourgeoisie to create viable national political entities grows, the leadership shifts to socialism. An earlier edition appeared in 1954.

2509. Zwitter, Fran.  Narodnost in politika pri Slovencih (Nationality and politics among the Slovenes). Zgodovinski časopis (Historical review) (Ljubljana), v. 1, 1947: 30-69 (with résumés in Russian and French).

A significant Slovenian literature began to develop during the second half of the 18th century, mainly under the direction of a clergy hostile to "pagan nationalism" (nationalism with political goals). The bourgeoisie, on the other hand, was German or Germanized. After the appearance of a Slovenian bourgeoisie around 1848, the peasants continued to support the clergy because the liberals lacked a people's program. Austro-Hungarian Social Democracy then diverted many Slovenes from their goal of national liberation by its emphasis on cultural autonomy. For an extensive treatment of the Slovene national movement since the French Revolution, see *Zgodovina slovenskega naroda: najnovejša doba* (History of the Slovene people: most recent era), by Josip Mal (Celj, Družba sv. Mohorja, 1929-1939, 1213 p.). For English treatments of the Slovenes, *see*:

Arnez, John A.   Slovenia in European Affairs. New York, League of CSA, 1958. 204 p. (Studia Slovenica, 1)

Barker, Thomas Mack.    The Slovenes of Carinthia. New York, League of CSA, 1960. 302 p. (Studia Slovenica, 3)

## 3. The Yugoslav Idea

2510. Haumant, Émile.    La formation de la Yougoslavie (XVᵉ-XXᵉ siècles). Paris, Éditions Bossard, 1930. 752 p. Illus., maps. (Institut d'études slaves de l'Université de Paris. Collection historique, 5)
*See also* entry no. 2376.

Useful sections on the French and Serbian revolutions, formation of the Serbian state, Illyrian movement, revolution of 1848, demographic crisis among Hungarian Serbs, pan-Croatian ideology, the Yugoslav idea, "trialism," and formation of the Yugoslav state. For other friendly views toward Serb-Croat-Slovene unity and for the thesis of transformation of the South Slavs between the Reformation and close of the Enlightenment from a subject peasantry and "nation without history" into a people conscious of its destiny, see: *Der Kampf der Südslawen um Freiheit und Einheit* (Frankfurt am Main, Frankfurter Societäts-Druckerei, 1925, 798 p.), and *Aus dem südslawischen Risorgimento* (Gotha, Verlag Friedrich Andreas Perthes, 1921, 199 p.), both by Hermann Wendel. For parallel views see: *Jugoslovenska misao: istorija ideje jugoslovenskog narodnog ujedinjenja i oslobođenja od 1790-1918* (The Yugoslav idea: a history of the notion of Yugoslav national unification and liberation, 1790-1918) by Ferdo Šišić (Beograd, Izdanje Balkanskog instituta, 1937, 280 p.).

2511. Novak, Viktor, *comp.*    Antologija jugoslovenske misli i narodnog jedinstva 1390-1930 (Anthology of the Yugoslav idea and of national unity, 1390-1930). Beograd, 1930. 931 p.
*See also* entry no. 2380.

Novak posits the thesis of a dual basis of Yugoslav nationalism — biological-linguistic (at both conscious and unconscious, or preconscious, levels) originating in pre-Balkan times and political-ideological, with a history since the end of the 14th century but with a dynamism only since the close of the 18th century and especially since 1830. Both were seriously weakened, however, by a dual cultural orientation and domination during the last thousand years: on the one hand, Byzantine, Greek, Orthodox, Turkic, and Ottoman; on the other, Roman, Germanic, Catholic, Hungarian, and Habsburg. Novak offers very few documents on the period before 1830, but the role of elites in diffusion of the Yugoslav idea since that time stands out clearly.

## 4. Realpolitik: Theory and Practice

2512. Jovanović, Slobodan.    O državi; osnovi jedne pravne teorije (The state: foundations of a legal theory). 3d rev. and enl. ed. Beograd, Geca Kon, 1922. 448 p. Bibliographies.
*See also* entry no. 2404.

Serbian historian Jovanović regards the state as the chief instrument of national formation. So long as the primary basis of nationality was religion, states made use of "confessional absolutism" to further the cause of state power. Following the Enlightenment and the French Revolution, the primary basis of nationality shifted to language. Finally, in the 20th century, the notion spread that nationality requires not only common language and literature and a common state but one *culture*: common education, common way of life, common ways of speech, common world view. The aim of democrats is to raise the cultural level of the masses, and so they resort to cultural absolutism, concentrating on the development of watered-down "extensive culture" instead of fortifying the former "intensive culture" of the elites. *See* section on "The Nation," p. 109-126.

2513. Jelavich, Charles.   Serbian Nationalism and the Question of Union with Croatia in the 19th Century. Balkan Studies (Thessalonike), v. 3, 1962, no. 1: 29-42.

Croats split into advocates of Greater Croatianism and supporters of Yugoslavism, whereas the goal of the Serbian government, church, army, middle class, intelligentsia, and peasantry alike was the liberation of all Serbs. Creation of the Kingdom of Serbs, Croats, and Slovenes was thus much more the result of *Realpolitik* than of ideological goals. On the growth of secular and bourgeois nationalism, *see* "The Call to Action: Religion, Nationalism, Socialism" by Charles and Barbara Jelavich, *Journal of Central European Affairs* (Boulder), v. 23, no. 1, Apr. 1963: 3-11. In his *Tsarist Russia and Balkan Nationalism: Russian Influence in the Internal Affairs of Bulgaria and Serbia, 1879-1886* (Berkeley and Los Angeles, University of California Press, 1958, 304 p.), Charles Jelavich shows how Russia's policy of spheres of interest (Bulgaria in the Russian, Serbia in the Austro-Hungarian sphere) culminated in a conflict between Bulgarian nationalism and Russian foreign policy.

2514. Sugar, Peter F.   The Southern Slav Image of Russia in the Nineteenth Century. Journal of Central European Affairs (Boulder), v. 21, no. 1, Apr. 1961: 45-52.

Between 1848 and 1860, Slavism yielded to regional nationalisms. Less able thereafter to take advantage of Slavism, Russia placed greater reliance on Orthodoxy as the symbol and agent of collaboration. But many South Slavs were not Orthodox, and religion itself had been weakened by secular nationalism. Even Orthodoxy was therefore less effective than it once had been, and it tended to lose its effectiveness still further whenever a South Slavic people was politically successful. At the same time as the author shows in "The Nature of the Non-Germanic Societies Under Habsburg Rule," *Slavic Review* (Seattle), v. 22, no. 1, Mar. 1963: 1-30 and 44-46, the economic backwardness of Serbia and religious differences between Orthodox Serbia and largely non-Orthodox South Slavs of the Habsburg Monarchy reduced the appeal of Serbia as a national nucleus.

2515. Seton-Watson, Robert W.   The Southern Slav Question and the
Habsburg Monarchy. London, Constable, 1911. 463 p. Map. Bibliography: p. 445-452.
    *See also* entry no. 2384.
        The Southern Slav question, 1849-1910. Believing that "Croato-
    Serb unity outside the Habsburg Monarchy can only be attained
    through universal war and a thorough revision of the map of Eu-
    rope" (p. 338), Seton-Watson advocates "trialism," or the union of
    South Slavs within the framework of the Habsburg Monarchy, as
    "Austria's mission." In a chapter on "Magyar Railway Policy," he
    shows Hungary pursuing a policy of railroad building inimical to
    Croatia. On the nationality problem in the Habsburg Monarchy
    *see also* Robert A. Kann, Arthur J. May, Oscar Jászi, Hugo Hantsch,
    a work by Fran Zwitter in collaboration with Jaroslav Šidak and
    Vaso Bogdanov, the *Austrian History Yearbook* (Houston, 1967-
    1968), and an anthology on nationalism in East Central Europe
    edited by Ivo J. Lederer and Peter F. Sugar (in preparation).

2516. Lederer, Ivo J.   Yugoslavia at the Paris Peace Conference: a Study
in Frontiermaking. New Haven, Yale University Press, 1963. 351 p.
Ports., maps. Bibliography: p. 317-329.
    *See also* entries no. 2391, 2429, *and* 2551.
        Discusses diplomacy, politics, and national ambitions of individual
    politicians and of the Yugoslav government in general in the making
    of Yugoslavia's frontiers. For a biographical sketch of Serbian prime
    minister Nikola Pašić see: *Pachitch et l'union des Yougoslaves* by
    Carlo Sforza (Paris, Gallimard, 1938, 253 p.). Sforza depicts Pašić
    not as a narrow Serb but as a statesman who sought to preserve and
    extend the Serbian union so long as institutionalization of the Yugo-
    slav Idea appeared impracticable. On Ante Trumbić, a Dalmatian
    lawyer important in the Serb-Croat Coalition and the London Yugo-
    slav Committee, in the negotiation of the Corfu Pact, as foreign
    minister and delegate to the Paris Peace Conference, and as an
    opponent of "Serbian hegemony," see: *Dr. Ante Trumbić: problemi
    hrvatsko-srpskih odnosa* (Dr. Ante Trumbić: problems of Croato-
    Serbian relations) by Ante Smith Pavelić (München, Knjižnica
    Hrvatske revije, 1959, 333 p.).

### 5. Markets and the Urge to the Sea: Colonial versus
### Metropolitan Economics

2517. Vucinich, Wayne S.   Serbia Between East and West; the Events
of 1903-1908. Stanford, Stanford University Press, 1954. 304 p.
Bibliography: p. 269-283. (Stanford University Publications, University Series. History, Economics, and Political Science, v. 9)
    *See also* entry no. 2338.
        Discusses regicide and the return to power of the Karađorđević
    dynasty, Serbian views of the Macedonian problem, and Serbian at-
    tempts to achieve economic emancipation. Austria-Hungary retali-

ates against the projected Serbo-Bulgarian customs union by the "pig war" and annexation of Bosnia-Hercegovina, while Serbia seeks and finds new markets and envisions a Danube-Adriatic railway.

2518. Đorđević, Dimitrije.   Izlazak Srbije na Jadransko more i Konferencija ambasadora u Londonu 1912 (Serbia's outlet to the Adriatic Sea and the Ambassadors' Conference in London in 1912). Beograd, 1956. 160 p. Maps. Bibliography: p. 153-158.

Serbia's maritime urge and aim to acquire a southern Adriatic port in a territory ethnically Albanian, close to western European markets. The Ambassadors' Conference excludes Serbia from the Adriatic. For other comments on this subject and on "national revolutions" of the Balkan peoples, which lead to the disruption of two empires (Ottoman and Habsburg), *see* the author's *Révolutions nationales des peuples balkaniques, 1804-1914*, translated by Margita Ristić (Beograd, Institut d'histoire, 1965). For the view that Serbia cannot free itself from the economic tutelage of Austria-Hungary by alienating Albanians, see *Srbija i Arbanija: Jedan prilog kritici zavojevačke politike srpske buržoazije* (Serbia and Albania: a contribution to the critique of the politics of conquest of the Serbian bourgeoisie) by Dimitrije Tucović (Beograd, Socijalistička knjižara, 1914, 119 p.), reprinted in 1946 by Kultura with a preface by Milovan Đilas.

## 6. Primitive Rebels and Millenarians

2519. Dedijer, Vladimir.   The Road to Sarajevo. New York, Simon and Schuster, 1966. 550 p. Illus., map, ports. Bibliography: p. 517-529.
*See also* entry no. 2372.

A study of millenarian aspects of nationalism in Austro-Hungarian Bosnia-Hercegovina. Dedijer views the nationalism of this province as a reaction of the young against "primitivism," or archaic forms of state, school, church, town, and family, and as a struggle between a "metropolitan" and a "colonial" people. Coming from a primitive milieu, the young rebels react in primitive fashion by resorting to "direct action" — the assassination of governors, of other officials, and of the Archduke Franz Ferdinand. One of the chapters is thus aptly entitled "Primitive Rebels of Bosnia." Moreover, many portions of Dedijer's study lend themselves to psychoanalytical interpretations. On the general subject of "primitive rebels," see *Primitive Rebels: Studies in Archaic Forms of Social Movement in the Nineteenth and Twentieth Centuries* by Eric J. Hobsbawm (Manchester, University Press, 1959, 208 p.).

## 7. Frontiers of Culture and National Minorities

2520. Moodie, Arthur E.   The Italo-Yugoslav Boundary, a Study in Political Geography. London, George Philip, 1945. 241 p. Illus., maps, diagrs. Bibliography: p. 233-238.
*See also* entries no. 2219 *and* 2552.

A study from Roman times to 1945 of the Julian region, both barrier and connecting link between the Adriatic and the middle Danube. Touches on ethnic distribution of Slovenes, Italians, and Serbo-Croatians in the Istria and Julian regions and delimitation of the Italo-Yugoslav boundary following the First World War. The author favors transfer of the region from Italy to Yugoslavia. Another geographic study, *La Croatie occidentale; étude de géographie humaine* by André Blanc (Paris, Institut d'études slaves de l'Université de Paris, 1957, 498 p.), shows that the traders of Karlovac and the Sava axis favored the linguistic reforms of the Illyrian movement — relatively unified Serbo-Croatian language — while Zagreb, the center of the "estates" conception of society and of domination by the aristocracy and the clergy, demurred. In *The Slovenes of Carinthia: a National Minority Problem* (New York, League of CSA, 1960, 302 p.), Thomas M. Barker portrays the Klagenfurt basin and Carinthia in general as an area of slow recession of Slovenian nationality in response to the competition of a politically and heretofore economically and culturally favored nationality — the Austrian Germans.

2521. Rothenberg, Gunther E.    The Croatian Military Border and the Rise of Yugoslav Nationalism. Slavonic and East European Review (London, v. 43, no. 100, Dec. 1964: 34-45.

A study of nationalism — Illyrian, Croatian, Serbian, and Yugoslav — in the Croatian Military Border and the decline of the area as a stronghold of loyalty to the Habsburg dynasty (*Kaisertreue*), 1804-1881. *See also*: "The Struggle over the Dissolution of the Croatian Military Border, 1850-1871," *Slavic Review* (Seattle), v. 23, no. 1, Mar. 1964: 63-78, and *The Military Border in Croatia, 1740-1881: A Study of an Imperial Institution* (Chicago and London, University of Chicago Press, 1966, 224 p.), both by Gunther E. Rothenberg. On the Croatian Military Border, Croato-Hungarian dualism (1102-1526), Habsburg rule, second Croato-Hungarian dualism (1868-1905), movement toward the third dualism (Croato-Serbian, 1905-1941), Ustaša state of Croatia, and a view of the struggle between Croats and Serbs during the Second World War as a fight of Croatiandom against "Yugoslavism and Communism," see *Die Kroaten: Schicksalsweg eines Südslawen-volkes* by Rudolf Kiszling (Graz-Köln, Verlag Hermann Böhlaus Nachf., 1956, 266 p.).

2522. Wilkinson, Henry R.    Maps and Politics; a Review of the Ethnographic Cartography of Macedonia. Liverpool, University Press, 1951. 366 p. Illus., maps, diagrs. Bibliography: p. 333-349.

*See also* entries no. 713 *and* 2229.

Ethnographic maps of Macedonia published between 1821 and 1946 (one in 1730) as symbols of national conflict and as instruments of political warfare. For a study of the Macedonian dispute, the Internal Macedonian Revolutionary Organization, Axis occupation of Macedonia during the Second World War, and rival communist (Yugoslav, Bulgarian, and Greek) views of the proper solution of the Macedonian nationality problem, see: *Macedonia, Its Place in Balkan Power Politics* by Elisabeth Barker (London and New York, Royal Institute of International Affairs, 1950, 129 p.). On nationalities of Macedonia and national identity of Macedonian Slavs, *see also* the pertinent writings by Victor Bérard, Henry N. Brailsford, Đoko Slijepčević, Dimitar Vlahov, Nikolaos P. Andriōtēs, and Evangelos Kofos.

## 8. The National Market and the Socialist Economy

2523. Mittelman, Earl Niel.   The Nationality Problem in Yugoslavia; a Survey of Developments, 1921-1953. Unpublished Ph.D. dissertation, New York University, 1954.

Largely on the Serbo-Croatian national problem and on relations between party politics and national struggle. Interesting chapters on Yugoslav communism, and particularly on the new attitude toward the national question in the Fundamental Law of 1953: Yugoslav Federation should no longer be regarded as only a union of nationalities and of their states; it will henceforth be the creative agent of an integrated socialist community.

2524. Raditsa, Bogdan.   The Yugoslav Intelligentsia: East and West; Old and New Nationalism. Journal of Central European Affairs (Boulder), v. 23, no. 4, Jan. 1964: 473-484.

Drawing on Dvorniković (*see entry* 2504) and Croatian writer Miroslav Krleža, Raditsa emphasizes the incomplete synthesis among Yugoslavs of Slavic (sensitivity), Balkan (dynamism), Central European, and Mediterranean characteristics. He proceeds to show how national antagonisms have persisted or been revived in communist Yugoslavia, with Slovenian Marxists regarding nationality as supranational or non-class category and certain Serbian Marxists ready to declare federalism obsolete and opt for a Serbo-Croatian cultural center, around which, it is hoped, other Yugoslavs would rally. Official communist policy seeks to promote understanding among Yugoslav subnationalities by building socialism and developing an integrated national market.

2525. Fisher, Jack C.   Yugoslavia, a Multinational State; Regional Difference and Administrative Response. San Francisco, Chandler Publishing Co., 1966. 244 p. Illus., maps. Bibliography: p. 223-231.

*See also* entries no. 2207, 2488, *and* 2619.

A basic factor in the resurgence of "national" tensions and sectional rivalries in communist Yugoslavia: continued cleavage between political and economic power, the first centered at Belgrade and turned toward the Danube and the south, including the southern Adriatic, and the second centered at Zagreb and oriented toward the north, including the northern and middle Adriatic. Post-1948 industrialization and urbanization have not removed traditional regional differences, and economically advanced republics of Croatia and Slovenia are making more rapid economic progress, maintains the author, than the others. The federal government seeks a solution to regional and "national" conflicts by encouraging social and economic development of the "commune." The author proposes outward expansion of transportation networks from the Sava axis (Belgrade-Zagreb-Ljubljana) as a way to hasten spatial integration.

2526. Stojković, Ljubiša, *and* Miloš Martić.   National Minorities in Yugoslavia. Belgrade, Publishing and Editing Enterprise "Jugoslavija," 1952. 226 p. Illus.

Discusses numerical strength and geographic distribution of national minorities (peoples other than Croats, Serbs, Slovenes, and Macedonian Slavs) in Yugoslavia, participation in or opposition to the Yugoslav national liberation struggle on the part of various minorities during the Second World War, territorial and cultural autonomies, and participation of minorities in the economy. For Yugoslav policies towards minorities in the decade since 1952 — encouragement of bilingualism, separation of the question of autonomous regions from the nationalities question, and promotion of social mingling of minorities with Yugoslav nationalities — *see*: "Yugoslavia's National Minorities under Communism" by Paul Shoup, *Slavic Review* (Seattle), v. 22, no. 1, Mar. 1963: 64-81. On the general subject of education and nationalities, *see* Gabor Jánosi's *Prosveta i kultura narodnosti u Jugoslaviji* (Education and culture of nationalities in Yugoslavia) (Beograd, Međunarodna politika, 1965, 42 p.).

2527. Shoup, Paul.   Communism and the Yugoslav National Question. New York, Columbia University Press, 1968. 308 p. Bibliography: p. 281-299.

A thoughtful and well-documented treatment of a complex subject.

## D. THE AGRARIAN QUESTION
## (HISTORICAL, POLITICAL, SOCIAL ASPECTS)

*by Traian Stoianovich*

### 1. Agrarian Order, Medieval to Ottoman: Progression or Regression?

2528. Novaković, Stojan.   Selo (The village). *In* Srpska Kraljevska Akademija. Glas (Beograd), v. 24, 1891: 1-261.

The village and other forms of rural settlement in Serbian lands in the Middle Ages, with data on some aspects of rural life as late as the 19th century. Special topics include rural social differentiation, forced labor and other forms of work organization, deserted villages, migratory habits, 14th and 18th century rural demography, rural craft specialization, and the declining cultural level of the village from the 15th century to the middle of the 18th century. Novaković pictures the 14th century as a period of agricultural expansion and pastoral contraction and regards the *zadruga* (extended family) as, in large measure, a post-14th century phenomenon arising from the recrudescence of pastoralism under Ottoman rule. For other views (some questionable) on Serbian medieval peasantry, see *Die agrar-rechtlichen Verhältnisse des mittelalterlichen Serbiens* by Milan Wlaïnatz (Jena, G. Fischer, 1903, 311 p.).

2529. Ninčić, Momčilo. Istorija agrarno-pravnih odnosa srpskih težaka pod Turcima. v. 1. Ranije doba (A history of the agrarian-legal situation of Serbian peasants under the Turks. v. 1. Earlier period). Beograd, Geca Kon, 1920.

Ottoman law was more lenient toward the peasant than had been Serbian law of the late Middle Ages. On the other hand, agricultural domains had been better organized, labor had been more abundant, and agricultural techniques had been at a higher level in medieval Serbia. The early phase of Ottoman rule was socially liberating but harmful to agricultural production. In the later period, the social situation of the peasantry deteriorated.

2530. Truhelka, Ćiro. Historička podloga agrarnog pitanja u Bosni (The historical foundations of the agrarian question in Bosnia). Glasnik Zemaljskog Muzeja u Bosni i Hercegovini (Herald of the Provincial Museum in Bosnia and Hercegovina) (Sarajevo), v. 27, 1915: 109-218.

Until the 18th century, few countries had a better regulated agrarian regime than the Ottoman Empire. The Ottomans perpetuated and improved the Bosnian medieval agrarian order, which the author assumes to have been less harsh than that of Serbia. For a different view of the Ottoman agrarian regime in Yugoslav lands, closer to that of Branislav Đurđev, *see* "Pogled na osmanski feudalizam sa naročitim obzirom na agrarne odnose" (A look at Ottoman feudalism, with special reference to agrarian relations) by Nedim Filipović, *Godišnjak Istoriskog Društva Bosne i Hercegovine* (Annual of the Historical Society of Bosnia and Hercegovina) (Sarajevo), v. 4, 1952: 5-146.

2531. Đurđev, Branislav. Prilog pitanju razvitka i karaktera tursko-osmanskog feudalizma — timarsko-spahiskog uređenja (A contribution to the problem of the evolution and character of Turco-Ottoman feudalism, or the Timariot-Spahi régime). Godišnjak Istoriskog Društva Bosne i Hercegovine (Annual of the Historical Society of Bosnia and Hercegovina) (Sarajevo), v. 1, 1949: 101-167.

———. O uticaju turske vladavine na razvitak naših naroda (The influence of Turkish rule on the development of our peoples). Godišnjak, v. 2, 1950: 19-82.

Ottoman feudalism led to the revival of seminomadism and to a decline in agricultural production. But in *Istoriski Glasnik* (Historical herald) (Beograd, no. 1/2, 1950: 187-202), Sergije Dimitrijević holds that by replacing labor rent with rent in kind the Ottoman state for a time raised peasant labor productivity. *See also* "The Yugoslav Lands in the Ottoman Period: Postwar Marxist Interpretations of

Indigenous and Ottoman Institutions," by Wayne S. Vucinich, *Journal of Modern History*, v. 27, no. 3, Sept. 1955: 287-305.

2532. Busch-Zantner, Richard. Agrarverfassung, Gesellschaft und Siedlung in Südosteuropa unter besonderer Berücksichtigung der Türkenzeit. Leipzig, Otto Harrassowitz, 1938. 158 p. (Beihefte zur "Leipziger Vierteljahrsschrift für Südosteuropa," Heft 3)

The *čiftlik* as a village of the 16th, 17th and 18th century colonization. Advantages and disadvantages of a plantation economy. For the relationship between the development of export crops (grains, cotton, tobacco) and the *čiftlik* regime and for the tendency of *čiftliks* to spread along coastal plains and river basins (Vardar, Morava, Maritsa, and Danube) and in the vicinity of towns, see "Land Tenure and Related Sectors of the Balkan Economy, 1600-1800," by Traian Stoianovich, *Journal of Economic History*, v. 13, Fall 1953: 398-411. For *čiftlik* in Macedonia during a later period, see *Agrarnite otnosheniia v Makedoniia prez XIX v. i nachaloto na XX v* by Khristo Khristov (Sofiia, Bŭlgarska Akademiia na naukite, 1964), with resumé in English: "The Agrarian Problem in Macedonia in the 19th and at the Beginning of the 20th Century."

## 2. From Archaic, or Pure, Peasant Society to Mixed Peasant Society

2533. Blanc, André. La Croatie occidentale: Étude de géographie humaine. Paris, Institut d'études slaves de l'Université de Paris, 1957. 498 p. Illus., maps. (Travaux publiés par l'Institut d'études slaves, 25) *See also* entry no. 2202.

Problems of human geography in an "archaic rural region": western Croatia, or the basin of Kupa, from the Middle Ages to the 20th century. Traditions of collective and private property, the *zadruga*, or extended family, house types and character of the Croatian village, relations between town and country, pastoralism, the economic role of the forest, the "Vlach" (Serbian) colonization of the seventeenth and eighteenth centuries, viticulture, the rise of maize cultivation and of cereal economy, the archaism of rural tools and techniques, the decline of pastoralism, the growth of agricultural cooperatives, and population expansion and emigration. For conditions of land tenure in Slavonia from the Middle Ages to 1848, see *Agrarni odnosi u Slavoniji* (Agrarian relations in Slavonia) by Josip Bösendorfer (Zagreb, Izdavački zavod Jugoslavenske Akademije znanosti i umjetnosti, 1950).

2534. Đorđević, Tihomir R. Iz Srbije Kneza Miloša: Stanovništvo, naselja (From Prince Miloš's Serbia: Population, settlements). Beograd, Geca Kon, 1924. 314 p. Illus.

Two chapters on the Serbian village between 1815 and 1839, with data on rural churches, taverns, inns, stores, village types, and the institutions of village mayor and village assembly (then called *selo* [village], *narod* [people], *veliko i malo* [the great and the small], or *kmetovi veliki i mali* [peasants great and small]). For comments on the Serbian village before, during, and following the Serbian revolution by a contemporary, see *Danica* (Morning star), by Vuk Stefanović Karadžić (Vienna), No. 2 (1827). Karadžić also provides data on the *čiftlik* (or *čitluk*) system of land tenure in prerevolutionary Serbia.

2535. Trouton, Ruth.  Peasant Renaissance in Yugoslavia, 1900-1950. London, Routledge and Kegan Paul, 1952. 344 p. Bibliography: p. 325-330.

*See also* entry no. 2674.

Transition after 1830, and chiefly after 1900, from a "pure peasant society" — a society in which the main social groups are family household and village and in which each family has enough land for its needs, produces nearly everything it requires, and consumes nearly everything it produces — to a "mixed peasant society" with market economy and cities. Class structure, bureaucracy, education, rural basis of communist revolution, and Yugoslav peasantry under socialism. See also *Peasant Life in Yugoslavia* by Olive Lodge (London, Seeley, Service, 1941, 332 p.). For a refinement of the theory of a peasant economy, *see* Aleksandr V. Chaianov's writings and articles by Daniel Thorner in *Deuxième conférence internationale d'histoire économique, Aix-en-Provence, 1962*, II (Paris, The Hague, Mouton, 1965), p. 287-300, and in *Annales, économies, sociétés, civilisations*, v. 21, no. 6, Nov.-Dec. 1966: 1232-1244.

### 3. Social Revolution and Peasant Insurrection

2536. Mirković, Mijo.  Ekonomska historija Jugoslavije (Economic history of Yugoslavia). Zagreb, Ekonomski pregled, 1958. 443 p. Illus. (Biblioteka Ekonomskog pregleda, 6)

*See also* entry no. 2591.

Chapters on economic and social institutions of village life, historical manifestations of various forms of collective property rights, feudal tenure and the seignorial regime, rural economy in Ottoman times, and the transfer of property between 1804 (Serbian insurrection) and 1953 (Yugoslav Fundamental Law) from foreigners and other privileged groups to the newly ascendant nationalities and especially to their peasantries. Pervading theme: close intertwining of national and social revolutions.

2537. Nedeljković, Branislav.  Istorija baštinske svojine u novoj Srbiji od kraja 18. veka do 1931 (A history of real property in new Serbia from the end of the 18th century to 1931). Foreword by Živojin M. Perić. Beograd, Geca Kon, 1936. 348 p.

A study of such changes in property relationships and in social distribution of property as occur "by leaps." The Ottoman conquest brought down the harsh feudal (seignorial) systems of the medieval Serbian states but the *čiftlik* system of land tenure introduced a new form of exploitation that had the disadvantage of hindering the development of capitalism. Transformation of Serbia between 1750 and 1850 into a "land of freedom" — *Slobodija* — to which peasants fled to escape oppression. Acts of national liberation (1804, 1833, 1878, 1912, 1918) were followed by redistribution of property in favor of the underprivileged peasantry of rising Serbian (and later Yugoslav) nationality and together constituted "a sort of bourgeois revolution" grafted upon a peasant revolution.

2538. Čulinović, Ferđo.   Seljačke bune u Hrvatskoj (Peasant rebellions in Croatia). Zagreb, Seljačka Sloga, 1951. 185 p. (Naučna knji-žnica, 7)

Peasant insurrections and popular movements in Croatia and fringe provinces from the 14th century to 1921. For similar movements in nineteenth century Bosnia-Hercegovina, see *Agrarno pitanje i turski neredi za vreme reformnog režima Abdul Medžida (1839-1861)* (The agrarian question and Turkish disorders in the reform era of Abdul Mejid [1839-1861]) by Vasilj Popović (Beograd, Srpska akademija nauka, 1949, 323 p.). *See also* numerous articles in *Godišnjak Istoriskog Društva Bosne i Hercegovine* (Annual of the historical society of Bosnia and Hercegovina) (Sarajevo).

2539. Jackson, George D., Jr.   Comintern and Peasant in East Europe, 1919-1930. New York, Columbia University Press, 1966. 339 p. Bibliography: p. 321-328.

*See also* entry no. 645.

In the chapter entitled "The Effete Party: Comintern Policy in Yugoslavia, 1924-1929" (p. 215-236), the author discusses the unsuccessful Comintern efforts to take advantage of Yugoslav peasantism, and especially of the Croatian Peasant Party, in order to achieve a "workers' and peasants' revolution" in Yugoslavia.

### 4. Agrarian Reform

2540. Ivšić, Milan.   Les problèmes agraires en Yougoslavie. Paris, Rousseau et Cie Éditeurs, 1926. 376 p. Maps, tables, bibliography.

Geological-geographic foundations of land tenure, history of land tenure in the various Yugoslav provinces (not altogether reliable), and post-1918 agrarian reforms and Yugoslav policies of internal colonization. Statistical tables show fluctuations in size patterns of farms in the northern provinces between 1850 and 1924. The author attributes the weakening of the economic capacity of various provinces in the early 1920s, as compared to the prewar decade, to the sudbdivision of large estates. He admits, however, that the decline in agricultural production was also a consequence of wartime devastation, especially of heavy losses in cattle. For comparison of Yugoslav reforms with those in Czechoslovakia and Romania, see *Die Agrarreform in Yugoslawien* by Josef Matl (Berlin und Breslau, H. Sack, 1927, 137 p.).

2541. Frangeš, Otto von.   Die sozialökonomische Struktur der jugoslawischen Landwirtschaft. Berlin, Weidmannsche Verlagsbuch-handlung, 1937. 288 p. (Schriften der Internationalen Konferenz für Agrarwissenschaft)

The former minister of agriculture criticizes post-1918 agrarian reforms, especially the subdivision of large properties in the northern Yugoslav areas (Slovenia, Croatia-Slavonia, and Vojvodina). Reasons: accumulation of capital is more difficult if not impossible on tiny properties; subdivision results in the creation of a rural proletariat, or peasantry, with insufficient land; subdivision provokes lowering of farm efficiency, or peasant labor productivity. The historical section is based in part on Čiro Truhelka. For a critique, see Jozo Tomasevich's *Peasants, Politics, and Economic Change in Yugoslavia* (entries no. 2389, 2436, 2543, *and* 2638). In "Agrarverfassung und agrarische Umwälzung in Jugoslawien" in *Die agrarischen Umwälzungen im ausserrussischen Osteuropa*, edited by Max Sering (Berlin, Leipzig, de Gruyter, 1930, 439 p.), Ludwig Fritscher agrees that the reforms of the 1920s caused a decline in Yugoslavia's ability to place its farm goods on the world market, but contends that this made industrialization more imperative than ever.

2542. Warriner, Doreen.  Urban Thinkers and Peasant Policy in Yugoslavia, 1918-59. Slavonic and East European Review (London), v. 38, no. 90, Dec. 1959: 59-81.

Criticism of urban thinkers and administrators of all political shades for regarding the peasants as a category. This view is modified somewhat by the author's awareness that the interwar and post-1945 agrarian reforms were both large in scope. An article in *Yugoslav Survey* (Beograd), v. 2, no. 6, July-Sept. 1961: 785-791, sets the total number of families benefiting from post-1945 reforms at 316,415, thus indirectly supporting Warriner's contention that interwar agrarian reforms were twice as extensive. In *Agrarna reforma u Jugoslaviji 1918-1941 god.* (Agrarian reform in Yugoslavia, 1918-1941) (Sarajevo, Veselin Masleša, 1958, 547 p.), Milivoje Erić acknowledges the importance of the interwar agrarian reforms but criticizes them for not achieving a more substantial subdivision of large properties.

## 5. Crisis Economy, Market Economy

2543. Tomasevich, Jozo.  Peasants, Politics, and Economic Change in Yugoslavia. Stanford, Stanford University Press, 1955. 743 p. Maps, tables. Bibliography: p. 703-726.

*See also* entries no. 2389, 2436, *and* 2638.

Social and economic history of the Yugoslav provinces from the Middle Ages to 1941, with special stress on the impact of the market and money economies on the Yugoslav peasantries since 1830. Systems of land tenure, peasant rebellion, bureaucracy, uneven struggle between "peasant moccasin" and "city coat," *zadruga* or extended family, rise and transformation of peasant parties, natural resources base of Yugoslav agriculture, demography, interwar agrarian reforms, size patterns of farms, rural technology, crops, animal husbandry, nutrition, health, marketing, agricultural credit, and peasants as taxpayers. For collectivization of the peasantry between 1945 and 1953 *see* "Collectivization of Agriculture in Yugoslavia," by Jozo Tomasevich, in *Collectivization of Agriculture in Eastern Europe*, edited by Irwin T. Sanders (Lexington, University of Kentucky Press, 1958), p. 166-192.

2544. Goranović, Maksim.   Poljoprivredni dohodak Jugoslavije (Agricultural income of Yugoslavia). Arhiv Ministarstva poljoprivrede (Beograd), v. 9, 1937.

See also his *Profesionalna i socijalna struktura sela u Jugoslaviji* (Occupational and social structure of the village in Yugoslavia) (*ibid.*, v. 12, 1938). Goranović shows a rising per capita income between 1918 and 1925, followed first by a slow decline as a result of the international agricultural crisis and then by a precipitous decline in 1931, with a very low income level until the minor economic revival of 1936. The period 1926-1935 was one of a massive return to a "natural economy" among the peasantry, which ceased to be a regular buyer of anything but salt (and less importantly matches, soap, kerosene, and occasionally coffee). The tempo of industrialization during the '20s was altogether inadequate to absorb the growing "surplus" rural population.

2545. Pertot, Vladimir.   Die Weizenregulierungen in Jugoslawien. Weltwirtschaftliches Archiv (Jena), v. 45, no. 3, May 1937: 628-659.

Between 1930 and 1936 Prizad (The Privileged Export Corporation) exercised an effective monopoly over the export of wheat. The purchasing operations of Prizad may have aggravated the lot of the Yugoslav peasantry. Because poor peasants lacked storage facilities and needed cash, they sold their grains in autumn, when prices were low. When their supplies ran out in spring, they had to reenter the market as buyers of wheat, precisely when prices were very high. Prizad and well-to-do traders, on the other hand, bought in autumn, when wheat prices were low, and sold in the spring, when they were high.

2546. Bilimovich, Alexander D.   Agriculture and Food in Yugoslavia Before, During, and After World War II. *In* Zagoroff, Slavtcho D., and others. The Agricultural Economy of the Danubian Countries, 1935-45. Stanford, Stanford University Press, 1955. p. 289-366.

Formerly professor at the universities of Kiev and Ljubljana, Bilimovich presents a well-integrated study of the interwar rural economy of Yugoslavia, wartime destruction of this economy, and UNRRA measures of relief. Data are given on post-1918 agrarian reforms and on food industries, nutrition, food prices, and curtailment of food supplies during and immediately after the Second World War.

2547. Kostić, Cvetko.   Changement de structure du village en Yougoslavie. Cahiers internationaux de sociologie (Paris), v. 23 (n.s., v. 4), July/Dec. 1957: 142-156.

See also his Seljaci industriski radnici (Peasants as industrial workers) (Beograd, Rad, 1955). In both studies Kostić deals with the phenomenon of a peasantry in disarray. As of the mid-1950s the Yugoslav working class was made up of a small number of persons with a relatively long urban and industrial tradition, while a large number was comprised of persons who had left the village to settle in some town and had ceased to be peasants before fully mastering the "style and technique of industrial labor." But half the industrial working class was then made up of "peasant-industrial" workers: peasants who worked in towns but continued to live and do some work in their villages, "hybrids" who lived in town during the workweek but returned to their village homes on weekends, and peasants from backward villages who found occasional work in towns.

2548. Leng, Earl R.   Agronomic Problems of Southeastern Europe. In Laird, Roy D., ed. Soviet Agricultural and Peasant Affairs. Lawrence, University of Kansas Press, 1963. p. 190-203.

An article devoted in large measure to Yugoslav agriculture since 1945: climate as it relates to the practice of growing corn and wheat in rotation, rises in yield levels of crops, development of early-maturing but disease-resistant and high-yielding corn hybrids, and mechanization. For further evidence of rising crop yields and for evaluation of post-1945 agriculture, see Yugoslavia: The Theory and Practice of Development Planning by George Macesich (Charlottesville, University of Virginia Press, 1964, 227 p.). For a comparison of Yugoslav and other East European agricultures, see Soviet and East European Agriculture, edited by Jerzy Karcz (Berkeley, Los Angeles, University of California Press, 1967, 445 p.).

## E. DIPLOMACY AND FOREIGN RELATIONS

### by John C. Campbell

### 1. The Settlement Following the First World War

2549. Alatri, Paolo.   Nitti, d'Annunzio e la questione adriatica, 1919-1920. Milano, Feltrinelli, 1959. 543 p. Ports., map, bibliographical footnotes. (I fatti e le idee, 18)

Best available study, from the Italian point of view, of the Italian-Yugoslav disputes arising out of the First World War.

2550. Baerlein, Henry P. B.   The Birth of Yugoslavia. London, L. Parsons, 1922. 2 v. Map.

A mixture of history and personal observations, by an English traveler and publicist, containing a wealth of information. The second volume deals with the aftermath of the war.

2551. Lederer, Ivo J.   Yugoslavia at the Paris Peace Conference; a Study in Frontiermaking. New Haven, Yale University Press, 1963. 351 p. Ports., maps. Bibliography: p. 317-329.

*See also* entries no. 2391, 2429, *and* 2516.

A fundamental study of the peace settlement of 1919-1920, based on careful use of available published and unpublished material, including documents from French, Italian, and U.S. archives and the Trumbić papers in Zagreb.

2552. Moodie, Arthur E.    The Italo-Yugoslav Boundary, a Study in Political Geography. London, G. Philip, 1945. 241 p. Illus., maps. Bibliography: p. 233-238.

*See also* entries no. 2219 *and* 2520.

Comprehensive treatment of the problem up to the beginning of the Second World War.

2553. Paresce, Gabriele.    Italia e Jugoslavia dal 1915 al 1929. Firenze, R. Bemporad, 1935. 326 p. Bibliography: p. 323-326.

Systematically covers relations between the two countries during the period indicated.

2554. Sforza, Carlo, *conte.*    Jugoslavia, storia e ricordi. Milano, Rizzoli, 1948. 210 p.

Count Sforza bases his study on extensive experience with Yugoslav affairs, using his own papers as a background. Much of the material was also included in his earlier *Pachitch et l'union des Yougoslaves* (Paris, Gallimard, 1938, 253 p.), translated into English as *Fifty Years of War and Diplomacy in the Balkans* (New York, Columbia University Press, 1940, 195 p.).

2555. Smith Pavelić, Ante.    Dr. Ante Trumbić; problemi hrvatsko-srpskih odnosa (Dr. Ante Trumbić; problems of Croatian-Serbian relations). München, Knjižnica Hrvatske revije, 1959. 333 p. Ports., illus. Bibliography: p. 317-320. (Knjižnica Hrvatske revije, knj. 3)

*See also* entry no. 2360.

A documented history of the politics and diplomacy of the Croatian leader, in connection with the formation of Yugoslavia and the settlement following the First World War.

## 2. The Interwar Period

2556. Akademiia nauk, SSSR. *Institut slavianovedeniia.*    Istoriia Iugoslavii (History of Yugoslavia). v. 2. Edited by L. B. Valev, G. M. Slavin, and I. I. Udal'tsov. Moskva, Izd-vo Akademii nauk SSSR, 1963. 430 p. Illus., facsims, maps, ports. Bibliography: p. 333-389.

*See also* entry no. 2378.

A standard Soviet interpretation of the period from 1917 to 1945. The bibliography is especially valuable for Soviet and Yugoslav publications.

2557. Avakumović, Ivan.    History of the Communist Party of Yugoslavia.

v. 1– Aberdeen, Aberdeen University Press, 1964– Bibliographies. *See also* entry no. 2482.

The first volume (207 p.) covers the party's history up to the beginning of the Second World War; includes some important material on the subsequent international relations of Yugoslavia. For the official history of the party, see *Pregled istorije Saveza komunista Jugoslavije*, edited by Rodoljub Čolaković and others (Beograd, Institut za izučavanje radničkog pokreta, 1963, 570 p.), which includes the postwar period.

2558. Avramovski, Živko.    Sukob interesa Velike Britanije i Nemačke na Balkanu uoči drugog svetskog rata. (The clash of interests between Great Britain and Germany in the Balkans on the eve of the Second World War). *In* Institut društvenih nauka. *Odeljenje za istorijske nauke*. Istorija XX veka; zbornik radova II (History of the 20th century; collection of writings, II). Beograd, 1961. p. 5-158.

Makes use of Yugoslav archival material and a wide variety of published works.

2559. Belgrade. Institut za međunarodnu politiku i privredu. *Odeljenje za međunarodno pravo*. Pregled razvoja međunarodno-pravnih odnosa jugoslovenskih zemalja od 1800 do danas (Survey of the development of international-law relations of the lands of Yugoslavia from 1800 till today). Beograd, 1962. 2 v.

The first volume lists chronologically pertinent treaties and agreements for the period from 1800 to 1918, and the second volume for 1918 to 1941.

2560. Hoptner, Jacob B.    Yugoslavia in Crisis, 1934-1941. New York, Columbia University Press, 1962. 328 p. Bibliography: p. 308-313. *See also* entries no. 2394 *and* 2425.

A competent study of Yugoslavia's foreign relations during the regency of Prince Paul, using *inter alia* his unpublished papers. *Jugoslawien am Scheidewege, das serbo-kroatische Problem und Jugoslawiens Aussenpolitik* by Milutin Čekič (Leipzig, F. Meiner, 1939, 138 p.) may also be consulted.

2561. Maur, Gilbert in der.    Die Jugoslawen einst und jetzt. Leipzig, J. Günther, 1936-1938. 3 v. Maps. *See also* entry no. 2375.

The second volume, devoted to international relations, contains a wealth of detail on the period 1919-1935. It is based on contemporary material, but there is no citation of sources. The third volume extends this coverage somewhat.

2562. Mehmedbašić, Sulejman M., *ed.*    Iz istorije Jugoslavije, 1918-1945; zbornik predavanja (From the history of Yugoslavia, 1918-1945; collection of lectures). Beograd, Nolit, 1958. 444 p.

Covers many aspects of international relations as well as domestic affairs. Among the authors are Milan Bartoš, Bogdan Krizman, and Jovan Marjanović.

2563. Yanochevitch, Milorad.   La Yougoslavie dans les Balkans. Paris, Les Éditions internationales, 1935. 283 p. Bibliography: p. 273-279.

Diplomatic history giving particular attention to the Little Entente and Balkan Entente. See also *La politique extérieure de la Yougoslavie* by Lazar Marković (Paris, Société Générale d'Imprimerie & d'édition, 1935, 344 p.).

### 3. The Second World War and Its Aftermath

2564. Castro, Diego de.   Il problema di Trieste. v. 1. Genesi e sviluppi della questione giuliana in relazione agli avvenimenti internazionali (1943-1952). Bologna, Cappelli, 1952. 679 p. Bibliographic footnotes, maps.

A detailed account of the Trieste dispute in its many aspects; indispensable for further study of the question, although coverage of Yugoslav sources is weak.

2565. Clissold, Stephen.   Whirlwind; an Account of Marshal Tito's Rise to Power. New York, Philosophical Library, 1949. 245 p. Maps.

To date, about the best account in English of the wartime developments in Yugoslavia and their international aspects.

2566. Dedijer, Vladimir.   Pariska konferencija (The Paris Conference). Zagreb, 1948. 439 p. Illus. (Biblioteka "Trideset dana")

The only detailed account of Yugoslav matters treated at the Paris Conference of 1946. The interpretations are strongly slanted along the official Yugoslav line of the time.

2567. Fotitch, Constantin.   The War We Lost; Yugoslavia's Tragedy and the Failure of the West. New York, Viking Press, 1948. 344 p.

*See also* entry no. 2450.

Wartime diplomacy is discussed by the royal Yugoslav ambassador to Washington. Contains useful information, despite the author's strong views on the Mihailović-Tito affair and his disillusionment with Western policy. The defense of Mihailović is also the theme of David Martin's *Ally Betrayed; the Uncensored Story of Tito and Mihailovich* (New York, Prentice-Hall, 1946, 372 p.).

2568. Martin-Chauffier, Jean.   Trieste. Paris, Hartmann, 1947. 199 p. Maps. (Centre d'études de politique étrangère. Section d'information. Publication No. 18)

A brief but useful account of the Trieste dispute from the liberation of Venezia Giulia to the conclusion of the Italian peace treaty in 1947.

2569. Plenča, Dušan.   Međunarodni odnosi Jugoslavije u toku drugog svjetskog rata (International relations of Yugoslavia during the Second World War). Beograd, Institut društvenih nauka, 1962. 425 p. Bibliographic footnotes.

*See also* entry no. 2463.

The most complete and scholarly account of wartime diplomacy regarding Yugoslavia published by a Yugoslav historian. The sources are mainly Yugoslav documents, but the principal foreign publications are also used.

## 4. International Relations of Tito's Yugoslavia

2570. Armstrong, Hamilton Fish.    Tito and Goliath. New York, Macmillan, 1951. 312 p.

An analysis, by the editor of *Foreign Affairs*, of Yugoslavia's break with Moscow in 1948 and its significance for the communist world. May be supplemented by Harry Hodgkinson's *Challenge to the Kremlin* (New York, Praeger, 1952, 190 p.).

2571. Barker, Elisabeth.    Macedonia, Its Place in Balkan Power Politics. London, New York, Royal Institute of International Affairs, 1950. 129 p. Maps.

*See also* entry no. 160.

A concise and balanced survey, still useful although more material has since become available and the problem has entered new phases. It may be supplemented, largely for background, by Asen I. Krainikovski's *La question de Macédoine et la diplomatie européenne* (Paris, M. Rivière, 1938, 339 p.).

2572. Bass, Robert H., *and* Marbury, Elizabeth, *eds.*    The Soviet-Yugoslav Controversy, 1948-58: a Documentary Record. Introduction by Hans Kohn. New York, Published for the East Europe Institute by Prospect Books, 1959. 225 p.

A convenient collection of public documents, speeches, and press articles presenting Soviet and Yugoslav positions on matters in dispute from the initial break to the controversy over revisionism. A further collection on the controversy of 1958 is *The Second Soviet-Yugoslav Dispute*, edited by Vaclav L. Benes, Robert F. Byrnes, and Nicolas Spulber (Bloomington, Indiana University, 1959, 272 p.).

2573. Campbell, John C.    Tito's Separate Road: America and Yugoslavia in World Politics. New York, Harper & Row, 1967. 173 p.

A discussion of Yugoslav-American relations in the world context from 1948 to 1966.

2574. Dedijer, Vladimir.    Jugoslovensko-albanski odnosi, 1939-1948 (Yugoslav-Albanian relations, 1939-1948). Zagreb, Borba, 1949. 225 p. Illus.

*See also* entry no. 357.

Written to present the Yugoslav case against Albania, this book is nevertheless important as the only detailed account of relations between the two countries and their communist parties during a critical period; includes facsimiles of documents.

2575. Dedijer, Vladimir. Tito. New York, Simon and Schuster, 1953. 443 p.
    *See also* entry no. 2474.
    An official biography, significant for its revelations concerning Soviet-Yugoslav relations during and after the Second World War. Additional light is thrown on this subject by Milovan Đilas in *Conversations With Stalin* (New York, Harcourt, Brace & World, 1962, 211 p.). *See also* Dedijer's *Izgubljena bitka J. V. Stalina* (J. V. Stalin's lost battle) (Sarajevo, Svjetlost, 1969, 435 p.).

2576. Halperin, Ernst. The Triumphant Heretic; Tito's Struggle against Stalin. London, Heinemann, 1958. 324 p.
    The work of a talented journalist and expert in communist affairs, this is more an account of the Tito regime, especially in international affairs, than a personal biography. Originally published as *Der siegreiche Ketzer* (Köln, Verlag für Politik und Wirtschaft, 1957, 390 p.).

2577. Hoffman, George W., *and* Fred W. Neal. Yugoslavia and the New Communism. New York, Twentieth Century Fund, 1962. 546 p. Maps, tables. Bibliography: p. 511-527.
    *See also* entries no. 2190, 2490, *and* 2604.
    Portions of this comprehensive study of postwar Yugoslavia deal with foreign policy.

2578. Kardelj, Edvard. Socialism and War; a Survey of Chinese Criticism of the Policy of Coexistence. New York, McGraw-Hill, 1960. 238 p. Bibliography.
    The Yugoslav leadership's authoritative reply to communist China's attacks on the Yugoslav government and Communist Party.

2579. Maclean, Fitzroy. The Heretic: The Life and Times of Josip Broz-Tito. New York, Harper, 1957. 436 p. Illus.
    The second half of this biography deals extensively with Yugoslavia's foreign relations between 1945 and 1955. The author headed a British mission to Tito during the Second World War and maintained his friendship and contacts with Tito after the war. Maclean's wartime experience as Churchill's emissary in Yugoslavia is described in his earlier *Eastern Approaches* (London, J. Cape, 1949, 543 p.), published in the United States as *Escape to Adventure* (Boston, Little, Brown, 1950, 419 p.).

2580. Međunarodni politički leksikon (International political lexicon). Compiled by Marijan Hubeny, Branko Kojić, and Bogdan Krizman. Zagreb, Novinarsko izdavačko poduzeče, 1960. 592 p.
    A general lexicon with numerous entries pertaining to Yugoslavia.

2581. Meier, Viktor. Yugoslav Communism. *In* Griffith, William E., *ed.* Communism in Europe; Continuity, Change, and the Sino-Soviet Dispute. v. 1. Cambridge, Mass., M.I.T. Press, 1964. p. 19-84.

> Analysis by a Swiss journalist long conversant with Eastern Europe. Foreign relations, especially with the Soviet Union, are emphasized.

2582. Savez komunist Jugoslavije. *5. Kongres, Belgrade, 1948.* V Kongres Komunističke Partije Jugoslavije, izveštaji i referati. (The 5th Congress of the Communist Party of Yugoslavia: statements and reports) Zagreb, Kultura, 1948. 575 p.

> The official reports of the fifth congress, held after the break with the Cominform in 1948, contain much material relating to Yugoslavia's international position. The main reports are by Tito, Kardelj, Ranković, and Đilas. A speech by Kardelj later in 1948 appeared in English translation as *Yugoslavia's Foreign Policy* (Belgrade, Jugoslovenska knjiga, 1949, 61 p.).

2583. The Soviet-Yugoslav Dispute; Text of the Published Correspondence. London, New York, Royal Institute of International Affairs, 1948. 79 p.

> *See also* entry no. 2470.

> The basic documents concerning the crisis of 1948, translated from texts published at the time under Soviet and Yugoslav auspices.

2584. Ulam, Adam B.   Titoism and the Cominform. Cambridge, Mass., Harvard University Press, 1952. 243 p. (Russian Research Center Studies, 5) Bibliography: p. 235-236.

> *See also* entry no. 2496.

> A careful study of the Soviet-Yugoslav dispute, based largely on the published documents available at the time. A summary account through 1955 is R. Barry Farrell's *Yugoslavia and the Soviet Union, 1948-1956: An Analysis with Documents* (Hamden, Conn., Shoe String Press, 1956, 220 p.). See also *National Communism and Soviet Strategy* by Dinko A. Tomašić (Washington, D.C., Public Affairs Press, 1957, 222 p.), worth consulting because of its wide use of Yugoslav sources, although its interpretations may be questioned.

2585. White Book on Aggressive Activities by the Governments of the USSR, Poland, Czechoslovakia, Hungary, Rumania, Bulgaria and Albania towards Yugoslavia. Belgrade, Ministry of Foreign Affairs, 1951. 481 p.

> An official collection of documents issued in support of the Yugoslav government's case against the Cominform countries being presented in the United Nations and to world opinion. Issued in several languages.

2586. Zalar, Charles.   Yugoslav Communism; a Critical Study. Washington, D.C., U.S. Government Printing Office, 1961. 387 p. Bibliography: p. 307-358.

*See also* entry no. 2499.

Questions may be raised about the objectivity of this study, but it is full of interesting details and is based on a wide range of sources.

## F. MASS MEDIA AND PUBLIC OPINION

### by Wayne S. Vucinich

2587. Belgrade. Jugoslovenski institut za novinarstvo. Štampa, radio, televizija, film u Jugoslaviji (Press, radio, television, film in Yugoslavia). Edited by Nikola Kern and others. Beograd. 1964. 198 p.

The organization of and legislation concerning the Yugoslav media of communication. For a later survey in English see *Press, Radio, Television in Yugoslavia* by the same sponsoring agency (Belgrade, 1966, 129 p.).

2588. Damjanović, Mijat, *and others.* Jugoslovensko javno mnenje o privrednoj reformi 1965 (Yugoslav public opinion concerning the economic reform of 1965). Beograd, Institut društvenih nauka, 1965. 177 p.

A symposium containing 25 papers on a variety of subjects concerning the popular reaction to and understanding of the Economic Reform of 1965. Also discussed are public opinion and economic crime, employment abroad, the cost of living, and other problems. This publication appeared in the monographic series *Jugoslovensko javno mnenje* (Yugoslav public opinion), published under the auspices of the Center for Public Opinion Research of the Institute of Social Sciences in Belgrade.

2589. Gledić, Petar, *and* Zoran Pandurović. Jugoslovensko javno mnenje o aktuelnim ekonomskim i socijalnim pitanjima 1965 (Yugoslav public opinion on current economic and social questions, 1965). Beograd, Institut društvenih nauka, 1965. 218 p.

Discussion of a variety of topics relating to public opinion on the economic situation, such as the price freeze, increase of productivity, and private versus socialized agriculture.

2590. Nuhić, Muhamed. Sloboda štampe i njeno ostvaranje u društvenim uslovima u Jugoslaviji (Freedom of the press and its realization under Yugoslav social conditions). Beograd, Jugoslovenski institut za novinarstvo, 1964. 52 p.

The organization and function of the press in Yugoslavia. For more recent English-language surveys of the subject *see*:

Olson, Kenneth E. The Press of Yugoslavia. *In his* The History Makers. Baton Rouge, Louisiana State University Press, 1966. p. 414-428.

Vatovec, Fran. The Development of the Slovene and Yugoslav Periodical Journalism. Ljubljana, Visoka šola za politične vede, 1968. 106 p. Bibliography: p. 100-106.

# 49

# the economy

*by Benjamin N. Ward*

## A. ECONOMIC HISTORY

2591. Mirković, Mijo. Ekonomska historija Jugoslavije (Economic history of Yugoslavia). Zagreb, Ekonomski pregled, 1958. 443 p. Illus. (Biblioteka Ekonomskog pregleda, 6)

See also entry no. 2536.

2592. Stelè, Melitta (Pivec). La vie économique des provinces Illyriennes (1809-1813). Paris, Editions Bossard, 1930. 359 p. Maps. Bibliography: p. i-lxvii. (Institut d'études slaves de l'Université de Paris. Collection historique, 6)

A large collection of economic data with annotated bibliography and discussion of relevant archival collections.

2593. Sugar, Peter F. Industrialization of Bosnia-Hercegovina, 1878-1918. Seattle, University of Washington Press, 1963. 275 p. Maps, tables. Bibliography: p. 247-257.

See also entry no. 2370.

A careful monograph, based on an exhaustive search of the relevant archives combined with stimulating interpretations of the data. Kemal Hrelja in his *Industrija Bosne i Hercegovine do kraja prvog svjetskog rata* (The industry of Bosnia and Hercegovina up to the end of the First World War) (Beograd, Savez društava ekonomista Jugoslavije, 1961, 195 p.) covers similar ground less intensively.

## B. SURVEY STUDIES; ORGANIZATION OF THE ECONOMY; PERIODICALS

2594. Belgrade. Ekonomski institut Narodne Republike Srbije. Proizvodne snage NR Srbije (Productive capacities of the People's Republic of Serbia). Beograd, 1953. 631 p. Tables, bibliographies.

Essays and collections of data on resources and performance of various sectors of the Serbian economy with emphasis on the postwar period.

2595. Belgrade. Univerzitet. *Seminar za društveni sistem i međunarodne odnose FNRJ.* Ekonomska politika FNRJ (The economic policy of the Federal People's Republic of Yugoslavia). Beograd, Rad, 1958. 2 v. Illus.

A collection of essays on the performance and organization of various sectors of the economy, attention being concentrated on the three or four years up to 1957 and policy implications. A similar approach dealing with the succeeding years can be found in *Privredni sistem i ekonomska politika Jugoslavije* (The economic system and economic policy of Yugoslavia), 2d ed. (Beograd, Rad, 1962, 432 p.).

2596. Berković, Eva. Ekonomski problemi ishrane u SFR Jugoslaviji (Economic problems of food in Yugoslavia). Beograd, Savez ekonomista Jugoslavije, 1964. 212 p. Illus. (Ekonomska biblioteka, 21)

General analysis of food and economic development with a survey of Yugoslav consumption by region and projections to 1980.

2597. Bilandžić, Dušan. Management of Yugoslav Economy (1945-1966). Beograd, Yugoslav Trade Unions, 1967. 138 p.

Translation of *Upravljanje jugoslavenskom privredom (1945-1966).*

2598. Bobrowski, Czesław. La Yougoslavie socialiste. Paris, Librairie A. Colin, 1956. 237 p. (Cahiers de la Fondation nationale des sciences politiques, 77)

An analysis of the Yugoslav economy by a leading Polish economist.

2599. Byrnes, Robert F., *ed.* Yugoslavia. New York, Praeger, 1957. 488 p. Maps, tables. Bibliography: p. 447-469. (East Central Europe Under the Communists. Praeger Publications in Russian History and World Communism, no. 23). Bibliography: p. 447-469.

*See also* entries no. 2165 *and* 2485.

A collection of descriptions of early postwar Yugoslavia by sectors published under the sponsorship of the Mid-European Studies Center of the Free Europe Committee.

2600. Čobeljić, Nikola. Politika i metodi privrednog razvoja Jugoslavije, 1947-1956 (The policy and methods of the economic development

of Yugoslavia, 1947-1956). Beograd, Nolit, 1959. 378 p. Illus.,
bibliography. (Ekonomska biblioteka, 10)
>A stimulating analysis of factors determining growth by one of
Yugoslavia's leading "centralists."

2601. Conrad, Gisela J.   Die Wirtschaft Jugoslawiens. Berlin, Duncker
und Humblot, 1952. 176 p. Illus. (Berlin. Deutsches Institut für
Wirtschaftsforschung. Sonderhefte, n.F. Nr. 17. Reihe A: Forschung)
Bibliography: p. 172-173.

2602. Ekonomika Jugoslavije (The economy of Yugoslavia). Edited by
Jakov Sirotković and Vladimir Stipetić. Zagreb, Informator, 1967-
1968. 2 v. (Ekonomska biblioteka, 3 kolo, br. 4-5, 8-9)
>A detailed and up-to-date university text by a team of economists
writing on a wide variety of aspects of Yugoslavia's economy. *See
also*:
>Sirotković, Jakov, *ed.*   Suvremeni problemi jugoslavenske
privrede i ekonomska politika (Contemporary problems of the Yugoslav economy and economic policy). Zagreb, Informator, 1965. 250
p. (Ekonomska biblioteka, I kolo, broj 10)

2603. Hočevar, Toussaint.   The Structure of the Slovenian Economy,
1848-1963. New York, Studia Slovenica, 1965. 277 p. Map. (Studia
Slovenica, 5) Bibliography: p. 273-277.
>A broadly based survey of the data relevant for discussion of eco-
nomic change in Slovenia.

2604. Hoffman, George W., *and* Fred W. Neal.   Yugoslavia and the New
Communism. New York, Twentieth Century Fund, 1962. 546 p.
Maps, tables. Bibliography: p. 511-527.
>*See also* entries no. 2190, 2490, *and* 2577.
>Still the most useful survey in English of economic and political
institutions during the '50s.

2605. Kubović, Branko.   Regionalni aspekt privrednog razvitka Jugoslavije (The regional aspect of the economic development of Yugoslavia). Zagreb, 1961. 234 p. Map. Bibliography: p. 221-234.
(Biblioteka Ekonomskog pregleda)
>The author constructs and applies an index of economic develop-
ment to Yugoslav territorial units.

2606. Macura, Miloš.   Stanovništvo i radna snaga kao činioci privrednog
razvoja Jugoslavije (Population and labor as factors in Yugoslavia's
economic development). Beograd, Nolit, 1958. 373 p.
>*See also* entry no. 2245.
>Analysis of population structure and change in the first postwar
decade and their relation to other changes in Yugoslavia.

2607. Miljević, Đorđe, *and others.* Razvoj privrednog sistema FNRJ (Development of Yugoslavia's economic system). Beograd, 1954. 259 p.

A useful account of economic organization and its consequences during the administrative period and the early years of the new system. Later editions have omitted the data on the administrative period. For more recent surveys *see:*

Samardžija, Miloš. Privredni sistem Jugoslavije (The economic system of Yugoslavia). Beograd, Naučna knj., 1965-1966. 2 v. Illus.

Twenty Years of Yugoslav Economy. Belgrade, Međunarodna štampa-Interpress, 1967. 289, 78 p. Illus., map.

2608. Privreda FNRJ u periodu od 1947-1956 godine (Yugoslavia's economy in the period from 1947 to 1956). Beograd, Ekonomski institut FNRJ, 1957. 396 p. Illus., maps.

Essays and data collections on the performance of various sectors of the economy in the first postwar decade.

2609. Šefer, Berislav. Životni standard i privredni razvoj Jugoslavije (Standard of living and economic development in Yugoslavia). Zagreb, Informator, 1965. 205 p. Illus. Bibliography: p. 195-199. (Ekonomska biblioteka, II kolo, broj 2)

2610. Savez komunista Jugoslavije. *Centralni komitet. Plenum.* Aktuelni problemi borbe Saveza komunista Jugoslavije za sprovođenje reforme (Problems in the struggle of the League of Communists of Yugoslavia toward the implementation of [economic] reform). Beograd, Komunist, 1966. 352 p.

For an English-language treatment of the subject see *The Economic Reform in Yugoslavia* (Belgrade, Socialist Thought and Practice, 1965. 95 p.).

2611. Stajić, Stevan. Realni nacionalni dohodak Jugoslavije u periodima 1926-1939 i 1947-1956 (Real national income of Yugoslavia 1926-1939 and 1947-1956). *In* Ekonomski problemi; zbornik radova (Economic problems; collection of data). Beograd, Ekonomski institut FNRJ, 1957. p. 7-58. (Serija III: Ekonomika FNRJ)

Offers one of the best collections of national accounts data available for an interwar underdeveloped economy.

2612. United Nations. *Economic Commission for Europe.* Economic Survey of Europe for 1953. Geneva, 1954. p. 106-122.

Very useful annals and analyses by the United Nations have appeared periodically. *See also* the *Economic Survey of Europe for 1962,* part II, 1965, p. 1-17; *Economic Survey of Europe for 1965, 1966,* p. 96-102; *Economic Bulletin for Europe,* v. 10, no. 3 (Geneva, 1958), p. 43-62.

2613. Vasić, Velimir. Ekonomska politika Jugoslavije (The economic policies of Yugoslavia). 4th rev. and enl. edition. Beograd, Savremena administracija, 1967. 371 p.

A textbook for law school students.

2614. Vinski, Ivo. Procjena rasta fiksnih fondova Jugoslavije od 1946 do 1960 (An estimate of the growth of fixed assets in Yugoslavia from 1946 to 1960). Zagreb, Ekonomski institut NRH, 1962. 107 p.

For other studies of the capital stock, *see* Vinski's *Nacionalno bogatstvo Jugoslavije* (National wealth of Yugoslavia) (Zagreb, Ekonomski institut NRH, 1957, 144 p.); and also *Investicije na području Hrvatske u razdoblju između dva svetska rata* (Investments in the territory of Croatia in the period between the two world wars) (Beograd, Ekonomski institut FNRJ, 1955, 72 p.).

2615. Yugoslavia. *Biro za organizaciju uprave i privrede.* Novi privredni propisi (New economic regulations). Beograd, Rad, 1954. 364 p.

A collection of essays and questions and answers evaluating the new organization of the economy introduced in 1952-1953, edited by Aleksandar Adašević and others. Proceedings of a seminar held in Belgrade in March 1954.

2616. Zagreb. Ekonomski institut. Bibliografija ekonomske literature (Bibliography of literature in economics). Zagreb, 1962–

So far two volumes have appeared (1962: 156 p.; 1963: 315 p.). *See also*:

Jugoslovenski bibliografski institut. Organizacija i poslovanje privrednih organizacija (Organization and operations of economic organizations). Beograd, 1966. 2 v. Lists over 7,000 books and articles.

2617. The leading economic periodicals are:

Ekonomist (Economist). 1948– Beograd. Quarterly. Organ of the Association of Yugoslav Economists.

Ekonomski pregled (Economic review). 1950– Zagreb. Monthly. Organ of the Association of Economists of Croatia.

Socijalna politika (Social policies). 1951– Beograd. Monthly.

Statistička revija (Statistical review). 1951– Beograd. Quarterly. Issued by the Yugoslav Statistical Society.

## C. ECONOMIC THEORY, PLANNING, STATISTICS

2618. Černe, Franc. Planiranje in tržni mehanizem v ekonomski teoriji socializma (Planning and the market mechanism in the economic theory of socialism). Ljubljana, Cankarjeva založba, 1960. 369 p.

A survey and critique, including some Yugoslav theories. *Savremene buržoaske teorije vrednosti i cena* (Contemporary bourgeois theories of value and price) by Zoran Pjanić (Beograd, Institut društvenih nauka, 1965, 280 p.), provides a more technical analysis of the underlying ideas and of recent developments in the West.

2619. Fisher, Jack C. Yugoslavia, a Multinational State; Regional Difference and Administrative Response. San Francisco, Chandler Publishing Co., 1966. 244 p. Illus., maps. Bibliography: p. 223-231.
*See also* entries no. 2207, 2488, *and* 2525.
A statistical analysis of regional policies.

2620. Horvat, Branko. Ekonomska teorija planske privrede (Economic theory of the planned economy). Beograd, Kultura, 1961. 314 p. Illus., bibliographies.
A challenging and original Marxist interpretation of economic development in the 20th century. A slightly modified English translation appeared as *Towards a Theory of Planned Economy* by Branko Horvat (Belgrade, Yugoslav Institute of Economic Research, 1964, 244 p.). For an earlier Yugoslav reinterpretation of Marx, see *Marxov zakon vrednosti* (Marx' law of value) by Aleksander Bajt (Ljubljana, 1953, 362 p.).

2621. Korać, Miladin, *ed.* Problemi teorije i prakse socijalističke robne proizvodnje u Jugoslaviji (Problems of the theory and practice of socialist commodity production in Yugoslavia). Zagreb, Informator, 1965. 207 p.
A collection of essays discussing the "income-prices" theory. A useful discussion of this and other Yugoslav theories of price, markets, and planning is contained in *Planning and the Market in Yugoslav Economic Thought* by Deborah C. Milenkovitch (New York, Columbia University [Ph.D. dissertation], 1966).

2622. Pejovich, Svetozar. The Market-Planned Economy of Yugoslavia. Minneapolis, University of Minnesota Press, 1966. 160 p. Illus., bibliographies.

2623. Sirotković, Jakov, *ed.* Ekonomika Jugoslavije (The economics of Yugoslavia). Zagreb, Informator, 1964. 2 v. (Ekonomska biblioteka, I kolo, broj 4) Bibliography: v. 1, p. 241-245.

2624. Waterston, Albert. Planning in Yugoslavia. Baltimore, Johns Hopkins, 1964. 109 p.
An "official" description of the planning process. For a more detailed account, see *Sistem planiranja u jugoslovenskoj privredi* (The system of planning in the Yugoslav economy) by Borivoje Jelić (Beograd, 1962, 266 p.). *See also* "Yugoslav Planning" by Savka Dapčević-Kućar in *Planning Economic Development*, edited by Everett Hagen (Homewood, Ill., Irwin, 1963), p. 183-220.

2625. Yugoslavia. *Savezni zavod za privredno planiranje.* Metode bilansiranja strukturnih proporcija u planu privrednog razvoja (Methods of balancing structural proportions in the plan of economic development). Beograd, 1965. 165 p. (*Its* Studije i analize, 22)
Presentation and analysis of a 29 sector input-output model for

1962. A model for 1955 was presented in *Međusobni odnosi privrednih delatnosti Jugoslavije u 1955* (Mutual relations of economic activity in Yugoslavia in 1955), published by Savezni zavod za statistiku (Beograd, 1957, 39 p.). For a theoretical analysis of input-output models containing occasional reference to Yugoslavia see *Međusektorska analiza* (Intersectoral analysis) by Branko Horvat (Zagreb, Narodne novine, 1962, 224 p.).

2626. Yugoslavia. *Savezni zavod za statistiku.* Jugoslavija, 1945-1964; statistički pregled (Yugoslavia 1945-1964; statistical survey). Beograd, 1965. 373 p. Illus., map.
   *See also* entry no. 2250.

## D. AGRICULTURE, INDUSTRY, LABOR, TRANSPORT

2627. Aćimović, Miroslav R. Bibliografska građa o radničkom samoupravljanju u Jugoslaviji . . . (Bibliographic information on the workers' self-management in Yugoslavia . . . ). Beograd, Institut društvenih nauka, 1966. 855 p.

2628. Bajt, Aleksander. Produktivnost rada i društveno-privredni uslovi njenog povećanja (Labor productivity and the socioeconomic conditions of its growth). Beograd, Nolit, 1960. 330 p.
   A general analytic discussion with some analysis of Yugoslav data.

2629. Bakarić, Vladimir. O poljoprivredi i problemima sela; govori i članci (Agriculture and problems of the village; addresses and articles). Edited by Slavko Komar. Beograd, Kultura, 1960. 589 p.
   For other readings on various economic aspects of agriculture *see*:
   Brašić, Branko M. Land Reform and Ownership in Yugoslavia. 1919-1953. New York, Mid-European Studies Center, 1954. 169 p. Bibliography: p. 157-169. (Mid-European Studies Center. Publication no. 17)
   Markovitch, Tihomir J. Le revenu agricole en Yougoslavie. Genève, Droz, 1967.
   Matić, Milan. Samoupravljanje u poljoprivrednim preduzećima (Self-management in agricultural enterprises). Beograd, Institute društvenih nauka, 1967. 143 p. Summaries in French and Russian.
   Milanović, Petar. Formiranje i raspodela dohotka seljačkih domaćinstava u svetla najnovijih procesa na selu (Formation and distribution of income of peasant households in the light of the most recent developments in the village). Beograd, Zadružna knjiga, 1966. 174 p. Diagrs.
   Popović, Svetolik. Agricultural Policy in Yugoslavia. Beograd, Međunarodna politika, 1964. 55 p. Translation of *Agrarna politika Jugoslavije.*
   Vasić, Velimir. Putevi razvitka socijalizma u poljoprivredi Jugo-

slavije (Paths of development of socialism in Yugoslavia's agriculture). Beograd, Rad, 1960, 267 p. Illus.

2630. Elias, Andrew.   The Labor Force of Yugoslavia. Washington, D.C., Bureau of the Census, 1965. 41 p. (International Population Statistics Reports, Ser. P-90, no. 22)

2631. Farkaš, Vladimir.   Ekonomika jugoslavenske industrije (The economics of Yugoslav industry). Zagreb, Informator, 1965. 269 p. Illus., bibliographies. (Ekonomska biblioteka. I kolo, broj 6)
A survey of postwar organization and policy.

2632. International Labour Office.   Workers' Management in Yugoslavia. Geneva, 1962. 320 p. Illus., map. Bibliography: p. 311-320. (ILO Studies and Reports, New Ser., no. 64)
*See also* entry no. 2683.
The most complete study of the workers' councils, including firsthand observation of some 20 factories during 1959-1960. For a history of the development of the councils in Yugoslavia see *Razvoj sistema radničkog samoupravljanja u FNRJ na području radnih odnosa* (Development of the system of worker self-management in Yugoslavia in the area of labor relations), by Ivan Perić (Zagreb, Institut za društveno upravljanje, 1962, 187 p.).

2633. Kukoleča, Stevan.   Industrija Jugoslavije, 1918-1938 (Yugoslavia's industry, 1918-1938). Beograd, Balkanska stampa, 1941. 537 p.
A massive collection of statistical and textual material on the structure of industry and interwar changes.

2634. Matić, S., *and others*.   Aktivnost radnih ljudi u samoupravljanju radnom organizacijom (Activity of working people in self-management through the workplace organization). Zagreb, Institut za društveno upravljanje NRH, 1962. 208 p. Bibliography: p. 207-208.
Results of an interview survey of workers in factories in a small Yugoslav town (Varaždin). See also *Workers' Councils: The Yugoslav Experience* by Jiri T. Kolaja (New York, Praeger, 1966, 84 p.), which reports on interviews with workers and officials in two factories.

2635. Prva decenija radničkog samoupravljanja (The first decade of workers' self-management). Beograd, Rad, 1960. 499 p. Illus.
A collection of pertinent speeches, anecdotes, legislation, and statistics. To be supplemented by the following English-language translation of the Serbian original:
Marković, Dragan.   Factories to Their Workers. Chronicle about Workers' Management in Yugoslavia. Belgrade, Privredni pregled, 1965. 290 p. Tables, illus. Bibliography: p. 253-291. For the control aspects of enterprises *see*:
Krajčević, Franjo.   Kontrola i revizija poslovanja poduzeća (In-

spection and auditing of the business of enterprises). Zagreb, Školska knjiga, 1966. 228 p.

2636. Radnički savjet i upravni odbor; priručnik za kadrove (The workers' council and management board; handbook for cadres). Zagreb, Informator, 1957. 391 p.

A survey of relevant laws, sample statutes, and regulations of the bodies and evaluation of alternatives. For a detailed survey of the legal aspects of enterprise operation, see *Ekonomika preduzeća* (Economics of the enterprise), by Stevan Kukoleča (Zagreb, Informator, 1961, 2 v.). Later editions exist. The most recent collections of laws and regulations on the subject is contained in:

Yugoslavia. *Laws, statutes, etc.* Propisi o izboru i opozivu organa upravljanja u radnim organizacijama . . . (Regulations concerning the election and recall of management organs in workers' organizations . . .). Compiled by Julije Kovačić. Zagreb, Narodne novine, 1965. 240 p.

2637. Sturmthal, Adolf F.    Workers Councils; a Study of Workplace Organization on Both Sides of the Iron Curtain. Cambridge, Mass., Harvard University Press, 1964. 217 p.

The Yugoslav councils placed in a comparative context.

2638. Tomasevich, Jozo.    Peasants, Politics, and Economic Change in Yugoslavia. Stanford, Stanford University Press, 1955. 743 p. Maps, tables. Bibliography: p. 703-726.

*See also* entries no. 2389, 2436, *and* 2543.

The definitive work on interwar agriculture containing, in addition, a very useful survey of pre-World War I agrarian history.

2639. Vogelnik, Dolfe.    Urbanizacija kao odraz privrednog razvoja FNRJ (Urbanization as a reflection of economic development in Yugoslavia). Beograd, Savez društava ekonomista Jugoslavije, 1961. 311 p. Illus. (Ekonomska biblioteka, 13)

An empirical analysis of urban structure and change based largely on census data and covering both the interwar and postwar periods.

## E. MONEY, FINANCE, COMMERCE, HOUSING

2640. Bogoev, Ksente.    Lokalne finansije Jugoslavije (Local finance in Yugoslavia). Beograd, SEJ, 1964. 376 p. (Ekonomska biblioteka, 20)

A survey and analysis of organization and statistics, 1947-1960, including some discussion of the early '60s.

2641. Miljanić, Nikola.    Novac i kredit u procesu društvene reprodukcije (Money and credit in the process of social reproduction). Zagreb, Informator, 1964. 96 p. Illus. Bibliography: p. 89-91. (Ekonomska biblioteka, 1)

Survey and analysis of monetary circulation and its impact during the '50s and early '60s in Yugoslavia.

2642. Tišma, Toša.    Javne finansije (Public finances). Zagreb, Informator, 1964. 352 p.

A survey of taxes and expenditures of the Yugoslav government during the '50s and early '60s.

2643. Žuvela, Ivo.    Međunarodni ekonomski odnosi (Foreign economic relations). Zagreb, Školska knj., 1966. 331 p. Bibliographies.

A university textbook. For regulations governing foreign trade and exchange, *see*:

Yugoslavia. *Laws, statutes, etc.*    Zbirka spoljnotrgovinskih i deviznih propisa (Collection of regulations concerning foreign trade and foreign exchange). Beograd, 1967. 527 p.

Yugoslavia. *Laws, statutes, etc.*    Društveni plan Jugoslavije za 1965 godinu . . . (The social plan of Yugoslavia for 1965 . . .). Beograd, Izd. Službenog lista SFRJ, 1965. 83 p. Contains the law concerning the social plan for 1965 as well as projections through 1970.

# 50

# the society

*by Joel M. Halpern*
*(with the exception of section F)*

## A. OVERVIEW

2644. Adamic, Louis.   The Native's Return. New York, Harper, 1934. 370 p. Illus.

> Account of social conditions in Yugoslavia in the '30s, after a return visit by a Slovene immigrant to America, with interesting observations on the impact of the depression in Slovenia and on the growth of Belgrade.

2645. Auty, Phyllis.   Yugoslavia. *In* Warriner, Doreen, *ed.* Contrasts in Emerging Societies; Readings in the Social and Economic History of South-Eastern Europe in the Nineteenth Century. Bloomington, Indiana University Press, 1965. p. 281-387.

> Brings together valuable sources on rural life, including previously unpublished archival data. Together with Jozo Tomasevich's *Peasants, Politics, and Economic Change in Yugoslavia* (Stanford, 1955), provides basic historical information for understanding Yugoslavia's socio-economic structure.

2646. Balch, Emily Greene.   Our Slavic Fellow Citizens. New York, Charities Publication Committee, 1910. 536 p.

> Information on the social life of Slovenes, Croats, and Dalmatians

* See also chapter 46, section B.

in their home setting and their subsequent adaptation in the United States early in the 20th century.

2647. Barić, Lorraine.  Traditional Groups and New Economic Opportunities in Rural Yugoslavia. *In* Firth, Raymond, *ed.* Themes in Economic Anthropology. London, New York, Tavistock Publications, 1967. p. 253-278.

> Attempts to isolate social variables associated with low productivity and low investment in agriculture in Yugoslavia. *See also* Alexander Vucinich's "Rural Yugoslavia" in *Rural Sociology*, v. 12, 1947, no. 3: 237-245, for an assessment of the agrarian reforms in the immediate postwar period.

2648. Belgrade. *Institut društvenih nauka. Odeljenje za naučnu dokumentaciju.*  Bibliografska anotacija dela empirijskog karaktera iz oblast društvenih nauka (Bibliographic annotations on empirical works in the social sciences). Beograd, 1964. 294 p. (Mimeographed)

> Limited to Serbo-Croat materials in the postwar period. The Institut društvenih nauka, Centar za istraživanje javnog mnenja, in Belgrade, published between 1964 and 1966 a series of monographs on public opinion surveys of such topics as standard of living, work conditions, impact of mass communications, and economic reforms.

2649. Blagojević, Borislav, *ed.*  Collection of Yugoslav Laws. Belgrade, Institute of Comparative Law.

> *See* v. 1, Legal Status of Agricultural Land, 1962, 91 p.; v. 4, Family Law, 1962, 61 p.; v. 10, Inheritance Law, 1964, 78 p.

2650. Brown, Alec.  Yugoslav Life and Landscape. London, Elek, 1954. 196 p.

> A perceptive description of Yugoslav society by a writer who spent over 30 years in close association with the area.

2651. Coon, Carleton S.  Racial History. *In* Kerner, Robert J., *ed.* Yugoslavia. Berkeley, University of California Press, 1949. p. 24-32.

2652. Čulibrk, Svetozar.  Želje i strahovanja naroda Jugoslavije (Hopes and fears of the people of Yugoslavia). Grebo, Zlata. Želje i strahovanja Jugoslavenske žene (Hopes and fears of the Yugoslav woman). Beograd, Institut društvenih nauka, 1965. 354 p.

> These two related studies form part of an international survey on happiness and consider the relationships among factors of economic position, health, and social status and how they influence personal and national aspirations of individuals. Nationality differences are discussed. Brief English summary. The data are also discussed in Hadley Cantril's *The Pattern of Human Concerns* (New Brunswick, N.J., Rutgers University Press, 1965, 427 p.).

2653. Dedijer, Vladimir.  The Beloved Land. London, Macgibbon and Kee, 1961. 375 p. Illus.

A valuable biographical account particularly useful for insights into the Hercegovinian society from which the author stems.

2654. Edwards, Lovett F.   Introducing Yugoslavia. London, Methuen, 1954. 255 p.

A fine general account by a writer who lived in Yugoslavia more than 15 years. Contains a useful annotated bibliography of general works.

2655. Evans, Arthur J.   Through Bosnia and the Herzegovina on Foot during the Insurrection, August and September 1875. London, Longmans, Green, 1876. 435 p. Illus., map.

A valuable historical account of contemporary social conditions, by the distinguished archaeologist.

2656. Garašanin, M., *and* J. Kovačević.   Pregled materijalne kulture južnih Slovena u ranom srednjem veku (Survey of the material culture of the South Slavs in the early Middle Ages). Beograd, Prosveta, 1950. 239 p. Bibliography, illus.

A primary concern in this useful survey is the origins ("ethnogenesis") of the South Slavs. An excellent annotated bibliography lists 232 items. The subject is treated in a somewhat different perspective in *Etnologija naroda Jugoslavije. Materijalna kultura* (Ethnology of Yugoslavia's peoples. The material culture) by Petar Vlahović (Beograd, Filozofski fakultet, 1968, 192 p., bibliographies).

2657. Goričar, Jože.   On Some Problems of Methodology in Yugoslav Empirical Sociology. *In* Puhan, Ivo, *and* Seymour Gross, *eds.* Selected Problems of Social Sciences and Humanities; Papers From the Yugoslav-American Colloquium, Ohrid, 1962. Bloomington, Indiana University Press; Skopje, University of Skopje, 1963. 160 p.

Discusses the applicability of Western sociological concepts to Yugoslav problems. For related discussions of sociological theory in Yugoslavia *see* Predrag Vranički's "Socialism and the Problem of Alienation" in *Praxis*, v. 1, 1965: 307-317. In the same journal *see also* Mihailo Marković's "Man and Technology," v. 2, 1966: 343-352, and Vojin Milić's "A Contribution to the Theory of Social Conflict," v. 1, 1965: 536-550.

The viewpoint of a Yugoslav sociologist who is also an administrator is expressed in Anton Vratuša's "The Sociologists and the Policy Makers in Yugoslavia" in *Transactions of the Fifth World Congress of Sociology* (Washington, D.C., September 1962), v. 1: 45-58. Additional discussions of Yugoslav society by Yugoslav social scientists can be found in the journal *Socialist Thought and Practice* (Belgrade); e.g., in articles such as "Socialism and Class Change" by Miroslav Pečujlić (v. 27, 1967: 3-37), and "Revaluation of Intellectual Work" by Dušan Popović (v. 27, 1967: 38-53).

2658. Gt. Brit. *Naval Intelligence Division.*   Jugoslavia. Norwich, Eng.,

Jarrold and Sons, 1944-1945. 3 v. (*Its* Geographical Handbook Series)

> Useful background materials in volume two on the people (ch. 3), social conditions (ch. 4), and public health (ch. 7), and in volume three on growth and distribution of population (ch. 1).

2659. Kojić, Branislav.   Seoska arhitektura i rurizam (Village architecture and "rural urbanism"). Beograd, Građevinska knjiga, 1958. 204 p. Bibliography, illus., maps.

> Considers Yugoslavia and especially Serbia from the point of view of the human geographer and architect. Concerned with types of structures and settlement patterns in their overall socio-economic context. Many excellent diagrams, including plans for the future. The author's earlier *Stara gradska i seoska arhitektura u Srbiji* (Old urban and village architecture in Serbia) (Beograd, Prosveta, 1949, 190 p.) deals with the 18th and 19th centuries, with diagrammatic presentation of changing styles.

2660. Miličić, Mirko.   Nepoznata Dalmatija (Unknown Dalmatia). Zagreb, Arhitekt, 1935. 202 p. Illus.

> Study of Dalmatian house types, settlement patterns, and home industries. Many illustrations and diagrams.

2661. Tomašić, Dinko. Personality and Culture in Eastern European Politics. New York, George W. Stewart, 1948. 249 p. Map. Bibliography: p. 239-249.

> An émigré Croat sociologist's view of Yugoslav nationality questions. Useful annotated bibliography.

2662. Tornquist, David.   Look East, Look West; the Socialist Adventure in Yugoslavia. New York, Macmillan, 1966. 310 p. Illus.

> *See also* entry no. 2184.

> An account by an American writer who worked as translator for a Belgrade publishing firm in the early '60s, with interesting information on aspects of urban living conditions and on the operation of Workers' Councils in different kinds of enterprises.

2663. West, Rebecca.   Black Lamb and Grey Falcon; a Journey Through Yugoslavia. New York, Viking Press, 1941. 2 v. Plates, ports., maps. Bibliography: p. 1151-1158.

> *See also* entry no. 2185.

> The classic travel account of Yugoslavia in the interwar period, politically biased but sensitive and perceptive. Contains a short but useful bibliography.

2664. The Yugoslav Commune.   International Social Science Journal, v. 12, 1961, no. 3: 379-469.

> A general discussion with articles by Yugoslav social scientists. For an analytical appraisal viewing the commune as a device for resolving regional interests *see* Jack C. Fisher's "The Yugoslav Com-

mune" in *World Politics*, v. 16, 1964, no. 3: 418-444. Fisher discusses urban communes in "City Planning and Housing Administration in Yugoslavia" in *Urban Affairs Quarterly*, Dec. 1965: 1-13.

## B. RURAL LIFE AND PROBLEMS

2665. Bićanić, Rudolf. Occupational Heterogeneity of Peasant Families in the Period of Accelerated Industrialization. *In* World Congress of Sociology, 3rd, Amsterdam, 1956. Transactions, v. 4, 1956: 80-96.

A good survey of the situation of peasant-workers, i.e., those who own and work land while holding jobs in industry.

2666. Halpern, Joel M. Farming as a Way of Life: Yugoslav Peasant Attitudes. *In* Karcz, Jerzy, *ed.* Soviet and East European Agriculture. Berkeley, University of California Press, 1967. p. 356-391.

Evaluates economic and political factors involved in both forcing and attracting peasants off the land. For a discussion of the problems of the transitional status of the peasant-worker *see* the author's "Yugoslav Peasant Society in Transition — Stability in Change" in *The Anthropological Quarterly*, v. 36, July 1963: 156-182; for biographical accounts *see* "The Process of Modernization as Reflected in Yugoslav Peasant Biographies," Kroeber Anthropological Society (Berkeley), Special Publication, no. 1, 1967: 109-126.

2667. Halpern, Joel M. Peasant Culture and Urbanization in Yugoslavia. Human Organization, v. 24, Summer 1965: 162-174.

Considers the impact of peasant culture on urban life and also compares the growth and development of Zagreb and Belgrade. For similar problems discussed from the viewpoint of the urban geographer see Jack C. Fisher's "Planning the City of Socialist Man," in *Journal of the American Institute of Planners*, v. 28, no. 4, Nov. 1962: 251-265.

2668. Hrženjak, Juraj, *ed.* Društveno kretanje u naselju Jalžabet 1945-1961 (Social development of Jalžabet village 1945-1961). Sociologija, v. 4, 1962, no. 1-2: 283 p.

Entire issue devoted to a study of a north Croatian village, with articles on historical demography, agricultural economics, health, and social structure. A somewhat parallel study of another Croatian village in Istria, but with emphasis on historical and formal institutional structures is Vjekoslav Bratulić's *Rovinjsko selo* (Village in the Rovinj region) (Zagreb, Jadranski institut, Jugoslavenska akademija znanosti i umjetnosti, 1959, 206 p.).

2669. Kostić, Cvetko. Seljaci industriski radnici (Peasants as industrial workers). Beograd, Rad, 1955. 250 p.

Surveys the historical background of peasant involvement with industry, the reasons for earlier resistance to off-farm work, and the conflicts involved in residing in the village while working in a factory. A summary of these views appears in English in the author's "Peasant Industrial Workers in Yugoslavia," in *Man in India*, v. 39: 221-234. Also, the July-September 1953 issue (v. 1) of *Sociologija sela* is a valuable source for articles on the socioeconomic transformation of village life under the impact of industrialization.

2670. Lodge, Olive. Peasant Life in Yugoslavia. London, Seeley, Service, 1942. 332 p. Illus., map.

The standard English-language source on Yugoslav peasant life in the interwar period.

2671. Marković, Petar J. Strukturne promene na selu kao rezultat ekonomskog razvitka, 1900-1960 (Structural changes in the village as a result of economic development in the period 1900-1960). Beograd, Zadružna knjiga, 1963. 164 p. Illus. Bibliography: p. 153-155. *See also* entry no. 2246.

Sees a gradual enlargement of the social sector in agriculture and increasing peasant involvement with the market and social sector. Extensive use of statistical data. English summary.

2672. Martić, Mirko. Bibliografija sociološke i srodne literature o problemima sela i poljoprivrede (Bibliography of sociological and related literature on village problems and agriculture). Sociologija sela, v. 2, Oct.-Dec. 1963: 91-127.

Useful list of pertinent materials, with both Serbo-Croat and Western language sources.

2673. Stojadinović, Miloslav, *ed.* Naše selo (Our village). Beograd, Savremena opština, 1929. 604 p. Illus.

A collection of articles by professors and politicians, mainly on Serbia but also dealing with many other areas. A good reflection of the general status of the peasantry and the state of knowledge of village society at this time. Also discusses government plans for rural improvements.

2674. Trouton, Ruth. Peasant Renaissance in Yugoslavia, 1900-1950. London, Routledge and Kegan Paul, 1952. 344 p. Bibliography: p. 325-330. *See also* entry no. 2535.

Provides much helpful background information although the interpretations are somewhat journalistic.

2675. Vukosavljević, Sreten V. Istorija seljačkog druètva (A history of peasant society). Beograd, Naučna knjiga, 1953. 335 p. (Srpska akademija nauka. Posebna izdanja, 209; Institut za izučavanje sela, 1)

Concerned mainly with landed property and its inheritance, from an historical and legal viewpoint. The role of village level institutions and their relationship to the national state is a principal theme. Based on field data. A subsequent volume (Posebna izdanja, 390,

426 p.) deals with the physical dimensions of village life: settlement patterns, household units, architecture, and relationships to the local agricultural economy. French summaries.

## C. URBAN LIFE AND PROBLEMS

2676. Dobrović, Nikola.   Urbanizam kroz vekove; (v. 1) Jugoslavija (Urbanism through the centuries; [v. 1] Yugoslavia). Beograd, Naučna knjiga, 1950. 416 p. Illus.

Relates the urban evolution of several hundred Yugoslav towns, in many cases beginning in medieval times. There is a detailed section on Belgrade and a consideration of future planning. Profuse illustrations.

2677. Fisher, Jack C.   Urban Analysis: A Case Study of Zagreb, Yugoslavia. *In* Association of American Geographers. Annals, v. 53, Sept. 1963: 266-284.

An historical case study, including a discussion of current city planning in Zagreb.

2678. Günther, Horst.   Die Verstädterung in Jugoslawien. Darstellung und Probleme. Wiesbaden, Harrassowitz, 1966. 224 p. Maps. Bibliography: p. 220-224.

*See also* entry no. 2208.

2679. Ilić, Miloš.   Socijalna struktura i pokretljivost radničke klase Jugoslavije (Social structure and mobility of the Yugoslav working class). Beograd, Institut društvenih nauka, Odeljenje za sociologiju, 1963. 542 p.

A basic study on geographic and occupational mobility in the postwar period. The sample included some 5,000 workers from all the republics. English summary, p. 395-406. For a more recent overview *see* Vojin Milić's "General Trends in Social Mobility in Yugoslavia" in *Acta Sociologica*, v. 9, 1965: 116-136.

2680. Kolaja, Jiri T.   Workers' Councils: The Yugoslav Experience. New York, Frederick A. Praeger, 1966. 84 p.

Observations based on a 1959 study of two factories in the vicinity of Belgrade.

2681. Kremenšek, Slavko.   Kulturna podobna železničarskega naselja na robu Ljubljane pred prvo vojno (Cultural configuration of the railway workers' district of Ljubljana prior to the First World War). Etnološki pregled, no. 6/7, 1965: 81-88.

A unique sociological study of an urban community of peasant origin, maintaining that railroad men, somewhat better off than other groups of workers, had more of a sense of community.

2682. Maksimović, Branko.   Urbanizam u Srbiji, osnivanje i rekonstrukcija varoši u 19om veku (Town planning in Serbia; the founding and reconstruction of towns in the 19th century). Beograd, Građevinska knjiga, 1962. 197 p. Illus., maps.

> Documents the efforts at planning during the period of the emergence of the Serbian state when a new urban society was created. English summary, p. 189-192.

2683. International Labor Office. Workers' Management in Yugoslavia. Geneva, 1962. 320 p. Illus., map. (ILO Studies and Reports, New Series, no. 64) Bibliography: p. 311-320.
    *See also* entry no. 2632.

> A general description with detailed bibliography. For more detail see chapter four of Adolf Sturmthal's *Workers' Councils; a Study of Workplace Organization* (Cambridge, Harvard University Press, 1964, 217 p.), which deals with Yugoslavia.

## D. FAMILY, WOMEN, YOUTH

2684. Barić, Lorraine. Levels of Change in Yugoslav Kinship. *In* Freedman, Maurice, *ed.* Social Organization. London, Cass, 1967. p. 1-24.

> Maintains that the extent of communications through kin links brings a wider variety of bilateral kin and affines into day-to-day contact than when kin group, work group, and local community largely coincided.

2685. Burić, Olivera, *and* Anđelka Zečević. Family Authority, Marital Satisfaction, and the Social Network in Yugoslavia. Journal of Marriage and the Family, May 1967: 325-336.

> Presents data to support the conclusion that the higher the social position of the husband, the lower his traditional authority in the family, and the more advanced his education, the lower the wife's satisfaction with marriage. *See also* Olivera Burić's "Attitudes Regarding the Status of Women in Yugoslavia" in *International Social Science Journal*, v. 14, 1962, no. 1: 166-174.

2686. Burić, Olivera, *and* Željka Perak. Bibliografija radova o Jugoslavenskoj porodici 1956-1960 (Bibliography of works on the Yugoslav family, 1956-1960). Sociologija, v. 3, 1966: 137-148.

2687. Đurić, Suzana, *and* Gordana Dragičević. Women in Yugoslav Society and Economy. Translated by Anđelija Vujović. Beograd, Međunarodna politika, 1965. 35 p.

2688. Erlich, Vera St. Family in Transition, a Study of 300 Yugoslav Villages. Princeton, Princeton University Press, 1966. 469 p.

> A useful prewar survey of family relationships, based on material collected from village teachers; substantially a translation of the author's *Porodica u transformaciji* (Family in transition) (Zagreb, Naprijed, 1964, 490 p.). *See also* Raymond E. Crist's "The Peasant

Problem in Yugoslavia" in *Scientific Monthly*, May, 1940: 385-402, for economic background on roughly the same period.

2689. Filipović, Milenko S.    Nesrodnička i predvojena zadruga (The zadruga of nonrelatives and the split zadruga). Beograd, Smiljeva, 1945. 61 p.

Considers the role of nonrelatives in the formation of household units in the culturally different regions of Yugoslavia.

2690. Filipović, Milenko S.    Symbolic Adoption among the Serbs. Ethnology, v. 4, 1965, no. 1: 66-71.

Treats a form of ritual kinship in which an individual substitutes for a deceased person in assuming fictive bonds of kinship with the family of the latter.

2691. Filipovič, Milenko S.    Vicarious Paternity among Serbs and Croats. Southwestern Journal of Anthropology, v. 14, Summer 1958: 156-167.

Considers institutional forms whereby barren women can conceive by men other than their husbands.

2692. Hammel, Eugene A.    Serbo-Croatian Kinship Terminology. *In* Kroeber Anthropological Society. Papers, no. 16, Spring 1957: 45-75.

Collates terminology from 10 sources (informants and literature) on Serbia, Croatia, and Slavonia.

2693. Mosely, Philip E.    The Distribution of the Zadruga Within South-Eastern Europe. *In* Jewish Social Studies. Publication, no. 5, 1953: 219-230.

Identifies three regional zadruga types.

2694. Mosely, Philip E.    The Peasant Family: The Zadruga or Communal Joint-Family in the Balkans and Its Recent Evolution. *In* Ware, C. F., *ed.* The Cultural Approach to History. New York, Columbia University Press, 1940. p. 95-108.

*See also* entry no. 225.

A very useful introduction to the South Slav extended family.

2695. Pušić, Eugene.    The Family in the Process of Social Change in Yugoslavia. Sociological Review, v. 5, Dec. 1957: 207-224.

Relates historical and legal factors to aspects of contemporary changes.

2696. Lodge, Olive. Socio-Biological Studies in the Balkans. Population, v. 1, Nov. 1934: 55-82; v. 2, Nov. 1935: 111-148.

Concerned mainly with infant and maternal mortality, with data based on visits to individual villages.

2697. Rašević, Miroslav.    Regionalno poreklo studenata Jugoslavije u

1961-1962 (Regional origins of Yugoslav [university] students in 1961-1962). Beograd, Institut društvenih nauka, Centar za demografska istraživanja, 1964. 126 p.

Correlates students' places of permanent residence and their place of education. English summary. A related work, also with English summary is Vojin Milić's "Socijalno poreklo učenika srednjih škola i studenata" (Social origins of secondary school pupils and university students) in *Statistička revija*, no. 1/2, 1959: 43-87.

2698. Rayner, Louise.    Women in a Village. London, William Heinemann, 1957. 247 p.

An Englishwoman's account of life in a village near Belgrade during the German occupation.

2699. Sicard, Émile.    La zadruga Sud-Slave dans l'évolution du groupe domestique. Paris, Éditions Ophrys, 1943. 705 p.

The most comprehensive study of the zadruga available, with a wealth of field observations and detailed historical data. The author worked in Yugoslavia from 1935 to 1941, returning after the war to prepare a second volume dealing with both urban and rural family groups: *Problèmes familiaux chez les Slaves du sud* (Paris, Éditions familiales de France, 1947, 207 p.). He also considers the zadruga in Serbian fiction in his *La zadruga dans la littérature Serbe, 1850-1912* (Paris, Éditions Ophrys, 1943, 137 p.).

2700. Silajdžić, Alija.    Some Problems of Family as a Factor in Upbringing. *In* Seminar on Social and Cultural Problems (sponsored by the University of Texas and the University of Ljubljana), Lake Bohinj, August 1961. Papers. Ljubljana, 1963. 432 p.

Deals mainly with illegitimacy and divorce. *See also* the author's empirical studies of court records relating to divorce, "Razvod braka na području okružnog suda u Dubrovniku" (Divorce in the area served by the Dubrovnik District Court) in *Godišnjak pravnog fakulteta*, v. 10, 1962: 33-58; and "Neka pitanja iz brako-razvodne prakse okružnog suda u Sarajevu" (Some questions relating to divorce practices in the Sarajevo District Court) in *Godišnjak pravnog fakulteta*, v. 2, 1954: 149-168.

For a statistical analysis of marriage and divorce on a national level in 1953 *see* Vojin Milić's "Sklapanje i razvod braka prema zanimanju" (Marriage and divorce correlated with occupation) in *Statistička Revija*, v. 7, Mar. 1957: 19-44, with English summary.

2701. Supek, Rudi.    Omladina na Putu bratstva; psiho-sociologija radne akcije (Youth on Brotherhood Road; psychosociology of the voluntary work movement). Beograd, Mladost, 1963. 344 p. Illus.

*See also* entry no. 2715.

Analyzes the behavior of the voluntary youth brigades in summer road construction projects, based in part on a questionnaire survey. French summary, p. 333-344.

## E. SPECIAL ASPECTS

2702. Georgeoff, John.   Nationalism in the History of the Textbooks of Yugoslavia and Bulgaria. Comparative Education Review, v. 10, Oct. 1966: 422-450.

Interesting comparisons, emphasizing the ways in which school texts present the history of their own country and virtually ignore that of the neighboring nation.

2703. Johnson, Chalmers A.   Peasant Nationalism and Communist Power: the Emergence of Revolutionary China, 1937-1945. Stanford, Stanford University Press, 1962. 256 p.

Interesting comparisons are made between the Chinese and Yugoslav experiences (p. 156-175).

2704. Kostić, Darinka M.   Promene u društvenom životu kolonista (Changes in the social life of colonists). Beograd, Institut društvenih nauka, 1963. 126 p.

Compares a group of colonists who migrated after the war from Montenegro to Vojvodina with others who remained in their place of origin. English summary. For specific studies of individual immigrant communities in Vojvodina *see* the several monographs published by Matica srpska (Novi Sad) and written by Branislav Bukovar (1957), by Branislav Rusić (1958), by Jovan Trifunoski (1958), by Milorad Vasović (1959); and for a general statement *see* Milenko S. Filipović's *Proučavanje naseljavanja Vojvodine* (Investigations of the settling of Vojvodina) (1958, 20 p.).

2705. Petrović, Aleksandar.   Banjane, Socijalno-zdravstvene i higijenske prilike (Banjane; public health and hygiene conditions). Beograd, Biblioteka Centralnog higijenskog zavoda, 1932. 160 p. (Zbornik zdravstvenih proučavanja i ispitivanja sela i narodnog života, v. 11)

An early public health study notable for its emphasis on village nutrition and peasant budgets. In the same series and by the same author are: *Raspored radnog vremena u jednoj seoskoj porodici u Rušnju* (Arrangement of work schedules in a Rušanj peasant family) (v. 14, 1934, 41 p.), and *Rakovica, Socijalno-zdravstvene i higijenske prilike* (v. 2, 1939, 169 p.). The latter is similar to the Banjane study but includes a useful new section on the medical and social-psychological problems of peasant women.

2706. Vukanović, T. P.   The Gypsy Population in Yugoslavia. Journal of the Gypsy Lore Society, v. 42, 1963, no. 1: 10-27.

Presents statistical data on the distribution and economic status of Gypsy groups in Yugoslavia in 1948 and 1953, based largely on census materials.

# F. PSYCHOLOGY

*by Josef Brožek*

## 1. Croatia

2707. Bujas, Zoran. Osnove psihofiziologije rada; uvod u industrijsku psihologiju (Foundations of the psychophysiology of work; introduction to industrial psychology). Collaborator, Boris Petz. Zagreb, Institut za higijenu rada Jugoslavenske akademije znanosti i umjetnosti, 1959. 420 p. Illus. Bibliography.

> Reprinted without change in 1964. For an appraisal, see *Contemporary Psychology*, v. 6, 1961: 316-317.

2708. Jugoslavenska bibliografija alkoholizma (Yugoslav bibliography on alcoholism). Prepared by Vladimir Hudolin and collaborators. Zagreb, Pliva, 1964. 190 p.

> Issued as a special supplement to the journal *Zdravstvo* (Health). Contains 2,858 entries, chronologically arranged in each of three sections: technical and popular articles; reviews of articles and books; and books, pamphlets, and other publications. There is an author index. The introduction is also given in English.

2709. Jugoslavenska akademija znanosti i umjetnosti. *Institut za medicinska istraživanja.* Institute for Medical Research, Incorporating the Institute of Industrial Hygiene. Zagreb, 1967. 43 p.

> This annual report for 1966 includes information on the activities of the Department of the Psychophysiology of Work, directed by Prof. Dr. Zoran Bujas (p. 22-24).

2710. Kongres psihologa SFR Jugoslavije. *2d, Zagreb, 1964.* Zbornik saopćenja i plenarnih predavanja (Contributed papers and plenary reports). Zagreb, Društvo psihologa SR Hrvatske, 1966. 258 p. Illus.

> Proceedings of the Second Congress of Psychologists of Yugoslavia, held in Zagreb on February 6-8, 1964. The papers are grouped by topic — industrial, social, educational, clinical, and general psychology. The plenary reports were presented by R. Supek (professional ethics), N. Rot (research on social processes), Zoran Bujas (tests of intelligence), and M. Rostohar (concepts of wholes and patterns in psychology).

2711. Zagreb. Univerzitet. *Psihologijski institut. Acta.* 1932– Zagreb. Irregular.

> A series of small monographs in experimental psychology. At first, articles were in French or German, but in recent years most have been in English. Issues 35-48, published as a single volume in 1964, were dedicated to the memory of the French psychologist, Henri Piéron.

## 2. Serbia

2712. Jugoslovensko udruženje za profesionalnu orijentaciju. Profesionalna orijentacija (Vocational guidance). Beograd, 1958. 122 p.

Proceedings of the first regular meeting of the Yugoslav Association for Vocational Guidance, held in Skopje on May 9-10, 1958. Contains 14 contributions, including a discussion of the use of tests (p. 81-86).

2713. Rot, Nikola. Opšta psihologija (General psychology). Beograd, Zavod za izdavanje udžbenika SR Srbije, 1966. 339 p.

A comprehensive textbook for students in teachers' colleges; includes chapters on industrial and clinical psychology.

2714. Rot, Nikola, *ed.* Stanje i perspektive jugoslovenske psihologije (The status and perspectives of Yugoslav psychology). Beograd, Jugoslovensko udruženje psihologa, 1965. 150 p.

These proceedings of the March 1963 conference of the Association of Psychologists of Yugoslavia are the best single source of information on contemporary psychology in Yugoslavia. A seven-year research plan, presented by Dr. Zoran Bujas, is included.

2715. Supek, Rudi. Omladina na Putu bratstva; psiho-sociologija radne akcije (Youth on Brotherhood Road; psychosociology of the voluntary work movement). Beograd, Mladost, 1963. 344 p. Illus.

*See also* entry no. 2701.

An important study in social psychology. Summary in French. For a review, see *Contemporary Psychology*, v. 10, 1965: 180, 182.

## 3. Slovenia

2716. Pečjak, Vid. Poglavja iz psihologije (Chapters in psychology). Ljubljana, Državna založba Slovenije, 1965. 211 p. Illus. Bibliography: p. 209-211.

An interesting presentation of selected topics. The references take into account works published in Serbo-Croatian and Slovenian.

2717. Podjavoršek, Albin, *ed.* Zbornik razprav in člankov o usmerjanju v poklice (Collection of essays and articles on vocational guidance). Ljubljana, Jugoslovansko združenje za usmerjanje v poklice, Sekcija za LRS, 1959. 140 p.

Proceedings of the meeting, held on April 13, 1958, at which the Slovenian section of the Yugoslav Association for Vocational Guidance was founded. Contains the editor's opening speech and 11 other contributions, including a tribute to Prof. Dr. Mihajlo Rostohar.

2718. Rostohar, Mihajlo. Osnove obče psihologije (Foundations of general psychology). Ljubljana, Državna založba Slovenije, 1964. 395 p. Illus., bibliographies.

Written for students of psychology, the work presents the scientific basis of the discipline, including a brief section on methodology, and describes the procedures of traditional experimental psychology. The selected bibliographies for each chapter include references to works in Slovenian and Serbo-Croatian.

# 51

# ıntellectual and cultural life

# A. LANGUAGES

## by Robert Auty

## 1. Serbo-Croatian

### a. General

2719. Belić, Aleksandar, *and others.* Jezik, srpskohrvatski (hrvatsko-srpski) (Language, Serbo-Croatian [Croato-Serbian]). *In* Enciklopedija Jugoslavije. v. 4. Zagreb, Leksikografski zavod FNRJ, 1960. p. 500-528.

> Covers the dialects and the literary language, especially in their historical aspects, with extensive bibliographies. Provides the best available general orientation in view of the absence of adequate and up-to-date reference works.

2720. Reiter, Norbert. Literaturbericht über die serbokroatische Sprachwissenschaft von 1925-1954. Zeitschrift für slavische Philologie (Heidelberg), v. 25, 1956: 405-424; v. 26, 1957/58: 174-209, 416-448; v. 27, 1958/59: 198-222, 425-435.

> Extensive critical bibliography of works on the Serbo-Croatian language published in Yugoslavia in the period reviewed.

### b. Periodicals

2721. Južnoslovenski filolog (The South Slav philologist). 1913– Beograd, Srpska akademija nauka i umetnosti. Annual.

> Articles on the Serbo-Croatian language as well as on other aspects of Slavonic philology. Includes full bibliographies of Yugoslav publications in the linguistic field. Can be supplemented by the more practically oriented journals *Naš jezik* (Our language) (1932–, Beograd, Srpska akademija nauka i umetnosti, Institut za srpski jezik) and *Jezik* (The language) (1953–, Zagreb, Hrvatsko filološko društvo).

2722. Jugoslovenska akademija znanosti i umjetnosti. Rad Jugoslavenske akademije znanosti i umjetnosti (Transactions of the Yugoslav Academy of Sciences and Arts). 1866– Zagreb.

> Appears frequently though at irregular intervals. Frequent articles on the language, especially on dialects and the history of the literary language. Linguistic articles of importance also appear in *Glas Srpske akademije nauka* (The voice of the Serbian Academy of Sciences), Odeljenje literature i jezika, n.s. (Beograd, 1951–).

### c. Dictionaries

2723. Rječnik hrvatskoga ili srpskoga jezika (Dictionary of the Croatian or Serbian language). Zagreb, Jugoslavenska akademija znanosti i umjetnosti, 1880– In progress.

> The most compendious dictionary of the language, based primarily on literature sources of the western (Croatian) variant. Volume 18, the latest published, has reached the word *tustošija.*

2724. Rečnik srpskohrvatskog književnog i narodnog jezika (Dictionary of the Serbo-Croatian literary and popular language). Beograd, Srpska akademija nauka i umetnosti, Institut za srpskohrvatski jezik, 1959– In progress. Bibliography: v. 1, p. xi-cx.

It is to be the most compendious dictionary of the eastern (Serbian) variant of the national language. Volume 4 (the latest) has reached the word *dugulja.*

Since both academic dictionaries are unfinished, it is still necessary to make use of two 19th century works, excellent in their time and still valuable: *Srpski rječnik istumačen njemačkijem i latinskijem riječima* (Serbian dictionary with German and Latin definitions) by Vuk Stefanović Karadžić (Beograd, Državna štamparija Kraljevine Jugoslavije, 1935, 880 p., facsimile reproduction of 3d ed. of 1898); *Rječnik hrvatskoga jezika* (Dictionary of the Croatian language) by Franjo Iveković and Ivan Broz (Zagreb, Štamparija K. Albrechta, 1901, 2 v.).

2725. Rečnik srpskohrvatskog književnog jezika (Dictionary of the Serbo-Croatian literary language). Novi Sad, Matica srpska, 1967–

Rječnik hrvatskosrpskog književnog jezika (Dictionary of the Croato-Serbian literary language). Zagreb, Matica hrvatska; Novi Sad, Matica Srpska, 1967–

An important lexicographic undertaking now in progress.

#### d. The Modern Serbo-Croatian Language

2726. Maretić, Tomislav.   Gramatika hrvatskoga ili srpskoga književnog jezika (Grammar of the Croatian or Serbian literary language). 3d ed. Zagreb, Matica hrvatska, 1963. 688 p.

This unchanged reprint of the second edition of 1931 is the best descriptive grammar of the modern language. Reference may also be usefully made to the best Serbo-Croatian grammar written in a West European language: *Grammaire de la langue serbo-croate* by A. Meillet and A. Vaillant (Paris, E. Champion, 1924, 302 p., Collection de grammaires de l'Institut d'études slaves, 3, bibliography: p. vii-viii; 2d ed. appeared in 1952). Also valuable is *Elementargrammatik der serbokroatischen Sprache* by M. Rešetar, 3d rev. ed., edited by E. Schneeweis (Halle/Saale, Niemeyer, 1957, 128 p.).

2727. Matica hrvatska, *Zagreb.*   Pravopis hrvatskosrpskoga književnog jezika s pravopisnim rječnikom (Orthography of the Croato-Serbian literary language with an orthographical dictionary). Zagreb, Matica hrvatska; Novi Sad, Matica srpska, 1960. 882 p.

Official orthoepic manual, incorporating the agreed forms, with variants, of the national language established by the Novi Sad Agreement of 1954. Separate Cyrillic and Latin-alphabet editions have been published, of which the former has *srpskohrvatskoga* (Serbo-Croatian) for *hrvatskosrpskoga* in the title.

#### e. Historical Grammars

2728. Belić, Aleksandar.   Osnovi istorije srpskohrvatskog jezika. I. Fonetika. Univerzitetska predavanja (Foundations of the history of the Serbo-Croatian language. I. Phonetics. University lectures). Beograd, Nolit, 1960– 172 p. Illus.

———. Istorija srpskohrvatskog jezika. II. 1: Reči sa deklinacijom. II. 2: Reči sa konjugacijom (History of the Serbo-Croatian language. II. 1: Declensions. II. 2: Conjugations). Beograd, Naučna knjiga, 1950-1951. 459 + 344 p.

> The text of Belić's lectures on historical phonology and morphology. The morphology can still be usefully supplemented by *Istorija oblika srpskoga ili hrvatskoga jezika do svršetka XVII vijeka* (History of the forms of the Serbian or Croatian language to the end of the 17th century) by Đuro Daničić (Beograd, Državna štamparija, 1875, 398 p.). Some indications of historical morphology may also be found in *Grammatik der serbo-kroatischen Sprache. 1. Teil: Lautlehre, Stammbildung, Formenlehre* by August Leskien (Heidelberg, C. Winter, 1914, 588 p.).

2729. Vaillant, André.   La langue de Dominko Zlatarić, poète ragusain de la fin du XVIᵉ siècle. Paris, Champion, 1928-1931. 2 v. Bibliography: p. xi-xviii. (Travaux publiés par l'Institut d'études slaves, 6)

> In the absence of full studies of the older language, this study of the phonology and morphology of the language of a single late 16th century Ragusan poet is of particular importance.

#### f. History of the Language

2730. Jonke, Ljudevit.   Književni jezik u teoriji i praksi (The literary language in theory and practice). 2d ed. Zagreb, Znanje, 1965. 471 p.

> Pages 7-175 contain a series of studies on the development of the Croatian variant of the literary language in the 19th century. The rest of the book discusses problems of contemporary usage.

2731. Knežević, Anton.   Die Turzismen in der Sprache der Kroaten und Serben, Meisenheim am Glan, Hain, 1962. 506 p. (Slavisch-baltisches Seminar der Westfälischen Wilhelms-Universität Münster. Veröffentlichungen, 3)

> Alphabetical list of the words taken from Turkish into the dialects of Bosnia, Hercegovina, and the Kosovo-Metohija region.

2732. Popović, Ivan.   Geschichte der serbokroatischen Sprache. Wiesbaden, Otto Harrassowitz, 1960. 687 p. Maps. (Bibliotheca Slavica)

> Discursive work containing a mass of material and concentrating mainly on the origins and early history of the language. The literary language is treated much less fully than the dialects and many of the author's hypotheses must be regarded with caution.

2733. Striedter-Temps, Hildegard.   Deutsche Lehnwörter im Serbokroatischen. Wiesbaden, Harrassowitz, 1958. 225 p. (Veröffentlichungen der Abteilung für slavische Sprachen und Literaturen des Osteuropa-Instituts an der Freien Universität Berlin, 18)

> Good historical study of the German loanwords of Serbo-Croatian.

2734. Unbegaun, Boris O.   Les débuts de la langue littéraire chez les Serbes. Paris, Champion, 1935. 84 p. Bibliography: p. 75-83.
>Admirable brief survey of the development of the Serbian literary language in the 18th century.

2735. Vasmer, Max.   Die griechischen Lehnwörter im Serbokroatischen. Berlin, de Gruyter, 1944. 154 p. (Abhandlungen der Preussischen Akademie der Wissenschaften. Phil.-hist. Kl. 1944/3)
>Important study of Greek loanwords taken over in the medieval period.

### g. Dialects

2736. Ivić, Pavle.   Die serbokroatischen Dialekte: Ihre Struktur und Entwicklung. I: Allgemeines und die štokavische Dialektgruppe. The Hague, Mouton, 1958. 325 p. Illus., maps, bibliographies.
>Best general survey of štokavic dialects, to be followed by volumes on the čakavic and kajkavic dialect-groups.

2737. Hrvatski dijalektološki zbornik (The Croatian dialectological compendium). 1956– Zagreb, Jugoslavenska akademija znanosti i umjetnosti.
>Series, appearing at irregular intervals. Volume 1 (1956) contains a complete bibliography, compiled by Mate Hraste, of publications on Serbo-Croatian dialects to that date.

2738. Srpski dijalektološki zbornik (The Serbian dialectological compendium). 1905– Beograd, Srpska akademija nauka.
>Series, appearing at irregular intervals, which includes important monographs on individual dialects.

## 2. Slovenian

### a. General

2739. Toporišič, Jože.   Jezik, slovenski (slovenački) (The Slovenian language). *In* Enciklopedija Jugoslavije. v. 4. Zagreb, Leksikografski zavod FNRJ, 1960. p. 495-500.
>Good general survey covering the history of the language, the dialects and the development of the modern standard language, with a brief bibliography.

### b. Periodicals

2740. Slavistična revija; časopis za literarno zgodovino in jezik (Slavic review; journal of literary history and language). 1948– Ljubljana, Slovenska akademija znanosti in umetnosti. Quarterly.
>Articles on the Slovenian language, especially its history and dialectology, and on other aspects of Slavonic philology. The earlier journals *Časopis za slovenski jezik, književnost in zgodovino* (Journal of the Slovenian language, literature and history) (Ljubljana, 1918-1931) and *Slovenski jezik* (The Slovenian language) (Ljubljana, 1938-1941) also contain some important articles on the language.

### c. Dictionaries

2741. Pleteršnik, Maks A.   Slovensko-nemški slovar (Slovenian-German dictionary). Ljubljana, Knezoškofijstvo, 1894-1895. 2 v.

Thus far the most extensive Slovenian dictionary, particularly valuable as the words are accented. For the language of today it will be replaced by the following forthcoming publication:

Slovenska akademija znanosti in umetnosti. Slovar slovenskega sodobnega jezika (Dictionary of the contemporary Slovenian literary language). Ljubljana, Državna založba Slovenije, 1969–. This massive lexicographic work is to appear in 5 volumes. Volume 1 is scheduled for publication in 1969 and will contain approximately 20,000 entries.

2742. Škerlj, Stanko, *and others.*   Slovenačko-srpskohrvatski rečnik (Slovenian-Serbo-Croatian dictionary). Beograd, Prosveta, 1964. 1302 p. *See also* entry no. 2725.

Good medium-sized dictionary of the modern language with definitions in Serbo-Croatian. Also, *Slovar slovenskega jezika* by Joža Glonar (Ljubljana, 1936) is still helpful.

### d. The Modern Slovenian Language

2743. Bajec, Anton, *and others.*   Slovenska slovnica (Slovenian grammar). Ljubljana, Državna založba Slovenije, 1956. 335 p. Illus., maps.

Normative grammar of the present-day language.

2744. Svane, Gunnar Olaf.   Grammatik der slowenischen Schriftsprache. Kopenhagen, Rosenkilde und Bagger, 1958. 151 p.

The best Slovenian grammar in a West European language. Also noteworthy is the grammatical sketch of Slovenian given on pages 363-434 of *Guide to the Slavonic Languages* by R. G. A. de Bray (London, J. M. Dent, 1951).

2745. Slovenska akademija znanosti in umetnosti, *Ljubljana.*   Slovenski pravopis (Slovenian orthography). Ljubljana, Državna založba Slovenije, 1962. 1054 p.

The official orthoepic manual issued by the Orthographic Commission of the Slovenian Academy of Sciences and Arts and prepared by Anton Bajec and others. Contains indications of accentuation and morphology as well as orthography.

### e. History of the Language

2746. Ramovš, Fran.   Kratka zgodovina slovenskega jezika (A short history of the Slovenian language). Ljubljana, Akademska založba, 1936. 246 p. Illus. (Akademska biblioteka, 3)

Contains a general introduction and the section on the development of the vowel system. No more was published.

2747. Ramovš, Fran.   Historična gramatika slovenskega jezika. v. 2. Konzonantizem (Historical grammar of the Slovenian language. v. 2.

The consonants). Ljubljana, Učiteljska tiskarna, 1924. 336 p. Bibliography: p. iii-x.
Deals with the development of the Slovenian consonant system. Of this work only volumes 2 and 7 were published.

2748. Ramovš, Fran.  Morfologija slovenskega jezika (Morphology of the Slovenian language). Ljubljana, Državna založba Slovenije, 1952. 170 p.
The text of Ramovš's lectures on historical morphology.

2749. Striedter-Temps, Hildegard.   Deutsche Lehnwörter im Slovenischen. Wiesbaden, Harrassowitz, 1963. 256 p. (Veröffentlichungen der Abteilung für slavische Sprachen und Literaturen des Osteuropa-Instituts an der Freien Universität Berlin, 27)
Descriptive and historical survey of the German loanwords in Slovenian.

2750. Tomšič, France.   Razvoj slovenskega knjižnega jezika (The development of the Slovenian literary language). *In* Legiša, Lino, *and* Alfonz Gspan, *eds.* Zgodovina slovenskega slovstva (History of Slovenian literature). v. 1. Ljubljana, Slovenska matica, 1956. p. 9-28.
Succinct general survey. The emergence of the modern language in the critical early 19th century period is the subject of two special studies: "The Formation of the Slovene Literary Language against the Background of the Slavonic National Revival" by Robert Auty, *Slavonic and East European Review* (London), v. 41, no. 97, June 1963: 391-402, and *Borba za individualnost slovenskega književnega jezika v letih 1848-1857* (The struggle for the individuality of the Slovenian literary language in the years 1848-1857) by Ivan Prijatelj (Ljubljana, Slavistično društvo, 1937, 134 p.).

#### f. Dialects

2751. Ramovš, Fran.   Historična gramatika slovenskega jezika. v. 7. Dialekti (Historical grammar of the Slovenian language. v. 7. Dialects). Ljubljana, Učiteljska tiskarna, 1935. 207 p. Map. (Znanstveno društvo za humanistične vede v Ljubljani, Dela 1)
Descriptive survey of all the Slovenian dialects.

### 3. Macedonian

2752. Koneski, Blaže.   Gramatika na makedonskiot literaturen jazik. Del I. Uvod. Za glasovite. Za akcentot (Grammar of the Macedonian literary language. Part 1. Introduction. Sounds. Accentuation). Skopje, Državno knigoizdatelstvo na NR Makedonija, 1952. Del II. Za formite i nivnata upotreba (Part 2. Forms and their use). Skopje, Prosvetno delo, 1954. Latest ed.: Skopje, Kultura, 1967. 552 p.
Normative grammar of the modern language. The introduction to part 1 includes valuable information on the history of the literary language. Also of value is the first Macedonian grammar in a western

language, Horace G. Lunt's *A Grammar of the Macedonian Literary Language* (Skopje, Državno knigoizdatelstvo, 1952, 287 p.). The official orthoepic manual *Makedonski pravopis so pravopisen rečnik* (Macedonian orthography with an orthographical dictionary) by Blaže Koneski and Krum Tošev (Skopje, Drž. kn-vo na NR Makedonija, 1950, 175 p.) is now a little outdated.

2753. Koneski, Blaže.   Istorija na makedonskiot jazik (History of the Macedonian language). Skopje, Kočo Racin; Beograd, Prosveta, 1965. 203 p.

Succinct survey of historical phonology, morphology, and lexicology. See also *The Macedonian Language in the Development of the Slavonic Languages* by the same author, which is a translation into English of the Macedonian original (Skopje, Kultura, 1968, 39 p.).

2754. Koneski, Blaže.   Jezik, makedonski (The Macedonian language). *In* Enciklopedija Jugoslavije. v. 4. Zagreb, Leksikografski zavod FNRJ, 1960. p. 492-495.

Brief descriptive and historical survey with select bibliography.

2755. Koneski, Blaže, *and others, eds.*   Rečnik na makedonskiot jazik, so srpskohrvatski tolkuvanja (Dictionary of the Macedonian language with explanations in Serbo-Croatian). Skopje, Institut za makedonski jazik, 1961-1966. 3 v.

Full normative dictionary of the contemporary language.

2756. Makedonski jazik (The Macedonian language). 1950– Skopje. Semiannual.

Contains articles in Macedonian on all aspects of the language. Frequency varies.

2757. Selishchev, A. M. Ocherki po makedonskoĭ dialektologii (Studies in Macedonian dialectology). v. 1. Kazan, 1918. 284 p.

Survey of the dialects with special reference to their phonology. Must now be supplemented by the dialect monographs appearing in two current series: *Diplomski raboti* (Theses) (1950–, Skopje, Filozofski fakultet na Univerzitetot, Katedra na južnoslovenski jazici) and *Posebni izdanija* (Monographs) (1953–, Skopje, Institut za makedonski jazik).

2758. Vidoeski, Božo.   Prilog kon bibliografijata na makedonskiot jazik (A contribution toward a bibliography of the Macedonian language). Skopje, Institut za makedonski jazik, 1953. 136 p. (Posebni izdanija, kn. 1)

Lists all publications on the language to 1952. Publications since that date are listed in the annual issues of the journal *Južnoslovenski filolog* (The South Slav philologist) (Beograd).

## B. LITERATURE

*by Albert B. Lord (sections 1, 2, 4)*
*and*
*David E. Bynum (sections 3, 5)*

### 1. Bibliographies, Serials, Surveys, Histories of Literature, Anthologies

2759. Barac, Antun.  Hrvatska književnost (Croatian literature). Knjiga I. Književnost ilirizma (Book 1. Literature of the Illyrian movement). Knjiga II. Književnost pedesetih i šezdesetih godina (Book 2. Literature of the '50s and '60s). Zagreb, Jugoslavenska akademija znanosti i umjetnosti, 1960-1964. 2 v.

The beginnings of a full history of modern Croatian literature that the author did not live to complete. Excellent surveys of the periods in question.

2760. Barac, Antun.  Jugoslavenska književnost (Yugoslav literature). 2d ed. Zagreb, Matica hrvatska, 1959. 331 p.

The only comprehensive history including Serbian, Croatian, and Slovenian literature. In 1955 the Committee on Foreign Cultural Relations of Yugoslavia published an English translation of this work by P. Mijuskovic.

2761. Bibliografija rasprava, članaka i književnih radova (Bibliography of essays, articles, and literary works). Chief editor, Mate Ujević. v. 1– Zagreb, Leksikografski zavod FNRJ, 1956–

*See also* entry no. 2090.

To date, eight volumes have appeared (the latest in 1965). The first large division, Nauka o književnosti (Scholarship about literature) includes (1) Literature in General, Theory of Literature, Comparative Literature; (2) History of Yugoslav Literatures; (3) History of Foreign Literatures; (4) Literary Periodical Publications; (5) History of Folk Literature; and (6) Literary Societies. The second large division is Jugoslavenska književnost (Yugoslav literature) and includes (1) Poetry. This division begins in volume four and ends in volume seven, in which the third division also begins, Strana književnost (Foreign literature), of which (1) Poetry is included in volume 7 in its entirety. Prose has been reserved for later volumes.

2762. Biblioteka antologija jugoslovenske književnosti (Library of anthologies of Yugoslav literature). Beograd, Nolit, 1955–

This series contains anthologies of Serbian and Croatian prose, modern Croatian lyric poetry, Serbian poets between the wars, Serbian folktales, Croatian drama and literary essays, Serbian literary criticism, Dubrovnik lyric poetry, and so forth. It is a useful companion to Antum Barac's *Jugoslavenska književnost* (*see* entry no. 2760).

2763. Djela hrvatskih pisaca (Works of Croatian writers). General editor, Dragutin Tadijanović. Zagreb, Zora, 1950–

> Includes the works of Croatian writers of the Illyrian movement as well as later realists such as Ante Kovačić, Josip Kozarac, Eugen Kumičić, Vjenceslav Novak, Ksaver Šandor-Đalski, and Dinko Šimunović. This series, together with the series *Stari pisci hrvatski* (Old Croatian writers), has in part been superseded by the series *Pet stoljeća hrvatske književnosti* (Five centuries of Croatian literature) (*see* entry no. 2773), but they still remain worthy of note.

2764. Hrvatska revija (The Croatian review). Godište 1-18. 1928-1945. Zagreb, Matica hrvatska.

> The main Croatian literary journal between the two wars, under the editorship of Branimir Livadić, later joined by Olinko Delorko.

2765. Ježić, Slavko.  Hrvatska književnost od početka do danas, 1100-1941 (Croatian literature from the beginning to the present time, 1100-1941). Zagreb, A. Velzek, 1944. 457 p.

> The only history of Croatian literature in Croatian that covers it for its entire length (at least to the Second World War).

2766. Jugoslavenska akademija znanosti i umjetnosti, *Zagreb*. Rad (Transactions). v. 1– 1867– Zagreb.

> Monographs on writers and works in all the periods of Yugoslav literature and on Yugoslav folklore are scattered throughout the more than 340 volumes of this venerable journal.

2767. Kombol, Mihovil.  Povijest hrvatske književnosti do narodnog preporoda (A history of Croatian literature before the national renascence). Zagreb, Matica hrvatska, 1961. 481 p.

> This is the classic history of Dalmatian, Croatian, and Slavonian literature before the 19th century. Especially valuable for the Renaissance and its antecedents, and for extensive bibliography.

2768. Koneski, Blaže.  Makedonska književnost (Macedonian literature). Beograd, 1961. 203 p. (Srpska književna zadruga, kniga 368)

———.  Makedonskata literatura vo 19 vek (Kratok pregled i tekstovi) (Macedonian literature in the 19th century [a short survey with texts]). 2d ed. Skopje, Državno knigoizdatelstvo, 1952. 92 p.

———, *ed.* Makedonska književnost (Macedonian literature). Beograd, Prosveta, 1968. 204 p.

2769. Legiša, Lino.  Zgodovina slovenskega slovstva (History of Slovenian literature). Ljubljana, Slovenska matica, 1956– Illus.

> Legiša is the general editor as well as author of several parts of this careful and authoritative set of volumes. Other authors included are France Tomšič, Boris Merhar, Milko Matičetov, Mirko Rupel, Anton Slodnjak, and Joža Mahnič. Thus far five volumes have been

published. For histories of Slovenian literature in Western languages
*see*:

Slodnjak, Anton.  Geschichte der slowenischen Literatur. Berlin,
Walter de Gruyter, 1958. 363 p.

Meriggi, Bruno.  Storia della letteratura slovena, con un profilo
della letteratura serbo-lusaziana. Milano, Nuova accademia editrice,
1961. 408 p.

2770. Ljubljanski zvon (The Ljubljana bell). 1881-1941. Ljubljana.
Monthly.

An important Slovenian literary and cultural journal. Contemporary with it and of the same kind and importance was: *Dom in svet*
(1888-1944, Ljubljana, monthly). For easy access to the materials in
*Ljubljanski zvon* see:

Kodela, Rudolf, Jože Munda, *and* Niko Rupel.  Bibliografsko
kazalo Ljubljanskega zvona 1881-1941 (A bibliographic directory
to Ljubljanski zvon, 1881-1941). Ljubljana, Slovenska akademija
znanosti in umetnosti, 1962. 419 p.

2771. Lunt, Horace Gray.  A Survey of Macedonian Literature. *In* Harvard Slavic Studies, v. 1. Cambridge, Mass.. Harvard University
Press, 1953. p. 363-396.

A concise treatment of Macedonian writers and writings in Macedonian dialects from the beginnings to the fall of 1951.

2772. Matica hrvatska, *Zagreb*.  Hrvatska književna kritika (Croatian
literary criticism). Zagreb, 1950-1966. 10 v.

Contents: v. 1, Od Vraza do Markovića (From Vraz to Marković),
and v. 2, Razdoblje realizma (The period of realism), edited by Antun
Barac. v. 3, M. Marjanović, edited by Petar Lasta. v. 4, A. G. Matoš,
edited by Marijan Matković. v. 5, Nehajev i suvremenici (Nehajev
and his contemporaries), edited by Šime Vučetić. v. 6, Miroslav
Krleža and v. 7, Antun Barac, edited by Petar Lasta. v. 8, Tin Ujević,
edited by Miroslav Vaupotić. v. 9, Kritika izmedju dva rata (Criticism
between the two wars), edited by Petar Lasta. v. 10, Suvremena
kritika (Contemporary criticism), edited by Šime Vučetić.

An excellent series under a numer of expert editors.

2773. Pet stoljeća hrvatske književnosti (Five centuries of Croatian literature). Zagreb, Matica hrvatska, Zora, 1962–

This well edited series is published in cycles of 12 volumes.
Authors published so far have included among others Marin Držić,
Ivan Gundulić, August Šenoa, Krklec, Milutin Nehajev, P. Zoranić,
J. Baraković, Novak, Dinko Šimunović, Vladimir Nazor, August
Cesarec, and Ivo Vojnović. There are, in addition, such special
volumes as *Zbornik stihova XVII stoljeća* (Anthology of verses of
the 17th century), *Komedije XVII i XVIII stojeća* (Comedies of the
17th and 18th centuries), and *Hrvatski narodni preporod* (The Croatian national awakenings) (two volumes).

2774. Popović, Bogdan. Antologija novije srpske lirike (Anthology of newer Serbian lyric poetry). 10th ed. Beograd, Srpska književna zadruga, 1956. 296 p.

First published in 1911 this anthology played an influential role in the history of Serbian literature. Among the poets represented were Đura Jakšić, Jovan Jovanović Zmaj, Lazar Kostić, Vojislav Ilić, Aleksa Šantić, Jovan Dučić, and Milan Rakić.

2775. Prilozi za književnost, jezik, istoriju i folklor (Contributions to literature, language, history, and folklore). knj. 1– 1921– Beograd, Državna štamparija.

Since its foundation this journal has remained the chief Serbian forum for learned work on Yugoslav literary history and folklore.

2776. Šicel, Miroslav. Pregled novije hrvatske književnosti (A survey of newer Croatian literature). Zagreb, Matica hrvatska, 1966. 308 p.

Brief, sensible essays on the development of Croatian literature from Illyrianism to the dominant writers of the present generation. The essays are followed by lists of writers and their works including outstanding critics and cultural historians as well as numerous writers of original literature ignored in other such surveys.

2777. Skerlić, Jovan. Istorija nove srpske književnosti (History of modern Serbian literature). Edited by Radojka Radulović. Beograd, Prosveta, 1967. 582 p. Ports., facsims. (*His* Sabrana djela, 13)

First published in 1914, with two other editions in 1921 and 1953, this work remains the standard literary history for the 19th century.

2778. Skerlić, Jovan. Srpska književnost u XVIII veku (Serbian literature in the 18th century). Edited by Miraš Kićović. Beograd, Prosveta, 1966. *(His* Sabrana djela, 9)

First published in 1909 and revised and edited by Vladimir Čorović in 1923, this work is still a valuable survey of the period.

2779. Srpska književnost u književnoj kritici (Serbian literature in literary criticism). Beograd, Nolit, 1956–

Each volume is a collection of essays or studies by various scholars past and present. The series forms a kind of history of Serbian literature, with a stress on criticism. The titles of the volumes speak for themselves: *Stara književnost* (Old literature), *Narodna književnost* (Folk literature), *Od baroka do klasicizma* (From baroque to classicism), *Epoha romantizma* (The age of romanticism), *Epoha realizma* (The age of realism), *Pesništvo od Vojislava do Bojića* (Poetry from Vojislav to Bojić), *Književnost između dva rata, I i II* (Literature between the two wars), *Savremena poezija* (Contemporary poetry), *Savremena proza* (Contemporary prose), *Drama* (Drama), and *Književna kritika* (Literary criticism).

2780. Srpska književnost u sto knjiga (Serbian literature in a hundred volumes). Novi Sad, Matica srpska, Srpska književna zadruga, 1957–

This excellent series includes, among others, Branko Radičević, Prota Matija Nenadović, Ivo Andrić, Laza K. Lazarević, A. Šantić, Svetozar Ćorović, Iva Ćipiko, S. Matavulj, Jovan Dučić, Jovan Jovanović Zmaj, Vojislav Ilić, Janko Veselinović, Branimir Ćosić, Dobrica Ćosić, Branko Ćopić, Isak Samokovlija, Dušan Matić, and Rastko Petrović. There are, in addition, valuable special volumes on *Naučnici* (Scholars) (from Đuro Daničić to Aleksandar Belić); *Novinari* (Journalists); *Stara srpska književnost* (Old Serbian literature) (two volumes); *Antologija starije srpske poezije* (Anthology of older Serbian poetry) (18th and 19th centuries); *Pripovedači* (Short story writers) (four volumes); *Književni istoričari i kritičari* (Literary historians and critics) (three volumes, 19th and 20th centuries); *Memoari XVIII i XIX veka* (Memoirs of the 18th and 19th centuries); and *Pesnici* (Poets) (four volumes, from Jovan Ilić to the present).

2781. Srpski književni glasnik (Serbian literary herald). Old series, no. 1-33, 1901-1914; new series, no. 1-62, 1920-1941. Beograd. Semimonthly.
Not published July 16, 1914 to Sept. 20, 1920. Discontinued after 1941. The main Serbian literary journal from the beginning of the century to the Second World War.

2782. Vienac, zabavi i pouči (The wreath; pleasure and instruction). God 1-35. Zagreb, 1869-1903.
The main Croatian literary journal of the latter part of the 19th century. Its publication was taken over by the Matica hrvatska, and its editors included such figures as Gjuro Deželić, the first editor; August Šenoa, perhaps its most distinguished; and Ksaver Šandor Gjalski.

## 2. Medieval Literature

2783. Danilo II, *Arhiepiskop*.   Životi kraljeva i arhiepiskopa srpskih (Lives of the Serbian kings and archbishops). Translated by Lazar Mirković, with an introduction by Nikola Radojčić. Beograd, 1935. 305 p. (Srpska književna zadruga. Izdanja, kolo 38, br. 257)
Modern Serbo-Croatian translation.

2784. Domentijan, *hieromonach*.   Životi svetoga Save i svetoga Simeona (The lives of Saint Sava and Saint Simeon). Translated by Lazar Mirković with an introduction by Vladimir Čorović. Beograd, 1938. 335 p. (Srpska književna zadruga. Izdanja, kolo 41, knj. 282)
A modern Serbo-Croatian translation. The originals may be found in *Život svetoga Simeuna i svetoga Save, napisao Domentijan* (The life of St. Simeon and St. Sava, as written by Domentijan), edited by Đuro Daničić (Beograd, 1865, 345 p.).

2785. Marulić, Marko (Marcus Marulus).   Judita (Judith). Edited by Vjekoslav Štefanić with an introduction by Mihovil Kombol. Zagreb, Zora, 1950. 159 p. Port., plates.
An excellent edition of a significant work, with helpful notes,

glossary, and sketch of Marulić's language. A bibliography of all Marulić's works and of books and articles about him and his writings, as well as some of his Latin poems both in the original and translation and articles about his style and versification can be found in *Zbornik u proslavu petstogodišnjice rođenja Marka Marulića, 1450-1950* (Festschrift in honor of the 500th anniversary of the birth of Marko Marulić, 1450-1950), edited by Josip Badalić and Nikola Majnarić (Zagreb, Jugoslavenska akademija znanosti i umjetnosti, 1950, 345 p., illus., facsims. Djela Jugoslavenske akademije znanosti i umjetnosti, knj. 39).

2786. Murka, Matthias (Matija). Geschichte der älteren südslawischen Litteraturen. Leipzig, C. F. Amelung, 1908. (Die Litteraturen des Orients, Bd. 5, Abt. 2) Bibliography: p. 220-225.

*See also* entry no. 242.

Strong on the Glagolitic literature of the Croatian littoral.

2787. Mošin, Vladimir. Ćirilski rukopisi jugoslavenske akademije (Cyrillic manuscripts of the Yugoslav Academy). Zagreb, Jugoslavenska akademija znanosti i umjetnosti, 1952-1955. 2 v. Illus.

Volume 1 contains descriptions of the manuscripts; volume 2 provides reproductions. Examples of other Cyrillic manuscripts can be found in the same author's *Paleografski album na južnoslovenskoto kirilsko pismo* (Paleographic album of South Slav Cyrillic writing) (Skopje, Kočo Racin, 1966, 164 p.).

2788. Pavlović, Dragoljub, *comp. and tr.* Iz naše književnosti feudalnog doba (Excerpts from our literature of the feudal period). Translated into Modern Serbian, with notes and introduction by Dragoljub Pavlović. 2d enl. ed. Sarajevo, Svjetlost, 1959. 414 p.

A very useful anthology in the modern language, with long enough excerpts of prose to give an adequate picture of the work as a whole. Đorđe Radojičić's *Antologija stare srpske književnosti (XI-XVIII veka)* (Anthology of Old Serbian literature [11th-18th centuries]) (Beograd, Nolit, 1960, 373 p.), includes greater variety, especially in verse, but somewhat shorter selections.

2789. Radojičić, Đorđe Sp. Tvorci i dela stare srpske književnosti (The creators of Old Serbian literature and their works). Titograd, Grafički zavod, 1963. 423 p. Plates (Biblioteka studija, kritika i eseja, 2)

A fine selection of Radojičić's articles in the '50s and '60s. This is an excellent companion volume to his anthologies. Another book by the same author, *Razvojni luk stare srpske književnosti* (Novi Sad, Matica srpska, 1962, 309 p.), combines texts and commentaries in a very imaginative and erudite way and also contains a valuable bibliography.

2790. Ramovš, Fran. Brižinski spomeniki; uvod, paleografski in fonetični prepis, prevod v knjižno slovenščino, faksimile pergamentov (The monuments of Freising; introduction, paleographic and phonetic transcript, translation into literary Slovenian, facsimile of the parchments). Ljubljana, Akademska založba, 1937. 31 p.

A facsimile edition of the first Slovenian manuscript, the "Monuments of Freising," which is also the first Slavic manuscript in Roman script. The book contains its translation into modern Slovenian and a scholarly introduction by the linguist Fran Ramovš and the historian Milko Kos. The connection of the manuscript with the literature of Sts. Cyril and Methodius was proven by Franc Grivec in his work *Zarja stare slovenske književnosti; frizinški spomeniki v zarji sv. Cirila in Metoda* (The dawn of old Slovenian literature; the Monuments of Freising in the dawn of Sts. Cyril and Methodius) (Ljubljana, Ljudska knjigarna, 1942, 63 p.).

Another scholarly book about the Monuments of Freising is Václav Vondrák's *Frisinské památky* (Praha, 1896, 80 p.), which includes a photographic reproduction, a transliteration, a translation into Latin and an extensive introduction.

2791. Rešetar, Milan, *Ritter von, ed.*   Libro od mnozijeh razloga, dubrovački ćirilski zbornik od g. 1520 (A book of many occasions, a Dubrovnik Cyrillic miscellany of 1520). Sremski Karlovci, Štamp. u Srpskoj monastirskoj štampariji, 1926. 221 p. Plates. (Zbornik za istoriju, jezik i književnost srpskog naroda: 1. odeljenje, knj. 15)

An important medieval miscellany. A study of its contents and language can be found in Milan Rešetar's *Dubrovački zbornik od god. 1520* (The Dubrovnik miscellany of 1520) (Beograd, 1933, 296 p., Srpska kraljevska akademija, Belgrade. Posebna izdanja, knj. 100. Filosofski i filološki spisi, knj. 24).

2792. Šišić, Ferdo (Ferdinand).   Letopis popa Dukljanina (Chronicle of the Priest of Dioclea). Beograd, Zagreb, 1928. 480 p. Illus., facsims. (Srpska kraljevska akademija, Belgrade. Posebna izdanja, knj. 67. Filosofski i filološki spisi, knj. 18)

A full study of the documents with an edition of the Latin text, Orbini's Italian, the Croatian redaction, and Marulić's Latin translation of it. The latest edition of the Latin with a modern Croatian translation side by side and the Croatian redaction printed below is that of Vladimir Mošin, *Ljetopis popa Dukljanina* (Chronicle of the Priest of Dioclea) (Zagreb, Matica hrvatska, 1950, 109 p.). Mošin's introduction summarizes the scholarship, and his notes to the text are useful.

2793. Stare srpske biografije (Old Serbian biographies). Beograd, 1924-1938. 4 v. Illus., ports. (Srpska književna zadruga. Izdanja, kolo 27, 38, 39, and 41; broj 180, 257, 265, and 282)

See especially sv. 1 (1924, 251 p.), "Život Stefana Nemanje (Sv. Simeona)" (The life of Stefan Nemanja [St. Simeon], by St. Sava; "Život Stefan Nemanje" (The life of Stefan Nemanja), by Stefan Prvovenčani; Život svetoga Save" (The life of St. Sava), by Teodosije; and sv. 3 (1936, 164 p.), "Život Kralja Stefana Dečanskog" (The life of King Stefan Dečanski), by Grigorije Camblak; "Život Despota Stefana Lazareviča" (The life of Lord Stefan Lazarević), by Konstantin Filosof; "Život Cara Uroša" (The life of Tsar Uroš), by Paisije.

Sv. 1 provides modern Serbo-Croatian translations of Sava's and Stefan Prvovenčani's lives of their father Saint Simeon. Another modern translation of these two lives of St. Simeon with other writings of the two brothers is in:

Sava, *Saint, Archbishop of Serbia.* Spisi svetoga Save i Stefana Prvovenčanoga (Writings of Saint Sava and of Stefan Prvovenčani). Translated by Lazar Mirković. Beograd, Državna štamparija, 1939. 234 p. Plates.

The originals of these lives and of some of the other writings from which these translations were made may be found in:

Čorović, Vladimir, *ed.*  Spisi sv. Save (Writings of St. Sava). Beograd, Sr. Karlovci, 1928. 254 p. (Srpska kraljevska akademija, Belgrade. Zbornik za istoriju, jezik i književnost srpskog naroda. 1. odeljenje, knj. 17. Dela starih srpskih pisaca, knj. 1)

Čorović, Vladimir, *ed.*  Žitije Simeona Nemanje od Stevana Prvovenčanoga (The life of Simeon Nemanja by Stevan Prvovenčani). Beograd, 1939. (Srpska kraljevska akademija, Belgrade. Svetosavski zbornik, knj. 2)

Daničić, Đuro, *ed.*  Život svetoga Save, napisao Domentijan (The life of St. Sava, written by Domentijan). Beograd, 1860. This work was actually written by Teodosije.

### 3. Literature of the Renaissance and Reformation

2794. Brlek, Mijo.  Rukopisi knjižnice Male braće u Dubrovniku (The manuscripts of the Franciscan library in Dubrovnik). v. 1– Zagreb, Jugoslavenska akademija znanosti i umjetnosti, 1952– Illus.

Indispensable to textual research on the literature of the Dalmatian Renaissance. A companion volume of the same nature is Stjepan Kastropil's *Rukopisi Naučne biblioteke u Dubrovniku* (The manuscripts of the Scientific Library in Dubrovnik) (v. 1–, Zagreb, Jugoslavenska akademija znanosti i umjetnosti, 1954–, illus.).

2795. Dayre, Jean.  Dubrovačke studije (Dubrovnik studies). Zagreb, Matica hrvatska, 1939. 92 p.

An influential book of original historical essays on a number of literary persons and writings of the Renaissance in Dubrovnik.

2796. Despot, Miroslava, *and others.*  Djela Pavla Vitezovića, 1652-1952 (The works of Pavao Vitezović, 1652-1952). Zagreb, 1952. 49 p. Illus.

Compiled as a guide to a tercentenary exhibition of Vitezović's works, this book is the best bibliography not only of Vitezović's own numerous writings but also of works written about him from the 18th century onward.

2797. Građa za povijest književnosti hrvatske (Materials for the history of Croatian literature). Zagreb, Jugoslavenska akademija znanosti i umjetnosti, 1897–

Numbering more than 28 volumes, this invaluable archive contains texts, variants, notes and commentary on writings from all periods of Croatian literature. It is especially useful as a source of materials from the Dalmatian Renaissance.

2798. Gundulić, Ivan. Osman s dopunom Ivana Mažuranića (Osman, with the continuation by Ivan Mažuranić). Zagreb, Zora, 1955. 287 p.

This edition is especially useful due to the notes and glossary by the editor, Milan Ratković.

2799. Hektorović, Petar. Ribanje i ribarsko prigovaranje (Fishing and fishermen's entertainment). Zagreb, Jadranski institut Jugoslavenske akademije znanosti i umjetnosti, 1951. 91 p. Annotated, illus., music, map.

A model edition by Ramiro Bujas of Hektorović's famous idyll of the sea.

2800. Hrvatski latinisti (Croatian writers of Latin). v. 1– Zagreb, Jugoslavenska akademija znanosti i umjetnosti, 1951–

A continuing series containing texts of Croatian literature in Latin. Among the authors represented are the lyricists Ignjat Đurđević and Juraj Šižgorić.

2801. Murko, Matija. Die Bedeutung der Reformation und Gegenreformation für das geistige Leben der Südslaven. Prag, Česká grafická unie; Heidelberg, C. Winter, 1927. 184 p.

An important contribution to the subject. The book reprints articles published between 1925 and 1927 in the Czech linguistic review *Slavia*.

2802. Palmotić, Junije Džono. Dubrovnik ponovljen i Didone (Dubrovnik renewed and Dido). Dubrovnik, D. Prestner, 1874-1878. 5 fascicles.

The last of the long epic poems in the tradition of the Renaissance in Dubrovnik.

2803. Petković, Milivoj A. Dubrovačke maskerate (The masques of Dubrovnik). Beograd, Srpska akademija nauka, 1950. 178 p. (Posebna izdanja, knj. 166)

On the Renaissance dramatic tradition in Dubrovnik derived from masquerades at Shrovetide.

2804. Rupel, Mirko. Primož Trubar, življenje in delo (Primož Trubar, life and work). Ljubljana, Mladinska knjiga, 1962. 321 p. Illus., ports., fold. map, facsims. Bibliography: p. 288-296.

The standard work on the most significant figure of the Reformation in Slovenia.

2805. Rupel, Mirko, *ed.* Slovenski protestantski pisci (Slovenian Protestant writers). Ljubljana, Tiskovna zadruga, 1934. 328 p. Illus.

2806. Stari pisci hrvatski (Old Croatian writers). Knj. 1– 1869– Zagreb, Jugoslavenska akademija znanosti i umjetnosti.

This continuing series contains the standard scholarly editions of the major monuments of Croatian literature before 1830.

2807. Torbarina, Josip. Italian Influence on the Poets of the Ragusan Republic. London, Williams and Norgate, 1931. 243 p.

The best work in English on the Serbo-Croatian literature of the Renaissance in Dubrovnik.

2808. Zoranić, Petar. Planine (The mountains). Zagreb, Hrvatski izdavalački bibliografski zavod, 1942. 202 p. (Tekstovi i pregledi, sv. 5)

This is the best edition of Zoranić's 16th century pastoral romance, prepared with notes and glossary by Vjekoslav Štefanić.

## 4. Literature of the 18th and 19th Centuries

2809. Aškerc, Anton. Zbrano delo (Collected works). Edited and with notes by Marja Boršnik. Ljubljana, Državna založba Slovenije, 1946.

Critical works on Aškerc include:

Odbor za proslavo stoletnice Aškerčevega rojstva. Aškerčev zbornik (An Aškerc Festschrift). Edited by Vlado Novak. Celje, 1957. 283 p. Illus., port. Bibliography: p. 221-266. On the occasion of the hundredth anniversary of the writer's birth; articles and a full bibliography. For a prewar monograph on Aškerc *see* Marja Boršnik Škerlak's *Aškerc, življenje in delo* (Aškerc, life and work) (Ljubljana, Založba Modra ptica, 1939, 462 p.).

2810. Barac, Antun. August Šenoa; studija (August Šenoa; a study). Zagreb, Narodna knjižnica, 1926. 152 p.

2811. Demeter, Dimitrija. Teuta, tragedija u pet čina — Grobničko polje, pjesan (Teuta, a tragedy in five acts — The Field of Grobnik, a poem). Zagreb, Matica hrvatska, 1891. 185 p.

This edition of Demeter's play, which marks the beginning of the modern Croatian theater, has introductions by the poet's nephew Vladimir Mažuranić and by the romantic poet Franjo Marković.

2812. Gligorić, Velibor. Srpski realisti (Serbian realists). 4th rev. and enl. ed. Beograd, Prosveta, 1965. 444 p.

The standard work on 13 realists: J. Ignjatović, St. M. Ljubiša, M. Glišić, L. K. Lazarević, J. Veselinović, S. Ranković, St. Sremac, S. Matavulj, R. Domanović, B. Stanković, I. Ćipiko, P. Kočić, and Branislav Nušić.

2813. Gołąbek, Józef. Ivo Vojnović, dramaturg jugosłowiański (Ivo

Vojnović, a Yugoslavian dramatist). Lwów-Warszawa, Książnica-Atlas, 1932. 488 p.

This careful prewar study of Vojnović does not deserve to be forgotten, as it is the only monograph on Vojnović that has come to hand. A selection of Vojnović's works is included in *Pet stoljeća hrvatske književnosti* (*see* entry 2773), where there is also a very good bibliography. The only collected edition of Vojnović's works was that started by the publishing house of Geca Kon in Belgrade in 1939. Three volumes appeared, the last in 1941, but the collection was never finished. Volume one begins with an essay by Lujo Vojnović, "Spomeni o bratu" (Memories of my brother).

2814. Jovičić, Vladimir.    Laza K. Lazarević. Beograd, Nolit, 1966. 294 p. Illus. (Biblioteka portreti, 38)

2815. Karadžić, Vuk Stefanović    Sabrana dela Vuka Karadžića (The collected works of Vuk Karadžić). Beograd, Prosveta, 1965–
*See also* entry no. 2861.

The most recent biography of Karadžić is that of Miodrag Popović, *Vuk Stef. Karadžić, 1864-1964* (Beograd, Nolit, 1964, 479 p., illus.). The standard biography with complete bibliography and chronology is still Ljubomir Stojanović's *Život i rad Vuka Stef. Karadžića* (The life and work of Vuk. Stef. Karadžić) (Beograd, Geca Kon, 1924, 783 p.). For editions of Karadžić's collections of folk material *see* entry 2861.

2816. Kidrič, France.    Prešéren. Ljubljana, Tiskovna zadruga, 1936-1938. 2 v.

A splendid work from all points of view. A third volume was planned but never published. For a more recent edition and biography *see*:

Prešeren, France.    Poezije in pisma (Poetry and letters). Edited by Anton Slodnjak. Ljubljana, Mladinska knjiga, 1964. 366 p.

Slodnjak, Anton.    Prešernovo življenje (The life of Prešeren). Ljubljana, Mladinska knjiga, 1964. 327 p. Illus., facsims., ports.

2817. Koblar, France.    Simon Gregorčič; njegov čas, življenje in delo (Simon Gregorčič; his period, life, and work). Ljubljana, Slovenska matica, 1962. 433 p. Illus., facsims., ports. Bibliography: p. 419-423.

A splendid monograph on this important author.

2818. Kostić, Laza.    Izabrana dela (Selected works). Beograd, Narodna knjiga, 1963. 416 p. Bibliography: p. 413-414.

Although selected works with some bibliography are included in the two volumes of Laza Kostić in the series *Srpska književnost u sto knjiga* (*see* entry 2780), there are items in the bibliography of this selection that are ignored in the other. Some of his articles on literature and aesthetics not found easily elsewhere are in his *Ogledi* (Surveys), edited by Predrag Vukadinović (Beograd, Nolit, 1965, 196 p.). An unusual book, *sui generis*, is Stanislav Vinaver's *Zanosi i prkosi Laze Kostića* (The enthusiasm and the obstinacy of Laze Kostić) (Novi Sad, Forum, 1963, 568 p.).

2819. Logar, Janez, *ed.* Levstikov zbornik (A Levstik Festschrift). Ljubljana, "Slavistični klub" na Univerzi, 1933. 417 p.

In addition to articles by several writers, there is a fine bibliography by Stanko Bunc, arranged chronologically. For a more recent monograph on Levstik *see* Boris Paternu's *Estetske osnove Levstikove literarne kritike* (Aesthetic bases of Levstik's literary criticism) (Ljubljana, Slovenska matica, 1962, 336 p., Razprave in eseji, 2).

2820. Matavulj, Simo. Sabrana dela (Collected works). Edited by Vido Latković and Đuza Radović, with an introduction by Vido Latković. Beograd, Prosveta, 1953-1954. 7 v.

Vido Latković also made a separate study, *Simo Matavulj u Crnoj Gori* (Simo Matavulj in Montenegro) (Skoplje, Južna Srbija, 1940, 278 p.). It contains a bibliography of Matavulj's works to the end of 1889.

2821. Mažuranić, Ivan. Pjesme Ivana Mažuranića (Poems of Ivan Mažuranić). Edited by Vladimir Mažuranić. Zagreb, Tiskarski zavod "Narodnih novina," 1895. 245 p.

This edition by the son of the poet is well supplemented by the article on Ivan Mažuranić in:

Matica hrvatska, *Zagreb.* Matica hrvatska od godine 1842 do godine 1892 (The Matica hrvatska from 1842 to 1892). By Tade Smičiklas and Franjo Marković. Zagreb, Matica hrvatska, 1892. 338 p. For a later edition *see:*

Mažuranić, Ivan. Smrt Smail-age Čengijića (The death of Smail-Aga Čengijić). Edited by Antun Barac. Beograd, Jugoslovenska knjiga, 1949. 91 p.

2822. Mihailović, Georgije. Srpska bibliografija XVIII veka (Serbian bibliography of the 18th century). Beograd, 1964. 383 p. Facsims., maps.

*See also* entry no. 2108.

An indispensable work for anyone interested in the 18th century in Serbia. Entries are presented chronologically, and almost all are accompanied by a picture of the title page or other illustrations of the books listed. Summaries in Russian, French, and English.

2823. Njegoš, Petar Petrović (Petar II, Prince Bishop of Montenegro). Cjelokupna dela (Complete works). Beograd, Prosveta, 1951-1956. 9 v.

This edition has excellent and full notes by the best contemporary scholars. Of the books about Njegoš two deserve mention:

Sekulić, Isidora. Njegošu knjiga duboke odanosti (A book of deep devotion to Njegoš). Novi Sad, Matica srpska, 1961. 461 p. (*Her* Sabrana dela, knj. 6) First published in 1951 as no. 315 of the *Srpska književna zadruga* series.

Latković, Vido.    Petar Petrović Njegoš. Beograd, Nolit, 1963. 258 p.

2824. Novaković, Boško.    Stevan Sremac i Niš (Stevan Sremac and Niš). Sarajevo, Izdavačko preduzeće "Veselin Masleša," 1959. 175 p. Illus., ports.

2825. Obradović, Dositej.    Sabrana dela (Collected works). Introduction by Vojislav Đurić. Beograd, 1961–

An excellent translation of Obradović's autobiography with a long introduction giving a splendid account of the period is *The Life and Adventures of Dimitrije Obradović*, translated from the Serbian, edited and with an introduction by George Rapali Noyes (Berkeley, University of California Press, 1953, 340 p., map; University of California Publications in Modern Philology, v. 39). There is a journal entirely devoted to articles on Obradović and Karadžić, *Kovčežić; prilozi i gradja o Dositeju i Vuku* (The little coffer; supplementary information and works about Dositej [Obradović] and Vuk [Karadžić] (Beograd, Vukov i Dositejev muzej, 1958–). It is edited by Đuro Gavela.

2826. Popović, Jovan Sterija.    Celokupna dela (Complete works). Beograd, Narodna prosveta, 1928-1931. 5 v. Illus.

At the time of the one hundredth anniversary of Sterija's death the Srpska književna zadruga published in 1956 a volume of essays and studies by various scholars, *Knjiga o Steriji* (A book about Sterija), as volume 335 in their well known series. It contains a useful biographical and bibliographical chronology.

2827. Popović, Pavle.    Milovan Vidaković. Beograd, Geca Kon, 1934. 349 p.

Vidaković's works were very influential in the formation of Serbian literature in the first half of the 19th century. He is too often ignored.

2828. Preradović, Petar.    Djela Petra Preradovića (The works of Petar Preradović). Edited by Branko Vodnik. Zagreb, Tisak Hrvatskog štamp. zavoda, 1918-1919. 2 v.

The first critical edition of this Illyrian poet.

2829. Radičević, Branko.    Pesme Branka Radičevića, sa pismima njegovim i jednim spisom u prozi (The poems of Branko Radičević, with his letters and a document in prose). Edited by Branislav Miljković and Milivoj Pavlović, with an introduction by Pavle Popović. Beograd, Srpska matica, 1924. 502 p.

The lengthy introduction makes this the best full edition of Radičević's poems, invaluable for a comprehension of their background. A recent study of Radičević's language, Vojislav I. Ilić's *Pesnički jezik Branka Radičevića* (The poetic language of Branko Radičević) (Beograd, Matica srpska, 1964, 258 p.), has a useful bibliography.

2830. Šenoa, August.    Sabrana djela (Collected works). Edited by Slavko
Ježić. Zagreb, Znanje, 1963-1964. 12 v.
> Volume 12 contains a full study of the life and works of Šenoa
> by Slavko Ježić, with appendices and an invaluable bibliography.

2831. Vraz, Stanko.    Pjesnička djela (Poetic works). Edited by Slavko
Ježić. Zagreb, Jugoslavenska akademija znanosti i umjetnosti, 1953-
1955. 3 v.
> *See also* his *Slovenska djela* (Slovenian works), edited by Anton
> Slodnjak (Zagreb, Jugoslavenska akademija znanosti i umjetnosti,
> 1952, 2 v.).

2832. Vučenov, Dimitrije.    Radoje Domanović, život, doba i geneza dela
(Radoje Domanović, his life, times, and the genesis of his works).
Beograd, Rad, 1959. 520 p.
> An indispensable work for this author, with a good bibliography.

2833. Zbrana dela slovenskih pesnikov in pisateljev (Collected works of
Slovenian poets and writers). Ljubljana, Državna založba Slovenije,
1946–
> A series of the collected works of the classical writers of Slovenian
> literature. It includes such figures as Anton Aškerc (2 volumes, 1946-
> 1951), Ivan Cankar (6 volumes, 1967), Simon Gregorčič (4 volumes,
> 1947-1951), Josip Jurčič (9 volumes, 1952-1967), Simon Jenko (1
> volume, 1965), Prežihov Voranc (8 volumes, 1962-1965), Anton
> Tomaž Linhart (1 volume, 1950), Josip Murn (2 volumes, 1954),
> Janko Kersnik (5 volumes, 1947-1952), Fran Levstik (9 volumes,
> 1948-1961), Josip Stritar (10 volumes, 1953-1957), Ivan Tavčar (7
> volumes, 1951-1958), Janez Trdina (12 volumes, 1946-1959), and
> Oton Župančič (3 volumes, 1956-1959).

### 5. Literature of the 20th Century

2834. Andrić, Ivo.    Sabrana djela (Collected works). Zagreb, Mladost;
Beograd, Prosveta; Sarajevo, Svjetlost; Ljubljana, Državna založba
Slovenije, 1963. 10 v.
> Among the studies of this Nobel Prize-winning author should
> be mentioned:
> Džadžić, Petar, *ed.*   Kritičari o Andriću (The critics about An-
> drić). Beograd, Nolit. 1962. 249 p.
> Šamić, Midhat.    Istorijski izvori Travničke hronike Ive Andrića i
> njihova umjetnička transpozicija (The historical sources of Ivo
> Andrić's Travnik Chronicle and their artistic transposition). Sara-
> jevo, Veselin Masleša, 1962. 216 p.
> Đuric Vojislav, *ed.*   Ivo Andrić. Beograd, Institut za teoriju
> književnosti i umjetnosti, 1962. 342 p.
> Bandić, Miloš I.    Ivo Andrić; zagonetka vedrine (Ivo Andrić;
> riddle of serenity). Novi Sad, Matica srpska, 1963. 410 p.

Džadžić, Petar.   Ivo Andrić; esej (Ivo Andrić; an essay). Beograd, Nolit, 1957. 227 p.

2835. Cankar, Ivan.   Izbrana dela (Selected works). Edited with notes by Boris Merhar. Ljubljana, Cankarjeva založba, 1951-1959. 10 v. Illus., ports.

2836. Cesarić, Dobriša.   Izabrane pjesme (Selected poems). Zagreb, Matica hrvatska, 1960. 155 p.

Cesarić is widely regarded as the best Croatian lyricist of the 20th century. The corpus of his poetry is so small that it is well represented in this one volume. Other poetry by Cesarić is in a book of poetic translations from Russian and German:

Knjiga prepjeva (A book of poems in translation). Zagreb, Mladost, 1951. 153 p.

2837. Crnjanski, Miloš.   Sabrana dela (Collected works). Beograd, Prosveta, 1966. 10 v.

The works of this important 20th century Serbian writer gathered together for the first time, with a selected bibliography of essays and reviews devoted to Crnjanski by other prominent literary persons.

2838. Kranjčević, Silvije Strahimir.   Sabrana djela (Collected works). Zagreb, Jugoslavenska akademija znanosti i umjetnosti, 1958-1967. 3 v. Ports.

This distinguished edition by Dragutin Tadijanović (volumes 1 and 2) and Ivo Frangeš (volume 3) is definitive, with copious notes, indices, chronology, and commentary.

2839. Krleža, Miroslav.   Sabrana djela (Collected works). Zagreb, Zora, 1953-1967. 25 v.

Studies of and essays on Krleža's works may be found in:

Bogdanović, Milan.   O Krleži (About Krleža). Beograd, Matica srpska, 1956. 122 p.

Vučetić, Šime.   Krležino književno djelo (Krleža's literary works). Sarajevo, Svjetlost, 1958. 327 p.

Matković, Marijan, ed.   Miroslav Krleža. Zagreb, Jugoslovenska akademija znanosti i umjetnosti, 1963. 773 p. Contains an invaluable bibliography of Krleža's works by Davor Kapetanić.

Frangeš, Ivo, and Aleksandar Flaker, eds.   Krležin zbornik (A Krleža miscellany). Zagreb, Naprijed, 1964. 457 p. (Institut za nauku o književnosti Filozofskog fakulteta Sveučilišta u Zagrebu, knj. 1)

Đurić, Vojislav, ed.   Miroslav Krleža. Beograd, Prosveta, 1967. 451 p. (Institut za teoriju književnosti i umetnosti. Posebna izdanja, knj. 2) Contains Davor Kapetanić's indispensable bibliography of works about Krleža.

2840. Marinković, Ranko.   Kiklop (The Cyclops). Beograd, Prosveta, 1965. 508 p.

Other works of this contemporary Croatian master are in: *Ruke*

(Hands) (Beograd, Prosveta, 1956, 291 p.); *Poniženje Sokrata* (The humiliation of Socrates) (Zagreb, Naprijed, 1959, 247 p.); *Glorija*; *mirakl u šest slika* (Gloria; a miracle in six scenes) (Beograd, Nolit, 1966, 216 p.).

2841. Matoš, Antun Gustav.   Sabrana djela (Collected works). Edited by Dragutin Tadijanović. Zagreb, Jugoslavenska akademija znanosti i umjetnosti, 1953–

> Only two volumes (v. 1, 1953; v. 3, 1955) have so far appeared in this excellent edition. The latest complete collected edition is *Djela A. G. Matoša* (The works of A. G. Matoš), edited by Antun Barac and Julije Benešić (Zagreb, Binoza, 1935-1938, 17 v.). Three volumes of selected works edited by Dragutin Tadijanović and Marijan Matković have appeared as volumes 64-66 of the series *Pet soljeća hrvatske književnosti* (*see* entry 2773).

2842. Nazor, Vladimir.   Djela (Works). Zagreb, Nakladni zavod Hrvatske, 1946-1950. 15 v.

> The collected works of an outstanding Croatian literary factotum of the 20th century.

2843. Nehajev, Milutin, *pseud.* (Milutin Cihlar).   Djela (Works). Zagreb, Hrvatski izdavalački bibliografski zavod, 1944-1945?. 13 v.

> The works of a major 20th century Croatian author.

2844. Nušić, Branislav.   Sabrana dela (Collected works). Edited by Ljubiša Manojlović, Beograd, Jez, 1966. 25 v.

> Volume 25 contains a bibliography by Dragoljub Vlatković. A fuller bibliography by Vlatković is to be found in *Zbornik Muzeja pozorišne umjetnosti; Branislav Nušić, 1864-1964* (Miscellany of the museum of theater art; Branislav Nušić, 1864-1964) (Beograd, Muzej pozorišne umjetnosti, 1965, 415, 214 p.). One might note one item not included in the bibliography: Bojan Ničev's *Branislav Nušić* (Sofiia, Bŭlgarska akademiia na naukite, 1962, 290 p.). In Bulgarian with a German summary.

2845. Palavestra, Predrag.   Srpska i hrvatska poezija dvadesetog veka (Serbian and Croatian poetry of the twentieth century). Beograd, Savremena škola, 1964. 320 p.

> This anthology concludes with the work of the contemporary Serbian poet Branko Miljković, and represents the main contributors to Serbo-Croatian poetry since 1909.

2846. Pavletić, Vlatko, *ed.*   Panorama hrvatske književnosti XX stoljeća (The panorama of 20th century Croatian literature). Zagreb, Stvarnost, 1965. 866 p.

> This book treats its subject in three parts: the "Moderna" movement, the interwar period, and contemporary literature. There is also an essay on the use of dialect in this literature, and a good review of the literary journals between 1914 and 1963.

2847. Petrović, Veljko.    Sabrana dela (Collected works). Novi Sad, Matica srpska, 1954-1958. 6 v. Illus.

This 20th century Serbian poet and short story writer is among the best of the older generation.

2848. Pregelj, Ivan.    Izbrani spisi (Selected works). Ljubljana, Jugoslovanska knjigarna, 1928-1935. 10 v. Illus.

One of Slovenia's best 20th century authors. A supplementary volume (11), which includes Pregelj's shorter writings and a variety of biographic data, was published in 1954 (338 p.) by Slovenska kulturna akcija in Buenos Aires as *Moj svet in moj čas* (My world and my times). Some important pieces omitted in this edition are found in his *Izbrana dela* (Selected works) (Celje, Mohorjeva družba, 1962-1966, 5 v.).

2849. Rakić, Milan.    Izabrana dela (Selected works). Beograd, Narodna knjiga, 1964. 260 p.

Milan Rakić is widely thought to be the best Serbian lyricist of the first half of the 20th century. In addition to the canon of his poetry, this edition contains a selection of his critical writings, and essays about him by others. Other editions of his poetry include *Pesme M. M. Rakića* (Poems of M. M. Rakić) (Beograd, 1924, 93 p.) and *Pesme* (Poems) (Beograd, Milica M. Rakić, 1947, 126 p., port., facsim.).

2850. Ravbar, Miroslav, *and* Stanko Janež.    Pregled jugoslovanskih književnosti (A survey of Yugoslav literatures). Maribor, Obzorja, 1960. 606 p. Illus., facsims., fold. map.

This survey in Slovenian covers all the literature in all four languages of Yugoslavia from the beginnings in the Middle Ages to 1960. There is a chapter about the Slavs of Yugoslavia, their languages and dialects (with a dialect map), and another chapter on Oral Literature. The book is especially valuable for biography of recent, lesser-known writers and for its unusually full treatment of 20th century literature.

2851. Samokovlija, Isak.    Tragom života (In search of life). Zagreb, Nakladni zavod Hrvatske, 1948. 506 p.

This is an anthology of tales by the best of the exclusively Bosnian writers in the first half of the 20th century. For the whole of his prose see: *Celokupna dela* (The complete works) (Sarajevo, Svjetlost, 1951-1956, 3 v.).

2852. Selimović, Meša.    Derviš i smrt (Death and the Dervish). 2d ed. Sarajevo, Svjetlost, 1967. 389 p.

This novel is the best work of one of the best authors of the contemporary generation in Bosnia and Hercegovina. Other works by this author are *Tišine* (Silences) (Sarajevo, Svjetlost, 1961, 172 p.) and *Tuđa zemlja* (A foreign land) (Sarajevo, Veselin Masleša, 1962, 167 p.).

2853. Slovenske večernice (Slovenian evening readers). 1861– Celovec/ Celje, Družba sv. Mohorja. Annual.

Many works of Slovenian literature are found in the more than 117 volumes of this series which has been appearing for more than a century "za poduk in kratek čas" (for instruction and entertainment).

2854. Stanković, Borisav. Sabrana dela (Collected works). Beograd, Prosveta, 1956. 2 v.

Volume 2 contains a bibliography of the works of Stanković.

2855. Ujević, Tin (Augustin).    Sabrana djela (Collected works). Zagreb, Znanje, 1963-1967. 17 v.

The complete works of this prolific and influential Croatian writer, with notes and indexes.

2856. Župančič, Oton.    Dela (Works). Ljubljana, Mladinska knjiga, 1967. 5 v. Ports.

The poetry of the outstanding 20th century Slovenian poet. An earlier edition and one that observes the order of original publication is: *Zbrano delo* (The collected works) (Ljubljana, Državna založba Slovenije, 1956-1959, 3 v.). A discussion of this author with many translations of his poetry is:

Tesnière, Lucien.    Oton Joupantchitch, poète slovène; l'homme et l'œuvre. Paris, Les belles-lettres, 1931. 383 p.

## C. FOLKLORE

### by David E. Bynum

2857. Cepenkov, Marko K.    Makedonski narodni prikazni (Macedonian folk tales). Skoplje, Kočo Racin, 1958-1959. 3 v.

An important posthumously published collection edited with an introduction, biographical sketch of Cepenkov, glossaries of difficult words and idioms, and an index of subjects by the Macedonian scholar Kiril Penušliski.

2858. Gavazzi, Milovan.    Narodni običaji (Folk customs). *In* Enciklopedija Jugoslavije. v. 6. Zagreb, Jugoslavenski leksikografski zavod, 1965. p. 245-252.

Family, marital, funerary, calendrical, and other customs and their regional variations in Yugoslav ceremonial and ritual life.

2859. Hörmann, Kosta.    Narodne pjesme Muslimana u Bosni i Hercegovini (Folk songs of the Moslems in Bosnia and Hercegovina). Sarajevo, J. Kušan, 1933. v. 2.

This is the classic collection of Moslem epic poetry in Serbocroatian. An important supplement to it consisting of songs and synopses from Hörmann's literary remains is:

Buturović, Đenan, *ed.* Narodne pjesme Muslimana u Bosni i Hercegovini iz rukopisne ostavštine Koste Hörmanna (Folk songs of the Moslems in Bosnia and Hercegovina from the manuscript legacy of Kosta Hörmann). Sarajevo, Zemalski muzej, 1966. 230 p.

2860. Jovanović, Milka, *and others.* Narodna nošnja (Folk costume). *In* Enciklopedija Jugoslavije. v. 6. Zagreb, Jugoslavenski leksikografski zavod, 1965. p. 229-244. Illus.

Essays with bibliography on native dress and some of its ceremonial connotations, arranged by regions and districts.

2861. Karadžić, Vuk Stefanović. Sabrana dela (Collected works). Beograd, Prosveta, 1965–

*See also* entry no. 2815.

Basic collections of numerous genres of folklore, and writings which have shaped scholarly opinion on many topics, including oral epic, folktale, proverbs, customs, and beliefs.

An earlier edition of Karadžić's work on folksong is his *Srpske narodne pjesme* (Serbian folk songs) (Beograd, Štamparija Kraljevine Srbije, 1891-1902, 9 v.). This is the so-called State Edition, the *editio princeps* of the classic Serbian collection of Yugoslav folk poetry.

More recent editions, with annotation and glossary, as prepared by R. Aleksić and others, appeared as *Srpske narodne pjesme* (Beograd, Prosveta, 1953-1954, 4 v.; 2d ed. Beograd, Prosveta, 1958, 4 v.). This is the classic Serbian collection of folk lyric, balladic and epic poetry in the only fully annotated edition and with glossaries of difficult words.

2862. Latković, Vido, *and others.* Narodna književnost (Folk literature). *In* Enciklopedija Jugoslavije. v. 6. Zagreb, Jugoslavenski leksikografski zavod, 1965. p. 204-220.

Fourteen essays, each with its own bibliography, treating the history of collecting and publication, the genres, the style, the scholarship, and translation into other languages of Yugoslav verbal folklore.

2863. Lord, Albert Bates. The Singer of Tales. Cambridge, Mass., Harvard University Press, 1960. 309 p. Music. (Harvard Studies in Comparative Literature, 24)

This book is the main statement and demonstration of the Oral Theory, a major development of literary science in the 20th century which is based chiefly on evidence in Serbo-Croatian oral epic poetry.

2864. Ložar, Rajko, *ed.* Narodopisje Slovencev (The ethnography of the Slovenes). Ljubljana, 1944-1952. 2 v. Illus.

*See also* entry no. 2293.

The standard work on Slovenian ethnography and folklore. Copious bibliography.

2865. Matica hrvatska, *Zagreb.* Hrvatske narodne pjesme (Croatian folk songs). Edited by Ivan Broz and others. Zagreb, Matica hrvatska, 1896-1942. 10 v.

The basic published Croatian collection of folk poetry from Croatia, Dalmatia, Bosnia and Hercegovina, Slavonia, and the Vojvodina. Volumes 3 and 4 contain most of the published portion of Luka Marjanović's famous collection of long Moslem epics from Bosnia.

2866. Merhar, Boris.    Folklora in narodopisje (Folklore and ethnography). *In* Bernik, France, *ed.* Slovenska matica, 1864-1964. Ljubljana, Slovenska Matica, 1964. p. 116-140.

A concise critical survey of the many folkloristic and ethnographic studies and materials sponsored and published by Slovenska matica in Slovenia.

2867. Mikhailov, Pancho (Pančo Mihajlov).    Bŭlgarski narodni piesni ot Makedoniia (Bulgarian folk songs from Macedonia). Sofiia, Shtipsko blagotvor. bratstvo, 1924. 295 p. Illus., music, ports.

A collection of Macedonian songs with music is:

Tsŭrnushanov, Kosta, *ed.    Makedonski narodni pesni* (Macedonian folk songs). Sofiia, Bŭlgarska akademiia na naukite, 1956. 390 p.

2868. Miladinov, Dimitŭr, *and* Konstantin Miladinov.    Bŭlgarski narodni piesni (Bulgarian folk songs). Sofiia, Ministerstvo na narodnoto prosvieshtenie, 1942. 571 p. Ports.

This is the classic collection of Macedonian folk poetry. It appeared first in Zagreb in 1861; later editions were issued at Sofia in 1891, again in 1961, and at Skopje, 1961.

2869. Murko, Matija.    Tragom srpsko-hrvatske narodne epike; putovanja u godinama 1930-1932 (In quest of the Serbo-Croatian folk epic; travels in the years 1930-1932). Zagreb, Jugoslavenska akademija znanosti i umjetnosti, 1951. 2 v. Illus., ports., fold. map. (Djelo Jugoslavenske akademije znanosti i umjetnosti, knj. 41-42)

This is the fullest published report of a modern epic collector's field experience in Yugoslavia. An excellent modern monograph on the epic poetry itself is:

Schmaus, Alois.    Studije o krajinskoj epici (Studies on the epic poetry of the border). Zagreb, Jugoslavenska akademija znanosti i umjetnosti, 1953. 247 p.

2870. Narodna umjetnost (Folk art). Knj. 1- 1962- Zagreb, Institut za narodnu umjetnost. Illus., music, plates.

Contains materials, monographs and bibliography of current publications on all aspects of folklore in Croatia, including ethnomusicology.

2871. Parry, Milman, *comp.    *Serbocroatian Heroic Songs. Edited and translated by Albert Lord.    Cambridge, Mass., Harvard University Press; Belgrade, Serbian Academy of Sciences, 1953-

The volumes of this series appear in pairs, each volume of original texts and notes with a companion volume of English translations, synopses of variants, and commentary. Another volume of material from the Parry Collection outside this series is:
Bartók, Béla, *and* Albert B. Lord.   Serbo-Croatian Folk Songs. New York, Columbia University Press, 1951. 431 p. (Columbia University Studies in Musicology, no. 7) Contains texts, music, and translations.

2872. Šaulić, Novica.   Srpske narodne tužbalice (Serbian folk laments). Beograd, Narodna misao, 1929. 336 p.
The classic collection of folk elegies in Serbo-Croatian.

2873. Sbornik na narodni umotvoreniia i narodopis (Archive for folk arts and ethnography). Sofiia, Bŭlgarska akademiia na naukite, 1889–
Volumes 1-18 published by Ministerstvo na narodnoto prosveshtenie; volumes 19-26 by Bŭlgarskoto knizhovno druzhestvo. The title of volumes 1–26 is: *Sbornik na narodni umotvoreniia, nauka i knizhnina* (Archive for folk arts, science, and literature). This estimable series contains much material from the folklore of Yugoslavia.

2874. Schneeweis, Edmund.   Serbokroatische Volkskunde. Erster Teil, Volksglaube und Volksbrauch. Berlin, Walter de Gruyter, 1961. 218 p.
This is a second, revised edition of *Grundriss des Volksglaubens und Volksbrauchs der Serbokroaten*, published first in Celje, 1935, and the most valuable survey of these subjects in a non-Slavic language.

2875. Shapkarev, Kuzman A.   Sbornik ot bŭlgarski narodni umotvoreniia (Archive of Bulgarian folk art). Sofiia, Liberalnii klub, 1891-1894. 9 v.
Folklore from Macedonia. An excellent monograph on the collector and ethnographer Shapkarev is:
Dinekov, Petŭr.   Kuzman A. Shapkarev, sŭbirach na narodni umotvoreniia (Kuzman A. Shapkarev, collector of folklore). *In*: Sbornik na Bŭlgarskata akademiia na naukite, v. 34, 1940: 471-562.

2876. Slovenski etnograf, časopis za etnografijo in folkloro (The Slovenian ethnographer, a journal for ethnography and folklore). letnik 1– 1948– Ljubljana, Etnografski muzej. Illus., ports., maps, music. Annual.
Since its foundation this journal has been the major forum for Slovenian folklore studies. It succeeds:
Etnolog (The ethnologist). 1926-1944. 17 v. Ljubljana, Etnografski muzej v Ljubljani. (1940–, Etnografsko društvo v Ljubljani). Illus., ports.

2877. Srpska akademija nauka i umetnost, *Belgrade*.   Srpski etnografski zbornik (Serbian ethnographic archive). Knj. 1– 1894– Illus., maps part fold.), atlases.

> This is the major repository in Serbia for materials and monographs on all aspects of Yugoslav folklore.

2878. Štrekelj, Karl (Karel).   Slovenske narodne pesmi iz tiskanih in pisanih virov (Slovenian folk songs from printed and manuscript sources). Ljubljana, Slovenska matica, 1895-1923. 4 v.

> The basic published collection of Slovenian folk poetry. See also: Kuret, Niko.   Praznično leto Slovencev; starosvetne šege in navade od pomladi do zime (The Slovene yearly cycle of feast-days; traditional observances and customs from spring to winter). Celje, Mohorjeva družba, 1965–. Illus.

2879. Strohal, Rudolf, comp. and ed.   Hrvatske narodne pripovijetke (Croatian folk tales). Rijeka, Karlovac, 1886-1904. 3 v.

> The classic Croatian collection of folktales. An earlier important collection from another part of Croatia is: Valjavec, Matija Kračmanov.   Narodne pripovjedke skupio u i oko Varaždin (Folk stories from Varaždin and vicinity). Varaždin, Josip Platzer, 1858. 315 p. Reissued as Narodne pripovjesti u Varaždinu i okolici (Folk tales in Varaždin and its environs) (Zagreb, Knjižara Dioničke tiskare, 1890, 315 p.).

2880. Verković, Stefan I.   Narodne pesme makedonski Bugara (Folk songs of the Macedonian Bulgars). Beograd, Pravitelstvenom knigopečatnom, 1860. 373 p.

> A recent, more readily available, and modernized edition of this work is: Penušliski, Kiril.   Makedonski narodni pesni (Macedonian folk songs). Skopje, Kočo Racin, 1961. 356 p.

2881. Zbornik za narodni život i običaje južnih Slavena (Archive for the folk life and customs of the southern Slavs). Zagreb, Jugoslavenska akademija znanosti i umjetnosti, 1896– Illus., plates, maps, plans, diagrs. Annual (semiannual 1898-1916).

> This is the major repository in Croatia for materials and monographs on all aspects of Yugoslav folklore.

2882. Žganec, Vinko, and Božidar Širola.   Narodna muzika (Folk music). In Enciklopedija Jugoslavije. v. 6. Zagreb, Jugoslavenski leksikografski zavod, 1965. p. 223-229.

> On the ethnomusicology of Yugoslavia.

## D. THEATER, DRAMA, CINEMA

### 1. Theater and Drama

*by David E. Bynum*

2883. Andrić, Nikola.   Izvori starih kajkavskih drama (The sources of old kajkavian dramas). *In*: Jugoslavenska akademija znanosti i umjetnosti, Zagreb. Rad Jugoslavenske akademije znanosti i umjetnosti (Zagreb), v. 146, 1901: 1-77.

> Numerous of the plays discussed in this work are unpublished; it contains summaries, critical comment, and comparisons of these early Croatian plays with their German originals and models.

2884. Badalić, Josip.   Bibliografija hrvatske dramske i kazališne književnosti (A bibliography of Croatian dramatic and theatrical literature). Zagreb, Jugoslavenska akademija znanosti i umjetnosti, 1948. 318 p.

> An exemplary compilation covering the whole literature from before the Renaissance in Dalmatia to the end of the Second World War.

2885. Belgrade. Muzej pozorišne umetnosti N.R. Srbije.   Zbornik Muzeja pozorišne umetnosti (Archive of the Museum of Theatrical Art). 1– Beograd, 1962–

> A learned journal devoted entirely to the history of drama and theater.

2886. Cindrić, Pavao.   Hrvatski i srpski teatar (Croatian and Serbian theater). Zagreb, Lykos, 1960. p. 249. Illus., bibliography. (Svjedočanstva, br. 6)

> A popular history with a useful biographical list of playwrights, actors and other personalities.

2887. Cvetković, Sava V., *ed.*   Repertoar Narodnog pozorišta u Beogradu 1868-1965. Hronološki pregled premijera i obnova (The repertory of the National Theater in Belgrade from 1868 to 1965. Chronological survey of premieres and revivals). Beograd, Muzej pozorišne umjetnosti, 1966. 172 p.

> Issued for the hundredth anniversary of this company. Two other centenary memorial volumes of the same time contain historical essays, materials, and incunabula:
>
> Roksandić, Duško, *and* Slavko Batušić, *eds.*   Hrvatsko narodno kazalište. Zbornik o stogodnišnjici, 1860-1960 (The Croatian National Theater. A volume on its centennial, 1860-1960). Zagreb, Naprijed, 1960. 326 p.
>
> Yugoslavia, *Srpsko narodno pozorište.* Spomenica, 1861-1961 (Memorial, 1861-1961). Novi Sad, 1961. 626 p. On the Serbian National Theater in Novi Sad.

2888. Đoković, Milan, *and others.*   Dramska književnost (Dramatic literature). *In* Enciklopedija Jugoslavije. v. 3. Zagreb, Leksikografski zavod FNRJ, 1958. p. 72-79.

> Five pieces of varying length on the dramatic literatures claimed by each of the present national republics of Yugoslavia.

2889. Dotlić, Luka, *and others.*   Zbornik priloga istoriji jugoslovenskih pozorišta (A collection of contributions to the history of Yugoslav

theaters). Novi Sad, Srpkso narodno pozorište u Novom Sadu, 1961.
385 p.

A centenary memorial volume for the Novi Sad theatrical company, containing important essays on a wide range of unusual subjects from the modern revival of Dalmatian Renaissance theater to
the beginnings of dramaturgy in Yugoslav Macedonia.

2890. Gudel, Vladimir.    Stare kajkavske drame (Old kajkavian plays).
Zagreb, Published by the Author, 1900.

Only 48 pages long, this monograph supplements and criticizes
N. Andric's "Izvori starih kajkavskih drama" (see entry 2883).
Gudel supplies here considerable information about unpublished
and lost plays.

2891. Jevtić, Borivoje.    Deset godina sarajevskog pozorišta, kulturno
istorijska studija (Ten years of the Sarajevo theater, a cultural-
historical study). Sarajevo, Izdanje časopisa Pregled, 1931. 138 p.
Illus., ports. (Grupa sarajevskih književnika, knj. 9)

On the beginnings of theatrical and dramatic art in the capital of
Bosnia and Hercegovina.

2892. Koblar, France.    Dvajset let slovenske drame (Twenty years of
Slovenian drama). Ljubljana, Slovenska Matica, 1964. 2 v.

The history of drama and dramatic productions in Slovenia from
1919 to 1939.

2893. Maletić, Đorđe.    Građa za istoriju srpskog narodnog pozorišta u
Beogradu od godine 1835 do 1876 (Material for the history of the
Serbian National Theater in Belgrade from 1835 to 1876. Beograd,
Čupićeva zadužbina, 1884. 1044 p.

A large, detailed chronicle of plays and their production by the
Serbian national theatrical company during the years indicated.
Much of this work is description and criticism of unpublished plays
performed by the company, given with synopses and references to
other summaries and comment in the contemporary press, and unique
information about authors, dates of writing and revision, and other
literary data.

2894. Pavić, Armin.    Historija dubrovačke drame (A history of Dubrovnik
drama). Zagreb, Jugoslavenska akademija znanosti i umjetnosti,
1871. 198 p.

In spite of its age, still the standard work on Dalmation drama
from the early religious theater of Hvar and Split to the fall of
Dubrovnik in 1806. Contains synopses of outstanding plays in each
period.

2895. Petrić, Vladimir, ed.    Teatar Joakima Vujića (The theater of Joakim
Vujić). Beograd, Nolit, 1965. 173 p.

The editor contributes a preface, an historical note on Vujić and his travels, and a bibliography to accompany the text of two of Vujić's plays which are still occasionally staged: "Nabrežnoje pravo" (The right of salvage) and "Ljubovnaja zavist čerez jedne cipele" (Lovers' jealousy wrought by a shoe), a melodrama and a comedy respectively. For more about Vujić *see*:

Mihailović, Dušan.   Knjažesko-srbski teatr (The Royal Serbian Theater). *In: Politika* (Belgrade), Dec. 17-23, 1960.

2896.  Repertoar slovenskih gledališč, 1867-1967 (The repertory of Slovenian theaters). Ljubljana, Slovenski gledališki muzej, 1967. 759 p.
A catalog of all the recorded productions in Slovenia during the hundred years indicated.

2897.  Šumarević, Svetislav.   Pozorište kod Srba (Serbian theater). Beograd, Luča, biblioteka Zadruge profesorskog društva, 1939. 449 p.
Treats the origins and the growth of dramatic activity among the Serbs during the 19th century.

2898.  Tomandl, Mihovil.   Srpsko pozorište u Vojvodini (Serbian theater in the Vojvodina). Stari Bečej, Matica srpska, 1953-1954. 2 v.
This model of theatrical historiography provides an invaluable survey of the forces that shaped the drama in the Vojvodina. Volume 1: 1736-1868; volume 2, 1868-1919.

2899.  Wollman, Frank.   Slovinské drama (Slovenian drama). Bratislava, Filosofická fakulta University Komenského, 1925. 332 p. Bibligraphy: p. 304-306. (Spisy Filosofické fakulty University Komenského v Bratislavě, čis. 6)
An earlier work on the same subject is:
Trstenjak, Anton.   Slovensko gledališče; zgodovina gledaliških predstav in dramatične književnosti slovenske (The Slovenian theater; a history of Slovenian theatrical performances and dramatic literature). Ljubljana, Dramatično društvo, 1892. 197 p. Illus.

2900.  Wollman, Frank.   Srbochorvatské drama; přehled vývoje do války (Serbo-Croatian drama; a survey of development up to the war). Bratislava, Filosofická fakulta University Komenského, 1924. 408 p. (Spisy Filosofické fakulty University Komenského v Bratislavě, čis. 5)
Although this book is in Czech, it is the only study that deals with both Croatian and Serbian drama and with the aspects of their development which they have in common.

## 2. Cinema

*by Paul L. Horecky*

2901.  Katalog Jugoslovenskog dokumentarnog filma (Catalog of Yugoslav documentary and short films). 1960– Beograd. Annual.
A listing of Yugoslav film production in this field of endeavor,

published in Serbo-Croatian and major foreign languages in connection with the annual Festival of Yugoslav Documentary and Short Films.

2902. Volk, Petar. Balada o trubi i maglama (Ballad of the horn and the fog). *In* Belan, Branko. Sjaj i bijeda filma (Splendor and misery of the film). Zagreb, Epoha, 1966. p. 237-335.

A detailed survey of the film in Yugoslavia. For other materials on the subject *see*:

Brenk, France. Aperçu de l'histoire du cinéma yougoslave. Ljubljana, Académie de l'art dramatique, 1961. 77 p. Illus.

Novaković, Slobodan. 20 Years of the Yugoslav Film. Belgrade, Festival of Yugoslav Films, 1965. 49 p.

Yugoslav Features. Les films yougoslaves. Belgrade, Yugoslavia Film, 1959. 217 p. Illus. This catalog presents in chronological order a descriptive listing of Yugoslav feature films from 1947 through 1958. Text in English and French.

Filmska kultura (Cinematography). 1957- Nagreb. Bimonthly. The leading journal in the field, edited by S. Ostojić and others.

# E. HISTORY OF THOUGHT, CULTURE, AND SCHOLARSHIP*

## by Michael B. Petrovich

2903. Atanasijević, Ksenija. Penseurs yougoslaves. Belgrade, Bureau Central de Presse, 1937. 307 p.

.A brief survey of the history of Yugoslav thought, with separate chapters on Marulić, Petrić, Bošković, Bartulović, Obradović, Njegoš, Knežević, Petronijević, and Cvijić.

2904. Babić, Ivo, *and* Marijan Filipović. Scientific Institutions in Yugoslavia. Belgrade, Edition Jugoslavija, 1958. 148 p.

Interpreting the word "scientific" in its broad European sense, this directory presents a brief history of scholarship in Yugoslavia. Then it lists all scholarly institutions, libraries, learned societies, and their periodicals in Yugoslavia, and gives an adequate brief description of each. For another directory published in the same year, see *The Academies of Science in the Federative People's Republic of Yugoslavia*, published by the Akademski savet FNRJ (Belgrade, 1958, 74 p.). For an even more recent and complete directory, but in Serbo-Croatian, *see* the *Adresar naučnih institucija SFRJ* (Directory of scientific institutions in the SFRY) (Beograd, Savezna privredna komora i Institut za naučno-tehničku dokumentaciju i informacije, 1965, 310 p.).

2905. Belgrade. Univerzitet. Sto godina Filozofskog fakulteta (One hundred years of the Faculty of Philosophy). Beograd, 1963. 885 p.

A massive monument to the centenary of the Faculty of Philosophy

* For learned institutions, libraries, archives and museums see chapter 1, sections F and G.

of the University of Belgrade. After a history of the entire school, the book proceeds to describe in great detail the work of all three divisions — Philosophy (philosophy, sociology, pedagogy, psychology, history, history of art, archaeology, ethnology, classical philology), Philology (linguistics, languages, and literature) and the Natural Sciences and Mathematics. An encyclopedic survey of great value.

2906. Črnja, Zvane.   Kulturna historija Hrvatske (Cultural history of Croatia). Zagreb, Epoha, 1964. 748 p. Illus. Bibliography: p. 661-701.
     *See also* entry no. 2350.
         An abridged version was published in English in 1962 under the same title. The Croatian original is a massive compilation treating Croatian cultural history from earliest times to the present. The author claims no special professional competence as a cultural historian. The book is lavishly illustrated.

2907. Horvat, Josip.   Kultura Hrvata kroz 1000 godina (The culture of the Croats during 1000 years). Zagreb, A. Velzek, 1939-1942. 2 v. Illus., plates, ports.
     *See also* entry no. 2349.
         A massive and detailed survey, written from a patriotic point of view but including much valuable material.

2908. Jagić, Vatroslav.   Spomeni mojega života (Recollections of my life). Beograd, Srpska kraljevska akademija, 1930-1934. 2 v. (Posebna izdanja, 75, 104; Društveni i istoriski spisi, knj. 30 and 45)
         Memoirs of a leading Croatian philologist and linguist who was a pioneer in Slavic studies. Jagić lived from 1838 to 1923 and studied and taught in Zagreb, Odessa, St. Petersburg, Berlin, and Vienna.

2909. Kićović, Miraš.   Istorija Narodne biblioteke u Beogradu (History of the National Library in Belgrade). Beograd, 1960. 258 p. Illus., ports.
         A basic history, by a librarian and literary and cultural historian.

2910. Matica srpska, 1826-1926. Novi Sad, Matica srpska, 1927. 704 p.
         Twenty-one studies by leading scholars on every important activity of this distinguished Serbian cultural center.

2911. McCellan, Woodford D.   Svetozar Marković and the Origins of Balkan Socialism. Princeton, N.J., Princeton University Press, 1964. 308 p. Bibliography: p. 275-296.
     *See also* entry no. 2334.
         A solid piece of research by an American who has worked in the libraries of Berkeley, Moscow, Leningrad, Belgrade, and Novi Sad, as well as in Soviet and Yugoslav archives. The author concludes that Marković deserves more from present-day communists than to be condescendingly praised and belittled as a mere utopian socialist. For some Yugoslav works on Marković, *see* especially Jovan Skerlić's

*Svetozar Marković; njegov život, rad i ideje* (Svetozar Marković; his life, work, and ideas) (2d ed., Beograd, 1922, 248 p.); Slobodan Jovanović's *Svetozar Marković* (Beograd, 1920, 217 p.); Veselin Masleša's *Svetozar Marković* (Beograd, 1946); V. Gligorić's *O životu i delu Svetozara Markovića* (Life and work of Svetozar Marković) (Beograd, 1946, 52 p.); and Lj. Manojlović's *Svetozar Marković* (Beograd, Nolit, 1963, 232 p.). For Marković's own writings, see his *Sabrani spisi* (Collected works) (Beograd, 1960-1965, 4 v.) and the Russian anthology *Svetozar Markovich, izbrannye sochineniia* (Selected works) (Moskva, 1956, 919 p.).

2912. Prijatelj, Ivan.   Kulturna in politična zgodovina Slovencev, 1848-1895 (Cultural and political history of the Slovenes, 1848-1895). Edited by Anton Ocvirk. Ljubljana, Akademska založba, 1938-1940. 4 v.

The standard work on Slovenian cultural history during the latter half of the 19th century. Despite the reference to political history in the title, this is in fact a cultural and intellectual history and was inevitably linked with the Slovenian national movement.

For a collection of contributions dealing with various intellectual aspects of the Slovenian Reformation see *Abhandlungen über die slowenische Reformation* (München, Trofenik, 1968, 268, 84 p. with illus.).

2913. Raković, Branko.   Scientific Policy in Yugoslavia. Minerva, 1965. no. 2: 187-209.

The development of scientific and technical research and the organization of science and technology prior to 1957 are reviewed at some length and compared with the state of affairs between 1957 and early 1965. The current situation is surveyed on the basis of the explicit national science policy introduced in 1957 with the founding of the federal and republic research councils. The author treats the roles of the academies of sciences, the universities, industry, and government in scientific research and planning. The relation of the constitutional reform of 1963 to science policy is evaluated, and the financing of scientific research is discussed. For a recent treatment of the subject, consult *Science Policy and the Organization of Scientific Research in the Socialist Federal Republic of Yugoslavia* (Paris, UNESCO, 1968, 123 p.).

2914. Ravlić, Jakša, *and* Marin Somborac.   Matica hrvatska, 1842-1962. Povijest Matice hrvatske. Bibliografija izdanja Matice (The Matica hrvatska, 1842-1962. History of the Matica hrvatska. Bibliography of the Matica hrvatska). Zagreb, 1963. 434 p. Illus., bibliography. *See also* entry no. 2147.

This centennial history of the Matica hrvatska (Croatian matrix) deals with one of the most influential and active cultural centers of the Croatian nation at a time when much of the struggle for national political identity was linked with the cultural movement. In addition to Ravlić's history, the bibliography of 1,385 items by Somborac gives impressive testimony to the work of this institution. For an earlier work, see also *Matica hrvatska od godine 1842 do godine 1892; spomenknjiga*, by Tade Smičiklas and Franjo Marković (Zagreb, Matica hrvatska, 1892, 338 p., ports., facsims.).

2915. Smotra jugoslovanskih kulturnih društev (Survey of Yugoslav cultural societies). Ljubljana, 1911. 64 p.

Published by the Matica hrvatska in Zagreb, Slovenska matica in Ljubljana, Matica srpska in Novi Sad, and the Srpska književna zadruga in Belgrade, this work contains articles on cultural institutions, learned societies, theaters, and other cultural centers among the Serbs, Croats, and Slovenes.

2916. Yugoslav Scientific Research Directory, 1964. Belgrad, Nolit Publishing House, 1964. 590 p. (Published for the National Library of Medicine through the National Science Foundation)

A guide to scientific organizations in Yugoslavia, including institutions dealing with the organization and financing of scientific research, research organizations, academies of science, institutions of higher learning, archives, museums, libraries, and professional societies, as of February 1963. The address, name of the director, scope of activities, facilities, and names of the professional staff of each institution are cited. The texts of laws dealing with the organization and financing of research are included. There is an index of publications of scientific institutions, indexes of scientific institutions according to discipline, according to republics, and according to types of institutions, an alphabetical index of institutions, and an index of personal names. A survey of the development and status of scientific research in Yugoslavia is given in the introduction.

2917. Zagorsky, Vladimir.   François Rački et la renaissance scientifique et politique de la Croatie, 1828-1894. Paris, Hachette, 1909. 257 p.

A solid work on the great 19th century Croatian historian and cultural leader and his role in the Croatian national renascence.

2918. Zbornik na trudovi na Narodniot muzej, Ohrid; posebno izdanje po povod 10 godišninata na osnuvaneto na Muzejot (Symposium on the activities of the National Museum, Ohrid; special publication on the occasion of the 10th anniversary of the founding of the Museum). Ohrid, 1961. 244 p.

## F. RELIGION

*by Michael B. Petrovich*

2919. Draganović, Krunoslav S.   Croazia sacra. Roma, Officium libri catholici, 1943. 311 p.

Historical survey of Catholicism in the Croatian lands from the earliest times. Essays by Croatian scholars in Italian.

2920.  Đurđev (Djurdjev), Branislav.    Uloga crkve u starijoj istoriji srpskog naroda (The role of the church in the early history of the Serbian people). Sarajevo, Svjetlost, 1964. 239 p. (Biblioteka društvo i religija)

A small but important survey of Serbian church history in the Middle Ages and under Ottoman rule, by a critical Marxist historian who stresses the feudal character of the Orthodox church as well as its national cultural role.

2921.  French, Reginald M.    Serbian Church Life. London, Society for Promoting Christian Knowledge; New York, Macmillan, 1942. 64 p.

A brief description of Serbian church history, worship, religious ideas, holidays, rituals, and organizations, by an English observer.

2922.  Gavrilović, Andra.    Sveti Sava; pregled života i rada (Saint Sava; a survey of his life and work). Beograd, Državna štamparija, 1900. 220 p. Illus.

A biography of the Serbian Church's greatest national saint and founder of its autonomy. For other biographies, see *The Life of St. Sava*, by Nikolaj, Bishop of Ohrid (Libertyville, Ill., Serbian Eastern Orthodox Diocese for the United States of America and Canada, 1951, 233 p.), a popular presentation; *Sveti Sava* (Saint Sava) (Beograd, 1935, 123 p.), by the distinguished medievalist scholar Stanoje Stanojević; and two volumes of the *Svetosavski Zbornik* (Saint Sava miscellany) (Beograd, Srpska akademija nauka i umetnosti, 1936-1939; Posebna izdanja 114, 125).

2923.  Gavranović, Berislav.    Uspostava redovite katoličke hijerarhije u Bosni i Hercegovini 1881 godine (The establishment of a regular Catholic hierarchy in Bosnia and Hercegovina in 1881). Beograd, Filozofski fakultet Univerziteta, 1935. 394 p. Illus.

A detailed history of the establishment of a regular Catholic hierarchy in Bosnia and Hercegovina after the Austrian occupation.

2924.  Hadrovics, László.    Le peuple serbe et son église sous la domination turque. Paris, Presses universitaires de France, 1947. 168 p. Bibliography: p. 158-162. (Bibliothèque de la Revue d'histoire comparée, 6)

The best account in a Western language of the Serbian Orthodox Church under Ottoman rule, by a Hungarian scholar who is obviously at home with Slavic and non-Slavic sources. This all too brief book ends with the transfer of the Serbian patriarchate to Hungary and the suppression of the patriarchate of Peć by the Turks in 1766.

2925.  Herzog, Heinrich.    Die Verfassung der Deutschen evangelisch-christlichen Kirche Augsburgischen Bekenntnisses im Königreiche Jugoslawien. Leipzig, Weicher, 1933. 162 p. (Leipziger rechtswissenschaftliche Studien, Hft. 81)

Examination of the constitution of December 22, 1930. For the history of the German Lutheran church in Yugoslavia, *see* Balduin Saria's "Die Gründung der Deutschen evangelisch-christlichen Kirche A. B. im Königreiche Jugoslawien," in *Ostdeutsche Wissenschaft* (München), v. 7, 1960: 263-285.

2926. Hudal, Alois.   Die serbisch-orthodoxe Nationalkirche. Graz und Leipzig, U. Moser, 1922. 126 p. (Beiträge zur Erforschung der orthodoxen Kirchen, 1)

History of the Serbian Orthodox Church from the end of the ninth century to the end of the First World War.

2927. Kniewald, Dragutin.   Vjerodostojnost latinskih izvora o bosanskim krstjanima (The veracity of Latin sources regarding the Bosnian Christians). Zagreb, Jugoslavenska akademija znanosti i umjetnosti, 1949. 166 p. Illus.

A scholarly critique of Latin sources on the Bogomils of Bosnia. The author concludes that the "Bosnian Church" was Manichaean and heretical. For other Yugoslav accounts of the problem *see* Vaso Glušac's *Istina o bogomilima* (The truth about the Bogomils) (Beograd, 1941, 272 p.); L. Petrović's *Kršcani bosanske crkve* (The Christians of the Bosnian Church) (Sarajevo, 1953, 184 p.); and Jaroslav Šidak's *Crkva bosanska i problem bogomilstva u Bosni* (The Bosnian Church and the problem of Bogomilism in Bosnia (Zagreb, 1940, 163 p.). For an analytical guide to Yugoslav scholarship on the subject, *see also* Šidak's study "Problem 'bosanske crkve' u našoj historiografiji od Petranovića do Glušca" (*Rad Jugoslavenske Akademije*, 259, 1937: 37-182), and Franjo Rački's *Borba južnih Slovena za državnu neodvisnost; Bogomili i Patareni* (The struggle of the South Slavs for political independence; the Bogomils and the Patarenes) (Beograd, 1931, 599 p.).

2928. Lanović, Mihailo.   Konkordat Jugoslavije s Vatikanom (Yugoslavia's concordat with the Vatican). Beograd, Štamparija "Sv. Sava," 1925. 107 p. (Biblioteke savremenih religiozno-moralnih pitanja, knj. 15 i 16)

A discussion of various factors which were to play a role in the negotiations for a concordat between the Vatican and the kindom of Yugoslavia. For a favorable view during the political struggle of the mid-1930s over this question, as reflected in selected press opinions, see *Javno mnjenje o konkordatu* (Public opinion on the Concordat) (Beograd, 1937, 195 p.).

2929. Milaš, Nikodim, *Bishop of Dalmatia, ed.*   Spisi o istoriji pravoslavne crkve u dalmatinsko-istrijskom vladičanstvu, od XV do XIX vijeka (Documents on the history of the Orthodox Church in the Dalmatian-Istrian Diocese from the 15th to the 19th century). v. 1. Zadar, Tip. C. Artale, 1899.

The author was a Serbian orthodox bishop in Dalmatia as well as a historian. The documents he presents extend from 1412 to 1796 and are largely in Italian, with some in Slavic and Greek.

2930. Mousset, Jean.   La Serbie et son église (1830-1904). Paris, Droz, 1938. 523 p. Bibliography: p. 11-18.

A rare account of the position of the Orthodox Church in the principality, and later kingdom, of Serbia from 1830 to 1904. A doctoral dissertation at the University of Paris, this massive work is based on excellent Serbian and other secondary sources as well as some published primary sources.

2931. Novak, Viktor.   Magnum crimen; pola vijeka klerikalizma u Hrvatskoj (Magnum crimen; a half-century of clericalism in Croatia). Zagreb, 1948. 1119 p.

A caustic attack on the "clerofascism" of the Roman Catholic Church in Yugoslavia from the First through the Second World Wars. The author stresses the church's antinational role and its ties with the fascist Independent State of Croatia during World War II.

2932. Pattee, Richard.   The Case of Cardinal Aloysius Stepinac. Milwaukee, Bruce Pub. Co., 1953. 499 p. Bibliography: p. 498-499.

A documentary description of the background of the trial of Cardinal Stepinac by the Yugoslav Government in 1946, by an American supporter of the Cardinal. The author writes: "Up to the present, only the documents for the prosecution have been made public. Here, for the first time, the documents for the defense are made available." For another sympathetic account in English, see also Anthony H. O'Brien's *Archbishop Stepinac, the Man and His Case* (Westminster, Md., Newman Bookshop, 1947, 100 p.). The official case of the Yugoslav government has been presented in *The Case of Archbishop Stepinac* (Washington, D.C., Yugoslav Embassy, 1947, 96 p.).

2933. Popan, Flaviu, *and* Čedomir Drašković.   Orthodoxie heute in Rumänien und Jugoslawien. Wien, Herder, 1960. 190 p.

*See also* entry no. 2007.

Deals with the conditions of the Orthodox Church and with the state of Orthodox theology in communist Yugoslavia and Romania. For a collection of legal regulations governing religious activities, *see*:

Yugoslavia. *Laws, statutes, etc.*   The Legal Status of Religious Communities in Yugoslavia. Foreword by Petar Ivičević. Translated by Borivoje Ljotić and Boško Milosavljević. Beograd, Međunarodna štampa-Interpress, 1967. 86 p.

2934. Pospischil, Viktor J.   Der Patriarch in der Serbisch-Orthodoxen Kirche. Wien, Herder, 1966. 271 p.

A thorough study of the historical development and present legal status of the office of patriarch in the Serbian Orthodox Church, according to the constitutions of the Serbian Orthodox Church, 1931-1947. The constitution of May 19, 1947, in German translation, is included as an appendix.

2935. Radonić, Jovan.   Rimska kurija i južnoslovenske zemlje od XVI do

XIX veka (The Roman Curia and the South Slavic countries from
the 16th to the 19th century). Beograd, Naučna knjiga, 1950. 748 p.
(Srpska akademija nauka, Beograd. Posebna izdanja, knj. 155)
*See also* entry no. 2383.

Based on detailed original scholarship, this massive work describes
the efforts of the Roman Catholic Church after the Council of Trent
to counter Protestantism in the South Slav lands and to entice the
reluctant Orthodox into union with Rome, against a background
of the confrontation between Christendom and Islam and Habsburg
politics.

2936. Rupel, Mirko.  Primus Trubar. Leben und Werk des slowenischen
Reformators. Edited and translated by Balduin Saria. München,
Südosteuropa-Verlagsgesellschaft, 1965. 311 p. Illus., facsims., map.
(Südosteuropa-Schriften, Bd. 5)

The best study of Trubar's life and work from the Slavistic point
of view. Includes a list of Trubar's works and a rich bibliography,
brought up to date by Professor Saria.

2937. Ruvarac, Dimitrije.  Postanak i razvitak srpske crkveno-narodne
avtonomije (The origin and development of Serbian ecclesiastical
national autonomy). Sremski Karlovci, 1899. 286 p.

A pioneer work on the establishment and development of Serbian
Church autonomy in the Habsburg lands since 1690.

2938. Simić, Sima.  Vatikan protiv Jugoslavije (The Vatican against Yugoslavia). Titograd, Grafički zavod, 1958. 135 p.

A review of relations between the Vatican and Yugoslavia from
the First through the Second World War, based largely on newspaper
accounts, with a view toward demonstrating the pro-fascist tendencies of the Vatican. For other works on Vatican-Yugoslav relations,
see *The Vatican and Yugoslavia, Part 1; The Vatican's Relations
Towards the South Slav Peoples up to the End of World War I*
(Belgrade, Edition Jugoslavija, 1953, 172 p.), a chronology of Vatican-Yugoslav relations from ca. 874 to the end of 1918, presented
through excerpts of documents, translated into English; and *Tajni
dokumenti o odnosima Vatikana i ustaške "NDH"* (Secret documents
concerning the Vatican's relations with the ustashi "Independent
State of Croatia") (Zagreb, 1952, 143 p.), an exposé of relations
between the Vatican and the fascist Independent State of Croatia
designed to document their collaboration.

2939. Slipjepčević, Đoko M.  Istorija Srpske Pravoslavne crkve (History
of the Serbian Orthodox Church). Munich, 1962-1966. 2 v.

The first thorough scholarly survey of the history of the Serbian
Orthodox Church. The first volume extends from the conversion
of the Serbs to Christianity to the end of the 18th century; the second
volume includes the 19th century and the 20th century through the
Second World War. Though not always critical, it far surpasses its
only rival, the long standard work by Radoslav M. Grujić, *Pravo-*

*slavna srpska crkva* (The Serbian Orthodox Church) (Beograd, 1920, 220 p.).

2940. Spinka, Matthew. A History of Christianity in the Balkans; a Study of the Spread of Byzantine Culture Among the Slavs. Chicago, Ill., The American Society of Church History, 1933. 202 p. Bibliography: p. 189-191. (Studies in Church History, v. 1)
*See also* entry no. 256.

> A unique book by a noted church historian at the Chicago Theological Seminary. Of its seven chapters, three deal with the Yugoslav lands, especially those espousing Orthodoxy or Bogomilism; three with Bulgaria; and one with the Slavic Balkan lands in general.

2941. Stanojević, Stanoje. Borba za samostalnost katoličke crkve u nemanjičkoj državi (The struggle for the independence of the Catholic Church in Nemanja's state). Beograd, Srpska kraljevska akademija, 1912. 178 p.

> A study of the Roman Catholic Church and its position in the medieval Serbian kingdom under the Nemanja dynasty, by a distinguished Serbian medievalist who wished to show that Catholic influence in medieval Serbia was greater than supposed.

## G. EDUCATION

### by Michael B. Petrovich

2942. Belgrade. Ekonomski institut Narodne Republike Srbije. Ekonomsko-društvene osnove sistema školstva u FNRJ (The socioeconomic foundations of the school system in the Federal People's Republic of Yugoslavia). Beograd, 1955. 254 p. Tables. (Mimeographed)

> A critical official analysis of the educational system in Yugoslavia after the Second World War. Covers basic policy questions, especially economic.

2943. Belgrade. Institut društvenih nauka. *Centar za istraživanje društvenih odnosa.* Jugoslovenski studenti i socijalizam (Yugoslav students and socialism). By Miloslav Janićijević and others. Beograd, 1966. 380 p.

> A fascinating collection of studies, based on polls, concerning the attitudes of Yugoslav students toward a variety of subjects including politics, ideology, social values, religion, work, social life, and leisure. Includes English summaries.

2944. Crvenkovski, Krste. Škola — samostalna društvena institucija (The school — an independent social institution). Beograd, Savremena škola, 1962. 161 p.

> A collection of important articles and reports from the period 1958-1961 concerning various aspects of educational reforms and policies.

2945. Dogović, Janko, Branislav Dumić, *and others*. Školstvo u Jugoslaviji (The school system in Yugoslavia). Zagreb, Informator, 1961. 255 p.

A complete handbook and directory, covering all levels and categories of schools in Yugoslavia.

2946. Đorđević, Živojin S.  Istorija škola u Srbiji ,1700-1850 (The history of schools in Serbia, 1700-1850). Beograd, Štamparija "Privrednik," 1935. 87 p.

A brief but useful survey, with chapters on the 18th century, the period of the First Serbian Insurrection (1804-1815), and the reigns of Miloš and Mihailo Obrenović (1815-1842) and of Aleksandar Karađorđević (1842-1858).

2947. Franković, Dragutin, *ed.*   Povijest školstva i pedagogije u Hrvatskoj (The history of the school system and of pedagogy in Croatia). Zagreb, Pedagoško-književni zbor, 1958. 542 p. Bibliography.

Written by a team of Croatian scholars, this is an admirably complete history of schools in Croatia from medieval times to the mid-1950s.

2948. Jemuović, Rodoljub.   Obrazovanje i reforma (Education and reform). Beograd, Sedma sila, 1966. 100 p.

A discussion of the aims and objectives of the then current educational reforms in Yugoslavia.

2949. Hadži-Vasiljević, Jovan.   Prosvetne i političke prilike u južnim srpskim oblastima u XIX v. (Educational and cultural conditions in the South Serbian regions in the 19th century). Beograd, 1928. 457 p. Illus. (Društvo sv. Save, knj. 37)

A very important book on the cultural and political confrontation between Serbian and Bulgarian influences in South Serbia, the Kosovo-Metohija region, and especially Macedonia in the 19th century. Much of this struggle was fought through competition in the establishment of schools. This study extends to the Russo-Turkish War of 1877-78.

2950. Kićović, Božidar.   Schools and Education in Yugoslavia. Belgrade, Edition Jugoslavija, 1955. 45 p.

A useful pamphlet giving basic facts about all levels of Yugoslav schools from 1938-1939 to 1953.

2951. Kirilović, Dimitrije.   Srpske osnove škole u Vojvodini u 18. veku (1740-1780) (Serbian elementary schools in Vojvodina in the 18th century [1740-1780]). Sremski Karlovci, 1929. 101 p. Facsims. (Istorisko društvo u Novom Sadu. Posebna izdanja, knj. 1)

A history of Serbian and German elementary schools in 18th century Vojvodina, especially from 1740 to 1780, with emphasis on administration and textbooks. An appendix contains the German and Church Slavonic text of Empress Maria Theresa's School Statute of 1776.

2952. Kulakovskiĭ, Platon A.   Nachalo russkoĭ shkoly u Serbov v XVIII veke (The inception of Russian schooling among the Serbs in the 18th century). Sanktpeterburg, 1903. 176 p.

A standard work by a Russian scholar on the influence of Russia on Serbian schools in 18th century Vojvodina. It deals especially with the activities of M. A. Suvorov and other Russian teachers there.

2953. Leko, Ivan.   Društveno upravljanje u prosvjeti i školstvu (Social management in education and the schools). Zagreb, Naprized, 1958. 353 p.

A survey of educational administration in Yugoslavia after the Second World War. The first three chapters deal with the war period, the postwar period of "administrative direction," and the present system of "social direction." The final chapter describes the work of educational councils and school boards.

2954. Leko, Ivan.   Novi školski sistem (The new school system). Zagreb, Školska knjiga, 1961. 223 p.

A general survey of the new Yugoslav educational system (as of 1961), with chapters on basic principles, schools and society, types of schools, teacher education, and supervision.

2955. Ljubljana. Slovenski šolski muzej.   Šolski sistemi na Slovenskem od 1774-1963 (School systems in Slovenia from 1774 to 1963). Ljubljana, 1964. 48 p. Illus.
Illus.

A very handy outline of Slovenian school systems from 1774 to 1963, with English summaries.

2956. Ognjanović, Andrija M.   Graničarske narodne škole i njihovi učitelji na teritoriji Vojvodine od 1774 do 1872 godine (The borderland folk schools and their teachers on the territory of Vojvodina from 1774 to 1872). Novi Sad, Matica srpska, 1964. 103 p.

The history of almost a century of education in the so-called Military Borderland of Austria, more specifically in Vojvodina. This study, which is based on archival materials as well as secondary works, covers Serbian, German, Croatian, Romanian, Slovak, and other schools in the territory.

2957. Organization for Economic Cooperation and Development. *Mediterranean Regional Project*.   Yugoslavia. Paris, 1965. 143 p.

An official international report assessing various aspects of the Yugoslav educational system and including future projections of needs. The statistics, of which there are many, deal largely with the late 1950s and early 1960s. An indispensable survey.

2958. Petrović, Kosta.  Istorija Srpske pravoslavne velike gimnazije kar-
lovačke (History of the Serbian Orthodox Gymnasium in Karlovci).
Novi Sad, 1951. 422 p. Illus. (Matica srpska, Novi Sad. Naučna
izdanja, knj. 12)

A very thorough history, from 1792 to 1921, of the Serbian Gymnasium in Sremski Karlovci, the seat of the Serbian Orthodox Church
in the Habsburg Monarchy and a leading cultural center of the Serbs
for over two centuries. A companion work to Vasa Stajić's history
of the Gymnasium of Novi Sad (entry no. 2962).

2959. Savez narodnih sveučilišta Hrvatske.   Narodna sveučilišta u Hrvatskoj, 1941-1961 (Popular universities in Croatia, 1941-1961). Edited
by Aleksandar Kovačić, Anuška Novaković, and Mihajlo Ogrizović.
Zagreb, 1961. 176 p. (*Its* Dokumentacija, 3)

A survey of adult education in Croatia.

2960. Schmidt, Vlado.   Pedagoško delo protestantov na Slovenskem v
XVI. stoletju (The pedagogical activity of Protestants in Slovenia in
the 16th century). Ljubljana, Državna založba slovenije, 1952. 224 p.
(Pedagoški tisk, Sv. 6)

A history of Protestant education in 16th century Slovenia, especially from the time of Primož Trubar.

2961. Schmidt, Vlado.   Zgodovina šolstva in pedagogike na slovenskem
(The history of schools and pedagogy in Slovenia). Ljubljana, Državna
založba Slovenije, 1963-1966. 3 v.

A very useful survey of the history of schools and education in
Slovenia from earliest times. The first volume ends with 1805, and
the second with 1848.

2962. Stajić, Vasa. Srpska pravoslavna velika gimnazija u Novom Sadu
(Serbian Orthodox Great Gymnasium in Novi Sad). Novi Sad, Matica
srpska, 1949. 448 p.

An admirably thorough history of one of the most influential
schools in modern Serbian history, located in Novi Sad, the "Serbian
Athens." The account extends from 1731 to 1920 and describes the
environment which produced so many generations of educated Serbs
in Austria-Hungary.

2963. Steinman, Zora.   Obavezno školovanje u SR Hrvatskoj; demografski faktor, materijalne i kadrovske osnove (Compulsory education
in the People's Republic of Croatia; the demographic factor, material
and personnel foundations). Zagreb, Školska, knjiga, 1964. 119 p.

A study on the development and results of compulsory public
school education in Croatia after 1945, taking into account demographic factors, finances, teacher training, literacy, and other problems.

2964. Tomich, Vera.   Education in Yugoslavia and the New Reform; the

Legal Basis, Organization, Administration, and Program of the Secondary Schools. Washington, D.C., U.S. Department of Health, Education, and Welfare, Office of Education, 1963. 146 p. Bibliography.

> Originally prepared as the author's doctoral dissertation at the University of California in Los Angeles, this useful study also includes the author's translation of the "General Law on Education."

2965. Turosienski, Severin K.   Education in Yugoslavia. Washington, D.C., U.S. Government Printing Office, 1939. 146 p. Illus., map, bibliography. (U.S. Office of Education Bulletin, no. 6)

> A comprehensive survey of all levels of Yugoslav education, this is an indispensable guide to the Yugoslav educational system between the two world wars. Includes extensive statistics and charts.

2966. Yugoslavia. *Savet za nauku i kulturu.*   Education in the Federal People's Republic of Yugoslavia, 1945-46 to 1950-51. Belgrade, Savet za nauku i kulturu, 1952. 133 p. Illus.

> An official survey, in English and French, of all levels and kinds of schools. Includes many charts, statistics, and illustrations.

2967. Yugoslavia. *Savezni zavod za proučavanje školskih i prosvetnih pitanja.*   Gimnazija (The gymnasium). Beograd, Savremena škola, 1959. 236 p.

> An official study on secondary schools in Yugoslavia which served as the basis for reforms. Many aspects of the schools are discussed, with emphasis on curriculum. For a similar report on elementary schools prepared by the same office, see *The Elementary School in Yugoslavia* (Belgrade, Edition Jugoslavija, 1960, 265 p.).

2968. Yugoslavia. *Sekretarijat za prosvetu i kulturu.*   The Proposed System of Education in Federal People's Republic of Yugoslavia. Translated from the Serbo-Croatian. Belgrade, Edition Jugoslavija, 1959. 191 p.

> An official study drawn up by the Commission for School Reform and adopted, after revision, as the official government statement regarding the new system of education.

## H. THE FINE ARTS

*by Jelisaveta Stanojevich Allen*

### 1. Serials

2969. Arhitektura — urbanizam; časopis za arhitekturu, urbanizam, primenjenu umetnost i industrijsko oblikovanje (Architecture — city planning; journal for architecture, city planning, applied arts, and industrial design). 1960– Beograd. Illus. Bimonthly.

> Journal of the Association of Architects of Yugoslavia and of

the City Planning Association of Yugoslavia. Summaries in English and French.

2970. Mala likovna biblioteka (Little library of representational arts). 1957– Zagreb, Naprijed. Illus.

An unnumbered series of small monographs on contemporary Croatian artists.

2971. Peristil; zbornik radova za historiju umjetnosti i arheologiju (Peristyle; collection of studies in art history and archaeology). 1954– Zagreb. Illus.

A review published by Povijesno društvo Hrvatske (Society of Croatian Historians) with articles by leading Croatian scholars.

2972. Umetnički pregled (Artistic review). v. 1-5; 1937-1941. Beograd. Annual.

The most important art journal published in Yugoslavia before the Second World War. The editor was Milan Kašanin.

2973. Umetnost (Art). 1965– Beograd. Illus. Quarterly.

Publishes essays on modern art and artists, with summaries in French or English. Includes reviews of exhibitions, books, and periodicals, foreign as well as domestic. Edited by Stojan Ćelić.

Of related interest is *Umetnost; časopis za likovnu umetnost* (Art; journal of representational art) (1-3; 1949-1951, Beograd), which was issued by the Association of Representational Artists of Yugoslavia (Savez likovnih umetnika Jugoslavije).

2974. Zbornik za likovne umetnosti (Collection on the representational arts). 1965– Novi Sad. Illus. (part col.).

Scholarly serial issued by the Division for Art of the Matica srpska, publishing articles by leading Serbian art historians, with summaries in English, German, or French. May be supplemented by *Zograf, časopis za srednjevekovnu umetnost* (Icon painter; journal of medieval art) (1966–, Beograd), edited by Svetislav Mandić.

## 2. General

2975. Đuric, Vojislav J.   Icones de Yougoslavie. Introduction by Svetozar Radojčić. Belgrade, 1961. 141 p. Plates, bibliography.

Catalog of an exhibition held during the Twelfth International Congress of Byzantine Studies, held at Ohrid, this is the best selection of icons in Yugoslavia, with a full description and bibliography for each icon in the catalog. The introduction gives a concise account of icon painting in Yugoslavia from the 10th to the 19th century. A deluxe publication on the same subject is *Icones de Serbie et de Macédoine* (Beograd, Éditions Jugoslavija, 1961, 15 p., 84 plates), edited by Oto Bihalji-Merin and with text by Svetozar Radojčić.

2976. Enciklopedija likovnih umjetnosti (Encyclopedia of representational arts). Editor-in-chief, Andre Mohorovičić. Zagreb, Leksikografski zavod FNRJ, 1959-1966. 4 v. Illus., col. plates, ports., bibliographies.

> A well-produced work. Worldwide in scope, it has especially good sections on Yugoslav art and artists, documented with up-to-date bibliographies and good illustrations. Biographies include living persons. A basic reference work.

2977. Karaman, Ljubo.   Pregled umjetnosti u Dalmaciji, od doseljenja Hrvata do pada Mletaka (A review of the arts in Dalmatia, from the immigration of the Croats to the fall of the Venetian Republic). Zagreb, Matica hrvatska, 1952. 90 p. Illus. (Povijest likovnih umjetnosti)

> A concise account of architecture, sculpture, painting, and minor arts from the seventh to the end of the 18th century. The text is followed by 185 well-chosen illustrations. May be supplemented by *Umjetnost XVII. i XVIII. stoljeća u Dalmaciji* (Art of the 17th and 18th centuries in Dalmatia) (Zagreb, Matica hrvatska, 1956, 146 p.) by Kruno Prijatelj.

2978. Kašanin, Milan.   L'art yougoslave des origines à nos jours. Beograd, Musée du Prince Paul, 1939. 91 p. 168 plates (8 col.) on 88 l. Bibliography: p. 89.

> An attempt to create a synthesis of Yugoslav art from the 9th to the 20th century. The major works of each period and region are treated.

2979. Petrović, Veljko, *and* Milan Kašanin.   Srpska umetnost u Vojvodini, od doba despota do Ujedinjenja (Serbian art in Vojvodina from the period of the despots to the unification). Novi Sad, Matica srpska, 1927. 135 p. Plates (part col.), ports. (part col.), atlas.

> A survey of architecture, painting, and the minor arts in Vojvodina from the 15th to the end of the 19th century. May be supplemented, for the period 1700-1900, by *Dva veka srpskoga slikarstva* (Two centuries of Serbian painting), 2d ed. (Beograd, Jugoistok, 1943, 75 p.) by Milan Kašanin. The text is in Serbian and German.

### 3. Early and Medieval Art

2980. Belgrade. Narodni muzej.   Srpski spomenici (Serbian monuments). 1-7; 1922-1934. Beograd. Illus., plates.

Monumenta serbica artis mediaevalis. Stari srpski umetnički spomenici. 1-2; 1933-1941. Beograd, Srpska akademija nauka.

> These two series comprise monographs on important medieval monasteries in Serbia and Macedonia. Each monastery is treated in detail, with information given on its history, its architecture, and the iconography of its murals.

2981. Deroko, Aleksandar.   Srednjevekovni gradovi u Srbiji, Crnoj Gori i Makedoniji (Medieval fortresses in Serbia, Montenegro, and Macedonia). Beograd, Prosveta, 1950. 214 p. Illus., map. Bibliography: p. 213-214.

A historical survey of fortified cities is followed by a topographical study of individual monuments, including plans and elevations. Summary in French. A companion volume is the same author's *Monumentalna i dekorativna arhitektura u srednjevekovnoj Srbiji* (Monumental and decorative architecture in medieval Serbia) (Beograd, Naučna knjiga, 1953, 359 p.). This is a study of the architecture of Serbian churches from the 10th to the 15th century, with summaries in French and English.

2982. Fisković, Cvito.    Dalmatinske freske (Dalmatian frescoes). Zagreb, "Zora," 1965. 31 p. Col. illus. (Umjetnički spomenici Jugoslavije)

A deluxe publication of mural paintings in Dalmatia from the 11th to the 15th century.

2983. Hamann-MacLean, Richard, *and* Horst Hallensleben.    Die Monumentalmalerei in Serbien und Makedonien vom 11. bis zum frühen 14. Jahrhundert. Giessen, Schmitz, 1963. 39 p. Illus., plates. (Osteuropastudien der Hochschulen des Landes Hessen. Reihe II. Marburger Abhandlungen zur Geschichte und Kultur Osteuropas, 3)

Representative study of medieval Serbian painting.

2984. Millet, Gabriel.    La peinture du Moyen Age en Yougoslavie (Serbie, Macédoine et Monténégro). Album présenté par A. Frolow. Paris, E. de Boccard, 1954-1962. 3 v. Plates, bibliography.

Material which Millet collected through the years of his systematic study of Serbian art was published by his associates in these volumes.

2985. Radojčić, Svetozar.    Mileševa. Beograd, Srpska književna zadruga, 1963. 92 p. Illus. (part col.). (Umetnički spomenici Jugoslavije)

Đurić, Vojislav J. Sopoćani. Beograd, Srpska književna zadruga, 1963. 148 p. Illus. (part col.) (Umetnički spomenici Jugoslavije)

Comprehensive and well-documented monographs on two major monuments (both monasteries) of 13th century Serbian art. Both volumes have a list of illustrations and summary in English. Đurić's work has also been published in German (Leipzig, 1967).

2986. Radojčić, Svetozar.    Staro srpsko slikarstvo (Old Serbian painting). Beograd, Nolit, 1966. 356 p. Illus., plates (part col.). (Biblioteka Sinteze)

A history of medieval Serbian painting, from the 12th to the 15th century, written by the foremost authority on the subject. May be supplemented by Vladimir R. Petković's *Pregled crkvenih spomenika kroz povesnicu srpskog naroda* (A survey of religious monuments through the history of the Serbian people) (Beograd, Naučna knjiga, 1950, 1258 p.). Issued by the Serbian Academy of Sciences as v. 157 in its series *Posebna izdanja*, this is a topographical study of all churches, including those known only from literary sources.

2987. Stele, Franc.   Monumenta artis slovenicae. Ljubljana, Akademska založba, 1935-1937. 2 v. Plates, facsims. Bibliography: v. 1, p. 53-56.
Treats the history of painting in Slovenia. The first volume deals with the mural paintings of the Middle Ages, and the second is on baroque and romantic painting. Text in Slovenian and French.

2988. United Nations Educational, Scientific, and Cultural Organization. Yugoslavia: Mediaeval Frescoes. Preface by David T. Rice; introduction by Svetozar Radojčić. Greenwich, Conn., New York Graphic Society, 1955. 29 p. Illus., 32 col. plates. Bibliography: p. 33. (UNESCO World Art Series, 4)
Plates reproduce frescoes from the most representative churches and monasteries in Serbia and Macedonia.

2989. Wenzel, Marian.   Ukrasni motivi na stećcima. Ornamental Motifs on Tombstones From Medieval Bosnia and Surrounding Regions. Sarajevo, "Veselin Masleša," 1965. 460 p. Illus., maps. (Biblioteka Kulturno nasljeđe)
A systematic study of sepulchral monuments of the 14th and 15th centuries. Text in English and Serbo-Croatian in parallel columns. May be supplemented by *Srednjevjekovni nadgrobni spomenici Bosne i Hercegovine* (Medieval sepulchral monuments in Bosnia and Hercegovina) (Sarajevo, Zemaljski muzej, 1950–), with English summary. A popular treatment of the subject is *Bogomil Sculpture*, essays by Oto Bihalji-Merin and Alojz Benac, with photographs by Tošo Dabac (New York, Harcourt, Brace & World, 1963, 36 p., 80 p. of illus.).

2990. Zadnikar, Marijan.   Romanska arhitektura na Slovenskem (Romanesque architecture in Slovenia). Ljubljana, Državna založba Slovenije, 1959. 358 p. Illus., bibliography.
A survey of Romanesque churches in Slovenia, with details of architecture and sculpture.

### 4. 16th Century to the Present

2991. Babić, Ljubo.   Umjetnost kod Hrvata (The art of the Croats). Zagreb, A. Velzek, 1943. 247 p. Plates. (*His* Sabrana djela, kn. 1)
Surveys architecture, sculpture, and painting in Croatia from the beginning of the 19th century up to the Second World War. Includes chronological lists of artists and architects and of exhibitions held in Zagreb during the years 1901-1941.

2992. Bihalji-Merin, Oto.   Primitive Artists of Yugoslavia. New York, McGraw-Hill, 1964. 200 p. Illus. (part col.), ports.
Surveys contemporary Yugoslav primitive artists, grouped by regions, and traces the roots and traditions of primitive art in general. Of closely related interest is *Naive Art in Yugoslavia*, edited by Oto Bihalji-Merin and with text by Mirjana Gvozdenović and Siniša

Paunović (Beograd, "Jugoslavija," 1959, 144 p.). Both works were also published in Serbo-Croatian and German.

2993. Čelebonović, Aleksa.   Modern Yugoslav Painting. Edited by Oto Bihalji-Merin and Jara Ribnikar. Beograd, "Jugoslavija," 1965. 54 p., 192 p. of illus. (part col.). Bibliography: p. xliii-l.

Outlines the development of contemporary Yugoslav painting. Includes short biographical sketches of 201 artists. Issued also in Serbo-Croatian.

2994. Grum, Željko.   Ivan Meštrović. Photos by Tošo Dabac. Zagreb, Matica hrvatska, 1962. 189 p. (chiefly illus.).

Fully illustrated monograph on the best known Yugoslav artist. Meštrović's works are treated chronologically, and architectural projects are included. Another important publication on the same artist is *The Sculpture of Ivan Meštrović* (Syracuse, Syracuse University Press, 1948, 29 p., 158 plates, bibliography), by Norman L. Rice, which contains a brief account of the sculptor's life by Harry N. Hilberry.

2995. Kržišnik, Zoran.   Contemporary Yugoslav Graphic Art. New York, Shorewood Publishers, 1964. 144 p. (chiefly illus., part col.)

Includes works of and biographical notes on 42 artists. Also issued in Serbo-Croatian and German.

2996. Latter-Day Yugoslav Sculpture.   Text by Miodrag Kolarić. Photos by T. Dabac, M. Szabo, and Foto Moderna galerija Ljubljana. Beograd, Jugoslavija, 1961. 155 p. (chiefly illus., ports.)

A brief outline of the development of contemporary Yugoslav sculpture since Meštrović, including biographical notes on 43 artists. An earlier volume on modern sculpture is *Yugoslav Sculpture in the Twentieth Century* (Beograd, "Jugoslavija," 1955, 183 p.) by Oto Bihalji-Merin, in which the works of 52 sculptors are represented.

2997. Protić, Miodrag B.   Savremenici; likovne kritike i eseji (The contemporaries; criticisms and essays in the representational arts). Beograd, Nolit, 1955-1964. 2 v. Illus. (part col.).

Informative descriptions and criticisms of the work of numerous contemporary painters and sculptors, mostly those who are represented in the Moderna galerija in Belgrade, which is directed by the author. Biographical information on the artists is included. The introductory essay in the first volume sketches the development of modern art in Serbia from 1904 to 1952.

2998. Šijanec, Fran.   Sodobna slovenska likovna umetnost (Contemporary Slovenian representational art). Maribor, Obzorja, 1961. 550 p. Bibliography: p. 541-542. Illus. (Likovna obzorja, 1)

A comprehensive work on architecture, sculpture, painting, and graphic arts in Slovenia today. Includes biographical notes on artists. Summary in French.

# I. MUSIC

*by Miloš Velimirović*

## 1. Reference Aids

2999. Andreis, Josip, *ed.* Muzička enciklopedija (Encyclopedia of music). Zagreb, Leksikografski zavod FNRJ, 1958-1963. 2 v. Illus., ports., music, bibliographies.

> An excellent encyclopedia with invaluable information on musicians and musical institutions in Yugoslavia. Besides articles and biographical essays on composers and the history of musical styles, it contains a great deal of information on musicians from other Slavic countries, data not otherwise found in standard Western European biographical dictionaries and musical encyclopedias. In most instances includes excellent bibliographical data. The second volume contains addenda and corrigenda (p. 845-854). Unusually fine pictorial documentation.

3000. Andreis, Josip, *and* Slavko Zlatic, *eds.* Yugoslav Music. Beograd, Edition Jugoslavija, 1959. 158 p. Illus.

> An informative survey of the history of music in Yugoslavia, with added chapters on musical folklore, the organization of musical life in Yugoslavia, publishing activities, and thumbnail biographical sketches of Yugoslav composers and performing musicians as well as ballet dancers (p. 88-159). The only publication of its kind in English, prepared and distributed for information purposes. The full list of authors and collaborators on this volume is found in the preface (p. 3).

3001. Cvetko, Dragotin. Les formes et les résultats des efforts musicologiques yougoslaves. Acta Musicologica (Basel), v. 31, 1959: 50-62.

> An extremely thorough bibliographical survey of Yugoslav musicological publications from 1945 to 1958.

3002. Cvetko, Dragotin. Histoire de la musique Slovène. Maribor, Obzorja, 1967. 337 p. Illus., ports., facsims., bibliography.

> A most valuable paperback, published for the Congress of the International Musicological Society held in Ljubljana in September, 1967. Based on the author's Slovenian work, *Zgodovina glasbene umetnosti na Slovenskem* (A history of musical art in Slovenia) (Ljubljana, Državna založba Slovenije, 1958-1959, 2 v.).

3003. Cvetko, Dragotin, *and others.* Jugoslawien. *In* Die Musik in Geschichte und Gegenwart; allgemeine Enzyklopädie der Musik. v. 7. Kassel, Bärenreiter-Verlag, 1958. cols. 315-378. Bibliographies.

> This is the most comprehensive survey of music in Yugoslavia in a foreign language. The article is divided into two basic sections,

"Kunstmusik" (cols. 315-336) and "Volksmusik" (cols. 336-378), both with good bibliographies. The sections are subdivided by geographical area, each handled by a different author. The section "Kuntsmusik" includes the following subdivisions: 1. "Slovenien" (D. Cvetko); 2. "Kroatien" (J. Andreis); 3. "Serbien" (S. Đurić-Klajn); 4. "Mazedonien" (T. Skalovski); and 5. "Bosnien und Herzegowina" (M. Pozajić). The section "Volksmusik" is subdivided as follows: 1. "Slovenien" (Z. Kumer); 2. "Kroatien" (V. Žganec); 3a. "Serbien" (S. V. Lazarević); 3b. "Montenegro" (S. Đurić-Klajn); 4. "Mazedonien (Ž. Firfov); and 5. "Bosnien und Herzegowina" (C. Rihtman). D. Cvetko is also the author of brief surveys of Yugoslav music in the *Encyclopédie de la musique*, v. 3 (Paris, Fasquelle, 1961), p. 1001-1002, and in the *Enciclopedia della musica*, v. 2 (Milano, Ricordi, 1964), p. 513-514.

3004. Đorđević, Vladimir R.   Prilozi biografskom rečniku srpskih muzičara (Contributions to a biographical dictionary of Serbian musicians). Beograd, 1950. 71 p. (Srpska akademija nauka, Posebna izdanja, knj. 169; Muzikološki institut, knj. 1)

The first essay for a biographical dictionary of musicians in Serbia. Contains notes and data on 46 musicians who achieved some prominence in Serbia before the First World War. Essentially source materials of uneven value.

3005. Kovačević, Krešimir.   Hrvatski kompozitori i njihova djela (Croatian composers and their works). Zagreb, "Naprijed," 1960. 553 p. Music. Summaries in English.

This is, in fact, a biographical dictionary of 50 Croatian composers, with a listing of their main works and a descriptive analysis (often with musical examples and indications of duration of performance) of some of their best works. In the absence of modern critical monographs on Croatian composers, this volume remains for the time being one of the primary sources. This is especially the case for Josip Slavenski (p. 409-428), probably the greatest Yugoslav composer of this century, on whom there are no special studies yet available. A study of Slavenski's choral music by Petar Bingulac was recently published in *Zvuk; jugoslovenska muzička revija* (Beograd), no. 69: 535-557, and no. 70: 727-747.

## 2. Serials

3006. Coover, James B.   A Bibliography of East European Music Periodicals: XI. Yugoslavia. *In* Fontes Artis Musicae, v. 9. Kassel, Bärenreiter-Verlag, 1962. p. 78-80.

A rather thorough listing of some 36 music periodicals recorded as having been published in Yugoslavia as of 1959. Should be supplemented by reference to the names of individual periodicals listed in *Muzička enciklopedija* (Encyclopedia of music), v. 2. (Zagreb, Leksikografski zavod FNRJ, 1963), p. 255-256, where a special article devoted to musical periodicals may also be found. Consult also the article by Stana Đurić-Klajn, "Istoriski pregled jugoslovenskih muzičkih časopisa" (Historical review of Yugoslav musical journals) in her *Muzika i muzičari* (Music and musicians) (Beograd, "Prosveta," 1956), p. 79-93.

3007. Muzikološki zbornik (Musicological annual). 1965– Ljubljana. Annual.

> With the establishment in Ljubljana in 1962 of the first and so far the only chair for musicology at a Yugoslav university, its chairman, Prof. Dragotin Cvetko, decided to found a periodical publication for musicological studies. Three volumes have appeared so far, each with summaries in English. The first volume contains seven studies, with emphasis on the music of Slovenia. The second volume includes twelve essays; in addition to topics of local significance, studies in the general history of music and summaries (in Slovenian and English) of the first three doctoral dissertations defended in Ljubljana are presented. One of these appears to be the first modern critical study of Vatroslav Lisinski, an important 19th century Croatian composer.

3008. Zvuk; jugoslovenska muzička revija. 1955– Beograd, Savez kompozitora Yugoslavije. Frequency varies. Illus., music, ports.

> Successor to an excellent periodical of the same name which was published between 1932 and 1936 by Stana Đurić-Klajn (Ribnikar). Seventy numbered issues published between May 1955 and the end of 1966 (several as double issues). Numbers 1-66 edited by Stana Đurić-Klajn, and 67-70, by Vlastimir Peričić. Since January 1967, edited by Zija Kučukalić, with offices in Sarajevo. Publication is now on a regular bimonthly basis, but the journal is much thinner and lacks the previous bibliographical appendixes and occasional appended summaries in the Western languages.

> A special issue, no. 77/78, was published in September 1967, on the occasion of the Congress of the International Musicological Society, held in Ljubljana. This issue contains exclusively articles in English, French, and German, representing brief historical surveys of music in the various provinces and essays on the main centers of musical activities in Yugoslavia.

## 3. History and Special Aspects

3009. Andreis, Josip, Dragotin Cvetko, *and* Stana Đurić-Klajn. Historijski razvoj muzičke kulture u Jugoslaviji (The historical development of music in Yugoslavia). Zagreb, Školska knjiga, 1962. 724 p. Illus., ports., facsims., music, bibliographies.

> The only thorough and comprehensive history of Yugoslav music. The volume is divided into three basic sections: "Croatia," by J. Andreis (p. 11-277; brief bibliography); "Slovenia," by D. Cvetko (p. 281-527; extensive bibliography); and "Serbia," by S. Đurić-Klajn (p. 531-709; bibliographical footnotes only).

3010. Andreis, Josip, *ed.*   Rad Jugoslavenske akademije znanosti i umjetnosti, knjiga 337. Zagreb, Jugoslavenska akademija znanosti i umjetnosti, Odjel za muzičku umjetnost, 1965. 436 p.

This volume contains eight studies prepared under the direction of Josip Andreis, the most serious contemporary Croatian musicologist. Includes summaries in English, French, or German. The most substantial study is that by the late Albe Vidaković on Juraj Križanić's "Asserta Musicalia" (1656), with the full Latin text and a Serbo-Croatian translation. Of bibliographic importance is a study by Ivo Olup on music periodicals in Croatia.

3011. Cvetko, Dragotin.   Academia Philharmonicorum Labacensis. Ljubljana, Cankarjeva Založba, 1962. 237 p.

A superb monograph on the musical life in Ljubljana in the second half of the 17th century and in the 18th, analyzing in particular the role and influence of one of the first professional societies of musicians in Yugoslavia. Includes an extensive summary in French (p. 195-221).

3012. Cvetko, Dragotin.   Davorin Jenko; doba, življenje, delo (Davorin Jenko; his times, life, and works). Ljubljana, Slovenski knjižni zavod, 1955. 296 p. Illus.

This is a considerably revised edition, in Slovenian, of a monograph originally published in Serbian under the title *Davorin Jenko i njegovo doba* (Davorin Jenko and his times) (Beograd, 1952, 237 p. [Srpska akademija nauka, Posebna izdanja, knj. 201; Muzikološki institut, knj. 4]). Jenko was born in Slovenia but devoted most of his life to musical activities in Serbia; his work is thus of interest in both of these areas. The Slovenian edition lacks the musical examples and bibliographical footnotes of the Serbian edition, but deals in greater length with background information for Jenko's activities in the second half of the 19th century. The Serbian edition contains a brief summary in English (p. 209-214), and the Slovenian edition has a French summary (p. 281-288).

3013. Cvetko, Dragotin.   Odmevi glasbene klasike na Slovenskem (The echoes of classical music in Slovenia). Ljubljana, Državna založba Slovenije, 1955. 253 p. Facsims., bibliographical footnotes.

A monograph on developments at the end of the 18th century and during the first half of the 19th, particularly the contacts between Ljubljana and Vienna. Includes a summary in French (p. 221-238).

3014. Cvetko, Dragotin.   Zgodovina glasbene umetnosti na Slovenskem (History of music in Slovenia). Ljubljana, Državna založba Slovenije, 1958-1960. 3 v. Illus.

Owing to historical circumstances, Slovenia has always participated in the basic developments of the history of music in Europe; it is fortunate that Cvetko, the best Yugoslav musicologist, should have devoted his life to this extensive and masterful presentation of the history of music in Slovenia. The first volume covers developments through the middle of the eighteenth century. The second volume extends the survey through 1848 and the last volume, through 1918, when the Yugoslav state was created. Each volume contains extensive summaries in French (v. 1, p. 365-382; v. 2, p. 389-410; v. 3, p. 459-474).

3015. Helm, Everett.    Music in Yugoslavia. Musical Quarterly (New York), v. 51, 1965: 215-224.

A brief survey of some of the more recent works of young composers, including a discussion of their immediate models, especially in Yugoslavia.

3016. Konjović, Petar.    Miloje Milojević, kompozitor i muzički pisac (Miloje Milojević, composer and writer on music). Beograd, Srpska akademija nauka i umetnosti, 1954. 298 p. (Posebna izdanja, knj. 220; Odeljenje likovne i muzičke umetnosti, knj. 1)

A fine monograph on one of the first modern composers in Serbia, who was also the first musicologist and a fine essayist besides being the first professional musical critic. The author is himself a distinguished composer. Includes a summary in French (p. 257-267) and a full listing of Milojević's compositions and literary works. Some of Milojević's essays deal with reviews of the contemporary scene and music in Yugoslavia, as well as with the immediate history of music in Serbia, as may be seen in volumes one and two of his *Muzičke studije i članci* (Musical studies and articles) (Beograd, Geca Kon, 1926-1933). The third volume of this work (published posthumously by Milojević's daughter in 1953) contains only essays on Western European and Russian composers. It is regrettable that the talented essayist, Vojislav Vučković, did not write on the history of Serbian music.

3017. Konjović, Petar.    Stevan St. Mokranjac. Beograd, Nolit, 1956. 239 p. (Biblioteka Portreti)

An impressionistic monograph on one of the most important figures in Serbian music at the turn of the century, by one of the greatest Serbian composers who is also an erudite essayist. No bibliography or footnotes. Additional essays on Mokranjac by Konjović may be found in two of the latter's collections: *Knjiga o muzici* (Book on music) (Novi Sad, Matica srpska, 1947) and *Ogledi o muzici* (Essays on music) (Beograd, Srpska, književna zadruga, 1965). The latter book contains reprints of some essays and a few more recent articles. There is also a monograph on Mokranjac in Russian by Ivan Martynov: *Stevan Mokran'iats i serbskaia muzyka* (Stevan Mokranjac and Serbian music) (Moskva, Gos. muz. izd., 1958, 164 p., music; bibliography: p. 162-163). A special study on the most important works of Mokranjac is Milenko Živković's *Rukoveti St. St. Mokranjca* (Selected compositions by St. St. Mokranjac) (Beograd, Srpska akademija nauka i umetnosti, 1957, 137 p. [Posebna izdanja, knj. 283; Muzikološki institut, knj. 10]).

3018. Stefanović, Dimitrije.    The Serbian Chant From the 15th to 18th

Centuries. *In* Lissa, Zofia, *ed.* Musica Antiqua Europae Orientalis. Warszawa, Państwowe Wydawn. Naukowe, 1966. p. 140-163. (Acta Scientifica Congressus, Bydgoszcz, 1966)

The most comprehensive survey of available information on the history of church music in Serbia. Other contributions on Yugoslavia in the same volume are Stana Đurić-Klajn's "Certains aspects de la musique profane serbe de l'époque féodale" (p. 117-139); Dragotin Cvetko's "La musique slovène du XVI^e au XVIII^e siècle" (p. 164-199); and Krešimir Kovačević's "Die kroatische Musik des XVII. und XVIII. Jahrhunderts" (p. 200-220).

# Index

Includes names of authors, compilers, editors, translators, and sponsoring organizations; titles of publications; and principal subject headings. Titles of books are italicized, titles of articles and parts of books are in quotation marks, and subject headings are in capital letters. Numbers refer to entries, not pages. The letter *a* following an entry number indicates that the title is to be found in the annotation to that entry. In Greek words, the letter group Gk (at the beginning of a word) is rendered here as G; Mp as B; and B as V.